100-250   250 and over

THE SOVIET UNION
AND EASTERN EUROPE

A HANDBOOK

HANDBOOKS TO THE MODERN WORLD

Africa, edited by Colin Legum
Asia, edited by Guy Wint
Western Europe, edited by John Calmann
Latin America and the Caribbean, edited by Claudio Véliz
Australia, New Zealand and the South Pacific, edited by Charles Osborne

In preparation:
The Middle East, edited by Michael Adams
The United States and Canada, edited by Richard Fisher

THE SOVIET UNION
AND EASTERN EUROPE

A Handbook

Edited by
GEORGE SCHÖPFLIN

PRAEGER PUBLISHERS
New York • Washington

BOOKS THAT MATTER
Published in the United States of America in 1970
by Praeger Publishers, Inc., 111 Fourth Avenue,
New York, N.Y. 10003

Library of Congress Catalog Card Number: 70-100941
Printed in Great Britain

CONTRIBUTORS

Terence Armstrong
Richard Bailey
Michael Bourdeaux
J. F. Brown
Karel Brušák
Violet Conolly
K. F. Cviić
D. V. Donnison
John Erickson
William Forwood
George Gömöri
Philip Hanson
Brian Holmes
Peer Hultberg
Raymond Hutchings
Neil Hyams
D. Iliescu
Everett M. Jacobs
E. L. Johnson
Michael Kaser
John Keep
J. M. Kitch
Malcolm Mackintosh
S. E. Mann

Mervyn Matthews
Michael Montgomery
Peter Moravec
Frank Parkin
Vivian de Sola Pinto
Dimitry Pospielovsky
Gabriel Ronay
Jānis Sapiets
Mátyás Sárközi
Michael Scammell
George Schöpflin
Francis Seton
E. Steiner
Geoffrey Stern
Victor Swoboda
John Russell Taylor
A. Todd
Ossia Trilling
David Turnock
Margaret Vallance
Geoffrey Wheeler
Marcus Wheeler
Philip Windsor

v

CONTENTS

vi

MAPS

EDITOR'S PREFACE

THE purpose of this volume is to provide both basic information and comment about the Soviet Union and the communist-ruled part of Europe. It has been compiled with the aim of presenting an objective and up-to-date picture of areas which remain to some extent obscure to the outside world. This obscurity is increased both by the inaccessibility of much of the information—principally because of the language problem—and by the fact that the governments of these countries aften seek to cloak reality with a propaganda screen designed to prove the superiority of an ideology.

Apart from the Basic Information section, the treatment has not been on a country-by-country basis. Instead, general features of the various topics examined have been stressed to take account of developments throughout the area. The only apparent exception to this has been to analyse events in one particular country, where these might offer a better understanding of the entire area. However, there has been a tendency to treat the Soviet Union and Eastern Europe separately, given that in many instances the divergence is wide. Inevitably, there are certain gaps, due above all to lack of information. Further, comment on current affairs always runs the risk of being overtaken by events. In the case of this Handbook, the Czechoslovak crisis (January 1968—September 1969—if that is, in fact, the terminal date) has been just such a watershed in the history of the Soviet Union and Eastern Europe. The long term implications of the Czechoslovak crisis cannot yet be analysed with any confidence. Consequently, 1 January 1969 has been taken as the terminal date for the Handbook, though in one or two instances later developments have been included. This will have ensured that the immediate impact of the invasion of Czechoslovakia has not been ignored.

As a matter of policy, all the contributors live outside the communist world. Although the traffic between East and West has increased enormously in recent years, it was felt that no citizen of a communist state could be expected to provide the kind of objective analysis that a Handbook like this demands. Equally, the days of the cold war are long past and the approach to the subject has been one of sympathetic criticism.

A special problem in the case of Eastern Europe is that of the orthography of proper nouns in the nine languages written in Latin characters. All these languages use a complex system of diacritical marks, something which adds to their apparent outlandishness. It has been felt that these diacritical marks serve a useful purpose as a guide to pronunciation—an explanatory table has been included—and they have, therefore, been retained, as they would be with French in contrast to the usual practice in the English-speaking world. Languages written in Cyrillic have been transliterated according to the British system, with very minor modifications.

My thanks are due to Richard Natkiel, who prepared the maps; to William Forwood, who compiled most of the Basic Information section; to Julian

Cooper, who prepared the economics part of the Basic Information section and the Comparative Statistics; to Roger Pemberton, who prepared the index; and to my wife, who assisted me at various times with the preparation of copy and the correcting of proofs.

Among the various people whose advice I have sought, I must single out Peter Reddaway, who acted as a consultant on Soviet affairs. My thanks go to him for providing his valuable specialist knowledge at all times.

I am especially grateful to the three publisher's editors with whom I have worked during the editing of the Handbook—Antony Wood, Sarah Richardson (Lady Riddell) and Andrew Kimmens. Their patience, professional skill and ability to provide a non-specialist viewpoint have been a vital asset in the compilation of the Handbook.

November 1969   GEORGE SCHÖPFLIN.

PRONUNCIATION GUIDE

CZECH AND SLOVAK

ä is a long sound between *e* as in l*e*t and *a* as in c*a*t
c English *ts* in le*ts*
č English *ch* in *ch*urch
ch as in lo*ch*
ď English *d* in *d*uke
g as in *g*ave
j English *y*et
ľ English *l* in al*l*ure
ň English *n* in ten*n*ure
ř approximately as *rsh* or *rzh*
š English *sh* in *sh*ow
ť English *t* in *t*une
ů English *oo* in b*oo*t
ž English *s* in plea*s*ure, usually indicated by *zh*
y English *i* in h*i*t
ě English *ye* in yell
An accute accent on a vowel indicates length, thus *i* is pronounced as in h*i*t whilst *í* is as in b*ee*t; the stress is invariably on the first syllable.
ě, ř and ů are found only in Czech; ä only in Slovak.

POLISH

ą French *on* as in b*on*
ę varies between English en or em and French *en* as in *en*terrer
ó English *oo* as in b*oo*t but somewhat shorter
y as in Czech
sz as Czech š
cz as Czech č
ń as Czech ň
rz and ż as Czech ž
ł English *w* in *w*ait
ś English *s* in *s*ue
ć as Czech ť
c and j as in Czech
w as English *v* in *v*ictory

The stress in Polish is usually on the penultimate syllable.

HUNGARIAN

a is appx. English *o* in h*o*t
á is appx. English *i* in f*i*ve but without the 'y' sound
c and j as in Czech
cs as Czech č
g as in Czech
gy as Czech ď
ly as j in Czech
ny as Czech ň
ö as in German
ő is the lengthened form of ö
s as Czech š
sz English *s* in *s*it
ty as Czech ť
ü as in German
ű is the lengthened form of ü
zs as Czech ž

Acute accent and stress are as in Czech.

xi

c, č, j, š and ž as in Czech
ć as in Polish

RUMANIAN

ă English *er* in weath*er*
â English *e* in garm*e*nt
ş as Czech š
ţ as Czech c
j as Czech ž
c before o,a,u is pronounced as k; before e and i as Czech č; when ce and ci come
  before a,o,u the e or i is not pronounced.
ch before e and i as k
oa, ua English *wa* in *wa*s
g before a,o,u as g in Czech; before e and i, as English *g* in *g*eneral; gh as g in Czech,
  the h is not pronounced.

The stress in Rumanian varies. In general, these rules apply: words ending in a
consonant are stressed on the last syllable; words ending in a vowel on the penultimate
syllable, but there are many exceptions.

ALBANIAN

c as in Czech
ç as *ch* in English *ch*ur*ch*
dh as *th* in English *th*is
ë as *e* in English t*e*rm
gj as Czech ď
j as in Czech
l as Czech í
ll as Polish ł
nj as Czech ň
q as the initial sound in the English *q*ueue, something like ky
rr a trilled r
sh as in English
th as *th* in English *th*in
x as *dz* in English a*dz*e
xh as *j* in English *j*oin
y as ü in Hungarian
zh as ž in Czech
Stress is on the penultimate syllable, unless otherwise marked by an acute accent.

INTRODUCTION

THE SITUATION AFTER STALIN

GEORGE SCHÖPFLIN

PERHAPS the best approach to the recent history of the communist-ruled states of Europe is to regard it in the light of the changing relationship between the Soviet Union on the one hand and the East European states on the other. When Stalin died in 1953 this relationship was all too straightforward: the Kremlin treated its East European satellites as colonies to be exploited politically and economically in whatever way served the interests of the Soviet Union. Stalin's successors had neither the will nor the inclination to maintain the relationship on this footing. Quite apart from anything else, they were set on dismantling some of the totalitarian apparatus of the Stalinist era within the Soviet Union and this was bound to have its repercussions on Eastern Europe. Hence the new men in the Kremlin, above all Khrushchev, were constrained to put their relationship with Eastern Europe on a new and mutually more acceptable basis. In the thirteen years that have followed the Secret Speech of February 1956, the first major step in de-Stalinisation, the discovery of this mutually satisfactory relationship has persistently eluded the Soviet leadership.

In a sense, it is hardly surprising that neither the East Europeans nor the Soviet Union can find a satisfactory relationship with the other, for the natural interests of the two parties coincide in relatively few respects. Traditionally, the objective of the nations of Eastern Europe has been to maintain their independence and security against the two great powers, Russia and Germany, that threatened their existence. (The Ottoman Empire had ceased to be a real threat by the end of the 19th century.) With the defeat of Germany and the total exhaustion of the countries of Europe after 1945, it was inevitable that the resulting power vacuum should nevertheless be filled by the two powers—the United States and the Soviet Union—which now had the military and economic strength to dominate Europe. What was unfortunate for the states of Europe was not so much that the great power rivalry between the United States and the Soviet Union should have clashed directly in the centre of Europe, but rather that this rivalry should have been exacerbated by an ideological conflict. For the East Europeans would have fallen within a Russian sphere of influence in any event sooner or later; it was a mere accident of history that Russia was too weak in 1918 to take advantage of the fall of the Habsburg Empire and the stemming of the German *Drang nach Osten*, the centuries-old drive to the east. Thus the 20 years of independence enjoyed by Eastern Europe between the two World Wars was an illusion and this illusion was brutally dispelled by the advance of the Red

Army in 1945. Nonetheless, the period of independence did strengthen the East Europeans' conviction that independence of the great powers was possible and that they had a right to it. In the post-war period the drive to reassert this independence *vis-à-vis* the Soviet Union—just as in Western Europe the tendency towards throwing off what has come to be seen as American tutelage—has become one of the major characteristics of the Soviet-East European relationship.

The Soviet Union, on the other hand, was guided by a set of interests wholly different from those of the East Europeans. Russia has traditionally sought a secure western frontier and access to the open sea. The results of the post-war settlement, whilst denying the second, went a long way towards granting the first requirement. Not only had the Soviet Union acquired a glacis right along its western frontier—the Soviet–Norwegian Frontier being the only exception to this—but also, by dictating the terms of the settlement, the Kremlin ensured that this glacis stretched much further to the west than had inter-war Eastern Europe. Poland was shifted bodily westwards by the expulsion of the German population of the Oder-Neisse territories and the Soviet zone of occupation in the eastern third of Germany was consolidated into a communist-ruled satellite. Russian power had been extended further west than it had ever reached before. The interest of the Soviet Union in the post-war period was to maintain the security of this glacis and by 1947–8 it became clear that this was to be done in all cases bar one by establishing what amounted to Soviet governmental branch offices in every one of the states of Eastern Europe. The one exception, Finland, is a very special case, where the very unusual circumstances obtaining gave the Soviet Union the security it felt it needed without the imposition of a communist government.

The first challenge to this newly-acquired empire did not come, as was expected in the Soviet Union and Eastern Europe, from the Western powers, but from Jugoslavia. In the immediate post-war period Jugoslavia was something of an anomaly in Stalin's empire because, in contrast to all the other East European states (except Albania) the communists had won power in Jugoslavia very largely without the assistance of the Red Army. Hence Tito's adhesion to the communist bloc was a voluntary act, undertaken by a party and government which controlled the levers of power in its own country. As the general centralising proceeded, bringing the East European satellites into line with Soviet practice, it emerged that although the Jugoslavs were more Stalinist than Stalin in some respects, they objected to Soviet officials trying to run the country. This, in essence, was what the Soviet-Jugoslav quarrel of 1948 was about. The interests of the Soviet Union—as interpreted very restrictively by Stalin—had clashed with the interests which Tito still regarded as vital to the survival of his party. The threshold had been reached, as it was to be reached on a number of occasions subsequently in Soviet–East European relations and it was probably only because of the highly unstable international situation, and also the expectation by Stalin that Tito could not get away with his defection, that the Soviet Union did not launch a full scale military campaign to bring the Jugoslavs to heel. Tito's successful defiance of the Soviet Union was to have enormous consequence in later years for the other East Europeans. Jugoslavia, independent of the Soviet Union, proved that defection from the Soviet alliance did not mean an automatic reversion to capitalism and, further, the existence of an alternative form of communist ideology provided an essential competition to the increasingly sterile Soviet formulas which thoughtful East Europeans were finding so restrictive.

4

In the Stalinist period, then, the states of Eastern Europe suffered under a dual tutelage. The Soviet Union not only exercised its political and military power to the detriment of the East Europeans, but also insisted on (and enforced) a communist ideology as the ruling way of life for these states, regardless of the suitability of that ideology for local East European conditions. In many respects, that ideology, or more correctly, the precise Soviet version of that ideology, was indeed rather unsuitable, and although in the inter-war period Marxism had had little success in Eastern Europe, there was some familiarity with it. All the states in question had had communist parties—though only the Czechoslovak Party had been a serious political force—and for much of public opinion, the coming of the Red Army in 1945 had been a genuine liberation. Under Stalin, Soviet tutelage came increasingly to be resented, but the Marxist ideology which had been imposed by force began to gain adherents among the East Europeans, whether through sincere conviction or opportunism. But these new adherents or even the older pre-war party members were, also, resentful of the way in which local interests were subordinated to those of the Soviet Union and of the blanket insistence that Soviet experience in the building of socialism was the only possible road to socialism. Hence, by the time that de-Stalinisation began in the Soviet Union, there was a potentially explosive anti-Soviet resentment on the one hand and an acceptance by a significant section of public opinion in Eastern Europe on the other that some form of Marxist ideology would remain the leading force in the running of society.

For the Soviet Union after 1956 one of the criteria for determining the extent to which its security was threatened in its glacis was the degree to which the Soviet version of Marxism was practised. Any major deviation from the Soviet-inspired norm, whether in Hungary in 1956 or Czechoslovakia in 1968, was regarded as constituting a danger sufficient to warrant direct Soviet intervention. At the same time, however, more or less in harmony with domestic de-Stalinisation—or democratisation to use a term more acceptable to Marxist jargon—the Soviet leadership was ready to accede to a more flexible relationship with the East Europeans than what had existed under Stalin. The dilemma was and remains that this greater flexibility inevitably involves a wider area of choice for the East Europeans and they have tended on the whole to exercise that choice by pursuing their domestic interests. And as the interests of the East Europeans overlap only to a limited extent with those of the Soviet Union, sooner or later a decision taken in Eastern Europe will come into direct conflict with what the Soviet Union still considers the norm. At this point—the threshold—the Soviet Union feels constrained to intervene to protect its interests and it has always been able to do this because of its overwhelming power. The dilemma is further complicated by the fact that the threshold varies in both time and place. At different periods and with regard to different countries the Soviet Union has appeared to establish the threshold at a different degree. This search for the threshold and to extend the limits of threshold, which can also be seen as the search for a status of alliance by East Europeans rather than that of vassalage, sums up much of the history of the Soviet Union and Eastern Europe since 1956.

In that year, indeed, political movements in one country, Hungary, went so far as to cross what was then the threshold, whilst developments in another, Poland, managed to remain just inside. Briefly, the Secret Speech shook both the Hungarian and Polish parties to the core because, *inter alia*, it put into doubt the legitimacy of these parties' rule. In Poland the party remained united with the single overriding aim that direct Soviet tutelage over the country—symbolised by the presence of Marshal Rokossovsky, a Soviet general, as Poland's defence minister and seen as a kind of governor—must be ended. Władysław Gomułka, who had been disgraced as a Titoist in 1949, became the focus of this movement and the Polish party united behind him to stave off a Soviet effort to reassume political control over Poland. There are two points which emerge from the Polish events. One was that the Polish party was never in any real danger of losing control of the situation and, therefore, communism was never threatened. And second, by making Poland's security *vis-à-vis* Germany depend on the Soviet Union—the annexation of the Oder-Neisse territories did just this—the Soviet leadership could be certain that in the final analysis the Poles could not afford to cut themselves adrift.

In Hungary, on the other hand, the situation slipped from the grasp of the party leadership and rapidly went out of control altogether. When the weak but well-meaning Imre Nagy, the temporary head of the government thrown up by the revolution, announced that Hungary would leave the Soviet bloc and would return to a multi-party system, the Soviet Union decided that the threshold had been overstepped. The Red Army put down the revolution by force and imposed a more compliant government on Hungary. The Hungarians, indeed, had not had time to develop anything like a distinctive ideology of their own, but such indications as existed suggested that Hungary, free of Soviet tutelage, would have attempted to create the kind of Marxist-humanist society which was the aim of the Czechoslovak leadership in 1968. For the time being the Soviet Union seemed to be the unchallenged master of the communist world, both from the power-political and from the ideological point of view.

But if at the end of 1956 it appeared that the monolith had been firmly reestablished, this was soon proved to be an illusion. The next challenge to Soviet dominance was offered not in Eastern Europe, however, but in Peking. Mao Tse-tung saw himself as the legitimate heir to Stalin's claim to the ideological leadership of world communism. Peking was to be the new leading centre. However, the challenge was slow in unfolding and its impact on Soviet-East European relations was even more delayed. At the international conference of communist parties in November 1957, the communist parties present gave all the appearance of a restored monolith. Although Khrushchev's formal recognition of the right of each country to find its own road to socialism was not explicitly withdrawn, the final Declaration emphasised the primacy of the Soviet Union as the 'first and mightiest socialist power'. At the same time, the conference condemned nationalism and revisionism, specifically criticising the Jugoslavs for the latter sin. At this stage, there was no hint that Sino-Soviet relations were on any but the friendliest footing. However, within four years the quarrel between Moscow and Peking was a matter of public knowledge.

The issues between China and the Soviet Union are not directly relevant here, but the existence of the dispute and the policy pursued by the Soviet leadership to end the dispute were of great importance to the development of Soviet-East European relations. The Soviet Union was henceforth involved in an ideological dispute—which later became open rivalry between two great powers—with China and had, perforce, to devote more attention to maintaining the ideological unity of Eastern Europe. In the circumstances, it was open to the East Europeans to try to extract whatever concessions they could from the Soviet Union as a price for ideological loyalty.

In its relations with one of its erstwhile allies, the Soviet Union was actually forced into a position of defeat. This former ally was Albania, which lined up with China in the dispute and thereby preserved its independence from a (real or imaginary) threat from outside. The principal determinant in Albania's foreign policy was the triangular Soviet-Jugoslav-Albanian relationship. Number one enemy for Tirana has always been Jugoslavia. During the war the Albanian communist resistance was hardly more than a branch organisation of Tito's partisans. After the war, the Jugoslavs all but succeeded in absorbing Albania into the Jugoslav federation. The quarrel between Tito and Stalin saved Enver Hoxha, the Albanian leader, for the time being, but the first reconciliation between Moscow and Belgrade in 1955 put him in a very difficult position. Hoxha was saved again when de-Stalinisation in Poland and Hungary went too far and the situation froze again. In 1957 Soviet-Jugoslav relations deteriorated and Hoxha knew that for the time being he could breathe freely. However, Khrushchev was still intent on patching up relations with Tito and gradually the Albanians came to feel that the Soviet Union was no guarantee of their national integrity, as they might at any moment be sold out to the Jugoslavs. As the Sino-Soviet dispute progressed—it probably reached the point of no return in 1959—the Albanians increasingly came to take the Chinese side. Thereafter, the Albanians were openly seen to espouse the Chinese cause, presumably regarding China as a reliable protector but without any designs on Albania's territory. Albania's relationship with the Soviet Union rapidly took on the appearance of an ill-mannered slanging match. In June 1960, at the Third Congress of the Rumanian Party in Bucharest, where Khrushchev launched a major attack on the Chinese, the Albanians openly supported Peng Chen, the Chinese delegate. Later that year, at the World Conference of 81 Communist Parties (Moscow, November-December 1960), Hoxha and Mehmet Shehu, the Albanian prime minister, heaped abuse on Khrushchev and walked out of the Conference. During the first half of 1961 Soviet and East European aid was steadily withdrawn from Albania and in June of that year, the Soviet Union was forced to give up its submarine base at Vlorë (Valona). At the Twenty-second Congress of the CPSU in October Khrushchev attacked the Albanians by name—this was the beginning of the war of substitutes when the Soviet Union attacked Albania and China attacked Jugoslavia—and at the end of 1961 diplomatic relations between the Soviet Union and Albania were severed.

The case of Albania is interesting in the history of Soviet-East European relations in being one where the threshold was clearly passed without Soviet intervention. Obviously, there are a number of factors which help to explain why the Soviet Union did not seek to restore its influence in Albania, by, say, liquidating the Hoxha group and replacing it with its own nominees. One of these is the geographical; it would have been physically difficult for the Soviet Union to intervene in Albania, seeing that that country is totally isolated from any Soviet ally. Secondly, there was never any danger of the Albanian leadership's abandoning communism—the Albanians are heretics but not apostates in Moscow's eyes. Thirdly, even although relations with China were deteriorating steadily at the time, the Soviet Union had clearly no wish to make matters worse through a military attack on Albania, as that might conceivably have brought repercussions in Sino-Soviet state relations. And finally, what must also have contributed to Albania's successful defiance of the Soviet Union was its unimportance. Although Albania's defection was irritating, it was too small and too isolated a country to serve as an example to others—and in any event, the left-dogmatist line of the Albanian party would hardly recommend itself to any other East European party. Right-revisionism coupled with nationalism remained (and still remain) the greatest danger from the Soviet point of view.

It is possibly because only one of these factors—nationalism—has been present in Rumania's challenge to the Soviet Union that so far it has been successful. Since 1962, when the conflict between Moscow and Bucharest became acute, the Rumanians have managed to liberate wide areas of their foreign policy from the restraints previously imposed by Moscow and have, at the same time, succeeded in doing so without overstepping the threshold. The story of these seven years is one of a very high degree of diplomatic skill, in which the Rumanians have exploited to the utmost whatever advantages the situation at any one time may have offered. The roots of Rumania's independence lay in the early 1950s. Communist rule in post-war Rumania had been the work of a small group of Moscow-trained communists, who had returned to the country from exile in the Soviet Union with the Red Army in 1944. In 1952 Gheorghe Gheorghiu-Dej, a native communist, who had spent the war years in Rumania, came out on top in an internal party struggle and purged the Muscovite leadership of Ana Pauker. Although at the time this minor palace revolution made no difference at all to Rumania's policies, it did come to assume importance in later years, in that the communist leadership could claim to be a national one. Dej consolidated his ascendancy by purging two other potential rivals in 1957 and thereafter Rumania was ruled by a wholly united and well-disciplined group. The upheavals of 1956 left Rumania largely untouched and in view of the country's stability and presumed reliability, the Soviet units which had been stationed on Rumanian soil since 1944 were withdrawn in 1958. By these developments, the ground was prepared for Rumania's challenge to the Soviet Union.

When it came, in 1962, the confrontation was not over some political issue, but over economics. Khrushchev, supported by East Germany and Czechoslovakia, attempted to convert Comecon, the East European international trading organisation, into a supra-national planning body and the proposed economic order in Eastern Europe would have halted Rumania's industrialisation—or at least curtailed it—and left Rumania with the role of being a supplier of primary produce to the industrialised countries of the area. This was the issue on which the Rumanians chose to do battle with the Soviet Union and it was well chosen. By 1962 the Sino-Soviet conflict was far advanced, though it was still ideological and its power-political aspects were very much in the background. In these circumstances, the Kremlin presumably felt that it needed every ally it could raise, so that Dej was in a position to extract concessions. Furthermore, by deciding to fight within Comecon, the Rumanians gained a second advantage, namely, that the statutes of that organisation prescribed a unanimous vote, thus giving any member state an effective veto. The significance of the Comecon dispute was that the Rumanian leadership, having once challenged the Soviet Union, did not then give up. Instead, Rumania embarked on a policy that might best be described as one of 'de-Sovietisation'. All the external signs of Soviet dominance in Rumania were quietly removed: street names reverted to their former Rumanian names, the Soviet cultural institute in Bucharest was closed, Russian ceased to be a compulsory subject in schools. These and other measures gained the leadership considerable popularity with the Rumanian public, which now felt that its government was again pursuing a policy of 'Rumania first'. The ideological bases of Rumania's independence were outlined in a statement issued in April 1964—usually referred to as Rumania's 'Declaration of Independence'. The essence of this statement was that Rumania was a sovereign independent state and that no other state had any right to intervene in its affairs. Thenceforward, no Rumanian policy statement was complete without some reference to the principles of sovereignty, non-intervention and equality of rights.

In the years that followed, Rumania gave numerous demonstrations of its new-found independence. In its foreign trade, Rumania gradually realigned its commerce, so that by 1969 about a half of its trade was outside the communist world. In culture—a field intimately connected with national self-consciousness—the Latinity of Rumania was reemphasised. And in politics, Rumania diverged from the Soviet line on a number of major issues. (See below, pp. 269–78.)

However, despite the success of Dej and of his successor after his death in March 1965, Nicolae Ceauşescu, in maintaining Rumania's independence, the situation could not have been satisfactory for either the Rumanian or the Soviet leadership. Rumania's individual position remained precarious and particularly so after the Soviet-led invasion of Czechoslovakia in August 1968. That invasion was followed by a general tightening up of Soviet control in Eastern Europe and the so-called Brezhnev doctrine, put forward to justify the invasion, was a very real threat to Rumania should the Soviet leadership have chosen to enforce it. The Brezhnev doctrine proposed the formula that the socialist community as a whole had the right to determine when socialism was threatened in any one socialist country and to use any means to destroy that threat. Thus the doctrine was in direct contradiction to the April 1964 declaration and was attacked by Rumanian spokesmen in the autumn of 1968 and in 1969. It was clear in Bucharest in the months after the invasion that the winds blowing from the east were extremely chill and that the Rumanian leadership would have to move with great circumspection to maintain its existing gains, let alone attempt to extend its limits of independence.

The persistent tension caused by the unsettled Soviet-Rumanian relationship has had its effects on Rumanian domestic affairs. In an atmosphere of continuing crisis, the Rumanian leadership has had to exercise a very strict control over the population in order to ensure unity at home while dealing with its opponents abroad. As a substitute, Rumanian public opinion has been allowed a fair degree of nationalist self-expression. However, this cannot be the basis of a modern society, especially in economics, where the need for greater decentralisation is already making itself felt. The leadership, presumably, regards this as too great a risk as long as the acute confrontation with the Soviet Union lasts.

Equally, from the Soviet point of view, Rumania's nationalist policies have a considerable nuisance value. Although by no stretch of the imagination can Rumania represent a serious security risk in Soviet eyes, it is a factor of instability in Eastern Europe and a potential example to others. This is probably a situation where an agreement between the two sides could be reached—the Soviet-Rumanian relationship is potentially one of the easiest in Eastern Europe to settle—if only the Kremlin were prepared to make some concessions. However, after the invasion of Czechoslovakia, there was every sign that far from becoming more conciliatory, the Soviet Union was intending to tighten the bonds over Eastern Europe, so that the tension between Bucharest and Moscow seemed likely to continue.

The events of August 1968 were, in fact, a major watershed in the elusive search for a mutually acceptable relationship between the Soviet Union and Eastern Europe. Before 1968 there were a number of signs that gradually the Soviet Union was preparing to accept the upgrading of the status of its former East European satellites to that of allies—rather minor allies, it is true, but nevertheless with some standing when dealing with Moscow. Thus until 1968 it seemed that an East European country could deviate fairly widely in domestic affairs from the Soviet norm, especially in economic affairs (including trade with the West), without overstepping the threshold. However, the radical recasting of ideology in Czechoslovakia in the spring and summer of 1968 and the complete reform of the political and social order went so deep as to prove unacceptable to the Kremlin, which judged that the Czechoslovak experiment of 'socialism with a human face' infringed vital Soviet interests. The unique feature of the Czechoslovak crisis was that in that instance party and public opinion were wholly united behind the reform programme, so that the maintenance of communist rule was in no way endangered. Nevertheless, in the Soviet view the quality of that rule would have deviated so widely from the Soviet norm—the ultimate yardstick—that it could not have remained in being and especially not succeeded without the threat of its spilling over and providing encouragement to possible imitators in the Soviet Union itself. This possibility, however remote, could not be viewed with equanimity by a Soviet leadership which was facing the beginnings of political dissent at home—a dissent which questioned the legitimacy of its rule.

Yet the invasion solved no problems. It demonstrated that the power of the Red Army was such that it could execute an unopposed invasion with a considerable degree of military proficiency, but that was virtually all. No kind of political settlement that would truly 'normalise' the Soviet-Czechoslovak relationship has emerged at the time of writing (August 1969) and none seems remotely possible. Czechoslovak public opinion, despite the gradual elimination of the reformist leadership and of most of the reforms, refused to accept the *fait accompli* and turned instead to massive non-co-operation. Thus the very instability which, presumably, the Soviet leadership had sought to eliminate by the invasion, had returned in a new and potentially more dangerous form. Whereas under Dubček the chances of the security of the Soviet Union being imperilled by the policies of the reformers were minimal, the invasion and its aftermath created a mood of deep, and probably lasting, revulsion against the Soviet Union and possibly against socialism as well. The parallel with the post-1956 reconstruction in Hungary, where gradually Hungarian public opinion learned how to live with a not too unpleasant neo-Stalinist order, does not really apply. In Hungary there had been no time to start on the creation of a new order. In Czechoslovakia the new order had been begun and was seen by public opinion to be working and working well. Hence the dissatisfaction will unquestionably prove more difficult to overcome. The prospects for any kind of equitable settlement between the Soviet Union and Czechoslovakia seem to be impossible for a long time to come.

Nor can the situation be of great comfort to other East European leaderships. None of them has any desire to return to the system that obtained under Stalin, which is now seen everywhere in Eastern Europe as having been wasteful and inefficient. Yet the alternative, which just seemed possible in 1968, is for the time being excluded, thanks to the very restrictive interpretation of its vital interests by the Soviet Union. The basic dilemma of any East European leadership is that it must found its rule on consent and not on terror. Consent in this context requires a degree of identification with the national interests of the country by the leadership in question. These national interests will sooner or later come into conflict with those of the Soviet Union and at that point the leadership must decide in favour of one or the other. By choosing the national interest, as the Rumanians have done, the leadership will have to face a continuing trial of strength with Moscow. By choosing the Soviet interest, it will face growing unrest at home. Ironically a possible solution to this dilemma is already in existence in Finland. The settlement reached in 1948 between Finland and the Soviet Union permits the Finns a considerable latitude in the running of their domestic affairs, whilst largely though not wholly tying their foreign policy to the Soviet Union. However, Finland could not serve as a model for a working relationship between the Soviet Union and Eastern Europe, as in Moscow's eyes Soviet security is much more directly affected in the centre of Europe than in Scandinavia. Yet until some open or tacit settlement is reached, Eastern Europe will remain a potential or an actual factor of instability for the Soviet Union and probably a source of greater tension on the Soviet Union's western frontier than an Eastern Europe which had come to accept the necessary minimum Soviet presence in the area.

FURTHER READING

Brown, J. F. *The New Eastern Europe: the Khrushchev Era and After*. Frederick A. Praeger, New York, 1966; Pall Mall, London, 1967.

Lendvai, Paul. *Eagles in Cobwebs: Nationalism and Communism in the Balkans*. Doubleday, New York, 1969; Macdonald, London, 1970.

Schwartz, Harry. *Prague's 200 Days*. Frederick A. Praeger, New York; Pall Mall, London, 1969.

Ulam, Adam B. *Expansion and Coexistence: the History of Soviet Foreign Policy from 1917–67*. Frederick A. Praeger, New York; Secker and Warburg, London, 1968.

GEORGE SCHÖPFLIN, editor of this Handbook, was formerly Research Assistant at the Royal Institute of International Affairs and is currently working in the communist affairs Research Unit of the BBC External Services. He has specialised in the problem of nationalism and national minorities in Eastern Europe and has published several articles in this field.

COMPARATIVE STATISTICS

COMPARATIVE STATISTICS

Sources: *UN Statistical Yearbook, 1967.*
UN Monthly Bulletin of Statistics.
UN Annual Bulletin of Transport Statistics, 1966.
ILO Employment Yearbook, 1967.
FAO Agriculture Production Yearbook, 1967

Symbols used: — nil or insignificant
. not available
( ) estimated

POPULATION AND LABOUR FORCE
POPULATION, 1967

Country	Area (000 sq. km.)	Population (000)	Density (per sq. km.)
Albania	28·8	1,965	68
Bulgaria	110·9	8,309	75
Czechoslovakia	127·9	14,305	112
East Germany	108·0	16,001	148
Hungary	93·0	10,217	110
Jugoslavia	255·8	19,958	78
Poland	312·5	31,944	128
Rumania	237·5	19,287	81
Soviet Union	22,402·2	235,543	11
USA	9,363·4	199,118	21
UK	244·0	55,068	226

Source: UN Yearbook, 1967; UN Monthly Bulletin of Statistics, September 1968.

EMPLOYED CIVILIAN LABOUR FORCE BY MAIN SECTORS

Country	Year	Agriculture (000)	(%)	Industry (000)	(%)	Other (000)	(%)	Total (000)
Albania[1]	1963	45	18·0	118	47·3	87	34·7	250
Bulgaria[1]	1965	214	10·5	1,179	53·7	804	35·8	2,197
Czechoslovakia[1]	1966	1,360	20·5	3,090	46·8	2,158	32·7	6,608
East Germany	.	.	.	.	.	.	.	.
Hungary	1963	1,566	32·7	1,836	38·2	2,388	29·1	4,790
Jugoslavia	1961	4,748	57·0	1,834	22·0	1,758	21·0	8,340
Poland	1960	6,637	47·7	4,028	29·0	3,242	23·3	13,907
Rumania[1]	1967	570	11·8	2,438	50·3	1,834	37·9	4,843
Soviet Union[2]	1967	9,416	11·5	34,981	42·5	38,877	46·0	82,274
USA	1966	3,979	6	22,990	33	45,926	62	72,895
UK	1966	467	2	11,125	44	13,382	54	24,974

[1] Socialised Sector only.
[2] State sector only—excludes approximately 25 million collective farm workers.

Sources: Employment Yearbook, 1967 (ILO)
Statistical Yearbooks of Albania,
Bulgaria, Rumania and the SovietUnion.

NATIONAL PRODUCT

PER CAPITA NET MATERIAL PRODUCT AT MARKET PRICES 1960–6
(1963 = 100[1])

Country	1960	1961	1962	1963	1964	1965	1966
Albania	88	91	93	100	103	100	.
Bulgaria	87	89	94	100	109	116	128
Czechoslovakia	96	102	103	100	100	103	112
East Germany	94	97	100	100	104	112	118
Hungary	86	91	95	100	104	105	114
Jugoslavia	84	88	90	100	112	114	122
Poland	87	94	95	100	105	111	120
Rumania	81	88	92	100	111	121	132
Soviet Union	89	95	98	100	108	114	121
USA[2]	93	93	98	100	104	109	114
UK[3]	96	97	97	100	105	107	108

[1] Owing to varying weight-bases from country to country these figures should be interpreted with caution and taken to indicate general trends rather than precise annual changes.
[2] GDP at market prices.
[3] GDP at constant factor cost.

Source: *UN Yearbook, 1967*

ORIGIN OF NET MATERIAL PRODUCT 1966
(%)

Country	Agriculture	Industry	Construction	Transport and communications	Trade	Other
Albania	.	.	.	.	.	.
Bulgaria	35	45	8	4	6	2
Czechoslovakia	14	64	9	3	9	1
E. Germany	.	.	.	.	.	.
Hungary	22	56	10	5	6	1
Jugoslavia	30	35	7	7	16	6
Poland	22	52	9	6	9	2
Rumania	31	49	8	4	6	2
Soviet Union[1]	22	52	9	6	11	11
USA[2]	3	33	4	6	16	37
UK[3]	3	40	7	9	11	30

[1] 1965
[2] GDP at market prices ⎫ Not directly comparable with figures for Eastern Europe
[3] GDP at factor cost ⎭ which exclude all non-material production sectors.

Source: *UN Yearbook, 1967*

(Note: totals may not equal 100 because of rounding.)

EXPENDITURE ON NET MATERIAL PRODUCT 1966
(%)

Country	Individual consumption	Collective consumption	Net fixed capital formation	Increase in stocks	Net exports of goods and services
Albania	.	.	.	.	.
Bulgaria	64	7	16	19	—6
Czechoslovakia	65	19	12	12	4
East Germany	.	.	.	.	.
Hungary	73	3	13	9	2
Jugoslavia[1]	52	9	26	13	—1
Poland	64	10	18	8	0
Rumania	.	.	.	.	.
Soviet Union[2]	64	9	15	11	1
USA[3]	62	19	17	1	0
UK[3]	64	17	18	1	1

[1] GNP
[2] 1965
[3] GNP at market prices: Column 1: Private consumption. Column 2: General government consumption. Column 3: Gross fixed capital formation.

Source: *UN Yearbook, 1967*

WARSAW PACT DEFENCE EXPENDITURE, 1966–7

	Defence expenditure ($ million)	Defence expenditure per capita in $	GNP per capita	Defence expenditure as % of GNP in market prices
Bulgaria	208	25	630	3·9
Czechoslovakia	1270	89	1560	5·7
East Germany	975	57	1700	3·3
Hungary	300	29	1040	2·8
Poland	1589	50	940	5·3
Rumania	510	26	740	3·5
Soviet Union	29800	129	1450	8·9
Netherlands	782	63	1645	3·8

Source: quoted in Alastair Buchan, 'The Communist Military Potential in Europe', in *The Soviet Threat to Europe*, The Foreign Affairs Publishing Co. Ltd., Petersham, UK, 1969.

FOREIGN TRADE
EXCHANGE RATES OF COMECON CURRENCIES PER POUND STERLING

	Official Bank Rate	Official Tourist Rate	Free Market Rate (approx.)	Domestic Purchasing Power[1]
Albania (new lek)	12·00	30·00	—	—
Bulgaria (leva)	2·81	4·80	10	2·77
Czechoslovakia (kčs)	17·28	38·74	80–100	34·2
East Germany (ostmark)	10·00	10·00	—	—
Hungary (forint)	28·18	72·00	100–120	51·4
Jugoslavia (new dinar)	30·00	30·00	—	—
Poland (złoty)	9·60	57·60	200–250	53·3
Rumania (leu)	14·40	43·20	120–150	30·0
Soviet Union (rouble)	2·15	2·15	5–8	3·55

[1] Domestic purchasing power is calculated on the basis of figures given by the Deutsches Institut für Wirtschaftforschung in its *Wochenbericht* no. 24 of 12 June 1969 in the article 'Zur Kaufkraft einiger RGW-Länderwährungen'. The conversion into sterling was made at the rate of DM 1 = 2s 1d.

EXTERNAL TRADE 1967

Country	Imports $ million	Imports $ per head	Exports $ million	Exports $ per head	Balance[1] $ million
Albania	98[2]	.	60[2]	.	−38
Bulgaria	1,572	189	1,458	176	−114
Czechoslovakia	2,680	187	3,013	211	+333
East Germany	2,865[3]	179	2,898[3]	181	+33
Hungary	1,776	174	1,702	167	−74
Jugoslavia	1,707	84	1,252	61	−455
Poland	2,645	83	2,527	79	−118
Rumania	1,546	80	1,395	72	−151
Soviet Union	8,536	36	9,649	41	+1,113
USA	26,813	134	31,243	157	+4,430
UK	17,207	312	13,862	252	−3,345

[1] + denotes export surplus.
— denotes import surplus.
[2] 1964.
[3] 1966.

Source: *UN Monthly Bulletin of Statistics*, September 1968

TRADE OF THE SOVIET UNION, 1960 and 1967
(% of total)

Origin and destination	Imports		Exports	
	1960	1967	1960	1967
North America	1·3	2·4	0·5	0·6
Latin America	2·5	5·2	1·9	6·3
France	2·3	2·2	1·3	1·6
West Germany	3·6	2·1	2·2	2·1
Italy	1·6	1·8	1·9	2·5
All Common Market	8·3	8·0	6·8	7·8
UK	2·0	2·3	3·5	3·3
All EFTA	5·1	4·9	6·3	5·3
Rest of Western Europe	3·4	4·1	3·5	3·8
Total Western Europe	16·8	17·0	16·6	16·9
Bulgaria	5·3	9·1	6·1	8·3
Czechoslovakia	11·8	11·5	11·5	10·5
East Germany	16·7	16·6	19·2	15·4
Hungary	4·4	7·0	5·6	6·3
Jugoslavia	1·1	2·7	1·0	3·0
Poland	7·0	10·5	8·9	9·8
Rumania	5·0	5·1	4·9	4·2
Total Eastern Europe	51·2	62·5	57·2	57·5
Africa	3·2	2·8	1·8	4·3
Asia and Oceania	25·0	10·1	22·0	14·4
Total	100·0	100·0	100·0	100·0

Source: *UN Monthly Bulletin of Statistics*,
July 1968

TOTAL IMPORTS 1960-7
($ million[1], f.o.b.)

Country	1960	1961	1962	1963	1964	1965	1966	1967
Albania	81	72	65	71	98	.	.	.
Bulgaria	633	666	785	933	1,062	1,178	1,474	1,572
Czechoslovakia	1,816	2,024	2,070	2,160	2,429	2,672	2,736	2,680
East Germany[2]	1,981	2,047	2,212	2,133	2,377	2,546	2,865	.
Hungary[3]	976	1,026	1,149	1,306	1,495	1,521	1,568	1,776
Jugoslavia[3]	826	910	888	1,057	1,323	1,288	1,575	1,707
Poland	1,495	1,687	1,885	1,979	2,072	2,340	2,494	2,645
Rumania[3]	648	815	941	1,022	1,168	1,077	1,213	1,546
Soviet Union	5,630	5,828	6,455	7,059	7,736	8,058	7,913	8,536
USA	15,071	14,703	16,316	17,072	18,666	21,347	25,445	26,813
UK[3]	12,640	12,286	12,516	13,523	15,415	15,619	16,107	17,207

[1] Converted at a rate of 0·9 roubles per US dollar.
[2] Excludes trade with West Germany.
[3] Value c.i.f.

Source: *UN Yearbook, 1967;*
UN Monthly Bulletin of Statistics,
September 1968.

TOTAL EXPORTS, 1960–7
($ million[1], f.o.b.)

Country	1960	1961	1962	1963	1964	1965	1966	1967
Albania	49	49	41	48	60	.	.	.
Bulgaria	572	663	773	834	980	1,176	1,305	1,458
Czechoslovakia	1,930	2,046	2,194	2,462	2,576	2,689	2,745	3,013
East Germany[2]	1,966	2,062	2,167	2,470	2,666	2,776	2,898	.
Hungary	874	1,029	1,100	1,206	1,352	1,510	1,594	1,702
Jugoslavia	566	569	691	790	893	1,091	1,220	1,252
Poland	1,326	1,504	1,646	1,770	2,096	2,228	2,272	2,527
Rumania	717	793	816	915	1,000	1,102	1,186	1,395
Soviet Union	5,564	5,998	7,030	7,272	7,683	8,175	8,841	9,649
USA	20,412	20,791	21,446	23,104	26,280	27,189	30,013	31,243
UK	10,213	10,629	10,933	11,741	12,353	13,238	14,134	13,862

[1] Converted at a rate of 0·9 roubles per US dollar.
[2] Excludes trade with West Germany.

Source: *UN Yearbook, 1967;*
UN Monthly Bulletin of Statistics,
September 1968

c

INDUSTRY

INDICES OF INDUSTRIAL PRODUCTION[1], 1960–7
(*1963=100*)

Country	*1960*	*1961*	*1962*	*1963*	*1964*	*1965*	*1966*	*1967*
Albania	82	88	94	100	108	115	.	.
Bulgaria	73	81	91	100	111	127	142	162
Czechoslovakia	87	95	101	100	104	112	120	129
East Germany	85	90	96	100	106	112	119	127
Hungary	78	87	94	100	107	111	118	125
Jugoslavia	76	81	87	100	116	125	131	130
Poland	79	88	95	100	109	119	128	140
Rumania	68	78	89	100	114	129	143	163
Soviet Union	77	84	92	100	107	116	127	139
USA	87	88	95	100	106	115	126	127
UK[2]	95	96	97	100	108	111	112	112

[1] Excluding construction.
[2] Including construction.

Source: *UN Yearbook, 1967; UN Monthly Bulletin of Statistics*, September 1968

INDUSTRIAL PRODUCTION (MAJOR PRODUCTS), 1966
(*000 metric tons*)

Country	Pig iron	Crude steel	Aluminium	Cement	Cotton yarn	Plastics and resins	Paper (other than newsprint)
Albania	.	.	.	135	.	.	.
Bulgaria	874[1]	699	.	2,851	64	40	126[2]
Czechoslovakia	6,360[1]	9,128	62	6,130	112	145	642
East Germany	2,448	4,539	(50)	6,450	78	250	846
Hungary	1,641[1]	2,649	61	2,601	71	33	192
Jugoslavia	1,217[1]	1,867	42	3,232	93	62	372
Poland	5,856	9,850	55	10,040	193	132	764
Rumania	2,198	3,670	.	5,886	80	95	192[2]
Soviet Union	70,300	96,900	1,300	80,000	1,323	974	4,324
USA	85,278[1]	121,654	3,321	67,167	1,999	5,680	38,231[3]
UK	15,962	24,705	221	16,751	224	1,017	3,770[2]

[1] Including ferrous alloys.
[2] 1965.
[3] 1961.

Source: *UN Yearbook, 1967*

HOURS WORKED IN MANUFACTURING, 1961–6

Country	Period	1961	1962	1963	1964	1965	1966
Albania	.	.	.	.	.	.	.
Bulgaria	.	.	.	.	.	.	.
Czechoslovakia	w	40·7	40·7	40·5	40·8	40·8	39·6
East Germany	.	.	.	.	.	.	.
Hungary	m	179·1	178·2	178·6	179·2	178·6	179·3
Jugoslavia[1] [3]	m	199	198	204	206	201	196
Poland	d	7·8	7·7	7·9	7·9	7·9	7·9
Rumania	.	.	.	.	.	.	.
Soviet Union	w	40·3	40·3	40·2	40·4	40·1	40·3
USA[3]	w	39·8	40·4	40·5	41·7	41·2	41·3
UK[2]	w	46·8	46·2	46·8	46·9	46·1	45·0

[1] Less salaried employees.
[2] Males only.
[3] Hours paid for.

Source: *UN Yearbook, 1967*

(Note: d = per day, w = per week, m = per month)

ENERGY PRODUCTION, 1966

Country	Coal (000 metric tons)	Lignite (000 metric tons)	Crude petroleum (000 metric tons)	Natural gas (million cu. m.)	Electricity (million kwh)
Albania	.	300[1]	920	—	341[1]
Bulgaria	491	24,653	404	—	11,757
Czechoslovakia	26,728	74,108	190	851[1]	36,528
East Germany	1,987	249,040	—	116	56,866
Hungary	4,360	25,988	1,760	1,553	11,855
Jugoslavia	1,133	28,159	2,222	402	17,174
Poland	121,979	24,508	400	1,290	47,385
Rumania	4,822	6,649	12,825	18,616	20,806
Soviet Union	439,170	146,434	265,125	142,962	544,566
USA	492,548	3,521	409,170	487,239	1,248,232
UK	177,388	—	78	180	202,568

[1] 1965.

Source: *UN Yearbook, 1967*

AGRICULTURE

LAND UTILISATION, 1966

Country	Agricultural area (000 hectares)	Agricultural area (% of total area)	Arable land[1] (% of agricultural area)	Permanent meadows and pastures (% of agricultural area)
Albania[2]	1,230	42·8	40·7	59·3
Bulgaria	5,802	52·3	78·7	21·3
Czechoslovakia	7,144	55·9	75·2	24·8
East Germany	6,423	59·5	77·6	22·4
Hungary	6,927	74·4	81·5	18·5
Jugoslavia	14,716	57·5	56·2	43·8
Poland	19,947	63·8	78·6	21·4
Rumania	19,335	81·5	77·6	22·4
Soviet Union	614,100	27·4	39·2	60·8
USA[2]	440,201	47·0	40·9	59·1
UK	19,587	80·3	38·2	61·8

[1] Including land under permanent cultivation (orchards, vineyards, etc.).
[2] 1964.

Source: *FAO Production Yearbook, 1967*

AGRICULTURAL PRODUCTION, 1966
(000 metric tons)

Country	Wheat	Potatoes	Sugar beet	Milk	Meat	Eggs (million)
Albania	(115)	(31)	(160)	(187)	(47)	(70)
Bulgaria	3,193	421	(1,500)	1,501	356	1,438
Czechoslovakia	2,247	5,846	7,762	4,395	880	3,080
East Germany	1,521	12,823	6,611	6,887	(910)	3,894
Hungary	2,327	2,433	3,570	1,929	469	2,436
Jugoslavia	4,603	3,230	4,030	2,723	562	1,966
Poland	3,646	46,751	13,620	14,622	1,761	6,253
Rumania	5,065	3,323	4,368	3,854	580	2,814
Soviet Union	100,499	87,853	74,037	76,000	7,866	11,600
USA	35,699	13,921	18,454	54,535	14,786	66,456
UK	3,475	6,580	6,599	12,750	2,033	14,136

Source: *FAO Production Yearbook, 1967*

TRANSPORT

RAILWAYS, 1966

Country	Length of line (km.)	Passenger/km. (millions)	Ton/km. (millions)
Albania	151[1]	.	.
Bulgaria	4,094	5,119	11,449
Czechoslovakia	13,330	19,653	57,652
East Germany	15,730	17,386	45,743
Hungary	8,801	13,743	17,618
Jugoslavia	11,580	12,196	16,554
Poland	26,739	34,877	85,041
Rumania	11,007	14,652	34,541
Soviet Union	132,500	219,400	2,016,031
USA	340,400	27,620	1,090,162
UK	22,082	29,699	23,858

[1] 1965.

Source: *UN Yearbook, 1967*

MERCHANT SHIPPING, 1967
(*000 gross registered tons*)

Country	Total merchant ships	Of which, tankers
Albania	.	.
Bulgaria	470	134
Czechoslovakia	—	—
East Germany	756	.
Hungary	—	—
Jugoslavia	1,196	.
Poland	1,210	.
Rumania	245	—
Soviet Union	10,617	2,739
USA	20,333	4,544
UK	21,716	7,845

Source: *UN Yearbook, 1967*

INLAND WATERWAYS TRANSPORT, 1966

Country	Length of inland waterways in use (km.)	Ton/km. (million)
Albania	—	—
Bulgaria	471[2]	.
Czechoslovakia	473	.
East Germany	2,519[1]	2,556
Hungary	1,277	2,116
Jugoslavia	2,001	5,196
Poland	3,432	1,651
Rumania	1,673[2]	1,074
Soviet Union	142,700[1]	137,582[3]
USA	.	373,753[1]
UK	1,345	195

[1] 1965.
[2] 1964.
[3] 1961.

Sources: *UN Yearbook, 1967; UN Annual Bulletin of Transport Statistics, 1966*

CONSUMPTION

CONSUMER PRICE INDEX, 1960–6
(*1963 = 100*)[1]

Country	1960	1961	1962	1963	1964	1965	1966
Albania	.	.	.	.	.	.	.
Bulgaria[2]	94	95	98	100	100	100	100
Czechoslovakia	99	98	99	100	101	102	102
East Germany	99	99	100	100	100	100	100
Hungary	100	100	101	100	101	103	106
Jugoslavia	79	86	95	100	112	150	185
Poland	96	97	99	100	101	102	103
Rumania	.	.	.	.	.	.	.
Soviet Union[2]	99	98	99	100	100	99	99
USA	97	98	99	100	101	103	106
UK	91	94	98	100	103	108	112

[1] Owing to differences in bases of estimation these figures should only be taken as indicative of general trends.
[2] Index of state retail prices.

Source: *UN Yearbook, 1967*

INTERNAL CONSUMPTION OF BASIC PRODUCTS, 1966

Country	Primary energy[1] kg. per capita	Steel kg. per capita	Newsprint kg. per capita
Albania	331	.	.
Bulgaria	2,726	205	3·1
Czechoslovakia	5,641	545	3·1
East Germany	5,493	450	4·8[2]
Hungary	2,825	234	3·3
Jugoslavia	1,202	141	2·3
Poland	3,608	300	2·1
Rumania	2,072	213	2·7
Soviet Union	3,789	396	3·2
USA	9,595	667	41·9
UK	5,139	387	24·8

[1] Reduced to coal equivalent.
[2] 1965.

Source: *UN Yearbook, 1967*

SOCIAL STATISTICS

HEALTH SERVICES, 1965

Country	Doctors	Dentists	Pharmacists	No. of inhabitants per doctor
Albania	900	139	153	2,070
Bulgaria	13,593	2,882	1,725	600
Czechoslovakia	26,252	2,898	5,291	540
East Germany[1]	21,365	6,397	2,720	750
Hungary	16,162	2,040	4,066	630
Jugoslavia	16,240	3,544	3,310	1,200
Poland	39,613	11,510	10,072	800
Rumania	24,875	2,585	4,715	760
Soviet Union	485,000	25,500	.	480
USA	288,671	93,400	118,284	670
England and Wales	47,000	12,400	1,420[2]	.

[1] 1966.
[2] State Health Services only.

Source: *UN Yearbook, 1967*

HOUSING

Country	Year	No. of occupied dwellings (000)	Average no. of rooms per dwelling	persons per room
Albania	.	.	.	.
Bulgaria	1965	2,019	(3·2)	(1·2)
Czechoslovakia	1961	3,820	2·7	1·3
East Germany	1961	5,507	2·6	1·2
Hungary[1]	1963	2,844	(2·3)	(1·5)
Jugoslavia	1961	4,082	2·8	1·6
Poland[1]	1966	7,725	2·5	1·7
Rumania	.	.	.	.
Soviet Union	1960	(50,900)	(2·8)	(1·5)
USA	1960	53,024	4·9	0·7
England and Wales[1]	1966	14,977	5·5	0·6

[1] Results of sample survey.

Source: *UN Yearbook, 1967*

FACILITIES IN DWELLINGS

| Country | Year | % of dwelling units with | | |
		electricity	inside running water	bathroom
Albania	.	.	.	.
Bulgaria	1965	94·8	28·2	8·7
Czechoslovakia	1961	97·3	49·1	33·3
East Germany	1961	.	65·7	22·1
Hungary	1963	81·3	25·9	18·5
Jugoslavia	1961	54·5	.	.
Poland	1960	80·1	38·7	13·9
Rumania	.	.	.	.
Soviet Union	.	.	.	.
USA	1960	99·8	92·9	88·1
England and Wales	1966	.	98·7	85·1

Source: *UN Yearbook, 1967*

MOTOR VEHICLES IN USE, 1 January 1967

Country	Passenger cars	Commercial vehicles
Albania	.	.
Bulgaria	.	.
Czechoslovakia	.	151,500
East Germany	721,000	343,000[1]
Hungary	118,700	.
Jugoslavia	253,300	80,000
Poland	289,400	196,800
Rumania	.	.
Soviet Union[2]	926,000	3,465,000
USA	77,959,300	14,884,300
UK	9,867,300	1,764,300

[1] Including farm tractors.
[2] 1965.

Source: *UN Yearbook, 1967*

RADIOS, TELEVISIONS AND TELEPHONES IN USE,
1 January 1967

Country	Radio receivers (000)	Radio receivers (per 000 population)	TV receivers (000)	TV receivers (per 000 population)	Telephones (000)	Telephones (per 000 population)
Albania[1]	130	68	(1)	(0·6)	10[3]	6
Bulgaria	2,144	260	288	35	306	37
Czechoslovakia	3,827	269	2,375	167	1,583	112
East Germany	5,812	340	3,559	208	1,724	101
Hungary	2,485	244	996	98	597	59
Jugoslavia	3,200	162	800	41	452	23
Poland	5,593	176	2,540	80	1,411	45
Rumania	2,925	152	712	37	510	27
Soviet Union	76,800	330	19,000	81	6,600[2]	28
USA	262,700	1,330	74,100	376	98,789	502
UK	16,432	300	13,919	254	11,289	206

[1] 1965.
[2] 1964.
[3] 1963 (Source: *Albanian Statistical Yearbook*).

Source: *UN Yearbook, 1967*

NATIONALITIES IN THE SOVIET UNION: 1959 CENSUS.

TOTAL POPULATION OF THE SOVIET UNION 208,826,650.

S	Russians	114,113,579	F	Hungarians		154,738
S	Ukrainians	37,252,930		Gypsies		132,014
S	Belorussians	7,913,488				
				Peoples of the North		127,155
T	Uzbeks	6,015,416		*of which*		
T	Tatars	4,967,701	Tg	Evenki		24,710
T	Kazakhs	3,621,610	F	Nenets		
T	Azeris	2,939,728		(Yurak Samoyed)		23,007
O	Armenians	2,786,912	F	Khanti (Ostyak)		19,410
C	Georgians	2,691,950	A	Chukchi		11,727
O	Lithuanians	2,326,094	Tg	Eveni (Lamut)		9,121
	Jews	2,267,814	Tg	Nanai		8,026
O	Moldavians	2,214,139	F	Mansi (Vogul)		6,449
O	Germans	1,619,655	A	Koryaks		6,287
T	Chuvash	1,469,766	F	Selkups		3,768
O	Latvians	1,399,539	A	Nivkhi (Gilyak)		3,717
I	Tadzhiks	1,396,939	Tg	Ulchi (Olchi)		2,055
S	Poles	1,380,282	F	Lapps		1,792
F	Mordvins	1,285,116	Tg	Udegei (Udekhe)		1,444
T	Turkmens	1,001,585		Eskimo		1,118
T	Bashkir	989,040	A	Itelmen (Kamchatkan)		1,109
F	Estonians	988,616		Kety (Yenisei Ostyak)		1,019
T	Kirghiz	968,659	Tg	Orochi		782
	Daghestanis	944,213	F	Nganasan (Tavgy Samoyed)		748
	of which		A	Yukagir		442
C	Avars	270,394	A	Aleuts		421
C	Lezghians	223,129				
C	Darghins	158,149	T	Gagauz		123,821
T	Kumyks	134,967	O	Rumanians		106,366
C	Laks	63,529	M	Kalmycks		106,066
T	Nogay	38,583	C	Ingush		105,980
C	Tabasaran	34,700	T	Tuvinians		100,145
C	Tsakhur	7,321	T	Uigur		95,208
C	Rutul	6,723	F	Finns		92,717
C	Agul	6,709	T	Karachai		81,403
			C	Adyghei		79,631
F	Udmurt (Votyak)	624,794	C	Abkhaz		65,430
F	Mari (Cheremiss)	504,205	I	Kurds		58,799
F	Komi and		T	Khakass		56,584
	Komi-Permyak	430,928	T	Altai		45,270
	of which		T	Balkar		42,408
F	Komi (Zyryen)	287,027	T	Turks		35,306
F	Komi-Permyak	143,901	C	Circassians		30,453
				Chinese		25,781
C	Chechens	418,756	S	Czechs		24,557
I	Ossetes	412,592		Dungans		
S	Bulgarians	324,251		(Chinese Muslims)		21,928
	Koreans	313,735		Aisori (Assyrians)		21,803
O	Greeks	309,308	I	Iranians		20,766
M	Buryats	252,959	C	Abaza		19,591
T	Yakuts	236,655	F	Vepse		16,374
C	Kabardinians	203,620	T	Shorians		15,274
T	Karakalpak	172,556	S	Slovaks		14,674
F	Karelians	167,278		Tats (Mountain Jews)		11,463
				Arabs		7,987

31

I	Beludzhi	7,842	T	Tofalar (Karagass)	586
T	Karaim	5,727		Other nationalities	17,163
O	Albanians	5,258			
S	Jugoslavs	4,998			
C	Udin	3,678		KEY	
O	Spaniards	2,446	S	Slavic peoples	
I	Afghans	1,855	I	Iranian peoples	
M	Mongols	1,774	O	Other Indo-European peoples	
O	Italians	1,158	T	Turkic peoples	
F	Ingrians	1,062	M	Mongol peoples	
O	French	1,013	Tg	Tungusic peoples	
	Japanese	961	F	Finno-Ugrian and Uralic peoples	
	Vietnamese	838	C	Palaeo-Caucasian peoples	
			A	Palaeo-Asiatic peoples	

MINORITIES IN EASTERN EUROPE

Some of the countries involved do not publish exact figures; in these cases approximations have been used.

Albania

Greeks	35,000	Kutuzo-Vlachs	35,000

Bulgaria

Turks	747,000	Pomaks[2]	160,000
Macedonians[1]	200,000	Armenians	23,000

Notes: 1 The 1956 census gave 187,860 Macedonians; the 1965 census only 8,750.
      2 Pomaks are Bulgarian-speaking Muslims.

Czechoslovakia

Hungarians[1]	541,000	Poles	60,000
Germans	125,000	Ruthenes[2]	80,000

Notes: 1 Hungarian minority sources claim with some justification that the number
      of Hungarians in Czechoslovakia is nearer 700,000.
      2 Ruthene minority sources claim that all individuals of the Eastern Orthodox
      faith are assimilated Ruthenes and that their total number is about 150,000.

East Germany

	Sorbs	30,000

Hungary

Germans	220,000	South Slavs	100,000
Slovaks	110,000	Rumanians	25,000

Jugoslavia

Albanians[1]	1,100,000	Czechs	30,331
Hungarians	504,386	Turks	182,964
Slovaks	86,433	Bulgarians	62,624
Rumanians	60,682	Germans[2]	25,000
Italians	25,615	Ruthenes	40,000

Notes: 1 In 1961, the year of the last census, there were 914,760 Albanians. It has
      since been officially estimated that through very high birth rate their
      number has risen to the figure given above.

      2 The Germans are not officially recognised as a nationality, but it is estimated
      that there are between 20,000–30,000 still in Jugoslavia.

Poland

Ukrainians	200,000	Slovaks	25,000
Belorussians	200,000	Lithuanians	20,000
Russians	150,000	Czechs	5,000
Germans[1]	30,000	Greeks[2]	9,000

Notes: 1 West German sources claim some 140,000 Germans still in Poland.
     2 The Greeks are refugees from the Civil War.

Rumania

Hungarians[1]	1,602,604	Czechs, Slovaks	35,152
Germans[2]	376,752	Turks	14,329
South Slavs[3]	46,517	Tatars	20,469
Ukrainians	60,479	Bulgarians	12,040
Russians	38,731		

Notes: 1 The figures for Hungarians and Germans were taken from the 1966 census; figures for the other nationalities were not available, hence the 1956 census was used.
     2 There has been a steady loss of Germans through emigration to West Germany.
     3 Mostly Serbs, but includes a few Croats and Slovenes.

In addition to the nationalities mentioned above, there are still Gypsies and a considerable number of Jews in Rumania. It was not thought worth giving the 1956 figures for these, as those for Gypsies are notoriously inaccurate by reason of the Gypsies' nomadic habits and high birth rate and as regards the Jews, because there has been a steady decline through emigration to Israel.

BASIC INFORMATION

ALBANIA

GEOGRAPHY

Features: Albania, the smallest country in Eastern Europe and approximately the size of Belgium, is situated on the Adriatic coast of the Balkan Peninsula and is bounded to the north and east by Jugoslavia and to the south by Greece. Three-quarters of the territory is mountainous and there are elevations of over 8,000 ft/ 2,400 m. in the North Albanian Alps, the Korab Mountains and the Morava and Grámmos Ranges, all of which constitute a part of the Dinaric mountain system. Much of the marshy coastal plain is lacustrine in origin.

Animal grazing on the lower slopes has reduced the once prevalent forest (oak, beech, chestnut, pine), and sheep-rearing and the cultivation of maize, tobacco, wheat, sugarbeet and wine represent the chief economic activities of this predominantly agricultural country. There is a limited production of brown coal, chrome, oil and other minerals. The principal centres of settlement and industry are widely dispersed, but Albania's terrain inhibits both internal and external communication.
Area: 10,600 sq. miles/28,700 sq. km.
Mean max. and min. temperatures: Durrës (41°N, 19°E; 25 ft/8 m.) 79°F/26°C (July) 47°F/8°C (Jan.); Shkodër (42°N, 19°E; 30 ft/9 m.) 77°F/25°C (July) 39°F/4°C (Jan.).
Relative humidity: Durrës 81%; Shkodër 82%.
Mean annual rainfall: Durrës 43 in./1,090 mm.; Shkodër 57 in./1,450 mm.

POPULATION

Total population (1965 est.): 1,865,000.
Chief towns and populations: (1964 est.) Tirana (157,000); Durrës/Durrsi (It. Durazzo) (48,000); Shkodër/Shkodra (It. Scutari) (47,000); Vlorë/Vlonë (It. Valona) (47,000).
Ethnic composition: Gegs (in North Albania) comprise 65% and Tosks (in South Albania) 33% of the population. The largest non-Albanian minority are Greeks (0·5%).
Language: Albanian, the official language adopted in 1909, is based on the northern (Geg) and southern (Tosk) dialects of the country.
Religion: In the early 1960s about 65% of the population were nominally Muslim (Sunni and Bektashi), 25% Albanian Orthodox and 10% Roman Catholic, but public worship has been practically abolished with the official closure of churches and mosques.

RECENT HISTORY

Albania was liberated from the Italians in 1944 and the following year the Western allies recognised the provisional government under the communist Secretary-General, Enver Hoxha, on condition that it held free elections. Amidst a savage purge of anti-communists, the subsequent elections resulted in a communist-dominated assembly. The UK and the USA broke relations with Hoxha, and their veto of Albania's admission to the UN was not lifted till 1955. In 1946 Albania was declared a People's Republic and King Zog was formally deposed.

Until 1948 the Albanian communists were largely controlled from Jugoslavia and the two countries formed a monetary and customs union. But following the

37

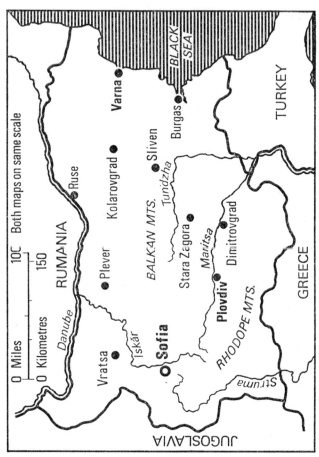

ALBANIA AND BULGARIA

Soviet-Jugoslav schism Albania aligned itself with the Soviet Union against the Titoist deviationists and executed pro-Jugoslav members of the party, incuding Koci Xoxe, chief of the secret police. By 1950 the Albanian-Jugoslav Treaty had been abrogated, diplomatic links severed and Jugoslav officials replaced by Soviet officials.

Of all East European states Albania has most resisted internal change and old Stalinists still constitute today's leadership. In 1956 Albania acceded to membership of the Warsaw Pact and was visited in 1959 by Khrushchev, but de-Stalinisation in Soviet bloc countries and the *rapprochement* between the Soviet Union and Jugoslavia drew a negative response in Tirana. In the late 1950s Albania increasingly aligned itself with China and after the Twenty-second Congress of the CPSU in 1961, at which Chou En-lai alone defended Albania, the Soviet Union withdrew economic and technical aid, evacuated its submarine base at Vlorë and broke off diplomatic relations. While Albania has ceased to be an effective member of Comecon and formally withdrew from the Warsaw Pact in 1968, it has received material aid from Peking in return for active support of Chinese interests at the UN and elsewhere. With its two neighbours contacts are minimal. Party rivalries deriving from Tito's post-war domination of the Albanian CP and the thorny issue of the Shiptar minority in southern Serbia (Kosmet) have so far precluded a reconciliation, and with the Greeks, who claim nearly one-half of its territory (as northern Epirus), Albania remains technically at war. Improved relations subsist nonetheless with some other countries of Europe. In 1963 Rumania reestablished relations, as did Italy in 1964 and France in 1965. Austria and Turkey also maintain ties.

Internally, however, Stalinism prevails in the persons of Party Secretary Hoxha and Prime Minister Mehmet Shehu and in their strictly orthodox administration of the economy, secret police and culture. China's Great Proletarian Cultural Revolution appears scarcely to have affected Albania, but in 1966 a campaign of Great Revolutionary Action was introduced to streamline administrative efficiency by means of ministerial reorganisation and limited decentralisation. With its high birth and death rates and extreme poverty, Albania is probably the least developed state in Europe.

Defence (1967): Military service is compulsory, for two years in the army and three years in the navy and air force. The rank system was abolished in 1966 (on the Chinese model) and political commissars reintroduced. Strength is estimated at: army 30,000, navy 3,000, air force 5,000, para-military forces 12,500. Albania formally withdrew from the Warsaw Pact in 1968 after six years of inactive membership. Naval and military agreements have been reached with China.

ECONOMY

Background: A backward agricultural country before World War II, Albania has since the break with the Soviet Union in 1961 steadily pursued an industrialisation policy with Chinese technical and financial assistance. From 1961 to 1965 national income increased on average by an annual rate of 5·7%. The current 1966–70 plan envisages a growth rate of from 7·4% to 8·2%; actual growth in 1966 was 9% and 7·5% in 1967, with a rise in industrial production of 12·8%. Priority is being given to agriculture, electricity generation, engineering and non-ferrous metallurgy. The Chinese have financed and equipped new power stations, a radio station, engineering works and a large copper wire factory at Shkodër. Elbasan is now the chief industrial town. In 1968 credit from China amounted to about 18% of national income.

Agriculture is almost entirely socialised with 80·5% of the cultivated area in the hands of collective farms and 18·1% as state farms. Production rose 5·2% annually for 1961 to 1965 and in 1967 by 12% following a record harvest in 1966. Main crops are maize, sugarbeet, wheat and potatoes. A large-scale land reclamation scheme is under way together with mechanisation and increased use of fertilisers, production of which expanded five-fold in 1967.

Foreign trade: Albania withdrew from Comecon in 1962 and now trades primarily with China. New export industries are being developed with Chinese aid, notably chrome, nickel and copper mining, petroleum products, timber and fruit and vegetables. In 1965 $11 million worth of goods were imported from Western Europe, mainly machinery and cereals. Albania exports craft products such as raffia work, handkerchieves and briar pipes.

Employment: Agriculture absorbs a large proportion of the labour force. Population is growing at the fastest rate of any European country (about 3 % a year) and the new demands for industrial labour should be satisfied. Technicians are being trained in China, and Chinese specialists are helping to train workers and managers in the new enterprises.

Consumption: Standards of living have risen substantially in recent years with a steady growth in retail trade turnover (7% increase in 1966). Supplies of consumer goods, especially textiles, foodstuffs and footwear have improved and there was a 13% gain in light industry output in 1967. However, per capita consumption of energy, ownership of consumer durables and availability of social services are the lowest in Eastern Europe. In February 1969 a 38% increase in military expenditure was announced; this burden must inevitably reduce prospects of advances in social expenditure in the coming years.

SOCIAL WELFARE

A new state Social Insurance Law came into force in 1967. Social insurance is non-contributory for all workers except lawyers and members of craft guilds and fishing cooperatives who are eligible for all benefits but on a contributory basis. All social security benefits are tax-free.

Health services: Notable improvements in Albania's health services have been made in recent years and the former chronic incidence of malaria, TB, trachoma and other endemic diseases has been radically reduced. There are 90 hospitals today. Free medical services are granted to all citizens. As sickness benefit most workers are entitled to 85% of average earnings if service has exceeded ten years (70% if less) while miners are entitled to 95% in the case of more than five years service (80% if less). In the case of occupational disease or injury the worker receives 95% of earnings (miners 100%) regardless of service record. Disabled workers, on the recommendation of the Medical Workers Committee, fall into one of four categories for which the disability pension is fixed at 85%, 70%, 60% and 40% of earnings respectively. Various bonuses are granted to special categories of invalid pensioner (e.g. a monthly supplement of 100 leks to the permanently incapacitated veteran of the 'War of National Liberation'). During the 84-day maternity leave the expectant mother is entitled to 95% of earnings if she has worked over five years, 75% if under five years. A worker, pensioner or student receives a bonus of 280 leks on the live birth of a child.

Pensions and other benefits: All employment since 1912 (save high-ranking administrative posts under former governments) counts as employment qualifying the worker for pensions. Also counted is work abroad of a 'progressive' kind and political exile or imprisonment during the Zog era. Time spent in the people's armed forces is counted as double time. Pensions and benefits are calculated on the basis of average monthly earnings, during the preceding year (or, at applicant's request, during any three-year period within the previous twelve years). For old-age benefits the pensionable age varies according to three categories of employment and length of service, but as a rule the age is 65 for men, 60 for women, and the pension calculated at 70% of earnings at the time of retirement (within the limits of 350 to 900 leks monthly). Partial old-age pensions (at not less than half the full retirement benefit) are granted to certain categories of men retiring at 60 and women at 55 and special merit pensions may be awarded to distinguished men retiring at 55 and women at 50, and to their dependants. Family pensions payable to non-working dependants of a worker who dies in (or within two years of) employment, range from 65% of earnings for families comprising three or more dependants, to 40% of earnings to one dependant. The orphan is entitled to a family pension computed on the basis of both parents' earnings. A worker attending a sick spouse or dependant is entitled to a compassionate leave benefit of 60% of earnings for up to three days (or ten days in each three months if the invalid is under seven years of age). A funeral allowance of 300 leks is paid to the family in the case of death of a worker or pensioner or of a dependant/spouse of his/hers.

Housing: Between 1945 and 1962 the state built 28,000 urban apartments and 47,000 rural dwellings. 20,000 new units were scheduled for the third five year plan (1961–5) at the cost of six-and-a-half million leks (or 75% more than during the second five year plan). State credits are available to cooperatives and to individuals and Albania claims to have the world's lowest rents.

EDUCATION

All educational institutions are ultimately supervised by the Ministry of Education and Culture, with the exception of the Higher Institute of Agriculture which comes under the Ministry of Agronomy. The executive committees of district people's councils provide administration at primary and secondary levels. Schooling is officially compulsory for children aged six to 13 but in more inaccessible areas is not easily enforced. The system has been greatly expanded since World War II. Education is free.

Primary education: This consists of compulsory seven-year school leading to the seven-year school leaving certificate.

Secondary and vocational education: This consists of four divisions: (a) the three to four-year general secondary school which forms the secondary extension of an eleven-year course and mixes academic studies with polytechnical training: (b) the three to four-year vocational school which emphasises practical and specialised instruction; (c) the four-year teacher-training school; (d) the three-year school of physical education. The first three categories provide leaving certificates or diplomas on the basis of which the pupil can proceed to higher institutions.

University and higher education: Albania's only university, at Tirana, was founded in 1957, and has seven faculties plus two associated institutes (of historical research and ethnology). There are in addition higher institutes of agriculture, fine arts, drama and music (Tirana), of zootechnics (Shkodër) and two teacher-training colleges (Tirana, Shkodër). The student at the university and higher institutes (excepting the two-year teacher-training colleges) takes four or five years to obtain his diploma. Written examinations in the area of specialisation are complemented by oral tests in general subjects.

Educational institutions (1965–6)

	Institutions	Staff	Students
Eleven-year primary/general secondary	3,404	392,511	14,169
Other secondary	51	927	23,991
Higher	8	959	12,761

Adult education: Basic and remedial courses for workers are provided at primary and secondary levels; the higher institutions organise evening and correspondence courses for those who have completed secondary school and are employed. In the latter case curricula are as for day students but require an extra year of study. Paid study leave is granted annually to all extra-mural students at the higher level.

MASS MEDIA

The press (1967): (Tirana).[1]

Dailies: Zëri i Popullit, Labour Party, 76,000; *Bashkimi,* Democratic Front; *Puna,* trade union.

Periodicals: Zëri i Rinisë (bi-weekly), Youth Union; *Ylli* (m), illustrated; *Drita* (irregular), literary/art; *10 Korriku* (w), military; *Hosteni* (irreg.), satirical; *Ekonomia Popullore* (w), economic; *Kultura Popullore* (m), cultural; *Letërsia Jonë* (m), literary; *Nendori* (q), literary; *Shqiptarja e Re,* woman's; *Llaiko,* Democratic Front, in Greek; *Shqipëria e Re* (f), Cttee. for Foreign Cultural Relations, in Chinese, Fren, Eng., Russian; *New Albania* and *Bulletin d'Information* (irreg.), govt. and Labour Pty.

[1] Circulation figures generally unavailable.

Broadcasting: The state-controlled radio, centred at Tirana, broadcasts from Kukësi, Shkodër, Korçë and Gjirokastër. Transmissions are also made in 13 foreign languages, and in Albanian for the Shiptar minority in Jugoslavia. There are experimental state TV broadcasts three evenings a week.

CONSTITUTIONAL SYSTEM

Constitution: The Soviet-type constitution of the People's Republic of Albania, revised in 1950, dates from 1946.

Legislature: The unicameral National Assembly which sits at least twice a year is the highest legislative organ and consists of 240 deputies (representing 8,000 inhabitants each) elected for four years by all citizens over 18 years of age. In the 1966 elections practically 100% of the electorate voted for the single-state candidates nominated by the Albanian Democratic Front. The Assembly appoints the nominally subordinate Praesidium, or collective presidency, comprising a president, three vice-presidents, a secretary and ten members. This includes (1968) the party leader and three other members of the party's Central Committee. It convenes the National Assembly and exercises the functions of the latter between sessions, represents the state in international affairs, interprets the law, issues decrees, ratifies treaties, grants pardon, awards honours, appoints diplomats, may declare war and hold referenda.

Executive: Highest executive authority is vested in the Council of Ministers which is elected by the National Assembly and theoretically responsible to it. Its members comprise (1968) a chairman, three vice-chairmen, twelve ministers and the president of the State Planning Commission. Six of these including the chairman hold concurrent membership of the party Central Committee. The Council directs state administration, may rule by decree and generally exercises considerable legislative power.

Local government: Albania is divided into 26 districts (*rrethe*) and the capital city of Tirana and subdivided into 140 communities (*lokaliteteve*). Each unit is administered by a people's council, directly elected in the districts for a three-year term and in the communities for two years. These appoint executive committees from amongst the council membership.

Judiciary: Civil and criminal justice is administered through the Supreme Court (whose judges are elected for four years by the National Assembly) and through the people's courts of districts and communities (whose judges and magistrates are locally elected for a three-year term and may be recalled). The lower courts are tribunals of first and second instance. The procurator-general and his deputies, appointed by the National Assembly, heads a separate body charged with supervision of administrative legality and with criminal prosecution. Forty-one offences are punishable by death.

Basic rights: These include social services and qualified freedom of speech, press, assembly, worship and artistic and scientific endeavour.

Party: Albania's sole party, the Labour (Communist) Party, has 67,000 members (1966). The first secretary of the praesidium of the party Central Committee is also president of the Democratic Front, a mass organisation which arranges elections and nominates candidates.

Leading government and party figures: Haxhi Lleshi (titular president), Mehmet Shehu (prime minister), Enver Hoxha (party first secretary and member of Praesidium), Beqir Balluku (defence minister and deputy prime minister), Haki Toska and Adil Çarçani (deputy prime ministers), Nesti Nase (foreign minister), Kiço Ngjela (foreign trade minister).

BULGARIA

GEOGRAPHY

Features: Bulgaria, one of the smallest of the communist countries, occupies the north-eastern part of the Balkan Peninsula and is divided in two by the Balkan Mountains (*Stara Planxina*) which extend on an east-west axis to the Sofia depression. The highest relief, however, comprises the Rila Range (Mt. Musala 9,590 ft/2,920m.) with its southern continuation, the Pirin Mountains and its south-eastern spur, the Rhodopes. Neighbouring states are Rumania, Jugoslavia, Greece and Turkey.

The Danubian Plain, or Bulgarian Plateau, stretches northwards to the Danube, which forms a political frontier with Rumania, and is dissected by loess-covered valleys. The Iskăr Valley in the west and Shipka Pass in the east provide the traditional crossing of the Balkan Mountains to the broad Maritsa Valley in southern Bulgaria. The climate is of the transitional continental-Mediterranean type.

Of the total land area, 41% is agricultural, 33% is forest and 26% unproductive. The two plains, north and south of the Balkan Range respectively, are extremely fertile. Wheat and maize (especially in the Danubian Plain) and tobacco, fruit and wines (notably in the Maritsa Valley) are the chief crops, but there is considerable cultivation of rye, barley, oats, vegetables and cotton. Wool, dairy and meat production are well distributed.

Lignite and some reserves of bituminous coal are mined in the Tvurditsa and Dimitrovgrad regions; oilfields have been found on the north-eastern coast.

The Sofia depression in the west forms the population, communications and manufacturing hub of the country, but Plovdiv, Pernik, Pleven and the port cities of Burgas and Ruse are industrially important. Tourism is being rapidly developed on Bulgaria's 150 m./250 km. of Black Sea coast, notably along the Dobrudjan shore around Varna.

Area: 42,800 sq. miles/111,000 sq. km.
Mean max. and min. temperatures: Sofia (43°N, 23°E; 1,805 ft/550 m.) 69°F/21°C (July) 28°F/–2°C (Jan.); Varna (43°N, 28°E; 115 ft/35 m.) 74°F/23°C (July) 34°F/1°C (Jan.)
Relative humidity: Sofia 82%; Varna 83%.
Mean annual rainfall: Sofia 25 in./635 mm.; Varna 19 in./485 mm.

POPULATION

Total population (1965 est.): 8,200,000.
Chief towns and populations (1965 est.): Sofia (801,000), Plovdiv (220,000), Varna (150,000), Ruse (120,000), Burgas (95,000).
Ethnic composition: 87% of the population are Bulgarian, 10% Turkish, 3% gypsies.
Language: The official language is Bulgarian.
Religion: About 87% are nominally Bulgarian Orthodox, 12% Muslim (of whom 10% are Turkish and 3% Bulgarian-speaking Pomaks).

RECENT HISTORY

Although Bulgaria had been at war with the UK and the USA since 1941, it retained diplomatic relations with the Soviet Union until the latter declared war on Bulgaria

(8 September 1944). At the very moment when a new pro-allied coalition under the Agrarian Party's Konstantin Muraviev was framing a democratic programme which would have reversed Bulgaria's axis alignments, a Soviet-supported grouping of communists and other left-wing parties, the Fatherland Front, was installed as a government under Kimon Georgiev (9 September 1944). Henceforth the Bulgarian forces operated against Germany under Soviet command and several key government positions became a communist monopoly. Special committees and a people's militia (under Anton Yugov) conducted the most ruthless purge of opponents, including several thousand executions. In consequence the communists and their allies within the Front obtained a majority in the 1946 general elections although the surviving opposition managed still to win 30% of the vote. King Simeon II having been deposed and exiled, the government of the new people's republic was placed in the hands of Georgi Dimitrov, a former secretary-general of the Comintern.

In 1947 the opposition Agrarian Union was in effect dissolved and its leader, Nikola Petkov, executed. In 1948 the smaller parties were either abolished or merged in the Fatherland Front with the Bulgarian Communist Party and the Agricultural People's Union. For 14 years Bulgaria was ruled by Stalinists and the tradition of a Russo-Bulgarian connexion based on linguistic, cultural and historical affinities reinforced by the closest party link.

Dimitrov died in 1949 and his brother-in-law the party secretary-general, Vălko Chervenkov, became prime minister until succeeded in 1956 by Yugov who, two years later, attempted an unsuccessful rapid industrialisation programme coterminous with China's Great Leap Forward. Both Chervenkov and Yugov were expelled from the party's Central Committee in 1962 when Todor Zhivkov, chief architect of Bulgarian de-Stalinisation and party first secretary since 1953, became prime minister; several hundred political prisoners were released. Zhivkov, a protégé of Khrushchev, has since had to contend with a number of party dissensions, including, in 1965, an allegedly pro-Chinese army conspiracy. But in the 1966 general elections the unopposed communist candidates and their allies were nonetheless returned to power under his continuing government and party leadership.

Of all East European states, Bulgaria can make the best claim to a special, if dependent, relationship with the Soviet Union, more recently bolstered by party allegiances and extensive Soviet economic and technical aid. Sofia was in 1964 the only East European capital not officially to question the manner of the removal of Khrushchev. Bulgaria's foreign policy has likewise reflected Soviet attitudes, especially within the Balkan context. Relations with Jugoslavia, so long exacerbated by the Macedonian problem, improved as a result of the 1956 *rapprochement* between Belgrade and Moscow and a more conciliatory approach to Greece (in such matters as war reparations and an Aegean sea-outlet) and to Turkey (concerning the Turkish minority in Bulgaria and trade) restimulated an interest in regional co-operation, at least until the invasion of Czechoslovakia (August 1968)—in which Bulgarian troops participated—reactivated certain regional tensions.

Defence (1967): Military service is compulsory for two years in the army and three years in the navy and air force. Strengths of the defence forces: army 125,000, navy 7,000, air force 22,000. Para-military forces number 20,000, people's militia 150,000. The 1966 defence expenditure was $208 million representing 3·9% of GNP. Bulgaria is a member of the Warsaw Pact and there are no Soviet divisions on Bulgarian territory.

ECONOMY

Background: The development of the Bulgarian economy is progressing at a rapid pace with most sectors responding to the new forms of economic management introduced gradually since 1965. National income increased by 11% in 1966 and 9% in 1967, higher than the average growth of 8·5%, provided for under the 1966–70 plan. The plan calls for a change of emphasis from agriculture to industry, transport and construction. Investment increased by 24% in 1966 and by 15·6% in 1967, when 35% of national income was invested. Ferrous metallurgy, energy production and engineering were the most dynamic branches of industry.

The reform has advanced more slowly than planned. Wholesale and retail trade units are being merged to form unified trade organisations which can enter into free contracts with producer units. Wholesale prices are being revised to bring prices into line with costs, and with world prices in export industries. Profitability is playing an increasing role as a performance indicator. Large vertically integrated trusts are also being established to assist with decentralisation of production and investment decisions.

Agriculture, although declining, is relatively important and continues to advance in output and productivity. Output rose by 15% in 1966 but only by 1% in 1967. A 5·4% average growth rate is envisaged in the current plan, accompanied by a 10% decline in the rural labour force. Main crops are wheat, sugarbeet, maize and potatoes. Wine growing and horticulture are both being expanded as major export branches. There have been signs of strain in the economy with raw material shortages and labour problems. Employment plans have been exceeded by wide margins and difficulties experienced in adapting rural labour to industrial conditions.

Foreign trade: Bulgaria is heavily dependent on trade with other Comecon countries (80% of all trade). Imports from Western Europe have risen substantially in recent years, however, mainly from Italy, West Germany and Austria. Sales of agricultural products account for one-third of Bulgarian exports. Problems have been met in expanding foreign exchange earnings and tourism is being promoted to facilitate purchases of Western machinery. In 1967 there were 1·8 million visitors compared with only 15,000 in 1960.

Employment: The industrial labour force has grown rapidly, by 7·4% in 1968 and 4·9% in 1967. A considerable labour reserve remains in the agricultural sector.

Prices and wages: Real wages rose by 9% in both 1966 and 1967. Agricultural workers have benefited from a preferential policy designed to equalise rural and urban earnings checking the outflow of rural labour. Productivity has improved, but has barely kept pace with wage increases.

Consumption: Recent advances in both industry and agriculture have led to improvements in living standards, although they are still low in comparison with other East European countries. Retail trade turnover increased by 8·4% and 11·5% in 1966 and 1967 respectively. Consumer durables are now more freely available with annual advances of over 40% in the supply of TV sets, refrigerators and cars. Money incomes have risen very sharply and problems of market equilibrium have become evident, as indicated by a marked rise in personal savings in 1967 and 1968. The existence of a large trade deficit with Western Europe has resulted in a diversion of food products to foreign markets accompanied by sharp price increases in 1968 and early in 1969.

SOCIAL WELFARE

The Central Council of Trade Unions directs all social security save health services (*viz.*) and pensions, which come within the jurisdiction of the Ministry of Finance. All contributions are paid by the employer enterprise, institution or organisation, except for the liberal professions, and their payment is included in the state budget.

The following data refer to 1967–8 unless otherwise stated.

Health Services: Public health is supervised by the Ministry of Public Health and Social Welfare, financed from state budget allocations and administered by the district people's councils through their departments of public health. Free health facilities are available to all citizens; patients pay only for medicine acquired in cases of out-patient treatment. After three months of service a worker is entitled to paid sick-leave. Compensation for accidents at work is paid immediately. For temporary disablement, indemnities range between 60% and 90% of the worker's wage, depending upon his length of service. Disablement benefits depend on the degrees of disablement and income and range between 35% and 100% of the worker's wage. Working women are entitled to 120 days of paid leave for pregnancy and childbirth.

Bulgaria possesses a total of 1,230 general and specialised hospitals and maternity homes. Out-patient aid and consultation are provided by polyclinics attached to city hospitals or organised on a regional basis in the countryside. In addition, a separate network of polyclinics and hospitals serves workers in industrial, mining, transport and building enterprises. Formerly endemic diseases such as malaria, typhoid and infantile paralysis have been practically eradicated.

Pensions and other benefits: Pension rates are determined on the basis of the remuneration received during three successive years in the last ten years of service. Old age pensions are granted according to the category of work. Workers in the first category, which includes the hardest jobs, are pensioned off after 15 years of service and at the age of 45 for women and 50 for men; those of the second category after 20 years of service and at the age of 50 for women and 55 for men; those of the third category after 20 years of service and at the age of 55 for women, and after 25 years of service and at the age of 60 for men. The rate of pensions ranges from 55% to 80% of wages and may be increased by 12% for years of service beyond the statutory work span. Dependants of a deceased insured worker are entitled to life insurance payment and a pension. The latter is paid to the amount of 50% for one dependant, to 75% for two dependants and to 100% for three or more dependants. Students are entitled to the whole or a part of the pension of the deceased until they reach 25 years of age, and in case they have done military service, up to the age of 27. Insured co-operative farm workers are also entitled to pensions, at the age of 55 for women and 60 for men, if they have been employed for 25 years in agricutlure. The monthly pension ranges from 10 to 40 leva. The pensions for permanent disability are 30, 20 and 10 leva per month for the three categories. Disablement pensions for general loss of health range from 10 to 15 leva per month. Farmers' pensions are financed by state-made contributions amounting to 6·2% of the co-operative farm's income and by additional taxes levied on the sales of alcohol and tobacco.

There also exist two further types of pension: pensions for special merits (granted to distinguished persons who have made 'an exceptional contribution' to national life) and national pensions (granted to 'fighters against fascism, reaction and capitalism'). Family allowances as well as lump-sum payments are granted at childbirth; these increase with the number of children. At the death of the insured, his family is entitled to a lump-sum payment.

Housing: As a rule housing construction is financed and directed by the state building organisations and individual industrial enterprises, but a co-operative system is also maintained: this allows citizens to acquire tenancy of individual flats in houses containing up to four units. The private sector is negligible. Since 1962 credits for housing construction and maintenance have been available from the Investments Bank as 25-year loans at an annual interest of 2%. Workers at machine-tractor stations and state farms are entitled to 20-year loans. For ordinary house-maintenance the Bulgarian citizen is entitled to a six-year loan. The maximum amount of state housing loans is 4,000 leva for towns and 3,000 leva for rural areas.

In the larger cities such as Sofia and Plovdiv much of the old Turkish housing has been cleared in favour of planned housing estates. High-rise housing is increasingly in evidence, especially in towns and along the holiday coast.

EDUCATION

The fast expanding educational system, which is free and coeducational, is generally the responsibility of the Ministry of Public Education, while immediate supervision is exercised by the district public education departments comprising two sectors, dealing with organisation and pedagogical guidance respectively. Since 1964, however, 80% of the vocational and technical secondary schools have been subordinated to the economic ministries. The performance and conduct of pupils are reviewed by the individual teacher's council, but there is stress on student participation in the life, order and extra-curricular activity of the school. Supplementary instruction is provided by the Pioneers and Dimitrov Youth Union. Education is compulsory from seven to 16.

Primary and general secondary education: Pre-school kindergarten (*detska gradina*) is mainly of an all-day type but some operate seasonally in case of parental absence and may offer boarding facilities. Primary and general secondary education provide, wherever possible, a unified twelve-year system in which the compulsory basic four-year course at primary school (*osnovno uchilishte*) leads to a subsequent four years of compulsory secondary education. Over 50% of pupils continue to the general secondary school (*gimnazia*). Matriculation for higher education takes place on the basis of final examination in the fourth year of gymnasium. The 1959 Statute for a Closer Link between School and Life (on the Soviet model of 1958) stressed the connexion between study and production training, and all primary and secondary education has since included elements of polytechnical instruction. Even in the gymnasia there is heavy emphasis on scientific subjects and on practical experience of 'labour training' in the workshop, farm, factory and enterprise. Grades 9 to 11 are given a preponderantly polytechnical curriculum and in grades 11 to 12 an 'elements of communism' course is obligatory. There is compulsory physical education.

Vocational and technical secondary education: 40% of all secondary pupils in 1966 were enrolled in vocational-technical schools (*sredno politekhnichesky uchilishta*) and 'technicums' (*teknikumi*) which follow on the 8th grade. The first of these train skilled workers by means of a two-year course and the latter combine skilled training with three-and-a-half to four-and-a-half-years of academic/polytechnical study. There are also special polytechnical language gymnasia where instruction is in Russian, English, French or German and the curriculum includes foreign trade, secretarial skills and tourist guidance.

Special education: There are free special schools for the mentally and physically handicapped at the kindergarten, primary and secondary levels.

University and higher education: All institutions of higher learning, with the exception of those in medicine and fine arts, which come under their appropriate ministries, are supervised by the Ministry of Public Education. Admission of students is on the basis of entrance examinations in two subjects related to the field of specialisation. Courses last from four to six years and include, in addition to the main subject, ideology and politics, foreign languages and physical education. Besides Sofia University there are 17 higher institutes in the country and separate academies of music, art, drama and ballet, each in Sofia. A university village is under construction near Sofia and will give facilities for 30,000 students.

Educational institutions

	Institutions	Staff	Students
Primary/general secondary	5,060	56,411	1,254,648
Other secondary[1]	285	9,275	187,274
Higher	26	5,905	84,467

Adult education: Evening and correspondence courses are popular with working people. Two-year 'semi-university' courses are offered in practical subjects such as library science, postal communications, etc.

MASS MEDIA

The Press (1967):

Dailies: (Sofia) *Rabotnichesko Delo*, CP, 630,000; *Narodna Mladezh*, youth, 170,000; *Otechestven Front*, Fatherland Front, 150,000; *Zemedelsko Zname*, Agrarian People's Pty., 130,000; *Vecherni Novini* (e), CP, 80,000; *Trud*, trade union, 65,000; *Kooperativno Selo*, agric., 55,000; *Narodna Armia*, military; (Plovdiv) *Otechestven Glas*, CP and Fatherland Front.

Periodicals: (Sofia) *Jenata Knes* (m), woman's, 370,000; *Septemvriiche* (w), youth, 250,000; *Naroden Sport* (3 per week), 85,000; *Radio-Televizionen Pregled* (w), radio, 64,000; *Literaturen Front* (w), lit., 50,000; *Narodna Kultura* (w), cult., 40,000; *Lov i Riholov* (m), hunting/fishing, 40,000; *Bălgarosăvetska Druzhba* (m), Soviet friendship, 40,000; *Dărzhaven Vestnik* (bw), Nat. Assembly, 29,000; *Nasha Rodina* (m), socio-polit., in Bulgarian 26,000; in Russian 30,000; *Novo Vreme* (m), CP, 27,000; *Septemvri* (m), lit., 15,000; *Slavyani* (m), Slav Cttee., 10,000; *Stărshel* (w), satirical; *Studenska Tribuna* (w), student; *Eiliulcu Çocuk* (w), Turkish; *Erevan* (bw), Armenian; *Evreiski Vesti* (bw),

---

[1] Incl. teacher-training.

Jewish; *Lefteria* (w), Greek; *Nov Put* (m), Gypsy; *Yeni Yaşik* (3 per week), Turkish; *Bulgaria* (m), illus., in Russian 97,000, in Chinese, 3,000.

Broadcasting: This is controlled by the government Committee for Culture and Art. There are ten radio stations. Foreign broadcasts are made in eleven languages and include transmissions for Jugoslav Macedonia. Two TV stations operate on six evenings a week.

CONSTITUTIONAL SYSTEM

Constitution: The Soviet-type constitution of the Bulgarian People's Republic dates from 1947.

Legislature: The supreme legislative body is nominally the unicameral National Assembly (*Narodno Săbranie*) elected for a four year term by universal suffrage (19 years and over) on the basis of one deputy for every 30,000 inhabitants. In the 1966 general elections, in which nearly 100% of the electorate participated, 99% of the votes were cast for the 416 single-slate nominees of the Fatherland Front. Meeting at least twice a year the Assembly enacts laws, determines the budget, approves the economic plan, may declare war and grant amnesty and elects the Praesidium, Supreme Court and chief procurator. The powerful Praesidium, or collective presidency, comprising a president, two vice-presidents, a secretary and 15 members, represents the state in international relations, appoints ministers nominated by the chairman of the Council of Ministers, appoints diplomats, ratifies treaties, decides on the general election date, convenes and adjourns the National Assembly, exercises the right of pardon, supervises ministerial activity and may repeal ministerial decisions which it regards as unconstitutional.

Executive: The Council of Ministers (*Ministerski Săvet*) is the supreme organ of government and consists of a chairman, deputy chairmen, ministers and the chairmen of key committees such as State Planning. The chairman is currently (1968) also party leader and his cabinet contains several prominent Politburo members. The Council of Ministers controls state administration and ensures the execution of the economic plan and the observance of laws.

Local government: This is exercised by the people's council (*narodni săvet*) at the levels of region (*okrăg*) and urban or rural municipality (*grad* and *selo*). Members of the people's council are directly elected for a three-year term and in turn appoint a standing committee (*postoyanen komitet*) as the executive branch. The 28 regions, dating from the territorial-administrative reforms of 1964, correspond to the economic subdivision. People's councils report annually to their electors.

Judiciary: Civil and criminal justice is administered through the Supreme Court (*Vărkhoven Săd*), 28 regional courts and 103 people's courts. The Supreme Court, whose judges are elected by the National Assembly for five years, supervises the judiciary and acts as the highest court of appeal while the lower courts, composed of a directly elected judge and two lay assessors (*zasedateli*), exercise original jurisdiction. The judiciary is deemed independent of government. There are also special courts such as military tribunals. A chief procurator (*glaven prokuror*), elected for five years by the National Assembly to which he is responsible, personally appoints and removes his subordinates. Procurators supervise the observance of legality by public bodies and citizens and prosecute in criminal cases. In 1961, on the Soviet model, comrades' courts (*drugari sădy*) were established to deal with minor offences in institutions and enterprises. Capital punishment is maintained.

Basic rights: These include equality, a broad scope of social services, cultural and educational rights for national minorities and qualified freedom of speech, press, assembly and religion.

Party: There are nominally two political parties, the Communist Party (BCP) and Agrarian People's Union (APU) which collaborate in the Fatherland Front (*Otechestven Front*), a mass organisation with a membership (1968) of 3,500,000 which alone nominates candidates. There is no parliamentary opposition. The BCP numbers (1966) 607,000, APU 120,000 and Dimitrov (Communist) Youth Union 1,100,000.

Leading government and party figures: Georgi Traikov (titular president), Todor Zhivkov

48

(prime minister and BCP leader), Zhivko Zhivkov (first deputy chairman of Council of Ministers), Ivan Bashev (foreign minister), Ivan Budinov (foreign trade minister), Gen. Dobri Dzhurov (defence minister), Dimiter Popov (finance minister), Apostol Pashev (chairman of State Planning Committee).

CZECHOSLOVAKIA

GEOGRAPHY

Features: Czechoslovakia is a medium-sized, inland state composed of the Czech lands of Bohemia and Moravia in the west and of Slovakia in the east. It is contiguous with Poland, East and West Germany, Austria, Hungary and, since World War II, the Soviet Union (which annexed Sub-Carpathian Ruthenia). Bohemia comprises a mountain-girt plateau (av. height: 1,600 ft/500 m.) diminishing towards the north where it is dissected by the R. Labe (Ger. Elbe) and its tributaries, on one of which, the Vltava (Moldau) stands Prague. The lower slopes and the low-lying plain of the Labe are fertile. In the west the frontiers with West and East Germany comprise the Český Les (Böhmer Wald) and Krušné Hory (Erzgebirge) respectively. In the north-east the Krkonoše Hory (Riesengebirge) form the highest range of the Sudetes (Mt. Sněžka: 5,259 ft/1,603 m.) and in common with the Sudetes (Sudeten) of Moravia and the Carpathians of Slovakia, constitute a political boundary with Poland. Moravia, which includes a small part of Silesia, is a mainly lowland region under 1,000 ft/300 m. and a water divide and a traditional crossing between north and south Europe. Slovakia covering half the land area of the country is two-thirds mountainous with parallel ranges of the Carpathians culminating in the High Tatra (Mt. Gerlachová: 8,737 ft/2,663 m.). In Slovakia fertile plains are confined to the Danubian Basin in the extreme south-west and basin of the R. Uh in the south-east. The climate of Czechoslovakia represents a transition from the maritime to the continental types.

Although the country is generally poor in minerals, it is one of the most industrialised in Eastern Europe. The chief mineral resources are brown coal and lignite (centred on Ostrava and Kladno), iron ore, uranium ore and magnesite. Heavy industry has been traditionally based in Bohemia and Moravia, in Prague, Plzeň (Pilsen), Brno (Brünn) and Ostrava. But the industrialisation of Slovakia has recently received priority.

About 40 % of the total area is cultivated, 30% forest and a further 16% is pasture. Intensive agriculture (maize, wheat, beets, fruit, potatoes, fodder crops) is practised in the fertile plains of the chief rivers, e.g. Danube, Morava, Vltava, Labe, Váh, Hron and Hornád. There are timber industries, but the hydroelectric potential (outstanding in Slovakia) is still largely untapped. Czechoslovakia's road and railway networks are dense and the Danube and lower reaches of the Vltava and Labe are navigable.

Area: 49,400 sq. miles/127,900 sq. km. (Bohemia and Moravia 78,900 sq. km.; Slovakia 49,000 sq. km.)

Mean max. and min. temperatures: Prague (50°N, 14°E; 660 ft/201 m.) 66°F/19°C (July) 30°F/–1°C (Jan.); Zvolen (48°N, 19°E; 980 ft/299 m.) 69°F/21°C (July) 29°F/–2°C (Jan.).

Relative humidity: Prague 82%; Zvolen 87%.

Mean annual rainfall: Prague 19 in./485 mm.; Zvolen 30 in./760 mm.

POPULATION

Total population (1966 est.): 14,240,000. Czech regions (Bohemia and Moravia): 9,826,000; Slovakia: 4,414,000.

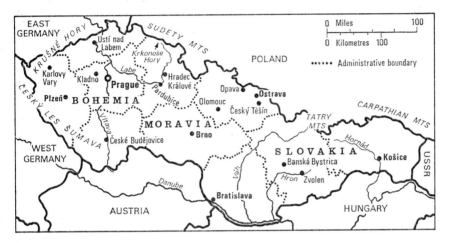

CZECHOSLOVAKIA

Chief towns and populations (1966 est.): State capital and capital of Bohemia, Prague, 1,028,000. Capital of Moravia, Brno (Brünn), 332,000. Capital of Slovakia, Bratislava (Pressburg), 274,000. Other major towns: Ostrava 268,000, Plzeň (Pilsen) 142,000, Košice (Kaschau) 109,000.
Ethnic composition: Czechs number 65%, Slovaks 29%, Magyars 4%, Germans 1%.
Language: Czech and Slovak are official languages.
Religion: 70% of the population are nominally Roman Catholic, 15% Protestant (mainly Reformed and Lutheran).

RECENT HISTORY

Czechoslovakia was not only the most industrialised country of Eastern Europe before World War II, it could also claim the longest tradition of parliamentary democracy. Betrayed by the West at Munich and subsequently dismembered by Germany, Hungary and Poland, it was liberated in 1945 by Soviet and American armies. The eastern province of Carpatho-Ruthenia was annexed by the Soviet Union while the Sudetenland, Těšín (Teschen) and the lost territories of southern Slovakia were restored to Czechoslovakia and a large proportion of the German and some of the Hungarian minorities expelled. President Beneš and many others believed that close relations with the Soviet Union were a guarantee of the nation's independence and the 1946 elections returned the communists as the strongest single party (38% of the vote). Its chairman, Klement Gottwald, became prime minister of the new National Front government. In 1948 twelve non-communist ministers tendered their resignation in protest against communist infiltration of the police, and in the subsequent elections the communists and their allies, who were unopposed, gained an 89% majority. The ailing Beneš himself resigned in June 1948 and was succeeded by Gottwald.

There ensued over a decade of totalitarian rule by a strictly Stalinist party. With non-communist leaders exiled or imprisoned, massive purges and show trials of party deviationists took place in the early 1950s, culminating (1952) in the show-trial of Rudolf Slánský, the party secretary-general. Under Soviet pressure, the economy from 1949 onwards was overwhelmingly geared to heavy industry and riots at Plzeň in 1953 were suppressed. On the death in the same year of Gottwald, Antonín Zápotocký became president and Viliám Široký prime minister. Khrushchev's secret speech at the Twentieth Congress of the CPSU in 1956 had no immediate repercussions in Czechoslovakia, unlike in Poland and Hungary, and a genuine opposition to the old Stalinist leadership was not felt until the 1960s. In 1957 party first secretary Antonín Novotný succeeded to the presidency, and was reelected in 1964. At the end of the second Five Year Plan in 1960, Czechoslovakia was proclaimed the first socialist republic in Eastern Europe and in 1963 the Czechoslovak-Soviet Treaty of Alliance was reaffirmed for a 20-year period.

A modest programme of de-Stalinisation was begun in the early 1960s. In 1963 prominent communists purged during the 1950s, including Vladimir Clementis and Slánský, were posthumously rehabilitated, while Prime Minister Široký was dismissed. Archbishop Beran and other ecclesiastics were freed. Under the new prime minister, Jozef Lenárt, Czechoslovakia also embarked on a new economic course, associated with Professor Ota Šik's radical system of management. Thus, until 1968, Novotný's orthodox leadership paradoxically presided over Czechoslovakia's New Economic Model and probably the most lively cultural ferment in Eastern Europe.

In January 1968 Alexander Dubček, Slovak party leader, replaced Novotný as first secretary of the Czechoslovak Communist Party and it was not long before the latter lost the presidency as well, to General Svoboda who, as a war hero, was equally respected by the reformers and by the Soviet leadership. Amidst a spate of suicides and defections (General Šejna, political chief of the army, escaped ironically to the USA), the remaining old guard was removed and its policies discredited. The 'action programme' of the new party and state leaders heralded seven months of political and economic reform, cultural efflorescence and personal freedom unknown in the country since 1948. The rehabilitation of party and non-party persons who had suffered during the Stalinist era, the reorganisation of the Czechoslovak Communist Party and revitalisation of other political parties, provisions for a Czecho-Slovak federation and the lifting of press censorship and of the ban on foreign travel were among the most remarkable of the innovations.

While a new Czechoslovakia was taking shape, its leaders took pains to stress their continued adherence to socialism and to membership of the Warsaw Pact and Comecon in particular. Support for Czechoslovakia's reforms and its position vis-à-vis the Soviet Union was soon received not only from most of the non-Soviet world but also from the Jugoslav, Rumanian and major Western Communist Parties; the stream of summer visitors included Tito and Ceauşescu, who were accorded a tumultuous welcome. Meanwhile, the remaining states of the Soviet bloc grew increasingly alarmed at this spectre of liberal socialism and, in meetings with Dubček at Dresden, Moscow and Prague, exerted diplomatic and economic pressures. Stalemate led to military pressures and Soviet and Polish troops assigned to Warsaw Pact exercises were not withdrawn from Czechoslovak soil. Moscow, East Berlin and Warsaw alleged West German 'penetration' of Czechoslovakia.

On 18 July the Soviet Union, Poland, East Germany, Bulgaria and Hungary despatched the so-called Warsaw Letter to Prague, stating that 'a determined struggle for the preservation of the socialist system in Czechoslovakia is not only your task but ours as well.' The Praesidium of the Czechoslovak Communist Party and the Polit-buro of the CPSU met in plenum at Čierna in Slovakia at the end of July, but neither this confrontation nor the subsequent meeting of the Czechoslovak leaders with the combined hierarchs of the Warsaw 'Five' at Bratislava satisfied the latter (in particular Ulbricht, Gomułka and Shelest, the Ukrainian party secretary). After a massive build-up in the frontier zones, the Soviet Union and its allies invaded Czechoslovakia without warning (21 August) and Dubček and others were temporarily arrested. Svoboda's mission to Moscow and the ensuing negotiations led to a repeal of the more liberal reforms and to an uneasy modus vivendi.

At the beginning of 1969 the Czechoslovak Federation came into being. As of January, 1969, a few of the reforms from the 'action programme' still remained intact, but the repeated removal of liberals such as Smrkovský, the reimposition of travel prohibitions, censorship and other bans on personal freedom, economic pressures from Soviet-bloc states and, above all, the continued presence of Soviet armed forces on Czechoslovak territory augur a lean and difficult period for the Czechs and Slovaks. The uneasy peace is disturbed by continual threats of workers' strike action and the self-immolation of students—symbols of mass resentment at the Soviet invasion.

Czechoslovakia's foreign policy, so long modelled on that of Moscow, evolved more freely during 1968 but is presently in flux. Its technical and economic role in developing countries, notably in Cuba, Egypt, Syria and Guinea is being maintained. *Defence (1968):* Military service is compulsory, for two years in the army and three years in the air force, and is followed by first reserve status till the age of 40, second reserve status till the age of 50. Strength is estimated at: army 175,000, air force 50,000, para-military forces 40,000. 1966 defence expenditure was $1,452 million representing 5·7% of GNP. The country is a member of the Warsaw Pact and until August 1968 was free of foreign troops. Since Soviet intervention, however, remnants of Soviet armed forces are maintained in the country. These are estimated (January 1969) at about six divisions.

ECONOMY

Background: The economic development of Czechoslovakia has been rather uneven and recently political events have overshadowed the economic. From 1950 to 1960 the national product increased at an annual average rate of 7·6%, but from 1960 to 1966 by only 3·3% with a trough in 1963 when national income actually declined by 2·2%. A 10·8% growth rate of national income was achieved in 1966 and 8% in 1967, but these figures conceal the fact that much of the increased industrial output went to enlarge stocks of unsold consumer goods and raw materials. The 1966–70 plan envisaged an annual average growth rate of around 4·25%. Investment has been at a rather low level compared with other East European countries. Engineering is the major branch of industry accounting for one-third of total output.

The economic reforms introduced over the last three years have run into serious difficulties. In 1967 a new wholesale price system was introduced, the aim being to eliminate subsidies and bring prices into line with world levels. On average, wholesale prices were expected to rise by 18%; in practice they rose by 30% as a result of monopolistic behaviour on the part of the large industrial trusts. Extremely high profits were earned and profit margins averaged 65% instead of the 22% planned. This put pressure on investment and consumer goods markets. Wages and prices, freed to some extent from central control, rose swiftly, wage increases outstripping productivity gains, partly because of greater freedom for the trade unions. These developments led to popular discontent and forced the government to resume control over most wages and prices. Investment was to have been largely decentralised so that bank credit accounted for 60% of investment finance and enterprise internal resources 25%, but progress has been cautious. A further cause of discontent has been the marked regional variations in industrial development and prosperity. Slovakia is much poorer than the Czech lands and the 1968 budget had to be changed to increase investment to Slovakia from one-quarter to one-third of the total. The economic reforms have continued since the Soviet intervention but with greater caution.

Agriculture has suffered from a persistent decline in the rural labour force and some neglect in terms of investments in machinery and fertilisers. Results have been satisfactory, however, total output increasing by 10·5% in 1966 and by 3·5% in 1967. Main crops are sugarbeet, wheat, barley and potatoes. Production of animal products is important and achieved a 5·8% improvement in 1967, to a large extent through improvements in yields.

Foreign trade: Czechoslovakia is extremely dependent upon raw material imports from the rest of Comecon. The Soviet Union alone supplies all Czech liquid fuels, two-thirds of all ferrous ores and nearly half raw cotton supplies. In return, Czechoslovakia exports engineering products, primarily machine tools, and accumulates a large surplus with Comecon, which accounts for 65% of its trade. Trade with Western Europe has expanded rapidly, especially imports of advanced engineering products and consumer goods, but is limited by a serious inadequacy of foreign exchange earnings. Full convertibility of the crown was an important aim of the reforms. Collaboration with Western firms has increased, however, Italy and West Germany playing a leading role.

E

Employment: Employment has increased by an annual average of about 2% in the 1960s with a steady rise in the proportion of women employed. In 1964 and 1965 about 1,300 factories were closed as part of a redeployment policy to develop export industries. After the reforms were implemented, growth of the industrial labour force declined and there are said to be up to half-a-million 'hidden unemployed'. Agriculture suffers from a shortage of labour and the labour force itself has an unfavourable age structure.

Prices and wages: Nominal wages have risen sharply since the reforms started, by 5·5% in 1967, and in the first quarter of 1968 alone by 9%, with a 20% rise for state farm workers. Output during this quarter rose by 7·6%. Prices have also shown a strong upward tendency resulting in little improvement in real incomes. Central control has been reextended to most retail prices.

Consumption: Standards of living are quite high on average in comparison with other East European countries, but there are substantial differences between regions and between town and country. Consumer goods are more freely available but are frequently ill-matched to demand. There were 64,000 cars sold in 1967, a 30% increase over 1966, but sales of TV sets and furniture showed a relative decline. Personal savings increased by 44·7% in 1967 alone, indicating the extent of frustrated demand.

SOCIAL WELFARE

Social insurance (1968) in Czechoslovakia is financed from state funds, administered locally by the national committees and (with the exception of health services) supervised by the Ministry of Social Security. The usual current working week is 44 hours covering six days, but a five-day 40-to-42-hour week should operate by 1970. Minimum annual paid leave is two weeks.

Health services: Health care is supervised by the Ministry of Health (which is directly responsible for research institutes, spas and special clinics) and by regional national health institutes responsible to regional national committees. Direct administration is the function of district national health institutes (responsible to district national committees) comprising at least one hospital plus polyclinics, specialist clinics, pharmacies, etc. Czechoslovakia's ratio of doctors per population is the third highest in the world. Free health facilities are available to all employees, apprentices, students, self-employed artists, members of producer cooperatives and, with some modifications, to members of farming cooperatives, together with their families. Sickness benefits for employees comprise 50% to 70% of average net earnings for the first three days of incapacity and 60% to 90% thereafter, the sum payable depending on length of service. Workers attending a sick member of the family are entitled to three to six days of special financial aid on a par with sickness benefits. During the 22-week maternity leave a mother is entitled to between 60% and 90% of her average earnings, according to length of service. On giving birth, the working woman (or wife of a worker) receives a bonus of 650 crowns. The employer is, on request, obliged to grant her paid leave (at 40% to 60% of average wage) till the child reaches the age of one.

Pensions and other benefits: Retirement pensions, covering all wage-earners, are tied to average income on a percentage scale according to length and type of employment. The three categories of occupation include (1) miners and air-crews, (2) persons working in hard conditions and (3) others. Given the prerequisite minimum of 25 years of employment, men are pensionable at 60, women at from 53 to 57 according to the number of children reared. Minimum retirement pension amounts to between 50% and 60% of average earnings during the preceding five or ten years (whichever is more favourable). In 1965 the average worker's retirement pension was 740 crowns (tax-free up to 700 crowns); the maximum pension (before tax deduction) is 2,200 crowns for the first category, 1,800 crowns for the second and 1,600 for the third. Disability pensions amount to a minimum 50% of earnings—or minimum 65% in case of work injury. Widows' pensions (amounting to 70% of pension due to the employee at the time of decease) are available for the first year of widowhood (longer for crippled women and mothers of dependent children). Orphans' pensions are between 25% and 50% of the late employee's pension. Workers in farming cooperatives (and their families) are also entitled to retirement, disability, widows' and orphans' pensions, which are computed on the basis of length of service and average earnings. Pensions of private farmers depend on their contributions. Family allowances, available for children till leaving school and for students under 25 are proportionate to a worker's earnings, and, in the case of a monthly income of (for example) under 1,400 crowns, range from 70 crowns monthly for one child to 1,210 crowns monthly for six children. Large families can also claim tax deductions, reduced nursery fees and lower rents. 360 crowns are awarded annually for every child taking lunch at school. On the death of a worker, the family is granted 1,000 crowns for funeral expenses; if a member of the family dies, the employee receives 200 to 800 crowns.

Housing: More than one million apartments were built between 1945 and 1966, providing accommodation for 25% of the country's population. Construction is financed by the state, cooperatives or individuals. State construction is geared to the needs of poorer families, dwellings being allocated by national committees on the basis of a waiting list. Cooperative housing construction is financed by members of housing and building cooperatives, which are founded by employees of individual enterprises, or by inhabitants of larger towns. The state provides a subsidy to the cooperatives and the state bank grants credit. Direct membership shares cover about 40% of the construction cost in towns, the remainder being met equally by credit and state subsidies. For working members of enterprise cooperatives the debt deriving from credits is gradually written off. Private housing is financed by owners from personal means or with a 20-to-30-year state loan. Units administered by the national committees are divided into four rent categories, in each of which rent is computed on the basis of floor space plus equipment. In cooperative units the relatively lower rent is on the basis of actual amortisation of credit and the cost of maintenance, repairs and administration. Tenants in private housing negotiate rent separately with the owner.

EDUCATION

The unified system of Czechoslovak education comes under the authority of the Ministry of Education and Culture. Immediate supervision and control of primary and secondary schools is exercised by the local national committees, each of which must, nonetheless, comply with ministerial directives. Tuition is free at all levels, books and materials free up to secondary schooling. The language of instruction is Czech or Slovak, but in primary and secondary schools established for Hungarian, German, Ukrainian and Polish minorities, pupils are taught in their mother-tongue and Czech or Slovak is a compulsory subject. Religious instruction is optional.

Primary education: Basic general education, which is compulsory, is provided by the nine-year school (*základní devítiletá škola*) for all children aged six to 15. Study is for six days a week and follows the same curriculum. Special emphasis is placed on the study of the mother-tongue, on basic natural and social sciences and on mathematics. Timetables include practical lessons in workshops and in factories or on farms. Study groups are maintained to help weaker pupils. For children with fully employed parents there are after-school-hours facilities. Extracurricular activities, often sponsored by the Union of Youth organisations, are encouraged. Attached to schools are parents' associations which provide contact between parents and teachers.

Secondary education: The nine-year school is followed by one of three main types of secondary school: (a) the three-year general secondary school (*střední vseobecné vzdělávací škola*) which concentrates mainly on preparing pupils for university education but includes a polytechnical syllabus; (b) the four-year vocational secondary school (*střední odborná škola*) which combines vocational secondary training with a wide range of academic subjects and which feeds the higher technical schools; (c) the three-year apprentice-training centre (*odborné učiliště*) which leads directly into either the three-year workers' secondary school (*střední škola pro pracující*) or five-year vocational technical and training schools for workers (*podnikový institut* or *podniková technická škola*), the latter being geared to higher technical positions and the former to general positions, or, in some cases, to further higher education. Matriculating pupils from all three main categories are, however, eligible for higher education. In the third category apprentice training is run by the enterprises and trade unions concerned together with the national committees.

Special education is available, with free tuition and treatment where necessary, for handicapped children at all levels.

Universities and higher education comprise six full universities (the Charles at Prague; Comenius at Bratislava; Purkyňová at Brno; Palacký at Olomouc; Pavla Jozefa Šafárika at Košice, founded in 1959; the 17 November University at Prague, founded in 1961, and offering foreign students courses conducted in Czech, Slovak, English and French, 16 technical universities and higher colleges (including the Prague School of Economics, Bratislava School of Economics, Prague, Brno and Slovak Technical Universities, Universities of Agriculture at Prague, Brno and Nitra, etc.), nine Academies of Music, Drama and Art (Prague, Bratislava and Brno) and several teacher-training colleges. The medical faculties are incorporated in the universities. Courses of higher education last five years except in teacher-training colleges and most art academies (four years) and for medicine, architecture and theatre science (six years). All higher studies are completed with examinations. First degrees granted are either *promovaný* (graduated) in the humanities and pure sciences or *inženýr* (engineer). There are two higher degrees.

Educational institutions, (1965–6)

	Institutions	Students
Primary	11,330	2,221,160
Secondary	374	112,928
Technical and teacher-training	645	297,654
Higher and university	38	144,990

Adult education: Secondary schools for workers offer evening and day courses. Curricula include most of the subjects taught in secondary schools and polytechnical training. Courses at university level usually last a year longer than normal courses.

Mass Media

The Press (1967):

Dailies: Rudé Právo, Prague and Bratislava (Czech and Slovak editions), Communist, 1,000,000; *Práce*, Prague, trade union, 350,000; *Pravdá* (s), Bratislava, Slovak CP, 270,000; *Mladá Fronta*, Prague, youth, 250,000; *Zemědělské noviny*, Prague, agricultural/forestry, 200,000; *Československý sport*, Prague, sport, 200,000; *Smena*, Bratislava, youth, 150,000; *Svobodné slovo*, Prague, Socialist, 134,000; *Lidová Demokracie*, Prague, Catholic, 130,000; *Rovnost*, Brno, CP, 130,000; *Práca*, Bratislava, Slovak trade union, 125,000; *Večerní Praha* (e), Prague, CP, 120,000; *Új Szó*, Bratislava, Hungarian; *Nová Svoboda*, Ostrava, CP; *Pravda*, Plzeň, CP; *Obrana lidu*, Prague, military; *Volkszeitung*, Prague, German trade union.

Periodicals: (Prague) *Vlasta* (w), women's illus., 630,000; *Mladý Svět* (w), youth illus.; *Svět Sovětů* (w), Soviet friendship, 210,000; *Květy* (w), illus., 200,000; *Literární noviny* (w), Writers' Union, political/cultural, 135,000;[1] *Kulturní tvorba* (w), CP political/cultural, 130,000; *Odborár* (f), trade union, 105,000; *Svět v obrazech* (w), illus., 100,000; *Nová mysl* (f), CP theory, 90,000; *Technický týdeník* (w), technical, 43,000; *Kulturní práce* (m), trade union cultural, 20,000; *Výtvarna práce* (f), art, 9,000; *Dikobraz* (w), satirical; *Mezinárodní politika* (m), internat. affairs; *Světova literatura* (f), for. lit.; *Národni divadlo* (m), theatre; *Filmový přehled* (w), film; *Katolické noviny* (w), Catholic; (Bratislava) *Život* (w), Slovak illus., 90,000; *Nové Slovo* (formerly *Predvoj*) (w), Slovak CP, 30,000; *Kultúrny Život* (w), Slovak cult.; *Slovenské Pohľady* (m), Slovak lit.; *Roháč*, Slovak satirical; *Ľud*, Pty of Slovak Revival; *Vychodoslovenské Noviný* (Košice).

[1] Suppressed in 1967 and replaced 1968 by *Literární listy*, 120,000. Other journals affected by Soviet intervention (1968) include *Politika*, *Reportér* and several student publications of which *Student* was the most influential.

Broadcasting: The state-run Czechoslovak Radio, based in Prague and Bratislava, maintains a national service and also regional services for Bohemia/Moravia and Slovakia, broadcasting in Czech and Slovak, and for limited periods in Hungarian,

German and Ukrainian. Foreign broadcasts are made in eleven languages. Czechoslovak Television, with studios in Prague, Bratislava, Brno, Ostrava and Košice, broadcasts daily for morning and evening periods.

CONSTITUTIONAL SYSTEM

Constitution: The Czechoslovak Socialist Republic, whose second communist constitution, of the Soviet type, was adopted in 1960 and extensively amended in 1968 (58 Articles out of 112), is a federal state of two nations possessing equal rights, the Czechs and the Slovaks. The status of 'Socialist Republic' presupposes the completion of a period of 'socialist construction'.

Legislative: The bicameral Federal Assembly sits in Prague. The two chambers of the Federal Assembly are the House of the People, with 200 deputies, and the House of Nationalities, composed of 75 Czech and 75 Slovak deputies. The term of office of the deputies is not constitutionally specified, but the two houses must be dissolved simultaneously. The two houses have equal powers and legislation must be approved by both. For most important matters, there must be a majority of both Czechs and Slovaks separately in the House of Nationalities, a provision intended as a safeguard for Slovak interests. A permanent body, the Praesidium of the Federal Assembly, composed of 20 Czech and 20 Slovak deputies, carries out the functions of the Federal Assembly when it is not sitting. Constitutional amendment and the election of the President of the Republic require a majority of three-fifths in the House of the People and three-fifths of Czechs and Slovaks separately in the House of Nationalities. The competence of the Federal Assembly is over federal matters and these are constitutionally defined as being those specifically delegated by the Czech and Slovak Republics. The following are within the exclusive jurisdiction of the federal authorities: foreign policy, national defence, material resources of the federation and protection of the federal constitution. In fairly wide areas, jurisdiction is divided between the federal and republican authorities. The legislature of the *Czech Socialist Republic* is the Czech National Council with 200 members and of the *Slovak Socialist Republic* it is the Slovak National Council with 150 members. The Slovak National Council, in common with all Slovak Republican organs, sits in Bratislava.

Executives: At the federal level, executive power is vested in the Federal Government, which is answerable to the Federal Assembly (in theory). Each federal minister is flanked by a state secretary and in each case, where the minister is a Czech, the state secretary must be a Slovak and vice versa. At the republican level, administration is exercised by the governments of the Czech and Slovak republics.

Local government: Czechoslovakia is divided into ten regions (*kraje*) and over 100 districts (*okresy*). Local government is vested in the national committee (*národní výbor*) at regional, district, municipal and local levels, while Prague has its central national committee and ten city district national committees. Candidates proposed by the National Front are elected directly for a four-year term. The national committees comprise a membership of 15 to 25 at local, 60 to 120 at district and 80 to 150 at regional or Prague central levels. Members elect councils whose function is to direct and co-ordinate the activities of the national committee.

Judiciary: There is a constitutional Court to decide potential legislative conflict between the Federal and Republican Assemblies and (in theory) to safeguard the right of the individual, as constitutionally guaranteed. There is, however, no right of individual recourse to the Constitutional Court. Otherwise, justice is administered through a Supreme Court (*Nejvyšší Soud*) and regional, district, military and local people's courts. Judges of the Supreme Court are elected by the National Assembly, of regional courts by regional national committees, of district and people's courts by citizens. The judiciary is independent. Supervision of the observance of laws by public bodies and by individual citizens rests with the procuracy (*prokuratura*). The procurator-general is appointed and removed by the president of the republic and is responsible to the National Assembly.

Party: Five political parties and several non-political organisations form the National Front (Národní Fronta) but this is dominated by the Communist Party and its allies, the remaining Socialist Party (middle-class intelligentsia), People's Party

(Catholics), the Slovak Revival Party and Slovak Freedom Party (both comprising former Democrats). In Slovakia the Communist Party of Slovakia is predominant. The Czechoslovak Communist Party is constitutionally designated as the guiding force in society and the state and has a membership of 1,700,000.

Leading political figures: Ludvík Svoboda (President of the Republic), Oldřich Černík (Federal Prime Minister), Josef Kempný (Czech Republican Prime Minister), Peter Colotka (Slovak Republican Prime Minister), Gustáv Husák (First Secretary of the Central Committee of the Czechoslovak Communist Party), Lubomír Štrougal (in charge of party affairs in the Czech republic—there is no separate Czech party), Štefan Sádovský (First Secretary of the Slovak Party), Dalibor Haneš (Chairman of the Federal Assembly).

EAST GERMANY

GEOGRAPHY

Features: East Germany, bounded by West Germany, Czechoslovakia, Poland and the Baltic Sea, has under half the size and one-third the population of West Germany. Formed from the post-war Soviet zone of occupation plus East Berlin, it covers much of the traditional German provinces of Brandenburg, Mecklenburg, Saxony, Saxony-Anhalt and Thuringia. Two-thirds of the territory comprise part of the glaciated North European Plain, 200 miles/124 km. broad at the Oder-Neisse frontier. This is characterised by low morainic ridges, marsh, numerous lakes, sand, clay and gravel heathland and north-flowing rivers rising in the upland third of the country. In the south-west a section of the German Central Uplands (*Mittelgebirge*) reaches altitudes of 3,500 ft/1,000 m. in the Thuringer Wald and Harz Mountains (Brocken 3,747 ft/ 1,142 m.) while in the south the Erzgebirge, serving as political frontier with Czechoslovakia, contain the state's highest peak, Fichtelberg (4,078 ft/1,214 m.). The R. Elbe drains most of the area and is separated from the Oder Basin by the Lausitz and Flaming heathlands. The Baltic coast is fringed with sandy islands, notably Rügen. The climate is continental with strong maritime influences.

Although lagging behind western parts of Germany, the pre-war territory was industrialised in relation to most of Eastern Europe. Generally poor in minerals, East Germany contains major lignite deposits, considerable potash and rock salt and small quantities of iron, copper and tin, and it is now one of the foremost industrial states of Europe. Industry is associated with the lignite and chemical producing regions of Saxony and the Middle Elbe, and with East Berlin, lignite being the major energy source. Forestry is concentrated in the mountain areas of the south. East Germany is not agriculturally self-sufficient but there is large scale cultivation of rye, wheat, barley, sugarbeet, potatoes and vegetables, and widespread animal husbandry.

Roads and railways, radiating from Berlin and Leipzig, and extensive inland waterways form the densest communications network in Eastern Europe, though Berlin's economic advantages as a pre-war transportation hub are nullified by partition. Four highways and four railways between West Berlin and West Germany constitute corridors across East Germany. Rostock is the only major port.

Area (incl. E. Berlin): 41,500 sq. miles/108,200 sq. km. (East Berlin 150 sq. miles/ 400 sq. km.)

Mean max. and min. temperatures: E. Berlin (53°N, 13°E; 190 ft/58 m.) 65°F/18°C (July) 30°F/-1°C (Jan.) Leipzig (51°N, 12°E; 410 ft/125 m.) 65°F/18°C (July) 31°F/-1°C (Jan.)

Relative humidity: E. Berlin 86%; Leipzig 85%.

Mean annual rainfall: E. Berlin 23 in./595 mm.; Leipzig 24 in./610 mm.

POPULATION

Total population (1965): 17,012,000, including East Berlin.

Chief towns and populations (1965): East Berlin (1,072,000), Leipzig (595,000). Dresden (504,000), Karl-Marx-Stadt (294,500), Halle (274,000), Magdeburg (265,000), Erfurt (190,000), Rostock (180,000).

Ethnic composition: There is a Serb minority of c. 30,000.

EAST GERMANY

Language: The official language is German.
Religion: Some 80% of the population are nominally Protestant (mainly Evangelical-Lutheran) and 10% Roman Catholic.

RECENT HISTORY

Following the unconditional surrender of Germany in 1945 the Tripartite Conference at Potsdam divided the central and western parts of the country into four zones of occupation, British, American, French and Soviet, providing for a four-power administration of Berlin. The Soviet zone included the *Länder* of Mecklenburg, Saxony-Anhalt, Brandenburg, Saxony and Thuringia (replaced in 1952 by 14 *Bezirke* or regions). Germany's present frontiers are in effect based upon a provisional allied demarcation pending the final peace treaty.

In 1946 the Soviet Union laid the foundations of a communist administration in the Soviet zone of occupation lying to the west of the rivers Oder and Neisse and, under Soviet aegis, a communist-dominated Socialist Unity Party (SED) was founded. In 1948 the Soviet Union blockaded Berlin from the west and in the subsequent 15-month siege only a massive Anglo-American airlift could prevent further Soviet encroachments on West Berlin. With the virtual breakdown of the Berlin Inter-Allied Control Commission, allied condominium of Germany ceased. Five months after the German Federal Republic had been established in the West, a Soviet-style constitution (October 1949) proclaimed the German Democratic Republic (DDR) in the East. The new state remained unrecognised outside the communist world. Wilhelm Pieck was appointed as president and Otto Grotewohl as chancellor while the secretary-general of the SED, Walter Ulbricht, became the latter's deputy. By 1950 the People's Chamber (*Volkskammer*) contained only SED members and their allies. A Stalinist system of terror and the Soviet military presence reinforced the communists' totalitarian rule. General rioting in several cities in 1953 was suppressed with Soviet army intervention and followed by ruthless reprisals but, despite some modest attempts at internal liberalisation, a stream of refugees, including thousands of young and skilled workers, flowed westwards during the 1950s. In 1955 the Soviet Union accorded East Germany full sovereignty.

President Pieck died in 1960 and the SED secretary, Ulbricht, was appointed chairman of the State Council, thus heading both party and government. For a while in 1961, at the height of the Cold War, it appeared that the Soviet Union, hinting at the conclusion of a separate peace with East Germany, was ready to relinquish direct control of West Berlin's corridors to the Federal Republic and in that year the Berlin Wall was built with the purpose of stopping East German migration and of further isolating West Berlin.

With the advent to power in 1963 of the liberal wing of the SED a two-year period of internal liberalisation, including dynamic economic reforms, and of conciliatory overtures towards West Germany was inaugurated, but after the removal of Khrushchev in 1964 the conservative faction led by Erich Honecker recaptured power at the Eleventh SED Plenum (1965). The liberal intelligentsia was drastically purged and there was a reversion to orthodoxy at home and a brake on *détente* with the West. In December 1965 Erich Apel, father of the New Economic System, committed suicide.

While the West has on principle refused to recognise East Germany, other non-communist states have so far been deterred by the Hallstein Doctrine, whereby Bonn threatens reprisals against countries which establish full diplomatic links with the Ulbricht government. Nonetheless, the Soviet Union and now Rumania and Jugoslavia possess embassies in both German states and Bonn's gradual *rapprochement* with other East European states serves to underline East Germany's isolation. This factor, together with the persistence of neo-Stalinist fears of the 'liberal infection', explains the notably assertive role of the East Germans in the military intervention of Czechoslovakia (August, 1968). West Germany's improved relationship with Israel has brought only marginal advantage to East Germany in Arab lands. On the other hand the East Germans maintain consulates in nine non-communist Afro-Asian countries and trade missions in twelve states of Western Europe, and their communist allies, notably the Soviet Union (for strategic and economic reasons) and Poland and

Czechoslovakia (for territorial reasons) clearly profit from the German *status quo* and are thus likely to continue underwriting the government in East Berlin.

East Germany's long-term problem of recognition is paralleled by the need to create a separate national identity and at the same time to preserve the ideal of Germany's ultimate reunification. Since 1963 the sporadic dialogue between West and East German politicians, intellectuals and churchmen has foundered on Bonn's refusal to recognise the East German government and on its claim to represent all Germany. What had promised to be a reconciliation between the SED and the West German Social Democrats, with prospects of a confederal solution, was negated in 1965 by East Germany's erosion of all-German institutions and exchanges. In 1967 the *Volkskammer* erased from the East German constitution the phrase 'There is only one German nationality'. Likewise the 1963 agreement between the East Germans and West Berlin Senate, allowing West Berliners to make holiday visits to relatives in East Berlin, was not renewed for Christmas 1967, and in that same year Chancellor Kiesinger's signal correspondence with the East German prime minister, Willi Stoph, proved unproductive.

Defence (1967): Military service is compulsory, for 18 months in the army and two years in the navy and air force. Strength is estimated at: army 85,000, navy 17,000, air force 25,000. Para-military forces include 70,000 security and frontier troops and 250,000 armed workers *(Betriebskampfgruppen)*. The estimate of 1966 defence expenditure was $975 million representing 3·3% of GNP. East Germany is a member of the Warsaw Pact and there are 20 Soviet divisions based on its soil.

ECONOMY

Background: The German Democratic Republic is the most heavily industrialised and prosperous of the East European countries. A steady rate of growth has been maintained in recent years; national income rose on average by about 4·5% from 1963 to 1966 and by 5% in 1967. Investment has been kept at a high level with increases in fixed investment of 7% and 9% in 1966 and 1967, representing 22·4% of national income in the latter year. Almost 10% of investment occurs in the remaining private sector. Engineering, energy production and chemicals have priority, and the stress now is on specialisation and quality, especially in the fields of machine tools, instruments and electronic equipment. Petro-chemicals are being developed on the basis of crude oil pumped directly from the Soviet Union. The transport system is undergoing modernisation; in 1966 84% of all rail traffic was carried by steam locomotives on average 35 years old.

Reforms are being introduced cautiously with experimentation before each innovation. A new wholesale price scale was introduced in January 1967 as part of the New Economic System, designed to bring prices into line with production costs and to reduce subsidies. Basic raw material prices were raised by from 40% to 70%. Plan indicators for enterprises were reduced in number. Specialisation is being encouraged by the creation of 'combinates' of enterprises. In July 1968 self-financing was extended to all state enterprises giving greater emphasis on internal sources of finance and bank credits.

Potatoes, sugarbeet and cereals are the main agricultural crops. Agriculture is advanced in comparison with other East European countries with crop yields up to Western standards. Mechanisation and the use of fertilisers are of particular importance as the rural labour force is steadily declining.

Foreign trade: Manufactured goods play a major role in East German trade forming 80% of exports to Western Europe. About 70% of trade is with Comecon, which provides basic raw materials for East German industry. Trade with the UK has rapidly expanded, benefiting from the marked decline in West Germany's share since 1966.

Employment: East Germany has had an almost static labour force for several years, increased industrial employment being almost wholly at the expense of agriculture. Consequently, much stress has been placed on labour productivity which in 1967 increased by 6·2% despite a reduction of one hour in the working week. Multiple shift working is widely practised.

Prices and wages: Real wages have risen by about 4% per annum in 1966 and 1967. The minimum wage was raised from 220 to 300 marks in July 1967 and social security benefits were improved. Retail prices have been stable throughout the 1960s.
Consumption: Standards of living in East Germany now compare favourably with those of Western Europe, although difficulties have been experienced in matching consumer goods' production and demands. Car ownership is being greatly extended. Housing is being given high priority with a move towards larger units. Education, health, social and cultural services account for two-fifths of total budget expenditure.

SOCIAL WELFARE

A unified social insurance system has since 1951 been operated by the Confederation of the Free German Trade Union to cover all workers except collective farmers, private craftsmen, owners of private enterprises and certain other classes, who are insured under the German Insurance Institution. The latter is also responsible for voluntary property and personal insurance. Social insurance is supervised by the Central Social Insurance Board and administered locally by enterprises. Workers make a compulsory contribution of 10% of gross earnings or a monthly maximum of 60 marks; employers contribute 10% (mining enterprises 20%) of gross earnings and an accident rate proportionate to danger; the state contributes the balance. In 1965 the state allocated 11,000 million marks to finance the workers' and office employees' social insurance system. University college and trade school students and pensioners are insured without contributions. The working week (consisting of 5/6 days in alternation) is limited to 45 hours. Annual paid holiday leave for workers is from twelve to twenty-four days.
Health services: Free health services, available to all insured and their dependents, include hospitalisation, medical and dental treatment, artificial aids and spa therapy. There are no prescription charges. Recent expansion of health services has strengthened the role of industrial and enterprise clinics and of rural outpatient dispensaries; there are (1967) 15 enterprise hospitals and 89 enterprise polyclinics. There have been amalgamations of institutions, such as the 1963 merger of 27 East Berlin hospitals into the Buch combine. The emigration of physicians before the construction of the Berlin Wall in 1961 increased the already serious shortage of medical personnel but the 1963 figure of 16,583 doctors is expected to double by 1970. The insured has the right to choose his doctor, on whose panel he remains for a minimum of three months. Sick workers receive wage equalisation payments from their place of employment for an annual maximum of six weeks. The two payments together total 90% of their net earnings. Hospitalised patients who maintain dependants receive household pension benefits of up to 80% of the sickness benefit. Special schemes exist for sick apprentices and miners, TB patients and victims of Nazism. The disability pension granted in the case of occupational injury or disease is 90% of average net earnings. A six-week pregnancy and eight-week confinement leave from work is available to women attending pre-natal consulting clinics, during which time their net earnings are paid from social insurance. In 1964 87% of expectant mothers attended welfare clinics and 95% gave birth in maternity clinics.
Pensions and other benefits: Due to war losses and emigration there are 32 old-age pensioners to 100 citizens of working age. Given at least 15 years of prior insurance men are pensionable at 65, women at 60 and those continuing in employment are granted both full pay and pension. Workers in certain vocations and victims of Nazism are pensionable at an earlier age. The monthly minimum pension was fixed at 150 marks in 1968. There are 883 old-age homes with a total of 55,600 places; the People's Solidarity and other mass organisations provide, free of charge, additional assistance to the aged. There is a state grant for every child born consisting of 500 marks for the first child, 600 marks for the second, 700 marks for the third, 850 marks for the fourth and 1,000 for every further child. A state children's allowance of 20 marks a month each is paid for the first, second and third child, 40 marks a month for the fourth child and 45 marks for each additional child.
Housing: The ravages of World War II, in particular as a result of allied bombing,

created grave housing problems above all in the cities. Housing construction reached a post-war peak in 1961 when 92,000 new or reconstructed dwelling units were built. In 1966 the construction figure was 65,300 units, of which 17,000 were co-operative dwellings. The state sector of housing is predominant; new state housing is allocated by the housing offices of local councils, operating in conjunction with housing commissions comprising three to five local citizens. Distribution of enterprise dwellings is influenced by enterprise management and trade unions. In older buildings the average rent of nationally owned units ranges between 0·60 marks per sq. metre (in rural communities) and 1·20 marks (in East Berlin). Large annual subsidies by the state have been necessary to meet construction costs of new housing and, as a result, a new rent tariff for state housing was introduced in 1966. Rent for new units let after this date is based on individual costs of construction, equipment and mainten-ance. In 1966 the average rent was 3·8% of the total expenditure of workers' and office employees' households. Cooperative dwelling units are built by the Workers' Housing Construction Cooperatives (AWGs) formed by workers in industry, trade, state administration, mass organisations and higher educational institutions. The AWGs are financed by interest-free state loans (of up to 85% of building costs), by the shares of members (one share=300 marks) which are proportionate to size of the housing unit, by workers' (optional) assistance in the construction or maintenance of the housing complex and by contributions from the cultural and social funds of the particular enterprise. The AWG system of allocation entitles one person to a one-room flat (excluding bathroom, kitchen etc), two or three persons to two rooms, three or four persons to three rooms, and four or five persons to three or four rooms. Cooperative rents are lower than state rents. The private sector includes mainly rural housing stock. East German construction usually takes the form of pre-fabricated high-rise multiple units; new large-scale townships include the Black Pump complex (at Hoyerswerda-Neustadt), Schwedt, Eisenhüttenstadt, Leuna II (at Halle) and Guben. Wartime damage to historically outstanding areas such as Gorlitz (in Dresden) has been made good.

EDUCATION

The Ministry of National Education is broadly responsible for education at all levels; immediate control is exercised by local organisations of government and the school boards representing staff and general public. The entire system is highly centralised.

Primary and secondary education: Elementary and secondary schools were replaced in 1959 by the unified general polytechnical school. After the municipally or industrially run optional kindergarten there is free and obligatory education for all children aged six to 16. Pupils must complete eight years' study at the ten-year general polytech-nical school (*10-Klassige allgemeinbildende polytechnische Oberschule*) whereupon there is transfer for a minimum period of two years to one of three secondary schools: (a) the four-year high school (*Erweiterte Oberschule*) with its university orientation and its division between humanities and sciences; (b) the three-year vocational secondary school leading to the *Abitur* examination (*Berufsschule mit Abiturabschluss*) open to those who have completed the ten-year school and which offers a mixed academic and polytechnical training: (c) the three-year polytechnical school (*Allgemeine Berufsschule*) for which completion of the ten-year *Oberschule* is again prerequisite and which prepares the student for specialised jobs or higher technical education. Matri-culation is by means of the *Abitur* (secondary school) certificate or *Facharbeiter* (skilled worker) certificate, but to qualify for an institution of higher education the student must pass an entrance examination (*Eignungsprüfung*).

University and higher education: Higher education is provided at Humboldt University, Berlin, the five other universities of Leipzig, Rostock, Greifswald, Jena and Halle, three universities of technology (*Technische Universitäten* and *Hochschulen*) at Dresden, Magdeburg and Leuna-Merseburg, 34 higher institutes (*Hochschulen* and *Hochschul-institute*) for specialised study in medicine, economics, art, architecture, political science, agronomy, forestry, sport, etc., and 183 technical colleges (*Fachschulen*). Many of these, including the eight teacher-training colleges, have been founded since

World War II. All establishments of higher education are legally government institutions and are centrally administered. In the more specialised *Hochschulen* and *Fachschulen* departments rather than faculties are the usual division. Student affairs are supervised by the Free German Youth movement (*Freie Deutsche Jugend*) which embraces the majority of students. 90% of the student body receives state scholarships based on merit and a means test, but monthly allowances are available to most others. In addition a monthly bonus may be awarded for outstanding performance; this is commensurate with the equivalent income from a job.

Educational institutions (1966)

	Institutions	Staff	Students
General polytechnical (primary/secondary)	7,780	n.a.	2,301,069
Extended general polytechnical (secondary)	303	n.a.	92,548
Vocational	1,145	15,115	446,200
Polytechnical	189	n.a.	119,326
Higher	44	n.a.	106,422

Adult education: Four 'faculties' provide basic and remedial secondary education (leading to matriculation) for more than 1,000 working people, and there are extramural courses at university level.

MASS MEDIA

The Press (1966):

Dailies: Neues Deutschland, Berlin, SED, 600,000; *Berliner Zeitung,* Berlin, SED, 500,000; *Berliner Zeitung am Abend,* Berlin, SED *Tribüne,* Berlin, trade union, 400,000; *Sächsisches Tagesblatt,* Dresden, LDPD, 68,000; *Liberal-Demokratische Zeitung,* Halle, LDPD, 55,000; *Der Morgen,* Berlin, LDPD, 50,000; *National-Zeitung,* Berlin, NDPD, 50,000; *Neue Zeit,* Berlin, CDU, 50,000; *Sächsische Neueste Nachrichten,* Dresden, NDP, 35,000; *Der Neuer Weg,* Halle, CDU, 33,000; *Thüringische Landeszeitung,* Weimar, LDPD, 32,000; *Thüringer Neueste Nachrichten,* Weimar, NDP, 31,000; *Der Demokrat,* Rostock, CDU, 25,000; *Märkische Union,* Dresden, CDU, 22,000; *Mitteldeutsche Neueste Nachrichten,* Leipzig, NDPD, 20,000; *Thüringer Tagesblatt,* Weimar, CDU, 20,000; *Norddeutsche Zeitung,* Schwerin, LDPD, 13,000; *Norddeutsche Neueste Nachrichten,* Rostock, NDP, 10,000; and the following SED organs (no statistics available): *Freiheit,* Halle; *Märkische Volksstimme,* Potsdam; *Leipziger Volkszeitung,* Leipzig; *Neuer Tag,* Frankfurt/Oder; *Das Volk,* Erfurt; *Die Volksstimme,* Karl-Marx-Stadt and Magdeburg.

Periodicals (no statistics available): Neue Berliner Illustrierte (w), Berlin, illus.; *Für Dich* (w), Berlin, woman's; *Forum* (w), Berlin, youth; *Sonntag* (w), Berlin, cult.; *Eulenspiegel* (w), Berlin, satirical; *Die Weltbühne* (w), Berlin, internat-affairs; *Sibylle* (f), Leipzig, fashion; *Pramo* (m), Leipzig, fashion; *Neue Deutsche Literatur* (m), Berlin, lit.; *Der Freie Bauer* (w), Berlin, agric.; *Die Wirtschaft,* Berlin, econ.; *Einheit,* Berlin, SED theory.

Censorship of publications: Acquisition of licences and newsprint is strictly regulated by the ministerially supervised *Presseamt* (Press Office), and since 1953 the *Allgemeines Deutsches Nachrichtenbüro* (ADN) news agency has been a state monopoly.

Broadcasting: The state Deutscher Demokratischer Rundfunk (German Democratic Radio) maintains three daily and continuous domestic transmissions through Deutschlandsender (23 hours), Berliner Rundfunk (23 hours) and Radio DDR I (24 hours of information and entertainment). A fourth, Radio DDR II, relays some of the latter's programmes in addition to its own (14 hours). A fifth, Berliner Welle, broadcasts daily but intermittently. Radio Berlin International broadcasts 364 hours a week in ten world languages. Radio Volga, based at Potsdam, transmits daily Russian programmes and Soviet relays for Soviet forces in East Germany. Deutscher Fernsehfunk (TV) broadcasts daily (72 hours per week). Unlike the rest of Eastern Europe, East Germany has not yet opted for the Franco-Soviet SECAM system of colour television. Broadcasting is financed by licence fees.

CONSTITUTIONAL SYSTEM

Constitution: The East German state, which was established in 1949 on part of Germany's Soviet-occupied territory, adopted in October 1949 a constitution superficially based upon the Weimar Constitution of 1919. East Germany was declared an indivisible German Democratic Republic (GDR) but the state has not been recognised *de jure* by any non-communist country. A new constitution was introduced in 1968.

Legislature: The highest legislative organ is in theory the unicameral *Volkskammer* (Parliament) elected for four years by universal franchise (18 years and over). It has 434 deputies representing 67 multi-member constituencies comprising from 130,000 to 240,000 electors. Its main functions include initiation and approval of legislation, approval of budget and the economic plan, ratification and abrogation of treaties, and election and dismissal of the State Council, Supreme Court judges and the procurator-general. In the 1963 elections the candidates sponsored by the National Front, a mass organisation, received over 99% of the vote, in which 99% of the electorate participated. The presidency was abolished in 1960 on the death of President Pieck and replaced by a collective presidency, the State Council. Elected by the *Volkskammer* for four years and officially responsible to it, the State Council consists of a president (who currently is also party leader), six vice-presidents, 16 members and a secretary. It appoints diplomats, ratifies treaties, confers honours, grants pardon, convenes the *Volkskammer* and may decide to hold a referendum. It can issue statutory decrees and interpret existing laws, is responsible for national defence and security and may order mobilisation.

Executive: Since 1952 the more senior ministers have formed a Praesidium within the Council of Ministers and this has largely superseded the ministerial body itself as the highest executive cabinet. The Praesidium, which supervises all ministries, includes the heads of key ministries and commissions such as Finance and State Planning, but excludes, among others, the ministers of justice, defence and foreign affairs. The minister for production material and the chairman of the Agricultural Council head two separate bodies. Members of the Council of Ministers represent theoretically separate parties, but the Socialist Unity Party predominates. Ministers are nominated by the State Council and approved by the *Volkskammer*. Willi Stoph, present chairman of the Council of Ministers, is also a vice-president of the State Council and a member of the party's Politburo.

Local government: In 1952 the five traditional *Länder* were replaced by 14 *Bezirke* (regions) each of which has its own Assembly (*Bezirkstag*) and Council (*Bezirksrat*). Berlin has separate administration. Each *Bezirk* is subdivided into 15 or 16 counties (*Kreise*) which in turn contain some 50 communes (*Gemeinden*) each.

Judiciary: In 1952 the system of courts was reorganised in accordance with the new territorial pattern. This provided for three kinds of court, the Supreme Court (*Oberster Gericht*), regional court (*Bezirksgericht*) and county court (*Kreisgericht*). The chief function of the Supreme Court, whose judges are appointed by the *Volkskammer*, is as the high court of appeal. First instance civil and criminal cases are heard at the regional and county levels by one professional judge and two lay assessors (*Schöffen*). Judges, who serve for four years, are officially independent and subject only to the constitution and law. The Soviet-style procurator-general (*Generalstaatsanwalt*) heads a body of procurators separate from the judiciary which both ensures observance of legality and prosecutes in criminal cases. Capital punishment is maintained.

Basic rights: These include equality, a wide range of social services, freedom of worship and conscience, of speech and assembly, and the right to emigrate. Press censorship is constitutionally forbidden.

Party: Of the National Front bloc, which issues a joint programme before general elections, the Socialist Unity Party (*Sozialistische Einheitspartei Deutschlands*, SED) heir to the former Communist and Social Democratic Parties, is predominant, with key positions in government and a current membership of 1,700,000. In the 1963 elections the SED was allocated 110 of the 434 seats in the *Volkskammer*. Most of the other parties are formally in league with the SED and include the Liberal Democrats (LDPD), National Democrats (NDPD), Christian Democrats (CDU) and Democratic Farmers' Party (DBD). There is no parliamentary opposition.

Leading government and party figures: Walter Ulbricht (titular President and SED first secretary), Willi Stoph (prime minister, vice-president of State Council and member of SED Politburo), Wolfgang Rauchfuss (chairman of Planning Commission), Otto Winzer (foreign minister), Horst Sölle (minister of foreign and inter-German trade), Erich Honecker (a leading 'conservative' member of SED Politburo).

HUNGARY

GEOGRAPHY

Features: Hungary is one of the smaller countries of Eastern Europe and is bordered by Austria on the west, Czechoslovakia on the north, Rumania on the south-east, Jugoslavia on the south and south-west and, since World War II, by the Soviet Union on the north-east. Only 2% of the total area exceeds 1,500 ft/400 m. and this falls entirely within the drainage basin of the Danube. A chain of mountains running south-west to north-east and reaching elevations of over 3,000 ft/1,000 m. in the Mátra, Bükk and Hegyalja Ranges, links the Alpine and Carpathian systems. Three-quarters of the country, however, comprises the very fertile loess-covered and alluvial Hungarian or Pannonian Plain (*Nagyalföld*) dissected by the Rivers Danube and Tisza. The largest lake in Central Europe, Balaton, is located in a tectonic basin of the upland region of Transdanubia. The climate is continental.

Hungary has always been preponderantly agrarian and the plains still lend themselves to the intensive cultivation of maize, wheat, beets, paprika, sunflowers and fodder crops. The upland regions support wine and timber industries and there is a widely distributed fruit cultivation. The once great deciduous forests are now depleted. Minerals include bituminous coal (in the vicinity of Pécs and Miskolc), lignite, ferrous metals, bauxite (largest deposits in Europe), uranium, petroleum and natural gas.

The chief centres of the important engineering, vehicle and chemical industries, Budapest, Veszprém, Miskolc, Debrecen, Szeged and Pécs are dispersed but enjoy easy intercommunication. The Danube and Lake Balaton are navigable.

Area: 35,900 sq. miles/93,000 sq. km.
Mean max. and min. temperatures: Budapest (47°N, 19°E; 395 ft/120 m.) 71°F/22°C (July) 30°F/-1°C(Jan.) Debrecen (47°N, 22°E; 430 ft/131 m.) 69°F/21°C(July) 27°F/-3°C(Jan.)
Relative humidity: Budapest 80%; Debrecen 85%.
Mean annual rainfall: Budapest 24 in./610 mm.; Debrecen 23 in./595 mm.

POPULATION

Total population (1966 est.): 10,160,000.
Chief towns and populations (1966 est.): Budapest (1,951,000), Miskolc (171,000), Debrecen (148,000), Pécs (135,000), Szeged (116,000).
Ethnic composition: Hungarians (Magyars) constitute 95% of the population but there are small German, Slovak, Jugoslav and Rumanian minorities.
Language: Hungarian.
Religion: Some 65% of the population are nominally Roman Catholic, 17% Hungarian Reformed, 6% Evangelical Lutheran and 2% Hungarian Uniate.

RECENT HISTORY

Having been occupied by German forces as late as 1944, Hungary was soon thereafter invaded and occupied by Soviet troops and in early 1945 an armistice was signed in Moscow between the allies and Hungary. In November free elections returned an overwhelmingly anti-communist majority and the Smallholders' Party emerged as

68

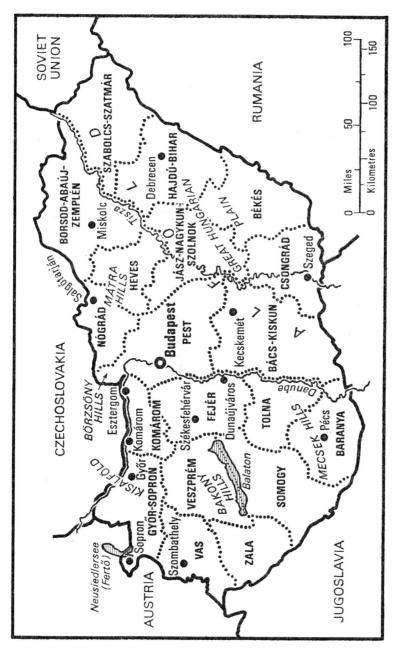

the largest unit in a coalition which, however, was obliged to fill key posts with communists. In 1946 a republic was declared with Zoltán Tildy as president and Ferenc Nagy (president of the Smallholders) as prime minister. By 1947 leading Smallholders and other non-communists were purged, many arrested or exiled, new elections were called and the Social Democratic Party was forced in 1948 to merge with the communists in the new Hungarian Working People's Party. The 1949 Soviet-type constitution declared Hungary a people's democracy and, in effect, a one-party state. There followed until 1953 a period of Stalinist terror and coercion enforced by the Mátyás Rákosi leadership. From 1952 to 1953 Rákosi combined both top party and government posts. The ferocious purge affected not only non-communist politicians and Catholic and Protestant churchmen, but also party dissidents like János Kádár and Gyula Kállai, who were imprisoned, and László Rajk, who was executed as a 'Titoist'.

After Stalin's death in 1953, Rákosi retained the party secretaryship but the appointment of Imre Nagy as new prime minister (till 1955) led to considerable relaxation, notably the release of a number of political internees and the partial decollectivisation of agriculture. The great revulsion to the Rákosi dictatorship reached its apogee, however, only in 1956, first in July when Rákosi was ousted from the party secretaryship (following a revolt of writers and the Petőfi circle of intellectuals) and then monumentally in October when a full-blown nationalist and anti-communist uprising took place. On 23 October a student demonstration in Budapest calling for free elections and national independence was fast joined by other sectors of society and by 30 October a new government under Imre Nagy promised a multi-party democracy and the negotiated removal of Soviet troops. On 1 November Hungary withdrew from the Warsaw Pact and requested UN and Western protection of the country's neutrality. There was no response from the West, and, two days later, one of Nagy's ministers, János Kádár, formed an alternative government, seeking Soviet support. Soviet forces entered Budapest and suppressed the uprising; Nagy and other ministers were abducted and later executed.

Disenchantment with the West and a massive retaliatory offensive on the part of the Kádár administration contributed to the anarchy and economic paralysis which beset Hungary for several years after 1956. Political apathy was to help rather than hinder the government; the party was reorganised and renamed the Hungarian Socialist Workers' Party, and in 1961 Kádár initiated a New Course of liberalisation and modernisation. Old Stalinists were dropped in 1962 and in 1963 a general amnesty affecting most detainees and refugees was declared. In 1965 Gyula Kállai became prime minister, Kádár continuing as party first secretary.

Despite, or because of, the shadow of 1956 the reforms of the 1960s have created a greater freedom, witness travel to the West and the 1964 accord with the Vatican, but a lasting *modus vivendi* with the Catholic Church, whose role is less significant than in Poland, is complicated by Cardinal Mindszenty's prolonged refuge in the US Embassy, and the continued presence of Soviet troops in the country serves to underline the government's dependence on Moscow. Hungary's foreign policy echoes the Soviet approach to most questions, although latterly there has been an awakened interest in cooperation between Danubian states. There is evidence that the Hungarian leadership, desirous of a more popular image at home, was embarrassed by its decision to support Soviet intervention in Czechoslovakia (1968). The fate of the Hungarian minority in Rumania is a potential source of friction.

Defence (1967): Military service is compulsory, for two to three years. Strength is estimated at: army 95,000, air force 7,000. Para-military forces comprise 35,000 security troops and border guards plus a workers' militia of more than 100,000. There is a 15-ship patrol flotilla on the Danube. 1966 defence expenditure was $313 million, representing 2·8% of GNP. Hungary adheres to the Warsaw Pact and accommodates four Soviet divisions.

ECONOMY

Background: Lacking raw materials apart from poor quality coal and bauxite, Hungary is highly dependent upon trade with the rest of Comecon for its economic viability. Economic growth has been rather erratic in the 1960s, falling to 1·1% in 1966 when a decline in agriculture coincided with a decline in industrial production, but rising to 8·4% in 1966 and 7% in 1967. Industrial output rose by 9% in 1967, considerably higher than planned, while investment increased by 15%; much of the gain stemming from higher productivity. Machine building, chemicals, building materials and light industry were the most successful branches. Fixed investment in 1967 represented 32·8% of national income, over 40% of this being allocated to industry and construction.

Hungary's New Economic Mechanism was introduced in January 1968 following almost three years' preparation. The aim of the reform was to restructure the economy for more effective participation in trade, especially with the West. New wholesale prices were implemented to eliminate most subsidies, except for basic raw materials, and at the same time, capital and supply allocation was decentralised. Eventually only 20% of investment finance will flow from the state budget; much of the remainder will be in the form of bank credits. Capital interest charges were extended and profitability became the chief success indicator. Enterprises are free to set output targets and the volume of employment, and to extend direct contracts with other units. The state sets overall guidelines and exerts control through the manipulation of credit, the centrally controlled prices and profit and turnover taxes. In the early stages the state retains control of wages.

The first year of the reform was not entirely successful in that its implementation was not as extensive as foreseen. Output rose by 5% despite a reduction of the working week to 44 hours, but enterprises made four times the planned profits and employment rose by about 4%. The excess profits put pressure on the investment goods and construction sectors, but retail prices did not rise as feared.

The new management system is also being extended to agriculture with new procurement prices designed to normalise relationships between agriculture and industry. Maize, sugarbeet, wheat, potatoes and rye are the main crops. Horticulture and dairy farming are important sources of export earnings. Agricultural output rose by 7·9% in 1966, following a 5·7% decline in 1965, and maintained progress in 1967 when improved yields were attained.

Foreign trade: Exports account for around two-fifths of Hungary's national income. Three-quarters of its exports are to Comecon countries, mainly in the form of manufactured goods. Convertibility has been a policy aim, since Hungary earns a surplus on trade with Comecon but is prevented from extending trade with the West by inability to earn sufficient foreign exchange. Special foreign exchange multipliers have been introduced as part of the reform, making it very unprofitable to import Western goods, but very profitable to export to the West. Exports to the West consist of fruit, vegetables, dairy produce, textiles and wine; imports, of machinery, chemicals and consumer goods. Vigorous efforts are being made to extend licensing and joint production agreements with West European countries.

Employment: Employment grew slowly until 1967, when there was a 2·1% rise, and 1968, when employment rose sharply (by 4% in the first three quarters alone) as enterprises were given greater autonomy. There is need for a radical redeployment of labour to export industries and services. Surplus labour and seasonality in the agricultural sector have led to an extension of auxiliary manufacturing activities on producer cooperatives.

Prices and wages: Real wages increased by around 3% overall in 1967 but by 8% to 9% for agricultural workers. This is partly a consequence of new price relationships and partly a result of measures to equalise rural and urban living standards. Retail prices have remained extremely stable for several years but have risen slightly since the reform began.

Consumption: Living standards have improved substantially in recent years, especially in the country. Retail trade turnover increased by 10% in 1967 when there was a minor boom in consumption in advance of the reforms. Car sales increased by 57% in 1966 and by over 65% in 1967, and there were advances in sales of TV sets, furniture and ready-made clothing.

SOCIAL WELFARE

In 1964 97% of Hungary's population enjoyed social insurance, which is supervised by the Ministry of Labour and the Insurance Council of the Central Council of Trade Unions and locally administered by the trade union committees based in principal county towns. Local authorities are empowered to allocate special grants beyond statutory limits. Per capita social insurance costs were 2,556 forints in 1957 and 3,865 forints in 1964. Benefits stated below refer to 1965–6, unless otherwise stated.

Health services: 13% of the state budget is allocated for sickness benefits. Free health facilities are accorded to all employees while employers contribute 6% of wages paid (excepting cooperative farms which pay a monthly contribution of six forints for each member). Sick pay for workers with over two years of service amounts to 75% of net earnings, 65% for workers with shorter service. If hospitalised, the worker receives 50% of average earnings as sickness benefit, or 80% if he/she maintains at least one relative. Sick pay is granted during the period of a worker's incapacity, to the limit of one year (two years in the case of TB). Continued or permanent disability entitles the invalid to a disability pension. Accident coverage is given to all workers and students sustaining work injury, employers contributing 8% of payroll. Women workers are entitled to 26 weeks of fully paid maternity leave and all women obtain at confinement a maternity bonus of 500 to 700 forints, provided the mother attends pre-natal consultation and where the husband is entitled to social welfare. As from 1 January 1967 an optional maternity leave of 30 months has been granted, at 600 forints (500 forints in agriculture) per month. Workers' families are eligible for most social insurance benefits including free medical treatment, also free drugs if received from a hospital; a prescription charge (15% of value) is otherwise payable. Certain drugs like protective vaccines, TB therapeutics and life-saving medicaments are always free. Dental treatment, including extraction, is free for workers and their families while dental prosthesis costs from four to twelve forints a tooth. Travel expenses in connexion with all socially covered therapy is free.

Pensions and other benefits: Costs of retirement pensions fall almost wholly on the employer, manual and clerical workers paying 3% of wages as contribution. Men are pensionable at 60, women at 55. Retirement pensions are generally fixed at 50% of the average net earnings in the last five years, supplemented by 1% for each year spent in work after 1929. Workers on cooperative farms obtain as a pension 35% of their average income and a further $\frac{1}{2}$% for each year of service after 1 January 1957. Pensions for members of farming cooperatives is supplemented by allowances in kind. Manual and clerical workers, members of handicraft cooperatives and students with two or more children are eligible for family allowances, which are set at a monthly 75 forints for a second child, 285 forints for a third and 120 for each other child (a single or widowed woman receiving 120 forints for each child). A special system operates for members of farming cooperatives with three or more children. A funeral grant is available to the family of the deceased consisting of a lump sum to cover the cost of the burial. There is no unemployment relief as such but allowances are payable by municipal councils and local employment offices following a means test.

Housing: The government's 15-year building programme (1961–75) scheduled one million new dwellings of which 285,000 were completed by 1966. Housing falls into public and private sectors, direct state investments for construction approximately 8% of the budget. State-built dwellings comprise cooperatives and freehold apartments both of which as a rule form multiple units on housing estates. Cooperative units are geared to large low-income families and their purchase price is fixed at about 80% of construction cost, towards which the new owner makes a 15% to 30% down-payment, the balance payable over 30 years. The construction of freehold apartments is state-financed through the National Savings Bank (OTP) the price being determined by actual building costs, although the amount of the cash deposit is not influenced by the size of the family as in the case of cooperative dwellings. The private sector accounts for one-third of housing construction; state building loans, amounting to around 75% of total cost and repayable over 20 years at 2% interest, are available. Private housing is prevalent in rural and outer suburban areas. Most new dwellings in larger towns have bathrooms while in villages 31% of new units contain a bathroom.

EDUCATION

Lower and higher education come under the general control of the Ministry of Education with the exception of all higher industrial and agricultural schools, and several commercial secondary schools, which are administered by the various industrial authorities or the Ministry of Agriculture. The Ministry of Health is responsible for the medical schools. More immediate control over the general primary and secondary schools in Budapest is exerted by the district, city and borough councils. In the small number of sectarian Catholic, Reformed, Lutheran and Jewish secondary schools which are staffed and administered by their respective denominations, the state curricular system is slightly modified. Primary education, which is free, is compulsory between the ages of six and 14. Those unable to complete the eight grades at 14 must attend school for an additional two years (*továbbképző iskola*). At higher levels tuition is free and over 90% of students obtain academic awards or else 'social scholarships' whereby the student is subsequently under contract to the donor institution, enterprise or organisation for the same number of years as his period of study.

Primary education: After voluntary kindergarten most six-year old children enter the general primary school (*általános iskola*), composed of four lower and four upper grades, and those successfully passing through the final grades can continue to any type of secondary school. Nearly half continue to gymnasia and a smaller fraction go to technical or specialised schools. In 1962 a revised curriculum put emphasis on practical aspects of 'modern' and 'socialist' education. Upper grade primary pupils must take two hours weekly of polytechnical instruction, and one foreign language (Russian). There are also over 100 music primary schools and 150 primary schools with special language divisions in which Russian, English, French or German are given particular stress from the third lower grade onwards. For children whose parents work, the schools provide after-school-hours facilities. Extracurricular activities, especially those of the Young Pioneers, are promoted.

Secondary education: There are three main types of secondary school, all of them divided into four grades: the gymnasium (*általános gimnázium*), the technical school (*technikum*) and specialised or vocational school (*szakközépiskola*). In the gymnasium the traditional academic orientation has been modified by the gradual introduction of the 'education for work' course and the so-called 'five plus one' system whereby the regular five-day school week is supplemented by a sixth day spent in a factory, farm or enterprise. All gymnasia follow the same general syllabus but there is specialisation in the upper grades. Two foreign languages are compulsory and a third, as also religion, is optional. The number of pupils in secondary technical schools has declined somewhat since the 1961 education reforms introduced polytechnical training into the gymnasium, but technical schools still provide instruction for over 50 branches of industry, commerce, transport, agriculture and administration. The specialised secondary schools also prepare the pupil for a vocation (technical, commercial, art, music, secretarial, etc.) but here four days are given to academic subjects and two to intensive practical training. Matriculation is by written and oral examination or, in the case of specialised schools, by a practical examination.

Special education is available to the physically and mentally handicapped; tuition, board and treatment are free.

Universities and higher education: There are nine main universities in Hungary, including four full universities, at Budapest, Szeged, Debrecen, Pécs and four separate medical schools in the same cities, also the Karl Marx University of Economics in Budapest. There are three technical universities, in Budapest, Miskolc and Veszprém, and the Universities of Building and Transport Engineering (Budapest), Agronomics (Gödöllő), Forestry (Sopron) and Veterinary Science (Budapest). There are four teacher-training colleges (Pécs, Szeged, Eger, Nyíregyháza) and one school eac of drama, music, fine arts and applied arts (all in Budapest). Other special institutions include one Reformed and one Lutheran Academy and a Jewish Seminary, in Budapest, each of which is autonomous. University courses last from five to six years; technical and agricultural colleges two to three years; teacher-training colleges two to four years.

Educational institutions (*1965–6*)

	Institutions	Staff	Students
Primary	6,036	62,167	1,413,500
Secondary	591	12,049	407,485
Higher	92	8,444[1]	93,957

[1] Excluding staff of teacher-training colleges.

Adult education has since 1945 allowed some one million working people to complete their primary, secondary and higher education through evening or correspondence courses at the Workers' General School and the Workers' Secondary School. In the correspondence courses standards are less strict, study plans more flexible and consultation occasional, but regular curricula are maintained.

Mass Media

The Press (1966):

Dailies: (Budapest) *Népszabadság*, HSWP, 750,000; *Népszava*, trade union, 256,000; *Esti Hírlap* (e), 157,000; *Népsport*, sport, 129,000; *Magyar Nemzet*, Patriotic People's Front, 99,000; (Provinces) *Dunántúli Napló*, Debrecen, 43,000; *Északmagyarország*, Miskolc, 45,000; *Kisalföld*, Győr, 45,000; *Hajdú-Bihari Napló*, Debrecen, 43,000; *Somogyi Néplap*, Kaposvár, 40,000; *Délmagyarország*, Szeged, 32,000; *Keletmagyarország*, Nyíregyháza, 27,000.

Weeklies: (Budapest) *Rádió és Televízió Újság*, radio/TV, 620,000; *Ludas Matyi*, satirical, 519,000; *Nők Lapja*, woman's, 446,000; *Szabad Föld*, rural polit., 436,000; *Ország-Világ*, illus., 257,000; *Magyar Ifjúság*, youth, 241,000; *Képes Újság*, illus., 191,000; *Élet és Tudomány*, pop. science, 190,000; *Pajtás*, children's, 180,000; *Film, Színház, Muzsika*, music/theatre, 168,000; *Füles*, illus., 158,000; *Hétfői Hírek*, polit., 124,000; *Képes Sport*, sport illus., 81,000; *Tükör*, illus., 70,000; *Magyarország*, foreign sociopolit., 68,000; *Lobogó*, polit., 66,000; *Élet és Irodalom*, let.; *Figyelő*, polit./econ.; *Új Ember*, Catholic; *Evangélikus Élet*, Lutheran, 10,000; *Új Élet*, Jewish; *Ludové Noviny*, Slovak; *Neue Zeitung*, German; *Narodne Novine*, Serbo-Croat.

Fortnightlies: (Budapest) *Magyar Mezőgazdaság*, agric.; *Szövetkezet*, cooperatives; *Református Egyház*, Reformed Ch.; *Foaia Noastră*, Rumanian.

Monthlies: (Budapest) *Kortárs*, literary; *Új Írás*, literary; *Nagyvilág*, literary; *Helikon Világirodalmi Figyelő*, world lit.; *Kritika*, criticism; *Nemzetközi Szemle*, internat. review; *Társadalmi Szemle*, polit.; *Akadémiai Közlöny*, acad.; *Magyar Tudomány*, science; *Közgazdasági Szemle*, econ.

Broadcasting: The state Hungarian Radio operates two domestic services, the Kossuth programme (continuous daily, with light material) and the Petőfi programme (intermittent daily, with serious material), based on Budapest but with five regional variations. Foreign broadcasts are made in nine languages. Hungarian television operates on one channel with five afternoon and evening programmes each week and three morning programmes.

Constitutional System

Constitution: The Hungarian People's Republic, whose Soviet-based constitution dates from 1949, is a state of workers and working peasants.

Legislature: The unicameral Parliament (*Országgyűlés*) is the highest legislative organ, theoretically exercising all rights deriving from the sovereignty of the people. It decides on the organisation, general course and conditions of government, upon the state budget and economic plan. It elects the Presidential Council, Council of Ministers, Supreme Court and procurator-general, can declare war, conclude peace and exercise the prerogative of amnesty. Parliament is elected for four years by universal franchise (18 years and over). The 349 deputies represent constituencies of 32,000 persons. 99% of the electorate participated in the last elections (March 1967) since which time more than one candidate may stand in each constituency. Parliament decides by a simple majority, but changes in the constitution require the approval of a two-thirds majority. The right of legislation is vested in Parliament, but legislation may be initiated by the Presidential Council, Council of Ministers or any deputy. A newly elected Parliament must be convened by the Presidential Council (*Elnöki Tanács*) within one month of elections. In turn Parliament at its first sitting elects from its members the Presidential Council (i.e. collective presidency) consisting of a president, two vice-presidents, a secretary and 17 members. This is empowered to call elections, conclude and ratify international treaties, appoint and recall diplomats, appoint higher officers of the civil service and armed forces, hold plebiscites on matters of national importance, supervise the local organs of state power, and to annul or modify any legislation enacted by central or local authority if this be deemed unconstitutional or detrimental to the interests of the working people. When Parliament is not sitting, the Presidential Council exercises full legislative functions.

Executive: The supreme organ of state administration is the Council of Ministers (*Minisztertanács*) (i.e. government) elected and removed by Parliament on the initiative of the Presidential Council and officially responsible to Parliament. Its members comprise a chairman (i.e. prime minister), vice-chairmen, 17 ministers and the presidents of the National Planning Office and the National Technical Development Committee. Central bureaus such as the Information Office and Bureau of Statistics come under their direct control. The Council of Ministers is closely associated with the upper hierarchies of the party and exercises considerable legislative as well as executive authority. It supervises ministerial functions, ensures law enforcement and the fulfilment of national economic plans, may issue decrees with the force of law and exercise direct control over any branch of the state administration. Its members participate in Parliament but are ineligible for election to the Presidential Council.

Local government: For administrative purposes Hungary is divided into 3,197 communities. Budapest has 22 subdivisions (districts) and the four towns of county status— Debrecen, Miskolc, Pécs and Szeged—have three or four each. There are 19 counties (*megyék*) consisting of a total of 121 districts and of 58 towns with district status. County councils are subordinate to the Council of Ministers, district councils to county councils, etc. All local councils, which function for four-year terms, elect from their membership executive committees presided over by a chairman.

Judiciary: Modelled on Soviet practice, justice is administered through a Supreme Court, county courts (in Budapest the Municipal Court is equivalent) and district courts. The president and judges of the Supreme Court (*Legfelsőbb Biróság*) are elected for five years by Parliament and judges of other councils elected for three years by local councils. Courts of first instance comprise one professional judge and two lay-assessors, while the three-member courts of appeal consist exclusively of professional judges. Special courts are provided for by the constitution. The procurator-general (*Legfőbb Államügyész*), whose office was instituted in 1953, heads a theoretically independent body of prosecutors on the county, municipal, district and town levels. Their task is to safeguard observance of legality and to prosecute in criminal cases. Capital punishment is maintained.

Basic rights: These include a wide range of social services, freedom of the press, of assembly, of speech, of worship and conscience, scientific and artistic activity compatible with working people's interests, equality and the right of national minorities to their own cultural life.

Party: Hungary is in effect a one-party state and there is no parliamentary opposition. The Hungarian Socialist Workers' Party (*Magyar Szocialista Munkáspárt*) is successor to the pre-1956 Working People's Party which had incorporated the Communist and Social Democratic Parties. The Patriotic People's Front (*Hazafias Népfront*), consisting of party and non-party members, recommends candidates for national and local elections. HSWP membership numbers some 585,000 (November 1966), while the Communist Youth Union (*Kommunista Ifjúsági Szövetség*) numbers 750,000 (1967).

Leading government and party figures: Pál Losonczi (titular president), Jenő Fock

75

(prime minister), János Kádár (first secretary of CC of HSWP), János Péter (foreign minister), József Biró (foreign trade minister), Imre Párdi (chairman of National Planning Office), Gyula Kállai (speaker in Parliament), Péter Vályi (finance minister), Lajos Czinege (defence minister).

JUGOSLAVIA

GEOGRAPHY

Features: Jugoslavia, a federation of six socialist republics (Serbia, Croatia, Bosnia-Hercegovina, Slovenia, Macedonia, Montenegro) including two autonomous provinces within Serbia (Vojvodina and Kosovo-Metohija), is situated on the Adriatic coast of the Balkan Peninsula and is contiguous with seven West and East European states (Italy, Austria, Hungary, Rumania, Bulgaria, Greece, Albania). Its geology and relief are exceptionally varied. The inland Pannonian Basin, drained by the Danube, is separated from the Adriatic coastline of Dalmatia by the Dinaric mountain system. In Slovenia, the Karawanken and Julian Alps contain the highest peaks in the country (Triglav 9,393 ft/2, 863 m.) and south of the Ljubljana basin continue as the Karst-type Dinaric Alps (av. height 5,000 ft/1500 m.) to the Kosovo-Metohija (Kosmet) Basin. From the Iron Gates of the Danube the north-east Serbian Mountains are ranged north-south and form a vertex with the Dinaric system in the Šar and Korab massifs of Kosmet and Macedonia (maximum elevations over 8,000 ft/2,400 m.). Glacial and Karst lakes are common and in the southern frontier zones, Lakes Ohrid, Prespan and Dojran are of tectonic origin. Much of the southern mountain system is faulted and subject to seismic disturbance. In Macedonia a low watershed between the Rivers Morava and Vardar (with outlets in the Danube and Aegean Sea respectively) permits of easy north-south connexions. The Dalmatian coast, always difficult for land access, is indented by several large bays, and only 60 of its 233 islands are inhabited. The coastal climate is Mediterranean, while conditions in the interior are of a continental type.

Of the total land area, over one-half is agricultural and one-third forest. Despite recent industrialisation the agrarian sector is still predominant. One-third of the arable land is located in the treeless fertile Pannonian Basin which, though liable to flooding and drought, produces half the nation's maize and wheat. Mixed farming is prevalent in the fertile regions of the Vojvodina, Serbia proper and Croatia. Fruit and vine production are widespread; citrus is confined to Dalmatia and sheep grazing is predominant in mountain regions. Timber of many types is exploited.

Jugoslavia possesses one of the widest ranges of mineral and fuel resources in Europe and is a leading world producer of copper, lead, mercury and bauxite. Serbia, Bosnia-Hercegovina and Macedonia have major sources of copper, lead, zinc and gold; mercury is mined in Slovenia; bauxite in Dalmatia and Istria and iron-ore in Bosnia, Serbia and Macedonia. Bituminous coal reserves, however, are poor but there is lignite in Bosnia-Hercegovina. Petroleum and uranium are also worked.

Heavy industry is centred in Ljubljana, Zagreb and Belgrade and at new sites in the Sava Valley. Iron-steel combines operate at Zenica (Bosnia), and Sisak (Croatia) and Skopje (Macedonia). Light industries are being promoted in the Vojvodina and Drava Valley. Stress is placed on the industrialisation of backward Bosnia-Hercegovina, Montenegro, Kosmet and Macedonia. Shipyards are located at the ports of Split (It. Spalato), Rijeka (Fiume) and Pula. Tourism, especially on the coast, is evolving fast. Hydroelectric potential is great and the current project at the Iron Gates, in cooperation with Rumania, is outstanding.

JUGOSLAVIA

Land relief impedes communication but road construction proceeds.
Area: 99,300 sq. miles/255,800 sq. km.
Mean max. and min. temperatures: Belgrade (45°N, 20°E; 450 ft/137 m.) 71°F/22°C
(July) 32°F/0°C(Jan.). Zagreb (46°N, 16°E; 540 ft/165 m.) 70°F/21°C(July) 32°F/0°C
(Jan.). Skopje (42°N, 22°E; 790 ft/241 m.) 73°F/23°C (July) 32°F/0°C (Jan.).
Relative humidity: Belgrade 80%; Zagreb 84%; Skopje 87%.
Mean annual rainfall: Belgrade 25 in./635 mm; Zagreb 35 in./890 mm.; Skopje
20 in./510 mm.

POPULATION

Total population (1966 est.): 19,741,000. Serbia: 8,048,000, Croatia: 4,314,000,
Slovenia: 1,662,000, Bosnia and Hercegovina: 3,667,000, Macedonia: 1,530,000,
Montenegro: 520,000.
Chief towns and populations (1966 est.): Federal capital and capital of Serbia: Belgrade
697,000. Capitals of republics: Zagreb (Croatia) 503,000, Skopje (Macedonia)
228,000, Sarajevo (Bosnia-Hercegovina) 227,000, Ljubljana (Slovenia) 182,000,
Titograd (Montenegro) 42,000. Capitals of autonomous provinces: Novi Sad
(Vojvodina) 126,000, Priština (Kosmet) 46,000. Other major towns: Rijeka 116,000,
Split 114,000, Niš 98,000, Maribor 94,000.
Ethnic composition (1961 census): Jugoslavia's five basic nationalities (Serb, Croat,
Slovenian, Macedonian, Montenegrin) account for 88% of the population, while
minority groups include Shiptars (Albanians) (915,000), Magyars (504,000), Turks
(183,000) and smaller groups including Slovaks, Rumanians, Bulgarians, Czechs and
Italians.
Language: Serbo-Croat, Macedonian and Slovene are official languages; Serbo-Croat
is the *lingua franca.* In Serbia, Bosnia-Hercegovina and Montenegro Serbo-Croat is

78

written in Cyrillic script, while in Croatia it uses a Latin script. Slovene uses Latin script; Macedonian is written in Cyrillic.

Religion: About 41% of the population are Serbian or Macedonian Orthodox (mainly in Serbia, Bosnia-Hercegovina, Montenegro and Macedonia), 31% are Roman Catholic (mainly in Croatia and Slovenia) and 12% Muslim (mainly in Bosnia). Protestants and Jews number less than 1% each.

RECENT HISTORY

The Jugoslav Partisans, under Josip Broz Tito, together with their Albanian colleagues, were the only communists in Eastern Europe to establish their post-war system without Soviet intervention. In the 1945 elections Tito won overwhelmingly, in part because the monarchists boycotted the ballot. The monarchy was subsequently abolished and the 1946 constitution declared a Federal People's Republic of Jugoslavia, consisting of six republics, which was soon recognised by the Great Powers. The government embarked on a ruthless purge of opposition factions, including the summary trial and execution of Serbian leader Mihajlović in 1946. In 1947 King Peter II and other members of the Karadjordjević dynasty were deprived of their nationality and their property confiscated. The Paris Peace Treaty with Italy provided for the cession to Jugoslavia of the greater part of Istria, although the fate of the Free Territory of Trieste was not settled till 1954 when the city of Trieste was finally awarded to Italy.

When in 1948 Tito refused to subordinate his party to Moscow, Jugoslavia was expelled from the Cominform and, alone among communist states, adopted a consistently independent programme, despite periods of reconciliation with Stalin's successors (1955 and 1961) and a frequent coincidence of view with the Soviet bloc. This independence allowed Jugoslavia to turn West for support in the early 1950s and, as an advocate of non-alignment, to play a disproportionately large international role. The first reconciliation with Moscow (1955–57) followed Khrushchev's visit to Belgrade and foundered on China's unrelieved hostility to Jugoslav 'revisionism' at a time when the Soviet leaders were making every effort to maintain good relations with Peking. The second reconciliation was highlighted by Tito's visit to the Soviet Union in 1962. The fortunes of more extreme liberals reflected changing Jugoslav-Soviet relations. Milovan Djilas, a former vice-president who had been dismissed from the Central Committee of the League of Jugoslav Communists, was imprisoned in 1956 for protesting about government inaction during the Hungarian uprising and for the implicit criticisms of the bureaucracy in his book *The New Class,* later published in the West. Djilas was again arrested in 1962 as a proponent of a two-party political system and the writer of another publication which subsequently appeared in the West, *Conversations with Stalin.*

In 1963 Tito was reelected president for the fourth time and a new constitution declared the state to be a Socialist Federal Republic. A reorganisation in 1966 of the League of Jugoslav Communists (LJC) abolished the Politburo and replaced it with a Praesidium and Executive Committee. Djilas was freed and in 1967 the vice-presidency formally abandoned now that the orthodox Aleksandar Ranković, a potential successor to Tito, had been dismissed from his posts as vice-president, co-secretary of the party and *de facto* head of the security police, but in the same year the young writer, Mihajlo Mihajlov, was imprisoned for disseminating hostile propaganda.

Jugoslavia's place, along with India, Egypt and Indonesia, as a leading neutral brought to Belgrade in 1961 a major conference of non-aligned countries, and despite the weakening of non-alignment as a world system and in spite of closer cooperation with the Soviet bloc countries, Jugoslavia still maintains today the most active and flexible foreign policy of all East European states, and Tito continues to make extensive journeys. Belgrade is an ardent proponent of European *détente,* has entered into diplomatic relations with West Germany and, with Rumania, eschewed a militantly anti-Israeli position in the Middle East crisis of 1967. Jugoslavia's unequivocal support for the Czechoslovak 'action programme' of 1968 earned Tito a hero's welcome in Prague, which he visited shortly before the Soviet invasion (August 1968). The subsequent indignation felt by Jugoslavs at the intervention, coupled with a certain nervousness about possible Soviet designs upon Albania and Rumania, as well as upon Jugoslavia, provoked a militantly defensive attitude on the part of politicians and populace alike. Relations with Moscow reached their lowest ebb since 1948.

Jugoslav aspirations in the Balkans are largely unfulfilled; Albania with her memories of party subordination to Tito during World War II and with an eye on the large Shiptar minority in southern Serbia (Kosmet) remains implacably hostile to Jugoslav overtures. Bulgaria is generally acquiescent in the Macedonian question but Greece, since the military coup of 1967, has scarcely promoted the ideal of a Balkan federation.

Internally, the principle of workers' self-government first introduced in 1950 has been reconfirmed by subsequent constitutions and the Jugoslav road to socialism has led to a drastic liberalisation of the economy, especially since 1965, and to significant administrative relaxations, symbolised by the departure of Ranković. There is now virtual freedom of movement, ready access to the ideas and commodities of East and West alike, and a breadth and depth of political discussion unequalled in the communist world. But the resurgence of constituent republican nationalism, notably among the Croats, poses serious problems for a federation which is economically and culturally centred on Belgrade.

Defence (1967): Military service is compulsory, for 18 months in the army and 24 months in the navy and air force. Strength is estimated at: army 220,000, navy 24,000, air force 20,000, para-military forces 19,000. 1965 defence expenditure was $352 million. Jugoslavia maintains no military alliance.

ECONOMY

Background: The Jugoslav economy has several unique features distinguishing it from the other European socialist countries. Since the break with the Soviet Union in 1948 Jugoslavia has steered a middle course between a fully centralised planned economy and a free market system. Small-scale private enterprises survive in many service industries and alongside the voluntary socialised units in the agriculture sector. Workers' councils exercise a strong influence on the pattern of management of enterprises.

Economic progress has not been smooth and much of the south of the country remains poor and underdeveloped. Recently the economy has been disrupted by the reforms introduced in 1965 and by the stabilisation policies accompanying them. Gross national product increased by over 12% in 1963 and 1964, by 3·4% in 1965, 8·6% in 1966 and by only 0·3% in 1967. From a peak in the first half of 1964, capacity utilisation, employment, productivity and industrial production have all declined. The reforms were designed to make the Jugoslav economy more competitive in world markets by changing prices and exchange rates and liberalising imports. Subsidies were removed and the tax structure adjusted to encourage self-financing by enterprises. To control the sharp rise in wages, which followed the reforms, and reduce liquidity the government arranged severe monetary restrictions, curbing bank lending to enterprises. This led to a starvation of working capital, reduction in output and unemployment. Output as a whole rose by only 1% in 1967 and the year ended with over 265,000 unemployed non-agricultural workers. In 1968 restrictions were eased somewhat, imports were controlled and incentives extended for export branches. This led to a slight improvement and a revival of investment, three-quarters of which was now financed by the enterprises themselves. A $16 million World Bank loan to ten industrial concerns for modernisation measures gave an added stimulus, but unemployment continued to rise.

The market mechanism plays a much greater role than in other East European countries and planning is of a more indicative nature. There have been moves to establish a capital market. In 1967 a law was enacted enabling foreign companies to invest in Jugoslav firms, participation being limited to 49%, and this has been successful in attracting West European investment over a range of industry.

Workers' control has played an important part in Jugoslav economic life although its effectiveness has varied widely. Much depends on the nature of the industry and the industrial experience of the workers. In theory enterprise directors are only answerable to their employees but, in practice, there is intervention by the state and by banks which control credit allocation.

Communications are an obstacle to levelling regional differences as the hilly terrain hinders railway development. A major motorway building project is now under way to ease this problem.

Agriculture has performed comparatively successfully, although there was a 2% decline in output in 1967, partly because of inadequate demand. One-third of the cultivated area is owned by part-time farmers who leave the land whenever terms of trade favour industry. Full collectivisation was abandoned in 1952. Wheat, potatoes and sugarbeet are important crops, but Jugoslavia is not self-sufficient in wheat.

Foreign trade: Around one-third of Jugoslavia's trade is with East European countries. Trade with Western Europe has been hampered by a payments deficit which stood at $287 million in 1967 for the Common Market alone, and an overall trade deficit in that year of $455 million. Efforts were made in 1968 to restrain imports of food-stuffs, vehicles and synthetic fibres and to some extent the liberalisation policy was reversed. From January 1967 over 2,000 products or product groups out of a total of 4,375 had been wholly or partly freed from controls. Exports rose by only 3% in 1967 compared with an 8% rise in imports. Tourism is a major source of exchange earnings and by 1970 Jugoslavia hopes to earn $400 million a year from it. Tourism has also provided new employment and a boom in hotel construction. Gold and foreign exchange reserves stood at $114 million in August 1968. Jugoslavia is a member of the IMF and has made approaches to the European Economic Community.

Employment: Unemployment has been a major problem for a number of years. Non-agricultural employment has been very erratic, rising by 6·4% in 1964, by 1·5% in 1965 and falling by 3% in 1966 and 0·5% in 1967. This is aggravated by seasonal unemployment in agriculture. In November 1968 a total of 9% of the whole labour force was without employment. The existence of small scale 'part-time' farming is a source of instability. Emigration has been on a large scale: 300,000 Jugoslavs are now working abroad. Labour demand in the private sector has been rising and drawing off some of the unemployed.

Prices and wages: Nominal wages have risen at a dramatic rate; by 26·8% in 1964, 38·5% in 1965, 38% in 1966 and by 15% in 1967. The retail price index has also shown substantial increases but not to such an extent as wages. Real wages have therefore risen despite the state of the economy; by 12·4% in 1966 and by 7·5% in 1967. Farm incomes have risen by more than industrial incomes. Productivity increases have fallen well below wage increases. Wage differentials have widened steadily for a number of years.

Consumption: Rural living standards have been advancing but there are still very great regional inequalities. Slovenia in the north is very prosperous with a per capita income higher than that of Italy. Although holding only 8% of the population it accounts for 16% of GNP and, with one car per 18 persons, has the highest car ownership rate of any socialist country. The richer republics do invest significant sums in the south but Serbia, Montenegro, Bosnia-Hercegovina and Macedonia remain comparatively backward. On average, per capita ownership of consumer durables, availability of social services and standards of living are low in comparison with other East European countries.

SOCIAL WELFARE

Due to the system of social and financial self-management the social security system in Jugoslavia differs markedly from systems operating elsewhere in Eastern Europe. Broadly supervised by the Federal Association of Social Insurance on a national scale, social security is administered locally by the associations of social insurance of each commune, which together form Republican Associations of Social Insurance. Each association is headed by assemblies elected directly by the insured persons. General social insurance covers all employees and self-employed while partial insurance of private farmers was introduced in 1962. Social insurance funds accrue from the contributions of enterprises and institutions, i.e. contributions levied on the personal income of the insured. Maximum contributions (health, retirement, disability pensions and children's allowances) are 19·5% of personal earnings and, fixed by the Federal Assembly of Social Insurance, are uniform throughout Jugoslavia. Local insurance associations may decree additional rates of not more than 2·5%. Separate funds for health insurance, for retirement and disability pensions are formed from the contributions of enterprises. All funds are independent. Social insurance expenditures in 1964 totalled 11% of the national income and are expected to exceed 13% by 1970. The constitution guarantees a 42-hour working week. In addition to a daily half-hour break and Sundays, all workers are entitled to paid annual leave of at least 14 working days (maximum 45 days). Women, and workers under 18 years of age, cannot be assigned to certain 'hard' categories of work and under-18-year-olds are entitled to an extra week of paid annual leave.

Health services: The health insurance system, compulsory for all workers and administrative employees, for the self-employed, and for their families, provides insurance against sickness, injury, work injury and disease and death. Since 1962 agricultural workers have, on a contributory basis, been partially insured. The share of expenditures on workers' health insurance as a proportion of national income rose from 3·30% in 1956 to 5·74% in 1965. Public health institutions are independent, being managed by their own organs of self-government and financed on the basis of contracts concluded with local associations of social insurance. Free health services, preventive and curative, are available to all workers including self-employed farmers, together with their families. Insured persons on health holidays will pay 20% to 50% of sanatorium board and lodging. A small prescription charge is levied on drugs obtained for home use. Insured persons treated at home receive the following sickness benefits: 80% of earnings for the first week of indisposition, up to 90% for prolonged leave and 100% after 61 days. Insured hospital patients receiving free board and treatment are entitled to between 60% and 100% of earnings, contingent on the number of dependents. Working women are entitled to 105 days of paid leave during confinement and after the birth of their child to a four-hour working day (at full pay) until the child is eight months old.

Pensions and other benefits: All employees are entitled to old-age pensions while the self-employed are insured on the basis of contracts concluded with the local association of social insurance. Insured persons qualify for a full retirement pension, which is equivalent to 85% of average monthly earnings during the last five years of employment, after a 40-year term of employment for men and 35-year term for women, regardless of age. The right to a pension is also acquired upon reaching 60 years of age (55 for women) and a 20-year term of employment, or 65 years of age and a 15-year term of service. Workers in certain 'hard' categories (mining, aviation, etc.) may retire earlier (eight months of employment counting as twelve). The initial pension acquired after 15 years of employment is equivalent to 35% of the pension basis and is raised for every other year spent at work until reaching 85% of the pension basis.

Disability pensions are granted to an insured person after at least five years in insured employment. A worker temporarily disabled due to occupational injury or disease is entitled to full pay. Other disabled persons acquire the right to a disability pension if one-third of their active life has been spent in regular employment. War invalids, victims of fascism and families of fallen combatants constitute a special category, their pensions being directly appropriated by the federal budget according to degree of incapacity and financial need. Family members of an insured person, including widows over 45, widowers over 65 and children registered at school, are entitled to a survivor pension. Widows younger than 45 qualify for a survivor pension if they look after children under 15. Survivor pensions amount to the following percentages of the basic pension rates: 70% for a widow, 80% for a family of two members, 90% for a family of three, and 100% for a family of four or more. In case of an insured person's death his family receives a cash payment (amounting to his last month's earnings) and a funeral allowance fixed according to local charges. Funeral allowances are also payable on the decease of any member of the insured's family.

There is no unemployment benefit as such, but in case of unemployment workers applying to the local labour exchange are entitled to compensation. All persons with an uninterrupted term of one year's employment, or 18 months with intervals, in the two years preceding unemployment are entitled to this compensation. Temporarily unemployed persons are entitled to health insurance and children's allowances.

Housing: In the 1956–64 period the total number of dwelling units rose by 650,000 (17%), and another 700,000 units were scheduled for the 1965–70 period (i.e. about 15% of Jugoslavia's total number of existing dwellings in 1965).

EDUCATION

The basic principles of Jugoslav education (including curricula) for all six republics have been determined on a federal scale. The republican Ministries of Education have ultimate responsibility for supervision and maintenance but schools are directly managed by their social communities through the school board, two-thirds of whose members are staff and one-third local citizens. Every school has its own statute outlining internal organisation, jurisdiction and procedure. The entire system is fast expanding and since 1961 the social communities, local enterprises and autonomous institutions have replaced the larger units as the main source of educational funds. Instruction is in the language of the republic except in the case of national minority schools.

Primary and secondary education: Primary instruction is the function of the eight-year elementary school (*osnovne škole*), free and compulsory for all children aged seven to 15. On completion of the primary course pupils may choose between one of the five types of secondary school, which are not compulsory: (a) the gymnasium (*gimnazija* or grammar school) with a four-year course in general and optional academic subjects and a quota of polytechnical training; (b) the technical/vocational school (*škole za srednji stručni kadar*) with two to four years of polytechnical and general instruction; (c) the vocational training school (*škole za kvalifikovane radnike*) whose predominantly practical three-year curriculum prepares the students for skilled work in such fields as agriculture, forestry, medicine, veterinary medicine, transport, business, library science and hydrometeorology; (d) four-year art school (*srednje umetničke škole*) and (e) five-year teacher-training school (*srednje škole za nastavni kadar*). Some gymnasia in larger cities offer more extensive instruction in traditional humanities. The majority of pupils graduating from secondary school proceed to higher education.

National minority education is provided at primary and secondary levels in the Shiptar (Albanian), Hungarian, Bulgarian, Turkish, Czech and Slovak, Rumanian, Italian and Ruthenian languages wherever there are large minority groups. Bilingual schools are established in some cases; one Jugoslav language is compulsory in all. The curricula of the national minority schools are similar to those in Jugoslav-language schools but include instruction in the national culture of the minority. In 1965–6 national minority institutions included, among others, 941 Shiptar-speaking primary schools with 176,723 pupils, 235 Hungarian-speaking primary schools with 45,311 pupils and 58 Turkish-speaking primary schools with 9,017 pupils. There were also 107 vocational schools and 37 general secondary schools for various national minorities with a total student body of 19,944.

Special education: Special schools exist for handicapped pupils at all primary and secondary levels. Tuition, board and treatment are free.

University and higher education: Under the 1954 Universities Law responsibility for university management was transferred from republican ministries to the universities and faculties themselves. Local autonomy was further reinforced in 1960. The faculties are independent of the universities but may unite in a university. Jugoslavia has six universities (at Belgrade, Zagreb, Ljubljana, Sarajevo, Skopje and Novi Sad), 93 faculties in 20 cities, 159 advanced institutes and higher schools and 14 arts academies. 16 of the advanced institutes, including the High Schools of Political Science in Belgrade and Ljubljana, the High School of Government Administration in Belgrade and the High Schools of Agriculture in Osijek and Zagreb, have faculty rank. Degrees from the 16 advanced institutes are recognised as equal to the diplomas received at the corresponding level of university studies. The majority of higher schools specialise in technical areas such as pedagogy, social work, hotel management, dentistry, railway engineering and leather technology. Separate from the other institutions are the three autonomous faculties of theology (Orthodox in Belgrade, Catholic in Zagreb and Ljubljana) and six Catholic seminaries. Most courses of higher education last four years but certain humanities and forestry (three years) and medicine (five years) are exceptions. Since 1961 a system of three levels of study has operated in several institutions so that some, especially technical, students may enter jobs and postpone later stages of study. In the universities and faculties attainment of the master's and specialist's degrees (equal first degrees) presupposes completion of third level study. Tuition is free; board for the great majority is covered by a 'children's allowance' (available to students up to 25 years of age with at least one employed parent) or by scholarships based on academic merit and/or inadequate parental aid. Student credit funds in each republic may provide study loans, repayment being related to the student's academic performance.

Educational institutions (1965–6)

	Institutions	Staff	Students
Primary	14,146	102,057	2,945,520
General secondary	388	8,658	177,000
Vocational secondary	1,349	17,630	434,000
University and higher	263	15,760	185,000

Adult education: In 1965–6 251 'workers' universities' and 247 'people's universities' provided vocational training for adults. Other schools gave remedial courses in basic subjects through seminars and lectures, at all primary and secondary levels.

MASS MEDIA

The Press (1966):

Dailies: *Politika*, Belgrade, ind., 310,000; *Večernje Novosti* (e), Belgrade, 260,000; *Borba*, Belgrade/Zagreb, Socialist Alliance of Working People of Jugo. (SAWPJ), 180,000; *Politika Ekspres* (e), Belgrade, ind., 124,000 (1965); *Vjesnik*, Zagreb, SAWPJ, 85,000; *Večernji List* (e), Zagreb, 85,000; *Delo*, Ljubljana, SAWPJ, 80,000; *Oslobodjenje*, Sarajevo, SAWPJ, 67,000; *Večer* (e), Maribor, SAWPJ, 44,000; *Sportske Novosti*, Zagreb, sport, 43,000; *Sport*, Belgrade, sport, 42,000; *Ljubljanski Dnevnik* (e), Ljubljana, 38,000; *Magyar Szó*, Novi Sad, SAWPJ, in Hungarian, 33,000; *Slobodna Dalmacija*, Split, SAWPJ, 29,000; *Nova Makedonija*, Skopje, SAWPJ, 28,000; *Dnevnik*, Novi Sad, SAWPJ, 28,000; *Večernje Novine* (e), Sarajevo, 22,000; *Privredni Pregled*, Belgrade, ind., 12,500; *Novi List*, Rijeka, SAWPJ, 11,000; *Glas Slavonije*, Osijek, SAWPJ, 8,500; *Rilindja*, Priština, SAWPJ, in Albanian, 8,000; *La Voce del Popolo*, Rijeka, SAWPJ, in Italian, 3,000.

Weeklies: *Arena*, Zagreb, illus., 330,000; *Male Novine*, Sarajevo, children's, 312,000; *Vjesnik u Srijedu*, Zagreb, info., 290,000; *Ilustrovana Politiki*, Belgrade, illus., 226,000; *Svet*, Belgrade, illus. 172,000; *Politikin Zabavnik*, Belgrade, children's comic, 170,000; *Komunist*, Belgrade, communist, 169,000; *Nedeljne Informativne Novine* (NIN), Belgrade, info., 140,000; *Pionir-Kekec*, Belgrade, children's, 134,000; *Studio*, Zagreb, broadcasting/arts, 130,000; *Pobjeda*, Titograd, SAWPJ, 115,000; *Rad*, Belgrade, trade union, 110,000; *Tedenska Tribune*, Ljubljana, info., 110,000; *Mladost*, Belgrade, youth, 96,000; *TV Novosti*, Belgrade, TV, 91,000; *Sport i Svet*, Belgrade, sport, 90,000; *Svijet*, Sarajevo, illus., 75,000; *Lovačke Novine*, Novi Sad, practical, 62,000; *Tovariš*, Ljubljana, illus., 51,000; *Zadruga*, Belgrade, coop., 53,000; *Globus*, Zagreb, illus., 50,000; *Ekonomska Politika*, Belgrade, econ., 9,000; *Književne Novine* (f), Belgrade, lit., 7,500; *Narodna Armija*, Belgrade, milit.; *Medjunarodna Politika* (f), Belgrade, internat. affairs; *Socijalizm* (m), Belgrade, Communist theory.

Broadcasting: Jugoslav Radiotelevision (JRT) is a federal association of the state broadcasting institutions of the six republics and two autonomous provinces. While all-nation relays are used, each unit maintains its own programmes of which Belgrade and Zagreb have three, Ljubljana, Skopje and Novi Sad two, Sarajevo, Titograd and Priština one each. Length of programmes varies from 33 hours per day in Belgrade to 16 hours per day in Titograd. The units also broadcast regionally through a network of 41 local stations, with special programmes in Shiptar (Albanian), Hungarian, Italian and Turkish. Radio Priština broadcasts a longer programme in Shiptar and Radio Novi Sad broadcasts mostly in Hungarian and also in Slovak. The all-nation TV network has stations in the republican capitals and broadcasts in the official republican languages. Over half the population is served. Some 6% of TV programmes consist of public advertising. Jugoslavia is a member of the European Radio Union (incl. Eurovision) and is in association with Intervision. Broadcasting is financed by revenue from subscriptions and advertising.

CONSTITUTIONAL SYSTEM

Constitution: The country's third post-war constitution (1963) declared Jugoslavia to be a Socialist Federal Republic based on the federal union of the six socialist republics. Each constituent republic maintains its own constitution in accordance with the the federal constitution. These differ from other socialist constitutions in several respects.

Legislature: The 670-member Federal Assembly in Belgrade (*Savezna Skupština*) is the highest organ of government and social self-government of the federation. It comprises the Federal Chamber (*Savezno Veće*), elected by universal franchise (18 years and over) on the one hand and four Chambers (Economic, Education and Culture, Social Services and Health, Political Organisation) elected by the Working Councils (*Radnički Saveti*) at the various territorial-administrative levels. These all contain 120 deputies each. Members of the Federal Chamber elected by the six Republican Assemblies and assemblies of the two autonomous provinces constitute the 70-member Chamber of Nationalities (*Veće Naroda*) (ten from each republic, five from each autonomous province) which functions as the guardian of the rights and equality of the federated peoples and republics. Deputies are elected for a four-year term; half the members of each chamber are elected every second year. No deputy may sit simultaneously in the Federal Assembly, a Republican Assembly or in two chambers of the same assembly, but a member of the Chamber of Nationalities keeps his seat in the republican or autonomous provincial assembly. Republican and Autonomous Provincial Assemblies are also subdivided into five chambers. Assemblies are elected on the same basis at the level of federation, republic, autonomous province, district and commune. The Federal Assembly at a joint meeting of all Chambers elects the president of the republic who constitutionally may be reelected only once, with the exception of the 'historic person' of Marshal Tito who holds office for life. The vice-presidency was abolished by constitutional amendment in 1967. The Federal Assembly legislates, approves the budget and annual financial statement, ratifies treaties, elects and removes members of the Federal Executive Council, Supreme Court, Constitutional Court and Supreme Economic Court. It exercises political supervision over other federal bodies, calls for a referendum, grants pardon, may declare war and generally determines internal and foreign policy. The 1963 constitution served to strengthen the office of the president of the Republic by entrusting him with the appointment of a deputy to the offices of presidency of the Federal Executive Council and by reconfirming his right to stay any decision of the latter body and place the matter in question before the Federal Chamber. The president is in addition commander-in-chief of the armed forces and may convene the Federal Executive Council.

Executive: The constitutional changes of 1963 provided for a separation of the offices of president of the republic and president of the Federal Executive (*Savezno Izvršno Veće*) and hence a more efficient division of work, but the president may preside over sessions of the Federal Executive Council and place matters on its agenda. The

85

G

competence of the Federal Executive Council was reduced; it could no longer appoint secretaries of state, federal secretaries or the federal procurator-general nor could it, in usual circumstances, issue decrees. The Federal Assembly's powers of appointment and recall of members of the Federal Executive Council and of supervision over that body underline the limitations placed on the chief organ of federal administration. While on the one hand the powers of the presidency of the republic and of the Federal Assembly have been officially reinforced, there has been a general devolution of legislative and executive power from the federal to the republican level. In 1967 the Secretaries of Health, Culture, etc. ceased to function at the federal level and their ministerial role was relegated to the republics. Now only the most important Secretariats (Foreign Affairs, Defence, Finance, Foreign Trade) remain within federal jurisdiction and their functions are explicitly coordinative.

Local government: Self-government (*samoupravljanje*) by the citizens in the commune (*komuna* or *opština*) is the political foundation of the socio-political systems in Jugoslavia. The supreme communal organ of communal government is the assembly whose members are elected for a four-year term (half the members being elected every second year). Executive bodies are appointed from within the assembly. An assembly comprises a communal chamber (*komunalno veće*) and a chamber of working communities (*veće radnih zajednica*). There are at present 516 communes. Larger towns comprise more than one commune and these may discharge their functions jointly. In all except the Slovene and Montenegrin republics another unit exists between commune and republic, namely the district (*srez*) whose precise competence varies according to republic but which discharges affairs of common concern to two or more communes. Members of district assemblies are elected by the communal assemblies from among their members. There are currently 24 districts. Within a given enterprise workers' self-government finds expression in the workers' council (*radnički saveti*) whose members are directly elected for a two-year term and which determines the plan, programme and development of the enterprise. It generally appoints a managing board (*upravni odbor*) for a term of one year.

Judiciary: Courts of general jurisdiction are the communal courts, county courts, Supreme Courts of the republics and the Supreme Court of Jugoslavia (*Vrhovni Sud Jugoslavije*). The latter decides on appeals against decisions of the Supreme Courts of the republics and directs application of federal laws. Its judges are elected and removed by the Federal Chamber of the Federal Assembly; Supreme Courts of the republics (*Vrhovni Sudovi Republika*) decide on appeals against decisions of county courts. Their judges are elected or removed by the republican assemblies. District courts (*sreski sudovi*) and communal courts (*opštinski sudovi*) comprise, except in certain single-judge cases determined by law, a judge (*sudija*) and two lay-assessors (*porotnici*) elected and removed by the assembly of the corresponding socio-political community except for some courts which may be directly elected by the citizens of that community. Court hearings are public save where the safeguarding of secrets or the protection of public decency are involved. Proceedings are held in the national language of the republic but provision may be made for interpreting. The Constitutional Court of Jugoslavia (*Ustavni Sud Jugoslavije*), consisting of a president and ten judges elected for a term of eight years, decides on the conformity of law with the federal constitution and on the conformity of republican law with federal law; it also resolves conflicts between courts and federal organs on the territories of two or more republics. Economic cases and other forms of litigation concerning the economy are heard by district economic courts (*sreski privredni sudovi*), higher economic courts (*viši privredni sudovi*) and the Supreme Economic Court (*Vrhovni Privredni Sud*). Special courts include military tribunals and courts of arbitration. The judiciary is independent. The Public Prosecution (*Javno Tužilaštvo*) is an autonomous organ entrusted with criminal prosecution and also with ensurance of the uniform enforcement of law and protection of legality. This is headed by the Federal Public Prosecutor (*Javni Tužilac Jugoslavije*) who is appointed and removed by the Federal Assembly. Capital punishment is maintained.

Party: There is only one political party, the League of Jugoslav Communists (LJC) with a current membership of 1,046,000, and there is thus no parliamentary opposition. The six republics maintain separate Communist Parties. The Federation of

Jugoslav Youth numbers at least 2,034,000. The Socialist Alliance of the Working People of Jugoslavia, which is a mass organisation rather than a political party, contains 8,126,000 members.

Leading government and party figures: Josip Broz Tito (president of republic and secretary-general of LJC), Mika Špiljak (president of Federal Executive Council), Milentije Popović (president of Federal Assembly), Marko Nikezić (foreign minister), Vasil Grivčev (foreign trade minister), Janko Smole (finance minister), Gen. Nikola Ljubičić (defence minister).

POLAND

Features: Poland lies in the geographical centre of the European continent and is the largest country in Eastern Europe after the Soviet Union. The Oder (Pol. Odra) and Neisse (Pol. Nysa) Rivers in the west, the River Bug in the east, the Sudetes Range in the south-west and the Carpathians in the south-east constitute the nation's post-war political boundaries, while in the north there are 320 miles/520 km. of Baltic sea coast. As a result of World War II Poland lost nearly half its pre-war territory to the Soviet Union but acquired from Germany parts of east Prussia and Brandenburg, much of Pomerania and Silesia and also the free city of Gdańsk (Ger. Danzig). Poland's present neighbours are thus East Germany, Czechoslovakia and the Soviet Union. Universal *de jure* recognition of these frontiers is still pending a final German Peace Treaty.

Of present Polish territory, one-half is drained by the Vistula and tributaries, and one-third by the Oder which, entering Poland by the Moravian Gate, divides the Sudetes on the west (max. height 5,000 ft/1,500 m.) from the Alpine-featured High Tatra section of the Carpathians on the east (max. height 8,200 ft/2,500 m.). The upper basins of the Oder and Vistula are separated by the Little Polish (*Małopolska*) Tableland (1,600 ft/500 m.). The fertile loess-covered Silesian lowlands, centring on Katowice, together with the upper basin of the Vistula, contain some of the world's richest coal, copper and sulphur deposits, also natural gas. Two-thirds of the country, comprising part of the North European Plain, is glaciated lowland, agricultural and forested. In the north the plains of Pomerania and Mazowia, west and east of the Vistula respectively, are of sand, clay and gravel composition and are characterised by numerous lakes, marsh, forest and morainic ridges giving way on the Baltic coast to lagoon-and-bar formations. The continental climate of the country is subject to maritime influences in the west.

Poland is one of the more industrialised countries of Eastern Europe. Its industrial heartland is based on the bituminous coalfields of Silesia. The chief manufacturing centres for metallurgical, chemical, textile, cement and food industries are Warsaw, Cracow, Wrocław (Ger. Breslau), Łódź, Poznań (Posen) and Gdańsk. There is lignite mining near Łódź and shipbuilding at Gdańsk and Gdynia which, together with Szczecin (Stettin), are major ports. More than half the land is agricultural, the main crops being rye, wheat, oats, barley and potatoes. Fruit cultivation and forestry are important. Some hydropower is harnessed, especially in the upper Oder region.

Area: 120,400 sq. miles/312,500 sq. km.

Mean max. and min. temperatures: Warsaw (52°N, 21°E; 395 ft/120 m.) 65°F/18°C (July) 25°F/-4°C(Jan.) Cracow (50°N, 20°E; 720 ft/219 m.) 67°F/19°C(July) 27°F/-3°C(Jan.) Gdańsk (54°N, 18°E; 35 ft/10 m.) 63°F/17°C(July) 29°F/-2°C(Jan.)

Relative humidity: Warsaw 86%; Cracow 87%; Gdańsk 80%.

Mean annual rainfall: Warsaw 22 in./560 mm.; Cracow 29 in./745 mm.; Gdańsk 21 in./545 mm.

Total population (1966 est.): 31,551,000.

Chief towns and populations (1965 est.): Warsaw (1,268,000), Łódź (745,000), Cracow

POLAND

(525,000), Wrocław (Ger. Breslau) (477,000), Poznań (Posen) (440,000), Gdańsk, (Danzig) (324,000), Szczecin (Stettin) (314,000), Katowice (287,000), Bydgoszcz (258,000), Lublin (206,000).

Ethnic composition: The largest minorities (1963) are Ukrainians (180,000) and Belorussians (165,000).

Language: The official language is Polish.

Religion: About 95% of the population are nominally Roman Catholic. Of the 13 other religious denominations, the Polish Orthodox Church is the largest.

RECENT HISTORY

In 1945 the Moscow-oriented Polish provisional government established in Lublin was supplemented by members of the London-based government-in-exile and recognised by the Western allies, but opponents of the communists and their allies were soon liable to fierce persecution, arrest, deportation to the Soviet Union and extermination. Most of Poland to the east of the Curzon Line had been occupied by Soviet troops since the 1929 Ribbentrop-Molotov Pact, while the liberation of the German-occupied regions now placed the rest of the country under Soviet control. The Teheran Conference (1942) had confirmed the Soviet annexation of 1939 and at Potsdam in 1945 the Great Powers sanctioned Polish suzerainty over former German territories east of the Rivers Oder and Neisse and over the larger part of east Prussia including Gdańsk.

After the 1947 elections at which the Peasant Party opposition under Stanisław

Mikołajczyk was subjected to coercion and police intimidation, the communist leadership inaugurated a decade of totalitarian rule based upon the closest dependence on Moscow and a Stalinist system of terror. In 1947 Bolesław Bierut, a Pole with Soviet citizenship, was elected the country's president and Mikołajczyk and other anti-communists fled to the West. In 1948 Władysław Gomułka, secretary-general of the Polish Workers' (Communist) Party and deputy prime minister was purged as a Titoist. The campaign against the Catholic Church was intensified and by 1953, when the primate of Poland, Cardinal Wyszyński, was arrested, several hundred clergy had already been imprisoned. In the same year the Polish Workers' Party and Socialists were merged in the Polish United Workers' Party (PZPR) and in 1949 the new United Peasant Party absorbed the remnants of the old Peasant Party. Significantly the Soviet Marshal Konstantin Rokossovsky was appointed as Poland's commander-in-chief and minister of defence. When the presidency was abolished (1952) in favour of a State Council, Bierut, while retaining his secretaryship of the PZPR, became prime minister, to be succeeded by Józef Cyrankiewicz in 1954.

The year 1956 represented for Poland, as for Hungary, a turning-point. Bierut died in March and the following June workers and students in Poznań demonstrated against one-party rule and Soviet domination. Profiting from a national mood of protest, anti-Stalinist party members staged a bloodless coup, the 'Polish October', and the resurgent Gomułka was elected Secretary-General of the PZPR. For several months the government's reforms suggested a Titoist departure from Stalinism, involving as they did a liberalisation of culture, improved church-state relations, decollectivisation of agriculture, the dismissal of Rokossovsky and other Soviet military personnel, economic aid from the USA and growing contacts with the West. But the lesson of Hungary in 1956 and Gomułka's political conservatism combined to disappoint the advocates of change. The 1957 elections returned Cyrankiewicz as prime minister and Aleksander Zawadzki as chairman of the State Council (to be succeeded on his death in 1964 by Edward Ochab). A state of political apathy, bureaucratic immobilism, economic stagnation and cultural anarchy has since prevailed; church-state rivalry and relations with the West have become a substitute for intra-party or inter-party debate. In a country where religion is so emphatically equated with national identity the Catholic Church has assumed a quasi-political force and in 1966 the PZPR was obliged to find a counter-attraction to the church's millenary celebrations. The Polish episcopacy was accused of interfering in the nation's foreign affairs when, as a conciliatory gesture, it invited West German bishops to Poland, and Western ecclesiastics including the pope were refused entry. The personal intransigence of both Gomułka and Cardinal Wyszyński symbolise the current impasse. Anti-Semitism was rife in 1968 and appeared to enjoy the support of the nationalist wing represented by Gen. Moczar.

Poland's foreign policy generally follows the Soviet line and since, for the first time in history, it has treaty arrangements with all its neighbours, it is firmly committed to present German frontiers and in 1950 secured East German recognition of the Oder-Neisse Line. In 1956 Foreign Minister Rapacki proposed a Central European denuclearised zone to include both parts of Germany, but the territorial issue impedes better relations with Bonn. As further proof of the increasingly reactionary nature of Poland's political leadership, Polish troops participated in the invasion of Czechoslovakia (August, 1968). Poland is otherwise a proponent of *détente* and it is significant that the USA and China maintain their only diplomatic links through a regular dialogue of their ambassadors in Warsaw.

Defence (1967): Military service is compulsory, for two years in the army and three years in the navy and air force. Strength is estimated at: army 185,000, navy 15,000, air force 70,000, para-military forces 45,000. 1966 defence expenditure was $1,589 million, representing 5·3% of GNP. Poland is a member of the Warsaw Pact and accommodates two Soviet divisions.

ECONOMY

Background: The second largest country of the East European socialist bloc, Poland has several unique economic features, notably a predominantly private agricultural sector. In the 1960s growth of national income has been quite steady at around 6% to 7%, with a drop from 7·2% to 6% from 1966 to 1967. Investment has been maintained at about 28% of national income: in 1967 44·2% of fixed investment was in industry and construction. Signs of strain appeared in 1967 when there was a high level of investment activity and import demand, but a declining growth in agricultural supplies and virtual stagnation in several branches of the consumer market. Despite the plan producer goods' output expanded at the expense of consumer goods. Engineering, metallurgy and chemicals all progressed well but food processing output increased by only 1·7% and textiles by 3·8%.

Reform has been undertaken cautiously in Poland and has been less sweeping than in neighbouring countries. More power is being extended to 'trusts', each responsible for a branch of industry, which are becoming semi-autonomous, self-financing bodies with their own investment and incentive funds. Some prices have been adjusted to reflect costs more closely and world prices have been adopted in export branches. Centralised price fixing remains, however, together with centralised supply allocation. Greater use is being made of bank credit for investment finance: 60% of all investment is to be financed from this source in the period 1966–70 compared with 5% for 1961–65. Plan indicators have been revised giving priority to profitability, and restrictions on employment have been lifted.

Agricultural production has failed to keep pace with rising demand. Total output rose by 5·4% in 1966 and by 2·7% in 1967 when 1·9 million tons of grain had to be imported. Main crops are potatoes, sugarbeet and grain; dairy farming is important as a source of foreign exchange earnings. The state owns only 14% of the land, collectivisation having been abandoned in 1956. The distribution of land is not conducive to efficiency as there is a considerable fragmentation of holdings (over 50% of less than 5 hectares) many in the hands of aged farmers and one-third run by women. These small scattered holdings are poorly supplied with fertilisers and machinery, and horses are still a major source of power. In January 1968 legislation was introduced to speed up consolidation of private holdings into state farms and cooperatives.

Foreign trade: One-third of Poland's trade is with the Soviet Union and a quarter with the rest of Comecon. In 1966 and 1967 efforts were made to reduce a large trade deficit and trade with Western Europe has been hampered by inability to earn adequate foreign exchange. In October 1967 Poland became a full contracting member of the General Agreement on Tariffs and Trade and agreed to increase imports from the West by 40% over five years. Incentives to export industries have been extended. Britain is Poland's largest West European trading partner importing £56·2 million worth of goods from Poland in 1967, including £21 million of meat. Imports from the West are primarily of machinery, non-ferrous metals and textiles; exports of meat, timber, dairy products, chemicals and fruit and vegetables. Cooperation with Western firms is being sought, especially for car production.

Employment: Since 1960 the expansion of employment has been almost 70% with a corresponding increase in the wage fund. Problems have been experienced in raising productivity and absenteeism has increased in the last two years. The workers' councils set up in 1956 give workers some influence in enterprise management.

Prices and wages: The overfulfilment of employment plans has resulted in an above plan expansion of money incomes and strain in the consumer goods markets. Real incomes rose by 3·3% in 1966 and by about 2·5% in 1967; the cost of living rose by 1·2% to 1·5% in these years. Peasants' real wages have tended to increase more rapidly than industrial wages. Per capita real income has risen faster than average real wages because of the expansion of employment and the steady decline in the rate of growth of the population which dropped from almost 2% in the mid-1950s to 0·9% in 1967.

Consumption: There has been rather a bottleneck in the supply of consumer goods during the last few years with a high level of demand for imported products. Some of the frustrated demand has been absorbed by the service sector; expenditure on services increasing by 19% in 1966 and by 10·3% in 1967. Retail trade turnover rose by 6·3% and 7·5% in these years. In 1967 meat supplies seriously failed to satisfy demands (partly because of the high level of meat exports) and the authorities were forced to raise prices, on average, by 17%. Investment in food processing, textiles and light industry is being expanded in an effort to restore market equilibrium.

SOCIAL WELFARE

Social insurance, which is supervised by the Ministry of Health and Social Welfare and financed from state budget allocations, covers all working people. Benefits mentioned below refer to 1966 unless otherwise stated.

Health services: Free health facilities are available to all workers (or pensioners) and their families, and to students and servicemen. Emphasis is placed on separate clinics for industrial enterprises and on a network of outpatient clinics, health co-operatives and mobile units in rural locations. A worker is entitled to sick pay amounting to 70% of earnings if during his incapacity he remains at home and receives treatment in an outpatient clinic. In case of hospitalisation he receives benefits fixed at 14% of average net earnings (50% if he has at least one dependant). A working mother is eligible for allowance amounting to 70% of earnings for the care of sick children under 14 years of age (payable for 30 days per annum) provided she forgoes her salary. An infectious disease allowance (70% of earnings) is payable to the worker compelled to miss work because of infectious illness at home. Special benefits are available to TB patients (from 35% to 70% of earnings) for periods of up to one year. Maternity benefits comprise a twelve-week confinement allowance (fixed at 100% of earnings if birth is given at home, and 20% to 50% of earnings if in a medical institution) and an allowance for breast-feeding mothers (amounting to one free litre of milk daily for the period of breast-feeding).

Pensions and other benefits: Since 1954 a uniform system of pension benefits has operated for workers, with separate schemes available for certain categories (miners, railwaymen, militia, armed forces, since 1964 lawyers and since 1965 artisans). Annual expenditure for old-age pensions grew from 2,800 million zlotys in 1955 to 13,000 million zlotys in 1963. The pensionable age for most workers is 60 for men, 55 for women. The old-age pension amounts to 75% of net earnings if these did not exceed 1,200 zlotys monthly; in the case of higher earnings, the worker receives an additional 20% of the sum in excess of 1,200 zlotys up to 2,000 zlotys, and 15% of the sum in excess of 2,000 zlotys. Disability pensions may be claimed by victims of occupational injury or disease and of certain 'social accidents' such as those sustained while risking life in the public interest; these vary according to category of employment, disability and total income. Family insurance, introduced in 1947, now benefits the families of 3,400,000 workers, annual expenditure on this exceeding one-third of the total social insurance budget. The family allowance, payable only to the fully employed parent or guardian, averages 12% of regular earnings. Monthly cash payments are fixed at 50 zlotys for one child, 175 zlotys for two children, 310 zlotys for three children and 150 zlotys for each additional child. The worker is entitled to a family allowance for his wife if she is not gainfully employed and rears at least one child under eight, or if she is 50 years of age or over, or incapacitated. A working woman is entitled to a family allowance of 30 zlotys monthly if her husband is wholly dependent. Funeral allowances, primarily intended to cover funeral costs, are paid to the family in the event of a worker's death, and amount to seven weeks' wages of the deceased. In the event of the death of a family member, the worker receives an allowance fixed at three weeks' earnings. Since officially unemployment is no longer a large-scale phenomenon (between 1955 and 1962 the number of unemployed in any single year never exceeded 50,000[1]) there is no unemployment insurance. Any incidental needs of the unemployed are met from other funds.

Housing: Poland in World War II lost per capita more housing stock than any country in the world. This factor, coupled with an extremely dynamic post-war demographic growth and a doubling of the urban population during the 1950s caused an acute housing shortage which is only now being substantially alleviated. Today's chief problems stem from a lack of separate one-family flats and the resultant necessity to

[1] Later figures not available.

maintain strict systems of rent control and allocation of dwellings. Of the three broad sectors, state, private and cooperative, the latter now shows the fastest growth and under the 1966–70 plan will include 57% of all new housing. As a rule the local people's councils allocate state housing to lower income groups, cooperative dwellings to middle and higher income groups. In the state sector the principal investors are the municipal people's councils and various industrial establishments whose building projects are financed from their own budgets, in turn subsidised by grants-in-aid from the state budget. Cooperative housing is administered by the Central Housing Cooperatives Union, which is responsible for its own investment services and design institutes. Prospective tenants contribute 15% to 25% of construction costs, the remainder being financed by state credits over a 40-year period whereas the state may grant additional aid by annulling up to one-third of the loan. To meet the cost of his contribution, a member of a housing cooperative can also obtain an additional personal loan of up to 10% from his place of employment. Construction of private housing, which is concentrated in rural and suburban areas, is supported by state credits averaging 50%, and never exceeding 75%, of construction costs, available for a period of up to 25 years. In Polish housing the emphasis is put on prefabrication and multiple units containing shopping precincts. Large-scale developments include the postwar renovation of Warsaw's Old Town, the planned reconstruction of the Muranów district (formerly Warsaw's Jewish ghetto) and the creation of new towns such as Nowa Huta and Nowe Tychy.

EDUCATION

In Poland's unified and secular system of education, primary, secondary and most higher institutions come under the Ministry of Education and Higher Education while medical schools are controlled by the Ministry of Health and Social Welfare. Fine arts colleges fall under the Ministry of Culture and Art, military colleges under the Ministry of National Defence and colleges of physical education under the Central Committee for Physical Culture. Since 1961 several reforms have raised the compulsory school-leaving age to 15, strengthened the polytechnical element in primary and secondary schooling, expanded West European language programmes and extended the system of higher learning. Russian is taught at primary and secondary levels while religion may be taken as an extra-mural option. There are two autonomous theological academies in Warsaw and a private Catholic University at Lublin. Extracurricular activities are promoted and boarding facilities in hostels or private accommodations are provided for pupils in need of them. Officially, the illiteracy rate was reduced to 3% in 1960.

Primary education: The free and optional kindergarten, which is run by the state, by institutions or communities, in 1964–5 provided pre-primary schooling (*przedszkola*) for 22% of children aged three and over. Eight-year primary education is free and obligatory for children aged seven to 15 and in cases of failure to complete this course, the compulsory school age limit is raised to 17. By 1967 the basic eight-year primary schools (*szkoły podstawowe*) replaced the earlier seven-year system and added such subjects as workshop activities, aesthetic and civic training, music and physical drill to the traditional academic syllabus. In 1965 78% of those leaving primary school continued to secondary schools. Of this number some 80% proceeded to vocational schools while the remainder went to general secondary schools. Admission to secondary schools is by entrance examination.

Secondary education: The four-year general secondary schools (*licea ogólnokształcące*) complete the uniform twelve-year general education programme on the combined primary and secondary levels. Between 1965 and 1967 the curriculum was broadened to include more mathematics, natural science, current affairs and also polytechnical elements. In addition to compulsory Russian, the study of either English, French, German or Latin is required. Over 2,000 pupils attend schools where the medium of instruction is a foreign language. Matriculation is by means of examination in Polish, mathematics, history, one language and a science and entitles the pupil to higher education.

Vocational education is organised on two levels. The lower vocational schools (*zasadicze szkoły zawodowe*) admit primary school leavers aged 15 to 17 and include two-to-three-year training schools for industry (*szkoły przysposobienia zawodowego*) and agriculture (*szkoły przysposobienia rolniczego*) in which basic vocational instruction is closely related to enterprises and cooperatives and may take the form of direct apprentice-ship or workers' refresher courses. At a higher level are the one-to-three-year technical schools (*technika zawodowe*) for graduates of general secondary schools; three-to-six-year technical schools (*technika zawodowe*) for graduates of the primary system who wish to combine practical with general education; five-year teacher-training schools (*licea pedagogicznee*) and five-year schools of arts and applied arts (*licea i technika artystyczne*). Eligibility for further vocational training at teacher-training schools for secondary school teaching (*technika przemysłowo-pedagogiczne*), post-secondary teacher-training courses (*studia nauczycielskie*) and nursing schools (*szkoły pielęgniarskie*), is based on completion of two to five years of previous secondary education.

Special education: For the handicapped there are special schools in the primary, general secondary and lower and higher vocational categories. Board is provided for chronic cases such as orphans, and treatment and tuition are free.

University and higher education: The institutions of higher education include eight universities (Jagiellonian Univ. at Cracow, Warsaw, Poznań, Wrocław, Lublin, Łódź, Toruń, Catholic Univ. of Lublin), nine Technical Universities (in major cities), ten Medical Academies (some in association with the universities), seven Agricultural Colleges (incl. Warsaw Central Agric. Univ.), seven Schools of Econo-mics (incl. Central School for Planning and Statistics, Warsaw), a Foreign Service College at Cracow, two Theological Academies, 16 art and music schools and four Pedagogical High Schools. Courses leading to the first (master's) degrees of *magistra* and *magistra inżyniera* last five years, while the degree of *lekarza* follows on six years for medicine and five-and-a-half years for veterinary medicine. Art and music school dip-lomas are awarded after five or six years of study. Approximately one-third of all those enrolled in higher institutions are extra-mural students otherwise employed; those in certain sciences take degree courses of six rather than five years.

Educational institutions (1965–6)

	Institutions	Staff	Students
Primary	26,539	171,745	5,176,588
General secondary	867	15,848	426,846
Vocational	n.a.	49,700[1]	1,670,800
Higher	76	21,600[1]	251,900

[1] Represents 1964–5.

Adult education: Approximately 45% of all pupils at lower vocational secondary schools and 25% at upper vocational schools are full-time workers who take vocational day or evening courses as students enrolled in the 'people's universities' and 'rural univer-sities'. These 'universities', of which there are almost 3,000, are set up as regular study groups for a minimum of 30 persons over the age of 17 who have completed primary school. Most courses last one or two years and include programmes of general culture and practical training. In addition various communities and educational organisations run highly popular correspondence courses, especially in foreign languages, at both secondary and higher levels.

Mass Media

The Press (1966):

Dailies: *Express Wieczorny* (e), Warsaw, ind., 500,000; *Trybuna Robotnicza*, Katowice, PZPR, 350,000; *Trybuna Ludu*, Warsaw, PZPR, 300,000; *Dziennik Ludowy*, Warsaw, ind.; *Express Ilustrowany*, Łódź, ind.; *Życie Warszawy*, Warsaw, ind., 210,000; *Słowo Powszechne*, Warsaw, Catholic, 150,000; *Dziennik Zachodni*, Katowice, ind., 145,000; *Echo Krakowa*, Cracow, ind., 125,000; *Głos Pracy*, Warsaw, trade union, 120,000;

Dziennik Łódzki, Łódź, ind., 107,000; *Głos Wielkopolski*, Poznań, ind., 106,000; *Sztandar Młodych*, Warsaw, youth, 103,000; *Kurier Polski*, Bydgoszcz, Democratic Party, 100,000; *Dziennik Bałtycki*, Gdańsk, econ./shipping, 100,000; *Słowo Polskie*, Wrocław, ind., 88,000; *Dziennik Polski*, Cracow, ind., 85,000; *Express Poznański*, Poznań, ind., 60,500; *Kurier Szczeciński*, Szczecin, ind., 51,000. (Each *województwo* has its own daily paper.)

Periodicals: Przyjaciółka (w), Warsaw, woman's, 1,960,000; *Gromada-Rolnik Polski* (3 per week), Warsaw, 600,000; *Kobieta i Życie* (w), Warsaw, woman's, 550,000; *Przekrój* (w), Cracow, illus., 450,000; *Panorama* (w), Katowice, illus., 370,000; *Kulisy* (w), Warsaw, review, 260,000; *Nowa Wieś* (w), Warsaw, rural illus., 260,000; *Dookoła Świata* (w), Warsaw, youth, 250,000; *Polityka* (w), Warsaw, polit., 180,000; *Twoje Dziecko* (m), Warsaw, mother's, 170,000; *Przegląd Sportowy* (4 per week), Warsaw, sport, 150,000; *Sport* (4 per week), Katowice, sport, 140,000; *Film* (w), Warsaw, film, 130,000; *Poznaj Świat* (m), Warsaw, geogr. illus., 120,000; *Radio i Telewizja* (w), Warsaw, radio, 120,000; *Morze* (m), Warsaw, maritime, 110,000; *Spilki* (w), Warsaw, satirical, 105,000; *Świat* (w), Warsaw, illus., 100,000; *Żołnierz Polski* (w), Warsaw, military, 100,000; *Chłopska Droga* (2 per week), Warsaw, rural polit., 80,000; *Robotnik Rolny* (w), Warsaw, agric. union, 73,000; *Sportowiec* (w), Warsaw, sport, 70,000; *Głos Nauczycielski* (w), Warsaw, teacher's, 70,000; *Przyjaźń* (w), Warsaw, Soviet friendship, 63,000; *Wrocławski Tygodnik Katolików* (w), Catholic, 60,000; *Życie Litterackie* (w), Cracow, lit., 50,000; *Problemy* (m), Warsaw, pop. science, 50,000; *Nowe Drogi* (m), Warsaw, polit., 50,000; *Przyjaciel Żołnierza* (w), Warsaw, military, 40,000; *Stolica* (w), Warsaw, cult., 40,000; *Życie Gospodarcze* (w), Warsaw, econ., 30,000; *Nowa Kultura* (w), Warsaw, lit., 25,000; *Nowe Czasy* (w), Warsaw, internat. affairs, 10,000; *Teatr* (f), Warsaw, theatre, 8,000; *Ekonomista* (6 per year), Warsaw, econ., 7,000; *Sprawy Międzynarodowe* (m), Warsaw, internat. affairs, 3,000; *Folks Sztyme* (4 per week), Warsaw, Yiddish.

Broadcasting: Polish Radio and Television, a state monopoly controlled by the Committee for Radio and Television, maintains three daily radio programmes, Programme I (24 hours, general), Programme II (19 hours, serious) and Programme III (evenings), broadcast by 23 stations. Foreign transmissions are made in ten languages. Television emits daily morning and evening programmes.

CONSTITUTIONAL SYSTEM

Constitution: The Polish People's Republic, whose Soviet-type constitution dates from 1952, is termed a people's democracy in which power belongs to the working people of town and country. The presidency was abolished in 1952 in favour of a Council of State.

Legislature: The unicameral *Sejm* (Diet or Parliament), convoked at least twice a year, is theoretically the supreme legislative organ, empowered to initiate and pass legislation, adopt the budget and national economic plan, declare a state of war, appoint and recall ministers, elect members of the State Council (*Rada Stanu*) and exercise control over the work of other organs of state authority and administration. The *Sejm* is elected for a four-year term by all citizens over 18 years. 460 deputies represent constituencies of 60,000 persons each. 97% of the electorate participated in the last elections (May 1965). Candidates are nominated by organisations strictly controlled by the Polish United Workers' Party (PZPR). Nominally subordinate to the *Sejm* is a 17-member collegiate body, the State Council, whose extensive powers include the convocation of the *Sejm*, the holding of general elections, the appointment and recall of diplomats, the ratification and abrogation of international agreements, the awarding of honours, the nomination of higher civil and military officers, the right to grant pardon, the definitive interpretation of laws and the issuance of statutory decrees such as martial law and mobilisation. It also supervises the people's councils. There is no constitutional provision for the recall of its members. Also responsible to the *Sejm* is the Supreme Chamber of Control which supervises the legality and functioning of legislation and administration at all levels and is required to make an annual report on the execution of the national economic plan. It is officially independent, with a chairman appointed and dismissed by the *Sejm*.

Executive: The highest executive and administrative body is the Council of Ministers (*Rada Ministrów*) whose members are appointed and recalled by the *Sejm*. It is responsible to the *Sejm* or, when the latter is not sitting, to the State Council and is composed of a chairman (i.e. prime minister), vice-chairmen, 23 ministers and the four chairmen of special commissions such as Economic Planning. It coordinates the work of ministries, frames and submits in the *Sejm* the annual budget and the draft of the national economic plan, ensures the execution of laws, establishes the annual conscription quota and directs the activities of the praesidia of the people's councils.

Local government: Poland is divided administratively into 17 voivodships (*województwa* or provinces) and five cities, with voivodship status (Warsaw, Cracow, Wrocław, Łódź and Poznań). These are subdivided into 317 districts (*powiaty*), 74 towns with district status, 710 towns, 5,238 communities and 102 settlements. Larger towns, moreover, together contain 39 boroughs. In each of these units government is exercised by the people's councils (*rady narodowe*) whose executive and administrative branches are the praesidia. The latter are assisted by departments of the praesidium, as, for example, departments of finance, health, agriculture, education.

Judiciary: Justice is administered through a Supreme Court (*Sąd Najwyższy*) and regional courts at the level of voivodship and district. The Supreme Court, which acts as both ordinary and extraordinary court of review, is elected for a five-year term by the State Council while the regional courts, consisting of one judge and two lay assessors, are elected by the People's Councils. District courts act as courts of first instance in most civil suits and less important criminal cases. Voivodship courts act as courts of appeal but also handle more serious cases. There are constitutional provisions for special courts, most of which (such as military tribunals) are outside the judicial system. The procuracy, based on the Soviet model, is separated from the judiciary and the procurator-general, appointed by the State Council, heads a body of prosecutors theoretically independent of local government. Their functions are both to enforce observance of socialist legality and to prosecute in criminal cases. Capital punishment is maintained.

Party: There are in theory three main political parties which collaborate in the National Unity Front, namely the Polish United Workers' Party (*Polska Zjednoczona Partia Robotnicza, PZPR*) which is the ruling party, the United Peasants' Party (*Zjednoesone Stronnictwo Ludowe, ZSL*) and the Democratic Party (*Stronnictwo Demokratyczne*). The PZPR is predominant. A small clandestine pro-Peking Communist Party has existed since 1966 with its base in Albania. The PZPR had (1967) 1,871,000 members and the ZSL (1966) 365,600.

Leading government and party figures (1969): Marshal Marian Spychalski (president of the State Council, i.e. head of state); Józef Cyrankiewicz (chairman of Council of Ministers, i.e. prime minister); Stefan Ignar, Piotr Jaroszewicz, Eugeniusz Szyr (vice-premiers); Stefan Jędrychowski (foreign minister); Kazimierz Switala (home minister); General Wojciech Jaruzelski (defence minister); Józef Kulesza (chairman of Economic Planning Commission); Marian Dmochowski (acting minister of foreign trade). First secretary of Central Committee of Polish United Workers' Party (PZPR): Władysław Gomułka; leading members of Politburo and party Secretariat: General Mieczysław Moczar (rep. radical 'right'), Edward Gierek (rep. radical 'left'), Marshal Marian Spychalski, Józef Cyrankiewicz, Stefan Jędrychowski, Piotr Jaroszewicz.

RUMANIA

GEOGRAPHY

Features: Rumania is a symmetrically shaped country adjoining four other communist states—the Soviet Union, Bulgaria, Jugoslavia and Hungary. Its north-eastern and southern political frontiers comprise in large measure the Rivers Prut and Danube respectively. It has 150 miles/250 km. of coast on the Black Sea. The country may be subdivided into three almost equal parts: plains, mountains and hilly plateaus. The southern ranges of the arcuate Carpathian chain reach heights of over 7,000 ft/2,000 m. in several regions. The Transylvanian and Someş plateaus lie inside the semicircle of the Carpathians, whilst the Moldavian and Wallachian lowlands (or Rumanian Plain) radiate to the east and south. The basins of the Tisza, extending westwards into Hungary and Jugoslavia, and of the Danube, are low-lying and of recent lacustrine origin. The climate is continental with the transitional character peculiar to south-eastern Europe, and is relatively uniform.

Despite the accelerated growth of industry in the last decade, unparalleled in Eastern Europe, Rumania is still primarily agricultural. With very fertile soils, especially in the Wallachian and Moldavian Plains, it supports a wide range of crops and is agriculturally self-sufficient. With 26% of its area forested, it has a well-developed timber industry, and the reed resources of the Danube Delta are exploited on an industrial scale. Rumania is well endowed with mineral and fuel resources, including the second largest oilfields in Europe (in the Ploieşti and Băcau regions), methane gas in Transylvania, lignite and black coal, especially in the Jiu Valley and hydroelectric power, generated in several regions. The hydroelectric plant at the Iron Gates of the Danube, built in cooperation with Jugoslavia, will be one of Europe's largest. A wealth of other minerals, including ferrous and non-ferrous metals, manganese, bauxite and rock-salt contribute to a variety of widely dispersed industrial complexes. Bucharest, Ploieşti, Braşov, Hunedoara, Cluj, the Banat, Galaţi and Constanţa are chief centres of the iron and steel metallurgical, chemical and petro-chemical, textile, construction and light industries. Communications are easy in lowland areas and facilitated in the mountainous fringes of Transylvania by several low passes. The Danube is navigable. Constanţa and the Danubian city of Galaţi are chief ports. New resorts, such as Mamaia and Eforie, serve the rapid evolution of tourism on the Black Sea coast.

Area: 91,700 sq. miles/237,500 sq. km.
Mean max. and min. temperatures: Bucharest (44°N, 26°E; 270 ft/82 m.) 74°F/23°C (July) 27°F/-3°C(Jan.) Cluj (47°N, 24°E; 1,285 ft/392 m.) 68°F/20°C (July) 24°F/-4°C (Jan.) Constanţa (44°N, 29°E; 15 ft/5 m.) 71°F/22°C(July) 31° F/-1° C(Jan.)
Relative humidity: Bucharest 87%; Cluj 85%; Constanţa 83%.
Mean annual rainfall: Bucharest 23 in./595 mm.; Cluj 24 in./610 mm. Constanţa 15 in./ 380 mm.

POPULATION

Total population (1966): 19,105,000.
Chief towns and populations (1966): Bucharest (1,382,000) Braşov (236,000), Cluj (207,000). Ploieşti (177,000), Constanţa (174,000), Timişoara (171,000), Iaşi (160,000), Craiova (151,000).

97

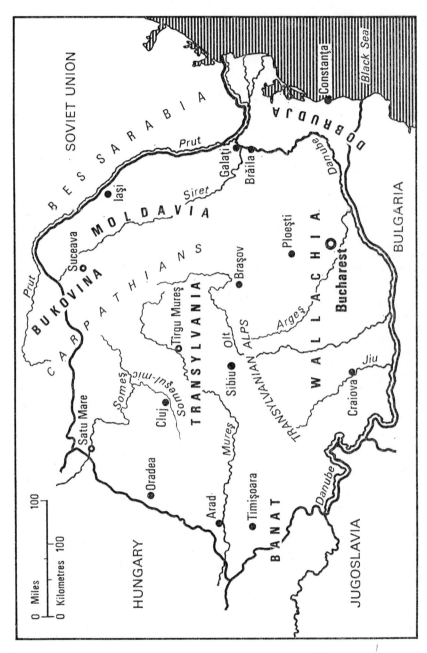

Ethnic composition: Rumanians number 87%, Hungarians 9%, Germans 2%. Other minorities include Turks, Greeks and Serbs.
Language: Rumanian is the national language but Hungarian and German have official parity.
Religion: Some 82% of the population are nominally Rumanian Orthodox and 9% Roman Catholic. Religious minorities include Protestant, Serbian Orthodox and Muslim groups.

RECENT HISTORY

After the invasion of Rumania by the Red Army in August 1944, King Michael led a coup d'état which removed the Fascist Antonescu government and allied the country to the Soviet Union and the Western allies. Elections in 1946 confirmed communists under Petru Groza in the key posts of a National Democratic Front government, even though in 1944 the party had only numbered 900 adherents, and in 1947 Groza, with Soviet support, conducted a mass purge of political opponents. The king abdicated and the country was proclaimed a People's Republic. The 1947 Paris Peace Treaty assigned to Rumania the frontiers of 1 January 1941 (i.e. leaving Bessarabia and northern Bukovina to Soviet control and southern Dobrudja under Bulgarian administration) with the exception of the frontier with Hungary which was restored to the pre-war configuration, Rumania thus retaining all of Transylvania.

In 1948 the Rumanian Communist Party and its subordinate Social Democrats merged to form the Rumanian Workers' Party with Gheorghe Gheorghiu-Dej as its secretary-general. Gheorghiu-Dej in 1952 succeeded Groza as prime minister, Groza becoming titular head of state. Certain deviationists including the veteran communist and foreign minister, Ana Pauker, were dismissed but in general Rumania suffered fewer purges than the other states of Stalinist Eastern Europe. Until the 1960s, nonetheless, Rumania remained a model ally of Moscow and there were few reverberations of Hungary in 1956. In 1958 the Soviet army was quietly withdrawn from the country while the role of agricultural and petroleum producer assigned to Rumania as a member of Comecon was throughout the 1950s loyally performed.

The 1960 Party Congress in Bucharest, at which Khrushchev was to air the developing Sino-Soviet dispute, marked the beginning of Rumania's increasingly independent line. It could profit from bloc disunity and at the same time advocate conciliation. In 1964 the RCP proposed a tripartite meeting, with Rumania as intermediary, to settle Sino-Soviet differences. In the 1960s it has put national objectives first and rejected a 'breadbasket' function within Comecon, embarked on a programme of rapid industrialisation and evolved a highly individual foreign policy, with the result that it is the most independent of all Soviet-bloc countries. After 1962 a policy of de-Russification was promoted; the Maxim Gorky Institute and Russian book-shops were closed, street names changed and the languages and culture of the West reinstated.

Gheorghiu-Dej died in 1965 and was succeeded as titular head of state by Chivu Stoica. Nicolae Ceauşescu was elected secretary-general of the RCP and a new constitution (superseding those of 1948 and 1952) declared Rumania a Socialist Republic. Ceauşescu succeeded Stoica in December 1967, thus to head both the party and government apparatus. Today's political leadership has inherited from the Stalin era a high degree of orthodoxy, and the paradox of Rumania's *volte-face* in foreign, economic and cultural affairs is to be explained by the identification of the party with national independence, be it from the supra-national planning of Comecon and the Warsaw Pact or from bloc ideological conformity.

The fostering of a Latin consciousness, the irredentist issues of Bessarabia and northern Bukovina and the creation of a unitary state despite the vexed question of the large Hungarian minority in Transylvania serve to consolidate the nation, while Rumanian foreign policy is directed at a denuclearised Balkan region exclusive of great power influence, at a maximum of manoeuvring within present economic, defence and ideological groupings, and at increasing economic cooperation with the non-communist world. At government level, Rumania is the East European pacesetter in contacts with the West; it retains a lukewarm link with China, in 1963 reestablished diplomatic relations with Albania, in 1967 exchanged ambassadors with West Germany, refused to join the anti-Israel chorus in the Middle East crisis and is, with Jugoslavia, reluctant to attend any Soviet-dominated conference of Communist Parties. In recognition of this independence, the UN General Assembly elected in 1967 the Rumanian foreign minister as its chairman, the first communist to fill such a position.

Rumanian sympathy with the Czechoslovak reformers (as opposed to reforms) suggested in 1968 the revival of a Little Entente relationship with Czechoslovakia and Jugoslavia but, soon after the Soviet intervention in Czechoslovakia (from which Rumania was conspicuously absent), Ceauşescu moderated his support in the face of massive pressures from Moscow. Nonetheless, Rumania has so far succeeded in retaining a large measure of independence and there is no doubt that Ceauşescu's nationalist postures draw a warm response from the great majority of Rumanians— and even from the Magyar, German and Serb minorities of Transylvania, whose loyalty has of late been carefully nurtured by the political leadership.

Defence (1967): Military service is compulsory, for one year in the army and two years in the navy and air force. Strength is estimated at: army 150,000, navy 8,000, air force 15,000, para-military forces 50,000. 1966 defence expenditure was $510 million, representing 3·5% of GNP. Rumania is a member of the Warsaw Pact; Soviet troops were withdrawn in 1958.

ECONOMY

Background: Rumania has experienced several years of rapid economic growth and made much progress in industrialisation. Between 1960 and 1966 net material product grew on average by 9·2% per annum. In 1967 national income increased by 7·5%, largely as a result of a 9·4% rise in output per man. Leading sectors are energy production, machine tools and plastics. Chemicals have received a high proportion of investment but have not yet produced the hoped for results. Industry receives almost 60% of total investment funds and fixed industrial investment increased by 10·2% in 1966 and by 17·1% in 1967. Despite the emphasis on the producer goods sector, light industry has performed well, recording a 14% growth in output in 1967.

Moves towards decentralisation began cautiously in 1967, but since then much progress has been made in reorganisation. Enterprises are being grouped into 'associations' which form the basis of 40 new regional units, each responsible to a ministry. The associations will have a high degree of autonomy in drawing up plans, allocating materials, encouraging specialisation and fostering relationships with foreign firms and trade organisations. The price system is being altered to bring prices more into line with costs and world prices, but greater central control is maintained over prices and wages than in other East European countries.

Agriculture, employing over half the working population, accounts for one-third of national income and a fifth of exports. It has progressed in recent years but suffers from a lack of fertilisers, irrigation and mechanisation. Main crops are maize, wheat, potatoes, sugarbeet and sunflower seeds. In 1967 the 340 state farms and 290 Machine Tractor Stations went on to the 'full accounting' system. The majority of the agricultural labour force work in the 4,678 producer cooperatives.

Foreign trade: Trade is vital to Rumania. Comecon's share has fallen throughout the 1960s and now stands at about 50%. West Germany is now the second most important trading partner after the Soviet Union. Rumanian imports from Western Europe are predominantly (89%) of manufactured goods. Difficulties have been experienced in raising foreign exchange earnings to pay for imports, but considerable efforts are now being made to develop links with Western companies for trade and technical cooperation. In 1967 Rumania ordered £11 million worth of British aircraft. France is playing a major part in developing the motor industry and, in 1968, a nuclear cooperation pact was signed with the USA.

Employment: The level of employment has risen steadily with increases of 3·3% in 1966 and 3·7% in 1967. Labour productivity gains have been a vital source of growth. A substantial labour reserve exists in the agricultural sector.

Prices and wages: Real wages increased by 6% in both 1966 and 1967. The average wage is now 1,215 lei per month with a minimum wage of 700 lei. Money incomes have risen more rapidly, leading to a sharp rise in personal savings and some strain in the consumer goods' market.

Consumption: Living standards improve steadily with advances in organisation and light industry. Retail trade turnover rose by 9·8% in 1967 with large gains in the supply of consumer durables. However, per capita consumption of cars, TV sets, refrigerators, etc. is still very low in comparison with other East European countries.

Social Welfare

Since 1967 social security, which is financed from the state budget, has been the responsibility of the Ministry of Labour.

Health services: Free medical assistance is available to all citizens in hospitals, sanatoria and polyclinics. Free medicine is granted to wage-earners, pensioners and the members of their families, children, school children, students, pregnant women, and to the members of handicraft co-operatives and their families. Co-operative farmers and their families benefit from free medical aid and a 50% reduction on the average charge in hospitals and specialised treatment. Maternity leave for working mothers is 112 days and may be taken from two months before childbirth.

Pensions and other benefits: Pensions are administered locally by the *judeţ.* Old age pensions are granted according to the category of work. Workers in the first category, which includes the hardest jobs (e.g. underground mining, ballet dancing) are entitled to retire at an age as low as 45, but the general retirement age is 62 for men and 57 for women. The average monthly old age pension is 1,400 lei; the lowest statutory pension is 700 lei per month. Pension schemes are basically non-contributory but since 1967, in order to correct the imbalance between wages and pensions, a contribution of 2% of earnings has been payable, repayable at the appropriate pensionable age. In co-operative farming, where men are pensionable at 65 and women at 60, old age pensions are financed from the individual co-operative's special pensions fund, which is set at 2% of annual income. 'Fighters against fascism' are entitled to a monthly pension of 2,000 lei, drawn from a separate fund. Invalidity pensions, which are related to the degree of invalidity, are granted till old age pensions are applicable.

Family allowances are set at a monthly bonus of 100 lei for all families with a monthly earning capacity not exceeding 2,000 lei. For the third child a mother is entitled to a sum of 1,000 lei at childbirth. The funeral allowance, distributed from trade union funds, is granted for the funeral expenses of a deceased industrial worker or functionary, and ranges from 500 to 800 lei.

Housing: Between 1948 and 1966 the urban share of the population increased from 23% to 33% and over one-third of all present urban housing was built in that period. However, structural deficiencies, lack of building materials and a serious decline in the private sector prompted the authorities in 1966–7 to draw up plans (implemented during the 1966–70 Five-Year Plan) for the improvement of urban and rural housing, for the expansion of the private sector through better credit facilities and a new rent scheme. There are three sectors of housing—state, co-operative and private. While formerly all state dwellings were centrally allocated, individual enterprises are now empowered to finance housing for their own employees. Co-operative units, which are increasingly sought after and financed on the basis of co-operative members' contributions and savings bank credits, may also include privately owned dwellings. Private housing is purchasable through state grants at 1·5% interest and guaranteed by a mortgage; the system of purchase includes three categories of loan according to personal income. For category I (basic monthly earnings up to 1,500 lei) the credit is for 25 years and the down-payment represents 20% of total cost; for category II (1,500–2,000 lei) 20 years and 25%; for category III (over 2,000 lei) 15 years and 30%. As a rule credit for private construction is granted only to residents of the respective town, except where a citizen's new locality has fewer inhabitants than the usual town of residence. Private ownership is confined to one dwelling only (excepting

H

holiday houses). In both the state and private sectors special purchasing arrangements are available for technical and intellectual workers employed in rural areas. The rent tariff enforced in 1968 is standard throughout the country and for all types of ownership. Differentiated according to the tenant's earnings, the basic monthly rent per sq. metre is fixed at 1·80 lei (when earnings are under 800 lei), 2·20 lei (when earnings are 801–1,000 lei) and 2·50 lei (when earnings exceed 1,000 lei). Most new urban housing (including private dwellings) takes the form of multiple units on housing estates. About two-thirds of state-owned units feature central or stove-gas heating and individual bathrooms.

EDUCATION

The Ministry of Education administers and supervises the school system as a whole but local organisation of education is entrusted to the regional and district people's councils which each contain an education section. Art schools are controlled by the State Committee for Art and Culture. All institutions of higher education are directly administered by the Ministry of Education. All tuition is free; at the level of higher education two-thirds of students receive state scholarships. Extracurricular activities, frequently sponsored by the Young Pioneer and Communist Organisations, are fostered on a broad scale.

Primary education: Crèches (for one-to-three-year-olds), controlled by the Ministry of Health, are set up in institutions, enterprises and communities. Following an optional pre-school kindergarten (ages four to seven), primary schooling consists of the compulsory eight-year school (*şcoală de 8 ani*) for all children aged seven to 15. The curriculum has a unitary structure and includes humanistic, scientific and polytechnical subjects. In 1965 there were, in addition, 731 national minority eight-year schools in which 225,000 pupils were taught in Hungarian, German, Serbian and Ukrainian.

Secondary education is of five types available to all who have completed the eight-year school. The general secondary school (*şcoală medie de cultură generală*), entrance to which is on the basis of an examination in Rumanian and mathematics, provides further general education for pupils aged 15 to 18. The curriculum is standardised in the first year; subsequent specialisation is in humanities or science, in both of which the polytechnical element is stressed. Every school maintains laboratory, workshop and sports facilities. 75% of the pupils proceed to specialised and technical schools or to universities. There were in 1965 13 general secondary schools numbering 22,700 pupils, in which tuition was in a minority language. National minority pupils may also receive lessons in their mother-tongue where Rumanian-language schools are the rule. The pressing need for trained technical workers resulted in a new law, taking effect in 1966–7, which established over 150 specialised technical/vocational secondary schools (*şcoli profesionale de ucenici*), of which 50 are industrial, 59 agricultural, 41 economic/administrative and 26 pedagogical. These schools offer both day and night classes, free of charge to pupils graduating from the eight-year school, also to older citizens in need of basic or remedial training. The course lasts four to five years and the curricula include both the main subject and a general education. Practical instruction is emphasised. The secondary art school (*şcoală medie de artă*) instructs in music, fine arts and choreography but in structure and curriculum otherwise resembles the general school. The physical education secondary school (*şcoală medie de educaţie fizică*) follows the pattern of the general and specialised school but gives special physical training. There is also the teacher-training secondary school (*şcoală pedagogică de învăţători* and *şcoală pedagogică de educatoare*) with six-year courses towards kindergarten and primary teaching. Matriculating pupils from all five systems may proceed to higher education. Boarding maintenance is given in special cases.

Special education: There are two types of school for handicapped children: general and vocational. Tuition, board and medical treatment are free. A research unit in the Cluj Institute of Pedagogy studies the problems of the handicapped.

University and higher education: An annual intake quota is imposed by the Ministry of Education in accordance with state planning. There are five universities, at Bucharest,

Cluj, Iaşi, Timişoara and, since 1966, at Craiova. Foreign language study (French, English, German or Russian) is compulsory for all university students in their first three years. Examinations are usually held three times in the first three years. Higher education is being rapidly expanded and 50 higher institutes include an Institute of Foreign Languages at Bucharest and Polytechnic Institutes in the capital, Cluj, Galaţi, Iaşi, Braşov and Timişoara. The usual higher education course is five years, but institutes for art and medicine (six years), drama (four) and teacher training (three) are exceptions.

Educational institutions (1966–7)

	Institutions	Staff	Students
Primary and General Secondary	15,513	143,610	3,327,856
Vocational secondary	905	19,215	308,271
Higher	181[1]	13,404	136,948

[1] Faculties

Adult education in post-war years aimed at the elimination of illiteracy; this objective was officially reached in 1956. Evening classes are now held in secondary schools for 60,000 pupils, and in 1967 30 'people's universities' provided further and remedial courses for 25,000 students.

MASS MEDIA

The Press (1966)[1]:

Dailies: (Bucharest) *Scînteia*, Communist Pty. (RCP), 880,000; *Munca*, trade union; *Informaţia Bucureştului*, RCP and People's Council (PC); *România Liberă*, PC; *Scînteia Tineretului*, youth; *Elöre*, Hungarian; *Neuer Weg*, German.
(Provincial) *Făclia*, Cluj, RCP and PC; *Igazság*, Cluj, RCP and PC, in Hungarian; *Drum Nou*, Braşov, RCP and PC; *Flacăra Iaşului*, Iaşi, RCP and PC; *Flamura Prahovei*, Ploieşti, RCP and PC; *Dobrogea Nouă*, Constanţa, RCP and PC; *Vörös Zászkeó*, Tîrgu Mureş, RCP and PC, in Hungarian.
Periodicals: (Bucharest) *Sportul Popular* (four per week), sport; *Femeia* (m), woman's illus.; *Contemporanul* (w), polit./cult./social, 70,000; *Lupta de Clasă* (m), RCP theory, 65,000; *Lumea* (w), internat. affairs; *Flacăra* (w), lit./art illus.; *Gazeta Literară* (w), lit.; *Tînărul Leninist* (m), youth polit.; *Viaţa Economica* (w), econ.; *Probleme Economice* (m), econ.; *Luceafărul* (w), lit.; *Urzica* (f), satirical; *Teatrul* (m), theatre; *Programul de Radio şi Televiziune* (w), radio/TV; *Viaţa Românească* (m), lit.; *Munkásélet* (w), trade union, in Hungarian; *Pravda* (3 per week), in Serbo-Croat; *Romanian Review* (q), lit., in English etc., 12,000.
Broadcasting: Rumanian Radio and Television, which is a state monopoly controlled by the Radio and Television Committee, operates, through 16 stations, two daily radio programmes and a third on Sunday evenings, with five regional variations that include programmes in Hungarian, German and Serbo-Croat. Foreign broadcasts are made in 13 languages. There are single-channel TV emissions, daily except Monday, from a network of nine main centres and 17 relay stations. Broadcasting is financed by subscriptions.

CONSTITUTIONAL SYSTEM

Constitution: The 1965 constitution, largely based on the Soviet model, declared Rumania to be a Socialist Republic, a sovereign, independent and unitary state of the working people of the towns and villages.
Legislature: The unicameral Grand National Assembly (*Marea Adunare Naţională*) is theoretically the sole legislative organ, with the following main functions: adoption of the constitution, regulation of the electoral system, approval of the budget, organi-

[1] Readership figures for most organisations unavailable but annual circulation (1966) of all newspapers and magazines exceeded 1,000 million copies.

sation of the Council of Ministers and ministries, of courts, the procuracy and people's councils, the framing of foreign policy, the declaration of war, the appointment and recall of the supreme commander of the armed forces, the proclamation of a state of emergency and the election and control of the State Council. The GNA is elected for four years by universal franchise (18 years and over). The 465 deputies (*deputaţi*) represent constituencies of 40,000 persons. Since December 1965 one or more candidates may stand in each constituency. 99% of the electorate participated in the last elections (March 1965). Officially subordinated to the GNA is the State Council (*Consiliu de Stat*) or collective presidency, consisting of president, three vice-presidents, a secretary and 15 members. This is a permanent body with executive functions which include the establishment of election dates, the appointment of military chiefs and diplomatic representatives and the right of pardon and commutation of punishments. Party control of both the GNA and State Council is decisive, although non-party members have occasionally been elected to head the State Council (formerly Praesidium). In 1967 Nicolae Ceauşescu, the party leader, was appointed its president.

Executive: The Council of Ministers (*Consiliu de Ministri*) is the supreme body of state administration whose sweeping powers include the conduct of foreign affairs, the achievement of national economic plans, general management of the economy, defence and control of subsidiary government organs. The Council of Ministers consists of a chairman, vice-chairman, ministers and the chairmen of the State Planning Committee, State Committee for Culture and the National Council for Scientific Research. Its chairman and vice-chairmen form a Permanent Bureau. It coordinates ministerial activity and is in theory responsible to the GNA. The majority of its members are active in the Central Committee of the RCP.

Judiciary: Justice is administered by the Supreme Court, 16 regional courts (and Capital Court in Bucharest) and people's courts. There are also special courts such as military and railway workers' tribunals. The Supreme Court (*Tribunal Suprem*) directs the judicial activity of all courts, is elected by the GNA and is responsible to it but has no power to review the constitutionality of statutes. It functions mainly as the highest court of appeal but can act as a court of first instance in special cases. People's Courts (*tribunale populare*) whose lay assessors are elected for four years, are the usual first instance tribunals but regional courts handle both appeal and first instance cases. The procuracy, introduced in 1952 and based on the Soviet model, is independent of the judiciary and headed by a procurator-general who is elected by the GNA for the term of the legislature and is responsible to it. The subordinate procurators not only maintain the procuratorial function of supervising state administration but act as prosecutors in criminal cases. There is capital punishment.

Basic rights: The state guarantees equality, many social services, freedom of speech, assembly, deomonstration (though these 'cannot be used for aims hostile to the socialist system and to the interests of the working people'), freedom of religion and conscience, the right to personal property and inheritance and the right of ethnic minorities to their own cultural self-expression and education in their own language.

Party: Rumania is a one-party state and there is no parliamentary opposition. In 1965, following the March general elections in which 99·6% of the electorate participated, the Rumanian Workers' Party was renamed the Rumanian Communist Party (RCP). Electoral candidates are nominated by a mass organisation, the Popular Democratic Front; the electoral law of December 1966 authorised nomination of more than one candidate in each constituency. The RCP has a membership of 1,700,000. The party leader is currently head of state.

Local government: Until early 1968 Rumania was subdivided into 16 regions (*regiuni*), two cities with regional status (Bucharest and Constanţa), districts (*raioane*), towns and communes, but a new system now operates and is based on 39 counties (*judeţe*), 46 city municipalities and, at a lower level, towns and communes. Bucharest is further subdivided into sectors. Each unit has its people's council (*consiliu popular*) with an executive branch. The executive committees at the city municipality level are subordinate to their county equivalents, with the exception of Bucharest, which is centrally supervised. Members of people's councils are elected for four years except at commune level where the term is two years.

Leading government and party figures: Nicolae Ceaușescu (titular president and secretary-general of RCP), Ion Maurer (prime minister), Corneliu Mănescu (foreign minister), Ilie Verdeț (first deputy chairman of Council of Ministers), Gheorghe Cioară (foreign trade minister), Alexandru Boabă (oil minister), Maxim Berghianu (chairman of State Planning Committee).

SOVIET UNION

GEOGRAPHY

Features: The two most salient features of Soviet geography are size and latitudinal location. The Soviet Union stretches almost halfway around the world covering 17% of the inhabited surface of the globe. Of this territory, one-third lies in Europe, two-thirds in Asia. Its total size is three times as large as the USA (including Alaska) and the European part is seven times the size of France. The distance from the Baltic Sea to the Pacific is 6,000 m./9,600 km., and from north to south 3,000 m./ 4,800 km. There are eleven time zones. The following states are contiguous with the Soviet Union: Norway, Finland, Poland, Czechoslovakia, Hungary, Rumania, Bulgaria, Turkey, Iran, Afghanistan, China, Mongolia and N. Korea.

The latitudes of much of the Soviet Union are comparable to those of Canada, Scotland and Scandinavia, Moscow being on a par with Edinburgh, and Leningrad with Oslo and southern Alaska. The Caucasus and Central Asia, however, are on the same latitudes as Italy or Utah.

Topographically outstanding is the generally low relief of the western half of the Soviet Union. Only at the southern periphery of this region and in the eastern sector are there extensive and high mountain ranges. In the western sector, the Great Russian Plain never reaches altitudes of more than a few hundred feet, the chief elevations being the Podolian Plateau, the Central Russian Uplands, Donets Ridge and Volga Heights. These have affected stream patterns of rivers which, like the Dnieper and Volga, are largely navigable. The Pripet marshes provide especially poor drainage in the west. The Ukrainian sector of the European Soviet Union is bounded in the south-west by the Carpathians (elevations above 6,000 ft/1,850 m.) and in the south by the Black Sea where the Crimean Peninsula contains elevations of over 5,000 ft/1,500 m. The north-western sector (i.e. RSFSR and Baltic republics) has a frontage on the Baltic, Barents and White Seas. It was in the Great Russian Plain that the Russian state historically evolved; it is this core area of the Soviet Union which still contains three-quarters of the Soviet population and two-thirds of its national production.

As an extension of the fault system rising in the Crimea and continuing under the Sea of Azov, the Greater Caucasus, ranged between the Black and Caspian Seas, attains heights of more than 18,000 ft/5,400 m. The Lesser Caucasus merge in the frontier zones of Turkey and Iran with the Armenian Plateau. At the geographical division of Europe and Asia, the plain is interrupted by the glaciated ridges of the Ural Mountains (av. height 2,000 ft/610 m.) These are sufficiently broken in places to allow unimpeded movement, settlement and industry. From the south-eastern shore of the Caspian Sea the Kopet Dag Range forms an eastern frontier with Iran and, at the political borders of Soviet Central Asia, Afghanistan, Pakistan, India and Chinese Sinkiang, the Pamirs, a north-western spur of the Himalayas, contain the highest peak in the Soviet Union (Communism Peak 24,700 ft/7,500 m.) and together with the Tien-Shan to the north reach several heights well above 20,000 ft/ 6,000 m. The massive physical barrier represented by these ranges is broken occasionally by east-west valleys such as that of the River Ili and the Dzungarian Gate.

To the north of the high ranges of Central Asia lies the arid Turanian Basin, drained by rivers such as the Amu Darya (Oxus) and Syr Darya (Jaxartes) with outlets in three inland bodies of water, the Caspian and Aral Seas and Lake Balkhash. Extreme high summer temperatures are recorded here. The black-earth (*chernozem*) steppe of the Kazakh Virgin Lands constitutes a transitional stage between Central Asia and the forest and tundra regions of Siberia. Western Siberia, bounded on the west by the Urals and on the east by the River Yenisey, centres on the waterlogged basin of the River Ob, emptying northwards into the Arctic Ocean. In its south-eastern sector, western Siberia includes the Kuznetsk coal-basin (Kuzbas).

From the Yenisey eastwards to beyond the Lena (both of which rivers attain nearly 3,000 m./4,800 km.) lies eastern Siberia, covering one-third of the Soviet Union's territory, yet supporting only 4% of its population. In the middle of this region the immense desert-filled Central Siberian Plateau reaches an average height of 2,000 ft/610 m. while to the south is a series of much higher, more complex ranges, the Sayan, Yablannovy and Stanovoy Mountains. At its southern fringes lies the tectonic basin of Lake Baykal (5,700 ft/1,750 m. deep). From this lake rises the River Angara with its incomparable hydropower.

Finally, between the Lena and the Pacific Ocean, is the Soviet Far East. Its several mountain ranges (notably the Verkhoyansk, Chersky and Anadyr Mountains) extend offshore in a series of islands and peninsulas. The Kamchatka Peninsula has 100 active volcanoes (including Klyuchevskaya 16,000 ft/4,800 m.). Only in the extreme southern part is there significant population, communications and economic development: in the valleys of the Amur and Ussuri Rivers and the petroliferous, coal-producing island of Sakhalin. The Soviet Union's important Pacific sea-port, Vladivostok, is largely icebound in winter (as are the main ports of the Baltic and Black Seas; Murmansk remains ice-free).

The climate of the Soviet Union has all the characteristics of extreme continent-ality, ranging from Arctic conditions in the far north to Mediterranean-type in the Crimea, subtropical in the southern Caucasus, arid in Central Asia and monsoon-type in the Soviet Far East.

Although there is not, for climatic, soil and topographical reasons, a good correlation between size and cultivable land, the Soviet Union possesses a diverse agriculture and is a major world producer of wheat, maize, sugar-beet and sunflower-seed. Grain is confined mainly to the European sector and to new steppe lands of Kazakhstan and Western Siberia; sugar-beet to the Ukraine and the central part of European Russia. There is localised production of potatoes, vegetables, flax, hemp and tobacco (European sector), vines (Moldavia, Caucasus, Central Asia), cotton (Central Asia), tea and citrus (Caucasus) and rice (Central Asia and Far East). There is varied and extensive pasture. Nonetheless some nine-tenths of the country remains at present uncultivable on a commercial basis. Nearly one-half of the Soviet Union comprises forest; providing for the world's greatest timber industry. Hydroelectric potential is unequalled.

Whilst inaccessibility is a major problem, the Soviet Union's overall fuel and mineral resources are the richest on earth. They include an estimated 58% of the world's coal deposits, 59% of its oil, 41% of its iron ore, 88% of its manganese, 54% of its potassium salts and 32% of its phosphates. The well established industrial areas are the Central Industrial Region (centring on Moscow and Gorky), Leningrad, the Donbas-Dnieper complex, the Middle Volga cities, Baku and the Urals. Recent emphasis is placed on new centres east of the Urals, along the axis of the Trans-Siberian railway and its branches as far as Lake Baykal. These include Karaganda, east Uzbekistan, the Novosibirsk-Kuzbas complex and Baykal. The Amur and Ussuri Valleys comprise the manufacturing hub of the Soviet Far East.

Area of Soviet Union: 8,600,000 sq. miles/22,402,200 sq. km.
Area of union republics:

RSFSR 6,569,000 sq. miles/17,075,400 sq. km.; Kazakh SSR 1,102,300 sq. miles/ 2,715,100 sq. km.; Ukrainian SSR 231,100 sq. miles/601,000 sq. km.; Turkmen SSR 187,000 sq. miles/488,100 sq. km.; Uzbek SSR 153,000 sq. miles/449,600 sq. km.; Belorussian SSR 80,000 sq. miles/207,600 sq. km.; Kirghiz SSR 76,150 sq. miles/

Soviet Union: Europe

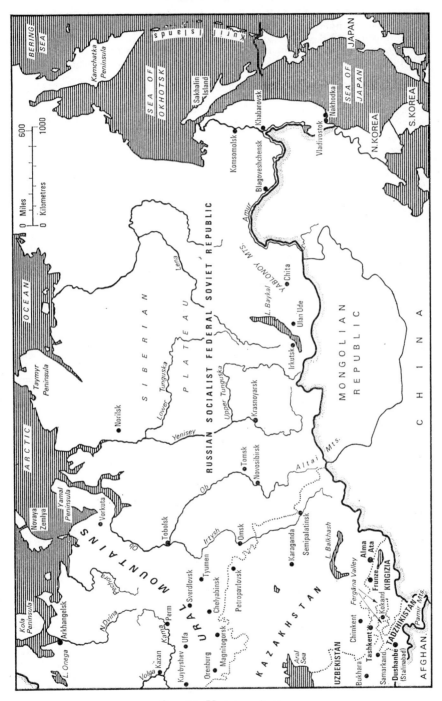

SOVIET UNION: ASIA

198,500 sq. km.; Tadzhik SSR 54,600 sq. miles/143,100 sq. km.; Azerbaidzhan SSR 33,400 sq. miles/86,600 sq. km.; Georgian SSR 27,700 sq. miles/69,700 sq. km.; Lithuanian SSR 25,000 sq. miles/65,200 sq. km.; Latvian SSR 24,600 sq. miles/63,700 sq. km.; Estonian SSR 17,300 sq. miles/45,100 sq. km.; Moldavian SSR 13,000 sq. miles/33,700 sq. km.; Armenian SSR 11,540 sq. miles/29,800 sq. km.

Temperature, Relative humidity, Precipitation

Station	Height in ft	Position	Temperature (Mean max. and min.)	Relative humidity	Mean annual rainfall
Moscow (European Russia)	505	55°N, 37°E	July 66°F/19°C Jan. 15°F/–9°C	84%	25 in./635 mm.
Riga (Baltic)	65	56°N, 24°E	July 64°F/18°C Jan. 25°F/–4°C	86%	22 in./559 mm.
Pechenga (Kola Peninsula)	35	69°N, 31°E	July 54°F/12°C Jan. 15°F/–9°C	83%	17 in./432 mm.
Odessa (Black Sea)	215	46°N, 30°E	July 72°F/22°C Jan. 25°F/–4°C	80%	14 in./356 mm.
Sevastopol (Crimea)	75	44°N, 33°E	July 72°F/22°C Jan. 35°F/ 2°C	79%	12 in./305 mm.
Batumi (West Caucasus)	10	41°N, 41°E	July 74°F/23°C Jan. 42°F/ 6°C	82%	96 in./2438 mm.
Lenkoran (East Caucasus)	60	38°N, 48°E	July 76°F/24°C Jan. 37°F/ 3°C	86%	49 in./1245 mm.
Astrakhan (Lower Volga)	45	46°N, 48°E	July 77°F/25°C Jan. 19°F/–7°C	80%	6 in./152 mm.
Sverdlovsk (Urals)	895	56°N, 49°E,	July 62°F/17°C Jan. 0°F/–18°C	82%	17 in./432 mm.
Dudinka (Central Siberia)	140	69°N, 87°E	July 55°F/13°C Jan. –22°F/–30°C	82%	8 in./203 mm.
Verkhoyansk (East Siberia)	330	67°N, 133°E	July 59°F/15°C Jan. –58°F/–50°C	74%	4 in./102 mm.
Tashkent (Central Asia)	1570	41°N, 69°E	July 78°F/26°C Jan. 29°F/–2°C	71%	15 in./381 mm.
Vladivostok (Far East)	25	43°N, 131°E	Aug. 69°F/21°C Jan. 7°F/–14°C	80%	21 in./533 mm.

POPULATION

Total population of the Soviet Union (1967 est.): 234,401,000.

Population by union republic, with capital cities (1967 est.): Azerbaidzhan SSR (Baku) 4,802,000; Armenian SSR (Yerevan) 2,253,000; Belorussian SSR (Minsk) 8,744,000; Georgian SSR (Tbilisi/Tiflis) 4,611,000; Estonian SSR (Tallinn) 1,294,000; Kazakh SSR (Alma-Ata) 12,413,000; Kirgiz SSR (Frunze) 2,749,000; Latvian SSR (Riga) 2,285,000; Lithuanian SSR (Vilnius/Vilna) 3,026,000; Moldavian SSR (Kishinev) 3,425,000; Russian SFSR (RSFSR) (Moscow) 127,312,000; Tadzhik SSR (Dushanbe) 2,654,000; Turkmen SSR (Ashkhabad) 1,971,000; Ukrainian SSR (Kiev) 45,966,000; Uzbek SSR (Tashkent) 10,896,000.

Chief towns and populations (1967 est.): Greater Moscow 6,507,000; Greater Leningrad 3,706,000; Kiev 1,417,000; Tashkent 1,241,000; Baku 1,196,000; Kharkov 1,125,000; Gorky 1,120,000; Novosibirsk 1,064,000; Kuybyshev 992,000; Sverdlovsk 961,000; Tbilisi/Tiflis 842,000; Donetsk 841,000; Chelyabinsk 835,000; Kazan 821,000; Dnepropetrovsk 817,000; Perm 796,000; Odessa 776,000; Omsk 774,000; Minsk 772,000; Rostov-on-Don 756,000; Volgograd 743,000; Saratov 720,000; Ufa 704,000; Riga 680,000; Yerevan 665,000; Alma-Ata 653,000; Voronezh 611,000; Zaporozhe 596,000; Krasnoyarsk 576,000; Lvov 512,000; Krivoy Rog 511,000; Frunze 396,000; Tallinn 340,000; Dushanbe 332,000; Vilnius/Vilna 317,000; Kishinev 302,000; Ashkhabad 238,000.

Ethnic composition: The 1959 census identified 108 distinctive nationality groups. Of these some 50 are recognised politically in administrative units ranked as union republic (SSR), autonomous republic (ASSR), autonomous region (AO) or national area (NO) in which a particular nationality is officially predominant, although (as in the case of Kazakhstan) it may be numerically inferior. The 15 SSRs comprise the 15 largest nationalities. Of the total population of the Soviet Union, Russians constitute 55%, Ukrainians 18%, Belorussians 4%. The remaining 23% are non-Slav nationalities. In the RSFSR 83% of the population is Russian but there are numerous other groupings of which some 30 are organised in ASSR, AO or NO sub-units. The largest minorities with special administrative status in the RSFSR are the Tatar (4%), Chuvash (1%), Mordvin (1%) and Bashkir (1%). Russians form large minorities in several non-Russian SSRs: Kazakhstan (52% including Ukrainians), Kirgizia (30%), Latvia (27%), Estonia (20%), Turkmeniya (18%), Ukraine (17%), Tadzhikistan (15% including Ukrainians), Uzbekistan (14%), Azerbaidzhan (14%), Moldavia (10%), Lithuania (9%) and Belorussia (8%). Ukrainians form minorities of 15% in Moldavia and 6% in Kirgizia. Other large minorities in SSRs include Uzbeks (23% in Tadzhikistan, 11% in Kirgizia, 8% in Turkmeniya), Armenians (12% in Azerbaidzhan, 11% in Georgia), Azerbaidzhanis (6% in Armenia) and Tatars (5% in Uzbekistan). The several minorities historically associated with territories outside the Soviet Union include Poles (9% in Lithuania, 7% in Belorussia), Kurds (2% in Armenia), Germans and Jews (each constituting approximately 1% of the Soviet Union) while Finns (including Karelo-Finns), Bulgarians, Persians, Koreans and others each form less than 1% of the Soviet Union's population.

Language: There are over 120 languages in the Soviet Union. Russian is the official language and *lingua franca* of the union. All SSRs and most of their constituent national subdivisions have, in addition to Russian, national languages with official status. Most of these languages are written in variations of Cyrillic, notable exceptions being the Baltic languages (Latin script); Georgian and Armenian use their own scripts.

Religion: Nominal adherents are estimated as following: 160,000,000 Orthodox (Slavs, Moldavians, Georgians); 30,000,000 Muslims (mainly Sunni in Central Asia and Shia in Azerbaidzhan); 4,000,000 Roman Catholics and Uniates (Lithuanians, Poles, west Ukrainians, west Belorussians); 4,000,000 Lutherans (Estonians, Latvians, Germans); 2,500,000 Armenian Christians; 2,300,000 Jews, 3–4,000,000 Baptists, Evangelical Christians, Mennonites; 400,000 Buddhists (Kalmyks, Buryat Mongols, Tuvans).

RECENT HISTORY

The Soviet Union's two primary objectives at the end of World War II were to reconstruct the severely damaged home economy and to consolidate the territorial and ideological gains that had accrued to it. These goals have been largely realised though often at the expense of individual liberties and of pacific relations with other states. The 1945 Potsdam Conference of the Soviet Union, USA and UK practically sanctioned the wartime incorporation within Soviet borders of most of Poland east of the 1919 Curzon Line, of part of Finnish Karelia, of Bessarabia, northern Bukovina, Carpatho-Ruthenia, Lithuania, Latvia, Estonia and the northern part of east Prussia. Peace with Japan likewise brought concessions in Manchuria, Port Arthur and northern Korea, the possession of the Kurile Islands and reincorporation of southern Sakhalin. Tannu Tuva was annexed in 1944. The Soviet military presence in most East European countries subsequently formed the basis for the establishment of communist governments in eastern Germany, Poland, Hungary, Bulgaria and Rumania. Liberated Jugoslavia was to maintain, till 1948, a close alignment with Moscow, while in 1948, a predominantly communist government was formed in Czechoslovakia. These, with Albania, were to be termed the satellite states of the Soviet Union. In 1949 they were conjoined in Comecon (Cema), the Soviet answer to the US Marshall Plan in Western Europe.

Europe was now divided by an 'Iron Curtain' running from Stettin to Trieste and, though the Soviet Union was a founder member of the UN, its former alliance with the Western Powers was converted into a Cold War. Several major events were soon to reinforce the growing bipolarisation of the world into Eastern and Western, communist and non-communist, Soviet- and American-oriented power blocs. In 1946 UN pressures forced the withdrawal of Soviet troops from Iranian Azerbaidzhan. In 1948–9 the Soviet attempt to blockade West Berlin was defeated by an airlift undertaken by the Western allies. In Germany cooperation between the Soviet Union and the West had come to a virtual standstill and the formation of a German Federal Republic in western Germany was promptly countered (1949) by the establishment of a German Democratic Republic in the zone of Soviet occupation.

When NATO was instituted (1949) as a means of containing Soviet expansionism in Europe, the Soviet Union responded by establishing the Warsaw Pact whose members included the Soviet Union and all the communist states of Eastern Europe except Jugoslavia. In the same year Mao Tse-tung obtained full control of mainland China and an 'eternal friendship' between the Soviet Union and People's Republic of China was proclaimed. The Western Powers were now faced by the apparent monolithic unity of a much enlarged communist bloc and from 1950 to 1953 war between the Sino-Soviet supported North Korean troops which had crossed the 38th parallel and the combined forces of South Korea and the UN posed the threat of a head-on collision between a Sino-Soviet alliance and the West. The 1951 defence pact between the USA and Japan, the admission to NATO of Greece and Turkey (1951) and of West Germany (1955), the creation of anti-communist defence systems on the Asian periphery of China and the Soviet Union (SEATO in 1954 and the Baghdad Pact/CENTO in 1955) and the detonation in 1953 of the Soviet Union's first thermo-nuclear device further served to intensify the Cold War. Summit conferences at Geneva in 1955 and 1959 failed to solve the German problem but in 1955, nonetheless, the Austrian Peace Treaty secured a Soviet signature.

This early post-war period was marked at home by the strengthening of the totalitarian system. Stalin's personal control of key positions in the party and government, of the secret police and army, of the judiciary and propaganda ensured the survival of his person and position, but after his death in 1953, the problem of succession was not immediately resolved. G. M. Malenkov succeeded as chairman of the Council of Ministers until 1955, to be replaced by N. A. Bulganin. In a secret speech to the Twentieth Congress of the CRSU in early 1956, the party first secretary, Nikita Khrushchev, made the first strong denunciation of some of Stalin's 'crimes', and this led to a cultural thaw. The trend towards de-Stalinisation had already begun in 1953 when several of Stalin's associates were purged, some, like Beria, to be executed, but now new personalities were to be matched by cautious modifications of the system itself. The cult of personality among political leaders was officially denounced and the use of terror was reduced. But few relaxations were tolerated in the East European countries of the Soviet bloc, for the example of Tito was easily recalled. In 1956, partly in response to de-Stalinisation in the Soviet Union riots in the Polish city of Poznań and subsequent events of the 'Polish October' led to a temporary liberalisation of the system within Poland, but a major uprising in Hungary was, with the help of Soviet troops, ruthlessly suppressed. Soviet action was condemned by the UN and much of world opinion. In 1958 Bulganin, through his association with the discredited 'anti-party group' was replaced as premier by Khrushchev who now held preeminent posts in both party and government. Collective leadership reasserted itself again in 1964 when the party's Central Committee removed Khrushchev. He was succeeded as first secretary of the CPSU by Leonid Brezhnev and as premier by Alexey Kosygin who, while upholding one-party dictatorship and other pillars of totalitarian rule in the face of an increasingly restless populace demanding more political, religious and cultural freedom and a higher standard of living, have reaffirmed the reforming principles symbolised by Khrushchev, especially in the economic sphere. In 1965 N. Podgorny was elected seventh president of the Soviet Union in succession to A. I. Mikoyan.

Soviet foreign policy since Stalin has been characterised by an increasing emphasis on the formula of peaceful coexistence with the West and with foreign capitalism, by growing trade and contacts with the entire non-communist world, by a corresponding deterioration in relations with Peking (based on ideological, national and territorial differences) and by an unprecedented ideological and economic involvement in third world countries, especially Cuba, India, Egypt, Syria, Algeria, Guinea and, formerly, Indonesia and Ghana. A direct conflict of interests has, nonetheless, brought the Soviet Union and the West to the brink of war, as in the Middle Eastern crises of 1956, 1958 and 1967, in the Cuban missile crisis of 1962 and currently in Vietnam. In addition to conventional diplomacy, the Soviet Union uses the inter-national network of communist parties and front organisations in its pursuit of external policy, but its support of 'national liberation' movements has been none too successful.

In 1961 another Berlin crisis led to the construction of the Wall, but since then the growth of nationalism and polycentrism in Eastern Europe together with Soviet preoccupations elsewhere have somewhat reduced Soviet domination of that region, but ideological ties of the party, regional integration within the Warsaw Pact and Comecon and the retention of Soviet troops in three East European states guarantee the preservation of a Soviet hegemony. Cooperation with the West, symbolised by the 1963 Nuclear Test Ban Treaty, in combination with a general East-West *détente*, must at the same time lessen the risk of war in Europe and thus further en-courage the Soviet Union to concentrate on domestic requirements.

At home the post-Stalin era has been notable for a decline in emphasis on heavy industry in the evolution of the economy, for the development of vast new regions, particularly in Siberia, Kazakhstan and Central Asia, for alternate thaws and freezes in the cultural and political climate and for major contributions to science, especially in aerospace and military technology, nuclear power, medicine and transportation. In 1957 the Soviet Union launched the world's first space satellite; in 1961 Yuri Gagarin manned the world's first space flight. In 1965 the first man walked in space from Voskhod 2, and in 1966 Russians could claim the first soft land-ing on the Moon (Luna 9) and the establishment in orbit of the Moon's first artificial satellite (Luna 10). In early 1969 two manned Soviet space-craft made a successful rendezvous in space (Soyu 4 and 5).

As a result of the Czechoslovak reform programme initiated in early 1968 the Soviet Union, together with its 'hard-line' allies (East Germany, Poland, Bulgaria and Hungary) invaded Czechoslovakia in August 1968 in an attempt to enforce ideological conformity in the Czechoslovak party and government. The liberal leadership of that country, supported by the overwhelming majority of Czechs and Slovaks, had far-reaching plans to adapt socialism to its own needs and it is clear that Moscow feared not only the strategic consequences of a 'Czech road to socialism' (there were allegations of West German infiltration) but even more the infection of 'heretical' policies which had already won the explicit sympathy of the Jugoslav, Rumanian and Western communist parties and of world opinion as a whole. This event, together with a renewed campaign against dissident intellectuals at home, has led many foreign observers (including friends of the Soviet Union) to question Moscow's professed interest in *détente* and humanitarianism.

Defence (1967): Military service is compulsory, ranging from two years in the army to four years in the navy. Strength is estimated at: army two million, navy and naval air force 465,000, air force 505,000, para-military forces 250,000. Present total defence expenditure, including items related to defence but not in the declared defence budget was estimated at $29,800 million, representing 8·9% of GNP (in market prices). In 1955 the Soviet Union signed the 20-year Warsaw Treaty of Friendship and Collaboration with Albania, Bulgaria, Czechoslovakia, East Germany, Hungary, Poland and Rumania. 20 Soviet army divisions are stationed in East Germany, two in Poland, four in Hungary and, reportedly, five or six in Czechoslovakia. While Albania formally abrogated her defence agreements with the Warsaw Pact countries in 1968 and Jugoslavia prepared herself, following Soviet intervention in Czecho-slovakia (August 1968), for a period of isolation, the build-up of Soviet naval forces in the Mediterranean attained a peak of 50 warships in the autumn of 1968.

ECONOMY

Background: Over 40 years have passed since the Soviet Union embarked on a course of intensive industrialisation and adopted a centralised planning system. Today the population is predominantly urban and living standards are quickly catching up with those of the advanced capitalist countries. High rates of growth were maintained throughout the 1950s; net material product achieved a 10·2% annual average growth rate between 1950 and 1960, resulting in an 8·4% growth of per capita product. Growth has declined to some extent during the 1960s, but remains high in comparison with Western countries. Between 1960 and 1965 annual average growth of national product was 6·5%. In 1965 the Kosygin reforms were introduced and in 1966 a new plan period started. National income was planned to increase by from 6·6% to 7·1% a year during the period: in fact, national income increased by 6·7% in 1967 and by 7·2% in 1968. In the latter year consumer goods' production expanded at a faster rate than that of producer goods for the first time. Investment remains at a high level, having averaged around 24% of national income since 1960. Emphasis has been laid on the development of new technology, specialisation and automation. Engineering and chemicals continue to advance strongly with particularly rapid development in motor vehicles, instrument making, electronic equipment and household appliances.

Total industrial output has risen by 29% since 1966, against 26% to 27% planned for this period and, in October 1967, the projected rate of growth of output was amended to give a 53% increase over five years instead of the original 47% to 50%. By 1970 it is planned to produce 670 million tons of coal (595 million tons were produced in 1967), 127 million tons of steel (over 100 million tons for the first time in 1967) and 350 million tons of oil. Construction is receiving high priority but results have been disappointing, with only a 4% increase in 1968; serious shortcomings in labour organisation and planning have been admitted and attempts are being made to raise the level of mechanisation in the industry. Production of motor vehicles now has high priority, 322,000 being produced in 1968. The target for 1970 is around 800,000 and for 1975, two million. Twenty-two enterprises are being built or modernised for this purpose with substantial Western technical assistance, notably at Togliattigrad where Fiat are assisting in the development of a factory to produce 660,000 vehicles a year.

The reforms introduced in 1956 now cover 27,000 enterprises (out of a total of 44,000) responsible for 72% of industrial output and 80% of profits. The main points of the reforms were a restoration of the ministerial system of administration, replacing the former territorial system, and greater independence for enterprises with a reduction of plan indicators from almost 40 to eight, including volume of realised production, wage fund, volume of capital investment, profit and rate of profitability (in relation to assets). Profit based incentive funds were introduced to improve the motivation of management and workers. A small capital charge was also adopted to reduce wastage of capital resources. In 1967 a new wholesale price system was introduced to bring prices more into line with costs and to eliminate subsidies, giving an average profit rate of 15%. The overall rise in industrial prices was 8%, but the rise was larger for basic fuel and materials, for example, 78% for coal. To equalise diverse natural conditions as a determinant of costs in extractive industries, a differential rent element was incorporated in the new prices. It is not easy to assess the success of the reforms because they were applied first in the more progressive enterprises, but in 1968 the volume of output of reformed enterprises increased by 8·3% (compared with an overall increase of 8·1%), labour productivity by 5·6% (5%) and profits by 15% (14%). There is evidence that the content of the reforms has been diluted as they have been extended, and there seems to have been rather less freedom to make direct contracts between enterprises and marketing organisations, especially for consumer goods, than was envisaged. Discussion continues on the question of more radical reform of the entire planning system to make more use of computers and scarcity pricing.

Agriculture still employs around one-third of the total labour force. State farms have been increased in number at the expense of collective farms. In 1968 there were 12,783 farms and 36,800 collective farms. Results were exceptionally good in 1966 when an all-time record harvest was gathered. Output was maintained in 1967 and increased by 3·4% in 1968. A high rate of investment was envisaged in the 1966–70 plan but this was later cut back by 5,000 million roubles. Good progress has been made, however, in mechanisation and in the application of fertilisers, production of which is to double in the plan period. Main crops are wheat, sugarbeet, cotton, sunflower seeds and potatoes; rice is gaining importance. In 1968 there was a reduction in the number of cattle, associated with a decline in private peasant holdings but steady advances in yields have maintained the level of production. State farms are now transferring to the new management system; the 800 enterprises on the new system achieved above-plan profits of 8% in 1968. A decree of September 1967 allowed the setting up of subsidiary enterprises on farms, for the production of consumer goods, food products, building materials, etc., partly in an attempt to absorb pockets of rural unemployment and partly to improve consumer goods' supplies. Progress has been hampered by difficulties in obtaining necessary supplies of materials. Subsidiary private holdings have declined in importance as working conditions have improved on collective farms, and the free *kolkhoz* market is no longer vital as a source of income.

Marked regional inequalities still exist in the Soviet Union. The RSFSR is highly developed in comparison with the north and eastern Siberia. This inequality is being tackled by large-scale investments and above-average wages and salaries. Siberia is rich in coal, iron ore, natural gas, timber and diamonds, and has excellent potential for hydro-electric power.

Foreign trade: Around 60% of Soviet trade is within Comecon. The Soviet Union imports manufactured products and exports raw materials but total imports represent only 3% of national income. Recently terms of trade for primary goods have deteriorated, worsening the Soviet trade position with respect to the rest of Comecon. Prices within Comecon are determined contractually or in relation to average world market prices during a preceding period.

Trade with Western Europe and the developing world has increased, but rather slowly; trade with Canada and Latin America has risen sharply in the 1960s. A major shift of trade within the socialist world occurred after 1960, when trade relationships with China were severed. Industrial cooperation between Western companies and Soviet industry have extended, especially for the production of cars, synthetic fibres, electricity supply equipment and machine tools. Britain has been the major West European trade partner, although replaced by Finland in 1968. Quotas for Anglo-Soviet consumer goods trade were raised by 60% in 1968. The Soviet Union is a major gold producer and gold has been used to cover exchange difficulties.

Employment: The Soviet population now stands at 239 millions (1 January 1969), women forming 54% of the total, whilst over 55% of the population are now classed as 'urban'. The industrial labour force has increased at over 3% a year in the 1960s, partly through absorption of surplus rural labour. The agricultural labour force has an unfavourable age structure as young workers tend to leave for the towns, and a very high proportion of female labour. It is expected to decline at an average annual rate of 4% between 1966 and 1970. Regional distribution of the agricultural labour force is rather uneven with areas of acute scarcity and areas of labour surplus. High priority is being given to measures to improve the mobility of the industrial labour force, with retraining to meet the needs of new technology, and the education system is biased towards the production of technologists and engineers. Management education is receiving more attention.

Prices and wages: Rural workers have benefited most from developments in recent years. Collective farmers now receive a guaranteed monthly wage related to state farm rates, in place of the old system of payment according to days worked, from the annual residual net income of the farm. Real incomes of collective farm workers rose by 13% in 1965, by 8% in 1966 and by 7% in 1967 and per capita peasant incomes are now equivalent to four-fifths of industrial incomes. Real incomes of the population as a whole have risen by an annual average of around 6% since 1965. Nominal wages have risen more rapidly, especially since the reforms were introduced, but retail prices have been held fairly stable. In 1965 average monthly earnings stood at 112·5 roubles, but indirect benefits from public consumption funds raised this to 151 roubles (compared with 140 in 1967). Minimum wages were raised in January

1968 from 40 roubles to 60 roubles per month. Labour productivity rose by 7% in 1967 and by 5% in 1968.

Consumption: The good performance of agriculture and above-plan output of consumer goods in 1966 and 1967 greatly improved deliveries of consumer goods. In 1966 output of consumer goods advanced by 9%, whereas in 1967 both this and the food processing branches excelled; the output of the former improving by 11% and of the latter by 7%. Moreover, the output of consumer durables increased by 15% in 1967 and services have much improved. Stocks of consumer goods have been run down, partly as a result of increased rural purchasing power. The 1968 plan called for an expansion of consumer goods output by 8·6%; in fact 8·3% was achieved. Over three million refrigerators were produced and almost 600 million pairs of shoes, but demand for clothing, footwear and household appliances was not fully satisfied. Savings deposits have risen on average by 20% a year since 1965 reflecting the above-plan increases in nominal wages, but also the success of an official savings drive. Housing has been much improved, 2,300 thousand units being completed in 1968, although in that year the urban population increased by almost three million. The next few years should see a rapid extension of private car ownership and greater availability of luxury products.

SOCIAL WELFARE

Social insurance (excluding medical services) is supervised by the USSR Central Council of Trade Unions, the central committees of trade unions and local trade union organisations. Trade union organs draft and approve estimates for social insurance, determine specific expenditure and help formulate social insurance policy. The social insurance budget is a part of the Soviet Union state budget. Pensions, sick pay, maternity benefits and accommodations at holiday therapy centres are the main expenditure items of social insurance, which is financed from compulsory payments by plants, factories, enterprises and institutions. All citizens are constitutionally guaranteed welfare in old age, free medical attention and compensation for industrial disability. A five-day week was introduced in 1967 and the average working week (1965) was 41 hours for most industrial and administrative workers, 36 hours for special categories. In 1968 the minimum paid holiday was fixed at 15 working days.

Health services: Free health services are available to the whole population. All expenditure on public health comes out of the state budget and the funds of state bodies or cooperatives, trade unions and other mass organisations. In 1965 the state's health allocations amounted to 6,700 million roubles (or 28·9 roubles per capita). Industrial enterprises and *kolkhozy* provide buildings and equipment and bear the maintenance costs of their own health units. Under the 1966–70 plan the number of hospital beds is to increase by 455,000 and pharmaceutical production by 70%.

Supervision over health services (including pharmaceutical industries) is exercised by the USSR Ministry of Health and its subordinate republican Ministries of Health. The *kray, oblast* and city public health departments of local soviets, subdivided into medical, maternity/paediatric and hygiene departments and subordinated both to the local soviet and to the higher public health body, are headed by physicians. Operational units are based on the *oblast*, city and *rayon* and are further subdivided into health districts. The *rayon* hospital offers comprehensive and integrated health care for in-patients and out-patients, is responsible for health screening of the *rayon*'s population and is aided by a network of peripheral units ranging from the district unit proper, headed by a district doctor, to the smallest local health unit, the feldscher-midwife station. As a rule district units possess small hospitals, maternity homes and health stations in rural areas. A 24-hour emergency medical service based on larger towns deals with an average 30 million calls a year and mobile health units are available for emergencies in remote locations. While expansion of facilities has included rapid growth of urban medical institutions and services there has been a tendency towards amalgamation or elimination of earlier establishments in rural areas, except in such developing regions as the Kazakh Virgin Lands where new wide-area hospitals with some 300 beds are the rule. The basic health philosophy in the Soviet Union is one of prophylaxis by health protection and public hygiene; formerly endemic diseases such as plague, cholera, smallpox and malaria have been eradicated.

Since 1968 all employees with a record of over eight years' service are entitled to full earnings during sickness leave, those with five to eight years of service receiving 80% of earnings. Disabled workers receive allowances of up to 90% of their pay, depending on length of service. In the event of occupational injury or disease the worker is, on the recommendation of his trade union, entitled to disability pension equalling full pay. Incapacity persisting over four months is subject to board review and further benefits. According to age and length of service the monthly minimum disability pension is 36 roubles, maximum 120 roubles. Fully paid maternity leave is granted for 112 days; post-natal leave with full pay is extended by 14 days after the birth of twins, or in case of complicated delivery. Gynaecological and legal counselling is available to all mothers, and psycho-prophylaxis is employed in a majority of childbirths. Mothers of large families and unmarried mothers receive monthly allowances.

The Soviet Union now has the world's lowest mortality rate (1965: 7·3 per 1000 population). Cardiovascular diseases are responsible for over 30%, and cancer for between 15% and 20% of deaths. Average life expectancy is 70 years (1963).

Pensions and other benefits: Pensions are paid by the state from funds annually allocated in the Soviet Union's budget. Citizens eligible for various pensions simultaneously are granted one pension of their choice; pensions are not taxable. Pensioners in 1967 composed 15% of the population (1940, 2%; 1959, 10%). Males engaged in industrial and administrative occupations and (since 1968) in collective farming are eligible for old-age pensions at 60 (with a record of 25 years service), females at 55 (with 20 years service). For certain categories of work (e.g. underground mining and Arctic services) men are pensionable at 50 or 55, women at 45 or 50. Pensions are computed on the basis of average monthly net earnings during the last twelve months of work, or, if the applicant requests, for the optimum five-year period out of the last ten years preceding application. Old-age pensions average 60% to 70% of earnings. Pensioners in ordinary work categories are entitled to monthly benefits ranging from 30 roubles (where monthly earnings did not exceed 35 roubles) to 55 roubles (where earnings exceeded 100 roubles). The minimum statutory retirement pension is 30 roubles, maximum 120 roubles monthly. Favourable adjustment is made for workers in 'hard' categories. Employees with insufficient service are ineligible for an old-age pension if they continue working; employees retiring before qualifying age are ineligible for pension till attaining that age. A pensioner with dependants is entitled to a maximum bonus of 30% of pension. Dependants bereaved of a working parent are eligible for pensions ranging from 16 roubles monthly (for one dependant) to 120 roubles monthly (for three or more dependants of an employee deceased as a result of occupational injury or disease). Since 1930 when the labour exchanges were abolished there has officially been no unemployment in a planned economy which 'guarantees the continuous expansion of production'. There is thus no unemployment relief.

Housing and resettlement: Since 1917 the devastating internal upheavals and two World Wars caused a chronic housing deficit. In World War II, 1,710 towns and industrial settlements and 70,000 villages were destroyed by the enemy, and some 25 million persons were rendered homeless. Such cities as Stalingrad (Volgograd), Minsk, Voronezh, Sevastopol and Smolensk had to be reconstructed after 1945. During the period 1959–65, 84 million persons obtained new housing and at the end of the current Five Year Plan (1966–70) over 60 million more persons will have moved into new or improved dwellings. Housing is still inadequate and overcrowded by Western standards. Despite increased urbanisation (the 1959 census indicated 25 cities with populations over 500,000 and between 1939 and 1959 Moscow grew by 20%), current emphasis on rural construction should help relieve a shortage especially acute in Siberia and the Far East. For the 1966–70 period, 75,000 million roubles from the state budget were allocated for housing construction, estimated at 5,166 million sq. ft. Cooperative units, increasingly popular, are purchased by the cooperative member on a ten-to-15-year credit covering 60% of total cost, a 40% down-payment

J

being required. For lower income brackets state housing, financed by city, town and enterprise authorities, is still predominant; here rent is fixed at between 4% and 5% of monthly wages. As a rule new Soviet housing comprises multiple, multi-storey units, largely prefabricated, incorporated in 'microdistricts', i.e. self-contained neighbourhood complexes. While much rural housing remains rudimentary, experimental schemes in the Far North (e.g. at Aikhal and Norilsk) have, through use of glass and heating, suggested a pattern of the future.

Resettlement grants are awarded as a stimulus to settlement and economic exploitation of new areas. Heads of families moving to *kolkhozy* and *sovkhozy* in the RSFSR and Kazakhstan are entitled to 60 roubles and members of their family 20 roubles each (corresponding sums for Kamchatka are 300/60 roubles; for the Amur area 130/27 roubles). Workers volunteering for work in eastern and northern areas, following a public appeal, draw double the allowance fixed for workers contracting with ordinary recruitment organisations. Grants are the responsibility of the enterprise to which the worker is transferred. Workers who are officially transferred and young persons graduating from higher educational institutions or from certain secondary schools are entitled to immediate housing on arrival. As compensation for the harsher conditions and higher cost of living in Arctic and certain Siberian areas (where price levels may be 80% higher than in temperate zones) all workers and office employees of government, cooperative and public organisations and enterprises receive an increment on their monthly earnings (e.g. in several Arctic areas 10% after a year's employment with a 20% rise for each successive year) and up to 18 days of extra paid holiday. Travel costs of all officially sponsored work-transfers are borne by the receiving enterprise.

EDUCATION

All but the oldest generations of Soviet citizens are products of an education which differs radically from Western systems. Over 70 million, or nearly one-third of the Soviet Union's total population, are currently enrolled in some educational institution. Education is uniform and highly centralised with ultimate control of primary and most secondary institutions vested in the 35 SSR and ASSR Ministries of Education while some higher and all secondary specialised schools are placed under the USSR Ministry of Higher and Specialised Education. Vocational-technical schools come under the State Committee of the USSR Council of Ministers on Vocational-Technical Education. The RSFSR Ministry of Education in effect sets the pace and standards for the development of the entire structure and curricula of schools, whether Russian or non-Russian. Soviet and national patriotism, revolutionary pride, party loyalty and *grazhdanstrennost* ('civic-mindedness') are the chief elements of communist morality inculcated at the earliest stages, and at every phase of administration the CPSU ensures ideological orthodoxy through its control of general educational policy and of local educational organisations, through its sponsorship of personnel and formulation of the curricula, through parent-teacher consultations, Pioneer and Komsomol activities and media of information and guidance such as the teachers' journal, *Uchitelskaya gazeta*. A feature of today is the growing role of polytechnical and practical elements in the curriculum and the consequent expansion of vocational and specialised schools. Production training has become as integral a part of secondary education as traditional science and humanities, although this trend received a set-back after the fall of Khrushchev in 1964. Other characteristics include coeducation at all levels (half the students in higher education are women), the emphasis on comprehensive-type primary and secondary education, the evolution of the boarding-school, the increasing use of the Russian language in non-Russian republics, and the development of schools for specially gifted children.

Language policy: The Russian language is the mother-tongue of half the Soviet Union's population and as a federal language has wide and growing application outside the RSFSR itself. Complete instruction is in theory available at all educational stages in Russian and the languages of the 14 non-Russian SSRs, although in rural areas there is often no choice. In major ASSRs primary and some secondary education is provided in the native tongue; in minor ASSRs and NOs schooling in the vernacular is seldom available above primary level. Other national minorities may or may not receive native language instruction at the lower grades. The non-Russian SSRs also support Russian-language schools which educate not only Russian residents but also, increasingly, non-Russians. These schools must however teach the SSR language. There also some 700 primary-secondary type schools in which many subjects are taught in English, German or French. Similar establishments are planned for Spanish, Chinese, Arabic, Hindi and Urdu. English, German and French are the most popular foreign languages at every level, and in higher institutions over 80 Soviet and foreign languages are taught.

Pre-school education: The non-compulsory crèches (*yasli*) for infants aged three months to three years and kindergartens (*detsky sad*) for children aged three to seven, run by Ministries of Health, individual factories, farms, enterprises or other bodies, are fee-paying institutions organised on an annual or seasonal basis and at present catering to approximately 25% of the total pre-school age group.

Primary education: Universal compulsory primary education was introduced in the 1930s; in 1952 a basic seven-year compulsory system was instituted and this was extended to eight years in 1958. The current Five Year Plan (1966–70) provides for the introduction of a universal compulsory primary-secondary (ten-year) education and this has already been realised in many large cities. The current eight-year school (*vosmiletnyaya shkola*), compulsory for all children aged seven to 15 (except those in special education), is divided into elementary and middle grades (*nachalnaya shkola* and *srednyaya shkola*) of four years each. In the middle grades the curricula include a foreign language (usually English, German or French), production training, basic physics, chemistry and biology and a high content of mathematics as well as Russian language, literature, history, geography and physical training. Labour training for girls includes elements of domestic science. In non-Russian schools the Russian language is taught as a second tongue. Pupils successfully completing eight years receive a certificate (*svidetelstvo*).

Secondary education: The compulsory eight-year school course is followed by one of four main types of secondary schooling: (a) the three-year secondary general poly-technical school (*srednyaya obshcheobrazovatelnaya politekhnicheskaya shkola*) which forms a three-year extension of the continuous primary-secondary system (eleven-year school, *odinadtsatiletnyaya shkola*) and combines academic courses with vocational training (in factories, farms, enterprises) leading to a school-leaving certificate (*attestat*); (b) the four-to-five-year secondary specialised school (*srednee spetsialnoe uchebnoe zavedenie*) which mixes a predominant proportion of vocational training (for some 400 professions) with general curricula, leading to a diploma (*diplom*); (c) the three-year vocational-technical school (*professionalno-tekhnicheskoe uchilishche*) which supplements institutionalised apprenticeship with a minimal academic course leading to a certificate (*udostoverenie*). Students here are paid at apprenticeship rates; (d) the three-year secondary general evening/shift school (*vechernyaya/smennaya srednyaya obshcheobrazovatelnaya shkola*) offering part-time or correspondence courses at the general polytechnical level to students unable, for reasons of employment, distance, etc., to enroll in day school. This also leads to the *attestat*. In theory graduates from all four categories are entitled to apply to higher institutions but those from secondary general polytechnical schools enjoy obvious advantages.

Special education is of three kinds, with eleven-year courses where possible: (a) schools for the handicapped and run by either Education, Health or National Insurance Ministries provide free treatment and general polytechnical tuition for the mentally or physically deficient; (b) children showing particular artistic promise may forgo the usual polytechnical and production training and combine general education with professional instruction at schools attached to music conservatories, ballet companies, etc. Since 1958 a few selective schools for the scientifically talented have also been established; (c) military schools, which give preference to children of war casualties and combine military training with a general curriculum.

Boarding-school education: The coeducational boarding-school (*shkola internat*) system has been greatly expanded since 1956 to include several categories of deprived and dislocated children. Where applicable, parents are subject to a means test. A variant is the extended eight-year day school (*shkola prodlennogo dnya*) where pupils participate in supplementary daily extramural activities. About four million pupils studied in these two types of school in 1966–7.

University and higher education: Every institute of higher education (*vysshee uchebnoe zavedenie, VUZ, pl. VUZy*) has the power to confer diplomas and postgraduate degrees and to conduct research. Higher education is coordinated on an all-union scale by the USSR Ministry of Higher and Specialised Secondary Education which is also directly responsible for 29 major institutions. SSR and ASSR Education Ministries or Committees have jurisdiction over the majority of their VUZy. Certain institutions come under specific Ministries: transport VUZy are controlled by the USSR Ministry of Transport, communications VUZy by the USSR Ministry of Communications, agricultural, forestry, medical, art and trade VUZy are administered by their respective republican ministries as are all teacher-training colleges except in the Belorussian SSR where a composite Ministry of Higher Specialised Secondary and Vocational Education is responsible. Curricula are generally uniform throughout the Soviet Union. Admission to the VUZ is on the basis of successful completion of secondary schooling and of success in the competitive entrance examinations (taken in both general and specialised subjects) but may be facilitated by a reference from the Komsomol, etc. All tuition is free, and board for most students is covered by grants (*stipendii*) which are related to performance. Bonuses are awarded for excellence. Every student must attend classes in the theory and history of Marxism-Leninism, in the history of the CPSU and in scientific atheism, in addition to his speciality. Many specialised departments (e.g. medicine) operate independently of the universities and enjoy at least equal status. Courses last from four to six years and lead to the diploma (*diplom ob okonchanii VUZa*). Sixteen universities and several hundred other VUZy have been founded since 1945. The 45 universities are: Alma-Ata, Ashkhabad, Baku, Cheboksary, Chernovtsy, Dnepropetrovsk, Donetsk, Dushanbe, Frunze, Gorky, Irkutsk, Kaliningrad, Kazan, Kharkov, Kiev, Kishinev, Leningrad, Lvov, Makhachkala, Minsk, Moscow (2)[1], Nalchik, Novosibirsk, Odessa, Ordzhonikidze, Perm, Petrozavodsk, Riga, Rostov-on-Don, Samarkand, Saransk, Saratov, Sverdlovsk, Tartu, Tashkent, Tiflis, Tomsk, Ufa, Uzhgorod, Vilnius, Vladivostok, Voronezh, Yakutsk, Yerevan.

Adult education: Part-time evening and correspondence courses leading to certificates or diplomas are increasingly popular at every level. These are sponsored and organised by factories, farms, enterprises, communities, etc., in formal collaboration with existing educational institutions. Theoretical training is closely linked to production work. The system of extramural VUZ education (1967) consists of 29 correspondence and evening colleges and more than 1,000 departments with an enrolment of over 2,382,000 students (i.e. more than half the total number of students in higher education). Students are entitled to annual supplementary paid leaves during work-shop and examination sessions.

Educational institutions (*1966–7*)

	Institutions	Students
General (eight and ten-year)	210,000	48,168,000
Secondary specialised	3,969	3,979,000
Vocational-technical	3,803[2]	1,960,000
VUZy (incl. extramural)	767	4,123,000
Other professional courses	n.a.	14,338,000
Special schools for handicapped	n.a.	285,000

MASS MEDIA

The Press (*1968*)[3]:

Russian-language dailies: Izvestiya, Moscow (M), govt., 8,300,000; *Pionerskaya Pravda*, M, children's, 8,200,000; *Pravda*, M and major cities, CPSU, 7,000,000; *Komso-*

---

[1] One of these being the Patrice Lumumba People's Friendship University, founded in 1960 for students from Asia, Africa and Latin America.

[2] 1965–6 statistics.

[3] Circulation figures generally unavailable.

molskaya Pravda, M, youth, 6,800,000; *Selskaya Zhizn*, M, CPSU agric., 6,200,000; *Sovyetskaya Rossiya*, M, CP and govt. of RSFSR, 3,200,000; *Sovyetsky Sport*, M, sport, 2,200,000; *Trud*, M, trade union, 2,000,000; *Krasnaya Zvezda*, M, military; *Gudok*, M, communications; *Moskovskaya Pravda*, M, CP and city soviet; *Moskovsky Komsomolyets*, M, youth; *Leninskoye Znamya*, M, CP; *Leningradskaya Pravda*, Leningrad, CP and city soviet; *Pravda Ukrainy*, Kiev, Ukrainian CP and govt.; *Rabochaya Gazeta*, Kiev, Ukrainian CP; *Sovyetskaya Belorussiya*, Minsk, Belorussian CP and govt.; *Sovyetskaya Estoniya*, Tallinn, Estonian CP and govt.; *Sovyetskaya Latviya*, Riga, Latvian CP and govt.; *Sovyetskaya Litva*, Vilnius, Lithuanian CP and govt.; *Sovyetskaya Moldavia*, Kishinev, Moldavian CP and govt.; *Bakinsky Rabochy*, Baku, Azerbaidzhan CP; *Kommunist*, Yerevan, Armenian CP; *Zarya Vostoka*, Tbilisi, Georgian CP and govt.; *Kazakhstanskaya Pravda*, Alma-Ata, Kazakh CP and govt.; *Pravda Vostoka*, Tashkent, Uzbek CP and govt.; *Kommunist Tadzhikistana*, Dushanbe, Tadzhik CP; *Sovyetskaya Kirgiziya*, Frunze, Kirgiz CP and govt. (also in Kirgiz).

Non-Russian SSR language dailies: Radyanskaya Ukraina, Kiev, Ukrainian CP and govt.; *Zvyazda*, Minsk, Belorussian CP and govt.; *Rahva Haal*, Tallinn, Estonian CP and govt.; *Cina*, Riga, Latvian CP and govt.; *Tiesa*, Vilnius, Lithuanian CP and govt.; 250,000; *Moldova Socialiste*, Kishinev, Moldavian CP and govt.; *Kommunisti*, Tbilisi, Georgian CP; *Sovietakan Aiastan*, Yerevan, Armenian CP and govt.; *Kommunist*, Baku, Azerbaidzhan CP; *Sotsialistik Kazakhstan*, Alma-Ata, Kazakh CP and govt.; *Sovyet Uzbekistony*, Tashkent, Uzbek CP and govt.; *Tochikistony Sovyety*, Dushanbe, Tadzhik CP and govt.; *Sovyet Turkmenistany*, Ashkhabad, Turkmen CP and govt.

Periodicals: (Moscow) *Zdorovye* (m), pop. science, 5,000,000; *Ogonyok* (w), illus., 2,050,000; *Krokodil* (3 per m.), satirical; *Za Rubezhom* (w), foreign news, 700,000; *Sovyetsky Soyuz* (m), Soviet Union illus., 600,000 incl. 13 foreign languages; *Sovyetskaya Zhenshchina* (m), Soviet woman illus., 550,000 incl. 9 foreign languages; *Literaturnaya Gazeta* (w), CPSU econ.; *Zhurnal Mod* (q), fashion; *Komsomolskaya Zhizn* (f), youth; *Narodnoye Obrazovaniye* (m), education, 100,000; *Novy Mir* (m), progressive literary, 150,000; *Oktyabr* (m), conservative literary; *Kommunist* (18 per annum), CP theory; *Novoye Vremya* (w), foreign affairs, also in 6 foreign languages; *Molodaya Gvardia* (m), youth; *Yunost* (m), literary youth; *Ekonomika Syelskogo Khozyaistva* (m), agricultural; *Kolkhozno-Sovkhoznoye Proizvodstvo* (m), agricultural; *Zemledeliye* (m), agricultural; *Iskusstvo* (m), art; *Inostrannaya Literatura* (m), for. lit.; *Planovoye Khozyaistvo* (m), economic; *Sovyetskaya Torgovlya* (m), trade; *Vneshnyaya Torgovlya* (m), for. trade, also in English, French and Spanish; *Muzykalnaya Zhizn* (f), music; *Teatralnaya Zhizn* (f), theatre; *Sovyetsky Ekran* (f), film; *Moskva* (m), literary; *Nash Sovremmenik* (m), literary; *Russkaya Literatura* (q), literary; *Literaturnaya Rossiya* (w), conservative literary; *Sovyetskaya Meditsina* (m), medical; *Lesnoye Khozyaistvo* (m), forestry; *Rybovodstvo i Rybolovstvo* (m), fishing; *Sovyetskoe Kino* (m), film; *Futbol* (w), football; *Zhurnal Moskovskoy Patriarkhy* (m), Orthodox Patriarchate; *Bratsky Vestnik*, Baptist. (Other cities) *Neva* (m), Leningrad, literary, 235,000; *Zvezda* (m), Leningrad, literary; *Don* (m), Rostov-on-Don, literary; *Radyanska Zhinka* (m), Kiev, woman's illus., in Ukrainian, 800,000; *Ukraina* (w), Kiev, illus., in Ukrainian, 180,000; *Raduga* (m), Kiev, literary, in Ukrainian, 15,000; *Literaturnaya Gruziya* (m), Tbilisi, literary, in Russian and Georgian; *Literaturnaya Armeniya* (m), literary, in Russian and Armenian; *Prostop*, Alma-Ata, literary, in Russian.

Broadcasting: Soviet broadcasting is supervised by the Committee on Broadcasting and Television under the USSR Council of Ministers and by similarly subordinate Committees in the SSRs. Radio Moscow with five programmes provides the bulk of relay material for the entire country, but each SSR and many lower units down to rayon level maintain their own stations. The total volume of daily broadcasting in 1966 was 970 hours. The SSR stations at Moscow, Baku, Dushanbe, Kiev, Minsk, Riga, Tallinn, Tashkent, Vilnius and Yerevan transmit foreign broadcasts in their own republican languages and also in a total of 53 world languages. In 1966 foreign transmissions were allotted 152 hours per day. Every SSR also has a regional (often bilingual) variation of Soviet television and in 1967 there were 748 TV centres and relay stations. Moscow, Leningrad and Kiev maintain three TV programmes every day, varying from ten to three hours, and Baku, Tallinn and Riga broadcast two TV programmes daily. Most other large population centres are served, often by means of communications satellite. Experimental colour TV transmissions began in Moscow in 1967, using the Franco-Soviet SECAM system.

CONSTITUTIONAL SYSTEM

Constitution: The Union of Soviet Socialist Republics is a socialist state of workers and peasants. All central and local power is vested in the soviets of working people's deputies. The constitution dates from 1936, with subsequent amendments.

Territorial-administrative divisions: The Soviet Union is a federal state formed on the basis of a voluntary union of 15 Soviet Socialist Republics (SSRs). Each SSR is a nominally sovereign republic possessing the right to secede from the Soviet Union, to maintain its own army and to have direct relations with foreign states—rights scarcely exercisable. The Praesidium of the USSR Supreme Soviet includes the 15 presidents of the SSRs in the capacity of vice-presidents; the USSR Council of Ministers includes the chairmen (prime ministers) of the SSR Councils of Ministers, and the USSR Supreme Court includes the chairmen of SSR Supreme Courts. Within the SSR the main subdivisions are the province (*oblast*), district (*rayon*) and rural localities. Cities are separately administered usually at the *rayon* level but the larger ones fall directly within SSR jurisdiction and themselves include a number of municipal *rayony*. There are also units theoretically based on autonomy for ethnic minorities. 19 autonomous republics (ASSRs) (of which 15 are inside the RSFSR) possess their own constitutions and state organs and send deputies to the Soviet of Nationalities of the USSR Supreme Soviet and one representative each to the Praesidium of the SSR Supreme Soviet. The nine autonomous regions or *avtonomnye oblasti* (AOs), are smaller subdivisions of the same type. Several large and remote areas within the RSFSR, classified as *kraya*, are administered like *oblasti* but can themselves contain *oblasti* or AOs. Finally there are ten national areas or *natsionalnye okruga* (NOs), all within the RSFSR, small national entities sending one deputy each to the Soviet of Nationalities in Moscow.

Legislature: The legislative structure consists of a pyramid of soviets (councils) reaching from the level of rural localities to the highest organ of state power in Moscow, the Supreme Soviet of the USSR (*Verkhovny Sovet SSSR*). The latter consists of two chambers having equal rights, the Soviet of the Union (*Sovet Soyuza*) and the Soviet of Nationalities (*Sovet Natsionalnostey*). The Supreme Soviet adopts and repeals the laws of the Soviet Union, supervises observance of the Soviet constitution, approves Soviet external and internal policy by turning decrees into laws, and regulates the functioning of state bodies. Formally speaking, it elects the USSR Praesidium (i.e. collective presidency), appoints the USSR Council of Ministers (i.e. government), elects the USSR Supreme Court and appoints the USSR procurator-general. In 1966 767 deputies (*deputaty*) were elected to the Soviet of the Union and 750 to the Soviet of Nationalities (representing 57 national groups). The Soviet of the Union is elected for a four-year term by all citizens of 18 years and over on the basis of one deputy for 300,000 persons. The Soviet of Nationalities is elected by the citizens of each national-administrative subdivision on the basis of 32 deputies from each SSR, eleven from each ASSR, five from each AO and one from each NO. Either chamber may initiate legislation; they sit simultaneously twice a year, and a bill becomes law when passed by a simple majority in both chambers. No vote to date has in fact been other than unanimous. Each chamber elects a number of standing commissions which meet between sessions of the Supreme Soviet, report to sessions and make recommendations to the Praesidium. The Praesidium of the Supreme Soviet of the USSR is elected at a joint sitting of the two chambers and is accountable to the Supreme Soviet. It consists of a president, 15 vice-presidents (the presidents of each SSR), a secretary and 16 members. It convenes and dissolves the sessions of the Supreme Soviet, issues decrees, interprets operative laws and discharges other functions of state administration.

The highest legislative organs in the SSRs and ASSRs are their single-chamber Supreme Soviets.

Election of deputies is conducted on the basis of universal, equal and direct suffrage by secret ballot; the electorate is offered a single slate of candidates, all of whom are elected unless any of them obtain less than 50% of the vote, something which has happened only occasionally and at the local level.

Executive: According to the Soviet Union's constitutional separation of powers, the USSR Council of Ministers (*Sovet Ministrov SSSR*), i.e. the Soviet government, has no official legislative authority and is responsible to the USSR Supreme Soviet or, in the intervals between sessions of the latter, to its praesidium. In reality much of the legislative as well as executive power is concentrated in the Council of Ministers, which operates in close association with the CPSU. It consists of a chairman (prime minister), first vice-chairmen, vice-chairmen, ministers, chairman of the State Planning Committee (Gosplan), chairman of the State Committee for Construction (Gosstroy) and chairmen of other state committees and agencies. The chief posts are held by prominent party members who form a praesidium within the Council of Ministers. Ministries are of three kinds: all-union, which have no equivalent in the SSRs; union-republic, which have counterparts in the SSRs; republic, which exist only in constituent republics and are formally subordinate to the Council of Ministers of the respective SSR all-union ministries and State Committees which administer affairs of all-union significance, e.g. communications.

Local government: The more than 47,000 soviets of working people's deputies constitute local organs of state power at the levels of *kray*, *oblast*, autonomous *oblast*, *okrug*, *rayon*, city and rural localities. The executive and administrative arm of the local soviet is the executive committee (*ispolkom*), elected by it and comprising a chairman, vice-chairmen, secretary and members. Local soviets are elected for two-year terms. In 1967 more than two million members were elected to them, of which nearly half were members of the CPSU, the others being 'non-party members'.

Judiciary: The highest judicial organ is the USSR Supreme Court (*Verkhovny Sud SSSR*) which is elected by the USSR Supreme Soviet. Each republic has its own set of courts. Subsidiary regional courts hear appeals and more important original cases but the latter function belongs mainly to the people's court (*narodny sud*) at the *rayon* level. There are also special courts, e.g. military tribunals and state arbitration bodies (*Gosarbitrazh*) which decide contract disputes between state enterprises. Courts are elected by respective soviets for a five-year period with the exception of the people's court which consists of a people's judge (*narodny sudya*) and two lay people's assessors (*narodnye zasedateli*), elected locally for five and two years respectively. The people's court functions as the first instance court for the majority of civil and criminal cases. The USSR Supreme Court acts as the ultimate court of appeal. This highest judicial organ, however, lacks the right to judicial review of legislation (a procedure non-existent in the Soviet Union) or the power to reverse the decisions of the CPSU or Council of Ministers. Judges, who are frequently CPSU members, are theoretically independent. In all courts cases are heard in public with the exception of cases where this is deemed prejudicial to the preservation of state secrets. The accused is guaranteed the right to defence, although the defence lawyer is appointed only after the indictment has been drawn up. Court proceedings are conducted in the language of the SSR, ASSR or AO, and interpreting facilities are made available.

The 200,000 comrades' courts (*tovarishcheskiye sudy*) which are now operating purport to instil a sense of civic duty (*grazhdanstvennost*) in individual and collective alike by combating anti-social acts and violations of labour discipline.

The safeguarding of 'socialist legality', supervision over the observance and application of laws by institutions, organisations and individuals, is vested in the procuracy (*prokuratura*) whose highest incumbent, roughly equivalent to the western ombudsman, is the procurator-general of the USSR (*generalny prokuror SSSR*). Elected for a seven-year term by the USSR Supreme Soviet, and never a member of the USSR Council of Ministers, he directs a system of subordinate bodies at the various republican, regional and city levels. Procurators, who act both as watchdogs over the bureaucracy and as prosecutors in criminal cases, are independent of local authority and subordinate only to their procuratorial superiors, and the procuracy, staffed as it is mainly by CPSU members, is in effect a strongly centralised and anti-federal institution.

The chief agent of public order is the people's militia but about 150,000 voluntary public order squads (*druzhiny*) currently function. Since 1950 capital punishment has been gradually restored for treason, espionage, sabotage, certain categories of murder, for terrorism, brigandage, certain economic crimes and, in particular circumstances, for attacks on militia and voluntary public order squads.

Party: The Communist Party of the Soviet Union (CPSU), whose supreme organ is the Party Congress (held in theory at least once in four years), purports to play the leading role in society and the state, unite the politically conscious sections of workers, peasants and intellectuals, lay the bases of communist society, raise the material and cultural level of the people, organise national defence and promote the solidarity of the international working class. The Soviet Union is a one-party state because its society is in theory morally and politically united. Its Central Committee (CC), elected by the Congress, meets at least twice a year and chooses a Politburo (currently numbering eleven members and nine candidate members), to direct the functions of the CC between plenary sessions. The party's structure at regional and local levels approximates to that of the state apparatus. It includes over 330,000 primary organisations. In 1966 the CPSU numbered over 11,700,000 members and the Young Communist League (*Komsomol*) (ages 15–28) 23,000,000.

Leading government and party figures: N.V. Podgorny (president), A.N. Kosygin (prime minister), A.A. Gromyko (foreign minister), N.S. Patolichev (minister of foreign trade), Marshal A.A. Grechko (defence minister), N. Baybakov (chairman of Gosplan), A. Poskonov (chairman of board of Gosbank), Yuri Andropov (chairman of KGB), S. Skachkov (chairman of Committee on Foreign Economic Relations), Mrs. E. Furtseva (Ministry of Culture), D.S. Polyansky and K.S. Mazurov (first vice-chairmen of Council of Ministers), G.I. Voronov (prime minister of RSFSR), A.F. Gorkin (chairman of USSR Supreme Court). Party figures: Leonid I. Brezhnev (general-secretary of CPSU); other full members of the Politburo of the Central Committee of the CPSU: A.P. Kirilenko, A.N. Kosygin, K.S. Mazurov, A.Y. Pelshe, N.V. Podgorny, D.S. Polyansky, M.A. Suslov, G.I. Voronov, P.E. Shelest, A.N. Shelepin. Candidate members of the CC of CPSU: P.N. Demichev, V.P. Mzhavanadze, V.V. Grishin, Sh.R. Rashidov, V.V. Scherbitsky, D.F. Ustinov, D.A. Kunayev, P.M. Masherov. First secretary of Komsomol: S.P. Pavlov.

PART ONE
HISTORICAL

RUSSIA AND THE
SOVIET UNION TO 1956

JOHN KEEP

INTRODUCTION

Two major themes run through the history of modern Russia and provide an element of continuity between the imperial and post-revolutionary epochs. One constant preoccupation of the Russian people, and more particularly of their rulers, has been the effort to overcome swiftly the country's historic legacy of backwardness *vis-à-vis* most Western nations. Forced industrialisation at a rapid tempo has involved a radical reshaping of the traditional social order and of men's attitudes to their environment. Their next most important concern has been the endeavour to adapt the political system to 20th-century conditions in such a way as to maintain an abnormally high degree of central control over the thoughts and deeds of individual citizens. In Russia the state authority has always loomed larger in people's lives than has been the case in countries with a democratic tradition. The Tsarist autocracy pursued aims of a quite conventional character, judged by the standards of the day. It sought to preserve the empire's external and internal security and to increase the national wealth insofar as this was compatible with political and social stability. The Soviet regime, on the other hand, has pursued much more far-reaching goals. Ever since the Bolshevik Revolution of October 1917 it has striven to effect a complete transformation of Russian (and international) society: to achieve socialism, and ultimately full communism, as defined by Marx and Lenin. The *raison d'être* of the Soviet Communist Party is to fulfil this ideological mission.

These two themes—socio-economic change and a tradition of political authoritarianism—are closely connected, as we shall see by examining each of them in turn.

SOCIO-ECONOMIC CHANGE IN RUSSIA

Russia's relative 'under-development' was the product of long-range geographic and historical considerations. Its vast size hindered communications and the exploitation of its rich mineral resources. Agricultural progress was impeded by the harsh climate and the poor quality of the soil in most areas of the country. Despite modern scientific and technological advances these factors remain important even today. So long as the bulk of the population lived close to the subsistence margin, it was difficult for autonomous social forces to emerge, strong enough to challenge the power of the state, which from the 15th century onward had been the architect of national unity. The Russian nobles preferred to follow careers in the state service, as officers or officials, than to make their mark as independent farmers or business men. Of the peasantry, the overwhelming majority of the population, a large element was economically passive or inert. Serfdom, abolished as recently as 1861, left deep traces upon the popular psychology. Russia conspicuously lacked an enterprising middle class able to take the initiative in modernising its economy, so that this role fell mainly to the state. After defeat in the Crimean War (1854–5) brought home the urgent necessity for economic progress, the government assisted private entrepreneurs to build railways and establish new mines and factories. An important part in this development was played by foreign capital, notably in the Ukrainian metallurgical industry and in petroleum extraction in Transcaucasia. To attract investors (predominantly French or British), the government stabilised the currency and built up a sizable gold reserve. From 1885 to 1900 Russian industrial output forged ahead, and in the last years of the 19th century its growth rate was second to none.

A business recession, war with Japan (1904–5) and consequent internal disturbances temporarily interrupted this progress, but it was resumed in the years before the outbreak of World War I. In 1913 Russia was the world's fifth largest industrial producer. In relation to its rapidly growing population, however, manufacturing output was very low. The per capita growth rate in the period 1885–1913 has been put at 1·25% per annum. Savings bank deposits rose twelve-fold between 1890 and 1913—eloquent testimony to increased popular well-being. Imperial Russia had yet to attain 'the take-off point for self-sustaining growth' (to use the modern jargon phrase), but it did have an industrial base in terms of equipment, manpower and technological knowhow upon which later Soviet planners could build.

There were two large blots on this happy picture. In the first place, labour obtained so little immediate benefit from Russia's industrial progress that social tensions in the cities were acute. The industrial wage-earners, some three million strong in 1913, earned more than most peasants, but wages lagged far behind newly aroused expectations. Working hours were long, factory conditions poor. Elementary protective legislation for women and juveniles was introduced in the 1880s, but the law had many loopholes and adult men often worked a 14-hour day. After 1905 some industrialists adopted more enlightened attitudes, but all too many behaved short-sightedly. Where ethnic and class discrimination was combined, as in factories employing highly paid foreign foremen, an explosive situation often resulted. World War I brought additional hardships for most groups of wage-earners.

The second major defect was the imbalance between industry and agriculture. To travel from the cities into the Russian countryside was to go back centuries in time. The *muzhik* had his virtues, notably an ability to withstand every kind of adversity with uncomplaining good humour, but his general cultural level was abysmally low. He obtained precious little uplift or enlightenment from the clergy or landowning gentry. The peasants lived in a world of their own, remote from authority, barely touched by modern influences radiating from the cities. Juridically they were free men, but until the early 20th century the village commune (*mir*) retained extensive administrative powers. It could allocate the heavy tax burden among the individual householders, penalising the thrifty to subsidise the idle or unfortunate. In Great Russia the commune held legal title to the land, which it redistributed periodically among its members according to their needs. This egalitarian system, highly regarded by some romantic intellectuals, was a serious disincentive to productive investment. Crop yields were extremely low, except on large estates; it was the latter which provided most of the surplus needed to feed the cities and for export. In areas of extreme over-crowding many peasants were dependent upon landowners who leased land at extortionate rates—as in Ireland or India.

These conditions explain why there was serious agrarian unrest in 1905. Thereafter the prime minister, Stolypin, embarked upon a major reform designed to create a strong class of individualistic peasant proprietors, who could reinforce the declining landed gentry as a bulwark of conservatism. Householders were encouraged to leave the commune and to gather their scattered strips into consolidated farms on the Western model. The reform evoked a good response in the more advanced regions of the country, but in Great Russia the results were modest. It was probably launched too late for it to have realised the government's high hopes. Greater success attended other measures taken to promote migration to new lands in Russian Asia: crop diversification, primary schooling in rural areas and farm mechanisa-tion. It was the regime's misfortune that this progress was disrupted by the outbreak of World War I in 1914. This led to widespread social dislocation and eventually to a turbulent revolution. In 1917, when authority in the countryside collapsed, the peasants renewed their ancient cry for a general distribution of the land, and embarked upon a new wave of violence from which not only the gentry but also their better-off fellows suffered. This spontaneous and anarchic agrarian revolution, sanctioned by the Bolsheviks, eliminated the more productive farms and turned Russia into a country of some 25 million smallholders, more addicted than ever to their communal traditions and eager to enjoy their new wealth free from outside interference. Such a situation posed intractable problems for any government, especially one committed to Marxist 'proletarian socialism'.

SOCIALIST ECONOMIC PLANNING

The Soviet regime inherited a grim legacy in the economic field. War and revolution had upset the whole pattern of international trade. From 1914 until the civil war ended in 1920 Russia was all but isolated from its normal markets and sources of supply. Industrial production was dislocated by terri-torial losses, lack of raw materials and fuel and by labour unrest. In 1918-9 the richest areas were outside Moscow's control altogether. Already in 1917 the transport system had broken down, serving as a potent stimulus to revo-lution in the famished cities. To escape starvation, many workers fled to the villages. The financial system, too, collapsed as successive governments covered their expenditure by issuing vast quantities of paper money. By 1920 the rouble had become practically worthless and trade had to be con-ducted in the form of barter. To add to the chaos, the new regime adopted doctrinaire socialist economic policies. All sources of wealth were nationalised and an attempt was made to replace the 'capitalist' profit motive by coercion coupled with moral exhortation. Some enthusiasts hailed the dying-out of trade and money as a sign that full communism was around the corner. Lenin was more realistic and inveighed against bureaucratic inefficiency, but his instructions on matters of economic policy were often ambiguous. Not until March 1921, when his regime was gravely imperilled by popular uprisings, did he persuade his colleagues to adopt a somewhat more rational approach.

The New Economic Policy (NEP) was construed ideologically as a compromise between socialism and capitalism, a transitional phase of unspecified duration. In practice it meant concessions to the peasant farmer and small private trader. The former was no longer subject to arbitrary and violent requisitions of allegedly 'surplus' produce, but had his dues fixed—at first in kind, later in cash—in relation to his property or earnings. Although crude, this arrangement did at least afford him some incentive to produce for the market. Ultimate ownership of the land remained vested in the state, but peasants were permitted to farm their land more or less as they wished, and even to employ hired labour on a limited scale. Meanwhile the top-heavy industrial bureaucracy was simplified. In less essential branches managers, often members of the old intelligentsia, were given wider decision-making powers, although within the factory they had to take account of the local trade union branch and party activists, and overall policy was still determined by the planners in Moscow. The 'controlling heights' of the economy—heavy industry and foreign trade—remained under close state control, but stress was now laid upon improving output and efficiency. As a result of these moderate policies agricultural, and later industrial, output within a few years reached and surpassed their pre-war level.

The next stage in economic strategy was the subject of intense debate within the party. The right-wing leaders, notably Bukharin, advocated a cautious policy: to conciliate the peasants by providing them with sufficient industrial consumer goods in exchange for their surplus produce. The left-wingers, notably Trotsky, took an alarmist view of the peasants' individualistic propensities, and urged that a policy of severe fiscal pressure be applied against the wealthier elements in order to obtain funds to promote rapid industrialisation, with the accent on producers' goods. In the event neither formula was adopted, since under Stalin it was politics that determined economics, not vice versa. Stalin first took an intermediate line, which won him support in the party; then, having suppressed his main opponents on the left and right, he embarked upon an ultra-leftist course more extreme than anything hitherto conceived.

First Five Year Plan

Stalin's first Five Year Plan (1929–33) anticipated Mao Tse-tung's 'Great Leap Forward'. By mobilising ideological enthusiasm and applying force on a massive scale, he sought to effect a drastic transformation of the economy. A large volume of capital, contributed by the population through heavy taxation, restrictions on consumption and cheap labour, was invested in the development of heavy industry. Production was boosted at a rapid tempo, regardless of the cost to working-class living standards. Fulfilment of targets assigned by the central plan became the prime legal obligation of all Soviet citizens. The peasants were cajoled or coerced into 'voluntarily' abandoning their independent properties and joining large mechanised collective or state farms, where their activities were subject to close administrative control. The collective farms had to meet heavy delivery quotas and other obligations before they could share out the residue of their income among their members. By 1936 90% of Soviet peasants had been brought within the new system of 'socialised agriculture'. The reform was carried through so violently, and with so little regard either for peasant interests or for economic rationality, that it was exceedingly unpopular. But those who protested (or were deemed likely to protest) were arrested and either shot as alleged *kulaks* or deported to forced-labour camps. Many of those who remained, threatened with loss of their property and mass starvation, slaughtered their horses and cattle. This was a contributory cause of the catastrophic man-made famine of 1932. Stalin himself later privately estimated the total loss of life at ten million, but in public claimed that his policies had succeeded. In a limited sense they had: the cities and the export market did get their surpluses, but at an incalculable human and material cost.

Wasteful and inefficient use of resources became one of the hallmarks of the Stalinist 'planned economy', in industry as in agriculture. The main incentive for all state employees, whether workers or managers, was fear of punishment for real or alleged shortcomings. At the same time, to provide a material stimulus, income differentials were widened, with privileges for 'shock workers' who exceeded their production norms or otherwise excelled. Educational opportunities were greatly improved. By the late 1930s a new managerial élite had come into being, a technologically-minded 'Soviet intelligentsia', which henceforward served as the principal bulwark of the regime. This stabilisation of Soviet society, and the high priority given to industries of significance for national defence, enabled the Soviet Union to meet the great test of war in 1941. The system of centralised planning was well suited to perform such tasks as evacuating entire factories to the rear and boosting production in new industrial areas (for example, the Kuzbas in western Siberia). The transport system, which had been extended and modernised, withstood wartime strains much better in 1941–45 than it had done in 1914–20. The population, accustomed to total mobilisation in peacetime, by and large accepted stoically the new burdens imposed upon them in order to defeat the invader. In the occupied areas, however, the artificial collective farm system swiftly collapsed.

POST-WAR ECONOMIC RECONSTRUCTION

When Stalin set about the formidable tasks of post-war economic reconstruction, he adhered to the well-tried system of priorities. Agriculture was once again starved of investment funds, while political controls over the farmers were reinforced. The prices paid for deliveries of produce were so low that many peasants earned little or nothing. The government feared that any concessions would encourage 'bourgeois individualist' tendencies. Instead it embarked upon grandiose schemes for 'the transformation of nature' which could not bring any short-term return. In industry the traditional emphasis on producers' goods was enhanced by the need to develop nuclear energy for military purposes.

Thus, when Stalin died in 1953 the Soviet economy suffered from striking disproportions. The Soviet Union had become the world's second largest military and industrial power. It disposed of ample resources of fuel (oil, coal, natural gas) and had developed a national electric grid. Production of steel, which in 1913 had been a mere 4·2 million tons, had by 1956 reached 48·6 million tons. New branches of industry, such as aircraft construction, as well as new regions, had been opened up. The GNP rose annually by an estimated 6·9% over the period 1928–55 (5·8% if population changes are taken into account). Yet in 1953 per capita agricultural production was less than it had been in 1928, and the consumer was badly served. The output of footwear, for example, sufficed to give each citizen only one pair of shoes or boots per annum. Clothing was expensive and shoddy in design. There were few private telephones, refrigerators or television sets and still fewer private cars. Much more serious from the standpoint of the average citizen were the deficiencies in his diet. Grain products played an inordinately large role, meat was an expensive luxury and even fruit and vegetables were scarce. The distribution service was so inefficient that the urban housewife might have to spend several hours accumulating the ingredients for a simple evening meal. Entertainment facilities were poor—except in Moscow, which was a showplace for visitors. Some 40 years after the Revolution, and 20 years after the achievement of socialism, life for ordinary working people was still monotonous and grim.

In such circumstances the new regime could hardly fail to adopt the path of reform. Yet energetic measures would bring into question some basic ideological assumptions: that in a socialist society the private pursuit of gain was amoral, and that economic choices were best made, not by individual consumers, but by government agencies on their behalf. Faced with this dilemma, the policy-makers fumbled. Collective farmers were given higher prices and the control system was simplified. However, less emphasis was placed upon improved incentives than upon extension of the sown area, introduction of new crops (for example maize) and employment of scientific agronomic techniques. Output of certain consumer durables rose appreciably, but producers' goods still enjoyed a high priority. The bureaucrats entrenched in Moscow resisted efforts to shift decision-making authority to local officials and industrial managers or to allow them to adapt their production plans to consumer preferences. Yet it was increasingly obvious that the notion of centrally fixed targets, expressed in physical units, was obsolete since the economy had now attained a relatively high level of sophistication, diversity and complexity. The planning system had to take more account of the market factors of supply and demand, and allow prices to find their own level—in short, to reintroduce the flexibility that had existed under NEP. But socialism was supposed to lead to communism, not to a new compromise with capitalism. Industrial maturity posed a threat to cherished Soviet political beliefs and institutions.

POLITICAL AUTHORITARIANISM

The political history of Russia before 1917 had been overshadowed by the monarchy's unwillingness to adjust itself to the demands of the modern world. The Tsar claimed the prerogatives of an autocrat. In practice his power rested upon loyal service by a phalanx of officials and a large standing army, which could be used for internal security duties in an emergency. Another bulwark of the imperial regime was the Orthodox Church, which had inherited from Byzantium a spiritual tradition that emphasised obedience to the temporal power. Although the church lost its hold over many educated Russians during the 19th century as secular influences penetrated from the West, religion remained a potent force in the lives of the common people, especially the peasants. The last Tsars, in particular Nicholas II (1894–1917), saw it as their sacred duty to resist any diminution of their power and strongly resisted the fashionable Western ideas of constitutional government, liberalism and democracy. Nevertheless the 'Great Reforms' of the 1860s did make two important breaches in the traditional political structure. Semi-autonomous elected councils were set up for local government and courts of law were made genuinely independent of the administration. These moves towards pluralism were bitterly resented by many conservatives, and often minimised by radical opponents of the regime. The latter, swayed by romantic myths posing as scientific social theory, argued that only violent revolution, not gradual reform, could ensure happiness for the Russian people. The government's heavy-handed efforts to suppress this dissent by press censorship and administrative interference in schools and universities, merely served to make radical ideas more plausible and attractive to the intelligentsia. By 1900 it had become plain that the autocracy would have to yield to the demands of educated 'society'.

The first explosion came in 1905 after the unsuccessful war with Japan. Nicholas II reluctantly consented to introduce a constitution (although the word was officially avoided). Under the new dispensation the Crown preserved extensive prerogatives, but laws ordinarily had to pass through a two-chamber legislature, in which the lower house (Imperial Duma) was elected on a limited and indirect franchise. This quasi-parliamentary system did not work smoothly, owing to accumulated mistrust on both sides. Political tensions mounted during World War I, when the administration assumed emergency powers and bypassed the legislature. Once again military defeat discredited the monarchy, which in March 1917 collapsed amidst general rejoicing.

THE BOLSHEVIK REVOLUTION

The takeover was almost bloodless, at least in Petrograd, but as the Bolsheviks extended their hold over the rest of the country, people came to realise that they were prepared to sacrifice democratic scruples and to apply ruthless terrorist methods in order to maintain their dictatorship. Opposition rapidly mounted and bitterness soon followed as the country was rapidly plunged into chaos. The undermining of traditional authority encouraged various segments of the population to press for immediate realisation of their demands for change. The provisional government, composed of inexperienced politicians with liberal and democratic socialist sympathies, was powerless to check this dissension, and forfeited public support by endeavouring to prolong the unpopular war. Upon this groundswell of mass discontent the Bolsheviks rode to power without much difficulty in October 1917.

Lenin's problem was to keep what he had so boldly seized. He saw his coup simply as the prelude to a general revolution of the war-weary proletariat in all the belligerent countries of Europe. He hoped that the victorious workers of the industrialised West would soon come to the rescue of the Russian Bolsheviks—a minority party of extreme left-wing socialists, with only a small working-class following, and even less among the property-conscious peasants. These expectations, however, remained unfulfilled. Europe turned its back upon communism, but the Bolsheviks were able against tremendous odds to consolidate their hold over Russia. By 1921, after the defeat of the White anti-Bolshevik forces which, with intermittent allied aid, vainly strove to resist Bolshevik rule, Lenin's party unexpectedly found itself master of most of the former imperial territories, a nominally socialist island amidst a capitalist sea. This situation forced its leaders to revise their ideological assumptions, and to try to 'build socialism in a single country' pending the outbreak of a new international revolutionary crisis which they could hope to exploit.

THE NEW SOVIET STATE

This meant that they had to improvise political institutions to govern the new 'Soviet state'. Such a state seemed to many of its followers a contra-

K

diction in terms, the denial of their innermost convictions. Naively, they had believed that the Revolution would lead to the speedy elimination of all public authority, enabling the masses to establish a new communist society run on ultra-democratic lines. The soviets (informal councils elected directly by workers and peasants) were seen as the symbols of this new order. In the early months of Soviet power these bodies were genuinely representative of mass opinion and exercised considerable influence. But the Bolsheviks, as devotees of organisation and discipline, could not tolerate this freedom, especially in a time of civil war, which necessitated maximum concentration of effort. There was thus a rapid drift towards administrative centralisation. The Red Army and the security police were two important instruments in this process. The soviets were subordinated to their central executive organ and to the government. The 1918 and 1923 constitutions formally vested supreme power in congresses of soviets, meeting at national and regional level, but in practice these deliberative assemblies were soon reduced to rubber stamps and the federal state structure had no real meaning. An increasingly important role came to be played by the Bolshevik Party, the only political grouping allowed to exist. It was organised on strict hierarchical lines. Decisions were taken in the Politburo, an inner organ of the Central Committee, and put into effect by a rapidly growing apparatus of full-time officials. In theory the party was independent of the state administration, and performed supervisory rather than executive functions. In fact these two roles were fused and many functionaries served simultaneously in both apparatuses. In this way the 'dictatorship of the proletariat' became the dictatorship of a small group—indeed, of a single individual: Lenin, succeeded on his death in 1924 by Stalin. The more idealistic communists were shocked by this development, which seemed to recreate in a new form the evils of autocracy; the more realistic, Lenin and Stalin included, understood that only in this way could the system be made to function.

THE STALINIST ERA

The party did not publicly acknowledge its usurpation of power from the people, but disguised the fact by propaganda fictions—for example, that the Soviet state was more democratic than any other since the masses took part in the execution of public policy. The divorce between the realities of Soviet political life and its official image widened appreciably after 1929, when Stalin consolidated his dictatorship in a monolithic totalitarian form. Totalitarian rule was designed to insulate Soviet society from hostile extraneous influences, to eliminate autonomous institutions and to subordinate the individual wholly to the all-encompassing demands of the state power. The 1935 constitution, promulgated after Stalin announced the achievement of socialism in the Soviet Union, embodied many long-cherished progressive principles, including guarantees of civil and political rights for every citizen. But the party leadership freely ignored these provisions whenever expedient since it considered itself above the law, responsible for its actions solely to history—to a discipline which was itself subject to crude manipulation, to make the record conform to current political requirements. In 1937 Stalin published an official textbook of party history from which all inconvenient facts and personalities were expunged. This became the new unchallengeable orthodoxy to which all thought and learning had to be adjusted. In consequence intellectual and political life atrophied since public affairs could no longer be discussed in a meaningful way. Instead men juggled with abstract ideological concepts or slogans, the continued repetition of which served to condition them psychologically to accept the *status quo*, or, like Pavlov's dogs, to react in the 'correct' manner to each new signal given from above. Writers and artists were required to suppress their individual consciences and to identify themselves wholly with party policies.

Stalin was remarkably successful in constructing a façade of total public conformity, but only at the price of sacrificing the communist movement's revolutionary dynamism. His efforts to reshape human nature were much too ambitious. By denying all freedom and insisting on absolute control, he forced people to be false to their true selves. Often they adopted a dual system of values: one for their public, another for their private conduct. Although the regime boasted of its overwhelming public support, it could not really trust the people and relied heavily upon its powerful machinery of coercion. There existed several interlocking bureaucratic hierarchies, upon whose natural rivalries Stalin skilfully played in order to maximise his personal power. Of these bodies the most important was the police, which maintained a vast network of secret agents. Their duty was to seek out and neutralise not only actual but also potential opponents of the regime. This 'prophylactic terror' produced a climate of fear and suspicion. Denunciation by one's closest associates for some allegedly 'counter-revolutionary' activity normally brought summary arrest, trial by an extra-judicial tribunal and a heavy sentence, such as exile to a forced-labour camp. These notorious establishments, administered by the police, held some ten million prisoners at the worst periods, many of whom died in them. Their very existence, however, was seldom acknowledged by the authorities. The camp inmates included entire categories of the population, such as persons of 'bourgeois' social origin or certain national-minority groups whose loyalty was suspect. About a million members of the new élite, the Communist Party, were also imprisoned in connection with the purges of 1935–39 and about half of these, including many in leading positions, perished in camps or were executed. 'The revolution devours its own children.' It is still unclear whether the purges were deliberately staged by Stalin as a preventive measure to ensure his paramountcy, or whether within the party apparatus there was indeed some organised opposition to his disastrous policies.

The terror eased slightly during the most critical years of World War II, but was subsequently resumed. Stalin was particularly afraid of soldiers, prisoners of war and others who had returned to the Soviet Union after gaining some experience of conditions abroad. An 'iron curtain' was lowered to limit contacts between Soviet citizens and foreigners and a campaign launched against 'bourgeois cosmopolitanism', which claimed many Jews among its victims. Stalin seemed to be on the point of preparing for a new bloody purge of his party when he died.

THE AFTERMATH

Once the great tyrant's controlling hand was removed, various pressure groups appeared within the establishment. A succession struggle developed in which the secret police soon lost power. In 1955 Khrushchev, who identified himself primarily with the party system, curbed the economic managers whose chief patron was Malenkov. Two years later he humiliated Marshal Zhukov, spokesman for the army, who had previously helped him defeat his opponents in the Praesidium.[1] The primacy of the party was thus estab-

---

[1] The Politburo bore the name of Praesidium from 1952 to 1966.

lished. Khrushchev may have decided that terrorist policies were counter-productive. In any case he found it politically expedient to dissociate himself in part from Stalin and his crimes. But the clumsy manner in which he did so at the Twentieth Party Congress in February 1956 produced a shock wave which temporarily imperilled the whole Soviet edifice in Eastern Europe. In the Soviet Union itself the regime lost credit and had to make certain concessions in an effort to regain popularity.

The party's hardest task henceforth was to bridge the gulf between ideology and reality and so to recover its pristine revolutionary *élan*, at a time when the Soviet public was becoming increasingly apathetic or sceptical towards official exhortations and promises. Among young intellectuals in particular, critical voices made themselves heard, calling for a clear break with the iniquities of Stalinism and a return to the humane libertarian ideals of the Revolution, as well as for closer relations with the West. But such demands could not easily be met without undermining the ideological foundations of the regime.

By the mid-1950s the communist dictatorship in the Soviet Union might be said, in economic terms, to have outlived its usefulness. It had provided a coercive political framework that had enabled the economy to develop rapidly, with a minimum of concern for the immediate well-being or funda-mental rights of the population. But increased prosperity made such func-tions no longer necessary. It was time for a return to a more pluralistic political system. However, the party had acquired both a vested interest in power and the technical ability to perpetuate its rule. Like the Tsarist autocracy, it was in no mood to surrender its prerogatives voluntarily; yet a totalitarian state, even an effete one, could not readily be overthrown by revolution. Far more likely was the prospect of gradual evolution towards a conventional non-ideological form of authoritarianism, the pace of which would be determined both by internal pressures and by the evolution of the world balance of power.

FURTHER READING

Bergson, Abram. *The Real National Income of Soviet Russia since 1928*, Harvard Univ. Press, Cambridge, Mass.; Oxford Univ. Press, Oxford, 1961.

Chamberlin, W. H. *The Russian Revolution, 1917–1921*, 2 vols. Grosset and Dunlap, New York, 1965.

Charques, R. *The Twilight of Imperial Russia*, Oxford Univ. Press, New York and London, 1967.

Conquest, Robert. *The Great Terror*, Macmillan, London, 1968.

Deutscher, Isaac. *Stalin: a Political Biography*, 2nd ed. (revised), Oxford Univ. Press, New York and London, 1967. *The Unfinished Revolution*, Oxford Univ. Press, New York and London, 1967.

Fainsod, Merle. *How Russia is Ruled*, 2nd ed. Harvard Univ. Press, Cambridge, Mass.; Oxford Univ. Press, London, 1963.

Jasny, Naum. *The Socialized Agriculture of the USSR*, Stanford Univ. Press, Stanford, Calif. 1949; Oxford Univ. Press, London, 1950.

Kolarz, Walter. *The Making of Modern Russia*, Jonathan Cape, London, 1962.

Moorehead, Alan. *The Russian Revolution*, Hamish Hamilton and William Collins, London, 1958.

Nove, Alec. *The Soviet Economy*, Allen and Unwin, London; Frederick A. Praeger, New York 3rd ed. 1962.

Schapiro, Leonard B. *The Communist Party of the Soviet Union*, Methuen, London; Vintage Books, New York, 1964.

Seton-Watson, Hugh. *The Russian Empire, 1801–1917*, Oxford Univ. Press, London and New York, 1967.

Shub, David. *Lenin: A Biography*, Penguin Books, London, 1966.

JOHN KEEP. Reader in Russian Studies at the School of Slavonic and East European Studies at London University. He has written *The Rise of Social Democracy in Russia*, 1963, edited *Contemporary History in the Soviet Mirror*, 1964, and is the author of a number of articles on Russian history and politics.

EASTERN EUROPE 1918-44

J. MICHAEL KITCH

ORGANISATION OF SOVEREIGN STATES

NOT until after World War I were all the lands and peoples of Eastern Europe released from imperial domination and organised into sovereign states. The dissolution of the Austro-Hungarian Monarchy in 1918 complemented the earlier decline of the Ottoman Empire and the eclipse of Germany and Russia prevented their succession to former Habsburg and Turkish domains. Pressures of war and revolution that crippled the imperial order gave rise in its place to a patchwork of small states fashioned by the Paris Peace Settlement in which the national principle found clear expression. Czechoslovakia and Jugoslavia were new states. Rumania doubled its area and population. Poland was restored and Albania confirmed in its independence. Hungary and Bulgaria were reduced to narrow ethnic limits. Despite much diversity among these states, all shared regional features which made for a fundamentally similar social, political and diplomatic experience.

Like the empires from which they grew these states were populated by diverse peoples coloured by disparate political and cultural traditions and living at different levels of social and economic development. The majority were peasants; 80% in Albania, 76% in Jugoslavia, 75% in Bulgaria, 72% in Rumania, 60% in Poland, 51% in Hungary and 33% in Czechoslovakia.[1] The peasants of Rumania, Bulgaria, Jugoslavia and Czechoslovakia, where land reforms distributed large properties among the peasantry, tilled their own small holdings. Those of Poland, Hungary and Albania, where large estates remained intact, owned only dwarf holdings or worked as landless labourers. As their architects hoped, land reforms staved off violent upheavals and lessened class antagonisms in the countryside, but they failed to improve the miserable lot of the peasantry. At bottom, the troubles of East European agriculture stemmed from low productivity perpetuated by mounting population pressure. On meagre and scattered lands the peasant proprietor, lacking technical knowledge and equipment, produced between three and four times less than the farmer of Western Europe. Productivity on the large estates of Hungary and Poland was only marginally higher than on the peasant properties in the reformed states. Meanwhile, the population explosion caused two to three times as many people to subsist on each unit of arable land in Eastern Europe as in Western Europe. Less marked on the vast estates of Hungary and eastern Poland, where peasant families limited themselves to one child, and the prosperous farms of Bohemia and Moravia,

[1] Wilbert E. Moore. *Economic Demography of Eastern and Southern Europe*, Geneva, 1945, p. 26.

138

rural over-population was widespread in regions given over to peasant proprietorship. One estimate calculated the 'surplus' rural population of Albania at 77%, of Jugoslavia at 62%, of Bulgaria at 53%, of Rumania and Poland at 51% and of Hungary at 22%; the figures of 39% for Slovakia and 58% for Sub-Carpathian Ruthenia stand out against the negative figure for Czechoslovakia as a whole.[1] Under such pressure small and unproductive plots were divided again and again until most were too small even to support a family. Within this vicious circle the peasantry lived in dire poverty, suffering all its symptoms. The disparity between industrial and agricultural prices brought about by the world depression lowered peasant purchasing power to depths from which it never recovered. Burdens of indebtedness and taxation were only slightly eased by belated government measures.

Surplus population could be drained off by emigration or absorbed by industry. Immigration barriers raised by the USA and the UK reduced emigration to a trickle. Industrialisation, on the scale and at the pace demanded, called for capital resources beyond the means of backward agrarian economies. Only Czechoslovakia, in Bohemia, Moravia and Silesia, and Hungary, in the Budapest region, possessed a sound industrial base. Other states pursued the phantom of industrialisation, frequently at the expense of peasant interests, with little success. Jugoslavia's experience was not untypical; from 1919 to 1939 the number of industrial vacancies grew by 185,000, the labour force by four million. After two decades of independence Eastern Europe retained its agrarian character, and the situation of a great proportion of the peasantry was no better, and sometimes worse, than it had been in the last years of imperial rule.

THE PROBLEM OF NATIONALITIES

The intermingling of different ethnic communities, usually possessed of a mature sense of identity, created serious tensions among and within countries whose frontiers and administration seldom resolved contradictory national aspirations. Except for Bulgaria, each state harboured groups who either disclaimed the national ideal upon which the state was founded or resented the manner in which this ideal was practised. To the first category belonged the German and Hungarian minorities, the most important of which lived in frontier areas contiguous to their own national states under the rule of their former subjects. Although all German governments rejected the new frontiers, the position and behaviour of the German communities was profoundly influenced by the establishment of the Third Reich. The 3·2 million Germans of the Bohemian-Moravian rimland first reluctantly accepted incorporation into Czechoslovakia and eventually participated in the government. However, after 1934 parties loyal to the state steadily lost ground to the *Sudetendeutsche Partei* which sought to break the state from within as Hitler destroyed it from without. Poland's one million Germans, concentrated in Pomerania, felt no attachment to the Polish state and, though forbidden political expression, National-Socialist attitudes spread quickly, even to the small enclaves of eastern Poland and Galicia. The smaller German settlements of Hungary, Jugoslavia and Rumania wrested concessions from governments anxious not to antagonise Berlin and became nations within nations.

The Hungarian communities, like the German, were encouraged by a

[1] *Ibid.* pp. 63-64.

government which openly espoused revision of the peace treaties and secretly aspired to the restoration of historic Hungary. Neither the Hungarians of Slovakia, who derived some benefits from Czechoslovakia's democratic institutions and prosperous economy, nor those of Vojvodina, who shared Jugoslavia's poverty and authoritarian administration, were ever reconciled to their new states. The economic misery and administrative chicanery that marred Rumanian life fell heavily upon the 1·4 million Hungarians of Transylvania who largely rejected Rumanian rule. As Rumanians and Hungarians alike regarded Transylvania as an integral part of their respective nations, the government and disposition of the province proved an insoluble problem. Attitudes similar to those of the Germans and Hungarians persisted among the Ukrainian populations of Poland and Rumania. However, since no Ukrainian state existed and Soviet rule had disadvantages, Ukrainians were at sea and divided. All asked for autonomy, but the most deprived groups of Volhynia and Bessarabia looked ultimately to the Soviet Union while those in Galicia clung to hopes of an independent Ukraine.

The Czech-Slovak and Serb-Croat controversies which bedevilled Czechoslovakia and Jugoslavia were of a different order. In Slovakia and Sub-Carpathian Ruthenia socio-economic discontent exacerbated resentment over administrative centralism in Prague and led to growing demands for regional autonomy within a federal structure. Likewise, the Croats pressed for federalism, accusing the predominantly Serb regime of perverting the Jugoslav ideal by managing Croatia as a colony of Greater Serbia. In Albania clan warfare was slowly eradicated, but religious and social antagonism continued in frequent clashes between Muslim landlords and Christian peasants. Rooted in history, these conflicts grew from a peace settlement which, inevitably, fulfilled the aspirations of some while frustrating those of others; it was hardly an atmosphere conducive to orderly development.

POLITICAL EVOLUTION

Against this background of social and national tensions the politics of the East European states took a tempestuous course. Except for Czechoslovakia, each country passed through three broad stages of political evolution: revolution, consolidation and reaction. The states emerged in a revolutionary setting marked by unprecedented mass participation in political affairs. The work of the national assemblies which met in nearly every state to establish fundamental laws and draft reform legislation witnessed the strength of the left drawn from widespread desire for change among the populace. Revolutionary tendencies, however, were curbed or crushed and there followed a period of relative stability during which new ruling classes emerged gradually to form conservative oligarchies. Although immediate financial and administrative difficulties were largely overcome in these years, more serious social and economic problems began to press upon the new regimes. When these problems grew acute, usually in the midst of the depression, there was a tendency towards reaction and dictatorship. In contrast to its neighbours, Czechoslovakia, thanks principally to a more balanced society and stronger liberal tradition, enjoyed essentially democratic government until the state disintegrated under external pressure.

Hungary

For five months in 1919 Hungary was a Soviet republic. By 1921 the counter-revolution was complete and the regime which ruled Hungary until 1944 was firmly in control. From beginning to end this regime was an uneasy partnership between conservative and right-radical elements presided over by Miklós Horthy. Throughout its first decade the regime was managed by the conservatives under Count István Bethlen. Without engaging in the crude excesses of total dictatorship, Bethlen's government robbed democracy of substance while chivalrously maintaining its forms. The depression forced Bethlen's retirement and in 1932 the right-radical element, scattered over a host of political and para-military organisations, took office in the person of General Gyula Gömbös. An admirer of Hitler and Mussolini, Gömbös saw himself as dictator of a one-party state, but the conservatives retained sufficient power to frustrate his ambitions. After Gömbös's sudden death in 1936 his successors tightened the bonds he had forged with Germany, though the conservatives preserved a measure of Hungary's independence. By 1941 the right-radicals and the army, backed by Germany, broke conservative resistance. Only Hitler's concern for a stable and reliable ally kept the Arrow Cross and other fascist organisations from seizing absolute power. The real dictatorship in Hungary was that of Horthy; its achievement was not to have been outflanked on the right.

Bulgaria
Bulgaria, the other defeated nation, also experienced an intense upsurge of revolutionary fervour followed by swift counter-revolution. In 1919 the agrarian leader, Aleksandăr Stamboliski, formed a government which then won massive endorsement at the polls. A 'dictatorship of the peasantry', Stamboliski's regime enacted social reforms and sought conciliation with Bulgaria's former enemies. Although Stamboliski had a popular mandate for his programmes, he recklessly alienated strong interest groups by using openly authoritarian methods and seeking *détente* with Jugoslavia on the Macedonian issue. Acting together, the army and the Internal Macedonian Revolutionary Organisation (IMRO) toppled the regime in 1923 in a bloody coup in which Stamboliski and scores of his followers were massacred. For the next nine years Bulgaria was held to ransom by IMRO whose campaign of terror had the support of the army and the acquiescence of the government. A second coup in 1934, engineered by authoritarian reformers, established a military dictatorship. After eliminating IMRO, the new government introduced financial and administrative reforms which brought some stability to the country. But King Boris was unhappy, for the coup had pre-empted his own plans for royal dictatorship. In 1935 he split the military regime and assumed the role of a dictator, maintaining his rule through favourites until his death in 1943.

Jugoslavia
Politics in Jugoslavia were dominated by the running feud between the Croats and Serbs. The source of the feud lay in the irreconcilable conception of the Jugoslav ideal held by the two peoples. Matters came to a head during the constitutional debate of 1921 when the centralist view of the Serbs, pressed by Nikola Pašić, prevailed over the federalist scheme of the Croats, championed by Stjepan Radić. A period of deadlock followed the adoption of the centralist constitution during which Radić's Croatian Peasant Party boycotted the Belgrade parliament and the Serbs took control of the administrative system. Attitudes eased with Pašić's death in 1926, then hardened when Radić was fatally wounded in parliament two years later. The king

intervened and, after vain attempts to reconcile the two parties, Alexander abolished the constitution, dissolved parliament and declared a royal dictatorship. In 1934 Alexander was himself assassinated by a Macedonian terrorist who was aided by Italy and Hungary, and Jugoslavia was momentarily united in the face of foreign dangers. But, Prince Paul, first regent and then new dictator, was slow to act and the moment was lost as extremism mounted on both sides. Authoritarian rule undermined the traditional parties whose followers increasingly turned to highly chauvinist organisations in both provinces. Growing opposition to his regime from all sides and menacing German encroachments into Eastern Europe drove Paul to accept the establishment of an autonomous Croatia in 1939. The arrangement pleased neither side and the bickering went on until the Germans partitioned the country in 1941, setting up independent client states in Croatia and Serbia.

Poland

The Polish state took its shape and character from the rivalry between the two national leaders, Roman Dmowski and Józef Piłsudski. Dmowski regarded Germany as Poland's chief enemy and urged expansion to the West; Piłsudski feared Russia and looked to the East. Dmowski favoured a unitary national state ruled from the centre; Piłsudski conceived of Poland as the dominant force in a confederation of peoples. Their compromise in 1918 produced expansion towards both West and East, incorporating large minorities who were subjected to Dmowski's policy of Polonisation. The constitution of 1921 was also Dmowski's work and, by limiting the presidential powers, it prompted his rival to withdraw from public life. Apprehensions about the state of the army and severe financial troubles brought Piłsudski out of retirement. In May 1926 he seized power and established a dictatorship. Piłsudski came to power with the help of the left and ruled with the support of the right, but ultimately lost the confidence of all political parties. Preoccupied with diplomatic and military affairs, he left domestic matters to the 'colonels', his comrades from the army, who introduced authoritarian rule by decree. Political disquiet and social discontent went hand-in-hand during the depression which increased hardship in the countryside. After Piłsudski's death in 1935 the 'colonels' split into rival factions and, losing all support, governed by fiat until the outbreak of war in 1939.

Rumania

In Rumania the post-war decade was marked by a struggle between the traditional political forces of the old kingdom and new forces arisen from the revolutionary climate and the incorporation of new lands. The Liberal Party of the *Regat* ruled from 1922 to 1928 and alone wrote the constitution which established centralised government over provinces whose union had been conditional upon a degree of autonomy. Opposition came from the National Peasant Party which expressed Transylvanian discontent over centralisation and the peasantry's desire for an extension of agrarian reform. Following the deaths of the Liberal leader, Ion Brătianu, and King Ferdinand in 1927, the party formed a reform cabinet under Iuliu Maniu. Measures were taken to redress the imbalance in the economy caused by the Liberal policy of placing the financial burden of industrialisation upon the peasantry. Export duties on cereals were repealed and restrictions on foreign investment eased. Before these measures bore fruit the depression struck. Amidst economic blight Maniu resigned over the return of King Carol's mistress. Carol proceeded to split the parties, establishing his own mastery over the country. In 1938 he set the seal to his royal dictatorship with a corporatist constitution which emasculated all political parties, including the fascist Iron Guard, skilfully used by Carol in his seizure of power. The partition of Rumania between the Soviet Union and the Axis two years later forced Carol to flee and his dictatorship was succeeded by another, headed by General Ion Antonescu. After using the Iron Guard to break Carol's power, Antonescu suppressed the movement when it carried violence to excess and threatened his own position. As a trusted, though not servile, ally of Hitler, Antonescu ruled Rumania until 1944.

Albania

Of all the countries of Eastern Europe, Albania was the least prepared for statehood. Occupied by several powers during the war and menaced by partition after it, Albania was not fully secure in its sovereignty until 1922. From 1920 to 1925 a bitter struggle for power was waged between Bishop Fan S. Noli, a Harvard-educated idealist, and Ahmed Zog, a ruthless *Realpolitiker*. A series of coups and counter-coups ended with Noli's exile to Italy and Zog's presidency of the Albanian republic. Zog at once crushed all opposition and assumed absolute power. From Italy he gained the financial assistance the country so desperately needed, but only in return for Italian direction of Albania's affairs. In 1928 Zog proclaimed Albania a kingdom and himself King. Italian influence increased throughout his reign and culminated in Albania's annexation in 1939. Zog fled, leaving his fallen crown to Victor Emmanuel III.

Czechoslovakia

Despite unsettling pressures generated by the problem of the nationalities, social balance, economic viability and political maturity made for stable and democratic government in Czechoslovakia. The direction of political affairs rested with the Pětka, a permanent committee representing the major Czech parties, which shaped successive coalition cabinets according to electoral results. The hold of the Czechs over politics and, more especially, administration was a source of disquiet among Slovaks and Ruthenes. The Administrative Law of 1927, establishing provinces with separate diets and governors, mollified Slovak and Ruthene opinion momentarily. But, as the social and economic position of the peasantry in the eastern provinces worsened, nationalist and radical parties profited from growing disenchantment with the coalition parties. Mgr. Hlinka's People's Party, which stood for autonomy, won a sizable following in Slovakia and the Communist Party, the only legal communist organisation in Eastern Europe, drew regular support in both provinces. Much of the tension in the situation was eased by the presidency of Thomas Masarýk, a man respected by Slovak and Ruthene moderates alike, and by the threat of frontier revision from Hungary and Germany. For after 1934 the German community, which was particularly hard hit by the depression, more and more threw its sympathies behind the separatist *Sudetendeutsche Partei*. As the Germans increased the pressure, Slovaks and Ruthenes extremists took advantage of the situation to press their demands for autonomy. Slovakia and Ruthenia became autonomous after the Munich Agreement of 1938 detached the German borderlands from the state. Upon being dismissed by the Prague regime, Mgr. Tiso's pro-German Slovak government appealed to Germany. In March 1939 the Slovak parliament reconvened with German backing and declared Slovakia independent. Now isolated, Ruthenia followed suit. Within 24 hours Hungary had annexed Ruthenia and later in the month Bohemia and Moravia became a German protectorate. Czechoslovakia was in ruins.

EASTERN EUROPE AND THE GREAT POWERS

The territorial division of Eastern Europe had been determined by the Paris Peace Conference which was dominated by the Western Powers, Britain, France and the USA, and from which the two remaining Eastern empires, Germany and Russia, were excluded. The peacemakers intended the national states as a barrier between expansionist Germany and revolutionary Russia, and all but Hungary and Bulgaria shared a common desire to preserve the territorial and political *status quo* established by the settlement. So long as Germany and Russia were too weak to reassert their traditional influence in the region, France and Italy made the running; France by constructing and supervising a set of alliances designed to bolster the *status quo* and Italy by fomenting dissension among the East European states to further its frustrated ambitions in the Adriatic. France entered alliances with Poland (1921) and Czechoslovakia (1924) aimed at containing Germany and French resources underpinned both the Polish-Rumanian Pact (1921), intended to safeguard each against Russia, and the Little Entente (1920–1) concluded between Czechoslovakia, Jugoslavia and Rumania to check Hungary. Italy's policy was directed primarily against Jugoslavia. Besides encouraging Hungarian revisionism, Mussolini tightened Italy's grip on Albania and lent support to Croatian separatism and Bulgarian terrorism. In response to Bulgarian intransigence Greece, Jugoslavia, Rumania and Turkey joined in the Balkan Entente (1934) which complemented the Little Entente in the Danube basin. All these alliances were based on the principle of collective security, embodied in the League of Nations, which in turn supposed that the Western Powers would defend the settlement they had imposed. The re-emergence of Germany as a great power shattered these illusions and led to the reassertion of imperial hegemony in Eastern Europe.

During the late 1920s Germany began to regain her position in Eastern Europe through a commercial drive welcomed by fragile economies which enjoyed limited trading relations with the West. Hitler accelerated this drive in 1934 with the plan of *Grossraumwirtschaft* (large territorial economy) by which Germany exchanged manufactured goods for food and raw materials on not altogether disadvantageous terms. Moreover, though none of the dictatorships were fascist, all were reactionary and some relied on groups which were inclined towards National-Socialism. When the Ethiopian and Rhineland crises revealed the League's impotence and France's irresolution, East European states, already dependent upon Germany economically and still wary of the Soviet Union, sought to come to an arrangement with Hitler. Germany began to press eastwards in 1938, and, with Hitler shrewdly playing on the antagonisms among states and the tensions within them, one by one they dropped their allegiances to one another and accommodated themselves to the new imperial power. The Little Entente was broken with the destruction of Czechoslovakia in which both Hungary and Poland took a hand. As in the past the partition of Poland provided the basis for a temporary Russo-German *détente*. Germany turned to face her enemies in the West; the Soviet Union set about strengthening her position in the East. Relations with Jugoslavia were opened and lands annexed by Rumania reclaimed. Eastern Europe again became the centre of Russo-German rivalry.

Posing as the protector of the Balkan states, Hitler collected Hungary, Rumania and Bulgaria as allies and crushed Jugoslavia in preparation for the invasion of the Soviet Union.

In June 1941 Hitler and Stalin took up the struggle for dominance in Eastern Europe broken off by the fall of the Hohenzollerns and Romanovs in 1918. Three summers later, when the Western Powers had only begun the liberation of France, the war in the East was decided. The Red Army had thrown back the *Wehrmacht* and was poised for its thrust into Eastern Europe. Of the four empires which ruled Eastern Europe three—the Ottoman, Habsburg and German—had passed; only Russia, now in radical guise, remained to claim the legacy.

FURTHER READING

Macartney, C. A. *October 15th: A History of Modern Hungary 1929–45*, Edinburgh Univ. Press, Edinburgh, 1961; Aldine, Chicago, 1962. With Palmer, A. W. *Independent Eastern Europe: A History*, Macmillan, London; St. Martin's Press, New York, 1962.

Roberts, Henry L. *Rumania: Political Problems of an Agrarian State*, Yale Univ. Press, New Haven, Connecticut; Oxford Univ. Press, 1951.

Rothschild, Joseph. *The Communist Party of Bulgaria*, Columbia Univ. Press, New York, 1959.

Seton-Watson, Hugh. *Eastern Europe Between the Wars. 1918–1941*, Shoe String Press, 1962.

Seton-Watson, R. W. *A History of the Czechs and Slovaks*, Hutchinson, London, 1943; Transatlantic, New York, 1944.

Stavrianos, L. S. *The Balkans since 1453*, Holt, Rinehart and Winston, New York, 1958.

Tomasevich, Jozo. *Peasants, Politics and Economic Change in Yugoslavia*, Stanford Univ. Press, Stanford, Calif., 1955; Oxford Univ. Press, London, 1951.

J. Michael Kitch. Assistant Lecturer in Rumanian History at the School of Slavonic and East European Studies, University of London. Preparing a D. Phil. thesis on Rumania and World War I. Educated in the USA at Duke and Indiana Universities. In 1965–8 carried out post-graduate studies at St. Anthony's College, Oxford.

EASTERN EUROPE 1944-56

GEOFFREY STERN

SOVIET INFLUENCE ON POST-WAR EVENTS IN EASTERN EUROPE

At one time, most Western commentators assumed that the Soviet Union's bloc of East European client states, fashioned in the late 1940s, was the result of a prearranged plan drawn up by Stalin during, or even before, World War II. Nowadays, however, many reject the conventional Western view in favour of the notion that the 'iron curtain' was to a large extent Stalin's response to a basically hostile international environment. Yet even supporters of this latter view grant that Stalin's influence on East European events was considerable, following on the advance of the Red Army in 1944.

In July 1944, for example, Moscow established its own Polish administration, the Lublin Committee, in the wake of the Soviet military thrust, and within two months Soviet-trained political agents were conveying instructions and financial assistance to communists in Rumania and Bulgaria, which had just capitulated. By the end of the war in May 1945, similar tactics were being employed to raise Communist Party fortunes in Hungary, Czechoslovakia and those parts of Austria and Germany which had fallen to the Red Army. In the meantime Stalin used as justification for his interference in the political life of the countries under Soviet occupation the wartime agreements of the Big Three. His voice was, of course, decisive in the redrawing of the East European map which was one of the outcomes of the Yalta Conference of February 1945.

By the time of the Potsdam Conference in July and August 1945, the Soviet Union's European borders had been expanded to resemble those of the Russian empire of 1914. Eastern Poland, the Baltic states, Bessarabia and northern Bukovina remained in Soviet hands. The former Czechoslovak territory of Sub-Carpathian Ruthenia, annexed by the Hungarians in 1939, went to the Soviet Union and likewise part of north-eastern Prussia. Meanwhile Stalin, in a move never formally accepted by the Western Powers, turned over to the Poles the area east of the Oder-Neisse line as compensation for their loss of territory to the Soviet Union.

Whether part of a long-term strategy or not, Stalin's subsequent treatment of his East European neighbours stemmed in large measure from his conception of the Soviet Union's security needs—a conception which was rooted as much in the Marxist dialectic as in Russia's historic experience. Basically Stalin believed that yet another conflict with a concert of 'capitalist' powers was inevitable, and that it was the Soviet Union's task to try and postpone the anticipated onslaught until it was no longer economically and technolo-gically retarded in comparison with its adversaries. In the meantime, for the Soviet Union's own safety, the governments of Eastern Europe had to be kept out of the hands of what remained of the pre-war generation of anti-Soviet and anti-communist leaders. At the same time Eastern Europe was to contribute to the Soviet economic and military advance by serving as both an economic reservoir and a strategic base for the deployment of Soviet troops. Sooner or later, however, it must have occurred to Stalin that these objectives would be difficult to achieve unless the countries in question were led by Soviet nominees, and before long it was clear that the Communist Party was to be Stalin's major instrument for effecting the requisite control.

In fact, however, Stalin behaved with extreme caution in the area in the months immediately after World War II. When, for example, certain Bulgarian communists sought to establish a one-party state after the libera-tion, Stalin despatched Molotov, the Soviet foreign minister, to persuade them to abandon the project. He was greatly annoyed with President Tito for establishing Communist Party rule in Jugoslavia in 1945 and for per-suading Enver Hoxha in Albania to follow suit in 1946. It is also worth noting that the communist insurgents in Greece received little or no Soviet assistance until some two years after the Greek communist revolt of December 1944.

Doubtless Stalin's main reason for attempting to temper his more over-zealous comrades in Eastern Europe was to avoid provoking the Western Powers into a 'holy alliance' with anti-communist forces in the region. But he had, in addition, to bear in mind the sheer administrative difficulty involved in turning over to communist control an area with such political, economic and social diversity. There may also be some validity in the view that the gradualist approach was designed to give Stalin time to reassert his authority over the more nationally orientated communist leaders, and especially those who, like Tito and Hoxha, had come to power largely without the aid of Soviet bayonets. In practice, at any rate, the East European countries amenable to Soviet influence seemed to be employing what the Hungarian communist leader, Mátyás Rákosi, termed 'salami tactics'—the technique of progressing slice by slice, as it were, to communist victory.

The Establishment of Communist Party Rule

At first the Communist Parties generally combined with Social Democratic, Liberal and other political elements on a relatively uncontroversial pro-gramme for reconstruction. At the same time they made strenuous efforts to win support by identifying themselves with popular aspirations. In Poland, for example, the party championed the cause of recreating the devastated capital, when others, more pessimistic, needed to be convinced of the feasibility of the undertaking. In Poland, Czechoslovakia and Hungary the party's campaign for the expulsion of nationals of German extraction had considerable appeal. Over such disputed areas as the Oder-Neisse territories, Transylvania, Macedonia, the communists of each country took an appro-priately 'patriotic' line.

At a later stage, however, the communist bid for popularity became secondary to their drive for increasing their control over political and economic life. During this period they infiltrated into the key Ministries of Security and Defence and established an extensive secret police network. They further enhanced their power by their penetration of political, econo-mic and cultural organisations and their sponsorship of frequent purges against 'fascists'—widely defined to include most of the Communist Party's influential opponents. Divisions within and among rival political groups were successfully exploited and soon the communists were able virtually to determine the leadership of the parties with which they nominally shared power. By the time of the Czechoslovak coup of February 1948 most of their political opponents had been either forced to toe the communist line or else rendered politically harmless by varying degrees of intimidation.

The transition to monolithic Communist Party rule did not occur at a uniform pace and there were significant variations from one country to another. Jugoslavia and Albania, both somewhat beyond Moscow's reach geographically and hence relatively independent of Soviet control, were, as we have seen, the first to attain the desired goal. Poland attained it more slowly, but at no time was there any semblance of a genuine coalition between parties. For even though in return for recognition the Western Powers managed to secure the inclusion into the Soviet-sponsored government of a few members from the London-based Polish government-in-exile, their protégés were in no position to resist communist demands. The non-communist leadership had been severely depleted by the heavy casualties sustained during the war at the hands of both German and Soviet invaders, and in the cabinet their representatives were outnumbered by 16 to 4. In 1947 the most distinguished of them, the Peasant Party leader, Stanisław Mikołajczyk, was forced to flee the country after the destruction of his party. Within a year, Communist and Socialist Parties had been merged into a Polish United Workers (i.e. Communist) Party and the others perpetuated in name only.

The Soviet Zone of Germany, likewise, produced no 'coalition of equals'. After the communists had failed to attract more than 20% of the votes cast in local elections in the autumn of 1945, the Soviet Union decided on the fusion of the Communist and Social Democratic Parties in the Zone and in April 1946 set up the Socialist Unity Party (SED.) under Walther Ulbricht's leadership. Almost immediately the other parties tolerated by the occupying power were rendered politically impotent, and soon most of the former Social Democrats in the SED hierarchy were removed from influential positions or deprived of effective power.

In the ex-enemy states of Rumania and Bulgaria, the 'genuine coalition' was of short duration. In March 1945, King Michael of Rumania yielded to a Soviet ultimatum and appointed Petru Groza, leader of the leftward-looking Ploughman's Front as premier of a new National Democratic Front government in place of the former coalition. All the vital posts in the new administration were held by communists and by November 1946 the Front, after much intrigue and intimidation, was able to obtain four-fifths of the parliamentary seats at a general election. Within a year the king had abdicated, the Communist and Socialist Parties had been merged, and all opposition had been eliminated.

But if there were some logic in the communist decision to curtail parliamentary activities in countries with a strong anti-communist tradition there was much less justification for treating Bulgaria in like fashion. After all, the Bulgarian Communist Party had enjoyed considerable popularity in the days before it was forced underground, and its Soviet connections were no obstacle in a country traditionally pro-Russian. On the other hand Bulgaria's pre-war political organisations had remained largely intact at the end of the war, and the communists felt that if they were to control the country their rivals had to be destroyed. In January 1945 the communists forced the resignation of a leading official in the Agrarian Union, the most influential group in the Fatherland Front Coalition, and increasingly the communists came to dominate the affairs of the Front. By October 1946 the government had been placed in the hands of the veteran communist, Georgi Dimitrov, after a communist-sponsored general election, and though a significant opposition remained for a while it crumbled after the execution in September 1947 of Nikola Petkov, leader of the Agrarian Union. Within two years all non-communist parties had been disbanded.

In Hungary, another ex-enemy state, but one whose experiences of a Soviet-type regime after World War I had rendered it strongly anti-communist, the parliamentary system was allowed to survive unfettered for somewhat longer. In November 1945 a general election in which the communists polled only 17% of the votes brought the Smallholders' (Peasants) Party to power, but their authority was soon threatened when the communists formed a leftist bloc with the Social Democratic and National Peasant Parties. In February 1947 Moscow ordered the arrest of the secretary-general of the Smallholders' Party and in May the Communists forced the prime minister, Ferenc Nagy, to resign. The ruling party disintegrated and the leftist bloc, having disenfranchised some 500,000 voters and intimidated others, was able to obtain a small lead over its opponents in a general election in August 1947. Within a year the socialists and communists had been fused into a single political organisation, and the last independent political party was dissolved in 1949.

It was in Czechoslovakia that the 'genuine coalition' lasted longest. Here the Communist Party, which had not been associated with the Munich 'betrayal' became the largest parliamentary party having obtained 38% of the votes at a free election in May 1946. With its leader, Klement Gottwald, as prime minister and a number of communists in the cabinet, it looked as if communist ambitions were being achieved by parliamentary means. But when the communists suffered reverses in local elections, the party began police operations against its rivals, and several non-communists resigned from Gottwald's cabinet in protest. The communists retaliated with strikes, demonstrations and the occupation of premises belonging to the non-communist parties, and on 25 February 1948 Gottwald staged his coup, creating a new administration which omitted all those opposed to communist rule. Soon the takeover was complete. On 10 March, Jan Masarýk, the non-communist foreign minister, died after a fall (possibly induced) from his office window, and in September President Beneš died, having resigned three months earlier.

STALINIST CONTROL OVER 'SATELLITE' STATES

However, while organised opposition to communism was crumbling, Stalin's hold over the Communist Parties of Eastern Europe was being tightened. In part this was Stalin's response to the gradual consolidation of the Western Powers into a bloc dedicated to the 'containment' of communism. And with each successive Western measure for greater economic and military security —the Truman Doctrine of aid to Greece and Turkey, Marshall Aid, the Brussels Treaty between Britain, France and the Benelux countries and the creation of NATO—Soviet control was further extended. In part, however, it was also an answer to the growing tendency of the communists in Eastern Europe to contemplate policies at variance with Stalin's conception of Soviet needs. To the interest shown by Polish and Czechoslovak communists in Marshall Aid, for example, Stalin took strong exception, and he was

L

suspicious of the projected Polish-Czechoslovak customs union and the proposed Balkan Confederation as conceived by Tito and Dimitrov. In order to crush such independent communist tendencies Stalin took measures to strengthen the Soviet Union's political, economic and military links with Eastern Europe.

The creation in September 1947 of the Cominform—an information bureau linking the Soviet Communist Party with the Communist Parties of Eastern Europe, France and Italy—was symptomatic of the new trend. But rather more crucial in the creation of a Soviet bloc of client states were the bilateral treaties of friendship and mutual assistance between the Soviet Union and its neighbours which legalised the stationing of Soviet troops in the area and served as a cover for the build-up of Soviet security forces. At the same time an iron curtain of barbed wire, watch towers and ploughed mine fields was erected between communist countries to keep each isolated both from the others and from the West. Meanwhile the reorientation of trade after the Western embargo on strategic goods to communist-dominated countries gave the Soviet Union a further level of control over its trade-dependent allies.

In actual fact Eastern Europe was, even after the tightening of Soviet control, never quite as monolithic as we are apt to assume. There were some variations in political and economic institutions, and of course the fundamental characters of these countries remained dissimilar. But in basic aspects of both internal and external policy their similarities far outweighed their differences. From 1948 a reign of terror was unleashed throughout the bloc (as in the Soviet Union itself) during which thousands of communists and non-communists were arrested, imprisoned or executed. The Hungarian minister of the interior, Rajk, a Bulgarian deputy prime minister, Kostov, the Czechoslovak foreign minister, Clementis, and the general-secretary of the Czechoslovak Communist Party, Slánský, were among those charged with 'national deviationism' and executed after carefully staged 'show trials'. Those arrested during this period included Władysław Gomułka, János Kádár, Gustáv Husák and Josef Smrkovský, who were to be prominent in post-Stalin East European politics. That more than 20 Bulgarian ministers were purged is sufficient indication of the extent of the upheaval.

Not surprisingly between 1948 and 1953 little was heard of 'independent roads to socialism'. Each country under Soviet control became a 'people's democracy'—a half-way house to socialism. Each became a mere replica of the Soviet Union in political, economic and cultural life and modelled its constitution on the Soviet constitution of 1936, ignoring, as did the Soviet leaders, its more liberal aspects. Most were headed by a dictator who developed his own 'personality-cult' alongside that of Stalin; as for example, Hoxha of Albania, Chervenkov of Bulgaria, Gottwald of Czechoslovakia, Rákosi of Hungary, Ulbricht of East Germany, Bierut of Poland and Gheorghiu-Dej of Rumania. All secondary schools were obliged to teach Russian, and a strict censorship was imposed on all forms of literature and art. Religious activities were placed under state control and several prominent churchmen were imprisoned. And following the Soviet Union's lead, the East European countries took to persecuting Jews under the pretext of fighting 'Zionism'.

The economies of Eastern Europe were reorganised to accord with Soviet requirements. Farming began to be collectivised, and industry and trade were nationalised and regulated by Soviet-style central planning techniques. The consumer sector was depressed and the planners emphasised heavy industry, especially steel production. Labour discipline was tightened, and trade unions became mere government agencies for increasing productivity.

Although little use was made of the Council for Mutual Economic Assistance (Comecon), created in January 1949 ostensibly for facilitating economic cooperation between bloc members, their economic relationships had been completely reorientated by the time of Stalin's death. Little more than a quarter of their total trade was done outside the bloc and they became increasingly dependent on Soviet technical knowhow, credits and raw materials. As these economic ties increased, so did the Soviet Union's economic exploitation of the region. That it was able to sell raw materials to Eastern Europe at prices above those on the world market whilst buying coal from Poland at about a sixth of the world price is an indication of how the Soviet Union profited from the terms of trade. The Soviet Union took the lion's share of the profits of the joint stock companies established to manage enemy property in East Germany, Rumania and Hungary, even though the East Europeans had contributed most of the capital. Finally, there were the heavy reparations exacted from ex-enemy countries which, in the case of East Germany, amounted in 1952 to nearly a quarter of its GNP.

Jugoslavia

However, the chain of 'satellite' states had one weak link—Jugoslavia, which, after President Tito had protested at Stalin's interference in and exploitation of his country, was expelled from the Cominform in June 1948. Once the Soviet Union had instituted a communist embargo on trade with Jugoslavia and had tried to engineer an anti-Tito coup, Jugoslavia virtually cut its East European ties and in 1952 joined Greece and Turkey (both NATO members) to form the Balkan Pact. Meanwhile, Jugoslavia was already creating a practical alternative to the Soviet type of communist regime. In place of Stalin's centralised bureaucracy Jugoslavia was pioneering a society of self-governing units and replacing the centralised planned economy with a decentralised socialist market economy. President Tito's approach to Marxism and Leninism became much more critical and he argued for the independence of each communist country and party as against Stalin's monolithic conception. Thus, even though it was not until 1956 that 'polycentrism' entered the political vocabulary, Tito was already indicating the possibility of independent centres of communist decision making and ideology.

POST-STALINIST THAW

After Stalin's death in March 1953 the Soviet Union's new leaders tried to establish a new relationship with the bloc. As at home so throughout Eastern Europe the power of the Soviet security apparatus was curbed, and many of its agents were recalled. At the same time economic exploitation was reduced and the Soviet leadership seemed willing to concede a measure of diversity in the region. From June 1953 to March 1955, for example, the Soviet government tolerated in Hungary a new course of economic and political development that was considerably more radical than that prevailing in the Soviet Union. During this period Imre Nagy, Hungary's prime minister, rejected the excessive concentration on heavy industry, terminated the forcible collectivisation of land, and allowed the peasants to set up their own small commercial undertakings. Legal procedure began to replace police despotism, and freedom of expression and movement gained ground.

However, the situation created by Stalin's death ushered in the unrest associated with all revolutions of rising expectations. In June 1953 there were workers' demonstrations in Plzeň and in other Czech and Slovak towns, and a revolt in East Berlin had to be put down with the aid of Soviet troops. Neither this, nor the creation in May 1955 of a formal East European alliance—the Warsaw Treaty Organisation—succeeded in silencing the dissidents. After Khrushchev's efforts to embrace Tito, his adoption of 'different forms of socialism' during his visit to Belgrade in May 1955 and his revelations about Stalin at the Twentieth Congress of the Soviet Communist Party in February 1956, the restlessness increased. After all, those communists punished only a few years earlier for their 'Titoism' had not yet been rehabilitated, and Stalin's nominees were still in power.

However, in Albania, Bulgaria, East Germany and Rumania, the party hierarchy rode the crisis by keeping a generally tight rein on their dissident elements and finding scapegoats to demote for their 'abuse of power' during the period of the personality-cult. In Czechoslovakia on the other hand, writers and students were for a time allowed more freedom to voice their criticisms, but events in neighbouring Poland and Hungary led the party to impose new restrictions in the summer of 1956.

In Poland the regime was already under heavy criticism as a result of the revelations of a security police chief, Colonel Swiatło, who defected to the USA in 1953. As the discontent spread, it appeared that only one man could restore the party's self-respect and earn the confidence of the country—Władysław Gomułka. But the Soviet government, which had come to think of Gomułka as an intractable 'national communist' was resolved to prevent his return to power. After the death of Bierut, the Polish communist leader, in March 1956, Khrushchev tried in vain to influence the choice of successor, and although Gomułka had not yet been summoned to lead the party, Ochab, the new party leader, was soon helping to extend liberalisation and preparing the ground for Gomułka's reinstatement. Significantly enough, the trial of workers whose strike in Poznań in June 1956 had turned into an insurrection was open to Western journalists and conducted with scrupulous fairness. Each of the accused had an able defence lawyer, and most were either acquitted or given lenient sentences.

Not surprisingly the Soviet government was alarmed by these developments and in October Khrushchev arrived in Warsaw together with Molotov, Kaganovich, Mikoyan and several Soviet generals to try to curb Poland's liberalisation and keep Gomułka out of power. The Poles, who had the Chinese and Jugoslavs on their side, refused to retreat and in the end it was the Soviet leadership that was forced to withdraw. Gomułka's return to the party leadership in October 1956 marked a turning point in Soviet relations with Eastern Europe since it constrained the Soviet Union to concede that Stalin's policy of holding Eastern Europe in total subjection was now out of date.

The Hungarian Uprising

Yet within two weeks of Poland's success, Khrushchev was to show that he set strict limits on the degree of autonomy to be permitted in the area. The test was to come in Hungary where there was no Gomułka to help the country win back its self-esteem in a way which was in keeping with political realities. By July 1956 the Hungarians, both outside the Communist Party and within it, had become so antagonistic to Rákosi, the party leader who had reversed the liberal tide after ousting Nagy from the premiership in March

1955, that Khrushchev had been forced to arrange for Rákosi's removal. But the substitution of Gerö, one of Rákosi's associates, had merely increased the country's frustration, and soon there were violent demonstrations in favour of Nagy, the end of Soviet domination and a free and independent Hungary.

When Nagy was allowed finally to return to the premiership in October, he bowed to popular pressure and proclaimed Hungary's withdrawal from the Warsaw Pact, the return of a multi-party system and his intention to secure the removal of Soviet troops from Hungarian soil. Since such policies threatened to undermine the whole basis of the Soviet bloc, the Soviet leaders could not allow them to be put into effect. Hence the tragic suppression by Red Army tanks of the Nagy administration and its supporters and the reinstatement of communist rule under János Kádár.

Hungary apart, there could be no return to the Stalinist relationship with Eastern Europe. For one thing, the Soviet Union's role in international society had enlarged since Stalin's day, and the Soviet leadership knew that without some revision of their approach to the bloc the country would be economically and politically ill-equipped in the competition with the Western Powers for the minds and sympathies of the newly emerging nations. Economically the Stalinist system did not make the best use of the area's resources; politically the exploitative relationship did not fit in with the new image Khrushchev wished to project abroad in support of his policy of 'peaceful coexistence'. In any case some of the political, economic and military factors enabling the Soviet Union to dominate Eastern Europe in Stalin's time no longer had quite the same force in the post-Stalinist 'thaw'. With a new generation of communist leaders coming to power, the widening of the Sino-Soviet rift and the easing of Cold War tensions in Europe in the years following this turbulent period, Soviet ties with the bloc were to become further relaxed until 1968.

FURTHER READING

Betts, R. E. (ed.) *Central and South-Eastern Europe (1945–48)*, Royal Institute of International Affairs, London, 1950.

Brzezinski, Z. K. *The Soviet Bloc*, Harvard Univ. Press, Cambridge, Mass.; Oxford Univ. Press, London, 1960.

Burks, R. V. *The Dynamics of Communism in Eastern Europe*, Oxford Univ. Press, London; Princeton Univ. Press, Princeton, New Jersey, 1961.

Byrnes, J. F. *Speaking Frankly*, Harper and Row, New York; Heinemann, London, 1947.

Calvocoressi, P. (ed.) *Survey of International Affairs (1947–51)*, Oxford Univ. Press, 1952–54.

Djilas, M. *Conversations with Stalin*, Harcourt Brace, New York; Rupert Hart-Davis, London, 1962.

Gluckstein, Y. *Stalin's Satellites in Eastern Europe*, Allen and Unwin, London; Beacon Press, Boston, Mass., 1952.

Halperin, E. *The Triumphant Heretic: Tito's Struggle Against Stalin*, Heinemann, London, 1958.

Leonhard, W. *Child of the Revolution*, Henry Regnery Co., Chicago, 1958; Collins, London, 1957.

Wolff, R. L. *The Balkans in our Time*, Oxford Univ. Press, London; Harvard Univ. Press, Cambridge, Mass., 1956.

GEOFFREY STERN. Lecturer in International Relations at the L.S.E. and a regular broadcaster on Communist affairs for the BBC's External Service and the Australian Broadcasting Commission. Publications include *Fifty Years of Communism*. He is writing on Soviet foreign policy at present.

PART TWO
POLITICAL

GENERAL

IDEOLOGY AND POLITICS

MARCUS WHEELER

THE role of 'ideology' in politics and society often appears mysterious to natives of the Anglo-Saxon countries. This is because the concept (which stems from Germany) is associated with a system-building style in philosophy which has largely been discarded in these countries in the last 50 years and with a totalitarian practice in politics which is felt to be still more alien. Yet anyone who has any interest in the Soviet Union or other communist states is likely to seek answers to such questions as 'What is the practical impact of the communist creed?' and 'Do the citizens of these states really believe in communism?' And this is what the study of communist ideology is about. Unfortunately, the simple essence of the matter is befogged by the special jargon employed by communist ideologists themselves, and any attempt to assess the function of ideology in the Soviet Union or other communist states today presupposes some understanding of the basis of their official creed—Marxism-Leninism.

THE PHILOSOPHY OF MARXISM

The core of the philosophical teaching of Karl Marx is what is known as dialectical materialism (or, in relation to the philosophy of history in particular, historical materialism). Marx opposed, on the one hand, the idealism of the German school led by Hegel which was in the ascendant in his own formative years and, on the other hand, what he called 'mechanical materialism'—in effect, the mainstream of French and British 18th-century philosophy. He sought to refute the former in much the same way as Dr Johnson thought that he had refuted the idealism of Bishop Berkeley—by suggesting simply that it contradicted common sense. As his friend and collaborator, Friedrich Engels, put it, Marx's achievement was to recognise

> the palpable but previously overlooked fact that men must first of all eat, drink, have shelter and clothing, therefore must work, before they can fight for domination, pursue politics, religion, philosophy, etc.

In short, *cogito quia sum* as opposed to *cogito ergo sum*—or, as Marx himself expressed it, 'it is not the consciousness of men that determines their existence, but, on the contrary, their social existence determines their consciousness'. From this observation springs the notion, which is central to Marx's thought and links his philosophy with his analysis of the politics and economics of his time, that the essence of social reality is productive activity. This idea also influenced Marx's opposition to the classical form of materialism, which portrayed reality as something both static and independent of the human percipient. And, although for Marx the basic reality was matter and not spirit, his criticism of this body of doctrine owed most of all to the Hegelian idea of 'dialectics'—hence the title *dialectical materialism*.

Dialectics is defined by Engels as 'the science of the general laws of the motion and development of Nature, human society and thought'. But this is an unilluminating account of a conception which amounts, crudely, to the following propositions: first, change or process is a universal feature of the world; second, the world-process comprises not random change but an advance from the less perfect to the more perfect; third, this progress is not direct but proceeds through tensions between conflicting forces and the resolution of these tensions. For Hegel, the development of the ultimate reality—Spirit, or the Absolute Idea—was manifested in the history of human society in the successive rise and fall of nations (from ancient China, through Greece and Rome, to his own Prussia). For Marx, however, the crucial 'unit' was the social class and the crucial conflict the struggle between classes which, at certain points in history, explodes as a result of an intolerable disharmony between means and methods of production and the property relations prevailing at that stage of society. But whereas from the conception of history as development through conflict and synthesis Hegel drew the conservative conclusion that the society of his own day and nation was the highest manifestation of the universal Spirit, Marx and his adherents saw in it on the contrary the justification for revolution. At least, one more cataclysm was scheduled, namely the decisive conflict between the two currently opposed classes—bourgeoisie and proletariat—which would result in the achievement of the final goal, the classless society. Why should this society be a *communist* society? Because, according to Marx, the new system of production ushered in by the Industrial Revolution was already a 'socialised' one, in which the product was the fruit of the pooled labour of the many and not, as in the old handicraft economy, of the special skill of one man— hence, individual ownership of this product, or appropriation of the market value thereof, was no longer in order. Moreover, the classless society which would result from the triumph of the proletariat would also neatly demonstrate another aspect of dialectics, the 'negation of the negation': as the system of private property had 'negated' the primitive communism which (according to the largely speculative anthropology of the mid-19th century) prevailed in early human society, so, in its turn, it would be 'negated' by communism of a higher type.

Mention should be made finally of one aspect of Marxian thought which springs directly from its Hegelian antecedents but which has resulted in the seemingly cynical indifference of some of Marx's followers to the choice of means in achieving their goal. This is his relativism with regard to values, which he expressed in the proposition that beliefs about good and evil (and, by implication, social, political, juridical and aesthetic values and concepts) are in no sense absolute but are inevitably a reflection of class interests. Marx did indeed criticise the French socialist thinkers of the early 19th century as 'Utopians' because their condemnation of existing society sprang from abstract notions of justice and injustice rather than from 'scientific' study of the 'laws' of social development; and, conversely, his advocacy of the interests of the proletariat was ostensibly based on an unsentimental conviction that history was on the side of that class. Marx's own life, however, to some extent belies his reasoning, in that he was clearly motivated by a humane detestation of the evils of the raw industrialised society of his time and by an idealistic longing for a better future for mankind.

MARXISM IN RUSSIA

In the movement of radical thought and of action against the Tsarist system which developed in Russia during the 19th century, Marxism was a foreign and unexpected growth. Until the last quarter of the century the economy of the vast Russian empire remained overwhelmingly agrarian. Industry was concentrated in two or three centres and, excluding certain special branches (such as the Tula armaments works and the Urals metal-working industry), the workers were recent immigrants from the country who remained solidly peasant in outlook. Moreover, among the radical intelligentsia who headed the movement for reform and later, disillusioned with the emancipation of the serfs and other reforms conceded from above in the 1860s, for more extreme action, a majority retained an uncritical faith in the peasant commune as the ready-made instrument for securing 'Russian socialism'. It is a measure of the insignificant impact made by the 'spectre of communism' that Volume I of Marx's *Capital* was able to be published in Russia in 1872 without let or hindrance from the Tsar's censors. The greater number even of the 'Westernist' intellectuals continued to believe that Russia could, with the aid of the commune, reach communism bypassing the capitalist stage (and, ironically, Marx himself gave qualified assent to this view). Debate about this question, however, was soon overtaken by events; the Russian Marxists, whose movement gained momentum rapidly after 1880 with the failure of attempts to 'revolutionise' the peasantry or to hasten change by individual acts of terror, rightly judged that capitalism had already arrived. As one of the early leaders, Georgy Plekhanov, put it:

> 'Is Russia to go through the school of capitalism?' We may answer: 'Why should she not complete the schooling on which she has already entered?'

What of Lenin's contribution to the communist ideology? The official present-day designation of the latter as 'Marxism-Leninism' may be misleading. For Lenin (1870–1924, real name: Vladimir Ilyich Ulyanov) made no appreciable addition to the philosophy of dialectical materialism. His great contribution lay in the field of political theory. in formulating the strategy of revolution and of the transition through revolution from capitalism to communism—a branch of the ideology now known as 'scientific communism'. The seminal elements of Lenin's thought are often obscured by the turgid style and polemical character of his voluminous writings, a large part of which took the form of *ad hominem* diatribes; but his most important theoretical statements are to be found in two works—*What is to be done?*, 1902 and *The State and Revolution*, 1917. In the former, he asserted (in opposition to the so-called 'economists') that the revolutionary movement must be guided by a revolutionary political theory and not reduce itself to an opportunist workers' struggle merely for improved economic conditions; and expounded his view of the revolutionary organisation as a tightly-knit clandestine party whose ranks must be limited to dedicated professionally-trained revolutionaries. In the latter, he expounded and expanded the views of Marx and Engels on the need for violence in bringing about the replacement of the bourgeois state by the proletarian state, on the functioning of the 'dictatorship of the proletariat' which was to ensure the suppression of the bourgeoisie on the morrow of the revolution, on the nature of 'socialist democracy', on the phases of the transition to full communism and on the eventual 'withering away' of the state. These are the doctrines which may properly be called 'Leninism'.

Ideology and Politics Today

With the passage of time since the death of Marx, Engels and Lenin and since the Russian Revolution the principles which constitute the communist ideology have undergone certain modifications—on the one hand, as a result of the pressure of external circumstances which its originators could not or did not foresee; on the other hand, as a result of what is euphemistically known as the 'creative development of Marxism-Leninism'. Lenin himself in 1921 sanctioned, albeit as a temporary expedient, a departure from ideology in initiating the New Economic Policy, which provided for a limited reintroduction of private economic enterprise. Stalin is considered in his later years to have jettisoned Marxist-Leninist principles in the administration of the country in favour of 'subjective' doctrines prompted by a paranoiac determination to maintain by whatever means his own personal power against enemies real or imagined. The posthumous condemnation of Stalin in 1956 was followed by a much-publicised reintroduction of 'Leninist norms' in the direction of the country's affairs; and Khrushchev in large measure rehabilitated ideological indoctrination as a substitute for terror. Yet he too, since his fall from office in 1964, has been charged with wanton tampering with hallowed Leninist principles. At each turn, it should be noted, it has been maintained that, whatever the excesses or aberrations of individual leaders, the party has remained corporately untarnished and true to the tenets of its founders.

How far does ideology at the present day impinge on the formulation of internal or foreign policy? How far does it affect the lives of ordinary people? Before an attempt is made to answer such questions, it should be noted that, in the Soviet Union, the term 'ideology' has a wider and a narrower meaning. In the former, more familiar sense, it connotes a whole body of philosophical, political, economic, ethical and aesthetic doctrine. In the narrower usage it relates to the application of such doctrine to day-to-day life. Thus, the Programme of the Communist Party of the Soviet Union adopted in 1961 specifies as the principal element of ideological activities 'the inculcation in all the working people of a spirit of high principle and of dedication to communism and of a communist attitude to work and the economy of the society, the complete overcoming of survivals of bourgeois views and *mores*, the all-round, harmonious development of the personality and the creation of a genuine wealth of spiritual culture'. Shorn of detail, this amounts to what is usually described as the 'formation of the new man'.

'Creative development of Marxism-Leninism' may be illustrated, at a fairly rarefied level, by the doctrine of phases in the building of communism and of the corresponding role of the 'dictatorship of the proletariat'. Marx, as far as can be discerned, saw the transition period between the overthrow of capitalism and the achievement of communism as a single phase. Lenin, however, developed the idea of two phases—the first, lower phase being the building of *socialism*, marked by the termination of private ownership, the conclusion of the struggle between 'antagonistic' classes and the stabilisation of society on the basis of the formula 'From each according to his ability, to each according to his work' (as opposed to the formula for *communism* of ' . . . to each according to his needs'). This milestone was deemed to have been reached in the Soviet Union in 1936. Nevertheless, authoritative documents continued until after the death of Stalin (in 1953) to lay down that the dictatorship of the proletariat shall remain in operation until the achievement of full communism. Khrushchev, however, inspired a new formula: the need for the dictatorship of the proletariat terminates with the achievement of *socialism* and thereafter gives way to 'the state of the whole people'. This change of formulation, although it was subsequently an important issue between the Soviet Union and China, belongs to an area of ideology which shades off, in one direction, into mythology, in another direction, into the language of public relations.

In other spheres—those of the sciences and the arts—the impact of ideology not only on policy but on ordinary human lives has been direct and palpable. In the case of the natural sciences, dramatic conflicts developed between freedom of research and constraints imposed by ideologists who assessed scientific work by reference to the nature of the society in which it was carried out. Leaving aside the bizarre episode of Lysenko and the condemnation of 'bourgeois' genetics, the rejection, while the Cold War lasted, of relativity theory and cybernetics as suspect 'pseudo-science' threatened at one point to jeopardise the Soviet defence and space research programmes. In this field, at least, the national interest, rationally appraised, appears to have won a resounding victory over ideological absurdity.

The freedom of writers and artists to experiment is less obviously related to national security and prestige, and their position is more complicated. In the Soviet Union, the Marxian tenet that the work of writers and artists necessarily reflects the interests and values of the class or society to which they belong was reinforced by the 19th-century tradition of 'civic' writing as a vehicle of political protest. It is open to question whether the Soviet rulers, or even the supervisors of cultural matters, attach a precise meaning to the mandatory formula of socialist realism (defined in the Statute of the Union of Soviet Writers as 'the truthful, historically concrete representation of reality in its revolutionary development'—a definition sometimes parodied as 'writing about life today as it will be tomorrow'); but they would certainly endorse the following admonition given by Khrushchev in 1963 in an address to a meeting of party leaders with Soviet writers and artists:

> It is the highest duty of the Soviet writer, artist, and composer, of every creative worker, to be in the ranks of the builders of communism, to put his talent at the service of the great cause of our party, to fight for the triumph of the ideas of Marxism-Leninism. We must remember that a sharp struggle is going on in the world between two irreconcilable ideologies—the socialist and the capitalist.
>
> It is the task of the artist actively to contribute by his works to the assertion of communist ideas, to deal crushing blows at the enemies of socialism and communism, and to fight against the imperialists and colonialists.

Since the early 1930s, strict control of the arts by the Communist Party has been maintained, with only brief intervals of relaxation in 1953-4, 1956-7 and 1962, and the situation has worsened since the fall of Khrushchev. The latter, despite his somewhat primitive and military-sounding conception of the duty of creative artists, personally intervened in 1962 to secure publication of the story, *One Day in the Life of Ivan Denisovich*, by Alexander Solzhenitsyn. This talented writer now occupies a position comparable with that of Pasternak in his last years, being debarred from publishing in his own country and charged with slandering the Soviet system.

During the past four years Soviet leaders have frequently and shrilly spoken of 'the exacerbation of the ideological struggle between capitalism and socialism'. Does this imply a panic fear on their part of contamination of decent Soviet minds by the works of Joyce, Proust or other decadent literary monsters? It is much more likely that they sincerely believe that their country is the target for a cultural offensive from the West of unprecedented strength.

163

In addition, they evidently believe that a removal of limitations upon freedom in the artistic sphere would be followed by dissemination of critical attitudes in the sphere of politics proper. As Khrushchev once put it:

> Let us see what would in fact happen in Soviet art, if the adherents of peaceful coexistence of various ideological trends in literature and the arts gained the upper hand. As a first step, a blow would be dealt at our revolutionary gains in the sphere of socialist art. By the logic of struggle, things would hardly end there . . .

In the eyes of communist ideologists, freedom in the arts is very closely related to freedom of the press—the penalties imposed on Sinyavsky and Daniel for unauthorised publication of their work abroad spring from the same logic as the restrictions imposed on the distribution of foreign newspapers and magazines (other than organs of foreign Communist Parties). It is hardly surprising that, from the Soviet point of view, one of the gravest 'errors' of the Dubček regime in Czechoslovakia was the removal of censorship of the press. This Soviet reasoning is probably not invalidated by the case of Jugoslavia, where over a number of years the availability of capitalist newspapers and the large measure of freedom accorded writers and artists (at least in matters of form) does not appear to have in any way undermined the regime; for the strength of Jugoslav communism rests in very large measure on nationalist sentiment and the special position of the country in relation to the 'socialist camp'.

What of internal affairs generally? Does the introduction of advanced technology, the implementation of limited but important economic reforms and the recognition of consumer choice as a legitimate aspiration betoken the end of ideology or imply that the leaders of the country or the people as a whole have become disillusioned with Marxism-Leninism? And, if so, are the continuing stress on indoctrination and the anathema on 'ideological coexistence' merely a last stand? To answer these questions, it may be helpful to draw a distinction between Marxism-Leninism as an ideology and communism as a political goal. Thus, Khrushchev was primarily a man of action, a somewhat crude expounder of doctrine, but a firm and sincere believer in the reality of the communist goal; so that he felt able, at the Twenty-second Congress of the CPSU in 1961, to offer a time-schedule for achievement of the 'material and technological basis of communism' and to proclaim that 'the present generation of Soviet people will live under communism'. No such promise has been repeated by his successors, but it would be quite wrong to conclude from this that they do not share the former leader's faith. It is rather that their 'style' is different: they are more cautious, less given to flights of fancy or of rhetoric, more concerned with the problems of today than with the distant horizon, more orthodox in their practices, less disposed to replace traditional governmental or legal organs by premature forms of 'communist self-government'—a mistake made, in their view, not only by Khrushchev but by the Chinese with their 'great leap forward' and 'people's communes' and by the Jugoslavs with their workers' self-management. The Chinese in particular have, as it appears to Soviet ideologists, sinned heinously against a fundamental tenet of Marxism-Leninism in giving the peasantry equal status with the workers as a revolutionary force and in allowing power to pass from the Communist Party to the army and the youth. Indeed, the kernel of the Soviet leadership's position is what may be called the dogma of party legitimacy: that is, that the party has an unquestioned right to a monopoly of power in the country. This dogma stands, so to speak, at the apex of the ideology; it is not itself part of it, but is a brute fact to be shored up by the ideology, for example, by the doctrine of 'intra-party democracy', according to which continued opposition to a party decision, once formally adopted, constitutes 'fractionalism' or, in effect, treason. It is instructive in this context to compare Article 3 of the Soviet constitution—'All power in the Soviet Union belongs to the working people of town and country in the person of the soviets of working people's deputies'—with Article 126, which describes the Communist Party as 'the directing nucleus of all organisations of the working people, whether voluntary or state organisations'. The unstated corollary of this is, of course, that no other party is permitted (other parties are permitted in some East European countries, but on condition that they adhere to a 'national front' and pledge loyalty to the socialist state). In this way opposition can be construed not only as a breach of an ideological principle but as a potential threat to the interests of the country. Hypothetically, the development of an opposition communist fraction would not jeopardise the Marxist-Leninist faith, but it would certainly threaten the dogma of party legitimacy. This is why the rival revolutionary parties in existence at the time of the Russian Revolution—the Mensheviks and the Socialist Revolutionaries—had to be suppressed; and this is why the split in the world communist movement, together with the formation in many countries of rival, schismatic communist parties, is, in the short term, seen as a greater threat than eventual disillusionment with communism as such. This explains also the rabid hostility of the CPSU to all forms of ideological 'revisionism', whether outright innovation—as in the case of the Jugoslav variant—or 'fundamentalist' criticism of alleged deviations by the Soviet Union itself, such as that prompted in Poland, Hungary and elsewhere by the retrospective campaign against Stalin and Stalinism.

Corresponding to the internal dogma of party legitimacy is a dogma—similarly unstated in formal documents—that the position of the CPSU, as the party of Lenin, is at any given moment the measure of orthodoxy. Here one may contrast the abstract doctrine of 'proletarian internationalism', as the guide to relations between the communist states, with what has come to be called in the West the 'Brezhnev Doctrine', effectively assigning to the Soviet Union the right to determine, as in the case of Czechoslovakia in 1968, what circumstances require collective action for the 'safeguarding of revolutionary gains' in any member-state of the socialist camp.

The interplay of ideological principles with the interests of the Soviet state, as interpreted by its rulers, and the modification of the former by reference to the latter, are strikingly displayed not only in relations between the Soviet Union and other communist states but in Soviet foreign policy generally. In the post-1945 period, the development of the hydrogen bomb and the emergence of the Soviet Union as one of the two super-powers, with the resulting global power stalemate, have resulted in the formulation that a World War between the socialist and capitalist systems is not 'fatally inevitable' (the related doctrine of 'peaceful coexistence' was not wholly new, being piously traced by Soviet apologists to Lenin). These factors have also conduced to the modification of Lenin's doctrine that the revolutionary process must necessarily involve violence. There has been, in addition, an oscillation in foreign policy between the 'ideological' aim of promoting revolution throughout the world and the 'political' aim of extending Soviet national influence through the cultivation of good relations with established non-communist regimes. This Jekyll-and-Hyde approach was always a factor in relations with the major Western powers but, since the death of Stalin, it has transformed policy towards the developing countries of the

M

third world. At various times the Soviet Union has pursued good relations with the governments of Middle Eastern, Asian, African and—most recently —Latin American countries with seemingly callous disregard for the interests and fate of local communists.

CONCLUSION

To sum up, it would be foolish to believe that the communist ideology is a rapidly waning force in the Soviet Union. It is at least probable however that, in its Soviet version, its impact is being diminished and its character modified by the following among other factors: the stabilisation of 'meritocratic' incentives (it would be premature to speak of a new class stratification); the increased attraction and availability of material luxuries; the chauvinism engendered by super-power status (but always latent in Russia); the inability of a sober-suited, trilby-hatted leadership and an arid jargon to kindle the enthusiasm of the younger generation—and, conversely, the appeal of new or revivified foreign interpretations of the communist ideal; the world-wide spread of nationalism, which has not only contributed to the proliferation of 'national' forms of communism but must inevitably, sooner or later, threaten the unity of the multi-national Soviet state; and—a factor involving simultaneously ideological, national and racial tensions— the prolongation and exacerbation of the conflict with China.

FURTHER READING

Berlin, I. *Karl Marx, His Life and Environment*, Oxford Univ. Press (Home University Library), London, 1963; New York, 1964.

Brzezinski, Z. K. *Ideology and Power in Soviet Politics*, Thames and Hudson, London; Frederick A. Praeger, New York, 1962.

Carew Hunt, R. N. *A Guide to Communist Jargon*, Geoffrey Bles, London, 1957.

Conquest, R. (ed.) *The Politics of Ideas in the USSR*, Bodley Head, London; Frederick A. Praeger, New York, 1967.

Fainsod, M. *How Russia is Ruled*, Oxford Univ. Press, London; Harvard Univ. Press, Cambridge, Mass., 1963.

Johnson, P. *Khrushchev and the Arts*, M.I.T. Press, Cambridge, Mass., 1965.

Keep, J. L. H. *The Rise of Social Democracy in Russia*, Oxford Univ. Press, London and New York, 1963.

Laqueur, W. Z. 'The Schism', *Survey*, 42, London, June 1962.

Lichtheim, G. 'On the Interpretation of Marx's Thought', *Survey*, 62, London, January 1967.

Meyer, A. G. 'The Functions of Ideology in the Soviet Political System', *Soviet Studies*, XVII, 3, Glasgow, January 1966.

Schapiro, L. *The Communist Party of the Soviet Union*, Methuen, London, 1963. With Boiter, A. (eds.) *The USSR and the Future*, Pall Mall Press, London; Frederick A. Praeger, New York, 1963. With Reddaway, P. (eds.) *Lenin: the Man, the Theorist, the Leader*, Stanford Univ. Hoover Inst. publication; Pall Mall Press, London, 1967.

Shub, D. *Lenin: A Biography*, Penguin, London, 1966.

The editors of *Survey*, London (eds.) *The State of Soviet Science*, M.I.T. Press, Cambridge, Mass., 1965.

Wesson, R. G. 'Soviet Ideology: the Necessity of Marxism', *Soviet Studies*, XXI, 1, Glasgow, July 1969.

Willetts, H. T. 'Khrushchev and the 22nd Congress', *Survey*, 40, London, January 1962.

MARCUS WHEELER. Formerly at the Foreign Office and the Royal Institute of International Affairs, is currently Professor of Russian at Queen's University, Belfast.

SECURITY SEEN FROM THE EAST

PHILIP WINDSOR

THE GERMAN PROBLEM

IF an American were asked what the chief problem of security was in the world today, he would almost certainly begin by talking about China and continue with a few ambiguous reflections about the Soviet Union. A West European would probably be torn between the Soviet Union, China and the evolution of the war in Vietnam. But an East European would certainly not mention the USA first, however strongly he condemned the war in Vietnam nor would he mention the Soviet Union first, whatever he thought about the Soviet invasion of Czechoslovakia and however much that had complicated his reflections. He would begin by talking about Germany. And concerned though he might be with China, Czechoslovakia, the evolution of US policy and the need for further *détente*, he would keep coming back to the paramount importance of settling the German problem once and for all.

This scale of priorities is fundamental to all discussions of security in Eastern Europe, including the Soviet Union. To the normal West European or American, it is puzzling; but it makes a certain sense within the context of policy decisions in Eastern Europe. For within this context, considerations of politics and of security are related more closely to each other than one is accustomed to in the West. This interaction will be discussed later; but first it is perhaps important to clear up a basic misconception about the East European view of Germany.

One hears it frequently argued that none in Eastern Europe, and certainly none in the Soviet Union, can seriously be *afraid* of Germany (meaning West Germany, of course). At the most, this argument runs, the East Europeans suffer from a pathological suspicion of Germany, which is perfectly understandable in view of what they suffered in the war, but which should surely not be taken seriously as a guide to policy-making. Those who argue in this way usually add, for good measure, that this suspicion generally applies to all Germans, East as well as West, but has not prevented other states in Eastern Europe from establishing close ties of friendship and interdependence with East Germany; indeed those ties are closest with some of the countries that suffered most at German hands during the war. In other words, the East European attitude is at worst official hypocrisy, at best a neurosis, understandable but unfortunate.

There is, of course, some truth in this argument. The experiences of the war have left hideous memories in the Soviet Union and much of Eastern Europe; and these memories would in any case make a *rapprochement* with West Germany difficult. But it is equally true that certain governments have not hesitated to exploit the memories of the war for their own political purposes. Is the official attitude, then, one of pure hypocrisy?

In the first place, however irrational it might appear, fear as well as distrust of Germany is an intensely powerful force in Eastern Europe. Clearly, this is not an empirical attitude, based on a detailed scrutiny of the contemporary political scene in West Germany. But nor is it quite so abnormal as it might sometimes appear in the West. It can, perhaps, be better understood with the aid of an analogy. Western Europe has, after all, never been occupied by Soviet troops and it is now a number of years since anyone expressed serious fear of Soviet 'aggression'. Yet the attitude is still normal in Western Europe and is still the basis of official policy, that unless the countries of the Atlantic Alliance continue to keep their guard up, the Soviet Union might revert to its old Stalinist ways and catastrophe could happen. This fear is based on a memory—and the memory is one of fearing events that never actually happened: a Soviet drive to conquer Europe, for which there was precious little evidence in the West, whatever happened in its Eastern part after the war. Yet it is still regarded as entirely reasonable. Now it might be objected that the Western view of the Soviet Union is at least based on the realities of power. It is a country which is stronger than Western Europe; the Atlantic Alliance is still necessary to ensure that the nations of the West *feel* protected—but the very strength of the Soviet Union should be enough to dispel all Eastern fear of Germany. The second power in the world, a country that could wipe out West Germany with a dozen missiles or so, should surely have nothing to worry about. This, however, is to misinterpret the nature of the fear—and of the analogy. At the height of the Cold War, when fears of Soviet intentions were at their most acute, the Soviet Union was very much weaker than the USA, so much so that if a war had occurred, European Russia would have been devastated whilst the USA would have escaped—literally—unscathed. But this was not really the point. It was rather that the Soviet leaders, Stalin in particular, were thought to be wicked or irrational enough not to be deterred; or that the situation might be ambiguous enough for them to think they could get away with it. Or, at least, that they could practically have devastated Western Europe before they acknowledged defeat. Precisely similar fears are voiced about Germany in Eastern Europe today. They are fears of irrational purpose or ambiguous situation—and they often go hand in hand with a contempt for the actual power of West Germany. It is worth recalling here that in 1941 Germany did not really stand a chance of defeating the Soviet Union, that it was even hopelessly irrational to attack, but that the attack happened and that 20 million Soviet citizens were killed before the *Wehrmacht* was thrown back. The existence of nuclear weapons has not really changed the nature of the fear: in fact, the fear of an ambiguous situation is now stronger than before. For now it is possible, in the Eastern view, that the Germans might make the fundamental miscalculation that since they are protected by the US nuclear umbrella, they can still hope to recover their former dominant position in Central Europe by the threat of physical pressure; at best create a profoundly unstable situation in Europe and at worst drag the world into war. This does not mean that the inhabitants of Poland, Czechoslovakia or Hungary are obsessed by a constant fear of what the Germans are up to; but it does mean that West Germany is still, so to speak, on probation, in very much the same way that the Soviet Union is when seen from the West.

The second point that needs to be made is this: that if one dismisses the Eastern attitude as so much hypocrisy, or a neurotic hangover from the experience of war, one implicitly admits that nothing can be done. Only time and the efforts of the people themselves can effect a cure. It might be that nothing can be done for the present: that the Eastern and Western approach to the problem of Germany and the problem of European security are too far apart to permit any fruitful initiatives. However, this does not mean that any attempts to frame a commonly acceptable understanding of what is involved demand a revision of assumptions on one side only. It is a political fact that the countries of Eastern Europe *are* preoccupied with the problem of Germany's future power and influence, and this preoccupation is based on a much more vivid and horrifying historical experience than anything the Western countries have to refer to in their own continuing distrust of the Soviet Union. Neither side can abandon altogether its own historical under-standing or scrap its preoccupations for the sake of creating international goodwill. The future power of Germany must be defined in any European system that would be acceptable when viewed from the East; just as the future role of the Soviet Union must be in any system that would be accept-able to the West.

But, granted that this is the basic underlying attitude to Germany in Eastern Europe, the question still remains: how does it affect the calculations that Eastern governments must make about their own future? To place this question within its context, one must first ask how their relations with Germany have developed, and how consistent their attitudes throughout Eastern Europe are as a whole.

The Development of Relations with Germany

At the beginning of this chapter, the phrase, 'settling the German problem' was used. This is very much a cant Eastern phrase and it has a particular meaning. The German problem is simply the fact that Germany has been too powerful in the past and cannot be trusted in the future. The settlement of the German problem is still more concise. When this form of words is used, it means that the only way to approach a solution is to recognise East Ger-many as a separate state. Soviet pronouncements on this matter, which have been followed closely by those of the other countries concerned, have been careful to include the possibility of ultimate reunification within the terms of the solution. But what they mean by reunification is some form of con-federation, which would leave East Germany as a still recognisable and influential entity, and one which would in some respects enjoy a power of veto over German policy as a whole. Otherwise, the relations between the two halves of the country are left obscure. Meanwhile an acknowledgement of the division of Germany is the only sensible step to take; what follows after can be left for the next generation or two to worry about.

This attitude is based upon the historical and psychological roots which have been sketched above. But these roots do not necessarily bear that kind of fruit. It is, in fact, the reverse of what Soviet policy was trying to achieve in the years after the war. For until the mid-1950s the Soviet Union made several attempts to prevent the division of Germany. Not that Soviet policy was consistently in favour of German reunification, but rather that until 1955 or so the Soviet leaders had never made up their minds what to do about Germany. For ten years after the war they tried several alternative policies, sometimes two or three at once. Almost immediately after the end of hostilities they began the establishment of a separate proto-state in their own zone of Germany. One of the paradoxes of the post-war situation was that, while

Soviet policy seemed for a while content to acknowledge that the country was being divided and even seemed to encourage this process, it was also clearly preparing for a time when the whole country could have been united—on terms, clearly, which would have made communist domination relatively easy. Hence the Soviet Union came into conflict with the Western Powers, not so much on the question of the separateness of development in the three Western zones, but about the growing tendency of the Powers to unite their zones administratively and politically. This conflict came to a head when currency reform was introduced throughout what is now the Federal Republic, and the blockade of Berlin began almost immediately thereafter. After the blockade East Germany was more than ever isolated from the West, and the *de facto* division of the country was more or less complete. But only a short time after, in 1952, Stalin began a new diplomatic offensive to press for reunification, and while East Germany continued to develop its own system, the East-West conferences continued on how to reunify the whole country; fruitless conferences, because each side posed conditions that were unacceptable to the other, but significant because they indicated that the Soviet Union was not yet reconciled to the division of Germany.

What changed the minds of the Soviet Union after all? Here, the answer is straightforward. West Germany joined NATO. As this prospect loomed, the Soviet Union made a series of attempts to prevent it: even at one point offering to join NATO and convert it into a collective security organisation. Once the decision was taken, the Soviet Union immediately began to insist that the division of Germany should be recognised by the Western Powers. When West Germany was about to be incorporated into NATO in 1955 the Warsaw Pact was established in Eastern Europe. East Germany was invited to become a member of the new Pact at the same time, and its own forces were integrated with the rest early in 1956.

So the first result of German rearmament—or, to be more accurate, of Germany's joining the Western Alliance—was the creation of a rival alliance system in the East: the German problem, from the very beginning, provided the focal point for the organisation of a general security system in Eastern Europe. Since then, the Soviet Union has been entirely consistent in its demand that the West should recognise East Germany as the first step towards a true relaxation of tension in Europe. What this means, in essence, is that Germany did not begin to become a security problem in Eastern Europe until it joined NATO. For the ten years between 1945 and 1955 it was a problem that was seen exclusively in political terms. During this period West Germany could not be said to provide any kind of threat to its neighbours and Soviet policy attempted (with varying degrees of finesse, and with whatever motives one cares to attribute) positively to bring German reunification about. From then on it was excluded. Why did this abrupt change come about?

The answer, surely, is that until then Soviet foreign policy had been conducted on a series of fairly simple assumptions. From then on it was much more ambiguous. In the first ten years, the policy itself was often complex enough—swinging between the Berlin blockade on the one hand and the Austrian Peace Treaty on the other—but its calculations were reasonably straightforward. These were that the only real threat to the Soviet Union lay in the air power of the USA; that the Soviet armies in Europe would be enough to hold this power in check, by the counter-threat they held against the nations of the West; but that within this context, it was the *political* outcome that was important. The essence of the political struggle was the future of Germany. Now this political struggle incurred the danger that the strategic power of the USA might be invoked—the early 1950s was after all the period of 'massive retaliation' in US policy, when the Soviet Union was gradually ringed with US bomber bases—but if a strategic attack could be avoided, communism was one day bound to triumph in Europe. And if Germany could be united on conditions which would leave it open to Soviet domination, this triumph could be immeasurably hastened. The result was that throughout this first period, the Soviet leaders looked on the USA as the chief enemy and one with whom they would have to be extremely cautious in dealing, but on Germany as their chief 'target'. Meanwhile, the other European countries, and particularly the UK were expected to act as some sort of restraining influence on the USA. All this changed when it became clear that West Germany was to become an integrated part of the Western Alliance. Since then the attitude has grown and become steadily more marked, that the chief function of the USA within NATO was to control 'the Germans'.

There is a basic paradox here. It is that, although the two Great Powers have been in fundamental disagreement about the future of Germany and the nature of a European settlement ever since 1955, they have nonetheless laid the basis for a *détente* in the division of Germany. Until then, when both were casting about for some form of reunification, they were in a position of inherent conflict: each wanted reunification on its own terms. But once Germany was effectively divided for the foreseeable future, it meant that on the one hand the Soviet Union had settled for less than it originally wanted; and that on the other, the USA had settled for a policy which in practice made reunification almost impossible to achieve. The USA, and the Western Powers in general, continued to pay lip service to the idea of reunification (and still do: early in 1968 an official study on the future tasks of NATO declared that this was still one of the objectives of the Alliance) but in practice it had become such a long-term notion that it was almost Utopian. In short, both sides accepted the actual situation for the time being. It meant that gradually each came to accept the other's sphere of influence in Europe, that each was reasonably secure about its own and that therewith the basis for a more general understanding, and for occasional specific agreements was laid. Clearly, all this did not happen overnight. Since 1955, there have been two major crises (Berlin and Cuba) and a number of less immediately dangerous ones (Suez, Hungary, the Lebanon and Jordan, Quemoy and Matsu, and so on). But these crises have not prevented a growing under-standing that both the Great Powers had too much to risk in approaching even the possibility of war, and that the area where they could least of all afford to take any risks was Europe. After the building of the Berlin Wall in 1961, this has really been the basis of their relations. Equally, it has been the basis of the *détente*.

This is what is meant in saying that Soviet policy became much more ambiguous after 1955. For on the one hand, the basis had been laid (in the Soviet view) for a European settlement, but on the other, the Western Powers and the USA refused to acknowledge that this was so. They insisted that the only way to resolve the tensions of Europe was to reunify Germany. It was (looking back, there seems to be no doubt at all) in order to make them abandon this claim and force them to acknowledge East Germany, that Khrushchev launched the Berlin crisis of 1958, which culminated in the building of the Berlin Wall in 1961. But this was the last time that the Soviet Union challenged the power of the USA (for the Cuban crisis was after all a

US challenge to Soviet power). Since then, it has tried to achieve the same results by more diplomatic means—but it is precisely this diplomacy which has been ambiguous. For in some respects, the USA is almost considered as an ally by the Soviet Union: not only in the common concern to avoid a nuclear war, but also in containing the power of West Germany. On the other hand, it is an opponent of the Soviet Union, in its refusal to recognise East Germany and in its tendency, which at least the Soviets discerned in the the early years of this decade, to accord West Germany a special position within NATO. The result has been an extraordinarily complicated series of diplomatic manoeuvres.

In particular, the Soviet leaders seem to want a NATO that is both strengthened and weakened. Strengthened in the sense that NATO is the best assurance they have that the very considerable military power of West Germany will continue to be under effective US control; weakened in the sense that on every occasion they have seen a danger that the USA might grant West Germany too much power inside the counsels of NATO—particularly the nuclear counsels—they have fought vigorously to prevent it. From the US viewpoint, such measures might only have been sensible precautions to prevent the disruption of the Alliance, but in the Soviet view, they opened the door to a dangerous and incalculable future. The most notable instance was the proposal for a multilateral force of nuclear missile-firing ships under NATO command, in which the Germans were expected to become a major partner and which was under active discussion between 1962 and 1964. Throughout this period, the two Great Powers were also discussing a treaty to prevent the spread of nuclear weapons to countries that did not possess them already—the Non-Proliferation Treaty which was finally tabled at Geneva in 1968. Throughout, the Soviet negotiators insisted that the Americans could not have both a multilateral force and a Non-Proliferation Treaty. They would have to choose; and negotiations only became serious from about 1965, when the USA allowed the multilateral force to drop and downgraded the alternative solutions that had been advanced to the problem of giving Germany a voice in nuclear planning to the point where these had become practically meaningless.

GERMANY AND EASTERN EUROPE

This was one clear instance of the ambiguous relationship which the Soviet Union developed with the USA, a relation compounded of conflicting purpose and common understanding in about equal proportions. In it the German question has played a predominant part. But this fact, though central, obscures another of great importance. That is, that the Soviet Union, however genuine its fears, has also *needed* a German problem. The reasons are obvious. Since the revolution in East European affairs which followed Khrushchev's denunciation of Stalin in 1956, and the consequent loss of Soviet authority in Eastern Europe, the question of Germany has served to hold the system together in the East and helped to perpetuate Soviet control over the Warsaw Pact. One must, indeed, go further: the Warsaw Pact has become a more important and a more effective military instrument in the East precisely during the period that NATO was falling into real disarray in the West. That is, since the first couple of years of this decade. Again the cause is clear. NATO stopped being an integrated military and political organisation and became instead a loose military alliance because the *détente* between the two Great Powers relieved the West European states of most immediate fears of a Soviet attack, and set their diplomacy free. However, for exactly the same reason the *political* threat to the East European system increased. The more free the West European nations were to negotiate new understandings in Eastern Europe, the greater the potential temptation for the Eastern states themselves to seek a new *modus vivendi* with their Western neighbours—and the greater, too, the prospects for a German diplomatic offensive to the East, based on the economic power of Western Germany, and offering fairly substantial rewards for any East European state that opened relations. This is, of course, what happened. Once Germany entered the ring, the Soviet Union was faced with a double threat. There was the threat on the one hand that German economic power could disrupt the Eastern system: it could offer alternative sources for long-term capital investment in the East, it could offer a much prized reserve of hard currency to those countries which developed extensive commercial relations, it could free them to a considerable extent from their economic dependence on the Soviet Union. This in turn could lead to a high degree of political emancipation. If the Soviet Union strove to prevent its allies from developing closer relations with Germany, it risked a serious split in the system anyway. Between these two threats, it settled at first for a compromise. It allowed a certain development of economic relations to go forward; but at the same time insisted that these economic relations should have no political importance.

To sketch the Soviet position in this way might seem to indicate that all the other states in the East have the same reactions to Germany. This would be quite inaccurate, for Eastern Europe itself is divided. The division is really between those states which, like the Soviet Union, need a German problem and those which merely have to take account of it in their relations with both the Soviet Union and the Western world. To the first category belong East Germany and Poland. To the second belong Hungary and Bulgaria. The reasons for the necessity of a German problem to the states in this first category are straightforward. Apart from the fact that Poland suffered horribly from German occupation, it is a country with a highly developed national consciousness and a strong anti-Russian tradition. To harness the forces of nationalism without turning them against the Soviet Union, the governments of Poland—and in the Novotný period, Czechoslovakia too—have constantly invoked the German danger. Even more, and again this applies particularly to Poland, a staunch anti-German line has enabled them to recover considerable diplomatic freedom of action in their relations with the West without alarming Moscow unduly. In the case of East Germany the reasons are still more straightforward: any attempt to justify the separate existence of East Germany to its own citizens, and to involve them to some extent with the development of their own country, has involved a continual campaign against West Germany. It must not be seen as a viable alternative to East Germany itself, either in terms of a more attractive society to live in, or in terms of standing a better historical chance of survival. East Germany must present itself not only as a society on the way to achieving the aims of socialism, but as the authentic custodian of German history, while West Germany continues to betray that history as the Nazis did before it.

Even this is to oversimplify. Czechoslovakia, for instance, has never been as straightforwardly anti-German as such an outline might indicate. There is strong evidence that the Slovaks were much more flexible in their attitude than the Czechs; equally, there have been many indications that the government and foreign ministry in Prague were deeply divided during the period between the beginning of West Germany's 'opening to the East' at the end of 1966 and the fall of the Novotný government in January 1968: divided in their attitudes to Germany and on the pragmatic question of how far it was possible for Czechoslovakia to go in relations with West Germany. Poland, on the other hand, underwent almost the opposite evolution. Between 1956, the year of Gomułka's coming to power, and about 1963 Polish foreign policy was fairly flexible and independent, Poland appeared to desire a new relationship with the Western world as a whole, and to be anxious to assert as far as possible its independence of the Soviet Union. This was the period of the Rapacki Plan (in its various versions) for a nuclear-free zone in the middle of Europe, for instance; and if one of the implications of the plan was a Western recognition of East Germany, it also showed little concern for East German susceptibilities or the Soviet desire to concert foreign policy for Eastern Europe as a whole. But in the last few years, Poland has aligned itself more and more closely with the Soviet Union and East Germany over most matters of European policy, and has supported East German attempts to swing other countries of Eastern Europe behind a united front against West Germany. This is in part a result of internal developments in Poland—of the conflict between church and state, and the conflict between generations—but it is also a reflection of the fact that since the building of the Berlin Wall in 1961, East Germany has become more secure, economically more powerful and diplomatically more important inside the Eastern bloc. Poland has obviously been unwilling to allow the development of an exclusive 'special relationship' between East Germany and the Soviet Union, and has instead allowed itself to be drawn into a kind of triumvirate which dictates policy between Eastern Europe as a whole and West Germany. This was the basis of a conference held at Karlovy Vary in Czechoslovakia in April 1967 in which, after the opening of diplomatic relations between Rumania and West Germany the other East European states were warned, more or less openly, not to follow suit.

THE NEW AMBIGUITIES

The difficulty was that from this point the interaction of politics and security became closer and more complex. Early in 1968 it could have been said that the Warsaw Pact consisted essentially of four states—the Soviet Union, East Germany, Poland and Czechoslovakia—with the rest as hangers-on, and with Rumania attempting to exploit the organisation for its own political purposes. But in August 1968 five members of the Warsaw Pact joined in the invasion of Czechoslovakia. What had happened in between, as is now becoming clear, was that the internal changes in Czechoslovakia were stimulating the controversies to which the parties in other countries were prone. In the end they found it impossible to resolve these political differences because the security of the whole communist system was thought to depend on a temporary fidelity to the *status quo*. The preparations for the invasion were continually justified by reference to the dangers of an increasingly close relationship between Czechoslovakia and West Germany. While this was nonsense, it did indicate that Germany had become a convenient and perhaps necessary, point of reference in communist debates about all kinds of issues, internal and external. More than this, it is probably true to say that the evolution of individual societies and of relations between states in Eastern Europe had become linked with the question of the German *Ostpolitik* and its future success. East Germany had made frantic and successful efforts throughout 1967 to persuade its allies not to enter into closer relationships with West Germany, and it was characteristic that when a treaty of friendship and mutual aid was signed with Bulgaria in September of that year, Ulbricht seized the opportunity to declare that whoever kept silent about the aggressive policy of the West German imperialists would make himself their accomplice.

In fact a nexus had been established between Germany, *détente* and the individual development of East European society. Czechoslovakia was the victim of this nexus—which was broken by the invasion of 21 August 1968. What this amounts to is that the Soviet Union was attempting to establish some kind of *status quo* in Eastern Europe when it decided on the invasion of Czechoslovakia. But in doing so it could not help changing the situation fundamentally, and it is now even more difficult and ambiguous than it was before. The situation that the act of invasion created—the continuing resistance of the Czechoslovaks themselves, the alarm and defiance of Rumania, the more ebullient defiance of Jugoslavia, not to speak of the muted apprehensions in the very countries which had taken part in the invasion—created the need for the Soviet Union to lay down a new set of rules. This set of rules has been summarised as the doctrine of 'limited sovereignty' or 'the socialist commonwealth' on which the Soviet leaders have been trying to insist ever since the end of September 1968. In essence it declares that the Soviet Union will not hesitate to intervene, by force if necessary, and that it will be justified in doing so, whenever it feels that 'socialism' or 'the interests of socialist states' are threatened. Needless to say, the Soviet Union remains the sole arbiter of what constitutes a threat to socialism or the interests of its socialist allies.

It would appear that such a doctrine might clarify the situation. At least the other states now know what their standing is *vis-à-vis* the Soviet Union; that is, they have no standing whatever. But, as one of the Czechoslovak leaders is reputed defiantly to have told a Soviet representative, it takes a Stalin to be a Stalin; and the other states in Eastern Europe have shown little sign that they are prepared to abandon their striving for at least a limited autonomy—and, in the case of Rumania and Jugoslavia, considerably more independence than that. The difficulty is that none of them will know how far it can go in its own internal reforms, or in pursuit of relations with the Western states without incurring the wrath of the Soviet leaders. In other words Moscow has now emerged as a threat to the security of the East European states themselves and it has done so by its own choice. Whereas before, and particularly during the period of Stalinism, they did indeed have to submit to the Soviet style and system of government, the evolution of the past 15 years had seemed to indicate that the Soviet Union was prepared to allow an increasing degree of latitude, and to maintain this within certain well defined limitations by reference to the threat from Germany. By an act of incredible shortsightedness the Soviet leaders have now thrown this away and presented their allies with a dilemma instead. The East Europeans now have two alternative threats to contemplate: that from the Soviet Union on the one hand and that from Germany on the other. The real risk that the Soviet leaders have created for themselves is that the threat from Moscow will come to appear more direct and more dangerous than the threat from Germany.

This certainly does not mean that the security position of Eastern Europe will change in any way in the near future. On the contrary the Warsaw Pact is likely to become more closely integrated than before and Soviet control will depend even more on maintaining the German threat. Again, it must be emphasised that for many countries this threat is still real.

The security of Eastern Europe as a whole is threatened by the unsolved German problem. The security of individual states is threatened by the Soviet Union. That is a somewhat epigrammatic way of putting it, but it is the essence of the situation which has now arisen. The real difficulty is that in the internal evolution of the individual states this dilemma might come to be felt more sharply as they make greater efforts to adapt to the world in which they live. There are two possible forms of hope in this situation: the first is a growing liberalism inside the Soviet Union. At present this is remote. The second is a greater *rapprochement* between the two German states, and this is much less remote. The implications of such a development would be that it was the Soviet Union itself which had to face the dilemma that it has at present imposed upon everyone else. Here it is at least conceivable, to put it no more strongly, that the Soviet leaders might perceive that their general interests require the development of a solution to the German problem even more than they require the maintenance of Soviet authority in Eastern Europe.

It is a curious fact that in August 1968, at the moment when the invasion of Czechoslovakia was more or less certain to take place, Ulbricht proposed an exchange of meetings at full ministerial level with West Germany. Did this indicate that now he felt secure from the threat of a faster evolution in other countries, he was prepared to go a long way himself in promoting better relations with West Germany? Is there a real conflict of interests here between the Soviet Union and East Germany? There is in any case no doubt that within the shaky coalition party (which is known as the SED) over which Ulbricht presides there are powerful forces pressing for increased contact and improved relations with West Germany. This evolution is partly the result of developments within the East German state, partly a consequence of the growing flexibility of West German policy. Ever since East Germany began a series of economic reforms at the beginning of 1963—the first country in Eastern Europe to take advantage of the economic debate inside the Soviet Union—it has become clear that Ulbricht was trying to hold his coalition together on a series of tactical steps. One of the most important elements in this coalition has been a group commonly referred to as technocrats, but who are really powerful and important political figures prepared to encourage a degree of flexibility in their attempt to promote technological innovation and economic growth. Some of them have put forward ideas, which bear a startling resemblance to those of Herbert Wehner in West Germany, on the possibility of thorough-going cooperation between the two German states in investment policies and the sharing of their benefits, and they have certainly not been silenced.

Much will depend here on the new coalition that forms once Ulbricht leaves the scene; but it is clear that a powerful new force is at work, which could transform relations between these hitherto implacable states.

Conclusions

Eastern Europe, then, is deeply divided about the German problem, and this division extends into East Germany itself. The future is extremely uncertain. The events in Czechoslovakia are likely to have profound effects on other states in the East as well. Even East Germany will one day be faced with the problem of Ulbricht's succession, and the nature of that country's future relations with West Germany is going to play a dominant part in decisions across a wide range of policies.

FURTHER READING

Brzezinski, Zbigniew K. *The Soviet Bloc*, Harvard Univ. Press, Cambridge, Mass.; Oxford Univ. Press, London, 1960. *Alternative to Partition*, McGraw-Hill, New York, 1965.

Buchan, Alastair and Windsor, Philip. *Arms and Stability in Europe*, Chatto and Windus, London; Frederick A. Praeger, New York, 1963.

Collier, David S. and Glaser, Kurt (eds.) *Western Policy and Eastern Europe*, Henry Regnery, Chicago, 1966.

Khrushchev, N. S. *The New Content of Peaceful Coexistence in the Nuclear Age*. Cross Currents Press, New York, 1963.

London, Kurt, (ed.). *Eastern Europe in Transition*, The Johns Hopkins Press, Baltimore, 1967.

Mackintosh, J. M. *Strategy and Tactics of Soviet Foreign Policy*. Oxford Univ. Press, London, 1962; Oxford Univ. Press, New York, 1963.

Sokolovsky, Marshall. (Garthoff, Raymond, L. translator). 'Introduction', *Military Strategy Soviet Doctrine and Concepts*, Frederick A. Praeger, New York; Pall Mall Press, London, 1963.

Windsor, Philip and Roberts, Adam. *Czechoslovakia 1968*, Chatto and Windus, London; Columbia Univ. Press, New York, 1969.

Wolfe, Thomas W. *Soviet Strategy at the Crossroads*, Harvard Univ. Press, Cambridge, Mass. 1964.

PHILIP WINDSOR. Reader in International Relations at the L.S.E. Read Modern History and did research on German History at Oxford and the Free University of Berlin. Publications include *City on Leave; Arms and Stability in Europe* (with Alistair Buchan), both 1963. *Germany and the Management of Détente* and *German Reunification: A Post-War History* are forthcoming.

THE MILITARY POTENTIAL OF THE WARSAW PACT COUNTRIES

JOHN ERICKSON

POST-KHRUSHCHEV POLICIES

SINCE the removal of Khrushchev from office and power (October 1964), the successor Kosygin-Brezhnev regime in the Soviet Union has carried out a major armaments programme. It has improved Soviet offensive capabilities, invested in defensive capacities, given increased priority to the naval forces, provided more equipment for the forces which might operate in a non-nuclear ('conventional') environment and, not least, augmented Soviet air- and maritime-lift resources for long-range movement. This programme has fallen into roughly two parts, a 'reconstruction period' (up to the end of 1965) devoted to curtailing the confusion and lifting the inhibitions which Khrushchev left in his wake, followed by a speedy build-up in strategic weapons and an attempt to bring some balance between the nuclear and non-nuclear forces in the whole Soviet arsenal and armoury. For that reason present Soviet policies cannot be explained satisfactorily without reference to the latter days of Khrushchev's rule; to his 'nuclear fetishism' or his over-riding preference for strategic nuclear weapons; to the decline in the credibility of the Soviet deterrent; to the growing strategic inferiority of the Soviet Union vis-à-vis the USA and the danger that this might become either unalterable or irreversible; to the neglect of the Soviet conventional forces and the rigidity imposed by thinking only of 'one-variant war' (namely nuclear war). What was permanent about Khrushchev's post-1959 military programme centred on the primacy of strategic deterrent power and on the ascendancy within the Soviet military establishment of the newly established strategic rocket forces, a transformation which produced much protest and prolonged furore but which has been maintained both in principle and in practice by the present leadership without substantial modification. The Soviet armed forces currently consist of five elements organised to conform with their roles or 'missions': the strategic rocket forces (operational ICBMs, medium-range and intermediate range ballistic missiles, MRBMs and IRBMs), the air defence command (PVO) with surface-to-air missiles (SAMs), anti-aircraft artillery and interceptor aircraft, the soviet navy with nuclear- and conventional-powered submarines, submarine-launched ballistic missiles (SLBMs), tactical ship-borne missiles and the naval air arm, the ground forces (Soviet army) with 140 divisions organised into tank divisions, 'motor-rifle divisions', airborne divisions and mountain troops, supported by tactical missile brigades and regiments and the air force with its long-range strike component (long-range aviation), tactical aviation of the tactical air force for close air support of ground operations, interceptor units of the air defence command and the naval air arm and air transportation units.

The primacy of 'deterrence' and the dominance of the nuclear forces have been carried over into present Soviet policies. However, the post-Khrushchev leadership has begun to search for more diversified military forces (though without cutting into the strategic elements) and is manifestly concerned to supply itself with several military options; conventional forces still have uses which might well expand, while in addition wide-ranging political commitments increasingly necessitate some long-range lift and intervention capability (signs of which are appearing in the build-up of transport and in the creation of amphibious units or 'special forces' suitable for this type of role). Such developments pose intricate and fundamental problems for the makers of Soviet strategy, who must decide upon the 'correlation of forces' (the strategic balance of power) best suited to Soviet interests, on the issue of land-power in relation to sea-power (moving away from the land mass and towards 'global' positioning), and not least on the relationship between the nuclear and the non-nuclear (or the strategic and the non-strategic) forces in the Soviet military system. Soviet strategy is now moving into a transitional phase, the third stage in its evolution since 1945. Under Stalin the overriding priority was to break the US nuclear monopoly and to hold Europe hostage to Soviet conventional military strength until the Soviet Union acquired nuclear weapons. Under Khrushchev these new weapons had to be worked into the Soviet military system in which new structures and new doctrines were introduced. Under the present leadership Soviet strategy has to be shaped amidst growing technological complexity and a political situation which becomes ever more intricate. This, therefore, forms the background to Soviet strategic ideas and the Soviet appreciation of the strategic environment, but the starting-point is that concern which has been common to and constant within all the Soviet leadership groups—the strategic balance between the USA and the Soviet Union, involving as this does fundamental and far-reaching decisions on offensive and defensive strategic weapons systems.

Soviet Offensive and Defensive Strategic Forces

Since 1966 the Soviet Union has speeded up improvements in the quality and the quantity of its ICBM force, which under Khrushchev never rose above 200 missiles. From October 1966 to October 1967 the strength of the Soviet ICBM force doubled, rising from 340 to 720, with an additional 300 ICBM launching silos reported to be under construction at the close of 1967. With the completion of these further sites (expected in 1970), the Soviet Union would for the first time enjoy numerical parity in land-based strategic missiles with the USA (with 1,054 ICBMs). Not less significant has been the improvement in the quality of the Soviet missile arsenal: the newer ICBMs are located in individual sites which are 'hardened' to afford protection against attack, improved fuels provide faster reaction times, while the Soviet command has paid close attention to the development of mobile land-based strategic missiles, thus contributing to the dispersal of the strategic delivery forces. More than once since 1965 the Soviet government has paraded a large three-stage rocket which has been announced as a 'global' or 'orbital' weapon—the fractional orbital bombardment system (FOBS) which has apparently undergone successful testing. Such a system could be used to

179

reduce the warning time available to radar defences. All these developments and innovations conform to the declared Soviet priority for 'the strategic missile forces and atomic missile-launching submarines'; towards the close of 1967 a new submarine-launched ballistic missile (SLBM) was paraded in Moscow, while on 30 July 1967 (Soviet navy day) Admiral Kasatonov (first deputy commander-in-chief of the Soviet navy) announced that the Soviet navy had become 'a global strike force', that the nuclear fire-power at the disposal of the navy gave it a new and vastly enlarged strategic role and that 'alongside the strategic rocket forces the navy has become the principal instrument of the Supreme Command'. The Soviet navy disposes of some 50 nuclear-powered submarines: 13 of the earlier types carried three missile-launching tubes, 15 E1 class submarines carried six launching tubes for six cruise missiles (with a range of some 300 miles), followed by the ten nuclear-powered E2 class submarines with eight launching tubes. It will be most likely that, once having achieved parity in land-based missiles with the USA, the Soviet Union will concentrate on building up major strength in nuclear-powered submarines capable of launching ballistic missiles while deeply submerged: the new Soviet SLBM displayed in 1967 bears some resemblance to the US missile, *Poseidon*.

Marshal N. I. Krylov[1] commands the strategic rocket forces, which include not only the ICBMs but also the MRBMs and the IRBMs, medium- and intermediate-range weapons, of which there are some 750 in the Soviet arsenal (a figure which shows no sign of increasing). The MRBM and IRBM installations are located in the Baltic states, western and south-western Russia, in the Caucasus, Soviet Central Asia and the Soviet Far East (extending also into Outer Mongolia), thereby covering strategic targets (and those of lesser magnitude) in Western Europe, Japan and now, apparently, in communist China. The Soviet MRBM (NATO code-name SANDAL) has a range of just over 1,000 miles, the IRBM (NATO code-name SKEAN) a range of 2,200 miles. The land-based 'deterrent' comes under the command of the strategic rocket forces, the Soviet navy commanded by Admiral S. G. Gorshkov disposes of the 'seaborne' submarine-launched missiles, while Air Marshal F. A. Agaltsov's long-range air force (the strategic air arm which operates for all practical purposes as an independent command) adds yet another element to Soviet long-range strike forces. The bulk of the strength of the long-range air force is located in western and south-western Russia and in the Soviet Far East: of its three 'air armies' two are in European Russia and one in the Soviet Far East, with staging bases and dispersal points distributed in the Arctic. The force of intercontinental bombers includes 110 M-4 (code-name BISON) four-jet machines, some 90–100 four turbo-prop TU-95 (code-name BEAR) aircraft capable of carrying two air-to-surface missiles: part of this force of aircraft is used as tankers to supply in-flight fuelling. Of the medium bombers, some 800 of them, the new supersonic TU-22 (code-name BLINDER) is intended as a replacement for the TU-16 (code-name BADGER), though the TU-16 has been refurbished with air-launched stand-off cruise weapons. The strategic bombers have an intercontinental reach, the medium-range bombers can cover the majority of targets in the European theatre.

The air defence command (PVO) under Marshal P. F. Batitsky, and latterly a form of anti-ballistic missile (ABM) defence, form the agencies and instruments of strategic defence. The PVO comprises an early-warning

---

[1] All military positions referred to as of January 1969.

system, the PVO air force (fighter-interceptor aircraft for identification and interception), surface-to-air (SAM) missile units and anti-aircraft artillery: the whole of the Soviet Union is divided into 'air defence districts' and the Soviet PVO is linked with similar air defence organisations in the East European countries which form the Warsaw Pact. The Soviet ABM programme employs the multi-stage, solid-fuel anti-ballistic missile (NATO code-name GALOSH) in installations sited around Moscow: the GALOSH system has a range of several hundred miles and carries a nuclear warhead of up to two megatons, providing some area defence of north-western Russia. So far there is no evidence of the GALOSH system being extended to other Soviet cities and it provides at the moment only a limited defence, penetrable by sophisticated missile aids. Compared with the prodigious progress made with strategic offensive missiles, the Soviet ABM programme has proceeded at but a moderate pace, thus suggesting that the Soviet response to any US ABM deployment is to press forward with improvements in the size and quality of their ICBM arsenal.

SOVIET NAVAL FORCES

This is the second largest navy in the world. It is thoroughly modernised with 19 cruisers, 170 destroyers and sea-going escort ships, 55 nuclear-powered submarines and 330 conventionally-powered boats, some 500 fast patrol boats (*Osa* and *Komar* class carrying short-range cruise missiles), 100 to 200 landing craft, 1,000 auxiliary vessels. The Soviet navy has no aircraft carriers but two helicopter carriers have been built and a third is reported to be under construction. The land-based naval air arm has some 800 aircraft, bombers (TU-22 and TU-16), long-range maritime reconnaissance aircraft, flying-boats and helicopters for anti-submarine warfare and some transport aircraft. The Soviet navy (including the air arm) has a strength of some 460,000 men and is organised into four main fleets, plus a few small flotillas: Admiral Lobov's northern fleet has 800 ships, Admiral Mikhailin's Baltic fleet has 750 ships, Admiral Chursin's Black Sea fleet has 700 ships (including the two new helicopter carriers), Admiral Amelko's Pacific fleet has 750 ships. Soviet missile submarines operate principally from the northern fleet and from the Pacific fleet areas. In addition to the submarine-launched ballistic missile (SLBM), Soviet surface units (and some submarines) carry cruise missiles for ship-to-ship action as well as surface-to-air missiles (SAMs): Soviet ship-to-ship missiles vary in range from 200 to 20 miles.

GROUND FORCES; TACTICAL AIR POWER

The Soviet ground forces (Soviet army) under the command of Army General I. G. Pavlovsky number some two million men, organised into 140 divisions: 26 divisions are maintained in Central and Eastern Europe, 60 in European Russia, 10 in the area east of the Urals, 15 in the Soviet Far East and 30 in the Caucasus and Soviet Central Asia. Soviet tank divisions, which go to make up about one-third of the ground forces, have 350 to 375 medium and heavy tanks: the 'motor-rifle division' has some 200 tanks and 10,500 men (tank divisions 9,000 men). Soviet airborne divisions have a strength of 8,000 men and there are presently some seven such divisions. The 'tank army' comprises three to four tank divisions, the 'all-arms army' three to five divisions (tank and 'motor-rifle' combined): tactical missile brigades and regiments, employing missiles on tracked and wheeled launchers with ranges

181

from 10 to 150 miles (and one cruise missile with a range of 300 miles), operate in support of armies and 'fronts' (the Soviet equivalent of an army group). The Soviet ground forces also operate their own air defence organisation, with anti-aircraft artillery and SAMs.

The tactical air force, with some 4,000 aircraft, accounts for just under half the total Soviet air strength (10,000 combat aircraft). Commanded by Aviation Marshal K. A. Vershinin, it is made up of twelve 'air armies' equipped with tactical bombers, ground-attack aircraft, interceptor fighters, transports, helicopters and special reconnaissance units. At the Moscow air show in July 1967 (Domodedovo airport) new aircraft were displayed, including a Soviet 'swing-wing' (variable-wing) machine. The older MIG-15 and MIG-17 interceptor-fighters are being replaced by MIG-19 and MIG-21: the new ground-attack Sukhoi SU-7 aircraft is being brought into service.

Manpower and Budgeting

The total manpower of the Soviet armed forces is in the region of three-and-a-quarter million men. The revised law on military service (October 1967), amending the law of 1939 and the 1950 modifications to it, reduced the period of compulsory service with the army and the air force from three to two years, and for the navy from four to three years. There will be henceforth two annual call-ups (instead of one) and educational deferment has been diminished. The call-up age has been lowered. The total effect will be to make more men available for military service, to increase the body of trained reserves and to increase the flow of men into military units by mobilising twice in the year.

In 1966 the declared Soviet defence budget amounted to 13,400 million roubles, a 5% increase on the previous year and bringing the declared military expenditure to just under 13% of the total budget. In 1967 the budget was again increased to 14,500 million roubles (equivalent to $16,000 million) and the present figure is 16,700 million roubles, representing some $13\frac{1}{2}$% of the total budget. This, however, is expenditure *publicly* revealed, so that 'defence-related items' (including research and development) could add appreciably to the declared sum. Current increases are due to the accelerated offensive missile and ABM programme, and it has been estimated that increases of up to 10% in the Soviet defence budget are likely up to 1970. It has also been estimated that more than 50% of the budget goes on the strategic nuclear forces and on the air defence command, followed by over 30% on the forces maintained in the Soviet Union itself and in Eastern Europe, the 'conventional' element in the Soviet establishment.

The Warsaw Pact: Organisation and Constituents

The treaty of Friendship, Mutual Assistance and Cooperation was signed on 14 May 1955 between the Soviet Union, Albania, Bulgaria, Czechoslovakia, East Germany, Hungary, Poland and Rumania. It was the first formal military alliance to be concluded between the Soviet Union and the East European states: Albania, having taken no part in its activities from about 1961 onwards, formally left the Pact in the aftermath of the invasion of Czechoslovakia in 1968. Until 1960–1 the Pact played little part in Soviet military planning, but under Khrushchev the Soviet Union pursued a policy of closer military cooperation with Eastern Europe. Khrushchev's policy of stressing Soviet nuclear weapons and reducing the place of conventional armament led to increased emphasis on the conventional forces of the Warsaw Pact member states. Greater military efficiency, closer military integration and political cohesion within the alliance became the foundation of Khrushchev's policy, which has been continued by the present regime.

The Warsaw Treaty Organisation has two main administrative bodies: the political Consultative Committee and the High Command of the United Armed Forces, both with their offices in Moscow. The political committee is made up of the first secretaries of the individual Communist Parties of the member states, the heads of government and both the foreign and defence ministers of member states: the committee has also a Joint Secretariat and a Permanent Commission, again both situated in Moscow. The commander-in-chief of the Warsaw Pact forces has always been a senior Soviet officer, since April 1967 Marshal Yakubovsky: the High Command of the Warsaw Pact enjoys complete authority over the forces assigned to it by the member states. The commander-in-chief is assisted by eight deputies who are the defence ministers or the individual national commanders-in-chief of the member states and is served by a staff manned by officers drawn from the general staffs of the member states, though the chief of staff of the High Command (who is also head of the Joint Secretariat) is and always has been a senior Soviet officer. Soviet control over the military and political organisation of the Warsaw Pact thus remains total and the Soviet monopoly of high posts is maintained.

To supplement the Warsaw Treaty itself there is also a complicated series of bilateral agreements, treaties of mutual aid, between the Soviet Union and individual East European states (with the treaty with East Germany signed in 1964), and parallel mutual aid treaties between member states (save for Albania, which has none with the contracting parties to the Warsaw Pact). The Soviet Union also has special agreements with Poland, Hungary, East Germany and Czechoslovakia to cover the stationing of Soviet troops in these countries: the agreement with Rumania on this lapsed in 1958 when Soviet troops withdrew. There are, therefore, two main collections of agreements, one multilateral and the other bilateral treaties, which govern Soviet commitments in and to the East European states, supplemented by the four special agreements on stationing of troops.

STRENGTH AND DEPLOYMENT

The preponderance of ground and air strength within the Warsaw Pact is Soviet. The group of Soviet forces in Germany (HQ Wünsdorf) consists of 20 divisions, half of them tank divisions, with a strength of some 480,000 men: these divisions are maintained at about 85% of their war establishment and the group is trained to fight in a nuclear environment. In addition, the two tank divisions and the four motorised rifle divisions of the East German army are subordinated to the Soviet group in Germany for operational purposes. One Soviet air army is attached to the Soviet group to provide tactical air support. Two Soviet divisions are stationed at Legnica in Poland (Soviet northern group) and there are four Soviet divisions in Hungary (Soviet southern group) with their HQ at Tököl, thus providing a total of 26 Soviet divisions in Central and Eastern Europe. (Soviet forces currently stationed in Czechoslovakia are dealt with below, p. 266).

The East European forces of the Warsaw Pact constitute some 60 divisions and represent over 900,000 men. For operational purposes, about half of these divisions are in a state of readiness and up to strength. The important distinction, however, is a regional one between what has been called the 'northern tier' of the alliance and the 'southern tier'. East Germany, Poland and Czechoslovakia comprise the 'northern tier' forces; Bulgaria and Rumania the 'southern tier', with Hungary occupying an intermediate position. Between them East Germany, Poland and Czechoslovakia have a paper strength of some 35 divisions: East Germany six (two tank, four motorised rifle), Poland 14 (five tank divisions, nine motorised rifle divisions) plus one airborne division, Czechoslovakia 14 divisions (four tank divisions, ten motorised rifle divisions). Between them Bulgaria and Rumania have 21 divisions (Bulgaria twelve, Rumania nine). Hungary has six divisions (one tank division, five motorised rifle divisions). Poland and Czechoslovakia dispose of considerable strength in tanks (3,000 and 3,300 respectively, principally types T-54 and T-55) while Rumania has less than half (1,200) including the older T-34s: East Germany possesses something under 2,000 tanks, the bulk of which are modern machines, T-54 and T-55.

WARSAW PACT AIR FORCES

As with the ground forces, the Soviet Union provides the backbone of the air power. In time of war it is assumed that the separate national air forces would come under Warsaw Pact High Command control; in addition to its tactical air force in East Germany (some 900 aircraft), the Soviet Union also maintains its home commands bordering on the Warsaw Pact area. The air defence systems and early warning systems in the Warsaw Pact area also come under the control of the Soviet air defence command (PVO). All strategic bombing capability and strategic missiles, as well as the MRBMs and IRBMs, are in Soviet hands. Although the member states of the Warsaw Pact have paraded tactical missiles, there is as yet nothing to suggest that they have received the appropriate warheads from the Soviet Union. The great bulk of the equipment in the individual Warsaw Pact air forces is Soviet, mostly ground-attack and interceptor-fighter aircraft, though some transport aircraft and tactical support helicopters have been supplied. Most of the member states employ the SA-2 surface-to-air missile as part of their air defences, which are being progressively improved.

The largest air force among the East European states is currently the Polish (*Polskie lotnictwo wojskowe*), with over 800 combat aircraft, light bombers (six squadrons), fighters (48 squadrons), ground-attack and reconnaissance (18 squadrons), supported by transports, helicopters and training machines: Soviet sources supply the combat aircraft but Polish industry has produced trainers (basic trainers and jet trainers), as well as helicopters. Recently the Polish air force has been accorded the status of an independent force, having operated previously under the command and control of the Polish general staff; PLW (Polish air force) headquarters will be at Poznań. The Czechoslovak air force ranks second in size after the Polish: *Československé letectvo* (Czechoslovak air force) has some 600 combat aircraft, half of them fighters (MIG-17 and MIG-19). Czechoslovak industry produces the L-29 DELFIN trainer, standard for all Warsaw Pact countries except Poland and East Germany. The East German air force (*Luftstreit-kräfte und Luftverteidigung*) has some 600 combat aircraft, the main strength being in interceptor-fighters, though there are ground-support and recon-naissance units, as well as an anti-aircraft division. The Hungarian air force, with less than 150 aircraft, is merged with the army, with which it operates in close support, although the Hungarian air component was reequipped with

MIG-21 supersonic machines after 1963. The Rumanian air force is slightly larger, with some 240 aircraft, the interceptor units operating with Soviet, Hungarian and Bulgarian squadrons for air defence and a small force for army tactical support. The Bulgarian air force is the same size as the Rumanian, 240 to 250 combat aircraft, with interceptor squadrons (MIG-17, MIG-19 and MIG-21), MIG-17 for reconnaissance and ground-support and a score or so of transport aircraft.

NAVAL FORCES

Poland, East Germany, Bulgaria and Rumania maintain naval forces (while Hungary operates a small 'Danube flotilla' made up of patrol craft), but the main force is represented by the 'allied Baltic Sea forces' (the Soviet Baltic fleet, the East German naval force and the Polish navy). The Soviet Baltic fleet disposes of, as its main units, 80 submarines, six cruisers and 35 destroyers. The Polish navy includes ten submarines, three destroyers and a score of minesweepers, supported by a fighter division of MIG-17 aircraft for naval cooperation: the East German naval force consists of light surface units (escorts and minesweepers), less than a dozen missile patrol boats and a marine brigade with landing craft. (An amphibious division has also been raised within the Polish forces.) The Bulgarian navy musters two submarines and small craft. The Rumanian navy is also without larger surface units and has no submarines.

In the Baltic, while the light forces can be used for coastal defence, the main power is supplied by the Soviet Baltic fleet: the Soviet Black Sea fleet performs the same function in the Black Sea. The presence, however, of Soviet, Polish and East German marine units suggests that amphibious operations might not be ruled out, and Soviet marines are trained to operate in a support role in any general nuclear campaign in Europe.

THE DEVELOPMENT OF MILITARY AND POLITICAL INTEGRATION IN THE WARSAW PACT

Since the dismissal of Khrushchev, the Soviet command has shown increasing interest in 'flexible response'—*gibkoe reagirovanie*, to use its Russian formulation—thus moving away from the idea of an automatic nuclear response in all situations. This goes some way to explain the revived Soviet interest in conventional and general purpose forces, which assume greater significance in any non-nuclear phase of operations and also help to increase Soviet options which are no longer confined to a single and diminishingly credible 'nuclear' retort. In Central and Eastern Europe, Soviet troops are trained primarily for nuclear war and their organisation and equipment (the high proportion of armour to infantry, the preponderance of tactical nuclear missiles) further suggest preparation for operations in a nuclear environment; the Warsaw Pact exercises of 1965 and 1966 were conducted in an environment presupposed to be nuclear, but one major exercise—*October Storm*—did open with a non-nuclear phase. Soviet military theorists now concede that 'local wars can take place *even in* Europe' and local wars will be conducted with non-nuclear forces. This in itself may provide one clue to the Soviet military investment of Czechoslovakia; the role of the Czechoslovak forces in any 'non-nuclear phase' was to hold the forward line for at least 72 hours, though it was far from clear how the Czechoslovak army would manage this. It was not simply a question of 'guarding' the frontiers but a matter of moving more diverse capabilities (principally conventional forces) further west; with only six Czechoslovak divisions effectively operational (as opposed to 20 Soviet divisions and six East German divisions in East Germany, as well as 14 Polish divisions plus two Soviet divisions in Poland), the Soviet case for further deployment in Czechoslovakia was both plausible and convenient. The movement of a Soviet mechanised corps up to the western frontier area immediately after the invasion of August 1968 was, therefore, not without some significance in this context.

The Soviet military intervention in Czechoslovakia involved some quarter-of-a-million men in all. Warsaw Pact forces had been massed at seven potential points of entry, while in East Germany two East German divisions, the Soviet 8th and 20th Guards Armies, the 1st Guards Tank Army and the 24th Tactical Air Army stood by. Elements of the Soviet 3rd Army invested the frontier with Czechoslovakia to the east, with a massive convoy on the alert inside Hungary; Bulgarian troops were also air-lifted to join this 'southern' concentration, to move alongside other token Warsaw Pact forces—Bulgarian, Hungarian, East German and Polish, in all. Some 14 to 15 Soviet divisions, with these token forces in their train, moved in from East Germany, the Carpathians and Poland, to be replaced by a second wave of Soviet formations drawn from Lithuania, Belorussia and the Ukraine, gaps here being filled in turn by the mobilisation of reserves. The actual investment of Czechoslovakia, carried out by formations under the command of General Pavlovsky, was speedy and efficient and a demonstration of the rapid movement of large bodies of men and large quantities of armour. While the bulk of these invading armies gradually seeped back to their original locations, the net Soviet redeployment produced by the move into Czechoslovakia has amounted to some 60,000 to 70,000 men (six or seven divisions), with the 'provisional stationing' of Soviet troops in Czechoslovakia provided for in the agreement of 16 October 1968 (though present signs indicate that the Soviet troops are prepared for a protracted stay). Against this 'gain' (if it is a gain) must be set the 'loss' of the 175,000 men of the Czechoslovak army, though the situation seems hardly as simple as that kind of rude calculation. In the very wake of the Soviet invasion, it was argued that this forward movement of Soviet troops had actually decreased the 'net threat' to NATO, since the Soviet command must reckon the Warsaw Pact as a whole less dependable, for Warsaw Pact forces would have to be committed to neutralise the Czechoslovak army and the Czechoslovak population along with it. The position of the Czechoslovak army is by no means wholly clear, but it did not suffer the fate of the Hungarian army in 1956, and quite recently Černík, the Czechoslovak prime minister, announced that plans were afoot to increase Czechoslovakia's 'defence capacity' and to develop the armed forces as 'a modern army of the socialist type'. This suggests that the Czechoslovak army cannot be wholly written off.

The 'northern tier' of the Warsaw Pact will continue to be of commanding interest and importance to the Soviet Union, with or without an effort at détente in Europe. At the same time, however, Soviet attention has been closely concentrated on the southern flank, involving both Bulgaria and Rumania. The shift so far has been less military than political, but an unmistakable consequence of the 'Brezhnev Doctrine' (the definition of the integrity of the 'socialist commonwealth' and the insistence upon limited sovereignty) is a modification in the whole concept of the Warsaw Pact. In spite of some earlier rumours, no Soviet formations have actually moved into or been stationed in Bulgaria; after some feverish weeks of tension, Soviet-

Rumanian relations cooled off and no Soviet troops appeared there, but Soviet interest in holding 'manoeuvres' in Rumania does not seem to have died away. Present activity related to 'strengthening' the Warsaw Pact seems to centre on setting up a much modified command structure, less on the lines of the 'rotating' command which the Rumanians earlier suggested but more in the direction of an 'international' command, which would have immediate rights over national armies and transcend national boundaries: such a 'supranational' command could decide not merely on the siting of 'manoeuvres' but also the location of troops, thus making further inroads on particular national sovereignties. This 'supranational' arrangement would not be any concession to East European national feelings; on the contrary, this major infringement of national sovereignty would be a potent measure for enforcing Soviet political control and would facilitate the proliferation of Soviet military presence in the whole Warsaw Pact area. This, rather than an 'invasion' on the Czechoslovak model, seems to be the current threat to Rumania's integrity and sovereignty and it is to be expected that such proposals will encounter stiff Rumanian resistance. But in addition to its several military functions, the Warsaw Pact has now come to occupy a major place in Soviet plans for political 'integration' in Eastern Europe.

FURTHER READING

'Air Forces of the World (Part 6): The Warsaw Pact Countries', *Interavia*, XXIII, London, February, 1968.

Herrick, Robert Waring. *Soviet Naval Strategy*, United States Naval Institute, Annapolis, Md., 1968.

McGwire, Cdr. M. K. OBE, RN (retd.). 'The Background to Russian Naval Policy', *Brassey's Annual*, The Armed Forces Year-Book, William Clowes, London, 1968. (See ch. XV).

Mackintosh, Malcolm. *The Evolution of the Warsaw Pact*, Adelphi Papers No. 58, June, 1969, Institute for Strategic Studies, London.

Mackintosh, Malcolm. *Juggernaut* (see Ch. 14), Secker and Warburg, London; Macmillan, New York, 1967.

The Military Balance 1968–1969, The Institute for Strategic Studies, London, 1968. (See Part I 'The Communist Powers' The Warsaw Pact pp. 1–8).

Strategic Survey 1967, The Institute for Strategic Studies, London, 1968. (See 'Eastern Europe' and 'The Soviet Union'.)

Wiener, Friedrich. 'Organisation-Taktik Waffen und Gerät', *Die Armeen der Ostblockstaaten*, Lehmanns Verlag, Munich, 1967.

JOHN ERICKSON. Professor of Politics (Defence Studies) at the University of Edinburgh. Previously Lecturer in Russian and East European History, University of St. Andrew's and Reader in Government, University of Manchester. Publications include *The Soviet High Command* 1918-1941 and the editorship of *The Military-Technical Revolution*.

THE SOVIET UNION

RUSSIAN NATIONALISM

NEIL HYAMS

'THE PRISON OF THE PEOPLES'

THE history of Great Russian[1] nationalism to be discussed here essentially concerns the use made for over a century by a centralised regime of nationalism for various reasons of state. The largely peasant mass of the Russian people, whose miseries did not automatically cease with the abolition of serfdom in 1861, was not itself noted for nationalistic or racialistic attitudes but in any case had little opportunity to influence the state's policy. Patriotic feelings, on the other hand, had been aroused among the Russian population at large by the Napoleonic invasion. Indeed, centuries of invasion and occupation of the Russian homeland had naturally left deep traces. Foreign observers of imperial Russia drew attention to attitudes still perceptible today. In his classic work *La Russie en 1839*, the Marquis de Custine declared, for instance:

> This Byzantine government, and indeed all Russia, have always looked upon the diplomatic corps and Westerners in general as envious and malevolent spies.

For most of the period that Russia has been a recognisable unitary state, its frontiers have been under pressure. Even today there is tension, particularly along the Sino-Soviet border. The borderlands have seen many struggles for supremacy (for example the Polish, Swedish, Turkish and Persian campaigns). Russian expansionism can at least in part be explained by a compulsion to acquire buffer areas, often in the teeth of protracted resistance.

During the reign of Nicholas I (1825–55), *narodnost*—the principle of Russian nationality—became part of the official ideology. The slogan of orthodoxy, autocracy and nationality had been devised by the Tsar's minister of education, Uvarov, in 1832 and it was to remain in force, theoretically at least, until the fall of the Russian monarchy. Actions were suited to words, and a deliberate process of Russification was initiated in the educational systems of parts of Poland, Belorussia and Lithuania. Simultaneously, the Orthodox Church increased its proselytising activities. The Jewish community, already restricted to the Pale of Settlement in the western and south-western provinces, was the hardest hit. Both enforced assimilatory (Jews were now also made liable to 25 years military service plus six in training establishments) and discriminatory measures were decreed.

---

[1] The term distinguishing Russians from other closely related East Slavs—the Ukrainians and Belorussians; not to be confused with the frequent Soviet reference to the 'great Russian people', in which the honorific adjective is reserved exclusively for Russians.

The concept of 'nationality' was elucidated in different ways, however. Officially it buttressed the idea of a divinely ordained autocracy, characteristic of Russia and superior to unstable Western institutions. Yet a wider and more influential interpretation, deriving from German romantic nationalism, gained ground among intellectuals, writers, journalists (two of the most influential being Russified Poles), officers and students. The contradictions between the legitimist concept, emphasising the preservation of the *status quo* and the 'intellectual' version with its undertones of revolutionary change and its messianic Pan-Slavist urgings, were most apparent in the sphere o foreign policy. Domestically the ethnocentric point of departure of exponents of both tendencies ensured a greater coincidence of aims.

A landmark in the complex relationship between Russia and the Ukraine was the arrest of the outstanding poet, Taras Shevchenko, in 1847 and his banishment to Siberia for ten years. Other members of the secret radical society to which he belonged were treated more leniently. Nationalism in those European parts of the Russian empire which bore the brunt of the Russian policy—particularly Poland—was itself being intensified. On the other hand, the path of Russification and advancement was open to such loyal subjects who were eligible.

Asiatic peoples were subjected to increasing colonisation but in general were left to their traditional Islamic education. Immigration of Russian settlers and rule by Russian bureaucrats naturally posed social problems familiar in other parts of the world.

The policy of Russification was further encouraged under Alexander III (1881–94) and his grey eminence, Pobedonostsev, whose name was a byword for reaction. Even peoples who had shown complete loyalty to the Russian throne like the Finns and Armenians were needlessly antagonised by Russian actions. Jews were subjected to pogroms, later instigated by organised proto-fascist groups known colloquially as the 'Black Hundred'[1], particularly active in the borderland areas where ethnic friction was highest. (The last Tsar, Nicholas II, was an honorary member of the best known such organisation.) Out of such conditions was born another nationalist ideology—Zionism.

Armenians also suffered through official connivance at pogroms. The Tatars of Azerbaidzhan were encouraged to attack them and the Baku riots of 1905 involved heavy loss of life.

Tsarism bequeathed certain techniques which were to reappear on a scale made possible only by a totalitarian state's command of every lever of power and every means of communication. Among them may be included an ideology celebrating Russian superiority, disseminated in schools and official publications; Russification of the educational system; a policy of divide and rule (such as the territorial division of Turkic peoples in the 1920s); and repressive measures such as deportation (inflicted on Crimean Tatars during the Crimean War and on the subjugated Chechens, for example, and used extensively by Stalin, particularly during World War II when entire peoples were deported). Moreover, general insensitivity towards local aspirations, characteristic of the Tsarist bureaucracy, lived on into the Soviet period as did the potentially violent reaction to anything incompatible with the Russian interest.

Many echoes of 19th-century Russian nationalism reverberated *fortissimo* under Stalin and his successors. Yet in the earlier period there was interaction between official and unofficial theorists, differences of emphasis and opinion

[1] Certain Stalinist *literati* are privately called the 'Red Hundred' by their colleagues today.

were expressed and genuine debate occurred despite the Tsarist censorship apparatus. Since the symbols of Russian superiority were artificially imposed in the 1930s in order to weld culturally disparate and even antagonistic peoples into a centralised industrial state, it has been impossible to gauge the true strength of nationalism among the Russian people. It can hardly be doubted, however, that the repeated acknowledgement over four decades of its primacy and its prowess in revolution, war and peace has had a potent effect on the Russian masses.

LENIN AND THE SECESSION ISSUE

Lenin was very alive to the exploitable discontent felt by non-Russians. From the outset he sought to gain their sympathy by stressing a nation's right of secession and self-determination. Nevertheless, he qualified this right. In his 1903 article, *The National Question in our Programme*, he subordinated it to the interests of the class struggle in each given case. Alliance was only permissible, he stressed, with the proletarian elements of nationalist parties. National movements assisting the bourgeoisie would have to be crushed. There was an element of expediency about his remarks in 1914:

> It is because and only because Russia and its neighbouring countries are experiencing this epoch (i.e. of 'bourgeois-democratic national movements' and attempts to establish independent national states) that we need a point on the right of nations to self-determination in our programme.

Nations temporarily seceding from the empire would, he believed, voluntarily 'merge' into the socialist state. After the fall of Nicholas II, however, nationalist governments and parties arose throughout the former empire. On seizing power, the Bolsheviks made several tactical gestures, avoiding the traditional Russian nationalism of their White enemies: for example, the issuing of a declaration concerning the 'rights of the peoples of Russia' and an appeal to Muslims; the banning of Russian settlement in certain areas and the return of historic and sacred relics to certain peoples.

Lenin was forced to abandon his objections to federation and the Soviet Union became composed of nominally independent states. However, he insisted on a single centralised party. The theoretical right of secession only applied (as it still does) to union republics, which by definition border on non-Soviet territory. Its worth can be gauged from Stalin's self-confessedly 'blunt' dictum in 1923 that 'the right of self-determination cannot and must not serve as an obstacle to the working class in exercising its right to dictatorship'.

CULTURE AND LANGUAGE

Lenin's detestation of Russian chauvinism was real enough: he declared 'war to the death' against it. He rejected the enforced use of Russian and supported education in local languages. Yet here again the class criterion was all-important and the content of education was to be determined by Marxism: clerical schools were thus an impossibility. He looked forward to the time when all national mistrust would disappear and nations would merge on the basis of an international proletarian culture. Various instructions by Lenin indicate his concern that non-Russian traditions and pride should not be trampled on and that the Russian political model should not be inflexibly imposed.

At the end of his life Lenin was pessimistic about the ability of Russian—and Russified—bureaucrats to administer the nationalities in the tactful spirit he had urged. He expressed strong disapproval of the rough treatment handed out in Transcaucasia by certain 'Russified non-Russians' (his chosen expert on the nationalities question, Stalin, among them) in notes dictated for circulation before the Twelfth Party Congress in 1923. They were not published until 1956 and little reference has been made to them since. He referred prophetically to freedom of secession turning out to be:

> a mere scrap of paper incapable of protecting the other nationalities in Russia from the inroads of that truly Russian type, the Great Russian chauvinist, essentially a scoundrel and bully, which is the typical Russian bureaucrat.

He differentiated between the nationalism of the oppressing nation and that of the oppressed:

> ... almost always in historical practice we, the nationals of the large nations, prove ourselves guilty of an endless amount of violence . . . and insults . . .

and demanded that the large nation should 'compensate' by actual 'inequality'.

Soviet claims to have solved the 'nationalities question' by the application of the 'Leninist nationalities policy' are common. The implication is that Lenin's precepts have been consistently applied.

Stalin

A frank discussion of Great Russian chauvinism (as Russian nationalism itself is termed) took place at the Twelfth Party Congress in 1923. Even Stalin in his report conceded that this factor was 'the principle force impeding the merging of the republics into a single union'. Anti-Russian nationalism was a defence against Great Russian chauvinism which 'was the cornerstone of the national question' and had to be combated by Russians themselves. A policy of establishing national cadres in the administration and economy with the intention of increasing native participation in Soviet rule was implemented from 1923–9. Native languages were encouraged and alphabets for peoples with no literary languages were devised. Certain national military formations were also established.

But the change of course in the 1930s was drastic. The new period was characterised by the elevation of the Russian people and things Russian to a position of preeminence, and in the subsequent heresy hunt innumerable non-Russians, party members, writers and common people lost their freedom or their lives.

In 1934 Stalin declared that the 'deviation against which we have ceased to fight' (i.e. non-Russian nationalisms), was 'the great danger'. Little has been heard from official sources of Great Russian chauvinism since then. The horrors of enforced collectivisation and the deliberate use of famine as a weapon, the increasing economic control from Moscow certainly aroused nationalist feelings, particularly in the Ukraine. A subsidiary factor was the resentment of Russian tutelage felt by local cadres. The later 1930s saw the establishment of the practice of installing Russian second secretaries in non-Russian party organisations. The national cadres created in the two previous decades were shattered, together with such 'national communists' as existed when the campaign against suspected officials reached its climax in 1937–9.

On the cultural front an indicative development affected those Soviet Asian peoples whose alphabets had already been changed from Arabic to Latin scripts (from anti-religious, as well as internationalist, motives). By 1940 these had all been changed yet again to the Cyrillic script. Words in certain categories had to be borrowed from Russian. In 1938 it was decreed that Russian would be a compulsory subject in all non-Russian schools.

The previous year another decree had been passed propounding the theory of the 'lesser evil': that whereas Tsarist annexation of non-Russian territories was evil, it was less evil than acquisition by other imperialist states would have been.

War and post-war

The line was considerably modified during the 'Great Fatherland War' as Nazi-Soviet hostilities were dubbed in a deliberate echo of the term applied to the 1812 Napoleonic invasion. In order to rally the Soviet peoples, and doubtless to divert separatist ambitions, concessions were made to nationalist sentiment. (The appeal to Russian tradition itself was reinforced by concessions made to the Orthodox Church.)

Certain non-Russian historians even publicly repudiated the 'lesser-evil' theory. But already towards the end of the war the line began to harden; in 1944–5, Tatar and Bashkir writers and historians were attacked for nationalism and for glorifying past struggles against the Russians. The attack broadened. Soon not only historians were being denounced but the very writings that stand at the heart of a people's culture—national epics.

Stalin's celebrated 1945 toast at a military reception to, 'the Russian people, because it is the most outstanding nation of all nations within the Soviet Union', heralded the period which has still not closed, in which non-Russians are officially called upon to acknowledge the leading role of their 'elder brother', to express gratitude to him for economic and cultural progress and to exalt the usefulness of his language—their 'second native language'. The contrast with Lenin's injunctions and early party resolutions could not be more complete.

Purges of 'nationalists' were reinstituted in several areas, particularly those 'reunited' with the Soviet Union. The obscurantist Zhdanov decrees (1946–8) rejected 'bourgeois' culture while claiming primacy for the Russians. The inculcation of 'Soviet patriotism' was a prime function of the arts. The Zhdanov period was followed by the anti-'cosmopolitan' witchhunt, largely aimed at Jews. The parallel with the most retrograde periods of Tsarist rule hardly needs mention.

The traditional fear felt by Russian rulers of infection from abroad culminated in the post-war years in an intensity of enforced xenophobia and chauvinism that only modern totalitarian means could have achieved.

KHRUSHCHEV

Immediately after Stalin's death in 1953, concessions were again made to the non-Russian nationalities. Some officials were charged with falsely accusing innocent people of 'bourgeois nationalism'. The (Russian) first party secretary of the Ukraine was demoted for introducing Russian as the language of instruction in West Ukrainian institutes of higher education and for other distortions of the 'Leninist-Stalinist nationality policy'. He was replaced by the first Ukrainian ever to hold this post in his native republic. Among other signs of relaxation was the granting of more economic rights to the union republics. By 1956 there was a partial rehabilitation of national literatures and—in Khrushchev's Twentieth Party Congress secret speech—of the Caucasian nationalities deported by Stalin. (The Volga Germans and Crimean Tatars had to wait until 1964 and 1967 respectively for such limited amends as were belatedly made.)

It is ironic, however, that a marked 'deviation' became discernible under

Khrushchev which even Stalin had specifically condemned in 1930: Great Russian chauvinists, the latter had said, considered that individual nations would begin to disappear in the Soviet Union and 'a single common language' would begin to develop 'within the borders of a single state'. This reflected the wish of the previously dominant nation's dying classes to regain their lost privileges. Under Khrushchev a theory was officially propagated according to which a *rapprochement* (*sblizhenie*) of peoples was under way prior to their eventual merger (*slianie*). The current (1961) party programme speaks not only of the development of 'an international culture common to all Soviet nations' but of the manner in which the 'boundaries of the constituent republics of the Soviet Union are increasingly losing their former significance'. In practice there had been many previous occasions when territorial changes or changes in status (even affecting a union republic—the Karelian—in 1956) were decided in Moscow. To oppose any such decisions would clearly have been foolhardy. When it came to another suggestion unofficially mooted under Khrushchev that national *languages* should merge, there was considerable controversy. Just how sensitive non-Russians feel on this issue was shown, after Khrushchev's downfall, even in published sources: a well-known Georgian writer and literary official vehemently denounced both 'the argument . . . over whether there should or should not be national languages' and the people who had waited 'with great impatience for the moment when all national cultures would merge into one whole'.

Khrushchev's economic decentralisation in 1957, involving the setting up of republican councils of national economy, led to charges of economic nationalism or 'localism'—another proof of continued resistance to central dictates when the opportunity arises. The imposition of a unitary pattern in other spheres continued. Thus in 1960 and 1963 CPSU Central Committee decrees intensified the relay of broadcasts from the centre. In areas where local newspapers were issued in Russian and a vernacular language, 'unified' editorial boards were set up in 1963. The 'friendship of the peoples, international education of the workers and mutual enrichment of cultures' were the themes of innumerable lectures and articles—as they are still today.

Immigration (particularly into the Virgin Lands of Kazakhstan), and the Russification of education and publishing continued increasingly. The 1958 theses on educational reform granted parents a choice between schooling in Russian or the vernacular. The proposal evoked different reactions in the union republics but was adopted by most of them. Certain social injustices resulted, however. Parents who wish to ensure their children's advancement are obliged to give them a Russian schooling, vital for entrance to most institutes of higher education and courses within them. Furthermore, ample provision is made for educating children of Russian migrants to non-Russian areas in their own tongue (a significant social factor when it is remembered that Russians favour settlement in towns—even the capitals of certain non-Russian republics contain more Russians than 'natives'); but reciprocal arrangements are not made for the children of the many migrants into the Russian republic (RSFSR).

THE POSITION TODAY

After Khrushchev's removal in 1964, there were indications of a slightly more tactful approach by the central authorities. The following year, the lapsed practice of publishing new laws passed by the USSR Supreme Soviet in languages of the republics was reinstituted. A certain liberty of debate was permitted. However, at the same time *Pravda* of 5 September 1965, echoing the party programme, warned against resisting 'a continuous exchange of trained personnel between peoples'.

Yet little has changed in basic essentials. Russians and Russified eastern Slavs continue to hold key party and government posts in non-Slav republics. The advantages, cultural and economic, past and present, of being linked with the Russian people are constantly publicised.

Particular sensitivity is shown in areas subject to frontier tension, as, for example, the Moldavian republic (previously part of Rumania)—where 'nationalist prejudices' were said by the first party secretary in 1965 to have 'become stronger in recent times', and the Far Eastern areas bordering on China. Pledges of their inviolability are given by Soviet leaders and scholars produce works emphasising their age-old links with Russia.

Russian insensitivity towards non-Russians emerges with force from Soviet publications themselves. Thus a session of the 'Russian section' of the Uzbek Writers' Union in 1968 heard complaints about 'disrespectful attitudes' (i.e. from Uzbek writers) and much insistence on rights for Russian-language book publishing which would certainly not be reciprocally vouchsafed to members of another nationality working in the RSFSR. This was despite the fact that, as in other republics, Russian books are published there in numbers quite disproportionate to the number of resident Russians. One speaker in fact revealed that many had to be pulped! According to the 1959 census, Uzbeks outnumbered Russians by five to one within Uzbekistan, yet the last full publishing figures show that in 1965, 983 books were issued in Uzbek while no less than 939 came out in Russian. Such figures are typical of the Soviet Union as a whole. All in all in 1966, 54,968 books and brochures were published in Russian compared to 15,579 in 63 other languages of the Soviet Union (many of them of course translations from the Russian); 3,481 magazines compared to 774 and 4,454 newspapers compared to 1,957. (The 1959 census showed that just over half the Soviet population was, or considered itself to be, Russian.)

The unfairness of this and other aspects of Soviet reality has inevitably alienated the many non-Russians who retain a sense of their own history and culture. It is rarely possible to express grievances directly in the face of the ever-watchful security police and the armed might which would instantly crush popular manifestations. (Some 300 Crimean Tatars were arrested in Chirchik, near Tashkent, in 1968 for peacefully defying a ban on celebrating Lenin's birthday on 21 April. It had been under Lenin's rule that a Crimean autonomous republic had been established. Stalin deported the whole people in 1944 and abolished their republic.)

Resentment finds many ways of expressing itself, from local refusals to 'understand' Russian to nostalgia for the past. Even such a prominent cultural functionary as O. Honchar, head of the Ukrainian Writers' Union, was heavily criticised in 1968 for a symbolic novel praising Ukrainian culture and traditions. The policy of imposing the Russian cultural model for reasons of political cohesion—according to Soviet figures, some 130 nations and nationalities inhabit the Soviet Union—can only be regarded as partially successful, to judge by the necessarily limited and circumspect reactions discernible in the press alone.

The manner in which selected nationalisms (Arab, Kurdish) are encouraged abroad for foreign political reasons must seem particularly cynical to many non-Russians. 'Imperialists' are not the only targets: broadcasts are also provocatively beamed at national minorities in China. The group

O

feelings of Baltic peoples, Armenians and others of the same stock as Soviet peoples who live abroad are exploited in an attempt to make them resettle in the Soviet Union. It is indicative that Soviet Ukrainians, for example, cannot subscribe to the Soviet magazines specially produced for their compatriots abroad. Nor, for that matter—a striking parallel with Tsarist practice—may they receive Ukrainian publications issued in Poland and Czechoslovakia.

Nationalism—in the Western sense—has discredited itself. Not surprisingly, ambiguous reactions are evoked when evidence of its continued existence comes from the non-Russian areas of the Soviet Union. Yet deep nationalistic feelings are frequently a product of adversity and of the denial of self-expression to an oppressed nation. It could be argued that latent tensions would be dispelled if the socially disadvantageous side of the relationship with the Russians could be openly discussed, or if non-Russians were no longer forced to regard the 'History of the USSR from the Most Ancient Times to Our Days'[1] from a Russian viewpoint. Yet the experience of Hungary and Czechoslovakia demonstrates how plastered-over national grievances can erupt into anti-Russian feeling when circumstances permit. Here as in other fields, the Soviet regime is all too aware of the dangers relaxation could bring.

FURTHER READING

Barghoorn, F. C. *Soviet Russian Nationalism*, Oxford Univ. Press, New York, 1956.

Conquest, R. *The Soviet Deportation of Nationalities*, Macmillan, London; St. Martin's Press, New York, 1960. (ed.) *Soviet Nationalities Policy in Practice*, The Bodley Head, London, 1967.

Dzyuba, I. *Internationalism or Russification?*, Weidenfeld and Nicolson, London, 1968.

Goldhagen, E. (ed.) *Ethnic Minorities in the Soviet Union*, Frederick A. Praeger, London and New York, 1968.

Holdsworth, M. 'Lenin and the Nationalities Question', *Lenin: The Man, The Theorist, The Leader—A Reappraisal*, (L. Schapiro, P. Reddaway and Paul Rotha, eds.), Pall Mall Press, London, 1967.

Riasonovsky, N. V. *Nicholas I and Official Nationality in Russia, 1825–1855*, Univ. of California Press, Berkeley and Los Angeles; Cambridge Univ. Press, Cambridge, 1959.

Seton-Watson, H. *The Russian Empire 1801–1917*, Oxford Univ. Press, New York and London, 1967.

NEIL HYAMS. A language teacher in a North London grammar school. Primary field of studies was art history. Specialisation in Soviet art of the 1920s led him into wider studies of Soviet cultural policy and society. Currently researching into problems of acculturation and assimilation among non-Russian peoples.

[1] The revealingly anachronistic title of a recent 12-vol. work.

NATIONALITIES IN THE SOVIET UNION

WILLIAM FORWOOD

INTRODUCTION

THE world's largest multinational state is the result of seven centuries of Russian expansion, a Slav-dominated land-empire in which political and economic integration, both forced and voluntary, has reached the point where the future of its non-Russian minorities is in doubt. According to the 1959 census, the Soviet Union possesses 108 distinct ethnic groups[1] of which several are the remnants of primitive peoples whose national cultures were barely developed before Soviet rule. If we include the Ukrainians, Lithuanians, Latvians and Estonians[2], the non-Russian minorities today amount to some 45% of the Soviet population. 15 nationalities, including the Russian, are organised territorially into union republics (SSRs) and most others into autonomous republics (ASSRs), autonomous regions (AOs) and national areas (NOs) but a number of widely dispersed nationalities such as Jews,[3] Poles, Germans, and Gypsies and several small peoples—including the majority of Palaeo-Asiatic and Tungusic groupings in Siberia and a few diminutive minorities in Caucasia—are directly administered by larger groups.

The nationalities of the Soviet Union are classified as follows. The Slav branch of the Indo-European family comprises the country's numerically greatest groups: Russian, Ukrainian and Belorussian, which together account for 77% of the Soviet Union's population. Not too distantly related to the Slavs are the Balts (Lithuanians and Latvians). To the Iranian branch of the same family belong the Tadzhiks (in Central Asia) and a scattering of isolated peoples in Caucasia (such as the Ossetes and Kurds) while the Armenians form an individual unit of the same phylum. Situated also in Caucasia are two major families, the so-called north Caucasian (notably the Chechen, Avars, Abkhaz, Kabardin and Cherkess) and the south Caucasian (or Ibero-Caucasian) of which the Georgians represent a majority. The Turkic family includes, of the more numerous peoples, the Uzbeks, Kazakhs, Turkmen, Kirghiz and Karakalpaks (all located in Central Asia), the Azerbaidzhanis (in Transcaucasia), the Tatar, Bashkir and Chuvash peoples (in the Volga-Urals area), the Crimean Tatars (mainly exiled in Central Asia) and the Yakuts, Altai, Shor, Khakass and Tuvinians (in Siberia).

---

[1] Unless otherwise stated, these are here defined by language rather than race.
[2] See chapter on the place of the Ukraine and the Baltic Republics in the Soviet Union.
[3] A Jewish AO was established in 1934 in the eastern RSFSR but its Jewish population is estimated at not more than 14,000.

Stretched over a wide arc from the Baltic to the Urals are peoples of the Finnic family—including the Estonians, Karelians, Lapps, Mordvin, Udmurt (or Votyak), Mari (or Cheremiss) and Komi, most of whom were historically engulfed by the successive tides of Slav migration, as were the related Ugrian groups of western Siberia, in particular the Khanty (or Ostyak) and Mansi (or Vogul), whose languages are related to Hungarian, and the small Samoyedic groups of the Far North. There is also a Hungarian minority in the Transcarpathian *oblast* of the Ukrainian SSR, the area marching with Hungary proper.

Geographically separated are the two Soviet branches of the Mongol family: the Kalmyks who migrated to the lower Volga, in the 17th century, and the Buryats of the Mongolian borderlands south of Lake Baykal. The rest of Siberia contains, in addition to the majority settlers (mainly Slav), Palaeo-Asiatic groups—including the Chukchi, Koryaks, Itelmen, Ainu and Gilyak, who variously show affinities with Amerindians, Koreans and Japanese—and the Tungusic family (Evenki, Even, Orok etc.) whose relatives are the aboriginal peoples of Manchuria.

Groups of Jews, Poles, Germans, Gypsies and Greeks are broadly dispersed and other peoples historically associated with foreign territories (Koreans, Bulgarians, Hungarians, Rumanians, Finns, Chinese, Turks and Czechs) are grouped mainly in frontier areas close to their ethnic brethren. In this category we can place the Moldavians who, though Rumanian, have SSR status and are classified in the Soviet Union as autochthonous.

There is no easy formula whereby nationality is equated with ethnic, linguistic or religious status, for the historic intermingling of the many Soviet peoples has blurred identities. It is enough to mention the examples of the Karelians, the Komi, Mari, Mordvin, Chuvash, Yakuts and (Turkish-speaking) Gagauzi—who are as a rule nominal members of the Russian Orthodox Church; or the Chinese-speaking Dungans and Georgian-speaking Adzhars—who are Muslim; or the Tats of Azerbaidzhan—who profess both Islam and Judaism.

A New Type of Colonialism

The present-day territorial map of the Soviet Union differs but little from the administrative organisation of the country made in 1924, which was based on a combination of Tsarist precedent, Leninist idealism and the expedients of economics and military strategy.

The constitutional right to national self-determination had in 1917 been formally guaranteed to all the peoples that had constituted the former Russian empire but this was in effect nullified the following year by Stalin's proviso that 'the principle of free self-determination . . . must be limited to the workers and refused to the bourgeoisie'. Following several short-lived experiments in sovereignty and federation (notably in Caucasia), all the non-Russian nationalities (save the Poles, Moldavians, Finns and Baltic peoples) were brought again under control. The Central Asian 'Basmachi' rebellion (1918–24), the 'pitchfork revolt' of the Tatars and Bashkirs (1919–20), Sultan Galiyev's abortive attempt in the early 1920s to create a socialist Muslim state on the middle Volga and the national uprisings of the Armenians (1921) and Georgians (1924) were only the most dramatic manifestations of national resistance. Between the civil war and 1940, however, the containment policy of the Great Powers and Moscow's domestic preoccupations prevented Soviet expansion across existing frontiers—except into Sinkiang, which was occupied from 1932 to 1943. But areas annexed during and after World War II (eastern Poland, parts of Finnish Karelia and east Prussia, Bessarabia, northern Bukovina, the Carpatho-Ukraine, the three Baltic states, Tannu Tuva, the Kurile Is and southern Sakhalin) were incorporated in the union, their peoples for the most part given varying degrees of nominal autonomy and set on the path of assimilation already trodden by other non-Russian nationalities, dissident elements being deported, often in thousands.

The pre-revolutionary imperial tradition was extended into the Soviet period through Moscow's initial adoption of the principle of 'nativisation' (or the creation of a socialist and Russian-oriented élite among the nationalities) and a policy of *divide et impera* whereby certain nationalisms, notably in the less developed areas of Caucasia, Central Asia, the Volga-Urals and Siberia, were deliberately fostered in order to forestall Pan-Turkic, Pan-Islamic, foreign irredentist and other anti-Russian, anti-Soviet coalitions.[1] Smouldering opposition was effectively extinguished in the purges of the 1930s and during World War II most of the peoples rallied to the new 'fatherland'. For alleged collaboration with the enemy, however, several small nationalities—the Karachay-Balkars, the Chechen-Ingush (whose homes were in the Greater Caucasus), the Buddhist Kalmyks and two larger groups, the Volga Germans (about 1 million) and Crimean Tatars (about 250,000)—were deprived of the symbols of nationhood and inhumanly deported to the Asian hinterland where they died in large numbers, while other peoples, in particular the Ukrainians, were held in suspicion by the central authorities.

The pattern of conquest and coercion followed by the Soviet heirs to Russian imperialism thus differs little outwardly from that of other imperialisms. Nonetheless, up to 50 years of centralised rule has resulted in a new type of colonialism in which the colonies, for all their cultural distinctiveness, are more efficiently integrated on the whole than was the case of the overseas empires of the European Powers. There is no doubt that the more backward peoples of the Soviet Union (such as the recently feudal Central Asians and the tribal societies of Siberia) have profited substantially from Slav supremacy in terms of economics, communications, social welfare and literacy and it is a fact that material advances in non-Russian areas have often surpassed those in many regions of Russia itself.

Nationalities Policy

Against this background of repression and forcible integration, of national stimulus and material progress, a consistent post-war nationalities policy is not easily discerned. The frequent changes of emphasis in fact reflect the ambiguity of simultaneously national and multinational evolution and the conflicting priorities of local and all-union affairs. De-Stalinisation in 1956 seemed to augur a happier epoch for the nationalities and indeed Khrushchev was quick to award a significant number of senior posts to non-Russians and to denounce his predecessor's deportation of small Caucasian peoples and Kalmyks (though at the time the Volga Germans and Crimean Tatars went unmentioned); but in the aftermath of the Hungarian uprising, with the defeat of the 'anti-party' group and the incipient rift with China, all-union interests were put first and enshrined in the resolutions of the Twenty-first CPSU Congress (1959). Since then the party has officially favoured a policy

[1] For an analysis see Zenkovsky, S. A. *Pan-Turkism and Islam in Russia*, Harvard Univ. Press, Cambridge, Mass.; Oxford Univ. Press, London, 1960.

of *sblizhenie* or 'drawing together' of the country's nationalities leading to their *sliyanie*, or merging. Khrushchev declared at the Twenty-second CPSU Congress (1961):

> Communists do not wish to preserve and perpetuate national distinctions. We depend on the natural process of an ever closer fusion of nations and nationalities . . . It is essential that we insist on the education of the masses in the spirit of proletarian internationalism and Soviet patriotism.

The cultural self-expression of the nationalities and intra-national (*mezhnatsionalnye*) relationships are expected to proceed within the supra-national framework of socialism and the Soviet state. Soviet culture should assimilate local cultures in such a way that Khachaturyan be regarded as a Soviet rather than Armenian composer and that Pushkin be as deeply cherished by the Komi or Kirghiz as by the Russians themselves. But how this synthetic 'supra-culture' should accommodate more than 100 languages, literatures, art forms, folk pantheons, mythologies and customs has never been satisfactorily stated.

While scholars and party theoreticians have, in the pages of journals such as *Voprosy istorii*, *Voprosy filosofii* and *Kommunist* debated the merits of *sblizhenie* through all-union planning of culture, national individuality has at the same time been strengthened, according to the formula 'national in form, socialist in content', through devolutionary measures such as the abolition of certain all-union institutions, for example, the all-union Ministries of Justice (1956) and Transport (1957)—abandoned in favour of SSR Ministries—and economic reforms such as the establishment (1957) of semi-autarkic *sovnarkhozy* (economic councils) and regional economic reorganisation (1962), which have served to enhance local independence. Some of these measures have, however, been reversed, the *sovnarkhozy* having been abolished in 1966. There is then an inherent contradiction between policies of *sblizhenie*, assimilation and centralisation on the one hand and national autonomy, federation and decentralisation on the other. Outweighing all theoretical possibilities, however, is the fact of Slav, especially Russian, preponderance—which may predestine all the minorities to merge gradually in a new, undoubtedly composite, culture, but one in which acculturation and ethnic convergence will necessarily favour the majority nation.

THE STATUS OF NATIONALITIES TODAY

How real is the sovereignty of nationalities in the Soviet Union? Politically their autonomy is little more than nominal. Just as SSRs are constitutionally entitled to secede from the union, so have they in theory the right (since 1944) to establish direct diplomatic relations with foreign states and to maintain their own armies. In reality the overall interests of state have precluded any meaningful exercise of these rights[1], and even the post-war Ukrainian and Belorussian membership of the UN has brought little gain except voting power for the Soviet bloc. Since 1957 SSRs have been empowered to form new *kraya* and *oblasti* on their territory but any change involving national units is subject to all-union authority.

Political participation of the nationalities in all-union affairs and within their own national units varies considerably. In all-union government the 1924 constitution awarded each SSR 25 representatives in the Soviet of

[1] See Aspaturian, V. V. *The Union Republics in Soviet Diplomacy*, Librairie E. Droz, Geneva, 1960.

Nationalities; in 1946 the SSRs were given representation in the Praesidium of the USSR Supreme Soviet, the republican presidents thus forming a collective vice-presidency of the all-union Supreme Soviet. Similar representation in the USSR Supreme Court was granted in 1957. Although an analogous formula of nationality quotas for senior party posts does appear to operate, national representation at the higher levels of the CPSU can be erratic, witness the favouritism shown by Stalin to fellow-Georgians (Ordzhonikidze, Beria, etc.), his purges of Jewish membership, Khrushchev's predilection for Ukrainians and a more recent tendency to overrepresent Belorussians. Thus, while several less developed minorities enjoy a minimum 'quota' representation in party and government organs, many larger nationalities such as Georgians, Armenians and especially Jews find the system restrictive. While, for instance, the Jews (constituting 1·09% of the Soviet population, according to official statistics) possessed in 1966 five deputies in the Supreme Soviet, the diminutive Abkhaz people of the northern Caucasus (representing 0·03% of the total Soviet Union population) sent seven deputies.[1]

At the republican level nationality participation in public affairs follows the rough pattern of representation according to ethnic composition of a given republic. By this standard, however, in 1964—to take but one example —Armenians were overrepresented and Estonians underrepresented in new admissions to their respective parties.[2] The republican first secretaryship of the party, a post more symbolic than real, always goes to a native, whereas the second party secretary is more often than not a Slav. Local party committees are of course wholly subordinate to the Moscow leadership, in the SSRs, ASSRs, AOs and NOs as well as at *oblast* level and below. Thus the Belorussian and Turkmen party committees have no greater rights *vis-à-vis* the USSR Central Committee than does the *obkom* of Leningrad or Vladivostok. The chairman of the republican Councils of Ministers and their first deputy chairmen are as a rule indigenous but the critical position of republican KGB chief is traditionally held by a Russian or Ukrainian. Despite lack of statistical evidence, there are clear indications that Slavs also hold a disproportionate number of important posts outside party and government, notably in SSR higher education, in large-scale agriculture (the Kazakh Virgin Lands), in the new industries of traditionally rural areas like Moldavia and in key industries such as Azerbaidzhani oil, Kazakh iron and steel and the Yakut coalfields.

SOVIETISATION OR RUSSIFICATION?

No more easily assessed is the national character of non-Russian cultures— because the ethnic homogeneity of a given national unit can range, as in the case of SSRs, from an 88% majority of the titular inhabitants (Armenia) to a 29·8% minority (Kazakhstan) and because the Soviet policy of *sblizhenie* attempts to shape a new supranational identity based on bilingualism (in the native tongue and Russian) and on the inculcation of neutralising ideas like Soviet patriotism, Soviet morality, 'partymindedness' and atheism. In theory Russian and non-Russian identities are expected to flourish on a horizontal base while constant interassociation will forge a transcendental Soviet consciousness.

[1] Bilinsky, Y. 'The Rulers and the Ruled', *Problems of Communism*, XVI, 5, Wash. D.C., 1967, pp. 23–4.
[2] *Ibid.*, p. 19.

How far has this enforced association affected national individualism? The Russian language, officially promoted as a 'second native tongue', has since 1938 been a compulsory study in all non-Russian general and secondary schools while Russian-language schools in the non-Russian republics have yet fully to implement a provision, confirmed in 1950, that resident Russians study the tongue of the SSR (though not ASSR, AO or NO). More Russians outside the RSFSR are, however, learning minority languages than ten years ago (Georgia and Lithuania being exceptions). Since the social and professional advantages of a complete education in Russian-language general and secondary schools outside the RSFSR are increasingly compelling, it is not surprising that a few nationalities have practically adopted Russian as their first medium. One can mention in this connexion first the Jews, Germans and Poles, who are too unorganised for effective resistance; second the Ukrainians and (especially) Belorussians whose cultures are, through historic contact, closely related to that of Russia (and from a Bashkir or Uzbek viewpoint are barely if at all distinguishable); and thirdly that complex, in the Volga-Urals area, of heterogeneous Turkic and Finnic peoples for whom Russian is a *lingua franca*. By contrast, the national languages of these peoples with a strongly articulated sense of nationhood (Georgians, Armenians, Azerbaidzhanis, Uzbeks, Tadzhiks, the Baltic peoples, etc.) are still the principal medium of commerce, local government, education and culture in their respective territories. Paradoxically, some recently illiterate nationalities like the Mari and Yakut have actually established national literatures under the Soviet aegis whilst for others, such as the Kazakhs and Kirghiz, the largely arbitrary demarcation of republican territories in the 1920s has tended to crystallise and focus local cultures which had previously suffered from diffusion and factionalism. Nonetheless, Russian alone among Soviet languages serves both as a *lingua franca* of the union and as a key to world culture. Bilingualism as an instrument of personal advancement is increasingly necessary for younger generations of non-Russian nationality—but this does not ineluctably spell the rapid decline of native languages.[1]

The viability of a nationality's institutions depends not only on the vigour of its culture but equally on the rights and status endowed upon it by the Soviet state and party. Obvious factors of assimilation and cultural denationalisation must include the imposition of the Cyrillic script upon non-Slav peoples (Armenia, Georgia, and the Baltic SSRs being the main exceptions); a disproportionate majority of Russian-language publications in the Soviet Union (in 1954, for example, 60% of all publications in Belorussia were in Russian, 40% in Belorussian. Corresponding figures for 1965 were 80% and 20%[2]); the proliferation of eleven-year Russian-language schools in the non-Russian SSRs and a general diffusion of Russian culture (through literary translation etc.). To a varying extent native languages have themselves been influenced by Russian, through the absorption of loan words, acronyms and even the Russian naming system. Another erosive element has been the anti-religious campaign, waged almost as intensively against Jews, Muslims, Buddhists, Georgians, Armenians and Catholics as against Russian Orthodoxy and the Russian-speaking Baptists.

[1] One Western analyst is optimistic about the survival of regional languages: H. Lipset 'The Status of National Minority Languages in Soviet Education', *Soviet Studies*, XIX, 2, Glasgow, 1967.
[2] N. P. Vakar, 'The Belorussian People between Nationhood and Extinction' in E. Goldhagen (ed.), *Ethnic Minorities in the Soviet Union*, New York and London, 1968, p. 222.

Personal association between Slav settlers and native peoples is almost invariably a one-way cultural process, although there have been historic cases of Russian political exiles who assume the language and living patterns of Tatars, Yakuts and Mongols. The impact of the Slav colonies in the republics has of course been long established in Russia east of the Urals, in the Crimea, Caucasia and Central Asia but pioneer-type colonies of the late 19th century have evolved during the Soviet period as prototypes of the new Soviet society, melting-pots in which various communities coexist and gradually merge, through daily contact, inter-marriage, common educational and professional forms and an increasingly collective identity. The Russianising trend is only slightly offset by such factors as the higher demographic growth of the nationalities in Caucasia and Central Asia, the reluctance of many natives (especially Muslims) to marry, reside or work outside their traditional milieux, and the tendency of many Slavs to treat the indigenous peoples as less than equal. (Slav segregation in cities such as Tashkent can sometimes even preserve a colonial flavour.)

Russian emigration to non-Russian republics is now such that Russians form a numerical majority in the Kazakh SSR and several lesser units; their propensity for urban settlement has given them, taking extreme instances, a 68% majority in the Kirghiz capital of Frunze and a comparable preponderance in the ASSR capitals of such peoples as the Udmurt and Chechen-Ingush. In many republics (Ukraine, Belorussia, Moldavia and Latvia) the urbanisation of native peoples brings a high degree of social mobilisation (of which Russification is an outstanding factor), and during the inter-census period from 1939 to 1959 the urban population of the Soviet Union as a whole in fact increased by 65%, a trend which is continuing.

THE LIMITS AND POSSIBILITIES OF NATIONALISM

Since a nationalist-organised opposition to the centripetal forces of all-union politics and economics is almost impossible, the expression of component nationalisms is limited mainly to the fields of economic bargaining (for example, over planning and budgetary distribution), cultural, linguistic and educational policy and personal intercourse. Racial discrimination is officially prohibited but there is no doubt that 'Great Russian chauvinism' persists at a personal level in many forms both inside and outside the RSFSR. Instances of professional favouritism towards Russians, of popular bias among settler groups against alien values and culture, of failure to learn the local language, are frequently cited. These may generate inter-racial animosities. At the same time the prevailing economic and cultural habits of a nationality may induce resistance to Sovietisation *per se*—of which Russianisation may or may not be a factor. Peasant hostility to collectivisation in the 1930s, certainly as fierce outside the RSFSR as within, finds a modern counterpart in rural opposition to heavy industry and the extreme reluctance of semi-nomadic peoples (Turkmen, Gypsies, Lapps) and isolated trappers and fishing folk (Evenki, Chukchi) to accept a market economy and sedentary habits.

Censorship and police surveillance work to guarantee the 'socialist content' of non-Russian literatures, and nationalists wishing to express a radical viewpoint must risk the perils of underground or foreign publication. As a rule, elements of local cultures accepted as 'progressive' thrive alongside others in their own territory, as a casual glance at the repertoire of any Central Asian opera house will indicate. The question of what constitutes a 'progressive' national culture is complicated by fluctuations in the party line. In matters of historical interpretation, for example, there have been four distinct periods, the first associated with M. N. Pokrovsky, the doyen of early Soviet historiographers, whose class theory of history focussed on the negative aspects of the Tsarist role in non-Russian territories; the war period after 1940 when epic national heroes (such as Shamil and Kenesary) of non-Russian peoples were rehabilitated in the interests of the Soviet fatherland; a post-war period of repudiation of the separate nationalities approach (leading to purges of nationalist intellectuals and artists) and a post-Stalin period of compromise in which the civilising influence of historic Russian conquest and settlement is considered complementary to the class strivings of the subject peoples.

Russia's 19th-century annexation of Central Asia is currently regarded as beneficent—by virtue of the fact that, by drawing the Central Asians into world markets it transformed their feudal society into a capitalist one and exposed them to the 'advanced culture of the Russian people and their revolutionary struggle'. Furthermore they were thus protected from British colonialism. Russian penetration of the Caucasus three centuries earlier likewise spared indigenous peoples from the 'military-feudal rule of the Ottomans and Safavids'. Similar arguments are advanced to exploit present-day Sinophobe sentiment among Kazakhs, Uighurs and other peoples of the Chinese borderlands, and nationalist issues involving foreign states can indeed serve the need for nationality consolidation. Soviet press response to China's sporadic references to *irredenta* in the Soviet Far East and Central Asia, Stalin's pretensions to Iranian Azerbaidzhan in 1946 and the anti-Turkish feelings manifested in 1965 by Soviet Armenians on the 50th anniversary of the Armenian massacres, are all authorised forms of a nationalism serving to bolster local support for Moscow.

But in the Soviet Union nationalism is a sword with a double edge. The independence of the Baltic, Polish and Finnish states after 1917 and the abortive experiments in Transcaucasia were based on what would today be termed national liberation movements, and more recent events in Jugoslavia (1948), Hungary and Poland (1956) and Czechoslovakia (1968) are proof of a determination to win maximum sovereignty in the outer orbit of Soviet power. The fate of the minority peoples who had assumed anti-Russian postures during World War II suggests just how sensitive the Kremlin is to the continuing existence of nationalist movements within its territory, and it is significant that while the Karachay-Balkars, Chechen-Ingush and Kalmyks were formally rehabilitated in 1957, the Volga Germans and Crimean Tatars were only partially exonerated (in 1964 and 1967 respectively) and have not since been allowed to settle in their former ASSRs despite strong 'underground' national campaigns. We have evidence of continued repression of Crimean Tatars in their Uzbek exile,[1] and their situation gives rise to speculation about that of other unrepresented nationalities such as the 20,000 Assyrians resident in the RSFSR and Armenia.

Nationalism among the bigger minorities is still more burdensome for the authorities. The riots that flared in Tbilisi after Khrushchev's denunciation (1956) of Stalin (who was one of Georgia's own) bore overtones of Georgian insurrection; the 1966–7 trial of the young journalist, Chornovil, and other intellectuals spotlighted the persistence of nationalism in the Ukraine, and the constant repression of organised Jewry is proof that Moscow fears the

---

[1] See *Problems of Communism*, vol XVII, No. 4, 1968, pp. 92–5.

voice of its most articulate minorities. Anti-Semitism has indeed since 1948 been implicit in the frequent purges of dissident Jewish intellectuals, in the gross suppression of religious freedom (Soviet Judaism suffers from a lack of a centralised administrative structure and, like other religions, from an almost total lack of religious literature), in the savage sentences imposed on Jewish economic speculators during the early 1960s and in the continued refusal to allow Jews to maintain their own schools and seminaries. Whilst Jewish membership of the Soviet intelligentsia is disproportionately high (forming 10% of the Academy of Sciences in 1962) and whilst Jews are third only to Russians and Ukrainians in the higher education bracket (in absolute terms), this minority of more than two million is politically underrepresented and permitted but two regular publications. It is therefore not surprising that Soviet Jews are the group with the smallest proportion (21·7%) claiming the language of their nationality (Yiddish) as their mother tongue. Only in Georgia, which boasts 20% of Soviet synagogues, is there a Jewish culture which may at present be depicted as flourishing, although stirrings are evident in Moscow, Leningrad and Vilnius.

It should be added, however, that inter-racial frictions involve not only the Russians. Georgian-Armenian rivalry is proverbial (Armenians constitute 11% of the population of Georgia and are the greatest minority in that SSR); Armenians have lately shown interest in absorbing the small ASSR of Nakhichevan which currently forms an enclave on their territory; Poles in the Ukraine and Belorussia show at least as much resistance to assimilation as Poles in the RSFSR and Central Asia, and anti-Semitism is as prevalent in Moldavia, the Ukraine and Belorussia (where of the total population Jews number 3·3%, 2% and 1·9% respectively) as in the RSFSR (where they represent 0·8%).

THE FUTURE OF SOVIET NATIONALITIES

Those minorities, like the Georgians, Armenians and Baltic peoples and possibly the Ukrainians, which have preserved their ancient and vital cultures and institutions (especially their prestigious churches) are likely to retain their identities in high degree. Central policy makers simply cannot afford to ignore them. The larger of the more recently defined peoples, especially the Central Asians, probably believe that on balance they benefit from their Soviet association. For them exist ready markets for primary products (Tadzhik cotton, etc.) and they are spared the cost of maintaining standing armies and other burdens of genuine sovereignty. It is the less cohesive non-Russian societies, the peoples least resistant to social mobilisation and Russification which are in danger of extinction. It could happen that within a few generations, if present policies are upheld, the Belorussians, Karelians, Ossetes, Yakuts and a host of smaller nationalities will find themselves devoid of anything more than a purely regional identity (like 'Crimean' or 'Siberian' today). For them even the symbols of nationhood will become meaningless.

FURTHER READING

Armstrong, T. *Russian Settlement in the North*, Cambridge Univ. Press, London and New York, 1965.
Conquest, R. *The Soviet Deportation of Nationalities*, Macmillan, London; St. Martin's Press, New York, 1960.
Dzyuba, I. *Internationalism or Russification?*, Weidenfeld and Nicolson, London, 1968.
Geiger, B. et. al. *Peoples and Languages of the Caucasus*, Mouton, The Hague; Humanities Press, New York, 1959.

Goldberg, B. Z. *The Jewish Problem in the Soviet Union*, Crown, New York, 1961.
Goldhagen, E. (ed.) *Ethnic Minorities in the Soviet Union*, Frederick A. Praeger, New York and London 1968.
Kolarz, W. *Peoples of the Soviet Far East*, George Philip, London, 1954.
Lang, D. M. *A Modern History of Georgia*, Weidenfeld and Nicolson, London; Grove Press, New York, 1962.
Matossian, M. *The Impact of Soviet Policies in Armenia*, Brill, Leiden, 1962.
Matthews, W. K. *Languages of the USSR*, Cambridge University Press, Cambridge, 1951.
Nove, A. and Newth, J. A. *The Soviet Middle East*, Allen and Unwin, London, 1967.
Pipes, R. *The Formation of the Soviet Union*, Harvard Univ. Press, Cambridge, Mass., 1964.
Problems of Communism, XVI, 5, Washington, D.C., 1967. (special issue, 'Nationalities and Nationalism in the USSR').
Shtepa, K. *Russian Historians and the Soviet State*, Rutgers Univ. Press, New Brunswick, N. J. 1962.
Wheeler, G. *A Modern History of Soviet Central Asia*, Weidenfeld and Nicolson, London, 1965.

WILLIAM FORWOOD. At present at the Council of Europe engaged on a survey of nationalism and minority problems in Europe and on a history of the Czechoslovak 'national idea'. Has done anthropological study in Bolivia, Peru and Argentina. Author of *Rumanian Invitation*.

THE UKRAINE

VICTOR SWOBODA

CONSTITUTIONAL SOVEREIGNTY

THE Ukrainian Soviet Socialist Republic has a territory of 234,000 sq miles and a population of over 46 million. This figure comprises one-fifth of the total population of all 15 republics of the USSR, and is second only to that of the RSFSR.

In theory, according to the constitution, the Ukraine, like all other republics, is a sovereign national state, belongs to the Union voluntarily and enjoys equality of rights, including that of secession, which right may be neither repealed nor restricted by the Union government. The Ukraine has the right, in theory, to establish its own international relations, which it has exercised only by its representation at the UN since 1958 (Belorussia is the only other Soviet republic also to be represented). The Ukraine also has the right, hitherto unclaimed, to establish its own military formations.

The Republic's sovereign power is theoretically vested in its Supreme Soviet, which appoints the Council of Ministers. Its sovereignty is, however, limited by the fact that all spheres of activity within the jurisdiction of the Union government are outside the Republic's control; a varying number of joint Union-Republican ministries are in fact under the Union's control. Their number had increased by the late 1960s to 24, and they included defence, foreign and internal affairs, trade, finance, the steel, building materials, chemical and food industries, light industries, communications, power, agriculture, health, culture, and higher and technical education. The Republic is solely responsible only for the Ministries of Roads and Road Transport, Housing, Communal Services, Education, and Social Insurance; of the various branches of the economy, only retail trading and public catering come entirely under the Republic's jurisdiction.

These considerable limitations of sovereignty are compounded by the fact that the Communist Party of the Ukraine (CPU) is accurately described in Soviet documents as 'the leading power of the society and State of the Ukraine'. As the CPU forms part of the CPSU, and has no programme or policy of its own, and is entirely controlled by the CPSU leadership, the supreme *de facto* power over the Ukraine rests with the CPSU leadership in Moscow.

ECONOMIC ROLE

The Ukraine has considerable natural resources. The Donbas coalfields have recently been expanded, and in the Lvov-Volynia region another has been discovered; oil, hitherto drilled only in the western Ukraine, has been struck in several eastern regions and in the Crimea. Vast natural gas sources have been discovered in the east. There is iron ore in Krivoy Rog and Kerch, and manganese in the middle Dnieper area.

The Ukraine has well-developed industries (the chemical industry has expanded particularly fast in the 1950s and 1960s) and a diversified agriculture. Gross output in the key industries approaches and, in certain cases, exceeds that of advanced European countries. In 1965 the Ukraine produced more pig-iron than any other European country, more steel than the UK or France, and was second only to the UK in coal mining. Per capita the Ukraine's production of iron, steel and iron ore leads the world.

The part played by Ukrainian industry within the Soviet Union is considerable; it accounts for some 50% of the pig iron, iron ore and coke output, over 40% of steel and nearly half of metallurgical equipment. The Ukraine also exports much agricultural produce. On balance, in various ways it contributes more to the USSR exchequer than it receives from it.[1]

PRE-SOVIET HISTORY

The Ukrainians, the southern branch of the Eastern Slavs, are descended from the inhabitants of the south-western regions of the 9th to 13th century Kiev state; these regions, comprising the Dnieper valley and the principalities of Kiev, Galicia and Volynia, passed in the 14th century to the Grand Duchy of Lithuania and the Kingdom of Poland, while the north-eastern principalities together with their future centre, Moscow, were subjugated in the 13th to 15th centuries by the Golden Horde.

From the 15th century growing numbers of peasants and serfs, as well as burghers and nobles, chiefly Ukrainians, chose the free life of hunting and fishing in the no-man's land of the south Ukrainian steppes. They had to fend off the Crimean Tatars' encroachments, and soon organised themselves into an independent military-political force. The Polish government attempted to put the Cossacks (as they came to be called) under its control, but in the 17th century they led a successful Ukrainian rebellion against the Polish overlordship, which was oppressive both socially and economically and because of the militancy of the Jesuits. The Cossacks were led by Hetman Bohdan Khmelnytsky, who set up the Cossack State and concluded a treaty with the co-religionist, Muscovy, in 1654. For the following 50 years the Cossack State was only loosely tied to Muscovy, and the elective Hetmans were virtually independent sovereigns. This independence was, however, gradually eroded by the Muscovite Tsars, and so in 1708-9 Hetman Ivan Mazeppa tried to break away by siding with Charles XII of Sweden, against Peter the Great; Peter's victory was the beginning of the end of Ukrainian autonomy.

The culture of the Ukraine followed on from that of the Kievan middle ages, but it was also subject to strong Western influences through Poland. In the 17th century the Ukraine contributed greatly to the education and culture of Muscovy, whilst its own population had a very high level of

---

[1] No complete balance sheets of the financial relationships between the Ukrainian SSR and the Soviet Union budget have been published; among the chief unknown quantities are the Ukraine's share of the Union administration and defence costs, of income from transport undertakings, and of 'hidden' payments in the form of the supply of goods to other republics at less than cost price. Nevertheless, comparison of incomplete balance sheets suggests that some republics receive more from the Union exchequer than they contribute, and others vice versa.

literacy. Educational standards were also maintained in the following century; in the 1740s there was one school with Ukrainian as the language of instruction for every 746 persons. The loss of autonomy was followed by increasing obstacles throughout the 19th century on printing and instruction which resulted in 1897 in a drastic drop in literacy to 13%. Some of these restrictions were imposed in reaction to the Ukrainian revival led by the poet, Taras Shevchenko (1814–61). Many restrictions were swept away by the 1905 revolution, but new repressions soon followed.

The Ukrainian Central Rada (Council), established on 17 March 1917, proclaimed on 20 November the independent Ukrainian People's Republic. The Central Rada did not recognise the Bolshevik regime recently established in Russia. On 25 December a Bolshevik Soviet government was formed in opposition to the Rada and proclaimed the Ukrainian People's Republic to be a federative part of, and actively supported by, the Russian Republic. This government was, however, unable to assert itself against a succession of national Ukrainian governments in a conflict that also involved occupation by the Central Powers, landings of allied expeditionary forces, the campaigns of Denikin's White Russian armies and in 1920 a Polish invasion. On 17 November 1918 a new provisional government of the Ukraine was formed in Moscow by the Central Committee of the Russian Communist Party (Bolsheviks)—RCP(B)—and a Red Army offensive was mounted. On 6 January 1919 the Ukrainian Socialist Soviet Republic was proclaimed, and on 10 March its first constitution was adopted, in which the Republic's independence was implied. On 1 June 1919, by Lenin's directive, a military alliance was formed between all the Soviet republics (Russia, the Ukraine, Belorussia, Latvia and Lithuania). The eventual frontier between the Soviet Union and Poland left a six-million strong Ukrainian minority in Poland.

The Soviet Ukraine: The Drive Against Ukrainian Nationalism

The Red Army had finally gained the Ukraine for the Bolsheviks by March 1920. When under pressure from Lenin the Comintern dissolved the Ukrainian Communist Party (UCP or Borotbists)—a national Communist Party founded in 1919 which stood for a completely independent communist Ukraine and whose strength rivalled that of the Communist Party (Bolsheviks) of the Ukraine or CP(B)U—a large section of it joined the latter party and contributed to its pursuance of policies directed towards the safeguarding of the interests of the Ukrainian Republic and its people and the policy of 'Ukrainisation'. The new Ukrainian government concluded a military and economic union treaty with the RSFSR in which the parties acknowledged their mutual independence and sovereignty. The Ukrainian SSR was a sovereign state, recognised by several European countries including the UK, and having diplomatic representatives in six.

The Soviet Union was formed, according to Lenin's plan, as 'a union of equals' on 30 December 1922, and the union treaty, at the Ukrainian SSR's insistence, included the right to secede for each member republic (Article 17 of the present constitution). Yet there were no provisions for redress against any violation of a republic's sovereignty, and CP(B)U delegates were unsuccessful in their demands for such at the 1923 RCP(B) Congress.

The industrialisation of the Soviet Union brought with it a speedy collectivisation of agriculture. In 1929 the Ukraine was selected 'to provide an example in the shortest time', and those who resisted were exiled, imprisoned or killed, in all 650,000 men, women and children, whilst another 350,000 fled from the villages. The speed of the collectivisation without the necessary machinery and the exorbitant demands for grain from Moscow culminated in the catastrophic famine of 1932–3. A Soviet Union law authorising the OGPU to shoot on sight anyone who attempted 'to steal socialist property' was applied throughout the Ukraine, sometimes against starving children. It has been estimated that not less than 10% of the population, some three to five million, may well have perished in the famine.

Collectivisation of agriculture was accompanied by increased attacks on 'Ukrainian bourgeois nationalism' with mass arrests, mostly secret trials and sentences to long terms in concentration camps. Most were accused of belonging to organisations (actually fictitious) working towards the restoration of a bourgeois-democratic independent Ukraine. Although lip-service was paid to Lenin's declaration that 'a distinction must necessarily be made between the nationalism of an oppressor nation and that of an oppressed nation', and although it was constantly reaffirmed at Moscow party congresses (attended by delegates from all the Soviet republics) until 1930 that Great Russian chauvinism was the chief menace to communism, in fact there were no prosecutions for Russian chauvinism, whilst thousands were deported on charges of 'Ukrainian bourgeois nationalism'. In November 1933 the party line was reversed, Ukrainisation was replaced by a drive to Soviet patriotism and Ukrainian nationalism declared to be the main threat to communism.

The OGPU terror of 1929–33 was not directed against non-communists alone; any manifestations of 'national communism' were also punished. When the CP(B)U leaders repeatedly appealed to Moscow to alleviate the 1932–3 famine by reducing grain delivery quotas from the Ukraine, the Central Committee of the CPSU(B) refused, accused the CP(B)U leadership of nationalism, blamed it for the non-fulfilment of the quotas, and a new wave of OGPU terror was unleashed. Between 1 June 1932 and 1 October 1933 75% of officials of local soviets and 80% of the local party committee secretaries were dismissed, and by late 1934 half of the CP(B)U's 520,000 rank and file were purged. Most were shot or exiled. There were also mass arrests amongst intellectuals. The OGPU fabricated charges of 'nationalism'[1] against the victims, while the real purpose of the terror was to exterminate even the potentially nationally minded leadership.

The secret police terror, after some slackening, intensified after October 1936 when Yezhov became its chief, reaching unprecedented proportions. By late 1938 nearly one million people in the Ukrainian SSR had been imprisoned, sent to concentration camps or shot. They were mostly Ukrainian intellectuals of the new Soviet school, officials, technicians, and others including many CP(B)U members. The highest CP(B)U bodies were wiped out; of the 115 Central Committee members elected in 1934, only 36 remained in May 1937, when the Thirteenth Congress elected a new Central Committee of 102 members; of these, only three remained in March 1938, while of the entire Politburo only one member survived in exile. The break in the continuity of leadership was absolute.

With Khrushchev, who arrived early in 1938 from Moscow with new men to fill the void, came a more militant policy of Russification, while the CP(B)U became merely a local branch of the CPSU(B).

[1] Though regularly punishable by death or concentration camp since about 1930, this offence has never been defined in Soviet law.

The Ukraine had barely begun to recover from one blood-bath before it was plunged into another with the devastation and losses suffered in World War II. Two million Jews were exterminated; deaths at the front and in German prisoner-of-war and forced labour camps, mass German reprisals against the civilian population and executions of resistance members and guerrillas accounted for at least another two million dead. These matched the 1930–38 'peacetime' human losses. Ukrainian nationalist partisans were destroyed both by the German army and, right into the 1950s, by the Soviet army.

After the war, Russification continued unabated. The Russian population of the Ukrainian SSR increased from 8·1% in 1926 to 16·9% in 1959; moreover, 6·5% of Ukrainians (who comprised 76·8% of the total population) gave Russian as their native language in the 1959 census, while non-Russian minorities are mostly Russian-speaking. Of the total Ukrainian SSR population, 73% gave Ukrainian as their native language and 24% Russian. Four-fifths of all Russians, and most other Russian speakers, live in cities and towns, where practically all administration, industry, trade and further education have been Russified. New campaigns against alleged Ukrainian nationalism were launched in 1946–7 and in 1951–53.

After Stalin's death the Central Committee of the CPU in June 1953 criticised Russification for the first time since the 1920s, and removed the first secretary, L. Melnikov, for having pursued it. A. Kirichenko was appointed in his place—the first Ukrainian to occupy this post since the founding of the CP(B)U/CPU in 1918. Protests against the Russification of education and culture penetrated—although only for a few months—into the Kiev press.

CONSTITUTIONALIST AND SECESSIONIST MOVEMENTS OF THE LATE 1950s AND 1960s

For the first time since the Ukrainian 'national communist' trends of the 1920s there were constitutionalist opposition attempts, all savagely suppressed by the KGB. In 1961, for example, seven men (three of them jurists, four CPSU members) who had planned the formation of a Ukrainian Workers' and Peasants' Union (UWPU) were tried for 'attempted separation of the Ukrainian SSR'. Their draft programme severely criticised, from the Marxist-Leninist standpoint, the party and government policies during the famine and the terror of the 1930s, the shortcomings of the post-Stalin period, economic bureaucracy, oppression of the peasants and the policy of Russification. It concluded that in order to develop normal statehood the Ukraine must secede by implementing Article 17 of the Soviet constitution. To this end the UWPU was peacefully and constitutionally to conduct secessionist propaganda and ask the Ukrainian SSR Supreme Soviet for a referendum. If the majority favoured secession, an independent Ukraine would still be a Soviet-type socialist state, staying within the socialist commonwealth and evolving towards communism; it would be a Ukraine 'in which all citizens could effectively enjoy their political freedoms and determine the direction of the Ukraine's economic and political development', and the UWPU's immediate aim was to be 'the gaining of democratic freedoms'. The draft's final words were: 'The triumph of Soviet law will also be our triumph'.

It seems from the data available (which may well be far from complete) that at least five or ten persons have stood political trial every year since 1956, some 70 in 1961–2, and 20 in 1966. There have been some death sentences, but most have ranged from between five and 15 years in prison camps. With the exception of two theoretically public trials early in 1966 and one in 1967, all the others have been secret, in complete violation of Soviet legislation.

Manuscript Literature

Since 1962–3 much literature, both signed and anonymous, has been circulating in manuscript in the Ukraine. It comprises a variety of genres: poetry, polemical pamphlets, transcripts of speeches at public functions, letters to editors and petitions to authorities (including those from political prisoners writing from prisons and camps). The authors protest against Russification and the breaking of Soviet laws by the KGB and the judiciary, and defend the rights of non-Russians to equality and independence. It was the production and dissemination of such literature which led to most of the charges of anti-Soviet nationalist propaganda in the 1965–6 arrests and trials of Ukrainian intellectuals. Arguments are usually based on Marxism-Leninism, the Soviet constitution and law. Among the most revealing and remarkable of such documents are *The Chornovil Papers*, a thorough examination of the 1965–6 arrests and trials; they expose numerous transgressions against 'Socialist legality' and condemn the trials themselves as anti-Soviet and anti-communist. For this protest, V. Chornovil was sentenced to three years' imprisonment, commuted under a general amnesty to 18 months. Another outstanding work is I. Dzyuba's *Internationalism or Russification?* originally submitted, following the same arrests, as a memorandum to the party and government in the Ukraine; it is an excellently documented indictment of the present-day Russian chauvinism, which, Dzyuba maintains, is a force working both against the principles of the Leninist nationalities policy and against present historical trends.

Russification of Ukrainian Culture

In the specifically national field of culture the Ukraine's position in the Soviet Union is decidedly inferior to that of most other republics. The disastrous effect upon literacy of the 19th-century restrictions on printing and teaching in Ukrainian has been mentioned; much was done after the creation of the Ukrainian SSR to establish education in Ukrainian at all levels, but since the mid-1930s Russification of all education has been under way. The process is least advanced in general education schools where the percentage of pupils in Ukrainian schools was 73% in 1958, being the same as the percentage of population who stated Ukrainian to be their native language in the 1959 census; but by 1965 only 66% of all pupils went to Ukrainian schools. This noticeable drop may be only partly accounted for by the continued trend in the Ukrainian population at large to adopt Russian as their native language, for this process could hardly have proceeded so fast; it is rather caused by administrative and economic pressures.

Schools in cities and towns are being Russified the most; Ukrainian schools which served solid Ukrainian settlements in other parts of the Soviet Union until the mid-1930s were liquidated under Stalin and have not yet been restarted. By contrast, Russians have more than ample numbers of Russian schools in every non-Russian republic. (Armenians are the only nationality partially to share this privilege outside Armenia.) All professional, secondary technical and higher education, about 50% Ukrainian in the early 1930s, has now been almost completely Russified (this, in varying degrees, also applies to other republics). A quota system, and possibly unofficial preferential measures, have the effect that throughout the non-compulsory sector of education the percentage of Russians and Estonians is always above, and the percentage of Ukrainians, Belorussians and Moldavians below their respective percentages of the total Soviet population. Thus in 1959–60 there were 482 students in higher education per 100,000 Ukrainians, and 732 students per 100,000 Russians. Moreover, in the Soviet Union there is inequality extending only within certain separate sectors of non-compulsory education (in addition to the five permanently 'most' and 'least favoured' nationalities just mentioned); the share of the following is in excess of their population ratio: the Lithuanians in secondary technical education, the Kazakhs, Georgians and Armenians in higher education, and in postgraduate studies all of these, except the Kazakhs, plus the Uzbeks, Azerbaidzhanis, Latvians, Kirgiz, Tadzhiks and Turkmens. And while the Ukrainians in the Soviet Union are far from enjoying the equality of opportunity in higher education, in 1967 30% of all students in the Ukraine came from outside the republic.

An objective indication of the position of a national culture may be found in its book publishing figures. In 1966, while 5·4 copies of books were produced per head of the population of the Soviet Union, the language ratios per head varied considerably between the republics. Thus, per Estonian in Estonia there were 9·3 books in his language; the Latvians with 7·5 were also well above average; the Lithuanians were only just below average, with 4·9 books per head; the others ranged between 3·9 (Georgians) and 2·3 (Kirgiz and Ukrainians), with the Belorussians lowest with 1·1. If it is assumed that book consumption in all republics (except Latvia and Estonia) is around the average, the lower figures quoted may be assumed to be made up by a correspondingly larger import of Russian books, and may be seen as a measure of the Russification of any given republic. Thus, by this criterion, Russification is most advanced in Belorussia and the Ukraine. Nor is the low number of Ukrainian books due to low readership demand: there are constant complaints about editions being insufficient and books sold out immediately upon publication. Editions are, in fact, kept artificially low by a central authority in Moscow allocating a disproportionately low total of paper to the Ukrainian SSR. Such discrimination has developed immensely since 1930; in 1966 only half the number of Ukrainian book titles and four-fifths of copies were published, compared with those produced in 1930, whilst the Ukrainian population of the Republic had meantime increased (mainly owing to the annexation of the Western Ukraine) by some 20%. During the same time, the total Soviet book production in all languages grew to 143% of book titles and 145% of copies. Russian-language figures, if analysed separately, would show an even steeper increase, thus reflecting, in conjunction with the drop in Ukrainian-language publishing, the progress of Russification between 1930 and 1966.

Ukrainian-language publishing compares unfavourably also with that of smaller and economically much less developed neighbouring communist states. Thus, in 1966 Poland produced 7,200 book titles, Rumania 6,400, Hungary 5,400, Bulgaria 3,500, while the Ukrainian SSR produced 3,021 titles in Ukrainian.

The Ukraine's membership of the Soviet Union, conducive to the development of Ukrainian culture until 1930, could well be argued to be against Ukrainian interests in the present conditions. The advances in economic development, education and contacts with the outside world are unavoidably generating increasing strivings towards greater freedom and demands for human rights, which are inseparable from national rights. These strivings to assert the national identity are particularly pronounced among the young post-Stalin generation of Ukrainians. The central Soviet authorities are responding to this with new repressions, since the CPSU is pledged to the principle of amalgamation, i.e. the *de facto* Russification of all non-Russians. These repressions may meet with increasing resistance and so snowball towards a Stalinist-type terror, although its extremes may well be avoided, even if only on account of the immense harm it would again produce by dangerously disrupting the life of important parts of the Soviet Union. What is at issue is the principle of the self-determination of nations, a principle advocated by Marxism-Leninism.

FURTHER READING

Armstrong, J. A. *Ukrainian Nationalism*, Columbia Univ. Press, New York and London, 1963.
Bilinsky, Yaroslav. *The Second Soviet Republic: The Ukraine after World War II*, Rutgers Univ. Press, New Brunswick, N. J., 1964.
Borys, Jurij. *The Russian Communist Party and the Sovietization of Ukraine. A Study in the Communist Doctrine of the Self-Determination of Nations*, Norstedt and Soner, Stockholm, 1960.
Browne, Michael (ed.) *Ferment in the Ukraine. Documents by V. Chornovil, I. Kandyba, L. Lukyanenko, V. Moroz and Others*, Macmillan, London, 1970.
Chornovil, Vyacheslav. *The Chornovil Papers*, McGraw-Hill, New York and London, 1968.
Dzyuba, Ivan. *Internationalism or Russification?*, Weidenfeld and Nicolson, London, 1968.
Goldhagen, Erich (ed.) *Ethnic Minorities in the Soviet Union*, Frederick A. Praeger, New York and London, 1968.
Kolasky, John. *Education in Soviet Ukraine. A Study in Discrimination and Russification*, Peter Martin Associates, Toronto, 1968.
Kostiuk, Hryhory. *Stalinist Rule in the Ukraine*, Stevens and Sons, London, 1960.
Kubijovyč, Volodymyr (ed.) *Ukraine: A Concise Encyclopaedia*, Univ. of Toronto Press, 1963.
Luckyj, G. S. N. *Literary Politics in the Soviet Ukraine, 1917–34*, Columbia Univ. Press, New York; Oxford Univ. Press, London, 1956.
Manning, C. A. *Twentieth Century Ukraine*, Bookman Associates, New York, 1951.
Reshetar, J. S. *The Ukrainian Revolution, 1917–20. A Study in Nationalism*, Princeton Univ. Press, Princeton, N. J.; Oxford Univ. Press, London, 1952.
Sullivant, R. S. *Soviet Politics and the Ukraine, 1917–57*, Columbia Univ. Press, New York, 1962.
'The Ukrainians', *Problems of Communism*, Washington, XVI, 5, September–October 1967 (Special Issue: 'Nationalities and Nationalism in the USSR').

VICTOR SWOBODA. Lecturer in Russian and Ukrainian at the School of Slavonic and East European Studies, University of London. Editor of T. Shevchenko's selected poetry, *Song Out of Darkness*, 1961 and contributor to reviews of Ukrainian studies, both in language and literature.

THE BALTIC REPUBLICS

JĀNIS SAPIETS

Up to 1918

As all countries situated at the crossroads between great and aggressive powers, the Baltic republics have had a turbulent history. Forming a natural gateway for the tidal waves of expansion from the East and West, they have been for centuries subject to almost unbearable political and cultural pressures.

The earlier history of Estonia and Latvia was dominated by the German crusading knights who established their rule over the pagan Estonian and Latvian tribes during the 11th and 12th centuries. The Estonians and the Latvians, denied all political rights, were gradually reduced to the status of serfs. Their languages were suppressed, and they were denied any participation in the administration of their local affairs. On the other hand, the harsh feudal rule of the Baltic barons and the complete lack of contact between the native population and their conquerors—described as fatal even by the Baltic-German historians—effectively prevented the assimilation of the Latvians and Estonians with their German masters. The native population retained its national consciousness—a factor which proved to be of decisive importance when, several centuries later, after World War I, the Baltic nations were given the opportunity to regain their independence. After a brief interlude of a much more enlightened Swedish rule in the 17th century, the Baltic provinces—Courland, Livonia and Estland—were finally annexed by Russia in the 18th century. Throughout this time and until World War I, the Baltic-German nobles retained, however, their political and economic power.

Lithuania, with a more highly developed ethnic-political community, was in a better position to show an effective resistance to the Teutonic knights and never experienced a direct invasion of its territory. In the 14th and 15th centuries, the Lithuanians captured a number of Russian principalities, and the Lithuanian state extended at one time from the Baltic to the Black Sea. In 1386 the Lithuanian monarch entered into a personal union with the Polish king and in 1410, at the Battle of Tannenberg, the combined Lithuanian, Polish and Russian forces completely annihilated the Teutonic order. Gradually, however, Lithuania came under Polish cultural and political influence, losing finally its independence in 1795 as a result of the division of Poland by Russia and the central German states. Thus, by the end of the 18th century, all the three Baltic nations found themselves under Russian rule.

The Period of Independence 1918–40

The national and social ferment of the 19th century did not leave the Baltic sector undisturbed. The Russian Revolution of 1905 found its violent expression in the 'Baltic provinces' under the red flags of the political parties of the left, but it was also an occasion for national struggle against the ancient oppressors, the Baltic barons. The demands for national independence, formulated and proclaimed towards the end of World War I, were the logical outcome of this struggle. When Germany and Russia crumbled in defeat and disorder, the Baltic nations were presented with a unique opportunity which they did not hesitate to grasp: in 1918, three independent Baltic states were established—Lithuania, Estonia and Latvia.

In 1920, the Soviet Union signed peace treaties with the three governments, forever renouncing all claims to these territories. As events proved, these promises were dictated more by expediency than sincerity.

Independence was greeted with an exuberant optimism which expressed itself in an almost unlimited political liberalism: the Baltic republics modelled their political systems on what seemed for them an ideal democracy. Proportional representation and powerful parliaments produced literally scores of small splinter parties, and this, in turn, resulted in weak governments. With the general tendency of some of the most powerful European states to gravitate towards the centralisation of power, and with two totalitarian giants on their borders, the Baltic republics discovered that the pressures were too great. In the face of these pressures, democracy crumbled and in the 1930s authoritarian regimes were established in all three Baltic republics.

The traditional orientation towards the Western democracies, especially the UK and France, was never in question. English and French were the principal foreign languages in secondary schools: in Riga, for instance, there was an English Institute for teachers, an English Grammar School and a French Lycée. In the bookshops one could obtain the latest London or Paris editions of best-sellers without any restrictions, and the central newspaper kiosks displayed on their stands publications from all over Europe, including the Moscow *Pravda* and *Izvestiya*.

Culturally the Baltic capitals were lively international centres, and Riga, true to its old Hanseatic traditions, remained one of the most important Baltic ports, a curious and stimulating mixture of national and international elements, of the past and the present.

The Western orientation of the Baltic republics was equally noticeable in the field of economics. After World War I and the Soviet invasion in 1918–9, the economic life of the countries was completely disrupted. Industries had to be built up practically out of nothing, and the new states had to prove themselves capable of competing on the European markets. In this they showed remarkable progress, especially with regard to agricultural production, and the export of dairy and meat products indicated a continuous tendency to expand. The main trading partners were the UK and Germany. In 1938, the direction of foreign trade was as follows: UK, imports 20%, exports 41·9%; Germany, imports 38·9%, exports 29·5%; USA, imports 6·3%, exports 1·4%; the Soviet Union, imports 3·5%, exports 3%.

Agriculture received a considerable boost as a result of radical land reforms in the early 1920s. The vast German estates were broken up and their lands distributed to the peasants. The social revolution, brought about by the land reform, may be seen from the following figures for Latvia.

TABLE 1

	Landowners and their families	Landless
	(%)	(%)
1897	38·8	61·2
1925	70·9	29·1
1930	76·8	23·2

Among the other exports, the most important were timber (up to 30% or 40% of the total export value) and flax. The Baltic industries were based on private enterprise, but the cooperative movement was well developed, and considerable sectors of export industries (i.e. timber) were state-controlled.

Given time and normal conditions of growth, the Baltic republics might well have reached the living standards of, for example, Denmark, but by now this is no more than speculation. World War II brought new invasions from East and West, reducing the Baltic states once again to the status of colonial provinces.

OCCUPATION 1940 AND AFTERWARDS

The Molotov-Ribbentrop Pact of 1939 gave the Germans a free hand in the West and allowed the Soviet Union to complete what the Soviet leaders had unsuccessfully tried to do 20 years earlier: to establish communist regimes in the Baltic republics.

In October 1939 the Soviet Union demanded the establishment of Soviet military bases in Estonia, Latvia and Lithuania, offering in exchange mutual assistance pacts to 'guarantee' Baltic independence. Unable to resist on their own and aware of their political isolation, the Baltic republics complied with the Soviet demands.

In June 1940 the Soviet Union accused the three Baltic governments of failing to implement the terms of the mutual assistance pacts. In ultimatums presented to the three governments on three successive days, the Soviet Union demanded the admission to their territories of as many troops as were required to ensure 'an honest implementation' of the mutual assistance pacts. Once again, the Baltic governments felt that they had no choice but to accept the demands. On 15 to 17 June, beginning with Lithuania, the Soviet troops moved in to occupy the three countries. The independence of the Baltic states was over.

The process of Sovietisation of the Baltic republics was interrupted by the German invasion in 1941, but continued after the reentry of the Soviet troops in 1944–5. Despite the changes in the social, political and economic structure since the loss of independence the Baltic nations have at the same time still preserved their national characteristics and their basically Western culture. For the 'real' Soviet citizen, born and brought up under the Soviet rule, travelling to the Baltic republics is like going abroad. This is probably what attracts so many Soviet tourists to Estonia, Latvia and Lithuania.

THE BALTIC ECONOMY

The development of the Baltic economy has been characterised by the speed of industrialisation. This, in turn, has changed the social structure of the nations. The formerly agricultural countries have now been transformed into highly industrial communities. Estonia and Latvia have at present the highest percentage of urban population in the Soviet Union. In 1939 34% of the Estonian population lived in towns; in 1965 the urban population was 64% of the total. In Latvia the corresponding figures are 35% for 1939, and 63% for 1967. The growth of the urban population in Lithuania has been somewhat slower: from about 30% in 1939 to 44·7% in 1966.

The immediate result of rapid industrialisation was a decline in agricultural production. Thus, the area under grain crops decreased in Lithuania from 65·6% in 1940 to 43·8% in 1958 and to 42·8% in 1965. In Latvia the corresponding figures were 57·6% in 1940 and 35·6% in 1958, showing a slight improvement (40%) in 1965. The production of grain crops fell in Latvia from 1·4 million tons in 1940 to a catastrophic 444,000 tons in 1958, rising again to 946,000 tons in 1965. It is true that during this time there was a considerable increase in fodder crop production (from 20·8% to 44·2% in Lithuania, and from 31% to 46·9% in Latvia), but it is clear that in the 1950s Baltic agriculture went through a difficult time. More recently much has been done to improve the situation, and the Soviet press has frequently praised Baltic farming. Estonia, in particular, has been singled out as the most efficient agricultural country outside the Soviet black-soil region.

There is little doubt, however, that the emphasis in the Baltic republics will be laid on the development of heavy and medium industries. According to the directives concerning the 1966–70 Five Year Plan, issued by the Twenty-third Congress of the CPSU, Lithuania is to increase her industrial output 1·7 times, and Latvia and Estonia 1·5 times. The rate of Baltic industrial development is already higher than anywhere else in the Soviet Union.

In Estonia, heavy industry is centred on oil shale production which provides 75% (15·8 million tons) of all Soviet oil shale, and 70% of the total Soviet artificial gas output. Fuel oil and petrol are among the other useful by-products. This industry has a special importance for the Soviet west and north-west where there are no deposits of oil, coal or natural gas, and where the development of hydroelectric power is lagging far behind the rest of the Soviet Union. Since oil shale provides fuel for power stations, Estonia is rapidly turning into a power base for the entire north-western region of the Soviet Union. Gas from Estonia is piped to Leningrad, and oil shale provides raw material for a number of chemical by-products: gasoline, sulphur, hyposulphate, phenol. Estonia supplies also electric power to Leningrad, Latvia and Lithuania.

Latvia, with no mineral deposits of its own, produces 130,000 tons of steel per year, 20% of all Soviet railroad passenger cars, 47% of all automatic telephone exchanges, 24% of all radio receivers, 47% of all motor-cycles, 12% of all washing machines and over 60% of all matches exported by the Soviet Union.

In Lithuania there is a similar range of industrial products, but a new and important item was added in 1968 in the discovery of oil in the district of Klaipēda. According to preliminary estimates, there is a large oil field under parts of Lithuania, Latvia, Kaliningrad region (formerly East Prussia), Poland and the Baltic Sea. If this is confirmed, it may well bring new and important industries to the Baltic republics.

These large-scale industrial developments require considerably more man-power than is available locally. By 1965 the number of industrial workers and white-collar workers employed in industries amounted to 15·8% in Estonia and to 15·1% in Latvia, compared to the 11·7% average for the Soviet Union as a whole. This demand for extra manpower has had a considerable effect on the population problems in the Baltic republics.

TABLE 2

POPULATION AND DEMOGRAPHIC CHANGES

Population (ooos)	1939	1959	1967
Estonia . .	1,052	1,197	1,273
Latvia . .	1,885	2,093	2,285
Lithuania . .	2,880	2,711	3,050

The above figures give no indication of the vast population changes which the Baltic nations have experienced during the 28 years from 1940–68. To obtain the true picture, one must take into account three main factors: mass deportations to the Soviet Union, emigration to the West, and the influx of Russians from the East. According to the available estimates, in 1941 and 1945–51 over half a million Baltic nationals were deported to Siberia as suspected enemies of the Soviet regime—mainly intellectuals, politically active workers and farmers considered to be unsuitable for integration in the collective farming system. Only a small percentage of these were allowed to return home in the 1950s.

After the war, about 250,000 Estonians, Latvians and Lithuanians elected to stay in the West where they had arrived as refugees in 1944 and 1945. At least as many, and possibly even twice the number, perished during the war or were put to death by the Nazis. This would mean a loss of over a million people out of the six million total. Even allowing for the natural population increase, the rise of the population figures to the 1967 levels can be explained only by a considerable population influx from outside. This deduction is even more inevitable when one remembers that the birth-rates in Latvia and Estonia are among the lowest in the world (3·8 and 4·2 per thousand, respectively, in 1965).

The demographic changes in the Baltic republics can be seen from the ethnic breakdown of population figures.

TABLE 3

ETHNIC GROUPS IN ESTONIA

	1934 (%)	1959 (%)
Estonians . . .	88·10	74·6
Russians . . .	8·20	20·1
Germans . . .	1·50	—
Swedes . . .	0·65	—
Finns . . .	—	1·4
Ukrainians . . .	—	1·3
Belorussians . . .	—	0·9
Latvians . . .	0·50	0·2
Jews . . .	0·40	0·5
Others . . .	0·65	1·0

Numerically, the Estonians have gone down from 992,000 in 1934 to 893,000 in 1959. The Swedes and Germans were evacuated to their respective countries during the war. The new Finnish minority is accounted for by the resettlement of Karelians in Estonia after World War II. The overall population loss has been more than offset, however, by migrants from other parts of the Soviet Union, particularly Russia.

TABLE 4

ETHNIC GROUPS IN LATVIA

	1935 (%)	1959 (%)
Latvians . . .	75·5	62·0
Russians . . .	12·0	26·6
Belorussians . . .	—	2·9
Poles	2·5	2·9
Jews	4·8	1·7
Germans . . .	3·2	—
Lithuanians . . .	1·2	1·5
Ukrainians . . .	—	1·4
Estonians . . .	0·4	0·2
Others	0·4	0·8

The pattern of population changes in Latvia is basically the same as in Estonia. The Germans were evacuated to Germany in 1939–41, and the Jewish minority suffered a considerable loss during the Nazi occupation. The total number of Latvians has decreased from 1,463,000 in 1935 to 1,298,000 in 1959, but the overall loss of population has been more than compensated by the influx of Russians and other immigrants from the Soviet Union (Belorussians, Ukrainians) who make up now one-third of the present population of Latvia. In Riga the native Latvian population constitutes now a minority of 45% (according to Soviet data of 1965).

TABLE 5

ETHNIC GROUPS IN LITHUANIA

	1936 (%)	1959 (%)
Lithuanians . . .	80	79·3
Russians . . .	—	8·5
Germans . . .	4	—
Poles	3	8·5
Belorussians . . .	—	1·1
Jews	7	0·9
Ukrainians . . .	—	0·7
Others	6	1·0

Lithuania is the only one among the Baltic republics which showed an actual population decrease according to the 1959 census—one more evidence of the heavy population losses during the war. The population loss is further emphasised by the fact that the 1959 figures include the population of Vilnius and its environs which became part of Lithuania in 1940. This accounts also for the increase of the Polish minority. The percentage of native Lithuanians has remained, however, almost unchanged, in spite of the Russian influx (considerably smaller than in Estonia and Latvia). The reasons for this can be found in the slower rate of industrialisation and in the higher Lithuanian birthrate—10·2 in 1965, even though this, too, is smaller than the 14·6 of 1958. Of the other ethnic groups, the Germans, as in the case of Estonia and Latvia, were repatriated to Germany in 1939–41, while the Jewish minority has all but disappeared.

Thus the industrialisation of the Baltic republics has been largely responsible for a sharp drop in the ratio of the native population. At this rate, the

Estonians and the Latvians may find themselves within a few decades minorities in their own countries, with Lithuanians barely holding their own.

RUSSIFICATION AND NATIONALISM

The increase of the Russian-speaking segment of population has naturally brought with it the danger of gradual Russification of the Baltic nations. The publication lists show, for instance, that in Estonia, from 1950–65, the number of Russian titles increased from 25% to 30% of the total for newspapers, from 14% to 25% for magazines, and from 15% to 30% for books. In Latvia this increase was even greater: from 25% to 35% for newspapers, from 24% to 43% for magazines, and from 26% to 45% for books. In Lithuania, the percentage of Russian titles was considerably lower (13% in 1950, and 14% in 1963 for newspapers).

The same tendency manifests itself in education. Not only are the school curricula identical with those in the rest of the Soviet Union, but special bilingual schools have been introduced in the Baltic republics, especially in Latvia. In these schools, classes are taught separately in Russian and in the native languages, but under the same roof. In 1967, there were 240 such schools in Latvia out of a total of some 1,500.

As for the cultural life in the Baltic republics, every effort is being made to root out all Western influences and to replace them by pro-Russian themes, both in art and in literature. The works of a number of pre-1940 writers have been banned or have appeared in heavily expurgated editions.

The net result of these pressures, however, has been the opposite of what the Soviet leaders probably expected: nationalist attitudes in the Baltic republics have not disappeared but have apparently infected even the younger generation, brought up on Soviet textbooks and deprived of all contacts with abroad.

The first secretary of the Central Committee of the Communist Party of Lithuania, Antanas Snečkus, has frequently condemned certain groups of the population 'who have not yet freed themselves from nationalist survivals'. In 1958 he warned the restless intellectuals that there was no third road: Lithuania must either remain in union with the Soviet Union or it would fall prey to the imperialists. A year later, the rector of Vilnius University, Juozas Boulavas, was dismissed from his post and expelled from the party for an alleged display of nationalist prejudices.

In Latvia Edvards Berklavs, at the time deputy chairman of the Latvian Council of Ministers, was dismissed in 1959 for advocating 'national isolation and economic self-sufficiency', thus weakening 'the bond of friendship' between the Latvian and Russian peoples. He and several other party leaders were replaced by Latvians born or trained in Russia. Among them were Arvids Pelše (now a member of the CPSU Politburo), Elmārs Bēmanis (born 1926 in Moscow), and the present first secretary of the Latvian Communist Party, Augusts Voss. The second secretary is a Russian, N. A. Belukha.

A similar purge took place in Estonia in 1950 when the first secretary of the party, Nikolai Karotamm, and several other officials, were dismissed for having displayed 'bourgeois nationalism'. Johannes Käbin, an Estonian from Russia, assumed the position of first secretary and has kept it ever since. The second secretary, Artur Vader, was born in Belorussia and first sent to Estonia in 1948. Another Estonian from Russia, Aleksei Muurisepp, is chairman of the Estonian Supreme Soviet. One of the few Estonians of non-Russian background holding a top post is the deputy chairman of the Estonian Council of Ministers, Arnold Veimer.

The pressure of Russification is reflected also in the party membership. In 1967 the Latvian Communist Party had a membership of 110,865. Of these only 49,559 (45%) were Latvians, while the majority was composed of Russians and others. The proportion of native nationals in Estonia and Lithuania is higher (about 60% and 70%, respectively), but still considerably below their population ratio.

These inner tensions and flashes of Baltic nationalism acquire considerable significance in the wider context of unrest in the Ukraine and in Eastern Europe. There is sufficient evidence to indicate that nationalism and the urge for self-determination in areas under the Soviet domination are not spent forces yet. It may well be that the political map of Eastern Europe, and this includes the Baltic republics, is due for some more changes in the years to come.

FURTHER READING

Consultative Assembly Report on the Situation in the Baltic States, Council of Europe, 1960.
Goldhagen, Erich. (ed.) *Ethnic Minorities in the Soviet Union*, Frederick A. Praeger, New York and London, 1968.
Raud, V. *Estonia: A Reference Book*, The Nordic Press, New York, 1953.
Rutkis, Janis. (ed.) *Latvia: Country and People*, Latvian National Foundation, Stockholm, 1967.
Spekke, Arnolds. *History of Latvia*, M. Goppers, Stockholm, 1951. *Latvia and the Baltic Problem*, Latvian Information Bureau, London, 1955.
Sprudzs, Adolf and Rusis, Armins (eds.) *Res Baltica* (A collection of essays in honour of the memory of Dr. Alfred Bilmanis), Sijthoff, Leiden, 1968.
Tarulis, Albert N. *Soviet Policy Toward the Baltic States, 1918–1940*, Univ. of Notre Dame Press, Notre Dame, Ind., 1959.
Vardys, V. Stanley. *Lithuania under the Soviets: Portrait of a Nation, 1940–1965*, Frederick A. Praeger, New York; Pall Mall Press, London, 1965.

JĀNIS SAPIETS. Born in Latvia, leaving during the Soviet takeover. Journalist and broadcaster. Studied modern languages at the University of Riga, theology at Bonn University, and Russian Language and Literature at London University. Publications include *Russia's Other Poets*, 1968.

SOVIET FOREIGN POLICY [1]

MALCOLM MACKINTOSH

SOVIET foreign policy can be analysed under three general headings: its guiding principles, the main areas of its activity and the conclusions which can be drawn from this activity. One preliminary factor should be mentioned: the Soviet Union is unique among the Great Powers in that neither the foreign minister nor the defence minister is a member of the real policy decision-making body, the Communist Party's Politburo. Foreign policy is therefore formulated on the advice of professional experts, but the decisions are taken by the eleven party leaders without the professionals' participation.

THE GUIDING PRINCIPLES

In a survey such as this it is inevitable that certain assumptions which cannot be proved must be made about the leadership of a foreign power. But it is probably true to say that the following principles guide the Soviet leaders:

(1) The survival of the Soviet Union as a state and as a world super-power, with some degree of parity with the USA.

(2) No military-strategic confrontation with the USA.

(3) No foreign commitments beyond the reasonable capability of the Soviet armed forces to fulfil them.

(4) Some degree of injection of communist ideology into foreign policy, especially within the world communist movement, where China represents an ideological threat.

(5) Wherever consistent with the first two principles, the general increase of Soviet political influence and prestige throughout the world. In a clash between survival and ideology or prestige, survival will always win.

(6) The retention of an active role in the UN, with the proviso that UN decisions which run counter to Soviet national or ideological aims will be unacceptable.

AREAS OF ACTIVITY

Relations with the USA

Historically there has always been a Russian urge to come to bi-polar terms with the world's strongest power—the Tsars with Napoleon and with Bismarck's Germany, and Stalin with Hitler. Today, such a relationship

[1] This material originally appeared in the June 1968 issue of *The World Today*, the monthly journal published by the Royal Institute of International Affairs, London.

with the USA helps to avoid a military clash through miscalculation; it ensures the acceptance of the Soviet Union's super-power status and it raises possibilities for Great Power deals and joint action to control unwanted crises. It also acts as a spur to the Soviet Union to formulate policies which could bring her nearer to parity with the USA; in the armaments field, this could mean either an arms race, or potentially, though less likely at the present time, arms control. While the Vietnam war was at its height, the Soviet Union could not be too eager for a deal with the USA, and the trend was towards keeping the bi-polar relationship to the minimum required for security and defence against miscalculation. In view of the ideological challenge from China and the Soviet Union's anxiety to retain the leadership of the world communist movement, it was essential to it to lead, and to be seen to lead, the aid programme to North Vietnam. If the negotiations in Paris bring an end to the Vietnam war, and peace returns to South-East Asia, it is likely that there will be a movement again towards important Soviet-US contacts over and above the essential and working-level links that have been in existence since Khrushchev's day.

Europe

The Soviet Union's prime requirements in the European sphere are to retain military predominance in Eastern Europe in order to cover the European part of the country militarily, and to reduce the amount of German manpower available to one German state, that is, to support the continued existence of East Germany. It needs the Warsaw Pact organisation as the instrument to carry out these tasks, and to counter-balance divisive trends in East European countries. The employment of the Warsaw Pact, politically and militarily, in this role was the main feature of Soviet foreign policy in 1968. For when the Czechoslovak Communist Party and government embarked on a programme of political, social and economic reform which offered the Czechoslovak people full information about, and genuine participation in the government of the country, and restored many of the basic freedoms which had been lost when the communists took power in 1948, the Soviet government became afraid that the Dubček regime meant the end of orthodox communist rule in Czechoslovakia. The Soviet leaders believed that the Czechoslovak programme would lead to a weakening of the country's links with the Soviet Union, a serious gap in the military solidarity of the Warsaw Pact and, perhaps equally dangerous, that it was infectious, and could easily spread to other East European countries and even to the Soviet Union itself. After many and varied attempts to dissuade the Czechoslovak leaders from their new course, and to intimidate them, the Soviet Union decided upon military intervention, using the forces of Poland, Hungary and Bulgaria (with nominal East German participation) alongside those of the Soviet army. The most important factor as far as timing was concerned was to act before the September 1968 Congress of the Czechoslovak Communist Party took place, and elected a Central Committee fully committed to the implementation of the Dubček reforms.

Since the occupation of Czechoslovakia and the establishment of a Soviet garrison in the country, the Soviet Union has slowly but relentlessly forced Czechoslovakia back into the mould of the traditional communist orthodox state, and although some elements of the reform programme may be enacted, the Czechoslovak leaders' freedom of manoeuvre has been severely restricted. The Soviet Union has shown that it will not tolerate divergence from communist orthodoxy in the Soviet bloc in Eastern Europe. It has proclaimed this view in terms of a doctrine raising the interests of the 'Socialist common-wealth' to a higher status than those of individual countries, and countries like Rumania, which had shown signs of independence from the Soviet Union, will be compelled to move more cautiously in the future.

Before the Czechoslovak crisis occurred, a particular Soviet interest in the European situation lay in some of the problems facing NATO on the eve of its 20th anniversary in 1969. The Soviet leaders seemed to feel that if they played their cards well, the initiative in Europe might fall into their hands and they might be able to influence the post-1969 European security scene. There were five main reasons for this: the US involvement in Vietnam; France's military withdrawal from NATO and its anti-American and, to some extent, anti-British policy; the new West German approach to Eastern Europe, and its decreasing rigidity towards East Germany (this was un-popular in Moscow, hence the Soviet attempts to discredit it and to distract attention from Bonn's new policy towards the East); the Greek-Turkish tensions, and the lowered prestige of the present Greek government; and last, the somewhat remote possibilities of revitalising certain West European Communist Parties, perhaps in the direction of forming popular fronts. This is an idea which seemed to appeal to Brezhnev, and the 1968 conference of Communist Parties in Budapest was a sign of this interest.

It is unlikely that the Soviet government had a firm and detailed plan for exploiting all these factors. It is especially unlikely that it now has serious hopes of bringing NATO to an end or of persuading the West Europeans to ask the Americans to leave Europe, especially in the wake of Soviet action in Czechoslovakia. There are, of course, credits for the Soviet Union as well as debits in a continued US presence in Europe; for one thing, it helps to cement the Soviet Union's status as a super-power. But the Soviet Union may still hope for a 'reduced' NATO in Europe; for example, a basic core of USA-UK-West Germany-Benelux-Italy; a passive 'political' Scandinavian membership; and serious inroads into the solidarity of the south-east Euro-pean membership, with either Turkey or Greece lessening its commitments to NATO. This, combined with an increased Soviet presence in the Mediterranean and the Middle East, could be a worthwhile target for the Soviet Union to aim at, and Soviet foreign policy will probably explore all these possibilities. In the field of diplomacy and propaganda, the Soviet Union will try to isolate West Germany and encourage other NATO members to follow the example of France.

The Middle East

The Soviet Union made a serious miscalculation in the Middle East at the time of the Arab-Israeli war in June 1967. There seem to be two main theories as to why it gave false information to the Arabs in May of that year: either to raise tension under Soviet control, with the aim of producing a demonstration of Arab military power, stopping short of war but rebounding to the credit of the Soviet Union as the Arabs' protector, or to bring pressure to bear on the unruly Syrians by frightening them, with the help of Egypt, into greater readiness to take Soviet advice. As a result of the Soviet information the Arabs reacted violently; the Soviet government lost control of the situation and, when war came on 5 June 1967 it was unable to aid the Arabs in their hour of need. Soviet policy since then has been based on the 'tactics of recovery', which were designed to blur the memory of the failure of Soviet help, to replace the losses of weapons, to show the Arabs that the Soviet Union is their only friend, and to spearhead the world-wide anti-Israel campaign, focusing on the generally accepted principle that annexations of territory should not follow military action, even in self-defence. This was one of the reasons for Soviet support for the British resolution in the UN Security Council. Lastly, Soviet policy aims to drive a wedge between those who need the Suez Canal and those who do not. While the Suez Canal is clearly of greater importance to the UK than to the USA, the Soviet aid programme to North Vietnam has made free passage through the Canal of increasing importance to the Soviet Union—a point which is probably not lost on the Israeli government.

One very important factor emerging from the Middle East crisis is the evidence of the stage which the Soviet Union has reached in its creation of a political-military intervention capability in peacetime; this began to appear in 1963–4. Although the Soviet naval presence was not used militarily during the June war, the Soviet Mediterranean squadron was quickly reinforced and used after the war in political operations, supporting itself without resort to permanent land bases. In addition Soviet air power was demonstrated in the arms airlift to the defeated Arab countries and a Soviet military presence even made a brief appearance in the civil war in the Yemen. The ultimate goal of Soviet policy in the Middle East cannot be predicted, but it is unlikely to involve an early resumption of the Arab-Israeli war (Israel is still too strong, Arab morale too low), or the establishment of permanent bases (as opposed to access to support facilities) in the Arab countries. But the area will continue to see a steady increase of Soviet political-military activity, which could be especially relevant to Soviet policy towards the NATO countries in the eastern Mediterranean. Much, however, of this activity could be of an experimental kind, allowing for speedy withdrawal in the event of a serious crisis.

Vietnam

The basic problem of Vietnam for the Soviet Union was the fact that the USA was at war with an established member-state of the communist camp. The Soviet Union had had mixed feelings on the war as such. On the credit side, it concentrated US attention and resources on an area far from the Soviet borders, it drained US power and raised confusion and doubt at home and overseas, and it offered the Soviet Union more freedom of action elsewhere, for example in the Middle East, the Mediterranean and Europe. But, on the debit side, war anywhere in the world in which a super-power is involved could lead to escalation, the US forces were becoming the most battle-experienced in the world and the Soviet air defence of North Vietnam was far from 100% effective.

On balance, the Soviet Union probably would like to see an end to the war, but not in terms of either a communist surrender or a complete US humiliation or defeat. One difficulty is that it has little influence in Hanoi, whose leaders are tough and independent. The practical Soviet conditions for sponsoring a negotiated settlement probably are: first, the end of US bombing of the north which was achieved in 1968 and led to the convening of preliminary discussions in Paris; second, the retention of the Vietnamese communist military-political power in South Vietnam, if necessary side by side with a US presence, at least during a truce period; third, acceptance by all parties (including China) that the Soviet Union should participate at the same level as the USA; and fourth, that contacts should be direct, without the good offices of smaller powers.

China

The present Soviet leaders are determined to confront China on all important issues. These issues are, first and foremost, territorial. There can be no compromise here; the Soviet Far East has been militarily reinforced since 1963 and Soviet troops are now in Mongolia. Second, there is the question of the leadership of the world communist movement. Again, no compromise is possible and the struggle to counteract Chinese activity in propaganda and subversion inside the movement and in the third world will continue. Third, Soviet prestige must be protected and the excesses of the Chinese cultural revolution will be exploited to underline Soviet moderation and dignity.

Soviet policy is likely to be to try to ride out the Mao era and hope for better successors. But one important factor in the long run could be the emotional fears traditionally aroused in the Soviet Union by China's numbers, so long as they are harnessed to one central authority.

The third world

Areas such as Latin America and Africa take second place in Soviet foreign policy considerations, partly because of distance and unfamiliarity, and partly because of unhappy Soviet experiences (in the Cuban crisis of 1962, the disturbances in the Congo, the overthrow of Nkrumah in Ghana and so on). The Soviet government will do what it can to keep Castro in Cuba, but will not commit itself to the support of his Latin American policy of guerrilla warfare. There is no Soviet master plan in the third world; Soviet policy is opportunistic. It will try to back potential winners (for instance, the federal government in Nigeria), and will step in where possible in countries newly opened to their influence, for example, the Sudan after the 1967 Middle East war. In any case, the Soviet Union is faced with a struggle on two fronts: against Western and against Chinese influence, and many African countries seem to be distrustful of Soviet long-term motives.

CONCLUSIONS

There are four main conclusions to be drawn from this survey. First, the Soviet Union is now ruled by men who are both pragmatic in terms of its survival and less flexible and impetuous than Khrushchev was. Basic security principles will not be tampered with and orthodox concepts will play an important part in foreign policy formulation. Some Soviet leaders, like Brezhnev, appear to believe that since the Cuban crisis of 1962 the USA has embarked on an offensive against 'the left'; they see evidence of this in the Cuban crisis itself, in the Dominican Republic, the Middle East, Vietnam, the emergence of what they saw as 'right-wing forces' in Czechoslovakia and even in the fall of pro-communist rulers like Sukarno and Nkrumah.

Second, the Soviet Union has probably set course for the achievement of a genuine intervention capability, designed ultimately to give it similar options to those of the UK or the USA in overseas policy. Already the Soviet navy may be capable of carrying out a small unopposed landing within reach of Soviet air power; in two to five years time, it could mount such an operation against light opposition. In strategic defence policy, the Soviet Union will probably achieve parity with the USA in numbers of ICBMs in the 1970s, and some measure of ballistic missile defence for Central European Russia.

Third, the Soviet Union probably hopes that, while no dramatic improvement of the world communist situation will occur, the West may suffer some defeats, for example, in Vietnam, and the Arab world, from which it can benefit. However, in Europe and in the context of NATO it is important to emphasise that, if Soviet initiatives fail, the Soviet Union's fall-back position is the *status quo* of today and not a more dangerous European confrontation.

This leads to the final point. Under no circumstances will the Soviet leaders allow their policy to lead to an all-out military confrontation with the USA, even after certain types of numerical parities have been reached in the 1970s. Probes and experiments there may be, some of them risky at the local level. However, as long as the West retains its ultimate deterrent, Moscow will not regard nuclear war as a feasible way of achieving the foreign policy goals which, according to the composition and convictions of the Politburo, they may set themselves now and in the years ahead.

FURTHER READING

Brown, J. F. *The New Eastern Europe*, Frederick A. Praeger, New York; Pall Mall Press, London, 1966.

Brzezinski, Zbigniew K. *The Soviet Bloc*, Harvard Univ. Press, Cambridge, Mass.; Oxford Univ. Press, London, 1960.

Dallin, David J. *Soviet Foreign Policy After Stalin*, J. B. Lippincott, Philadelphia, 1961; Methuen, London, 1962.

Erickson, John. 'The Military Factor in Soviet Foreign Policy', *International Affairs*, London, 6, 1963.

Goldwin, Robert A. (ed.) *Beyond the Cold War*, Rand McNally, Chicago, 1965.

Horelick, Arnold L. and Rush, Myron. *Strategic Power and Soviet Foreign Policy*, Univ. of Chicago Press, Chicago, 1966.

Ionescu, Ghiţa. *The Break-up of the Soviet Empire in Eastern Europe*, Penguin, London, 1965.

Mackintosh, J. M. *Strategy and Tactics of Soviet Foreign Policy*, Oxford Univ. Press, London, 1962 and New York, 1963.

Ulam, Adam B. *Expansion and Coexistence: the History of Soviet Foreign Policy, 1917–1967*, Secker and Warburg, London; Frederick A. Praeger, New York, 1968.

MALCOLM MACKINTOSH. Consultant to the Institute for Strategic Studies on Soviet Affairs, and has headed the BBC's Bulgarian and Albanian programmes. From 1945–6 he was Liaison Officer with the Soviet Army in Rumania and Bulgaria. Publications include *Strategy and Tactics of Soviet Foreign Policy*, 1962, and *Juggernaut: a History of the Soviet Armed Forces*, 1967.

EASTERN EUROPE

NATIONALISM IN EASTERN EUROPE

J. F. BROWN

HISTORY OF PRESENT-DAY EASTERN EUROPE

HISTORY has been unkind to Eastern Europe on a number of accounts, not least in its indiscriminate dumping of a large number of nations into its relatively small area. The area of Eastern Europe is about two-thirds the size of Western Europe, yet, whereas the one is almost exclusively covered by five large nations—British, French, German, Spanish and Italian—the other has more than 15 nations jostling within its boundaries. Nor are these nations compact units: all have sizable minorities of other nations in their midst and members of their own nation enveloped by others. The events which have produced this situation are complex and bitter and still influence the attitudes and actions of the East European nations today.

The history of the East European nations has largely been one of struggle for existence, against outsiders or against each other—or against both simultaneously. For the most part these nations themselves are not indigenous to Eastern Europe but settled there, through outside pressure, between the 6th and the 10th centuries. The peaceful Slavs, later to become divided into many nations, came from the interior of Russia and had by the year 1000 settled the area between the Elbe and Oder in the west and the approaches to the Byzantine empire in the south. The Hungarians, coming from the steppes of southern Russia, had finally been forced to settle in the central plain of Eastern Europe. Of the nations that inhabited Eastern Europe at the time of the Roman empire, the only three that survive today are the Wallachians of Rumania, the Albanians and the Greeks.

Between the beginning of the 11th century and the end of the 18th, these East European nations were subjected to constant pressures from literally all points of the compass. From the west came pressure, both warlike and peaceful, from the Germans, and from the Italians, particularly the Venetians in south-eastern Europe; from the south by the Turks; from the east, first by the Tatars, then by the Russians; even from the north, the Swedes in the 17th century made damaging incursions into Poland. Not all nations suffered the same degree of pressure or for the same period of time, but it was *the* constant factor in the existence of all of them and in the end all succumbed to it. Those states which the various nations of south-east Europe had created were the first to disappear. The Serbian and Bulgarian fell at the end of the 14th century, the Albanian shortly afterwards in the middle of the 15th century. Constantinople was finally overrun in 1453—all fell to the Ottoman Turks. Early in the 16th century, Moldavia and Wallachia (later to become Rumania) and most of Hungary fell also to the Turks. In central and north-eastern Europe different conquerors took the spoils. Early in the 17th century,

Czech independence was finally snuffed out for 300 years by the Germans; at the end of the following century it was Poland's turn, divided by Prussia, Austria and Russia in the course of three partitions.

However, it was during this period of what in retrospect is now seen as gradual inexorable liquidation that some of these nations—those which were to reappear again as states in the 20th century—had built up states and empires impressive in size and often in civilisation. This had been mostly done, not at the expense of those outside nations bearing down on them, but of other nations in the same area and under the same threat. Thus, in south-eastern Europe, first the Bulgarians and then the Serbs created empires between the 10th and 14th centuries which covered, in part, the same territory. Further north the Hungarian kings extended their domain to include territories inhabited not only by Magyars but by Rumanians and Slavs. (Much later, after the establishment of the Austro-Hungarian monarchy in 1867, Hungary was to reestablish its hold over these regions; from a subjugated nation it became an imperialist power.) Poland, at the height of its power in the 16th century, held sway over a vast conglomeration of non-Polish peoples.

These periods of greatness, mediaeval or modern, remained clearly in the minds of the successive generations of East European peoples submerged in the long night of foreign occupation. Their country to them was their country at the very peak of its power and when their long night ended in the course of the 19th century and at the beginning of the 20th, this was the country they claimed as both their heritage and their birthright.

PRESSURES ON THE NEWLY INDEPENDENT STATES

Thus, independence when it came usually meant not fulfilment, but at best only partial satisfaction; only too often it meant bitter frustration and resentment. Bulgaria, for example, at the very dawn of its independence from Turkey, considered itself cheated by the Congress of Berlin in 1878 because a large part of the territory it had gained a few months earlier was taken away by the great states in the interests of the 'balance of power'. In efforts to recover part or all of this territory from Serbia, Rumania and Greece, Bulgaria took the losing side in the second Balkan War, and the two World Wars. Poland, restored to independence after World War I, hankered after its frontiers of before the first partition of 1772 and Polish territorial dissatisfaction led to embittered relations with Germany, Soviet Russia and Czechoslovakia. This was in spite of the fact that the new Poland still contained several million non-Polish inhabitants. The case of Hungary was different in that it had been the one local imperialist power in the period before World War I. The treatment it received subsequently was extremely severe. As a result of the Treaty of Trianon, not only were large 'historic' territories lost but at least one-third of the Hungarian nation found itself outside the borders of the motherland, enveloped by peoples once its subjects, now its masters. Hungary became an embittered rump state, its foreign policy dictated by the desire to recover its lost territories and peoples.

Nor was this dissatisfaction, caused by nationalist and imperialist frustrations, confined to the inter-state level. The peace treaties after World War I created one binational and one multinational state in Eastern Europe: Czechoslovakia and Jugoslavia. Czechoslovakia was quite the most advanced state in Eastern Europe between the wars, but relations between Czechs and Slovaks deteriorated steadily largely because of Slovak frustration at Czech domination. In Jugoslavia the situation was much more explosive. Here the Croats and Slovenes, relatively advanced culturally and economically, formerly part of the Habsburg empire, were put into a state dominated by the Serbs, far less advanced and, to them, still showing unmistakable signs of over four centuries' membership of the Ottoman empire.

All these historical factors made a veritable witches' brew in Eastern Europe between the wars. Add to it the bubbling ingredient of ethnic minorities in every country, left in the wake of empires, invasions and emigrations, and one had a situation lacking almost every prerequisite for both internal and international stability. The Wilsonian concept of self-determination was certainly the wisest and the most equitable for Eastern Europe. But it posed almost as many problems as it solved and developments in the rest of Europe, leading inevitably on to World War II, soon made a peaceful solution of these problems impossible.

One important reason why the new problems could not be solved was that the old dangers remained. What the 20th century has shown is that the external pressures on Eastern Europe continued unabated. Up to and including World War II Italy, then Germany, then the new Russia reassumed their predatory interest. After World War II the Soviet Union assumed domination over the whole region. This it did partly by the reincorporation of those territories which had previously been part of Tsarist Russia (and some which had not)—the independent Baltic republics of Estonia, Latvia and Lithuania, large slices of eastern Poland, Sub-Carpathian Ruthenia, northern Bukovina and Bessarabia—but mainly by installing or engineering communist governments in Poland, Hungary, Rumania and Bulgaria. In Jugoslavia and Albania communist governments were installed largely without Soviet support. Finally, Czechoslovakia fell into the Soviet sphere through a brilliant coup in 1948 actively or tacitly supported by a large minority of the population.

SOVIET DOMINATION OF EASTERN EUROPE

The Soviet domination in Eastern Europe contained a historically new element in that most states affected did not lose their identity. They were not physically incorporated into the Soviet Union as previously Poland had been swallowed up by Russia, Prussia and Austria, or Bulgaria and Serbia by the Ottoman empire. The essential framework for nationalist expression—the state—was, therefore, preserved. But, according to communist theory, the factors that had caused the bitter nationalist and chauvinist enmities of the inter-war years had now been swept away. The old ruling class had gone and with it the old feudal and capitalist system. The new concept of proletarian internationalism now embraced the area. Previous antagonisms would be replaced by cooperation between governments of the same type, led by new leaders operating a new system that, by definition, precluded both inward exploitation and outward imperialism.

So much for the theory. The practice was quite different. For one thing, the Soviet Union economically exploited the Eastern European states to an extent that made the previous imperialisms look almost charitable. Countries like Hungary, Rumania and East Germany, which had fought against the Soviet Union in the war, had to pay grievously damaging war reparations, and states like Rumania and Bulgaria were also plundered of their mineral wealth by means of joint stock companies, owned 'equally' by the Soviet Union and the states concerned. Finally, all the East European states were subjected to a trading relationship which involved cheap exports to the Soviet Union and relatively expensive imports in return. For another, even with communist governments installed, national peculiarities soon appeared, and Stalin was hardly partial to any peculiarities except his own. There was also evidence that, proletarian internationalism or not, some communist states still heartily disliked others for reasons mainly based on the old rivalries. Finally—and most dangerous of all—some communist leaders were not prepared to accept the principle of exclusive Soviet control over their affairs. There were clear examples of this in Poland and Bulgaria, where Władysław Gomułka and Traicho Kostov, albeit convinced communists, were bent on policies conceived, first and foremost, according to the requirements of their own countries.

Jugoslavia

It was Jugoslavia, however, which brought to earth the ineffable claims of proletarian internationalism. Tito and the other Jugoslav leaders—again, convinced communists and at first blindly loyal to the Soviet Union—soon clashed with Stalin on how things were to be run in Jugoslavia. For these men, veterans of an epic struggle for communism in Jugoslavia, it was inconceivable that they could not be trusted with the effective government of their own country. Thus began the bitter dispute between Belgrade and Moscow which led to the break in June 1948. It was, therefore, the Soviet imperialism practised by Stalin that brought out the latent nationalism in Jugoslav communism and showed that nationalism was by no means incompatible with a creed that was supposed to make it irrelevant. Stalin's answer to the Jugoslav disaster—the only kind he knew—was not to relax the grip but to tighten it, to try to stamp out the signs of a reviving East European nationalism.

His organisational response to the danger was the Cominform (Communist Information Bureau) founded in September 1947. This was a harmless enough title for a body designed to check the centrifugal forces already at work in Eastern Europe, forces deriving their sustenance from national and historical peculiarities. It recalled, as it was designed to, the Comintern of the inter-war years, an organisation that Stalin soon perverted for Soviet rather than purely communist aims. Later, after the break with Jugoslavia, Stalin began the *Gleichschaltung* in earnest. Communist leaders, whose experience had been gathered mainly or exclusively in their own countries and were therefore suspected of 'nationalist deviations', were replaced by 'Muscovites', leaders who had spent long years of exile and education in Moscow. Kostov in Bulgaria and László Rajk in Hungary were executed after nightmare trials, Gomułka and Lucreţiu Pătrăşcanu in Rumania were publicly disgraced (the latter was eventually executed in 1954). Large-scale purges were carried out in all parties. Down to almost the last detail of public life, the Soviet model was the only one to be followed. The Stalinist era in Eastern Europe had begun in earnest.

It was only to last till Stalin died in March 1953. But during this short period, East European nationalism was effectively submerged under a thick layer of ice that gave the area east of the Elbe a blank appearance of uniformity and cohesion. It looked durable but was not; it could last only as long as Stalin. His was a system which could not be bequeathed because without him it was unworkable.

Stalin's successors, mainly Khrushchev as he elbowed his way to supreme power, fumbled towards a new policy that had two layers. First, the East

European satellites were to be granted more autonomy in running their own affairs and Moscow's economic exploitation of them, at least in its crudest forms, was to stop. Second, the governments of the satellites themselves were urged to make themselves more acceptable to the people they were governing. Both layers of this policy tended to encourage the reemergence of East European nationalism. The more autonomy the satellites received, the more diverse they again became and, if their leaders were to hope for any kind of consensus with the population, then they had, in some degree, to embrace— or pay lip-service to—the national sentiments of these peoples. Khrushchev's *rapprochement* with Tito in 1955, very much on Tito's own terms, gave considerable impetus to this national revival. It was a *de facto* Soviet recognition of the existence of national communism and could not fail to have a considerable effect throughout Eastern Europe as a whole. Nor could the significance of the abolition of Stalin's Cominform in April 1956 go unnoticed.

Poland and Hungary

The effects were not long in coming. In October 1956 a revolutionary situation in Poland resulted in the return to power of Władysław Gomułka, who had been purged in 1949 for resisting Soviet attempts at the complete domination of Poland. In Hungary an actual revolution, also in October 1956, succeeded for a few days in toppling the Stalinist regime and had to be crushed by the Soviet army. In the immediate sense, these outbursts were prompted by local dissatisfaction at local oppression. But, basically, they were nationalist outbursts against the system of empire Stalin created and were possible because that system was being deliberately dismantled.

After Poland and Hungary Khrushchev showed both courage and statesmanship by refusing to stop this dismantling process despite the near-disasters it had caused. But he was very much aware that the centrifugal forces were gathering pace. Reformer though he was, he was not prepared to preside over the dissolution of Soviet hegemony. He therefore cast about for a new and more viable means of cohesion and by 1958 it was obvious what he had in mind.

Comecon had been founded in 1949 as the communist bloc's (very ineffectual) answer to the Marshall Plan. It had been virtually ignored by Stalin and had never really assumed real importance after his death. Khrushchev now saw it, however, as an instrument for economic integration leading eventually to political integration. What he had in mind was indicated in a remarkable passage during a speech made in East Germany in March 1959. After referring to the future communist society and its benefits, Khrushchev went on:

> In these conditions the old concept of borders as such will disappear . . . In all likelihood only ethnic borders will survive for a time and even these will probably exist only as a convention. Naturally these frontiers, if they can be called frontiers at all, will have no border guards, customs officials or incidents . . . Speaking of the future, it seems to me that the further development of the socialist countries will, in all probability, proceed along the lines of consolidation of the single-world socialist economic system.[1]

The fact that Khrushchev, often a man of brilliant insights, could make a statement like that as late as 1959 showed how seriously he underestimated the extent to which nationalism had revived in the communist bloc since Stalin's death. Already by the time he made that speech his differences with

[1] *Pravda*, 27 March 1959: quoted by Zbigniew K. Brzezinski, *The Soviet Bloc: Unity and Conflict*, Harvard Univ. Press, Cambridge, Mass., 1960.

China had passed the point of no return. More relevant in this context, however, were his troubles in Eastern Europe, where Moscow had begun a serious dispute with one state, Albania, and where its relations with another, Rumania, were beginning to give cause for concern.

Albania

Albania's dispute with the Soviet Union was caused by its nationalist enmity with Jugoslavia and its fear that Moscow's *rapprochement* with Belgrade would lead to a fatal sacrifice of its interests or even its existence. The dispute with the Soviet Union was cloaked in Marxist-Leninist terms; Khrushchev had adopted a 'revisionist' policy and sold himself out to the Jugoslav renegades, etc. Behind all this was the almost paranoid anxiety of a precarious nation whose relations with Jugoslavia had always been bitter and the fact that there were nearly one million Albanians living in Jugoslavia—about one-third of all the Albanians in the world—only added to the bitterness and resentment.

The result of the Albanian dispute with Moscow is, of course, well known. Taking advantage of Moscow's rift with Peking, the Albanian leaders switched alliances, became China's bridgehead in Europe and the second European communist state, after Jugoslavia, to break with the Soviet bloc.

Rumania

Rumania's dispute with the Soviet Union was the direct outcome of Khrushchev's plan for a 'single-world socialist economic system'. As this plan unfolded it became clear that Rumania's role in it would be mainly as a supplier of raw materials and, to a nation bent on building up a many-sided industry, this was an affront both to national pride and aspirations.

As Bucharest's dispute with Khrushchev and his successors has progressed, the nationalist character of Rumania's entire policy, domestic and foreign, has become abundantly clear. Rumania remains a member of the Soviet alliance but only in the same way and to the same extent as France under de Gaulle remained a member of the Western alliance. Any proposal made by the Soviet Union or the other allies not considered in accord with Rumanian national interest is rejected, and this has led to the shelving of such cherished Soviet ideas as the strengthening of both Comecon and the Warsaw Pact. Any Soviet-inspired policy not to Rumania's liking is repudiated, such as the pro-Arab policy in the Middle East war, the cold front toward West Germany and the wish for a formal condemnation of China.

THE REVIVAL OF NATIONALISM AND OUTLOOK FOR THE FUTURE

Looking to the future, one may expect that, even among those East European states now less obviously affected by the revival of nationalism—Bulgaria and Hungary, for example—nationalistic influences will grow and make their mark. Throughout Eastern Europe a whole new generation is coming to positions of power. New leaders are emerging who, though communist, never experienced the long winters out of power when Moscow was the only beacon and guide, whose experience is largely confined to their own countries and its problems. Under these men, as the East European states enter the modern technological age, a new race of technocrats is emerging, little impressed either with the communist ideology or with the Soviet Union. As the windows to the West have opened, these men have had a chance to compare the economic, technological and managerial attainments of East and West and know which they prefer. If one adds to this the psychological and moral defeats the Soviet Union has suffered (the split in the communist movements, the revelations of her own inglories under Stalin, to mention only two) there is ample reason to assume that Moscow's problems in Eastern Europe will grow rather than subside. Repression, as in the case of Czechoslovakia, is only a short term answer to these problems.

One need not be a cold warrior or a 19th-century nationalist to approve the general development described in this essay. But one must not ignore its darker side. Between the two World Wars Eastern Europe was a hotbed of nationalism and chauvinism; this was a tragedy in itself and an open invitation to outside intervention. The horrors of World War II and the following submergence of all these states in the Stalinist system did in a sense produce a kind of unity for the first time in history, negative though it was. Many East Europeans began to realise that, however serious their previous rivalries and conflicts may have been, they were paltry compared with the predicament they now found themselves in. Thus the word 'unity' or 'association' came to have a pressing significance it never had before.

Certain preconditions for unity in the meantime were being created. The economic and social structure of Eastern Europe was radically changed; the differences of centuries were unceremoniously brushed aside. Before the war the area as a whole had been mainly agricultural. Still, there had been a world of a difference between relatively egalitarian Bulgaria and semi-feudal Hungary, between the well-balanced class structure of Bohemia and the dangerously uneven spread of wealth and rights in Poland. Now, the state controlled industry in every country and agriculture was being collectivised in most. Many of these economic measures were unwise and all too brutally implemented, but they had the potential of solving a vital problem of the future Eastern Europe.

Today, some of the old feuds between neighbours are reviving. Economic nationalism is perhaps the most conspicuous. This was the reef on which Comecon foundered, but it is also evident in bilateral relations. For example, one of the reasons for Czechoslovakia's economic depression in the early 1960s was the refusal of states like Rumania and Bulgaria to purchase Czechoslovak machinery (because of its inferior quality) in exchange for raw materials. But political nationalism is also rearing its head. Many Hungarians, for example, have never reconciled themselves to the loss of Transylvania and there is increasing resentment in Budapest over the Rumanian government's policy of assimilating the Hungarian minority within its borders. Recently, too, the age-old problem of Macedonia has flared up anew between Bulgaria and Jugoslavia. All this, besides being a tragedy in itself might one day present Moscow with the opportunity to *divide et impera* if the need arose.

However, as the case of Jugoslavia has shown, even federalism provides no immunity to the virus of nationalism. This is something the newly federalised Czechoslovakia must take into account. To adapt a pre-war saying, Jugoslavia is a state with six republics, five nations, four languages, three religions, two alphabets and one party. It is a federation with each of the six republics enjoying great and increasing self-government. But the old nationality question which so plagued the pre-war kingdom has returned to endanger the post-war communist republic, often in new economic guise. The Croats and Slovenes still despise the 'primitive' Serbs and the ghastly massacres during the war did nothing to endear the Croats to the Serbs. The country is also divided on a 'have-have-not' basis. The richer republics (Slovenia and Croatia) bitterly resent their income being used to subsidise economic growth in the backward republics like Montenegro and Macedonia, not to mention

Serbia. Tito,[1] the 78-year-old giant who holds the fabric together, has been persuaded that only further decentralisation can stave off disruption. One hopes he is right. The danger is that, especially after his death, decentralisation will lead to a deepening rift between the advanced prosperous Central European parts of the country (Slovenia and Croatia) and the backward poor Balkan parts (Serbia, Bosnia, Hercegovina, Montenegro, Macedonia and the large Albanian Kosmet region). The fire-bell is ringing in the night for Jugoslavia and it is Tito, the quintessential Jugoslav, who must hear it the loudest.

But, to end on a more cheerful note, despite the disruptive tendencies among and within states in Eastern Europe, there are other tendencies encouraging hope. In the economic sphere, sensible bilateral and regional schemes for cooperation can be found to weigh against the narrow nationalism referred to above. Socially, the astonishing development of tourism among the East European nations (for example, nearly 1,600,000 Czechoslovaks visited other East European states and the Soviet Union in the first nine months of 1967), while not contributing immediately to brotherly love, is at least doing something to overcome the complete lack of knowledge which the East Europeans proudly have about one another. Finally, and most important, the *awareness* that closer association between the East European nations is necessary and good in itself is still very much alive. Many communists, Georgi Dimitrov in the late 1940s, Tito himself, Imre Nagy and now János Kádár, the present Hungarian leader, have realised that closer cooperation is not something that proletarian internationalism will take care of. It is something that must be worked at, vision being tempered by patience and common sense. Kádár (only too aware that nationalism and irredentism in his country are not dead) has supported steps toward 'closer cooperation among the states of the Danube basin', stressing particularly Hungary, Austria, Czechoslovakia and Jugoslavia. Rumania and Bulgaria are urging the signing of a Balkan Pact. During the Dubček reform period, before the Soviet invasion, the idea of a new Little Entente was floated. It would have comprised Czechoslovakia, Jugoslavia and Rumania in the first place, but might later have been extended to Hungary as well.

The cynics may complain that we have heard all this before; perhaps so. But unless we hear it all again and unless something is done about it, the deep and swift current of East European nationalism will never be channelled for constructive ends. It will remain a destructive—a self-destructive—force distracting the talents and energies of these gifted nations from better and more lasting work.

FURTHER READING

Brown, J. F. *The New Eastern Europe: The Khrushchev Era and After*, Pall Mall Press, London; Frederick A. Praeger, New York, 1966.

Brzezinski, Zbigniew, K. *The Soviet Bloc—Unity and Conflict*, Harvard Univ. Press, Cambridge, Mass.; Oxford Univ. Press, London, 1960.

International Conference on World Politics, Johns Hopkins Press, Baltimore, 1965.

Kolarz, Walter. *Myths and Realities in Eastern Europe*, Lindsay Drummond, London, 1946.

Macartney, C. A. and Palmer, A. W. *Independent Eastern Europe—A History*, Macmillan, London, 1962; St. Martin's Press, New York, 1962.

Schöpflin, George, A. 'National Minorities Under Communism in Eastern Europe'. *Eastern Europe in Transition*, (ed., Kurt London), Johns Hopkins Press, Baltimore, 1966.

Seton-Watson, Hugh. *Eastern Europe between the Wars*, Cambridge Univ. Press, London, 1945.

[1] Born in May 1892.

J. F. Brown. At present chief political analyst at Radio Free Europe, Munich, and formerly Senior Fellow at the Research Institute on Communist Affairs, Colombia University. Publications include *The New Eastern Europe: The Khrushchev Era and After*, 1966, and he is working on a book tracing the development of Communist rule in Bulgaria.

NATIONAL MINORITIES IN
EASTERN EUROPE

GEORGE SCHÖPFLIN

INTRODUCTION

EASTERN Europe is renowned for its problem of national minorities. The ethnic complexion of the area has become very mixed over the centuries and hence the newly established nation-states which emerged from the Paris Peace Settlement (1918–20) were bound to include some national groups alien to the ruling nation. The difficulty of drawing just frontiers, ones drawn in such a way that the number of individuals separated from the main body of their co-nationals should be the lowest possible, is recognised; nevertheless, in a number of cases the professed principle of self-determination was blatantly disregarded by the peace-makers in favour of some other principle, such as the need to guarantee the security or communications of the new states. The post-World War I frontiers were left largely unaltered after 1945. The only significant change was that the powerful German minorities of Poland, Czechoslovakia and Jugoslavia were expelled, the majority to West Germany, whilst a few found their way to East Germany and Austria.

A distinction must be made between a minority proper and a co-equal nationality. Thus in a state which is multi-national in character, that is, made up of two or more constituent national groups (*Staatsvölker*), each of these constituent national groups enjoys full rights, precisely because it is one of the constituent national groups. The rights of a minority, on the other hand, tend to be more circumscribed. The question of relations between constitutionally equal national groups forming the state—as in Czechoslovakia and Jugoslavia—will not be treated in this chapter which is concerned only with minorities.

Minorities may be classified in a number of ways. For instance, they may be distinguished as minorities which are cut off from the main body of their co-nationals by an arbitrarily drawn state frontier; as minorities which live separated by a great distance from their co-nationals; and as minorities which are in effect a nationality of their own, having no co-nationals anywhere (only the Lusatian Sorbs of the Bautzen area of East Germany fall into this category in Eastern Europe; in Western Europe, the Bretons provide another example). However, for this chapter another classification has been thought more useful, namely, in terms of political power. Hence minorities are divided into those which are large enough to occasion political concern to the majority nationality and those which are not. A list of the latter, excluded from discussion in this chapter by reason of their lack of political importance, is given in an appendix. The former, which will be looked at in some detail,

EASTERN EUROPE: ETHNIC GROUPS

are the Hungarians in Czechoslovakia, the Turks in Bulgaria, the Albanians and Hungarians in Jugoslavia and the Hungarians in Rumania.

Official communist policies towards minorities stem from Lenin's belief that class was more important in practical terms than nationality. Lenin was fully prepared to support national demands where this suited his purposes, but for purely tactical reasons. Thus in framing his policies *vis-à-vis* Tsarist Russia, he accepted the demands of the non-Russian nationalities for autonomy or even independence. Once the Soviet state was established, minorities retained a fair measure of formal local rights, notably press and education in the local languages, but the basic philosophy of these institutions was that of communism. Essentially, Lenin saw the local languages as little more than the most intelligible and hence the most effective vehicle for communist propaganda. Subsequently all communist governments have professed the principle of local linguistic rights in the treatment of minorities—a principle which is often summed up in the slogan 'national in form, socialist in content'. In fact, theory and practice have diverged in a number of cases and where in a communist country the population suffered totalitarian rule, the weight of this bore especially heavily on the minority which found itself under a double pressure. With the growth of the national element in the policies of the communist states of Eastern Europe in the late 1950s and early 1960s, the pressure on the minorities tended to increase. On the other hand, where liberalisation had made a major breakthrough (as in Jugoslavia after July 1966), then the treatment of the minorities tended to improve parallel with other fields.

Czechoslovakia: The Hungarian Minority

According to the 1961 census, Hungarians in Czechoslovakia number 541,000 (about 12% of the population of Slovakia). They live in a compact group in southern Slovakia, in the areas bordering on Hungary. The majority of them are employed in agriculture, although the proportion working in industry is slowly increasing; it is, however, still well below the overall Czechoslovak average. Relations between Slovaks and Hungarians have been traditionally poor and this became, if anything, worse after 1945 after the brief interlude of Hungarian rule from 1938–45 over the Hungarian-inhabited southern marches of Slovakia. The post-war Czechoslovak government applied the principle of collective guilt against the minority. This policy was not reversed until the communists took power in 1948. From then until 1960 the Hungarians enjoyed moderately good treatment, given the otherwise oppressive policies of the Czechoslovak government in the Stalinist and neo-Stalinist periods. In other words, Hungarians were seldom subjected to extra discrimination on the grounds of their nationality alone, though there were individual instances of discrimination. Around 1960 there came a certain change in attitude towards the Hungarian minority. Possibly as a late reaction to the Hungarian revolution of 1956, which the Hungarians in Slovakia followed with sympathy, the Prague government, with the support of Bratislava, decided on a new policy towards the minority. The essence of this policy was to encourage as far as possible the assimilation of the Hungarians. As a first step, three changes were undertaken. Administrative boundaries were changed with the result that Hungarians were left in a majority in only two districts after the reorganisation (okres Dunajská Streda and okres Komárno). However, whatever its impact on the Hungarian minority, the reorganisation of local government districts did make local administration more efficient. Second, changes were initiated in education. Great emphasis was placed on the inculcation of a 'state patriotism', of absolute and overriding loyalty to the Czechoslovak nation-state in all fields. And third, a campaign was undertaken to induce the Hungarians to learn Slovak.

The Dubček reforms of 1968 did not leave the Hungarian minority untouched. On 12 March 1968 the Central Committee of Csemadok, the Hungarian Workers' Cultural Organisation, adopted a policy declaration which called for separate political organisations for the minority; for the reorganisation of local government districts in order to end the situation where Hungarians were in a minority in areas where they would have formed

244

the majority had Slovak-inhabited districts not been attached to Hungarian ones in 1960; for equality of opportunity in participating in all aspects of public life; for improved educational facilities and for full autonomy in culture.

On 27 October 1968, the Czechoslovak National Assembly adopted a new Minorities Statute, which guaranteed by means of legislation of constitutional authority, the position of the minorities and incorporated most of the demands of Csemadok. The willingness to do this on the part of the Czechoslovak authorities was without a doubt encouraged by the stand of the minority during the invasion of the country by Warsaw Pact forces. The Hungarian-inhabited area was garrisoned largely by troops from Hungary and contrary to their expectations, the minority remained absolutely loyal to the Dubček leadership, something which was recognised even by the most nationalistic Slovaks. The Minorities Statute came into force on 1 January 1969. It has been expanded by further legislation of the Slovak National Council, which has established a Commission for Nationalities Affairs, a *de facto* ministry (it does, of course, include the Ruthene-Ukrainian minority within its competence, but the minister, László Dobos, is a Hungarian). It remains to be seen in what spirit the Slovak authorities will apply the Minorities Statute. The Hungarians are hopeful, but the press polemics between them and the Slovaks in the summer of 1968 makes it clear that the national antagonism between the Slovak majority and the Hungarian minority is deep-seated and intense.

Bulgaria: The Turkish Minority

The Turkish minority in Bulgaria numbers about 750,000—about 12% of the population. The Turks live mainly in south-eastern Bulgaria and in the north, along the Danube. They are mostly employed in agriculture. The Turks in Bulgaria are in part the descendants of Turkish colonists and in part assimilated Bulgarians who have adopted Islam. There is no doubt that the Turkish minority has not reconciled itself at all to communism, especially, being devout Muslims, to its anti-religious policies and that the great majority of the Turks would wish to emigrate to Turkey. In 1950–1 the Bulgarian government announced that it would permit the emigration of 250,000 Turks and some 150,000 did leave, often under circumstances which were hardly different from expulsion. During the 1950s the Bulgarian authorities put considerable pressure on the minority to conform to its policies and, up to a point, to assimilate. At the same time, an effort was made to spread education among the Turks, with some success. With the improvement in relations between Bulgaria and Turkey in 1966, the question of the minority came under discussion and the Bulgarians agreed that those families which had been split in 1951 should be reunited. Some 30,000 Turks are to be permitted to leave Bulgaria for Turkey.

Jugoslavia: The Albanian Minority

The Albanian minority in Jugoslavia presents a particularly difficult problem for the Jugoslav authorities. The number of the minority is about 1·1 million and they form about 38% of all the Albanians, or, looked at in another way, over one-third of the Albanian nation lives outside the frontiers of the Albanian nation-state. The majority of Albanians in Jugoslavia (usually, though no longer officially, referred to as 'Shiptars') lives in the Socialist Autonomous Province of Kosovo and Metohija, known as the Kosmet. The distribution of the minority is the following (1961 census figures): 70·7% or 646,031 live in the Kosmet; 20% or 183,109 live in Macedonia, mostly in the areas marching with Albania itself; 5·7% or 51,173 live in the Vranje district of Serbia and a further 2·8% or 25,803 live in Montenegro. The discrepancy between these figures and the estimated 1·1 million total of Albanians in 1968 is an indication of the staggeringly high birth-rate among the minority. All these areas are without exception extremely backward economically and, by and large, the Albanians tend to form the poorest section of the population. The situation is not improved by the traditional and deep-rooted hostility between the Albanians on the one hand and the Serbs and Montenegrins on the other. In the Kosmet, where Albanians form 67% of the population, the Serbs are 23% and the Montenegrins are 4% (the remainder are mostly Turks), hence the Slavs form a substantial minority.

The history of the Kosmet—the other areas of Albanian population will not be treated in detail—fell into two main phases in the post-war period. The first ended with the liberalisation after the Brioni plenum (July 1966) and was marked by considerable oppression of the Albanians, whereas during the second, post-Brioni phase the minority has been feeling its strength politically and this has brought about a marked nationalist mobilisation among the Albanians.

In the pre-Brioni period the Serbs treated the Kosmet as a colony and the situation of the Albanians deteriorated, if anything, after 1957 when the quarrel between Jugoslavia and Albania intensified. The Albanians of the Kosmet were generally regarded by the Serbs and particularly among the secret police, the UDB, as potential agents of Enver Hoxha. Hence the fall of Ranković and the purging of the UDB brought to light a widespread reign of terror inflicted by the UDB, largely an agent of the Serb nationalists, on the Albanians. Much of this was catalogued by the Albanian-language paper *Rilindja*, published in Priština, the capital of the Kosmet. At the same time, considerable investment was channelled into the Kosmet in the pre-Brioni period, especially in education, and even if Serbs benefited from this out of all proportion to their numbers, the Albanians still gained something. In particular, for the first time in the history of the Kosmet something like an Albanian intelligentsia was beginning to emerge.

This combination of political liberalisation and growing expectations created a potentially explosive situation in the Kosmet. The political leaders of the Kosmet, for the most part Albanians, were fully aware of this and attempted to pursue a compromise policy of demanding equality, especially in the question of language, whilst opposing any separatist manifestations. In the matter of equality for the Albanians, the first objective appeared to be to detach the Kosmet constitutionally from the republic of Serbia and to establish it as the seventh constituent republic of Jugoslavia. By the end of 1968 the leaders of the Kosmet had achieved this in all but name. Second, direct contacts were taken up between Priština and Tirana in cultural matters. Third, accepting the principle that only one Albanian nation existed, the Albanians of the Kosmet adopted the literary language of Albania as their standard. Fourth, in the question of distribution of jobs, a number of senior posts were graded for bilinguals only; in the short term this would have had the result of improving the chances of Albanians, since few Serbs spoke both languages.

The chances are that the Albanian minority, whether in the Kosmet or outside it, will eventually reach an agreement with the Serbs, mainly because it has no real alternative. Even if Jugoslavia were willing to let the

Kosmet secede and join Albania, it is unlikely that Enver Hoxha's regime is attractive enough for the Kosmet Albanians—especially as agriculture is largely in private hands in Jugoslavia but fully collectivised in Albania—and in any event, this would still leave a considerable number of Albanians in Jugoslavia. The political difficulties of 1968 are without a doubt a reaction to the pre-Brioni policies of oppression and once the minority finds that its national existence is no longer under threat from the Serbs, it will probably reach a political equilibrium.

Jugoslavia: The Hungarian Minority

At the last census (1961) there were 504,368 Hungarians in Jugoslavia. The great majority of these, 442,560, live in the Vojvodina (forming roughly one-quarter of the population there), and the bulk of the remainder are in Croatia. In contrast to the Albanian minority, the Hungarians appear to be reasonably content with their treatment. In fact, of the three large Hungarian minorities, the one in Jugoslavia is undoubtedly the one which has accepted its separation from Hungary most completely. The policy of the Jugoslav government has unquestionably contributed to this, as has also the fact that the general political atmosphere is incomparably more liberal in Jugoslavia than in Hungary. After the war, despite the deplorable behaviour of the Hungarian authorities during the war in the areas of the Vojvodina annexed in 1941 (and returned to Jugoslavia after the war), the Jugoslav authorities made it very clear that no nationalist reprisals by Serbs would be tolerated; nor was there any attempt to apply the principle of collective guilt to the Hungarians. Nevertheless, it was admitted after the Brioni plenum that the Hungarians had suffered discrimination during the Ranković period and that every effort would be made to redress wrongs. In the event, although the Hungarians were not permitted to revive their cultural organisation which had been dissolved in 1954–7 (together with all nationally-based cultural organisations except that of the Italians), they had all the institutions necessary to maintain their cultural autonomy. This included schooling, higher education, book publishing, press, broadcasting and bilingual administration. In 1968 a Hungarological Institute was established with the objective of studying and furthering the cultural life of the minority.

Rumania: The Hungarian Minority

The Hungarians of Transylvania form the numerically largest minority in Eastern Europe, 1,602,604 according to the 1966 census. The overwhelming majority of Hungarians live in Transylvania, but the numbers emigrating to the Regat is on the increase. The number of Hungarians in Bucharest is now thought to be over 100,000. The greatest concentration of Hungarians is to be found in the so-called Szekler counties, lying roughly between Tîrgu Mureş and Braşov; the area marching with Hungary itself also has a Hungarian majority and there are considerabe pockets in the Banat. Until 1945 the Hungarians were in a majority in most towns in Transylvania and although they still constitute a substantial proportion of the urban population, they are in a majority probably only in Oradea as a result of the great influx of Rumanians from the countryside. (It is difficult to be precise on this as the detailed figures of the 1966 census have still to be released.)

The political fortunes of the Hungarians have gone through enormous fluctuations in the last 50 years. The rulers of Transylvania until 1918, they were incorporated into Rumania unwillingly and felt that they owed it little loyalty. About two-thirds of the Hungarian population of Transylvania again came under Hungarian rule in 1940 as a result of the Second Vienna Arbitration, only to be returned to Rumania in 1945 with the restoration of the 1918 frontiers. In the early years of communist rule the Hungarians enjoyed extensive political and cultural privileges, including a separate Hungarian-language university at Cluj and a Hungarian Autonomous Region comprising the Szekler counties. However, with the reemergence of nationalism as a force in Rumanian politics in the late 1950s, the privileges of the Hungarians were gradually suppressed. The Hungarian university was merged with the Rumanian one (1959), thereby effectively ending its role as an institution of Hungarian culture. Hungarian-language schools were merged with Rumanian-language schools, with the result that education became gradually Rumanianised, in spirit at least, The Hungarian Autonomous Region was first reorganised (1960) in such a way that its Hungarian population fell and its Rumanian population rose. At the end of 1967 it was abolished altogether in the territorial reorganisation. From about 1959 to 1966, the Hungarian minority was subjected to extensive discrimination, a judgment borne out by the report of the International Commission of Jurists (December 1963).

However, in about 1966 or 1967 there came a change in policy. It is difficult to pin-point it exactly, but it is certain that by the summer of 1968 the Rumanian leadership was in favour of accommodation with the Hungarians. Nicolae Ceauşescu, the Rumanian party leader, was for a long time regarded as an arch-nationalist and as a committed anti-Hungarian. Yet as early as 1966 he toured Transylvania and lost no chance of stressing the historical links between Hungarians and Rumanians. Certainly, among the Hungarians these speeches were regarded as window-dressing. Nevertheless, the situation did improve, or at least, the atmosphere of terror and intimidation which ruled in the early 1960s was being dispelled.

It seems not implausible that the Rumanian leadership was aware of disaffection among the minority and recognised that by promoting Rumanian nationalism against the Soviet Union, which in turn spilled over into hostility against the Hungarians, they had totally alienated the Hungarian minority. The handling of the territorial reorganisation at the end of 1967, which extinguished the Mureş-Hungarian Autonomous Province (actually it had only existed in name after the first reorganisation), was another indication of a greater sensitivity towards the minority. The new system of local administration created 39 counties out of the former 16 regions and in several of these the Hungarians are in a majority. Furthermore, each county with a large Hungarian population has been provided with a separate Hungarian-language daily paper.

On 27 June 1968 the Rumanian party leadership convened a meeting with the leaders of the Hungarian minority in order to discuss 'work in the scientific and cultural fields'. It appears that at this meeting the Hungarians told the Rumanians that they were frankly dissatisfied with their treatment and demanded radical changes. Ceauşescu, who was in the chair, seemed genuinely surprised, according to the reports, and promised to look into the Hungarians' grievances. The news of this meeting, and particularly that the plain speaking had brought no reprisals with it, spread and led to a further easing in the atmosphere. The situation was again improved, from the point of view of both sides, by the fear of invasion in the aftermath of the Czechoslovak crisis in August and September 1968. It was widely rumoured that the Soviet Union, had it chosen to invade Rumania as well, would have made use of units of the Hungarian army to occupy Transylvania in the hope that the Hungarian minority would side with its co-nationals. In fact, all reports agree, the Hungarian minority remained loyal to Rumania. Ceauşescu then offered further concessions to the Hungarians (as well as to the other minorities). On 24–25 October 1968 the Central Committee approved the creation of a Front of Socialist Unity, within which Councils of Nationalities would play an important role. What the functions of these Councils are to be is unclear at the time of writing (December 1968), but the establishment of institutions with a specific interest-group character is a major step.

Looking at the wider political perspective, some part of the stimulus for change in policy towards the minorities is clearly anxiety about the intentions of the Soviet Union. The Rumanian leadership is well aware that the Soviet Union would not hesitate to use the Hungarian minority as a lever against the unity of Rumania. At the same time, the discrimination felt by the Hungarians occurs not so much at the national level but locally, in dealings with Rumanian officials, who may be less inclined to pay heed to the national susceptibilities of the Hungarians. The memories of the policy of Magyarisation imposed on the Rumanians before 1918 have become part of the Rumanian national myth and are hence not easy to eradicate. Equally, the Hungarians are at fault in that, although they may have reconciled themselves to incorporation into Rumania, they continue to feel that they deserve a special status, that Transylvania is as much their *patria* as it is of the Rumanians and that they should not be treated as a minority, but rather as a full *Staatsvolk*—and a good case can be made out for this. The feeling of cultural superiority over the Rumanians still cherished by the Hungarians, that Hungarian culture is Western whereas Rumanian culture is not, often leads Hungarians to adopt an attitude of contempt towards everything Rumanian. Latterly, there has been considerable evidence that the Hungarians have retreated into an intellectual ghetto, a kind of internal emigration. It remains to be seen if more relaxed policies will encourage the Hungarians to take a less despondent view of their situation.

THE NATURE OF GOVERNMENT AND POLITICS IN JUGOSLAVIA

K. F. CVIIĆ

THE SPLIT WITH MOSCOW

WHEN after four years of bitter civil war and enemy occupation, Marshal Tito came to power in Jugoslavia in 1945, he did so as a dedicated communist wholly committed to the cause of international communism.

The conflict with Moscow, which broke out into the open in 1948, was not about the differences of opinion between the two Central Committees in such matters as the pace of the industrialisation programme or the 'correct' policy to be pursued in the countryside. Nor was it, as the Soviet side tried to make out, about the 'undemocratic' conditions inside the Communist Party of Jugoslavia (an odd complaint from a party led and dominated by Stalin). When a specially convened meeting of the Cominform expelled Jugoslavia from its membership in June 1948, it did so at Stalin's behest, not in order to cure an ideological deviation but to defeat a power challenge. Unlike other communist leaders in Eastern Europe, who were brought to power by the Red Army and were totally dependent on Soviet support, Tito had come to power at the head of a large and loyal partisan movement and an army with hundreds of thousands of supporters drawn from all of Jugoslavia's nationalities; Croats, Serbs, Slovenes, Montenegrins, Macedonians as well as the national minorities. Stalin feared and mistrusted his most successful pupil and when Tito showed signs of wanting to extend his influence in the Balkans and possibly to a still wider area, the axe fell; or it fell as far as membership of the Soviet bloc was concerned. Internally Tito's position was secure and he was able to accept Stalin's challenge. The manner of that acceptance showed that Tito and his colleagues were hoping for a reconciliation in the relatively near future. Jugoslavia's foreign policy remained pro-Soviet and anti-Western for over a year after the break. At home Jugoslav communists tried to prove their orthodoxy by introducing a number of ultra-left measures, including a new collectivisation campaign in the countryside.

As the propaganda war waged from Moscow and the satellite capitals became more intense, accompanied by attempts to subvert key personnel in the army and the security service and to stir up trouble among the national minorities, the Jugoslavs were forced to rethink their whole domestic and foreign strategy. In order to repair the damage done to their economy both by the Soviet economic blockade and their own mistakes, they were obliged to turn to the West for help. They quietly withdrew from the Greek civil war and began to distribute their own propaganda criticising Soviet foreign and domestic policies.

As an important concession to the country's peasant majority the drive towards collectivisation was abandoned in 1951, resulting in a rapid break-up of the majority of the country's already existing collective farms. Other more fundamental reforms and changes were to follow, but the important thing about all of them was that they were practical measures, imposed on the regime by the new political and economic circumstances and designed to help maintain its independent stand abroad and monopoly of power at home.

The First Reforms

One of the earliest, and to this day best known, innovations of the Jugoslav regime was the creation of the workers' councils (*radnički savjeti*). Launched in July 1950 in the middle of the economic crisis, the new institutions were designed to improve the abysmally low productivity in Jugoslav factories. The councils, elected by the workers, were to give the workers a say in all aspects of the factory's operations—choice of product, prices, wages, investment and distribution of surpluses. Initially the factory manager retained considerable power, and likewise the supervising local authority (which in practice meant the local Communist Party committee) with the result that the slogan with which the campaign was launched, 'factories to the workers', remained a dead letter for a number of years.

Most of the early restrictions were removed by measures of genuine decentralisation, political and economic, instituted in the late 1950s and the early 1960s. Yet, paradoxically, the councils are probably less important in Jugoslavia today than any other new institution introduced by the Tito regime.

The reason is to be found in the economic situation since the 1965 reform. The severe credit squeeze, the liberalisation of imports and other drastic measures designed to cure Jugoslavia's balance of payments problem, have resulted in the closure of numerous industrial and commercial enterprises and, inevitably, severe unemployment. Although over half-a-million Jugoslav workers have gone abroad to work in West Germany, Sweden, France and other West European countries, there is still unemployment at home. Over every worker hangs the shadow of dismissal. As one of the participants at a symposium on workers' councils put it: 'When a worker puts forward his view, he often comes into conflict with his superiors. And then, unfortunately, his livelihood comes into question.' In many enterprises workers have had to accept wage cuts. Those who want to fight have resorted to the old-fashioned weapon of the strike. Since the first post-war strike in a Slovene coal mine in 1958, the number of strikes has been rising every year.

An unexpected outcome of the new situation, which the authorities have now accepted, is the increasingly important role played by the trade unions (*sindikati*). For many years mere instruments of Communist Party control in factories and workers' councils, the unions have, under the new economic policy, been waging a vigorous battle to defend workers' living standards. So it is now the unions, more than the workers' councils, that appear as the champions of workers' rights.

That the workers' councils have not proved to be vital instruments of the new political strategy is probably in part due to the still very low educational level of the Jugoslav industrial labour force, which gives the better educated technical personnel a head start in any discussion. But despite their failure as a typical example of the new-style 'direct democracy' in Jugoslavia, the workers' councils have played an important role in educating hundreds of thousands of men and women in industry to fight for their rights by using the opportunities now provided by the decentralised system of government and politics which in turn evolved out of the workers' council experiment.

SELF-MANAGEMENT IN POLITICS

The first Jugoslav parliament elected in November 1945 was a typical communist rubber-stamp parliament modelled on the USSR Supreme Soviet. To begin with it contained a few pre-war political figures brought in by the communist regime to satisfy one of the provisions of the Yalta Agreement between Britain, the USA and the Soviet Union. Some of those politicians joined the Communist Party; others did not but played along with the wishes of the government. Those who showed any signs of independence were thrown out and imprisoned. The main role of the federal parliament and o Jugoslavia's six republican parliaments was to ratify decisions already reached by the Politburo of the party.

The picture began to change when in the early 1950s the conventional political parliamentary assemblies, elected by all voters in a constituency, were supplemented by a new type of assembly. These were elective at all levels, from that of the local district to that of the republic and then the federation, by all those working in industrial enterprises, in public services and institutions and in the collectivised sector of agriculture (private peasants were excluded). This new assembly, called the producers' council (*vijeće proizvodjača*) represented an attempt to extend the workers' management principle into politics.

However, the producers' councils did not become forums for fundamental political debate. The men elected into them were, like deputies of the conventional territorial assemblies, trusted members of the party. But there was one important difference. Those who were elected to the producers' councils from the very beginning felt themselves to be spokesmen for the new pressure groups that the decentralised economy tended to produce. Wine-growing interests from Croatia, the mining interests from Serbia and various interests in Macedonia, Slovenia and the other republics were able to make themselves heard.

An important step towards decentralisation was the establishment in 1955 of the new unit of local government—the commune (*komuna*)—which took over many of the administrative and economic functions formerly vested in the central or republican apparatus.

THE 1963 CONSTITUTION

The climax of this development was reached in the new constitution of 1963, which, together with a few important amendments passed in April 1967 and December 1968, represents the constitutional framework within which Jugoslavia is governed today. A document of great length and complexity, it is undoubtedly a major departure from the first Jugoslav constitution of 1946 (a faithful copy of Stalin's 1936 constitution) and is also a great improvement on the more liberal 1953 constitution passed in the early days of the reform.

The Federal and National Assembly in Belgrade consists of five chambers (instead of two as under the previous constitution). They are: the Economic Chamber, the Health and Welfare Chamber, the Culture and Education Chamber with 120 deputies each, elected indirectly by delegates of communal assemblies and corresponding enterprises and institutions. Then there is the Socio-Political Chamber, also with 120 deputies elected directly by voters in all the communes. (This chamber takes over the functions of two previous chambers abolished in December 1968: the Federal Chamber and the Administrative-Political Chamber.) Finally, there is the Chamber of Nationalities with 140 deputies—20 for each of the six republics and ten for each of the two Socialist Autonomous Provinces, the Vojvodina and Kosovo-Metohija (Kosmet). Any decision taken by a chamber of the National Assembly must have the approval of the Chamber of Nationalities, which is clearly designed to act as the guardian of the interests of the republics and provinces *vis-à-vis* the federation. This is emphasised by the fact that the deputies of the Chamber of Nationalities are elected by the republics and the provinces and act as their delegates.

This pattern, without, of course, the Chamber of Nationalities, is reproduced at the republican level and in the two autonomous provinces. The communal assemblies continue to have two chambers only.

Until 1963 the same people continued to be elected into parliamentary bodies and there were only as many candidates as there were seats to be filled. Now there has been a radical change. At the elections held in April 1967 seats for republican and federal assemblies were contested by two, three or even four candidates. Out of 60 newly elected members of the Federal Chamber in Belgrade (the other 60 had been elected in 1965), no less than 59 were new men. The principle of rotation introduced in 1963 forbids deputies to run again for seats in the same assembly. The same principle applies to holders of high posts in the federal government and the governments of the individual republics. Party leaders, who would like to alternate between parliament and government, are finding it difficult to be nominated or elected, as the 1967 election showed. A number of prominent party candidates were defeated by lesser known men. The nomination procedure, which has been relaxed still further since the 1967 election, makes it relatively easy for groups of citizens to put forward names of their own candidates, sometimes even against the wishes of the local party leadership. In a small town in Serbia, a former partisan general was elected in 1967 as the candidate of the local veterans' association despite official party opposition. It took many months of pressure, including direct intervention by the Central Committee in Belgrade, to have him unseated at the end of 1967. In another Serbian town, friends of one candidate mined a number of bridges in the constituency in order to prevent a rival candidate from addressing the voters. The election generated so many conflicts that cases were still being heard by the courts a year later.

PARLIAMENT AND GOVERNMENT

Once they are elected to parliament, deputies take part in vigorous and prolonged debates and frequently petition the government on a variety of issues. All assemblies, federal, republican, provincial and communal, meet frequently and their deliberations are fully reported in the press and on radio and television. A debate on an important financial bill led to the resignation of the Slovene republican government in December 1966. This resignation, subsequently withdrawn after a compromise was reached, has created a precedent. A year later the national press reported, in what was clearly a calculated leak, that the federal government had used the threat of resignation to force the passage of another controversial financial bill. The bill was passed but at least one dissatisfied government, that of Slovenia, has queried the final decision in the context of the rapidly developing debate on the rights of the individual republics in the federation.

The majority of deputies of federal assemblies are Communist Party members, likewise the republican deputies. At the communal level, however, there is an increasing tendency to elect non-party specialists and personalities. Although the party still retains the numerical predominance in all the really important bodies, this fact has in the new conditions lost a good deal of its former importance. For the truth is—and party leaders openly admit it—that the party is split from top to bottom and hardly exists as a united body.

In 1952 at the Sixth Party Congress in Zagreb, the Communist Party changed its name to the League of Communists of Jugoslavia (LCJ) and adopted new and more liberal party statutes, thus tempering the severity of the old Leninist 'democratic centralism' principle. Few could have predicted this development. When Milovan Djilas, one of the moving spirits behind the reform, advocated the formation of a 'loyal opposition' party he was clearly ahead of his time. His ideas were unacceptable to his colleagues on the Central Committee and they were rejected by the all-powerful local party leaders. Djilas lost his top party post, and later his freedom too. Today he lives in enforced retirement, but his ideas form the common currency of the ideological debate going on within the party.

Years of economic reform and political experiment have eroded the party's once all-powerful position. And the question being asked by younger party intellectuals is, 'does Jugoslavia need this type of party any more? And why not have two or more parties to ensure all-round competence and regular rotation on a more systematic basis.' The question was raised by Mihajlo Mihajlov, a young non-party intellectual in 1965. Mihajlov is still serving a prison sentence for attempting to publish an opposition newspaper. But the debate has continued, notably in the two main organs of the 'revisionist' Marxist intellectuals, *Praxis* in Zagreb and *Gledišta* ('Views') in Belgrade.

STRUGGLE WITHIN THE PARTY

Whether or not the regime allows the formation of an opposition party, which, on present evidence, seems unlikely for a number of reasons some of which will be dealt with below, there are inside the party a number of unofficial groups or wings which represent not one but several varying shades of opinion. For several years what might loosely be termed the 'liberal' wing has been represented by communist leaders from the republics of Slovenia and Croatia, the two most Westernised and industrially developed in the whole federation. Its leaders, the Slovene, Kardelj, and the Croat, Bakarić, have consistently advocated economic reform and political decentralisation which would give more power to individual republics. This tendency was opposed by another powerful group of leaders mainly from the less developed republics. The most prominent of these was Aleksandar Ranković, founder of Jugoslavia's security police (UDBA) and for years one of the secretaries of the Central Committee. Ranković and his friends opposed the liberals on the grounds that economic and political decentralisation would weaken still further the Jugoslav state and undermine the party's control in the country.

The conflict between the two wings came to a head over the question of the timing of the 1965 reform. Unable to secure its postponement, the 'conservatives' tried to sabotage its implementation. At the same time Ranković and his friends began active preparations for securing power in Jugoslavia. The security service put a number of top party leaders under surveillance and when Tito discovered a hidden microphone in his own bedroom he decided to act. A special meeting of the party's Central Committee was held in Brioni in July 1966 at which Ranković and his closest collaborator, the then head of Jugoslav security, Svetislav Stefanović, were charged and were subsequently deprived of their posts. Their defeat led to a wholesale purge of the security service and later to its reform. A drastic decentralisation of the service left the central security organs with responsibility for only such matters as counter-intelligence. Public security was placed in the hands of the republics.

The Party and Jugoslavia's Nationalities

Paradoxically, the liberals' victory has brought with it more problems than it has solved. In the aftermath of the July 1966 confrontation, it became a matter of the utmost urgency for the regime to begin seriously to tackle the problem of nationalism. Touched upon at the Eighth Congress of the party in 1964 and even earlier, the problem came into the open in the great 'investment debate' between the developed and undeveloped republics. The Croats and the Slovenes had for years resented Belgrade's policy of heavy investment in the less developed republics of Montenegro, Macedonia, Bosnia and Hercegovina and Serbia itself at the expense of their own development and modernisation. And when, under the economic reforms of 1961 and 1965, drastic action to close down uneconomic industrial enterprises became imperative the axe was bound to fall first on the 'political' factories of Montenegro, Serbia and Macedonia. The conservatives' defeat, which also meant the victory of the school which had advocated the concentration of investment in areas where it would bring maximum returns, i.e. in the developed republics, has led to further complications. Leaders from the less developed republics are now trying to influence the federal authorities in their favour, which in turn has led the republican authorities in Croatia and Slovenia to demand fuller sovereign rights for themselves *vis-à-vis* the federation.

Whilst this controversy gathers strength the party itself has become a battleground for bitter nationalist struggles. Basically, Jugoslavia now faces the same problems which eventually destroyed the first Jugoslav state before the war—that of relations between the Serbs and the other nations. The economic debate had brought to light the resistance of Jugoslavia's nations and national minorities to Serbian hegemony. When Ranković fell, it was disclosed that other Serbian security officials had been pursuing an oppressive chauvinistic policy against the Albanian minority in Kosovo-Metohija (see above p. 245). It was also disclosed that similar offences had been committed against the Croats and the Muslims in parts of Hercegovina, a mixed area historically claimed by both the Serbs and the Croats.

The regime has tried to rectify the situation, particularly among the Albanians in Kosmet, which borders on Albania proper. More encouragement has been given to various forms of cultural expression among the Albanians, who are the majority in the province. The Albanian flag has been permitted to fly and the Albanian language now enjoys fully equal status. The constitutional amendment passed in December 1968 gives the Kosmet authorities the right to plan their own economic and social development with full control of their financial resources, and within the framework of a separate provisional constitution for Kosmet.

The implementation of these far-reaching and long overdue concessions to the Albanians in Jugoslavia has undoubtedly been speeded up in order to contain the rising wave of Albanian nationalist propaganda in Kosmet and elsewhere in Jugoslavia. Riots in Priština and other major Kosmet cities in November 1968 and then again in Tetovo in western Macedonia, where there is a strong Albanian element are evidence of the strength of Albanian nationalism in Jugoslavia today and of the urgent need for constructive measures to prevent it from getting out of control.

These conciliatory moves to the Albanians accompanied by similar concessions to other national minorities have provoked a bitter counter-reaction among the Serbs. The 'political underground' in Serbia, now thoroughly nationalistic, is causing the regime a great deal of anxiety. Meanwhile, in Croatia there continues to be a strong nationalist reaction to Belgrade's centralism in the first two decades after the war, symbolised by the use of the Serbian language in the army and the central state institutions, the predominance of Serbs in diplomatic posts, key positions in the army, security service, etc. In Slovenia, too, anti-Belgrade spirit has been strengthened rather than weakened by Ranković's fall. Of the 'controversial' republics, only Macedonia appears to have remained calm. But the concessions to Macedonian nationalism, notably the formation of the autocephalous Macedonian Orthodox Church (previously a part of the Serbian Orthodox Church) in 1967, have provoked a bitter reaction in Serbia whose church has refused to recognise the new body.

The key problem facing Jugoslavia's leaders today is whether their deeply divided party can keep the country together when Tito has gone. There is no obvious successor in sight but even if one is found who would be acceptable to the majority of leaders from all the republics, he could not count on the automatic loyalty of the ex-partisans, who formed the backbone of Jugoslavia's establishment in the first two decades after the war. Many of those ex-partisans, who used to occupy key posts in industry, party apparatus, security service, and the army have in any case given way to younger and better-educated men whose loyalties are much more uncertain.

The Jugoslav federation is at the moment undergoing a process of profound change in the direction of the gradual strengthening of the republican governments and other organs at the expense of the once powerful federal government in Belgrade. The Jugoslav press, radio and television, for years the most independent in the countries of Eastern Europe, have been canvassing for some kind of reorganisation along the lines of a confederation. But such a move is at present unlikely; it would require a degree of unity and understanding among Jugoslav party leaders which does not exist. Serbian opinion in particular would bitterly oppose any move that would divide the population into three big groups: the main one in Serbia proper, and the important minorities in Bosnia, Hercegovina and Croatia. Any division of Bosnia would almost certainly be opposed by the Muslims, some of whom consider themselves to be Croats and some Serbs, whilst the majority has preferred, because of strong Serbian pressure after the war, to remain nationally uncommitted, a unique phenomenon in European politics. The large Serbian minority in Croatia, many of whose members took part in the partisan war, would also strenuously oppose any move that would separate them from other Serbs.

It is not surprising, therefore, that Tito and his closest collaborators have been increasingly turning to the army as the only force capable of preserving the state's unity. The army has received much more publicity recently than in past years. The communists in the army have been integrated into party organisations in their garrison towns, presumably to act as a stabilising element. Since the Middle East war in June 1967 the army's budget has been significantly increased, and changes in the army top commands have yet again emphasised the importance that President Tito himself attaches to the army's role. A thought which cannot have escaped him and the other party leaders is that the army still contains a larger proportion of Serbs and Montenegrins and that they are bound to support the unity of the state. The authorities' strenuous efforts to attract more Croats, Slovenes and Macedonians have had disappointing results. Army careers, despite high earnings, are less attractive in Slovenia and Croatia where they have to compete with better industrial and other available jobs. In the case of the Macedonians and the Slovenes, there is the additional problem of the language; the army uses the Serbian variant of the Serbo-Croat language. Significantly, the army's predominantly Serbian character was one of the targets of a declaration signed by 19 Croat cultural institutions in March 1967. This declaration, bitterly attacked by the official party leadership, demanded that Croat and Serb be proclaimed separate languages guaranteed by the constitution. Punitive measures were taken against the declaration's signatories but their demand was symptomatic of the state of public opinion on the nationalities issue.

Should there be a further sharpening of the national conflict in Jugoslavia coinciding with a leadership struggle after Tito's death, the army could decide to step in and take power into its own hands. Such a move might be popular with Moscow because a military dictatorship would probably be more amenable to Soviet wishes in return for Soviet military support. However, it would be deeply unpopular with all the peoples of Jugoslavia and could even result in a split within the armed forces themselves. Fortunately, Jugoslavia with its decentralised economy, decentralised political system and decentralised security service is not now a country which could be taken over easily or quickly.

The future remains uncertain. Some have compared Tito with the last Habsburg emperor, Francis Joseph, and today's Jugoslavia with a slowly disintegrating Austria-Hungary. Only the future can show whether the comparison is apt. However, it must be remembered that it took a world war to destroy Austria-Hungary and that the first royalist Jugoslavia collapsed only when attacked from outside by overwhelmingly stronger Axis forces in 1941.

Jugoslavia's Influence in Eastern Europe

Jugoslavia's innovations of the past 20 years have been widely studied, admired and occasionally copied in a number of countries. The theory and practice of workers' councils was said to have been of particular interest to Algeria and Indonesia, when those two countries were being run by Tito's close friends, Ben Bella and Sukarno. More recently, President Nasser of Egypt is said to have been influenced by the model of the Socialist Alliance, Jugoslavia's mass organisation formerly known as the People's Front, when refashioning his own mass organisation, the Arab Socialist Union. Even in the UK, sections of the Labour Party have shown a certain amount of interest in Jugoslavia's system of self-management.

But it is in Eastern Europe that Tito's Jugoslavia has exercised a profound and historic influence in the past 20 years. Tito's independent stand against Stalin in 1948 represented the first challenge to the hitherto undisputed principle of the 'leading role of the Soviet Union'. The bold affirmation by the Jugoslav communists of the new principle of 'equal relations between the socialist states' each pursuing its own 'road to socialism' was bound to find responsive listeners in the deeply nationalist countries of Eastern Europe, the majority of which had achieved their national independence only a few decades before.

Stalin lost no time in an attempt to eliminate potential 'Titoists' from the ranks of communist leaders in satellite countries. A number of prominent leaders, most of them 'home-grown' like László Rajk in Hungary, Traicho Kostov in Bulgaria, Koci Xoxe in Albania, were executed and many others, less well-known, with them. Władysław Gomułka in Poland was imprisoned; similarly thousands all over Eastern Europe were imprisoned or expelled from the party as suspected 'nationalists'. The spread of the 'Titoist' disease seemed to be checked temporarily.

But when in May 1955 Soviet leaders, Khrushchev and Bulganin, made their famous trip to Belgrade and in a joint declaration with Tito explicitly recognised Jugoslavia's right to her 'separate road to socialism', the pressure for greater independence in satellite countries became irresistible. Why should Tito be allowed to get away with what was forbidden to them?

For a while it seemed as though Soviet Union leaders recognised the force of this argument and would be prepared to see a certain measure of liberalisation take place within the bloc. This in itself was a tremendous moral victory for Tito and his colleagues who now felt entirely vindicated. Moreover, they hoped that they might be allowed to return to the pre-1948 situation and perhaps even be able to assist the Soviet Union in the task of reorganising Eastern Europe along more liberal lines. Tito's triumphant tour of the Soviet Union in the summer of 1956 represented the high point of these hopes. And reluctant satellite leaders began to show signs of slowly coming to terms with the situation.

However, when in the autumn of the same year the Polish Central Committee, acting in defiance of Soviet wishes, reinstated the 'Titoist' Gomułka, and the impatient students and writers of Budapest were making demands for neutrality and genuine internal democracy, the process of 'Titoisation' of Eastern Europe was halted abruptly. Tito and his ideas were out in the cold again. But the concept of 'separate roads to socialism', first propounded by Tito, lived on even after the guns of Budapest. A few years later, in the new conditions of the Sino-Soviet split, first Albania in 1961 and then Rumania in 1964, took their own separate roads, and in 1968 it was Czechoslovakia's turn to try and loosen the ties with Moscow.

Since 1956 Jugoslavia's economic policies have been followed very closely and critically in various East European countries. It was in Czechoslavakia in the period between January and August 1968 that Jugoslav political and economic ideas found their most sympathetic audience. Tito, for his part, warmly supported the Dubček regime from the beginning, and in the summer of 1968 Tito seemed to be on the brink of fulfilling his old dream: that of leading a group of moderate, progressive and, above all, independent communist nations in Eastern Europe.

The invasion of Czechoslovakia by Soviet and other Warsaw Pact troops in August of the same year put an end to any such hopes for a long time to come. Once again Jugoslavia finds itself in enforced isolation with only Rumania (now much more careful not to offend Moscow) to keep it company. However, frequent critical articles and broadcasts on Jugoslavia's politics and economy coming from Warsaw Pact countries are evidence of the fact that the ups and downs of the 'heretical' Tito regime will continue to be watched and interpreted with a mixture of hostility, fascination and perhaps a little envy. Meanwhile, in Jugoslavia itself the new sense of external danger from the East since August 1968 has created a new defiant mood which has certainly, for the moment, made a good deal easier President Tito's task of keeping the peoples of Jugoslavia under the same roof.

FURTHER READING

Auty, Phyllis. *Yugoslavia*, Thames and Hudson, London; Walker and Co., New York, 1965.

Bićanic, R. 'Economics of Socialism in a Developed Country', *Foreign Affairs*, Vol. 44, No. 4, July 1966.

Campbell, J. C. *Tito's Separate Road*, Harper and Row, New York, 1967.

Clissold, Stephen. *Whirlwind*, Cresset Press, London; Philosophical Library, New York, 1949.

Djilas, Milovan. *Conversations with Stalin*, Rupert Hart-Davis, London; Harcourt Brace, New York, 1962.

Halperin, Ernst. *The Triumphant Heretic*, Heinemann, London, 1958.

Hoffman, G. W. and Neal, F. W. *Yugoslavia and the New Communism*, Twentieth Century Fund, New York, 1962.

Jukić, Ilija. 'Tito's Last Battle', *East Europe*, 18, 4, April 1967.

Maclean, Fitzroy. *Disputed Barricade*, Cape, London, 1957.

Rusinow, D. 'Understanding the Yugoslav Reforms', *The World Today*, 23, 2, February 1967.

Shonp, Paul. *Communism and the Yugoslav National Question*, Columbia Univ. Press, New York, 1968.

Sylvester, A. 'Intellectual Ferment in Yugoslavia', *Survey*, 62, January 1967.

K. F. Cviić. Broadcaster and journalist on the affairs of Jugoslavia, where he was born. Has lived in Britain since 1954. Has spent three years studying recent Jugoslav history at St. Anthony's College, Oxford. Now on the staff of *The Economist*.

THE CZECHOSLOVAK EXPERIMENT

MICHAEL MONTGOMERY

The Toppling of the Old Order

Since early 1963, when a late de-Stalinisation began in Czechoslovakia, the increasing ferment in the country led the Stalinist Novotný regime to apply the characteristic 'stop-go' policies of enforced liberalisation. These policies were much the same as the neo-Stalinist line followed in the Soviet Union since the late Khrushchev era; the aim was to make life more tolerable where absolutely necessary by concessions in certain limited sectors, while at the same time retaining firm party control over everything. All over Eastern Europe, Communist Parties and governments were compelled now and again to give in to specific demands from below, but they were equally forced sooner or later to take repressive measures against the wave of boldness engendered by their concessions. In Czechoslovakia relaxation was later in coming than in any of Moscow's other satellites, with the exception of East Germany, and this reluctant de-Stalinisation moved too slowly for many Czechs and Slovaks, particularly for the liberal writers and economists and for the nationalists of Slovakia. Novotný, who had survived in high party office from the Stalin era and who still held the twin posts of party leader and head of state (a combination already obsolete in Eastern Europe, though subsequently revived by Ulbricht and Ceauşescu), was increasingly seen as a symbol of repression. By the summer of 1967 the tension between the party leadership and the intellectual and technocrat rank-and-file was becoming intolerable.

The intellectuals were disappointed by the lack of cultural as well as general civic freedoms, which were theoretically guaranteed by the constitution. Though there had been occasional periods since 1963 in which outspoken utterances were tolerated and the Czech and Slovak intellectuals had probably won a greater measure of freedom than their colleagues in most of Soviet-dominated Eastern Europe, the order of the day was firm party control. The writers above all realised that what freedom they had could be lost again in a moment and began pressing for their gains to be written into the law. In many fields, the right to discuss and criticise extended no further than minor everyday matters. But from mid-1966 on public calls for democracy, for free elections, for the correction of distorted history and for a less 'loaded' legal system were being voiced with increasing frequency, especially in the weekly of the Czechoslovak Writers' Union, *Literární noviny*, and in its Slovak counterpart, *Kultúrny život*. These suggestions, like most of those made later during the Dubček liberalisation, aimed at making the communist system more palatable and more consistent with its professed ideals, and not at destroying or replacing it. The reaction of the authorities to criticisms of this sort was erratic; sometimes the critics found themselves the victims of stern public or behind-the-scenes sanctions, sometimes no action was taken at all.

In the case of the Slovaks, there were added reasons for dissatisfaction. The political and constitutional status of Slovakia in the Czechoslovak state had never been a happy one in the 50 years of its existence. The status accorded them certainly failed to live up to the national aspirations of all but a minority of Slovaks. These aspirations had been satisfied only during the brief period of autonomy within the republic after Munich and during the six-year existence of the independent Slovak republic in the war years. Apart from this, the Slovaks were left with the feeling of being treated as second-class citizens in a state where they formed a third of the population. Two decades of communist rule had done little or nothing to set right their grievances against Prague 'centralism'. The few Slovaks who served in the central party and government organs in Prague were rarely popular in Slovakia as national politicians. On paper Slovakia had its own representative body, the Slovak National Council, but its powers were heavily curtailed in practice, as were the powers and functions of the Slovak Writers' Union and similar professional and interest groups. These organisations, like the Slovak Communist Party itself, were merely appendages of the corresponding nationwide —that is, Czechoslovak—bodies.

Nationalism has long been a moving force in the ethnic melting-pot of Central Europe, and the Slovak question was to prove the catalyst which set in train the process of de-Stalinisation in Czechoslovakia. Added to the broader Slovak national grievances was a feeling that Slovakia was being neglected economically by the central government in Prague and that too little was being done to raise it nearer the level of industrial development in the Czech lands of Bohemia and Moravia. Much Slovak frustration was channelled over the years into complaints on this score at party meetings. The greatest national grievance, however, concerned the trials of the Slovak 'bourgeois nationalists' in the early 1950s, which resulted from internal party conflicts with their roots in the closing years of the war. Within the space of a year or two most of the capable Slovak communist leaders had disappeared into prison or to the gallows for their alleged advocacy of a separate Slovak road to socialism or for deviations from the Moscow line of a joint nationwide Communist Party. Demands for the rehabilitation of these leaders were strong in Slovakia, and the party was eventually forced to order a review of the show trials in the early 1960s. The results of this judicial review were made known in August 1963: most of the Slovak victims, Gustáv Husák for instance, as well as Czechs who had suffered in similar trials, were rehabilitated. In the climate of change the Slovak intellectuals became more outspoken, and their example was soon followed by writers in the Czech lands.

These enforced rehabilitations and the general relaxation in the cultural field in response to heavy pressure from below coincided with the beginnings of a movement to free the run-down economy from the centralised 'command' system inherited from the Soviet Union as part and parcel of communist dogma. By 1962 the Czechoslovak economy—now well below its pre-war level of performance—was in dire need of drastic restorative measures if it was not to collapse completely. Inefficient central planning, apathy among the workers and enforced sales to the Soviet Union at dictated prices over 14 years of communism had reduced the economy to a shadow of its former self. A blueprint for economic recovery was worked out by a group of liberal economists led by Dr. Ota Šik, at that time head of the Economic Institute of the Czechoslovak Academy of Sciences as well as a member of the Central Committee. Like the similar, but more restricted, Liberman scheme in the Soviet Union, the Šik reform envisaged a system incorporating some principles of the market economy: a large measure of local autonomy would be given to individual enterprises, including the freedom to regulate their output according to consumer demand, and the guiding principle would no longer be dogma but economic profitability. In addition a freer system of trading with Western countries was advocated. The party leadership accepted the reform programme—some members of it with scarcely concealed reluctance—and plans were made for it to be phased into operation during 1966. But even before that some prominent party leaders appeared to be trying to sabotage the reform behind the scenes, and there was also widespread hostility among local party bosses (who stood to lose their jealously guarded dictatorial power in the factories) and also a certain amount of mild industrial unrest from workers who faced a probable reduction in wages coupled with a general rise in prices. These attempts at sabotage continued even after the new economic system became fully operative in January 1967. Vested interests within the party were reluctant to accept the new situation, which was further complicated by the emergence of other liberal economic schools of thought partially or totally opposed to Dr. Šik and full of ideas of their own on how to conduct the economic salvage operation. By the end of 1968 party spokesmen were attributing new economic difficulties partly to the Warsaw Pact invasion and partly to continued obstruction of the reform.

The essence of the Czechoslovak economic reform was the move away from rigid dogma in favour of greater pragmatism, and this shift corresponded to the rise of a new generation of technocrats, who had ideas—always within the communist system—of running the economy efficiently without the restrictions imposed by received communist doctrine. It did not require much imagination to extend this principle to the whole complex of government policies, in fact to all walks of life, rejecting dogmatic in favour of pragmatic solutions. It was this idea which lay broadly behind the various forces in the liberalising wave on which the Dubček leadership came to power in January 1968. The Dubček reform programme was the logical culmination of this rejection of dogma. It was argued that if the economy was on the verge of collapse because of a failure to face up to realities, then perhaps the general political apathy in the country—and particularly the lack of interest in politics among young people—had its roots in the same rigid attitudes in other spheres. Hence the attempt to humanise communism to make it more attractive by rejecting the worst aspects of its political creed. In this aim of presenting a new and competitive image, the Dubček leadership by and large succeeded. The liberalisation did not produce droves of new party members, but it made the population at large feel, despite a certain amount of popular suspicion and scepticism, that, for the first time in 20 years, the Communist Party was doing something for the good of Czechoslovakia and not merely obeying orders from Moscow. These sympathies were naturally heightened in the wave of national unity which followed the Warsaw Pact invasion in August 1968, but the suspicions also grew as the year drew to a close and the ambiguous political situation remained unsettled.

The latent dissatisfaction over the old Stalinist policies first erupted into open revolt at the Congress of the Union of Czechoslovak Writers in June

1967 where several younger writers, passing beyond the strictly cultural sphere, enraged the party leadership by their attacks on various aspects of the political set-up. The party's subsequent sanctions against the dissident writers and intellectuals only served to increase the discontent, which was now threatening to reach unmanageable proportions. Conversely, for the protesters, the party's dictatorial stance was also becoming intolerable. Opposition to the government's Moscow-orientated support for the Arab states in the Arab-Israeli war, and increasing Slovak restlessness were heightened by various incidents in the autumn of 1967: the shooting of escapees on the Austrian border, police brutality to Prague students demonstrating against the faulty electricity supply and bad food, and fisticuffs between President Novotný and Slovak party leaders during a presidential visit to Slovakia.

The liberals in the party's centres of power, however, were not yet sure of their strength and their ability to vote the old leadership out of office. Furthermore, there was no unified opposition to Novotný, but rather a loose alliance of people with different aims and interests—the economic reformers, the intellectuals, the Slovak nationalists and an increasing number of loyal party members who recognised the political sterility of the Novotný line. In addition, there were a number of opportunists who could be relied on to choose the winning side in the forthcoming battle. The winter months of 1967 were marked by calls for the replacement of Novotný as first secretary of the party. This campaign had been initiated by Dubček—then first secretary of the Slovak Communist Party—at a meeting of the Central Committee in October. Novotný is said to have branded Dubček a 'bourgeois nationalist' for this speech; the term was an unpleasant reminder of the past and only served to confirm the belief of the anti-Novotný faction in the justness of their cause. The issue of Novotný's replacement was again debated at two meetings of the Central Committee in December, but the vote was inconclusive. It was not until the first week of January 1968 at a renewed Central Committee session that Novotný was replaced by Alexander Dubček after a further vote. Novotný himself had forfeited some support by attempting to mobilise military forces against the reformers in the intervening period. The change from Novotný to Dubček, then a relatively unknown quantity, was achieved by almost democratic means, without the purges, trials and acts of vengeance which had usually accompanied changes of regime in the communist world in the past, at least until the fall of Khrushchev.

THE NEW LINE

The January meeting of the Central Committee also outlined the new policies of the party, and with this the word 'January', like 'May', which referred to a later meeting of equal significance, assumed an almost mystical meaning in the otherwise turgid vocabulary of Czechoslovak politics. The January declarations were followed by a wave of personnel changes designed to secure support for the new leaders. Over the next month or two the 'old guard' in the party leadership gradually disappeared from office, but a large number of conservative-minded communists remained in the Central Committee and in the National Assembly (both, of course, elected during the Novotný period), and Novotný himself retained his position on the party Praesidium and the figurehead post of president of the republic until March and his Central Committee membership until May.

The 'conservative' communists in positions of influence continued to pose a serious problem to the new party leaders as a potential source of obstruction. Dubček still had to reckon with an estimated opposition factor of between 30% and 40% in the Central Committee and the National Assembly. This pattern was repeated wherever there were men with vested interests in the old system. The new leaders had come to power on a very slender majority and the ever-present possibility that the Novotný supporters would succeed in swaying the opportunists against the liberal line made it necessary to remove the 'hard-liners' as soon as possible. It would, of course, have been possible to use Stalinist tactics and simply remove the opposition by 'administrative' methods, but Dubček was determined to introduce what he called 'socialist democracy'—a genuine involvement of the people in public affairs—instead of the previous dictatorship of a small party élite. After much public discussion, the May Central Committee meeting decided, somewhat against the inclinations of the leadership which wanted to proceed at a more cautious pace, to convene an Extraordinary Party Congress in September in order to elect a new Central Committee. In the event this congress was convened a fortnight earlier than planned, during the first days of the Soviet invasion, but subsequent events were to prevent the complete ousting of 'conservative' elements. Nonetheless, the Soviet leaders found few willing collaborators even among the opposition to Dubček.

Soviet interference must have seemed a remote possibility in the period of change, of open discussions and revelations that followed the January Central Committee meeting. On numerous occasions, not least in their charter of reform, the 'Action Programme', which was published in April 1968, the new Czechoslovak leaders reaffirmed that alliance with the Soviet Union remained the cornerstone of their foreign policy. Though the misgivings of the Soviet Union and of their neighbours were frequently made known to them, they believed that these objections would be overcome by argument and persuasion.

The Czechoslovak liberalisation was essentially very cautious in character. During its short-lived period of glory, the new regime was trying to steer a middle course between the conflicting claims of 'extremist' liberalisers, 'conservatives' with a vested interest in the old system, apprehensive allies and a population at first sceptical and lukewarm in its support of the new line. Although an unprecedented freedom of expression was permitted, with the abolition of prior censorship, and although the trappings of the Stalinist police state were slowly dismantled, party spokesmen were always at pains to disavow the demands of radical communists for a multi-party system, for greater trading freedom with the West and even for revision of the country's Warsaw Pact obligations. Broadly, the regime was out, in the words of Dubček, to give communism 'a human face'—to establish it as a competitive political system which would win adherents by its very essence instead of commanding obedience by police terror and repression. It was largely for this reason that the 'Czechoslovak springtime' won the support of the major Western Communist Parties, which saw it as a means of brightening their tarnished image and improving their electoral prospects.

The Czechoslovak Action Programme, which was approved by the Central Committee on 5 April 1968, gave a complete statement of the aims of the new regime. Previous party programmes for reform had never been so far-reaching; they were designed to grant a minimum of concessions and they never overstepped the bounds of neo-Stalinist orthodoxy. The new Action Programme contained many departures from orthodox doctrine. It opened by attributing the barrenness of Czechoslovak political life to inexperience, dogmatism, subjectivism and foreign practices and political concepts in the introduction of communism. It admitted that the party and government were responsible for the harm caused by violations of 'socialist legality'. According to the programme, the class struggle had ended, the country had to meet the challenge of the world technological revolution and the public must be allowed the widest possible participation in government and administration. This spontaneous 'self-criticism' by the Czechoslovak Communist Party was unprecedented. So too was the idea of mass involvement in politics which, though democratic principles are enshrined in every communist constitution, usually remain in the hands of a self-perpetuating power élite.

The Action Programme went on to outline the various reforms which would be undertaken in order to introduce 'socialist democracy'. In future the Communist Party would have to be seen to deserve the leading role which it traditionally accorded itself, and it would act by persuasion and not by repressive means. Dissenting minorities would continue to be bound by majority decisions of the party, but internal party discussions would be unrestricted. Guarantees of these new freedoms, including the freedom of speech as a check against the abuse of power, would be included in a new constitution. Party membership would no longer be a passport to a successful career; communists would now have to take their chances in free competition with non-communists. In setting up a more humane system of administration, state and party bodies were to be clearly separated, and past political injustices would be righted by the creation of a federal state of the Czechs and the Slovaks. The law courts were henceforth to play their proper role without party interference, prior censorship—already heavily cut down since March—was to be abolished and basic human rights, including the ownership of property, were to be guaranteed. In the field of foreign policy, apart from reaffirming the alliance with the Soviet Union, the Action Programme reiterated Czechoslovakia's adherence to the policy of peaceful coexistence and its determination to seek 'useful relations' with all states.

The part of the programme detailing the new internal policies represented so radical a departure from the Stalinist police state of Novotný with its small élite ruling by decree that at first there was little confidence among the public. Early public opinion polls showed that large sectors of the population remained sceptical about all or part of the reform. By the middle of 1968, however, public confidence had risen sharply. The measures already taken by way of rehabilitating past purge victims, ensuring freedom of speech and discussion and introducing less oppressive methods of administration, and the fact that Dubček always seemed to emerge successful from meetings with the apprehensive Soviet government convinced people that what had started as a 'palace revolution' was to be taken seriously.

Soviet Fears

The Dubček programme was a conscious break with a past that was acknowledged to have been evil. In part it did no more than introduce in practice what all communist constitutions guarantee in theory: freedom of speech, democratic involvement of the public in political life and a concern with human values and the development of society. In other points, however, the Action Programme deviated from orthodox communist doctrine to an extent which must have worried the ideological chiefs in Moscow. In addition, the whole reform was accompanied by unofficial proposals—usually disavowed by the party—for even more radical improvements than those contained in the programme itself. These included the creation of an opposition party or parties and the idea of neutrality as a solution to some of Czechoslovakia's problems. What must have irritated the Moscow ideologists most was the suggestion that the Soviet model of communism, imposed on Czechoslovakia in 1948, had been unsuitable because it was originally designed for a backward agrarian country and not for an advanced Central European state like Czechoslovakia. It was also a heresy to maintain that Czechoslovakia had outstripped the Soviet Union in various aspects of the building of 'socialism', so that the class struggle was over and progress could henceforward be made not on the basis of the working class ('the dictatorship of the proletariat'), but on the support and cooperation of all sectors of the population.

These heresies naturally worried the Soviet Union and Czechoslovakia's other Warsaw Pact allies, and Dubček had to account for himself at numerous meetings—at Dresden in March, Moscow in May, Čierna-nad-Tisou and Bratislava in the summer—and also in a number of bilateral confrontations with other communist leaders. On these occasions, just as in December 1967, when the Soviet party leader Brezhnev came to Prague after the first attempt to unseat Novotný, the Czechoslovak leaders appear to have convinced their doubting allies that they were simply engaged in a slightly more far-reaching form of neo-Stalinism (which was perhaps true of at least some of them). They made some concessions to the Soviet demands that press attacks on the Soviet Union should be stopped and promised to clamp down on the worst 'anti-socialist' excesses accompanying the liberalisation. Probably too, there was a degree of genuine misunderstanding; 'democracy' clearly had different meanings for the Czechoslovak and the Soviet leaders.

But it seems that ideological objections were only a cover for the deeper Soviet mistrust of Dubček. True, there was a danger of infection with liberal ideas for all the other East European countries. There was also the humiliation for Moscow of being challenged by a more popular form of communism in one of its satellites and perhaps even the vision of being superseded by Prague as a centre of communism. Public criticisms of the Moscow line were being published wholesale in Prague, as well as uncomfortable revelations about the role of Soviet agents there in the past. But the ideological objections were only part of the story; Moscow was moved equally, if not more, by practical reasons of power politics.

For, despite his assurances, there was always a danger that Dubček would lose control and that Czechoslovakia would turn neutral or, worse still, attempt to go over to the West. Even without this extreme development, there were untold opportunities for the 'imperialists' to use Czechoslovakia as a base for subverting the entire communist bloc. It was on this issue that Soviet, Polish and East German press attacks concentrated from April on. This fear of subversion and of a possible shift in the balance of power in Europe (and perhaps nuclear war, the prevention of which depends on that balance) lingered on in the Soviet leaders' minds. They continued to press Dubček for a toning down of the liberalisation in the meetings at Čierna and Bratislava. Although the absence of any significant revision of the Czechoslovak reform gave them good reason for irritation, what most likely lay behind the order to invade (the military side of the operation had obviously been prepared for months before) was the realisation that, with the Extraordinary Party Congress planned for 9 September, their last chance of pulling strings in Czechoslovakia would disappear as the Czechoslovak 'hard-liners' were voted out of office; Soviet secret police agents had already left the scene when the Ministry of the Interior was liberalised earlier in the year. Without any means of wielding influence, and with Dubček's control of the situation in some doubt, Moscow would have to rely solely on the Czechoslovak leaders to maintain the country's loyalty.

THE FATE OF THE REFORM

By mid-August 1968, when the Warsaw Pact invasion took place, the implementation of the Action Programme had not proceeded very far. Many of the individual points of the programme had been put into effect provisionally, pending the passing of appropriate legislation by the National Assembly. Thus the new-found freedom of speech, the demonstrations and the formation of political interest-groups, such as the 'Club of Committed Non-Party Members' (KAN) and K231, an organisation of former political prisoners, though sanctioned by the Party's Action Programme and by the government's subsequent policy declaration, were in fact in conflict with the existing law as well as with preceding practices. Dubček and his prime minister, Oldřich Černík, were cautious about the tempo of reform, knowing very well that anything too drastic might provoke an immediate crisis with the Soviet Union. The bulk of the legislation on the Action Programme was to be left in the hands of parliamentary drafting committees and introduced only after September when Novotný's supporters would be safely out of the way. In the meantime, by August the party had secured a large measure of popular support for the new policies. The most influential of Novotný's supporters had been removed. Freedom of speech and discussion reached unprecedented levels. Censorship ceased to exist for all practical purposes. Thorough investigations were started to rehabilitate and compensate the victims of past political injustices. History was reassessed and formerly taboo figures, like the founder-president of Czechoslovakia, T. G. Masaryk, and his son Jan, who died in mysterious circumstances shortly after the communists came to power, were publicly proclaimed as heroes. Interest groups abounded and banned organisations, like the scout movement, emerged again. For a brief period, it seemed that there could be no limit to freedom.

At the end of 1968, after the traumatic experience of the invasion and more than three months of occupation and pressure from Moscow (including attempts to drive wedges between Dubček and the other leaders), a surprising amount of the reform programme remained intact. The Czechoslovak leaders continued to profess adherence to the 'post-January policies', though Dubček sounded a more cautious note in a New Year broadcast, implying adherence to this line 'as far as possible'. Official speeches warned that unpopular steps might have to be taken in the near future. Censorship was reintroduced, but the Czechs and Slovaks saw to it that it was largely auto-censorship, and the press and broadcasting media still retained a large measure of freedom. The rehabilitations continued, but certain restrictions were again imposed on foreign travel. The more outspoken critics of the Soviet Union could no longer voice their views publicly. The future of the economic reform was in doubt, with its architect, Dr. Šik, in exile. And a mood of gloom and foreboding hung over the country as a power struggle developed within the party between Dubček's supporters and those more ready to compromise. But the federal reorganisation of the state was allowed to go ahead (though without a separate Czech Communist Party, which was vetoed by Moscow). Moscow clearly hoped to use this reorganisation as an opportunity to press for the dismissal of uncomfortable opponents and the introduction of the new federal system was observed by a Soviet delegation. Although the wave of public unrest and threatened strikes over the fate of the popular reformer, Josef Smrkovský, whose job as president of the National Assembly was destined for a Slovak in the new Federal Assembly, did not keep him in his post, it did bring home to the Czechoslovak leaders that, even under heavy pressure from other quarters, they could not neglect a public opinion which had had a foretaste of a better life unprecedented in the communist world.

FURTHER READING

Chapman, Colin. *August 21st. The Rape of Czechoslovakia*, Cassell, London, 1968.

Schmidt, Dana Adams. *Anatomy of a Satellite*, Little Brown, Boston, 1952; Secker and Warburg, London, 1953.

Schwartz, Harry. *Prague's 200 Days: The Struggle for Democracy in Czechoslovakia*, Frederick A. Praeger, New York; Pall Mall Press, London, 1969.

Weisskopf, Kurt. *The Agony of Czechoslovakia '38/'68*, Elek, London, 1968.

Windsor, Philip and Roberts, Adam. *Czechoslovakia 1968*, Chatto and Windus, London; Columbia Univ. Press, New York, 1969.

Zeman, Z. A. B. *Prague Spring: A Report on Czechoslovakia 1968*, Penguin, London, 1969.

The Action Programme of the Communist Party of Czechoslovakia, English text published by CTK (Czechoslovak News Agency), Prague, 1968.

MICHAEL MONTGOMERY. Writer on Central European topics, specialising in Poland, Czechoslovakia and Germany. At present on the staff of the BBC External Services.

RUMANIAN FOREIGN POLICY
AFTER 1945

GABRIEL RONAY

INDEPENDENCE AND AFTER

AFTER two decades of brilliant manoeuvring towards national independence, cautious strategic advances and well-timed tactical withdrawals, the Rumanians took a dangerously brave and uncompromising stand over the invasion of Czechoslovakia. President Ceauşescu openly challenged the Soviet Union's right to intervene and branded the use of Warsaw Pact troops as a 'bloc police force' as quite inadmissible. 'When the Warsaw Pact organisation was founded', he said, 'it was conceived as an instrument of collective defence. At no point was it visualised that the Warsaw Treaty could be used to justify interference in the internal affairs of other countries.' Rumania, although a Pact member, dissociated itself from the July 1968 Warsaw declaration of the 'hard-line' countries and did not take part in the five-nation armed invasion of Czechoslovakia.

However, Bucharest had, in fact, no choice: not to have affirmed at this critical juncture the inalienable right of every member nation of the socialist community to decide its own internal and external course, not to have asserted the principle of equality and non-interference would have resulted in the loss of its own painfully acquired independence. In short, Rumania would have been back under the Soviet thumb where it found itself after the liberation in 1944.

Vyshinky's *bon mot*—'Rumania is not a nation, it's a profession' (which amused Stalin) summed up their treatment after the war. Milovan Djilas, the former partisan leader and vice-president of Jugoslavia, described in his book, *Conversations with Stalin*, the immediate post-war situation in Rumania:

> Their wealth was being extracted in various ways, most frequently through joint-stock companies (*sovroms*) in which the Russians barely invested anything except German capital, which they simply declared a prize of war. Trade was not conducted as elsewhere in the world, but on the basis of special arrangements according to which the Soviet government bought at lower and sold at higher than world prices. We knew all that. And the spectacle of misery as well as our awareness of impotence and subservience among the Rumanian authorities could only heighten our indignation . . . We had already accepted it as a fact of life that the Russian treatment of the Rumanians was 'possible even in socialism' because 'Russians are like that'—backward, long isolated from the rest of the world, and dead to their revolutionary traditions.

The Soviet leaders who liberated Rumania from the German yoke behaved as befitting the victors of a conquered country and ruthlessly extracted the spoils of victory. The local communists were denied control and prevented from playing the decisive role in policy-making they had assumed would be their right after the liberation. Instead, they were treated as mere agents of the Soviet command and the 'Moscow exiles', who had spent the war years in the Soviet Union and returned to the country with the Red Army. The Soviet command made it plain right from the beginning that it would not countenance any Rumanian communist claim for the status of 'co-liberator'. The question as to whether the Soviet army liberated or merely supported the indigenous forces in liberating the country was not merely a legalistic point: the Soviet Union's right to interfere in the internal affairs of the defeated country was organically linked to it, and the mandate, claimed by the Rumanian communists to transform the social and political order of Rumania too, was based on the rights of liberators.

The actual historical facts of Rumania's liberation were, however, somewhat different. In the face of the rapidly approaching Soviet army, Rumanian officers and the non-collaborationist parties staged a swift coup on 23 August 1944, and on King Michael's personal order, Antonescu, the war time dictator of Rumania, was arrested. The purpose of the coup was to establish a coalition government, reverse alliances and assume the role of co-belligerent, thus denying the Soviet Union the right to impose a government of occupation of its own choice. Although the Rumanian communist leaders, freed from Antonescu's goals earlier in the spring, took part in the preparations for the anti-German armed uprising, the coup itself was staged without their knowledge. The communists, however, had, for a variety of tactical reasons, committed themselves to this common Rumanian effort to avoid the full consequences of a military defeat and incurred Moscow's displeasure. General Sănătescu included the communist Lucrețiu Pătrășcanu in his broad anti-fascist national coalition government and, as coalition partners, the communists took part in the military operations against the German troops in Rumania. Thus, while not actually the organisers of the 1944 armed uprising, they could rightly claim the title of co-liberator. Anything more would have been a physical impossibility, for the Rumanian party, undermined by the consequences of the Molotov-Ribbentrop Pact and decimated by Antonescu's secret police during the war years, could hardly muster a thousand members on the eve of the 1944 coup.

The Communist Party's Leading Role

The true significance of the stress laid by the Rumanians on the party's leading role in the liberation of the country emerged only later as Gheorge Gheorghiu-Dej began to loosen Moscow's grip on Rumania. Having accepted the inevitable satellite status in 1944 and shown abject subservience to the Soviet masters, Gheorghiu-Dej soon emerged as the leader of the national faction, which had spent the war years in Rumania, and was tolerated by the Soviet command as a liaison man with the Rumanian masses. Through masterful manoeuvres he managed to interpose himself between the Kremlin and the 'Muscovites' by 1947. As a zealous exponent of doctrinaire Stalinism and a vociferous supporter of the harsh 'class struggle' against the remnants of the bourgeoisie, intellectuals of all shades, peasantry and religious organisations, Gheorghiu-Dej had made himself sufficiently indispensable to the Kremlin to obtain Stalin's consent to purge the Jewish-cosmopolitan Muscovite group of Ana Pauker in 1952. The removal of the 'Muscovites' reduced Russia's ability to interfere directly in Rumania's affairs and ensured for the first time, even if through a narrow minority, Rumanian control over the party's Politburo and Secretariat.

To avoid Stalin's wrath for his open championing of Rumanian national interests in his battle with the Muscovites, Gheorghiu-Dej took a public oath of loyalty to Stalin and maintained a most rigid Stalinist order internally, ruthlessly purging all deviationists. Stalin's death in 1953 left Dej in an exposed position. To consolidate his position in the party he continued his role of guardian of Rumanian interests while maintaining his tight domestic control. But the changes in the Kremlin and the abandonment of the Cold War in favour of peaceful coexistence forced Gheorghiu-Dej to protect the interests of his Stalinist faction through a more independent Rumanian foreign policy.

New Course in Foreign Policy

In charting this new independent foreign political course, Gheorghiu-Dej exploited the first open cracks in the Soviet monolith and sought the protection of the Moscow Stalinists against the de-Stalinisers gathered around Khrushchev. His thorough Leninist training, however, prevented him from putting all his eggs in one basket and, as a reassurance, he began to build bridges to Peking, whose nationalist policies then espoused the same basic goals as Bucharest's. The concessions wrung by the Chinese from Moscow in 1954, 'complete equality of rights and mutual respect for the national interests of the two nations', summed up Rumanian foreign political aspirations. (The principal vehicle of these aspirations was a bold reinterpretation of the Rumanian Communist Party's role in the 1944 coup.) In August 1955, the eleventh anniversary of the coup, Gheorghiu-Dej stated in the presence of Khrushchev that the anti-German move, far from being undertaken by King Michael, was the work of the leading forces of the anti-Hitler Patriotic Front—the Communist Party of Rumania. He added that the king and his entourage were compelled to accept the plan of action which was established by the Rumanian Communist Party. The theme was further developed on all suitable occasions, and it was finally stated that in fact the Muscovite group had disapproved of the coup because it had prevented the final destruction of the Rumanian army by the Soviet Union and an immediate transition to the dictatorship of the proletariat. These efforts were crowned by Mao Tse-tung who, alone among the communist leaders, endorsed Gheorghiu-Dej's reassertion of the Rumanian party's decisive role as co-liberator of their country, and, indirectly, denied the Soviet 'right' to interfere in Rumania.

The sudden intensification of Rumanian external activities in search of allies for its 'Rumania first' policies resulted in a spate of economic and cultural agreements with such politically diverse countries as 'revisionist' Jugoslavia, left-wing 'deviationist' China and 'capitalist' France. But while these new contacts were designed to reduce Rumania's dependence on the Soviet Union, their ideological justification on grounds of peaceful coexistence with countries of differing social order could not be repudiated by Moscow without risking its own *rapprochement* with the West.

At the Second Congress of the Rumanian Workers' Party in 1955, Gheorghiu-Dej first spelt out in cautious Marxist phraseology that the socialist transformation of Rumania would not be subordinated to the interests of the socialist camp headed by the Soviet Union, and sought a mandate from the party to carry out this programme. Khrushchev's attempt to de-Stalinise the top echelon of the satellite parties posed a direct threat to

Gheorghiu-Dej and his domestic policies. The Rumanian leader, with his unrivalled ability to change policies without appearing to have switched positions, could no doubt have weathered this new challenge too. But Khrushchev's proposals for increased economic coordination of East European economies through Comecon—a move aimed at reimposing Soviet control through economic rather than military means—was justly considered by the Rumanians as a major threat to their independent course. The need for dissociation from the Soviet Union was imperative, for the Rumanian road to socialism required an independent economy not subordinated to Soviet interests.

RIFT IN RELATIONS WITH THE SOVIET UNION

Soviet attempts to force Rumania back into line and to replace Gheorghiu-Dej by a more amenable puppet were halted by the Hungarian uprising of October 1956. It not only saved Gheorghiu-Dej but justified his internal policies and, at the height of the Hungarian crisis, enabled Bucharest to wring further political and economic concessions and a definite commitment to withdraw all Soviet troops from that country. While Khrushchev refused to endorse Rumania's own road to socialism even in the post-Hungarian period, the growing schism between China and the Soviet Union offered new ground for Rumanian manoeuvring. The valuable Chinese support for Rumanian initiatives and 'the strengthening of fraternal ties with China' enabled Bucharest to continue its partial disengagement from the Soviet Union and to mend its fences in the West. The new markets acquired in Western Europe and among the uncommitted nations helped at the same time to reduce Rumanian economic dependence on the Soviet Union.

Khrushchev's blunt rejection of the Rumanian need to develop further the country's heavy industry as incompatible with Comecon plans for specialisation and economic integration, led to an open confrontation at the June 1962 Comecon conference in Moscow. Khrushchev, determined to 'break' the Rumanians, threatened economic sanctions, while Gheorghiu-Dej made it equally plain that he would resist all 'external interference'in Rumania's economic affairs, and would not subordinate Rumanian interests to bloc interests. An open collision between Moscow and its faithful East German and Czechoslovak allies on the one hand and Bucharest on the other, was only averted by the Soviet-US confrontation in Cuba. Exploiting to the full the tactical advantages of the Soviet Union's Cuban fiasco, Gheorghiu-Dej moved along the path to national independence at great speed and without the customary caution that characterised his earlier moves. He correctly assessed Moscow's unwillingness to split the socialist camp when in a relatively weak position.

The Rumanians secured their gains by taking up the role of internationally accepted mediator between the Soviet Union and China, whose quarrel had grown increasingly bitter. The correct Leninist analysis of the consequences of polycentrism in the socialist camp and Khrushchev's determination to expel the Chinese from the international communist movement prompted the April 1964 Bucharest statement formally proclaiming the Rumanian party's independence from Moscow. The statement, usually considered as the formalisation of Rumanian independence, branded Soviet interference in the internal affairs of others as inadmissible and reaffirmed the right of every nation to determine its own destiny. It affirmed that every party must be free to choose its own road to socialism and that sovereignty over the national plan is the prerequisite of national independence. The statement warned that, as all parties were equal, there could be no international centre entitled to issue instructions to parties in other countries, to depose or appoint party leaders, excommunicate or liquidate sovereign parties, determine what is true socialism or claim to be the sole interpreter of Marxism-Leninism.

The tenets expounded by the 1964 Declaration directly challenged the Soviet Union's leading role in the world communist movement and threatened Soviet hegemony in Eastern Europe. By embarrassing Moscow and adopting the position of an independent and neutral socialist country, the Rumanians thereby greatly strengthened their acceptability to the West. Rumanian foreign policy played a vital part in the consolidation of Rumanian independence, although Khrushchev's unexpected downfall and the inability of his successors to take effective steps against Bucharest in the aftermath of the coup was a godsend to Gheorghiu-Dej.

Building Bridges to the West

Nicolae Ceauşescu, who took over on Gheorghiu-Dej's death in 1965, continued his predecessor's policy of paying lip-service to the unity of the socialist camp while simultaneously seeking closer ties with France and the non-committed states of Asia. However, the growing involvement of the USA in Vietnam and the ensuing freeze in international relations deprived Bucharest of much of its earlier room for manoeuvre. With great realism Ceauşescu renounced Rumania's claim to Bessarabia and made several other tactical concessions to Moscow while at the same time reorientating his country's external policies. Instead of embracing an 'edited' version of Gomułkaism and Titoism, he sought to build more bridges to the West and to put relations between the Balkan countries on a new footing.

Operating under the ideologically impeccable doctrine of peaceful co-existence, the Rumanians sponsored a move in the United Nations aimed at improving good neighbourly relations between the small nations of different social systems living under the shadow of big powers in Europe. The *rapprochement* between Denmark, Belgium, Bulgaria, Hungary, Rumania, Finland, Sweden, Austria and Jugoslavia—the so-called 'Group of Nine'—master-minded by Corneliu Mănescu, Ceauşescu's foreign minister, cut right across bloc allegiances. By stressing what so naturally united the small nations of the Warsaw Pact and NATO, the Rumanians focused on the continent's attention on the anachronisms of bloc allegiances and their harmful effect on *détente*. Not surprisingly, the hard-line 'Northern Tier' Warsaw Pact countries—the Soviet Union, East Germany and Poland—saw the Rumanian move as 'a new intrigue to destroy the unity of the socialist camp'.

The concept of Balkan cooperation was regarded by Bucharest as another important stepping stone to disengagement and true independence. Mindful of the Soviet Union's morbid sensitivity whenever its spheres of interests appeared threatened, Rumanian diplomacy made good use of the Soviet-approved doctrine of 'regional cooperation' and 'Balkans—an Atom-free Zone'. The bilateral agreements with the NATO-member Turks and Greeks and the non-aligned Jugoslavs were complemented by an exchange of visits and stepped up cooperation with Sofia, for the Rumanians knew full well that without Bulgaria—the pillar of the Kremlin's Balkan policies—there could be no fruitful Balkan cooperation. But, whereas the Soviet leaders considered the regional cooperation concept to be a useful means of drawing away the Turks and Greeks from NATO, the Rumanians regarded it as a golden opportunity to end their isolation and, in the wider context of

Rumanian diplomatic activities, to demand the dissolution of all military blocs both in the East and in the West.

TIES WITH BONN

The establishment of diplomatic relations with West Germany in January 1967 in the face of strong Soviet opposition was the crowning event of all Rumanian efforts to this end and a major victory for their diplomacy. Rumanian national interest was put before bloc solidarity and the political differences between Bonn and Bucharest were pushed aside for the sake of mutual economic interest. Bucharest justified its move by pointing out that, as a result of the war, there were two German states and by establishing diplomatic ties with Bonn it was merely acknowledging this historical fact. 'The strengthening of cooperation on the basis of equality, the strengthening of political relations between all states, including the establishment of diplomatic relations with both German states, represents one of the most significant steps towards the development of cooperation between the states of Europe' a Rumanian statement said.

Soviet opposition to the Rumanian move was complicated by the fact that Moscow had recognised both East Berlin and Bonn, and could hardly deny the same right to the Rumanians. The fact that Rumania put its national interests before bloc interests and recognised Bonn without insisting on the three Warsaw Pact preconditions for improved relations—recognition of the Oder-Neisse line, recognition of East Germany and renunciation of nuclear arms by Bonn—caused a severe Warsaw Pact crisis. It brought into the open the underlying stresses and conflicting national interests and showed that the German revanchist bogey, the corner-stone of the Soviet Union's Central European policy, cut no ice with the 'Southern Tier' of the Warsaw Pact.

Bucharest's insistence that the establishment of normal relations with Bonn was its own affair, had nonetheless wider implications. It touched on the crucial question, whether a Pact member could be allowed to pursue its own interests, regardless of the possible consequences for its allies, or whether Pact interests must always have precedence over national interests. It also left East Germany, with its vested interest in the *status quo*, alarmingly isolated and in a dangerous mood. Ulbricht's rear-guard action and attempts to prevent other East European countries from resuming diplomatic relations with West Germany succeeded in stopping Hungary and Bulgaria from following the Rumanian example.

The Rumanian insistence on full equality of rights caused other stresses within the rigid pattern of the Warsaw Pact alliance. Ceauşescu repeatedly demanded an increased say in the deployment and possible use of nuclear weapons, raised the question of the cost of Soviet troops stationed in East Germany and asked for more command posts for officers of member countries instead of filling them always with Soviet generals. These 'Gaullist' demands, running counter to Soviet attempts to strengthen the Pact by closer integration of national military forces, made the East Germans, Poles and Soviets more intransigent, for they feared that any reorganisation would weaken the Warsaw Pact and leave them a prey to Bonn's 'revenge-seekers'. Thus, Bucharest's efforts to free itself from the subservient posture within the alliance by loosening the frame of the Warsaw Pact clashed with the interests of the 'Northern-Tier' countries bent on maintaining the *status quo*.

The attitude of the Rumanian delegate at the Geneva disarmament conference, where he repeatedly demanded safeguards for the non-nuclear small nations and spoke of the need for nuclear countries to give up their weapons, was another example of Bucharest's independent course in line with its own political interests. The Rumanian stance ignored narrow bloc interests, in the Soviet and US disarmament deal, and was calculated to please the uncommitted world. On the non-proliferation treaty communist Rumania is demonstrably closer to other European non-nuclear states, fearful of nuclear blackmail, than to the Warsaw Pact nations toeing the Moscow line.

These apparently gradual moves towards a more independent stand on world issues, always justifiable in Marxist-Leninist terms and never sufficiently provocative to trigger off a Soviet military reaction, were turned into a qualitative change in Rumanian foreign policy during the crisis of the Arab-Israeli war of 1967 when Moscow was once again in a weak position. Rumania, alone among the Warsaw Pact nations, dared to defy the Moscow-dictated pro-Arab bloc stand and did not break off diplomatic relations with Israel. The Rumanians refused to vilify Israel as the other East European countries did, bluntly criticised the Arab position as untenable and voiced their support for Israel's right to exist. By refusing to bow to Moscow's dictate, Ceauşescu not only demonstrated his country's independence but secured tangible political and economic gains. With acute perception and in the best Leninist tradition the Rumanians chose once again a world crisis, caused by Moscow's clumsy Middle East policies, as the opportunity for loosening the Soviet grip on their country. In December 1967 Bucharest signed a very favourable three-year trade agreement with Israel. It provided the opportunity Bucharest needed to break out of the Comecon orbit into a major new market without being excommunicated by the socialist camp, but the political and psychological significance of the move transcends the financial calculations.

During his stewardship, Ceauşescu developed Gheorghiu-Dej's erstwhile 'Rumanian way of dissent' into a coherent foreign policy capable of serving the vital national interests of the country. That he has succeeded in defying the Soviet Union on Albania, China, Germany, Comecon, European settlement, disarmament, Warsaw Pact integration and world communist summit plans without being invaded like Czechoslovakia, is the greatest praise for his statesmanship.

FURTHER READING

Brown, J. F. 'Rumania Steps out of Line', *Survey*, October, 1963.

Fischer-Galati, Stephen. *The New Rumania*, MIT Press, Cambridge, Mass., 1967.

Ionescu, Ghiţa. *The Politics of the European Communist States*, Weidenfeld and Nicolson, London; Frederick A. Praeger, New York, 1967.

London, Kurt (ed.) *Eastern Europe in Transition*, Johns Hopkins Press, Baltimore, 1967.

Montias, John Michael. *The Economic Development in Communist Rumania*, MIT Press, Cambridge, Mass., 1967. 'Background and Origins of the Rumanian Dispute with Comecon', *Soviet Studies*, XVI, 1964.

GABRIEL RONAY. A regular contributor to the *Sunday Times* on East European affairs, and writes the *Inside Russia* column of the *New Statesman* under the pen-name Gabriel Lorince. Born in Rumania, he studied Russian and Marxism-Leninism at Budapest University. Publications include *Gogol's Satire and its Influence on Modern Russian Literature*, 1968.

PART THREE

ECONOMIC

ECONOMIC PLANNING IN COMMUNIST SOCIETIES

FRANCIS SETON

ORIGINS

'FROM each according to his capacity, to each according to his need.' This was the Marxian vision of the communist society which was to replace capitalism in the fullness of time. It demanded a moral transformation of man, but even more a technological transformation of machines to create an era of material plenty. Without this, the 'non-utopian' visionaries could not admit the practical possibility of communism, as they saw irresistible pressures for expanding production perpetuating differential incentives, economic inequalities and rewards according to social class. Only when capitalism had exhausted all its potentialities for technological progress could society legitimately take the first steps towards communism. Conditions were ripe for this in highly developed economies—in the UK, France or Germany— but not in the backward East which would have to await rescuing operations from the victorious proletariats of the West.

Yet it was in the Tsarist empire of the East that the doctrine fell on the most fertile ground. The Russian intelligentsia had long cherished the dream of a socialist millennium in which the age-old traditions of human equality enshrined in the Russian village commune would coalesce with their own individualist aspirations and searching spirit—a marriage of Russia's soul with Russia's mind—to create a promised land of free and equal men. The Populist movement had called for such an alliance with messianic fervour and had urged its consummation in Russia *before* all other countries, *precisely* because Russia was backward and therefore uncorrupted by the virus of bourgeois capitalism which had already sapped the moral fibre of the West to the point of incapacity for socialism. Russia alone might still be able to escape the fatal infection if action were taken in time, and might yet save the world by her example. The utter failure of the Populist movement in the 1870s and 1880s created widespread disillusion and despair, but also immense receptivity for the more 'muscular' form of socialism which the Marxian doctrine seemed to offer.

First, however, the doctrine had to be adapted to Russian soil and to the needs of the Russian intelligentsia which would never reconcile itself to the role of a passive victim of backwardness condemned to wait for liberation at foreign hands. It was left to Lenin to perform this adaptation, and he performed it brilliantly. His theory of imperialism unveils a late and degenerative phase of capitalism dominated by financial power, monopoly and international cartels which had developed weaknesses and contradictions that

Marx could not have foreseen. In the place of a single powerful yoke, removable only by a massive proletariat at the peak of its strength, the new capitalism had forged a world-wide chain of exploitation which could best be broken at its *weakest* link. This weakest link was Russia where capitalism had entered only in its latest moribund phase and yet was having to struggle against the strong survivals of a feudal absolutist order. It was therefore the historic mission of the Russian proletariat and intelligentsia to set the spark to world revolution, in spite of their relative weakness and immaturity. What was lacking in the material preconditions for the survival of the revolution in Russia would soon be made good by the newly roused proletariats of more advanced countries who, once the revolution was won, would quickly come to its aid.

Lenin provided the strategy and tactics of revolution in Russia as well as its ideological justification. But even more crucial to an understanding of the origins of Soviet planning is his concept of the role of Soviet power in Russia as a holding operation while revolution spread throughout the world, a stewardship undertaken on behalf of an international proletariat which was still to rouse itself. There could be no question of realising communism in Lenin's Russia any more than a military base could aspire to turn itself into a new Jerusalem. The task was survival, resistance and consolidation.

In such conditions planning itself concentrated on the commanding heights of the economy, those areas which the regime must control to prevent a recrudescence of capitalism (foreign trade, banking, grain procurement and certain key industries). The rest of industry was put under a regime that came to be known as state capitalism, i.e. the retention of former owners in management functions, subject to surveillance from above and below, but without the requirement to work to a plan. In retail trade and on the land there was at first no substantial departure from private capitalism. Lenin justified this New Economic Policy as a tactical manoeuvre essential to the survival of the regime. Meanwhile the ground could be prepared for the eventual annexation of *all* sectors to the state by the creation of a network of central organs of planning and administration (State Planning Commission, established 23 August 1923, Supreme Economic Council, established 8 August 1918, etc.); and a long-term plan (GOELRO, 1920/1) to establish the technological preconditions for socialism within 15 years ('communism = Soviet power + electrification').

SOCIALISM IN ONE COUNTRY

When it became clear that world revolution was nowhere within sight, a longer-term accommodation had to be found. Moreover popular faith in Lenin's New Economic Policy and the mixed economy in general was soon to be rudely shaken. In 1923–4 the 'scissor crisis' erupted as a violent price-movement against the agricultural producer which threatened the country with a full-scale peasant 'withdrawal from the market' (into subsistence farming) and imminent starvation for the towns. The crucial link between agriculture and industry which the New Economic Policy had been invoked to save was now endangered by the very market forces which that policy had unleashed.

It was only now that planners found themselves face to face with the fundamental problem of planning: deciding the direction in which the economy *as a whole* was to move. A right-wing faction under the influence of Bukharin supported a policy of high and differential incentives to private farmers until such time as enough agricultural surplus had been created to sustain a voluntary movement of resources into industry.[1] The opposing faction, inspired largely by Trotsky, Preobrazhensky and Pyatakov, argued for the immediate and forcible transfer of those resources and took their stand on the need for industry to embark on the 'primitive accumulation' of capital through the deliberate exploitation of peasant agriculture—much as a metropolitan country exploited its colonies, or an emergent social order in the Marxian scheme of things was said to draw its initial fund of strength by parasitic action on the predecessor which it was about to supplant. The intellectual weapons of the contestants were historical analogy and dialectical materialism rather than the analytical tools of the professional economist, but the controversy found its reflection on a more technical level inside the State Planning Commission and other bodies where the economic and planning implications of alternative policies occupied the forefront of attention.

THE PLANNING CONTROVERSY

The older school of economists, led by such impressive figures as Kondratyev, Groman and Bazarov, advocated—and practised—what came to be known as 'geneticist' planning. Essentially, they took their starting point from a forecast of the harvest (as the least controllable variable in the economy) with the consequent surpluses available for urban consumption, and built around these estimates a balanced system of performance indicators (output, employment, investment, etc.) for the guidance of the urban and the rural economy alike. The indicators were presented as feasible ideals to be aimed at rather than binding targets, and their mutual consistency was tested by means of structural coefficients derived from the experience of normally functioning unplanned economies, including that of pre-revolutionary Russia. The opposing 'teleological' school, in which Strumilin was steadily gaining in prominence, rejected such procedures as a retreat from the 'conscious choices' made possible by socialism towards voluntary submission to the 'elemental forces' at work in lower-type economies, and advocated a method of planning which was to take its starting point from the final aims, rather than the initial possibilities, that characterised the period to be covered. It was the planners' task to single out the 'leading links' in the economy whose development was desired by the party on political or social grounds, and to draw up the concrete investment projects to serve them. From these were derived the targets for output or other performance which the rest of the economy would have to meet to support the postulated investment programme. Overall consistency was tested by a system of supply-and-requirements balances drawn up separately for each key commodity or commodity-group with the aid of technological input norms. If the original programme turned out to be unrealisable with existing resources, this was remedied by further shifts from consumption to investment, a tightening of input norms or, as a last resort, a lowering of the initial targets; but at each stage of the adjustment process the leading links were assured of absolute priority.

As the 1920s wore on, the annual economic plans or 'control figures' (which were issued from 1925/6 onwards) became more and more oriented towards the 'teleological' school, and by the end of the decade the advocates of 'geneticism' had completely lost out or disappeared in political purges.

[1] The industrialisation controversy was in full swing during the years 1925–27.

COLLECTIVISATION AND AFTER

Meanwhile the party leadership had veered abruptly to the left, and the country was radically transformed by the forced collectivisation drive of 1929–32. Henceforth the food surplus exacted from the peasants passed under the political control of the government, the risks of the harvest devolved entirely on the rural population, and the terms of trade between country and town could be dictated at will without endangering the supply situation, present or future. Accordingly, the crucial questions concerning the pace of industrialisation, the rate of investment and consumption, etc. ceased to be debated in *economic* terms (i.e. as choices between competing ends, given scarce means), and largely assumed the character of *technological* or *military* problems in which the ends were preconceived and unassailable, and only the means to their fulfilment remained open to choice.

This was the basic premise on which economic planning proceeded throughout the Stalinist period. The aims were unalterably given by the Stalinist understanding of the Soviet Union's historical setting. The economy was treated as a single gigantic factory in which agriculture provided man-power as a kind of raw material for industry. Industry itself gave little or nothing in return, and concentrated overwhelmingly on the production of capital equipment for its own use. Food and amenities were produced in quantities sufficient to keep the wheels turning, but consumer satisfaction as an end in itself had no place in the scheme of things. It is to this concept of an economy geared to the secular transformation of one basic resource into another (surplus peasant labour into industrial capital) rather than to the traditional optimum allocation of *given* resources, that the nature and pur-port of economic planning under Stalin must be linked.

THE MECHANICS OF INDUSTRIAL PLANNING

The great Five Year Plans[1] marked out the stages of the transformation process to be covered in each quinquennium. They were political documents setting out the major projects, production capacities, and output targets to be achieved. Their starting point was a set of party directives, usually published six to 18 months before the plan, in which the aims were given in rough outline. It was then the task of the Planning Commission (Gosplan) to translate this into concrete targets for the major branches of industry. Theoretically the Commission was supposed to reach its decisions after a form of dialogue with subordinate organs, dealing simultaneously with those in charge of the separate branches of industry (people's commissariats, later ministries) and with those responsible for separate geographic divisions (republican or regional planning commissions). These organs would receive an outline plan in the nature of a 'bid' from Gosplan and were required to answer with a 'counter-plan' which was to be at once a confirmation of feasibility (with corrections) and a pledge for the future. The counter-plans themselves were seen as the result of a lower-level dialogue proceeding mean-while between the branch authorities and their own executive organs, so that the ultimate source of the counter-bids and pledges reaching the Planning Commission would be the enterprises' own assessment of what they were able

[1] The great Five Year Plans: First FYP 1928/9–32/3 (declared fulfilled by end of 1932), Second FYP 1933–37, Third FYP 1938–40 (interrupted by war), Fourth FYP 1946–50, Fifth FYP 1951–55, Sixth FYP 1956–60 (superseded by Seven Year Plan), Seven Year Plan 1958–65, Eighth FYP 1966–70.

and willing to do. The Planning Commission was then required to coordinate, integrate and summarise these responses into the final plan document for submission to the political authorities as the 'concretisation' of the original directives.

Once the Five Year Plan was ratified, the State Planning Commission was required to retail its provisions once again as specific orders to subordinate organs who would then do likewise to the lower rungs of the hierarchy, until all industrial enterprises at the grass-roots of production had been provided with detailed targets.

A similar procedure (with minor variations) generated the annual plans which were in theory emanations of the Five Year Plans but soon took on a life of their own—and, indeed, could trace their historical ancestry to the yearly control figures which ante-dated the quinquennial plans by four to five years. It was the annual plans which eventually acquired the greater operational significance. Factory directors and ministers could expect rewards or sanctions according to the degree to which they fulfilled them, while their commitment to the Five Year Plans was at best moral and general.

The procedure, interaction and time-pattern of the plans has remained substantially unaltered to the present day. There were occasional departures of longer-term planning into three or seven year plans, and occasional extensions of an annual plan to cover a period of two years. Occasionally also the chain of command along which the planning dialogue and the eventual retailing of targets was conducted changed from the 'branch-principle' (economy/major sector of industry/subsector-enterprise) to the 'territorial principle' (economy/regional council/locality) and the two principles, when allowed to operate simultaneously, received different emphasis from time to time. More recently there were said to be experiments with 'rolling' Five Year Plans subject to annual revision as the new opportunities opened up by each year's achievement became clear. Nevertheless, the principle of political guidelines receiving progressively finer detail in a prescribed sequence of bid and counter-bid and culminating in a set of mandatory targets for all producing enterprises has not so far been departed from.

What has changed—and is still in the process of change—is the nature of the targets set and the kinds of incentives offered for their fulfilment.

TARGETS AND INCENTIVES

Up to the mid-1950s the overriding task facing each enterprise was fulfilment of the 'gross output' target expressed in physical units (tons, gallons, kwh., etc.) or in terms of constant prices. There were bonuses for fulfilment and often a steeply rising scale of management rewards for varying degrees of overfulfilment. Not surprisingly, the managers strove to excel in this at the expense of all other aspects of economic performance—quality, profits, productivity and costs—and the authorities were forced to devise more and more subsidiary targets (input-limits, cost-reduction, etc.) to minimise the damage done by 'output-fetishism'. As the number and complexity of targets multiplied it became increasingly difficult to secure a proper coordination between them, and soon the typical manager saw himself faced with a welter of contradictory targets and supplementary orders which it was impossible to fulfil. The only way out was a judicious choice between them according to the manager's assessment of the political pull behind each target and the ease or difficulty of simulating the required result. The upshot of this situation appears to have been the continued enthronement of the output target as by and large the most worthwhile task to be pursued.

Clearly, this cost the economy dearly as the structure of production shifted to needlessly output-biased assortments (heavy items where the target was in tons, long items where it was in yards, high-cost items where it was in value, etc.). Above all output was pursued regardless of its usefulness to the purchaser in the next link of the production chain, as the high output targets themselves created perennial shortages and a seller's market. There was no need to please the customer who would in any case take whatever he got, and the pipelines of production became choked with ill-adapted or unusable hardware. The emphasis on sheer output also resulted in serious backlogs in technology, as managers were reluctant to make room for innovations and new products which required retooling and irksome interruptions to the smooth flow of output. Some of the most spectacular technological revolutions of Western economies were missed or long delayed in the Soviet Union; for example, the shift from metals to plastics, from natural to artificial fibres, from steam traction to diesel locomotives, and from coal to oil and gas in general. Not all of this can be laid at the door of output-fetishism but the comparative absence of cost-consciousness and regard for allocative efficiency must bear the major share of responsibility. The fact that industry nonetheless developed at an unprecedented pace must be ascribed to its 'transformative' character, its lavish absorption of rural labour, and its tight hold on the consumer who was forced to sacrifice everything to investment.

The picture changed abruptly, however, when the potentialities of surplus labour were nearing exhaustion and further advances became dependent on the productivity of those already working in industry. From that time onwards low standards of living became a hindrance rather than a help. The need to keep a nucleus of skilled workers on the land enforced higher food prices, and the need to raise the skills of those in towns demanded higher consumer standards all round. Resources were no longer free to be fed into an undiscriminating sausage-machine, but had to be husbanded and judiciously allocated where they could do most good.

In such a climate the system of targets and incentives had to be thoroughly revised. Attempts were made to replace the output target by an overriding cost-reduction target, and later by sales and profit targets whose fulfilment depended to some extent at least on efficiency, quality and adequacy to consumer needs. In addition the number of targeted performance indicators was reduced and overambitious demands scaled down. There was also some shift towards greater rewards for *accepting* high targets with reduced bonuses for *overfulfilling* them, in the hope of eliminating the age-old cat-and-mouse game whereby managers would jockey for low and easily fulfilled targets.

PLANNING AND DECENTRALISATION

It is difficult to gauge to what extent these attempts have been successful. Management incentives have certainly improved as rewards became geared to sales or profits rather than gross output. But a vast bureaucratic phalanx with a vested interest in 'targetry' has been created over the years and now seems almost impossible to dismantle. In spite of party resolutions the ministries and departments do not reduce the number of indicators handed down to productive enterprises—or if they do so for a time, they soon slip back into their old habits. In some cases targets have been known to proliferate even more than before the reforms. Enterprises still complain they are being tied hand and foot and that remote officialdom continues to arrogate to itself the entrepreneurial functions and initiative which ought to thrive at the grass-roots of production.

The party and government are well aware of the problem, but have shown a certain ambivalence in their approach. Their basic desire to decentralise in the interests of greater efficiency is being frustrated at one and the same time by the entrenched bureaucracy and by the disruptive tendencies of managerial technocrats when given too much rope without guidance. Greater investment powers for factory directors, for example, has often brought increased frittering of resources on a multiplicity of projects and false starts, as overenthusiastic managers bit off more than they could chew and failed to overcome material shortages. The need to unfreeze resources and improve coordination between material supplies and financial allocations in its turn has led to creeping re-centralisation. But the supply problem is notoriously difficult to solve on centralist lines, as the number of production units to be tied in grows roughly with the *square* of industrial expansion. Practically all moves towards greater centralism in this sphere have resulted in intolerable delays, disorganisation and the development of an informal supply system along the old-boy network and the underhand trading of mutual favours.

The basic fact is, of course, that decentralisation requires for its permanent success a system of depersonalised signals like market prices, interest rates and freely disposable profits, which can push and pull individual managers in the desired direction without a constant string of detailed orders from the centre. The greater the complexity of the economy the greater the need for such a transformation in the forms of economic guidance. But while this need is widely felt in Soviet industry, the authorities still shrink from its implications in terms of shifts in economic power and control. Thus prices are revised, but not freed, and decisions fragmented, but not devolved. In spite of considerable improvements in the running of Soviet industry and construction the right combination of central control and local initiative still eludes the powers that be.

THE GROWTH AND STRUCTURE OF SOVIET INDUSTRY

The long persistence of output fetishism and rigid centralisation favoured rapid growth in terms of physical weight and volume. In the quarter century from the inception of the Five Year Plans (1925) to the mid-1950s Soviet industry was undoubtedly one of the fastest growing in the world. Opinions differ on the proper measure of this growth performance and the Soviets' own claims up to 1955 are rightly discounted by Western observers (not without some implied support from Soviet commentators). Nevertheless the annual growth rate of industry was probably comparable—and may have exceeded—those achieved by the most spectacular 'industrialisers', such as Japan (from the turn of the century to the early 1930s) and South Africa (from about 1910 onwards). With the approach to economic maturity industrial growth rates slowed down and by the early 1960s Soviet industry dropped well behind West Germany, Japan and Italy in the league table.

Table 1 below displays the record of different periods and compares Soviet manufacturing growth with that of the main developed nations of the West. The fall in official Soviet growth-rates up to 1966 is conspicuous, and would be more so if the first quinquennium of the 1960s were analysed year by year. Equally conspicuous, however, is the recovery in 1967 in the wake of the preceding bumper harvest and of the movement towards more rational planning and less ambitious targets. Indeed the planned growth targets show an even more conspicuous decline from year to year, but due to improved fulfilment the actual performance does not follow the trend so relentlessly.

TABLE I

ANNUAL GROWTH RATES OF INDUSTRIAL PRODUCTION
(%)

Industry:	Total (A)	Producer goods (B)	Consumer goods (C)	Lead of producer goods[1] (D)
1928–37	14·1[a] (18·2)[c]	(23·1)[c]	(13·4)[c]	(8·6)[c]
1951–55	9·4[b] (13·2)[c]	(13·8)[c]	(12·0)[c]	(1·6)[c]
1956–60	10·4	11·3	8·5	2·6
1961–65	8·6	9·6	6·3	3·1
1966	8·6	9·0	7·0	1·9
1967	10·0	10·2	9·0	1·1
1968[d]	8·1	7·9	8·6	−0·6
1968–70[e]	8·1	8·9	8·6	0·0

Manufacturing:	Total	Main producer goods[g]	Main consumer goods[h]	Lead of main producer goods[1]
USSR 1928–37[f]	16·0	21·8	11·1	9·7
,, 1951–5[f]	10·7	16·6	11·4	4·7
USA 1949–56	4·6	6·7	1·0	5·0
UK 1949–56	4·0	5·3	1·3	3·9
Germany 1949–56	14·5	16·8	12·1	4·2
EEC 1949–56	9·7	11·6	7·6	3·7

[1] Computed as $1 + \dfrac{D}{100} = \left(1 + \dfrac{B}{100}\right) \div \left(1 + \dfrac{C}{100}\right)$.

[a] Average of 3 Western estimates (National Bureau of Economic Research 10·7, D. Hodgman 15·7, F. Seton 16·0).

[b] Average of 3 Western estimates (National Bureau of Economic Research 7·7, D. Hodgman 9·9, F. Seton 10·5).

[c] Official claims.

[d] Annual plan.

[e] Required to fulfil current plan for 1970.

[f] Author's estimates.

[g] Basic metals, engineering and metal working, chemicals.

[h] Light industry, textiles, footwear and food industry.

Source: From official Soviet data unless otherwise stated.

The last column of the table has been added as a sensitive barometer of the hardness of economic policy. Throughout the Soviet period the doctrine that fast industrial expansion demanded the 'predominant growth' of producer industries has held undisputed sway. Its justification, though often speciously offered in terms of economic theory, has basically been ideological and political—the regime's unspoken apology to the hard-pressed consumer. It is clear (see lower half of the table) that for the most part the bias towards producer goods in the Soviet Union has equalled or exceeded that of the largest exporters of such goods who were able to compensate for this by the corresponding imports of consumer goods (as the Soviet Union is not). As the transformative phase of Soviet development drew to a close and a friendlier policy towards the consumer became necessary the bias gradually lessened, though not without periodic, and immediately damaging, relapses into the hard line.

As a consequence of this spectacular growth the Soviet Union has by now reached a level of industrial output which is variously estimated at one half to two thirds of US industry, though in terms of labour productivity she is probably still somewhat below the half-way mark. These bald statements naturally conceal wide variations in the comparative performance of different branches. No doubt in metallurgy, heavy engineering and similar easily integrated and planned sectors, the Soviet achievement comes closer to that of the USA: its output of steel is now 63% of the US figure, of tractors 76% and of cement nearly 90%. At the same time the Soviet Union produces only 50% of America's fertiliser output, 35% of its electric power, 25% of its chemical fibres and less than 8% of its motor vehicles.

Table 2 below compares the internal structure of Soviet industry and manufacturing with that of the USA and the UK. The chosen date is 1959 since this is particularly well documented in Soviet statistics thanks to the publication of a partial input-output table; only fragmentary data are available for later years. In spite of certain elements of arbitrariness in our attempts to secure a comparison, the broad picture which emerges may be taken as correct. Particularly striking is the high concentration of labour in construction and the relative neglect of electricity generation, gas, etc. The former reflects the Soviets' overriding concern with investment activities and the latter the comparatively undeveloped state of municipal services and rural electrification. We must, however, note the unusual capital intensity of electric power and gas production and the exceptionally high capital costs involved in Soviet extractive industries. This last fact has led the Soviet Union repeatedly to ask for special contributions (possibly in the nature of rental payments) from East European importers of Soviet ores and minerals over and above the world market price.

The structure within the manufacturing industry clearly reflects the long-standing bias in favour of large-scale and highly 'integrable' lines of production—branches which lend themselves easily to central planning and also pander to the 'investment first' ideology. In spite of a stunted motor car industry, the metals group absorbed over 40% of the total labour force in manufacturing, thus approaching the highly motorised and export-oriented countries of the West. The lag in chemicals is notable, both in the share of labour and of capital, and owes a great deal to the prolonged reign of the 'metal-eaters'. Equally striking is the very low capital intensity of textiles, clothing and other light industry, whose share in fixed capital is so much below their share in the labour force. This clearly reflects their technological backwardness and long years of neglect.

Since 1959 strenuous efforts have been made to modernise the structure of Soviet industry. The proportion of labour and capital resources flowing to the chemical industry and electric power stations has greatly increased, while constructional activities have been made rather less labour-absorbing than before. Textiles and other light industries have had their capital allocations increased, and the overall structure of manufacturing has undoubtedly shifted nearer to that of highly developed Western economies.

TABLE 2

A COMPARISON OF INDUSTRIAL STRUCTURE IN 1959 (ESTIMATED)
(%)

	Distribution of labour force			Distribution of fixed capital stock	
	USSR[1]	USA	UK	USSR[1]	UK(1958)
	(1)	(2)	(3)	(4)	(5)
Total industry and construction	25·6mn[a][b]	19·7mn[e]	11·1mn[c][a]	77·3rbl.bn[b][a]	27·1£bn[d][e]
of which:					
Mining and quarrying	7·4	3·4	7·5	15·2	4·8
Construction . .	23·5	14·1	12·8	7·1	2·6
Electricity, gas, etc. .	1·6	3·1	3·5	14·5	26·6
Manufacturing . .	67·5[b]	79·4	76·2[b]	63·2	66·0[e]
Within manufacturing:	100·0	100·0	100·0	100·0	100·0
Food . . .	12·6	9·4	9·0	14·7	10·6
Textiles, footwear, clothing . . .	20·5	16·2	18·5	8·2	12·3[e]
Light industry[f] . .	9·8	12·0	7·4	6·7	8·9
Chemicals . . .	3·1	9·0	6·1	7·1	15·1
Building materials .	8·9	3·5	3·9	9·3	3·4
Basic metals and prods.	10·0	17·2	13·1	} 43·0	} 49·7
Engineering . .	26·6[b]	18·3	20·9		
Transport equipment	3·9	10·7	17·8[b]		
Miscellaneous . .	4·6	3·7	3·3	11·0	0·0

[1] An attempt was made to ensure comparability by eliminating from the Soviet data the estimated contribution of timber-hauling and fisheries which are outside the purview of industry in Western statistics.

[a] Man-years worked.

[b] Including machinery repair shops (USSR) and motor repairers (UK).

[c] Wage-earners and employees.

[d] One billion = 1000 million USSR at initial cost, UK at replacement cost.

[e] Including estimate for textiles obtained by 'blowing up' data for footwear and clothing in proportion to labour force.

[f] Wood-working, furniture, paper, printing, and rubber.

Sources: Soviet. V. Treml in *Soviet Studies*, January 1967, pp. 293 *et seq.* adjusted for comparability, and Research Analysis Corporation (Typescript) October 1963.

US and UK. OECD, *Manpower Statistics, 1950–1960*, and CSO *National Income and Expenditure, 1968.*

THE SITUATION IN COMMUNIST EASTERN EUROPE

When Eastern Europe passed under Soviet influence it was at first so tightly clasped in the Stalinist embrace that few manifestations of genuine independence, or even local differentiation, could be expected in any field. For close on a decade (less in the case of Jugoslavia) there was no significant departure from the Soviet model in economic policy or openly expressed economic thought. When the heavy hand was finally lifted in the early or mid-1950s it was to liberate a considerable potential in pent-up criticism and original thought. In contrast to their Russian predecessors, the Marxist intellectuals of Poland or Jugoslavia had no need to justify or instigate the movement away from capitalism in their countries; nor did they need to consolidate their position in an isolated stronghold. Instead they were able and anxious to concentrate on operational blueprints and models designed to promote the material progress of the post-capitalist economy in their own surroundings of time and space.

These surroundings differed from Soviet experience in three main respects: (a) the longer tradition of personal land ownership among the peasantry, (b) the smaller size of the national unit and its consequent dependence on international trade, and (c) the closer acquaintance of sizable groups in the population with Western modes of life and thought. Each of these factors served in its own way to accelerate the *reductio ad absurdum* of the cruder Stalinist impositions and to sharpen the reaction against them.

Peasant resistance to collectivisation and the governments' enforced retreat in Jugoslavia, Poland and Hungary necessitated genuine incentive-prices in agriculture, followed by a drift towards incentive-wages in alternative urban occupations. The resulting cost-inflation in industry, sometimes reinforced by demand-inflation originating from the peasant sector, played havoc with the centrally administered price structure. Production units intended as a source of profit for central investment found themselves in need of state subsidies within a short time of every new price reform. This produced disincentive effects on management, calling for fresh adjustments and revisions. In proportions varying with the labour-intensity (i.e. proneness to inflation) of different industries, official selling prices ceased to reflect current costs almost as soon as they had been centrally determined, and as a consequence the planners' resource allocation and investment choices went widely and demonstrably astray.

Apart from agriculture, the classical instance of an economic sector resistant to central planning and control is foreign trade. Its decisive importance in the people's democracies injected further elements of uncertainty and confusion. Owing to rapid changes in foreign markets and political relations within the bloc, imported raw materials soon came to enter the domestic price structure at purely historic valuations, deviating both from the terms of trade at which they had been obtained and the relative costs at which they could be produced at home. It became increasingly difficult, if not impossible, to decide which goods should be exported and which retained for internal use.

The many instances of glaring and prolonged wastefulness which resulted provoked responsible intellectuals to turn to their own, often very extensive, knowledge of Western economics in search of analytic tools and operational practices which might be suitable for adaptation to the new environment. It was clear, however, that the resulting recommendations could not hope to avoid dangerous ideological overtones and might be identified as an open or implied protest against the Soviet impositions of the recent past.

The Jugoslav defection of the late 1940s and the Polish of October 1956 had a strong influence on economic thinking in Eastern Europe. In Poland a prolonged debate culminated in the famous *Theses* of the Economic Council (published in 1957) which laid down the desirable principles of price formation to be pursued. In the nature of things it could only touch the behavioural rules to be followed by the price commissions of the centre and could not advocate any devolution of price-forming functions to lower organs, let alone enterprise managers; but it was an important first move back to the scientific marginalism in economics which the Marxist orthodoxy had rejected for so long. It was in Poland also that the contribution of productive resources other than labour was first readmitted to a semblance of its right place in the formation of social value. By the early 1960s the economic legitimacy of interest rates, ground rents, etc.—at least as accounting categories—no longer 'raised any serious doubts' in Poland.

There were also stirrings of a more critical spirit in Hungary and János Kornai's book on *Overcentralisation in Economic Administration* crystallised the doubts in the minds of many. The abortive revolution of 1956 brought only a partial setback to overt criticism, and the greater analytic spirit of Hungarian economists soon took wing again in a flowering of the mathematical school.

In recent years Czechoslovakia came into the forefront of the economic reform movement and invested much sound theoretical thought in the construction of Ota Šik's model of a partially free economy.

The reform movements in Eastern Europe and the much less ambitious parallel changes in the Soviet Union are all long-delayed responses to a planning system which may have had some virtues in transforming a backward semi-rural and semi-autarkic economy into a modern industrial state, but was bound to become a strait-jacket in the context of fast maturing and highly complex economies where the direction of desirable development is no longer obvious for all to see, and where further progress depends on streamlining and efficiency rather than sacrifice and massive regimentation. That the Soviet Union and much of Eastern Europe are now entering this stage no one can deny. It remains to be seen whether the political power implications of the new economic climate will be accepted in good time.

FURTHER READING

Campbell, Robert W. *Accounting in Soviet Planning and Management*, Harvard Univ. Press, Cambridge, Mass.; Oxford Univ. Press, London, 1963.

Crankshaw, Edward. *Russia without Stalin (The Emerging Pattern)*, Viking Press, New York; Michael Joseph, London, 1956.

Grossman, G. *Economic Systems*, Prentice Hall, N.J., 1967.

Holzman, F. D. *Readings on the Soviet Economy*, Rand McNally, Chicago, 1962.

Jasny, N. *Soviet Industrialisation 1928–52*, Univ. of Chicago Press, Chicago, 1961.

Montias, John M. *Central Planning in Poland*, Yale Univ. Press, New Haven, Conn., 1962.

Nove, Alec. *The Soviet Economy*, Allen & Unwin, London, 1961.

Richman, Barry M. *Soviet Management*, Prentice Hall, N.J., 1965.

Spulber, Nicholas. *The Soviet Economy*, W. W. Norton, New York, 1962.

Wiles, P. J. D. *Communist International Economics*, Basil Blackwell, Oxford, 1969.

FRANCIS SETON. Official Fellow of Nuffield College, Oxford. Has written numerous articles on the economies of the Soviet Union and Eastern Europe.

PLANNED ECONOMIES UNDER REFORM[1]

MICHAEL KASER

Two Special Cases

The two countries of Eastern Europe which first adopted the Soviet style of central economic planning were also the first to dissociate themselves from the international political authority of the Soviet Union. Jugoslavia, and under its aegis, Albania, undertook a wholesale nationalisation of industry and trade as soon as the war ended, and set up controls after the Soviet model. Jugoslavia launched a Five Year Plan for 1947–51, the first emulation abroad of a Soviet long-term plan, paralleled, as it happened, by the start of a Five Year Plan in Mongolia, the Soviet Union's only associated state before the war. Both made every effort to reorient their commerce towards the Soviet Union: UNRRA supplies furnished unrequited exports from the West, but the countries' foreign-trade monopolies (established with similar promptness in the Soviet fashion of 1918) were given instructions to maximise trade with the East. The lack of concern with protecting the interests of foreign owners during nationalisation—executed with a harshness unequalled in the rest of Eastern Europe—and major diplomatic incidents (the Jugoslav quarrel over Trieste and the Albanian mining of a British destroyer in the Corfu Channel) rendered trade with the West still less attractive. Yet it is only Jugoslavia and Albania which today are outside the politico-economic bloc formed in the wake of the Soviet military victory of 1945.

Stalin's dispute with Tito in 1948, and Hoxha's alignment with Mao against Khrushchev in 1961, set Jugoslavia and Albania outside the pale of Soviet influence. Jugoslavia clung for four years to Soviet-type centralisation while its economy adjusted to the termination of trade with the East and its replacement by exchange with the West, and began experiments in 'market syndicalism' in 1952. The creation of workers' councils and the gradual repeal of price and investment controls set up a system in deliberate contrast to the centralisation which was the rule throughout the rest of Eastern Europe until 1964. The further Jugoslav economic reform begun in 1965 widened the distance almost as soon as it began to close, and included the freeing of banks to invest in productive enterprise, the admission of foreign capital, the issuance of debentures by enterprises to domestic savers, a substantial devaluation and the acceptance (by membership of GATT) of foreign access to the home market and a non-discriminatory tariff towards the bulk of the world trading community. But, though Jugoslavia by 1968 was operating a

[1] This is a revised version of an article in the December 1967 issue of *The World Today*, the monthly journal published by the Royal Institute of International Affairs, London. It takes account of developments to the end of 1969.

much more thoroughgoing market economy than any other East European government appeared to envisage, it demonstrated to them that decentralisation and intimate relations with capitalist concerns could be combined with the restriction of private capitalism. By retaining the socialist form of property, Jugoslavia had a significant effect upon the rest of Eastern Europe where the predominance of socialist ownership of the means of production was accepted as one of the most important tenets of Marxism. The penetration of market forms and of Western firms into Jugoslavia was, however, the feature of East European copying—however tentative, modest and controlled—which aroused the suspicion of the Soviet government, and must have been a contributory factor to its decision to convene some of its allies in the Warsaw Treaty Organisation to occupy Czechoslovakia in August 1968.

Albania—which formally withdrew from the Warsaw Treaty in consequence of that invasion—remained, in its economic system, at the other extreme from the Jugoslav. Its government in 1966 denounced the economic reforms elsewhere as 'revisionist' and maintained, subject to some simplification in 1966–1968, the practices of direct central control; its response to change was to launch in 1960 a drive to modernise the small-scale industry which had been slowly established (with credits successively from Jugoslavia, the Soviet Union and China) over the preceding two decades; and also to promote in 1969 a concept of 'workers' control' which owed much to the Chinese example of 'cultural revolution'. In so small an area as the territory of Albania and with relatively few enterprises to control, centralism posed few of the problems of dispersion and complexity found by the more developed states of Eastern Europe.

The Standard Practices of Eastern Europe

Six countries of Eastern Europe (Bulgaria, Czechoslovakia, East Germany, Hungary, Poland and Rumania) adopted the Soviet system of central planning around 1949, having at various dates over the preceding three years nationalised large-scale industry, all banks and other financial institutions and transport, submitted retail and wholesale trade to strict control (leading to the virtual extinction of private commerce), imposed a government monopoly of foreign trade, set up the first state and cooperative farms and adopted short-term economic plans. The Soviet Union itself had embraced its present system mainly during the course of the first Five Year Plan (1928–32), but the state foreign-trade monopoly had been established as early as 1918 and the collectivisation of agriculture was not effectively completed before 1937. Until 1955 the group of countries acted as one in the domestic policy to be implemented by central planning: because the Soviet Union had adopted one of self-sufficiency, the East European countries also tended to be autarkic. The establishment of the Council for Mutual Economic Aid (Comecon) in 1949 did nothing to attenuate the duplication and excessive cost of industrial capacity which such parallel programmes induced. The political disruptions of 1956 in the East and the signing of the Treaty of Rome in 1957 in the West led to serious reconsideration of industrialisation patterns; Comecon came to be used as the forum for the coordination of long-term plans and for the discussion of the respective product specialisation of members. The view that economic integration in Western Europe, within the EEC and EFTA, should be matched by a corresponding development in the East brought proposals for a 'supra-national' Comecon in 1962, which—largely due to the opposition of Rumania—were shelved during 1964–8.

In that period the domestic practices of each country began to diverge (economic reforms in Poland in 1956–58, in Hungary in 1957, and in Czechoslovakia in 1958, had been overwhelmed by 'creeping recentralisation'). East Germany was the first to devolve substantial management authority to groups of enterprises (the VVB) in 1964 and Rumania the last to do so in 1969; the Soviet Union joined the progress towards decentralisation in 1965, in which year both Bulgaria and Poland enacted measures devolving some of the detail of management to enterprise associations. Czechoslovakia, by a reform starting in January 1967 and Hungary, a year later, were making considerable advances towards interposing a market between state-owned enterprises, and this market the government would seek to influence rather than to direct explicitly. The occupation of August 1968 led Czechoslovakia in the following year to revert to the old system, but other governments in the area proceeded further.

The crucial elements in the economic reforms of 1964–68 were the administrative level at which transactions would be made and the criteria upon which such decisions should be based. Because the reforms concentrated upon the role of transactions in the general process of production, distribution and exchange, foreign trade was, by definition, affected. Of itself, the increasing importance accorded to profits per unit of capital employed as a yardstick for decision-making could lead to more intensive commercial relationships with Western countries, where the profit motive is a dynamic factor in the functioning of the market economy. For some time, however, political tensions may reduce the opportunities to benefit fully from the changes, which in any case must proceed slowly in view of the threat of inflation involved in a too rapid activation of a long dormant price mechanism.

PRODUCTION AND TECHNOLOGY

It need hardly be emphasised that the organisation of production, as distinct from transactions, is very similar in West and East European countries. The basic unit, the production plant, installs capital, absorbs raw material, pays labour and sells its product. A tendency dating from before the Russian Revolution, and accentuated by Stalin's industrial policy, led to the erection of larger plants than was common at the time in Western business practice. The post-war nationalisations in Eastern Europe and the deliberate neglect, save only in East Germany, by the new regimes to accord a place to private industrial enterprise, resulted in the closure of many smaller plants. Athough economic growth and the enlargement of markets (notably within the EEC) have enlarged the average sizes of plant in Western Europe in the recent years, the tendency in Eastern Europe and the Soviet Union is still for plant to be rather larger on average than in the West.

Increased size of plant, although accompanied by economies of scale, has not brought with it a higher average technology. A comparison of technology is extremely difficult—almost impossible—but it may be very roughly estimated that Soviet technique is now on the whole about where the USA was in the decade after World War II. Naturally, technology has a wide variation, from the advanced computer networks underlying the Soviet aerospace programme to the dilapidated textile mills of Ivanovo. Eastern Europe, for a decade or more, failed to take proper advantage of the rapid growth of investment and the replacement of war-damaged plant to embody new technology in its capital equipment. There were two reasons for this tendency—which was in surprising contrast to that, for example, in West

U

Germany or France, where reequipment and development was effected at a high level of technology. First, the presence in many countries of surplus agrarian labour made it appear cheaper to use labour-intensive techniques rather than the more modern methods which tended to be labour-saving. Second, no country had much chance, from about 1949 to the mid-1950s, to buy up-to-date equipment—that is, at the time when war damage and Soviet exactions were being replaced and when the investment drive was at its peak. Deliveries of sophisticated equipment were seriously limited from Western firms by the strategic embargo, then at its most restrictive. East European suppliers—and Czechoslovakia had a near-monopoly in many lines—did not have to compete with Western firms in this field and had little opportunity to learn of new advances in the West. It was cheaper to replicate the machine models which had been in production before and during the war than to spend on research and retooling. Only in the past decade have East European engineering plants had the facility to reequip themselves on contemporary lines, and, until the present reforms, they have been inhibited in this by centralised planning procedures. An enterprise which decelerated production to reequip was in most cases penalised for failure to pursue the rapid short-run expansion to which the plan gave priority; the higher profit which it eventually earned from the improved plant was, again in the majority of cases, surrendered to the ministry of finance as increment in profits tax.

If it may be said that the process of production is broadly the same seen from the standpoint of the production manager, it may also be suggested that the executive which directs him on the pattern of production and outlay is—in the East as in the West—operating to a plan. Large industrial corporations in the West have, in fact, developed techniques of planning and assessing implementation by their processing and manufacturing units, which are very similar to those employed by the industrial ministry and its directorates in an East European planned economy.

The Function of 'Enterprise'

The instructions handed down by a Western corporation or by a Soviet-type industrial ministry may be of the same form (to produce, for example, a certain output of certain product-mix, by month or year), but the transactions upon which those plans are based are essentially different. While no Western country may have entirely 'free' enterprise, the transactions which a company forecasts are those indicated by likely markets. In planning its purchases and sales, it is motivated chiefly by maximising profit. Although other motivations may predominate (for example, increasing sales turnover), or be planned on a longer-term basis in which the short-term profit is ignored, the standard operation of an industrial unit is expected to be at a current and capital cost exceeding the expected value of sales.

The corresponding standard of the unit in a centrally-planned economy is, however, output maximisation, subject (though by no means invariably) to the meeting of plant costs by expected sales. A normal profit (calculated as a small percentage of the wage bill plus depreciation) has often been added for administrative convenience, but the essence of the Soviet-type planning system has been to expand output in accordance with explicit 'indicators' communicated by the industrial ministry (and to the latter by the central planning office). In a Soviet-type economy, a failure by the ministry to forecast a price increase for a certain raw material would not be visited upon the producing plant: its financial plan would be adjusted, as in the case of unplanned excess costs in general, if they could be demonstrated to have occurred otherwise than through the mismanagement of the production unit. A similar rise in the price of materials by a free-enterprise firm would be borne by itself: either its profit would be reduced or it would seek a lower-priced substitute. The corresponding unit under central planning has little incentive to seek out a cheaper substitute because its profit plan or its planned subsidy would, by and large, be adjusted in consequence.

The Plan 'Indicator'

If the Soviet-style enterprise had to alter its product-mix to use a cheaper substitute, in response to a price rise in a material, it could well be checked in such a course by the need to fulfil an explicit task in the annual plan. The plan in the Soviet-type system, so far discarded only in Hungary, operates on 'indicators'—that is, according to instructions on output handed down by a plan authority. This conformed to the traditional type of central plan, which was constructed in physical-product terms (the so-called 'material balance'), although since the reforms, increasing reliance in achieving operational equilibrium is placed on the financial plan.

A central agency with adequate information and served by computers could, in principle, both construct a set of 'indicators' so that all production is assured a planned outlet (either as input to another unit or as sales to final consumers) consistent with maximum profitability (to ensure optimal utilisation of equipment, raw materials, inventories, etc.) and could also adjust this 'ideal plan' as often as external conditions warranted (for example, to comply with changes in consumer demand, in import or export prices, in wage rates, if these were uncontrolled by the planners, etc.). Some economists in the Soviet Union and Eastern Europe advocated computerisation to protect the central planning system in its old form. However, neither the data essential for this type of planning, nor the electronic equipment proved to be available; further obstacles were the conservative policy of certain central statistical offices, and the preferential supply of sophisticated computers to the aerospace sector. Without a computer network, the traditional 'manual techniques' constructed the balances needed for an annual plan in five months of paperwork and departmental negotiation; once it had been set up and no product was left 'unbalanced', adjustment to any of its 10,000 items— the Soviet figure—in the light of changing conditions during the year was so laborious as to be avoided so far as humanly possible. Indeed, to minimise the annual recomputations, the structure of such balances was kept as similar as possible from year to year: the tendency was for the relationship between products as inputs and outputs and between suppliers and consumers to be stable, and only the scale of production was changed. It is clear that technological progress has long been an incidental victim of this practice. To avoid the rigidity of this central planning procedure, the East European governments have, in general, now resolved to reduce the role of production targets, and to leave current transactions to the decision of the enterprise, or group of enterprises themselves. The 'indicators' in consequence are becoming predominantly targets for sales, cost, profit and return on installed capital. For these to replace physical planning, reforms have had to be made in the price system and in the motivation of the production unit.

Price Reform

Diagram

PRICE FORMATION FOR INDUSTRIAL CONSUMERS' GOODS EMBODYING AN AGRICULTURAL RAW MATERIAL

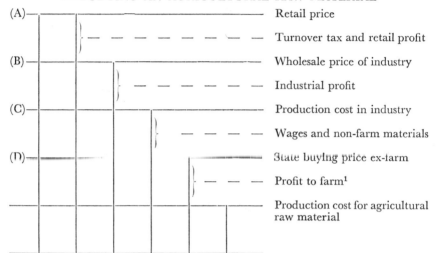

(A) — Retail price

— Turnover tax and retail profit

(B) — Wholesale price of industry

— Industrial profit

(C) — Production cost in industry

— Wages and non-farm materials

(D) — State buying price ex-farm

— Profit to farm[1]

— Production cost for agricultural raw material

[1] Losses were incurred at the level of prices paid under the Stalinist system, the farmers bearing the deficit from their private subsidiary production (the 'household plots', the produce of which is freely marketed).

Following the Soviet practice of the 1930s, the East European states in the 1950s adopted a 'four-tier' price system. In no tier was the relationship between one product and another necessarily the same. The highest tier was that of retail prices—(A) in the diagram; they were separated from wholesale prices—(B) in the diagram—by turnover tax, the indirect tax which accounted for the bulk of government revenue and paid for most centralised investment throughout the period of rapid industrialisation. Wholesale prices comprised two separate sets, one for industrial goods, the other for farm goods. The tier of wholesale prices for industrial goods was separated from a further tier, that of industrial costs—(C) in the diagram—the margin between these being formed by profits and subsidies; up to 99% of profits could legally be forfeited to the government, if wholesale prices exceeded costs, but a subsidy, paid from the budget or from an intra-industry equalisation account, was available if cost exceeded price. The wholesale prices paid to collective farms—(D) in the diagram—were extortionately low under Stalin in the Soviet Union (and during the corresponding periods in Eastern Europe), falling in some instances below cost of production. Deliveries were assured by compulsory procurement, and farm collectivisation, from which only Poland has exempted itself.

Costs themselves, as calculated in an industrial enterprise, were essentially the sum of materials, wages and depreciation. There was no charge for capital—finance, generally speaking, being assured by a budget grant—no rent, and relatively little depletion charge for minerals or other natural resources.

The initiative for the present reforms first showed itself in wholesale price reviews in Hungary as long ago as 1959 and a first round of such revisions was completed by July 1967 in the Soviet Union; these brought order—though not necessarily the best order—into the relationships between wholesale prices and costs in industry. Some rationalisation has been effected in farm procurement prices, but the economic reforms have, as yet, scarcely affected agriculture. The first stage of price reforms was accompanied by a revaluation, at current replacement cost, of the industrial capital stock. In sum, the price reforms made wholesale prices reflect 'costs' on the accepted Soviet definition. The second stage, which again began in Hungary in 1964, and has been accepted by all East European countries except Rumania, was to institute a charge for capital. This has been effected in two ways: first, by levying a tax on existing capital assets, according to their replacement cost and performance, and second, by requiring that the bulk of new capital be financed by profits or by reimbursable bank loan. The position varies with respect to rent and depletion charges from country to country, but even in the Soviet Union, where such charges were once dogmatically renounced as un-Marxist, their use is under active consideration. The third stage in the reform, and the most difficult, is to adjust such supply-determined prices in the light of demand. But the market has been so long in disuse that the balance of demand and supply cannot be struck by mere computation.

For this reason three states have authorised some derogation of their price-fixing powers. In Bulgaria the prices of all basic commodities remain centrally determined, but since the end of 1968 inter-enterprise contracts have set prices for a number of goods, subject to centrally-fixed ceilings or ranges; the prices board will, however, retain power to impose a price even in the contractual sphere. In January 1967, a few Czechoslovak prices were wholly decontrolled and a large number of others permitted to fluctuate within specified limits; during 1969, however, the government reimposed fixed prices, justifying itself on a real enough inflationary pressure, which it claimed had been generated by precipitate abandonment of 'indicators'; the latter were forthwith re-established, ostensibly as a temporary measure. The Hungarian authorities kept to their timetable for 1968–70, by the mid-point of which prices were free for 80 percent of capital goods, 40 percent of home raw materials and 30 percent of consumers' goods. In East Germany price revisions are taking place at frequent intervals, the view being that the price-control authorities can adjust as they go towards demand-supply equilibrium. In Poland a price revision scheduled for 1971 should permit a certain adjustment to demand (notably for new goods and for obsolescent lines) but there, as in the Soviet Union and in Rumania, central authority over prices remains absolute.

Only Hungary has ventured to carry its price reform into the retail level, but consumer-goods prices are so out of relation to their wholesale counterparts since the reforms that some adjustments, mainly upward, will have to be made everywhere. The price increments of 1966 in Hungary created a situation close to riot—though this was due in part to government mishandling—and other countries are being cautious in introducing such change. The inflationary situation is serious enough under the increased wholesale prices and a round of wage increases following the rationalisation of retail prices could well spark off wage demands leading to a further turn of the inflationary spiral. Turnover tax has hitherto been computed so as to skim off purchasing power (essentially the national wage bill plus farmers' sales) at the global level of retail sales, but has scarcely been used carefully to differentiate between products. It will remain the main factor in equilibrating retail with wholesale prices (and will thereby finance state administration, the social services and what will remain of centralised investment), and it is hoped that it can be turned to more sophisticated use in adjusting specific prices to the demand for individual goods. Furthermore, attempts are beginning to be made to shape consumer demands by advertising and other marketing techniques.

THE DANGER OF MONOPOLY

Governments trying to relax their hitherto tight control over pricing are in a dilemma. If they devolve too little authority for price-setting to the production units, prices will not find their proper level and the ensuing shortages could induce a return to central dictation. If, on the other hand, too much power is put into the hands of industrial enterprises, the latter may be tempted to act as a monopoly. Monopolisation is relatively easy because enterprises are large in relation to the national market, and because—for administrative and technical efficiency—governments are tending to transfer planning functions to enterprise groups rather than to the basic production units as such. This danger was foreseen by the author of the Czechoslovak reforms, Dr. Ota Šik, when he formulated his proposals in 1964, and he relied upon the threat of competitive imports as protection. Two factors make this an inadequate shield. First, the protection of domestic industry has been exercised in the past not behind customs walls (although some of the countries have refurbished their tariff legislation in recent years), but by mandatory instruction; that is, by constructing the material balances and the derived 'indicators' preferentially to utilise domestic sources. Enterprises can hence readily appeal against reducing this *de facto* protection on the grounds that they need time for adjustment, and that no tariff or single exchange rate could for some time reflect their true competitive position. Hungary became the first state to transfer protection to a tariff proper followed, though much more tentatively, by Bulgaria in 1969. Second, the trend to release competitive imports will be severely restricted by balance-of-payments difficulties. Indeed, it may be said that if the domestic condition for the success of the reforms is the containment of inflation, the external essential is a more favourable foreign balance.

The relevance of external trade is not entirely confined to the use of imports to combat monopoly, for the margin between domestic and export prices begins to assume significance in those countries which are members of GATT. Czechoslovakia has been a member since the foundation of the organisation; Jugoslavia was accepted in 1966 and Poland joined in 1967 and applications by Hungary and Rumania were under consideration at the end of 1969. These are all vulnerable to the complaints of other countries on dumping, as in principle are all the East European countries trading with states with anti-dumping legislation. It is, of course, an incidental of the relationship between state-trading nations and market economies that the extent of the tariff on imports and that of dumping in exports cannot be precisely determined. The group of experts convened by the UN Economic Commission for Europe, in which both sides were making progress in finding acceptable solutions, has, however, suspended its discussions, but, if membership of GATT is extended to nearly all the Eastern European group, that agency may become the appropriate forum.

THE LIMITS OF ENTERPRISE

The freedom to transact business in the light of profit has been least extended in the fields of capital, finance and foreign trade. As already indicated, governments have in principle renounced their willingness to hand out capital finance to production units as non-reimbursable grants. In its day, the allocation of funds to match those of equipment fitted the technique of the material balance, but it was patently more difficult to assure the best use of capital resources than of current resources. The institution, everywhere save in Rumania, of a capital charge has been accompanied by the channelling of state capital finance through the bank system. Together with the reinvestment of profits (in itself a significant incentive for enterprises to make profits), loan capital is intended to provide the bulk of investment funds. But the plan offices retain the authority to instruct the banks—which are, of course, state institutions—on the projects or industries to which they should give preference, and some projects, albeit a minority, will continue to be financed from the budget. Western exporters of capital equipment, therefore, will not in general be dealing with plenipotentiaries in negotiations with the East European end-user. Futhermore, where the foreign trade corporations retain their monopolistic position, the end-user will still not be an entirely free agent even as regards current goods.

With some exceptions, the extent to which producing enterprises (or their associations) have been given their freedom depends chiefly upon the balance of payments and the refinement of administrative technique. Thus, even if the authority of the Ministry of Foreign Trade in Czechoslovakia is, on paper, absolute, the domestic enterprise has in reality extensive powers of negotiation: Motokov, for example, may be formally a corporation subordinate to the Ministry of Foreign Trade but it functions as a marketing subsidiary of Škoda. In Hungary all firms and elsewhere certain industrial associations have been accorded import and export rights.

FOREIGN ECONOMIC RELATIONS

One of the functions of the foreign trade corporations in the past has been to siphon off the windfall profit, or to absorb the nominal loss, arising from the wide disparity of domestic and foreign-trade prices. Transactions with the West have always been denominated in the Western currency; transactions with other East European countries are at approximate 'world-market prices' denominated in 'transferable roubles'. The official exchange rates at which the Western currencies (or the 'transferable roubles') are converted into national monetary units are known to be still artificial. No single exchange rate could reflect a purchasing-power parity even when the price reforms discussed above have been completed. Consequently, either the foreign trade corporations will have to function as financial intermediaries, or the national bank will have to operate multiple exchange rates.

Even so, it would be administratively convenient if the official rates were brought down to that which minimises either the volume of equalisation payments through the Ministry of Foreign Trade (or Foreign Trade Bank) or the spread of the different exchange rates. Because Hungary is the most advanced in seeking to open its economy to international market forces— exports now reach 40% of the national product and domestic prices are to be modelled as nearly as possible on world relationships—it was the first to make a *de facto* devaluation (by altering domestic conversion coefficients in 1968); a similar, though smaller change, was made at the same time in Rumania, which faced a severe balance-of-payments deficit in convertible currencies in 1968.

A final limitation on foreign trade flexibility lies in commitments to other planned economies. Over the past decade, planned coordination within Comecon has been carried out on the basis of material balances, and by commissions paralleling the industrial ministries. At a 'summit meeting' of Comecon in April 1969 the USSR pressed its fellow members to promote economic integration in the wake of political consolidation, but encountered opposing views on means. Hungary and Poland thought it possible to open the region to world market forces by creating a form of free-trade area in which members' preference would be assured by differential customs duties; by the late 'seventies a competitive trading relationship could be further promoted by making their several currencies convertible. Other members favoured the elaboration of practices to which Rumania—now cautiously assenting—had objected in 1964, namely the concerted compilation of five-year plans so that new investment would be for products having guaranteed sales in member states. No decision being reached, a further meeting at the highest political level was scheduled for 1970.

FURTHER READING

Balassa, B. A. *The Hungarian Experience in Economic Planning*, Yale Univ. Press, New Haven, Conn., 1969.

Brown, A. A. and Neuberger, E. (eds.) *International Trade and Central Planning*, Univ. of California Press, Berkeley, Calif., 1968.

Csikos Nagy,B. *Pricing in Hungary*, Institute of Economic Affairs, London, 1968.

Feiwel, G. R. *The Economics of a Socialist Enterprise*, Frederick A. Praeger, New York; Pall Mall Press, London, 1965 (ed.) *New Currents in Soviet-type Economies*, International Textbook Co., Scranton, Penn., 1968.

Friss, I. (ed.) *Reform of the Economic Mechanism in Hungary*, Akademia Kiado, Budapest, 1969.

Gamarnikow, M. *Economic Reforms in Eastern Europe*, Wayne State University Press, Detroit, Mich., 1968.

Garvy, G. *Money, Banking and Credit in Eastern Europe*, Federal Reserve Bank of New York, New York, 1966.

Grossman, G. (ed.) *Money and Plan: Financial Aspects of East European Economic Reforms*, University of California Press, Berkeley, Calif., 1968.

Kaser, M. C. *Comecon: Integration Problems of the Planned Economies*, Oxford University Press, London and New York, 2nd edn., 1967.

Kaser, M. C. and Zieliński, J. G. *Planning in East Europe: Industrial Management by the State*, The Bodley Head, London, 1970.

Montias, J. M. *Central Planning in Poland*, Yale Univ. Press, New Haven, Conn., 1962.

Montias, J. M. *Economic Development in Communist Rumania*, M.I.T. Press, Cambridge, Mass., 1967.

Pryor, F.L. *The Communist Foreign Trade System*, M.I.T. Press, Cambridge, Mass., and Allen and Unwin, London 1963.

Pryor, F. L. *Public Expenditure in Communist and Capitalist Countries*, Yale Economic Growth Centre, New Haven, Conn., and Allen and Unwin, London, 1968.

Sirc, L. *Economic Devolution in Eastern Europe*, Longmans, London, 1969.

Wellisz, S. *The Economies of the Soviet Bloc*, McGraw Hill, New York and London, 1964.

Wiles, P. J. D. *Communist International Economics*, Basil Blackwell, Oxford, 1969.

MICHAEL KASER. Lecturer in Soviet Economics, Oxford University and Fellow of St. Anthony's College. Until 1963 staff member of the U.N. Economic Commission for Europe. Former Second Secretary in H.M. Embassy, Moscow. The first Western visitor to Comecon in 1955 and author of *Comecon: Economic Integration Problems of the Planned Economies*, 1967. Other publications include *Economic Development for Eastern Europe*, 1968. *Soviet Economics* in preparation.

THE EEC AND EASTERN EUROPE

GEORGE SCHÖPFLIN

EAST EUROPEAN REACTION TO COMMON MARKET

ONE suspects that the first private reaction of the East Europeans to the Rome Treaty was one of incredulity. On the one hand, they were accustomed to regarding political developments in the West according to Marxist principles, and these had preordained the speedy dissolution of the capitalist economies under the weight of their inner contradictions. On the other hand, their own experience of integration had been anything but happy; they were used to the Soviet interpretation of this concept, which during the Stalinist period had in practice meant ruthless economic exploitation. Consequently, they did not see how the European Economic Community could be made to work.

The East Europeans' official reaction to the Common Market was open hostility. Taking their cue from Soviet propaganda, they professed to see in the Community a dangerous plot against peace in Europe, an economic extension of NATO, which would rapidly subordinate Western Europe to the domination of American and German monopoly capital. Besides these arguments, the East Europeans disliked the EEC for economic reasons as well. They contended that a closely-knit economic community would crystallise the economic division of Europe, something for which, of course, the West Europeans were solely to blame. This contention seemed to be borne out when EFTA was established as a rival organisation.

This ostensible division of Western Europe into two competing economic groupings afforded communist publicists an excellent opportunity for exercising the 'inner contradictions of capitalism' type of argument. In particular, they focused on three principal issues. The first was the existence of the two trading blocs as a source of contradictions. The second involved the obvious divisions within the EEC between the richer and the poorer member states, which led the East Europeans to claim that Germany would rapidly dominate the others. And third, the East Europeans stressed the economic differences within individual Common Market countries, waxing eloquent on the theme of the 'pauperisation' of the working classes in Western Europe.

Under Soviet influence, all the communist countries except Poland and Jugoslavia adopted this approach at first. Poland in the immediate post-deStalinisation period, from about 1957 to 1959, was a partial exception to the chorus of woe, but from about 1960 onwards the Poles too began to toe the line with the hardening of the domestic situation and no doubt under the impact of the Berlin crisis. Nevertheless, Poland's criticism of the EEC remained comparatively muted—often the Poles restricted themselves to reprinting Western criticisms—and for a while they tended merely to emphasise the disadvantages accruing to Poland from the operation of the

Community policy. The current hard line in Warsaw dates only from the emergence of the close relationship with East Germany, a freezing of positions which has affected nearly everything in Polish political and economic life. Even so, the recent appointment of Franciszek Modrzewski as Poland's ambassador to Belgium, with an unofficial watching brief over the Community, suggests that the Poles are to some extent still interested in keeping open their options *vis-à-vis* the Six: Modrzewski has been deputy minister of Foreign Trade and is experienced in dealing with Western countries on economic matters.

JUGOSLAVIA'S PRAGMATIC APPROACH

The other exception, Jugoslavia, adopted and maintained a much more pragmatic approach to the Community. Although not ignoring political objections to the EEC, the Jugoslavs saw the Community primarily as a threat to their economic position. Furthermore the Jugoslavs found themselves in the unhappy situation of being exposed to potential trade discrimination from both the EEC and the Comecon.

The Jugoslavs were also anxious for political reasons. First, they were highly suspicious of the economic penetration by Community countries in Africa, as enshrined in the 1963 Yaoundé Convention of Association. Secondly, pursuing a neutral line themselves, they opposed all political blocs, which, as Tito put it in 1958, 'hampered integration in the wider sense'. In spite of Jugoslavia's early acceptance of the reality of the Community— something absent elsewhere in Eastern Europe at the time—the Jugoslavs were just as tardy in taking any practical steps which might allow them to come to terms with it. The reasons for this lay mostly in the internal political situation in Jugoslavia—the strength of the party conservatives, which remained unbroken until 1966—but partly in Tito's hopes of successfully organising the non-aligned countries of the world into a viable political force.

What can be regarded as the first phase of communist attitudes to the EEC—sterile hostility based on the reiteration of the dogma—lasted until about 1962, when evidence of the growing success of the Common Market constrained the East Europeans to reappraise their policies. In particular the Soviet Union began to recognise the power of attraction exerted by the Common Market on Eastern Europe and the third world. Likewise, Community tariffs began to affect East-West trade. The ideological response to this was to revise the thesis that the Common Market was about to disintegrate under the weight of its inner contradictions, and to accept the Community as a dangerous economic reality. On the political level, Khrushchev's scheme to convert Comecon into a supranational planning organ—a move predestined to failure because of the overwhelming economic predominance of the Soviet Union in Comecon and finally torpedoed by the Rumanians— was also in part dictated by the need to counter the growing economic and political strength of the Community.

FEW DIRECT CONTACTS

As far as the East Europeans were concerned, they echoed Moscow's ideological guidelines faithfully, but at the same time they began to concentrate their criticism of the Community on particular aspects of what they regarded as its discriminatory policies, rather than condemning it in its entirety. For instance, it was at this stage, about 1962, that a certain change could be discerned in Hungarian attitudes, although the new approach was very slow. Direct contacts with Brussels, however, remained few and limited. The Poles sent experts to Brussels as early as 1964, but their brief did not really go beyond technical questions, such as quotas for Polish agricultural produce.

The Rumanians, whose policies of noisy independence from Moscow began to attract increasing attention from about 1964, have always been rather conservative on the question of international integration. Whilst they favour trade with the West as a means of lessening their dependence on Soviet economic help and technical know-how, they have opposed integration in Western Europe unreservedly—but then they could hardly have done anything else, given the fact that they had opposed it in the East European context. In principle and in practice, the Rumanians have consistently praised the virtues of bilateral economic relations and rejected multilateral groupings.

The first really fundamental readjustment of policies towards the Community came from Jugoslavia. In December 1964 Tito explained that in his view Jugoslavia's relations with the West were good, save only for a few discriminatory measures by the Community. Shortly afterwards, in May 1965, the Jugoslavs began their attempt to negotiate a general and economic agreement with the Community, though without success; indeed success eluded the Jugoslavs on each subsequent occasion, in early 1967 and in March 1968. In May that year Vasil Grivčev, Jugoslavia's federal secretary for foreign trade, published in the Belgrade *Review of International Affairs* a detailed analysis of the highly prejudicial impact of the common agricultural policy on exports of Jugoslav agricultural produce. The article, which could be taken to represent the thinking of the Jugoslav government on the subject, hinted that Jugoslavia might have to initiate 'corrective measures'. In July 1968, however, the Community's Council of Ministers finally gave the Commission the go-ahead to open negotiations with Jugoslavia.

Economic Necessity

The more realistic and practical approach by the communist countries to the Common Market appeared to derive, unsurprisingly, from economic necessity. The two most trade-dependent countries of Eastern Europe, Hungary and Czechoslovakia, were the next to take steps to clarify their policies, steps that were perhaps easier once French policy had ensured that the Community would not become a supranational political bloc in the near future. On 23 February 1968, the Hungarian prime minister, Jenő Fock, stated categorically that the Common Market was now a reality and Hungary would not hesitate to negotiate with it, if this proved to be in Hungary's interest. These sentiments were repeated and expanded on 19 April, by Václav Valeš, Czechoslovak foreign trade minister, when he stated that Czechoslovakia would be willing to recognise the EEC, should that be to Czechoslovakia's advantage. He added that bilateral discussion had already been undertaken with France, West Germany and Italy, with a view to intensifying economic cooperation, and that these talks were going well.

This more businesslike attitude in Eastern Europe towards the Community did not appear to find a ready response in Brussels. As one Czechoslovak spokesman put it in an interview on 4 May 1968: 'We are now examining the impact of the Common Market on our economic relations with West European countries. I cannot give you more information at the moment, but we are interested. In general, we regard the Common Market favourably, but a great deal depends on the attitude of the Common Market countries.' The post-invasion confusion has, of course, affected this aspect of Czechoslovak foreign policy, so that no new initiatives are to be expected for the time being.

TRADE PATTERN

The pattern of trade between the Six and Eastern Europe helps to explain the Community's relatively lukewarm interest in Eastern Europe. From the Community's point of view, Eastern Europe is unimportant in economic terms. In 1965 Eastern Europe (without Jugoslavia) contributed a mere 6·5% of EEC imports, while taking 6·3% of EEC exports. East European exports to the Community, moreover, consist largely of agricultural produce and raw materials. Given the Community's own agricultural surpluses, it is understandable that the Six are less than enthusiastic about offering extensive trade concessions to East European imports. Until now the East Europeans have managed to avoid the worst effects of the restrictions deriving from the common agricultural policy by switching the content of their exports, but this kind of procedure is hardly conducive to good economic relations in the long run, and is not a substitute for a properly negotiated trade agreement.

TABLE I[1]

TRADE BETWEEN EASTERN EUROPE AND THE EEC

Imports from the EEC
($ US millions)

	1958	1966
Bulgaria	30	241
Czechoslovakia	122	225
East Germany	60	134
Hungary	73	206
Poland	138	240
Rumania	51	282
Soviet Union	222	473
Total	696	1801

Exports to the EEC
($ US millions)

	1958	1966
Bulgaria	25	127
Czechoslovakia	110	216
East Germany	41	102
Hungary	75	207
Poland	120	253
Rumania	56	218
Soviet Union	271	618
Total	698	1741

Notes: These figures do not include intra-German trade. Trade between the EEC and Albania is negligible.

[1] Sources for Tables 1, 2 and 3 are from foreign trade statistics published by the various countries concerned, the EEC and the Economic Commission for Europe.

TABLE 2

EEC TRADE WITH THE SOVIET UNION AND
EASTERN EUROPE AS A PROPORTION OF TOTAL EEC TRADE
($ *US millions*)

	1958	*1967*
Total EEC exports . . .	15,911	31,627
EEC exports to Eastern Europe .	696	2,102
Total EEC imports . . .	16,156	30,767
EEC imports from Eastern Europe	698	2,008

Note: These figures exclude intra-EEC trade.

TABLE 3

THE SHARE OF THE EEC MEMBER STATES OF
TOTAL EEC TRADE WITH EASTERN EUROPE, 1967
($ *US millions*)

	EEC exports	*EEC imports*
Belgium/Luxemburg .	155	136
France	438	361
West Germany . . .	883	666
Italy	445	686
Netherlands . . .	180	159

Note: These figures exclude intra-German trade and
trade with Jugoslavia.

MODERN MACHINERY NEEDED

On the other hand, although it now seems politically impossible, the East
Europeans do need to export more to the markets of the industrialised
Western countries, far more than the other way round. Between 15% and
20% of East European trade is with the Community, and this trade is
qualitatively as well as quantitatively much more important to Eastern
Europe than it is to the Six. The communist economies are in general faced
with the problem of equipping or reequipping their industries with modern
machinery, and to succeed they must have access to the more sophisticated
techniques in the West.

Should their foreign earnings fall as a result of the common agricultural
policy and other difficulties, then their already chronic shortage of convertible currency will be gravely accentuated. The UN Economic Commission for Europe's *Economic Survey of Europe 1967* stated clearly that tariff
discrimination on trade in manufactured products had hampered East
European exports to Western Europe (to EFTA as well as to the EEC), even
if this adverse impact had been mitigated by tariff reductions within GATT.
Indeed, although trade between the Six and Eastern Europe (Bulgaria,
Czechoslovakia, Hungary, Poland and Rumania only) increased from
$2151·3 million in 1966 to $2432·4 million in 1967, this rise was largely the
consequence of growth in East European imports from the Community and
was not balanced by a corresponding rise in their exports.

NO GENERAL AGREEMENT BY THE SIX

There is, nevertheless, a certain awareness in official circles in Brussels of the
relatively unfavourable position of the East Europeans. During a European

parliament debate on this subject on 12 March 1968, Jean-François Deniau, a member of the Commission, indicated that he recognised that the situation was changing and that trade between the Six and Eastern Europe had grown significantly in the last few years. On the other hand, he explained that the Commission could not at that stage formulate a guideline for trade with Eastern Europe. In the absence of a general agreement among the member states on the objectives of such a guide—and this he suggested was the case—it was extremely difficult to draw up any kind of regulation in this respect.

As Deniau saw it, there were three aspects to any such guideline. First administrative and legal: in spite of a considerable relaxation in matters like the lifting of strategic embargoes, trade with Eastern Europe still fell into a special category. Second, he touched upon the economic aspects; in this his analysis was substantially the same as that offered above: that the East Europeans were too dependent on agricultural exports and that he hoped to see a greater diversification into industrial goods. The third aspect mentioned by Deniau was the political. On this he insisted that the unity of the Community could not be put at risk, but at the same time the policies of the Six should move into a more active phase in expanding trade with Eastern Europe. In short Deniau expressed himself, though rather cautiously, in favour of a dialogue with Eastern Europe.

POLITICAL QUESTION

This debate was concerned with a report on trade between the Community and the 'state-trading countries' of Eastern Europe, presented to the European parliament by its rapporteur, Karl Hahn, German Christian Democrat. Hahn was considerably more enthusiastic and more outspoken in the debate than Deniau. He accepted that trading with Eastern Europe was in part a political question, and even though the difficulties of trading with Eastern Europe should not be underestimated, he strongly favoured a Community policy. In particular, Hahn suggested that it would serve no useful purpose to refuse to recognise that this trade involved agricultural imports and that this presented major problems for the countries of the Six. Essentially, the key to trading with Eastern Europe lay in formulating a common policy on imports and also in regulating credits. Finally, Hahn strongly criticised the Council of Ministers for having failed to do anything about trade with Eastern Europe, although proposals had existed since 1964.

Ultimately, the prospects are not particularly encouraging, from either point of view. So far as the communist countries are concerned, their trading structure—especially their totally irrational pricing systems—is the one main economic obstacle. On the other side, the Six have not been able to agree on a common trade policy, with the result that bilateralism tends to be perpetuated. In the present political situation, it is extremely difficult to predict how things will evolve; certainly the cautious optimism expressed in the debate in the European Parliament in March 1968 must have dissolved completely since the invasion of Czechoslovakia. For the moment, the political will to bring about a more rational trading structure between the Community and the East Europeans is significantly absent.

FURTHER READING

Wilczynski, J. *The Economics and Politics of East-West trade.*

SOVIET AND EAST EUROPEAN AID
TO DEVELOPING COUNTRIES

A. TODD

THE ORIGINS AND PURPOSES OF AID

Soviet Policy

WHEN Stalin died in May 1953, the Soviet Union was already a leading political, military and economic power and the leader of a group of communist-ruled states comprising a quarter of the world's population. Communism however, had made little progress among the poor backward countries of Asia and Africa which were then beginning to achieve political independence but were still bound by economic ties to their traditional markets and suppliers in the capitalist world. The new Soviet leaders decided that they could now afford to devote some economic effort to cultivating relations with these emerging countries, and with those of Latin America. Their political aim was to 'strengthen the independence' of the developing countries—that is, to weaken their traditional ties with the ex-colonial powers and the USA, and establish a competing communist presence. Subsidiary economic aims were to facilitate the Soviet Union's imports of tropical produce and to expand Soviet trade generally.

The resources available to support this new policy consisted chiefly of some surplus capacity in the Soviet engineering industry, especially for the production of capital equipment, and substantial surpluses of arms becoming obsolescent in the Warsaw Pact alliance. The Soviet Union had gained experience in organising and executing large development projects not only in its own underdeveloped regions but also in Eastern Europe and China. Its centralised administration enabled it to offer equipment and services for development in return for tropical produce, without making inroads on either party's reserves of gold or foreign currency. It could give fairly long credit and the interest rates were low. Priorities nearer home, however, required that its aid policy should be selective; it could not think of attacking world poverty on a broad front. Soviet policy makers could not, as the Americans have done, promise continuing large supplies of foodstuffs, nor lend convertible currency, nor give away large quantities of grant aid. They could, nevertheless, make a gift of a hospital, or a presidential VIP aircraft or food for emergency relief if this seemed expedient.

For many of the governments of the third world, with their insatiable demands for economic assistance, any new source of help was in principle welcome, and Soviet aid had distinctive attractions. The Soviet government showed a flattering regard for a new country's right to plan its own future and would not question the financial viability of a cherished development project, or the objectives underlying a keenly felt need for new armaments. A

Soviet-built factory, once the instalments were paid off, would become the absolute property of the recipient and its profits would not be expatriated to foreign shareholders; and repayment in produce promised a stable market for known quantities of exports over a relatively long period, and might help to keep up the prices to be earned from non-communist buyers as well.

There were, however, serious obstacles to the acceptance of Soviet aid. The dangers of giving communist advisers access to vital sectors of the host country's economic and administrative system were obvious. Soviet methods and products were unfamiliar; and the hazards of even a marginal transfer of trade from Western to Eastern partners sometimes seemed more formidable if it was imagined that the acceptance of Soviet aid in one field might provoke a withdrawal of Western support in others. The first countries to accept Soviet aid therefore had to have other reasons besides economic need for doing so; Afghanistan was the subject of peculiarly pressing attentions because of its geographic position bordering on Soviet Central Asia, India and two member countries of the Baghdad Pact; India and Indonesia were two of the largest and most vocal proponents of 'non-alignment' and Egypt, whose non-alignment was embittered by Western support for Israel, had come under the control of a revolutionary military government determined to use new methods of solving the country's internal problems and enlarging its role in world affairs. In all these cases Soviet offers of economic aid were the more readily accepted because of the accompanying offers of arms.

The role of Eastern Europe

The Soviet Union's fellow-members of the Warsaw Pact alliance and the Council of Mutual Economic Assistance shared, in varying degrees, in the Soviet desire to promote world communism and had the same economic motives for seeking to exchange their surplus industrial products for tropical raw materials. They also possessed, in varying degrees, experience of trading and contracting in the less developed countries dating back to their pre-war non-communist days. Their political and economic diversity and their modest military stature made them seem less dangerous to deal with than the Soviet Union. Therefore although their combined economic capacity for giving aid was only a fraction of the Soviet, they made a vital contribution, collectively and individually, to the total penetration effort.

Jugoslavia, moved by the same economic factors which led the minor Warsaw Pact countries to increase their activity in the third world, added a further element of variety to the communist repertoire. Like those countries, Jugoslavia gives credit less generously than the Soviet Union and deals rather in sales of machinery than in packaged project aid; but its political independence of the Soviet Union gives it an easier entrée to some countries prepared to deal on a trial basis with communists but not with members of the Warsaw Pact.

THE NATURE OF AID

We now consider the two main forms, military and economic, in which the Soviet Union extends aid to the underdeveloped countries and, briefly, the ancillary programmes of cultural and scientific cooperation.

Military aid

Soviet (or East European) military aid consists of the provision of equipment and training for the armed forces of the recipient country on credit terms broadly similar to those governing economic development aid, which is discussed below. It began in 1955 when the Egyptians, having been refused the arms they sought from Western suppliers because of the danger of an Arab-Israeli war, received them first from Czechoslovakia and Poland but subsequently from the Soviet Union. Soviet military aid is now extended to about half of the 35 countries receiving Soviet economic aid. In addition to the supply of equipment, with spares and ammunition, a military aid agreement provides for the loan of Soviet technicians to train the recipient forces in handling and maintenance of the new equipment, and sometimes for the acceptance of students at schools in the Soviet Union for longer training as, for example, aircrew or submarine crews, or on Staff College courses.

The Soviet Union does not insist that its customers change over completely to Soviet or East European equipment for all their forces; it will agree to provide infantry or artillery weapons or tanks, surface vessels or submarines, fighters or bombers or missiles as the customer (within reason) requires, and the range of equipment on offer varies from types obsolete in Eastern Europe to models still in use in the Warsaw Pact forces and in production in the Soviet Union. In accordance with non-proliferation policy, however, it shows no signs of willingness to supply nuclear weapons.

The political importance of military aid and the Soviet Union's interest in regulating the military production of its Warsaw Pact allies entail a higher degree of Soviet coordination over those countries' arms exports than over other forms of aid. There is some division of labour; Czechoslovakia produces a jet aircraft (the L29 'Delfin') which sells even in the Soviet Union as a trainer, Poland has a substantial share of the market in warships; the others have little to export except small arms and vehicles. But any military aid provided by a minor Warsaw Pact country may be regarded as part of the general Soviet policy.

Economic aid

Soviet economic aid consists mainly of tied development credits repayable in the produce of the recipient country. When the Soviet Union decides to help a project for a dam and power station, or an integrated steel plant, or a cotton mill, it agrees to supply all the materials and equipment which the recipient cannot produce, to plan and erect the factory and assemble the equipment and to train the labour force. The recipient provides the site, with suitable communications and services, and the unskilled labour. Payment may begin a year after the first consignment of Soviet equipment arrives, or some years after the whole project has been completed, and is made with interest at not more than 3%, by exports of the recipient's produce to the Soviet Union in instalments over a period of ten years or more.

The arrangements for project aid of this sort are usually embodied in an inter-governmental economic and technical cooperation agreement. Such agreements in the 1950s frequently promised large round sums (for example, $100 million as the value of the goods and services to be provided on credit) but the propaganda advantages of this method were quickly lost because of delays in the detailed negotiation and execution of individual projects. Some later agreements allotted specific sums to named projects or to the beneficiary's development plan. A more recent example, the economic cooperation agreement with the federal military government of Nigeria concluded in November 1968, is simply a framework agreement; the Soviet Union will provide on credit expert services, materials, equipment and training for projects to be agreed on in detail later.

The general form of Soviet project aid, which makes up four-fifths of all Soviet economic aid, has varied little since 1955. The main change is that, where the recipient proves unable to finance the local costs of preparing the site or hiring local labour the Soviet Union now sometimes provides goods on ten-years' credit to be sold by the recipient government, the proceeds being used to meet these local expenses.

A minor form of Soviet economic aid, but one which has a greater importance in East European practice, is the provision of machinery and equipment on less generous credit—five to ten years, with interest at 4% or 5%. Soviet trading organisations grant credit in this range without the political authority of an intergovernmental agreement—a fact which suggests that project aid is politically motivated and subsidised.

Cultural, educational and scientific aid

Under cultural cooperation agreements the Soviet Union and the East Europeans assist in the establishment of press and broadcasting services, the organisation of trade unions and the provision and training of teaching staff for schools, hospitals, technical colleges and universities. They provide full degree courses (at Lumumba University in Moscow and elsewhere) for students in science, medicine and economics who first undergo a thorough training in the Russian language. They provide scientists on loan to work in the developing countries on problems affecting the local agriculture or industry. The Soviet Union has further undertaken to provide a few specially favoured countries (India, the UAR, Indonesia, Iraq, Ghana and Afghanistan) with small nuclear research reactors, and to train staff in their use for research and in isotope production for local use; and a more extensive collaboration with India in the industrial nuclear field is planned. In general, however, these projects have proved too ambitious for the recipients and some have been abandoned. None of them conflicted with the Soviet policy of limiting the spread of nuclear armaments.

THE SCALE OF AID AND THE RECIPIENTS

Tables 1, 2 and 3 show, as rounded estimates, the total amount of aid promised since 1954 by the Soviet Union and the East European Warsaw Pact countries, and its distribution by donors and recipients. The Soviet Union itself is responsible for three-quarters of the total of $8,000 million, and Czechoslovakia and Poland together for more than half of the rest. Among the recipients, India ($1,900 million) and the UAR ($1,500 million) stand out as absorbing between them two-fifths of the combined total; Indonesia, Afghanistan and Iran share another 20% and the remainder is divided among some 35 countries of which 15 are in tropical Africa and four in South America; the shares of these latter areas are only one-tenth and one-twentieth of the whole.

Generally speaking, the earliest recipients were countries whose non-alignment had an anti-Western bias; the exceptions (Turkey, Argentina, Ethiopia) have made little use even yet of the promised credit facilities. By the early 1960s, the list included the Sudan, Pakistan and four of the newly independent tropical African countries; it now numbers 38 countries including one member of NATO and all three Asian members of CENTO, several Middle Eastern countries including three major oil producers (Iran, Iraq, Algeria), ten Commonwealth countries (seven of them in Africa) and a few others, like Senegal and Mauretania whose political leanings are by no means favourable to communism. The spread of communist aid in Africa illustrates the readiness of most developing countries nowadays to accept development assistance from any quarter; but the small size of most of the commitments probably reflects caution on both sides.

Among the present recipients the most striking current development is the effort being put into a project for a steelworks in Iran, to be paid for in natural gas, and the progress towards making use of a large credit promised to Turkey in 1965. But concurrently with detailed planning under existing agreements the search for new clients continues.

Promise and performance

It can be deduced from Soviet statements that only about $3,000 millions' worth of goods and services had actually been delivered by the end of 1967 out of the $8,000 millions' worth promised since 1954; the undelivered arrears amount to some $3,600 million for the Soviet Union and $1,500 million for Eastern Europe. Part of this backlog is due to large block allocations made to development plans still in progress, and part to aid programmes now in suspense, as in Indonesia and Ghana; but most of it represents a failure to agree on the details of suitable projects or to make reasonable progress with their implementation. The fault lies partly with the donors' concern to meet the recipients' wishes, however unrealistic, and partly with the recipients' overambitious planning and ineffectual execution.

It was, therefore, not surprising that 1967 and 1968 should have seen a sharp drop in the amount of new commitments undertaken from the high levels of the two preceding years. There are, however, some signs that the rate of deliveries may also have slackened somewhat; this is not due to any economic inability of the Soviet Union or the East Europeans to provide the aid they have promised, but rather to the difficulties of effective cooperation between donors and recipients.

Aid and trade

According to Soviet statistics, Soviet exports to the third world increased ninefold, from $140 million to $1,330 million between 1955 and 1967, and imports from it quadrupled from $195 million to $770 million. From statistical discrepancies it can be inferred that half of the exports in 1967 were deliveries of aid, probably civil and military in roughly equal proportions; the amount of aid repayment included in the 1967 imports was probably at least $150 million, and the net outflow of aid was something like $500 million in that year. During the aid period Soviet exports to the third world on trade account (excluding aid), have increased fivefold and imports from it (excluding aid repayments) trebled. The aid programme undoubtedly played a part in bringing about this increase in non-aided trade; but the limited capacity of the developing countries to increase their exports to the Soviet Union reflects the failure of aid to stimulate their economic growth as quickly as had been hoped. On the other hand, two of the Soviet Union's important trading partners (Argentina for wheat in bad years, and Malaysia for rubber every year) have not yet been brought into the ambit of Soviet aid, and purchases from them have to be paid for in convertible currency.

A note on Cuba

The only communist country geographically separated from the Soviet Union and China did not become communist due to Soviet economic inducements but to local insurrection; but since 1960 it has been sustained by Soviet economic as well as diplomatic and military aid. Promises of development aid starting in that year have now reached a total of over $600 million, of which three-quarters have come from the Soviet Union and deliveries so far amount to about one-half of this (a larger proportion than is usual among non-communist recipients). In addition, however, the severance of trade ties with most of the American continent has so seriously affected the Cuban economy that the Soviet Union has felt obliged since 1962 to accept responsibility for keeping Castro afloat by providing imports on credit to an annual value which now exceeds $300 million. Thus the actual delivery rate of Soviet economic aid to Cuba is not far short of the total rate of Soviet deliveries to all non-communist recipients in the underdeveloped parts of the world. This is more than the Kremlin bargained for in 1960. There have been repeated disappointments at Cuba's failure (despite their help) to fulfil its plans for sugar production and exports; but the Soviet Union cannot afford, politically, to see an economic collapse in Cuba. The thought that any major non-communist clients might one day ask for a similar measure of support must be somewhat disquieting.

CONCLUSION

Soviet and East European economic aid, measured by current gross annual delivery rates, amounts to rather less than UK governmental aid, about a fifth of US aid and about six times that of communist China.

This aid has given the Soviet Union and its allies a position of real importance in the economic life of a few recipients, and a degree of acceptance in some 30 others which seemed improbable 15 years ago. They have acquired, on balance, a considerable measure of prestige, and have made contacts with élite groups in these countries (service officers, administrators, students) which could give them powerful indirect influence over the general policies of the recipient countries. Their aid has strengthened the anti-capitalist and anti-imperialist tendencies of many of the emerging countries. The rapid increase in trade, stimulated largely by their aid policy, has correspondingly diminished the preponderance of Western trade ties.

On the debit side, they have had to accept defaults and reschedulings from a few countries, and increasing demands from others. Like other donors, they have had disappointments over the slow response of the developing economies to the stimulus of aid. Recipients take the claim that Soviet aid is 'without strings' so seriously that they publicly castigate any aspect of communist policy that meets with their disapproval; it seems likely that if there were strings, and if they had in fact been pulled there would have been louder complaints than have in fact been heard. Such influence as its aid policy may have given the Soviet Union is used, if at all, with great discretion.

The Soviet Union and the East Europeans (whatever the differences among themselves) are undoubtedly keeping up their aid effort, both by trying to make existing programmes more effective and by looking for new customers. It is hard to judge whether this is because they are, broadly speaking, satisfied with the results they are already achieving or because of some ulterior objective which is not yet in sight. On balance, they seem to be content at present with displaying the merits of their system as widely as possible and gaining goodwill rather than seeking to promote revolution; they may still think that their aid will help the prospects of creating communist governments in a few important developing countries in the longer term.

TABLES

SOVIET AND EAST EUROPEAN AID
DONORS, COMMITMENTS AND RECIPIENTS, 1954–67

Note on the tables

The figures given in these tables are estimates based on published statements, which are often imprecise and ambiguous, of the amount of economic aid (mainly development project credits) promised by the Soviet Union and the East European Warsaw Pact countries to non-communist developing countries. (Cuba is treated separately in the text.)

The tables give the amounts promised to each recipient, and the minor donor countries (Bulgaria, Czechoslovakia, East Germany, Hungary, Poland and Rumania) are identified by initials.

All money figures are equivalents in millions of US $.

TABLE 1

ASIA
(*$ US millions*)
Cumulative commitment

Recipient		Date of first agreement	Soviet Union	Eastern Europe donors	Eastern Europe amount	Total
Afghanistan	.	1954	575	C, P	10	585
Burma	. .	1956	10	G, P	25	35
Cambodia	.	1957	25	C	5	30
Ceylon	.	1958	30	G, P	50	80
India	. .	1955	1,585	B, C, H, P, R	330	1,915
Indonesia	.	1956	370	B, C, G, H, P, R	275	645
Laos .	. .	1962	10		—	10
Nepal	.	1959	20		—	20
Pakistan	.	1961	180	C, P	55	235
Area total	.		2,805		750	3,555

TABLE 2

MIDDLE EAST AND NORTH AFRICA
(*$ US millions*)
Cumulative commitment

Recipient		Date of first agreement	Soviet Union	Eastern Europe donors	Eastern Europe amount	Total
Iran .	. .	1963	350	B, C, H, P, R	155	505
Iraq .	. .	1959	190	B	10	200
Syria	. .	1957	230	B, C, G, H, P	145	375
Turkey	. .	1957	230		—	230
UAR (Egypt)	.	1956	1,000	B, C, G, H, P, R	505	1,505
Yemen (Arab Republic)	.	1956	85	C, G, H	15	100
Algeria	. .	1963	230	B, C	70	300
Morocco	. .	1962	40	P	35	75
Sudan	.	1961	20	B, C	50	70
Tunisia	. .	1960	35	B, C, P	20	55
Area total	.		2,410		1,005	3,415

TABLE 3
TROPICAL AFRICA
($ US millions)
Cumulative commitment

Recipient	Date of first agreement	Soviet Union		Eastern Europe donors amount	Total
Cameroun .	1963	10		—	10
Congo (Brazzaville)	1964	10		—	10
Ethiopia . .	1959	100	B, C	15	115
Ghana . .	1960	95	B, C, G, H, P	95	190
Guinea . .	1959	100	B, C, G, H, P	30	130
Kenya . .	1964	50		—	50
Mali . .	1961	70	B, C, P	20	90
Mauretania .	1967	5		—	5
Nigeria . .	1965		C	15	15
Senegal . .	1964	10		—	10
Sierra Leone .	1965	60		—	60
Somali Republic	1961	70	C	5	75
Tanzania .	1964	20	G	5	25
Uganda .	1964	15		—	15
Zambia . .	1967	5		—	5
Area total .		620		185	850

FURTHER READING

Wiles, P. J. D. *Communist International Economics*, Blackwell, Oxford, 1968.
Goldman, M. I. *Soviet Foreign Aid*, Praeger, New York and London, 1967.

A. TODD. Studied and concerned with international economic problems, notably those of the developing countries of the Third World.

MARKETING AND THE CONSUMER IN A COMMUNIST SOCIETY

PHILIP HANSON

PHILIP HANSON

INTRODUCTION

ACCORDING to the conventional Western view the production and marketing of consumer goods in Eastern Europe is done, on the whole, rather badly. The conventional Western view is right. Many East Europeans share it. There is, after all, every reason to be more impressed by Soviet rockets than by Soviet department stores. For all the Soviet Union's success in industrialisation one finds, in the late 1960s, a higher quality and greater variety of consumer goods in the shops of Athens, for example, than in those of Moscow, and this is not merely in shops catering for a wealthy minority. Yet the Greek economy as a whole is by most tests less developed than the Soviet economy. In other words, Soviet economic development has been, by Western standards, uneven. This is broadly true of all the communist countries of Eastern Europe.

However, the relative backwardness of the consumer sector in these countries is not necessarily a permanent feature. Many of the changes under way in the late 1960s are towards a more consumer-oriented system, and in time may well make our conventional view obsolete. This chapter will therefore follow the venerable Soviet practice of combining a critical review of the recent past with a certain optimism about the future.

CONSUMPTION LEVELS IN THE 1960s

How do East European living standards compare with those of Western countries? So far as private consumption is concerned, it is possible to make some broad comparisons of consumption levels. We can take these as a starting point, although global comparative figures of the annual volume of per capita private consumption of goods and services in different countries can indicate only rough orders of magnitude, and should not be taken too seriously.

One need do no arithmetic to see that consumption levels in Eastern Europe are generally below those of the UK and the EEC. It is equally obvious that there are wide differences between individual East European countries. To make specific comparisons for each country would require a great deal of research which has not yet been done. From various partial indicators one might hazard the guess that the most developed East European countries—Czechoslovakia and East Germany—have average levels roughly comparable to that of Italy, and that the least developed—Albania and Jugoslavia—have average levels probably below that of Greece. For the in-between countries we may cite, for example, an international comparison for 1960 which put Hungary on the same level as Greece and below the Soviet Union, and assigned to the Soviet Union a figure close to that for Spain and below that for Japan. For a more recent year, 1965, I have estimated real per capita personal consumption in the Soviet Union at about a half of the UK.

CONSUMPTION PATTERNS

Global comparative figures by themselves give little idea of what consumers in various East European countries actually get for their money. The best way to approach this is to review the major types of expenditure, generalising as much as we can for Eastern Europe as a whole but also picking out some major differences between countries.

To begin with, households in these countries are for the most part poorly, but extremely cheaply, housed. Contrary to what is generally supposed in the West, this is not simply the result of state ownership and control of the housing stock. It is true that private landlordism is illegal or restricted, though there is a good deal of subletting of public housing. But typically these countries have a large percentage of owner-occupied housing units. In the Soviet Union at the end of 1966 over a third of the urban housing stock in terms of floorspace, and possibly more in terms of dwelling units, was privately owned. For the rural population, which was then 45% of the total, private home ownership is probably predominant ('homes' in this case include tents in Central Asia and a large proportion of log cabins). Overall, the British owner-occupation percentage of around 50 is probably equalled in the heartland of socialism. The picture is broadly similar elsewhere in Eastern Europe. For example, over half the new dwelling units put up in Hungary in 1960–65 and in Rumania in 1965 and 1966 were private projects. In some affluent and thoroughly private-enterprise economies the percentage of owner-occupation is much lower—in Canada in 1967, for example, only about 20. Thus one reason why housing space is both meagre and cheap is that private people build very modest homes of their own and labour costs are in any case relatively low.

However, state control is still very important here. Control over the supply and price of building materials to private persons sets limits to private construction, and in the cities state and cooperative housing projects typically account for most new residential construction. Rents in state and cooperative housing are held down, typically with some element of state subsidy. And typically, again, there is an acute housing shortage and a great deal of overcrowding. The official Soviet figures for late 1966 show urban floorspace (including corridors, cupboards and everything remotely resembling a domestic floor) of 10 sq. metres per person. This is an improvement on the estimated 1913 level of 6·3, but only around half of what is normal in Western Europe. Most of the new state housing that is going up in the Soviet Union is in the form of self-contained two-room flats of 40 to 45 sq. metres floorspace, taking a family of four or so and therefore doing little to raise the average amount of floorspace from 1966 on. In general, Eastern Europe, in the process of rapid industrialisation, has faced a particularly rapid growth of urban population, and has not put enough resources into urban residential building to yield per capita housing space even approaching Western levels. This is despite a substantial housing drive in most of Eastern Europe since the mid-1950s. The housing drive has been fairly impressive in terms of dwelling units, but less so in terms of total space.

On the other hand, the cost of housing is much less of a burden in these countries. Housing and utilities (water, gas, electricity) were of the order of 5% of personal expenditure in the Soviet Union in 1965, whereas the UK *Family Expenditure Survey for 1960–2* showed an average of over 15%, with many families spending much more than this percentage. The provision of utilities is, however, generally worse in Eastern than in Western Europe. Much peasant housing in the Soviet Union is little different in character (though average size has probably risen) from pre-revolutionary days. A great deal of rural electrification has still to be carried out.

Food occupies a relatively large share of consumers' expenditures in Eastern Europe. Whereas food accounted for 30% of average UK household expenditure according to the *Family Expenditure Survey for 1960–62*, Hungarian official statistics for 1965 show a percentage of 36, for example, and I have estimated the comparable figure for the Soviet urban population in 1965 at 43%. The reason for this difference is not only that real incomes are generally lower than in Western Europe. It is also, in part, a reflection of the constrained low share of housing expenditure. In the Soviet Union, though not throughout Eastern Europe, it is also due in some measure to the fact that food prices are higher relative to the prices of manufactured goods than they are in Western Europe.

The food supply is generally adequate in terms of calories. Calorie intake per head of population per day is usually estimated at around, or somewhat above, West European levels. The quality of the diet, however, is relatively poor, with a heavy reliance on carbo-hydrates—bread, potatoes and the like. Whereas protein—meat, fish and animal products—generally accounted for about 42% of the calories in the UK food supply of the mid-1960s, some comparable estimates for Eastern Europe are Rumania (1963) 16%, Jugoslavia (1964) 18%, Poland (1960–62) 30% and Hungary (1965) 32%. For comparison, the Greek figure in 1963 was 23%.

East European countries vary considerably in their levels of consumption of manufactures. In both durables and non-durables they generally lag somewhat behind Western Europe, but there are wide differences between individual countries and a good deal of overlap with Western countries. Official data for East and West Germany in 1965, for example, show an identical rate of television ownership—201 sets per 1,000 population—though the figures may not be precisely comparable in coverage. The UK figure, for comparison, was 247, and that for France 131. The (approximately) equivalent figures for other East European countries were: Czechoslovakia 149, Hungary 82, the Soviet Union 68, Poland 66, Jugoslavia 32, Rumania 26, Bulgaria 21. For Albania, the calculated figure comes out at one half of a television set per thousand people. There are also very wide variations in the rate of ownership of other relatively 'new' durables, such as refrigerators and washing machines. Private car ownership, on the other hand, is generally much below West European levels. Clothing, though still well below West European standards in both quantity and quality, in the Soviet Union at least, has improved vastly in the last decade, and the bleak grey uniformity image, which Western visitors to Eastern Europe in the late 1950s unfailingly reported, is on the way out.

Expenditure on services is generally relatively small in Eastern Europe, partly because real incomes are relatively low but also because many services, such as laundries, repair services and so on, have been generally very much neglected, at least until about 1965, and there has tended to be an extremely meagre capacity to supply them.

In general, the patterns of consumption in Eastern Europe differ from those in Western Europe. They are in part what one would expect given the general income levels of these countries, but in part they are also influenced by the special circumstances of communist society. Thus an ordinary Soviet consumer may have quite 'Western' standards in terms of items such as watches, cameras, radios and even, to a lesser extent, the newer durables. However, he is extremely unlikely to have much housing space, or a car, or a good and interesting diet, and, particularly if he lives in a rural area, he may well lack some basic Western amenities, such as electricity, main drainage or piped water. He has certain advantages over his British counterpart: books, films, intra-city and inter-city public transport are mostly cheap and fairly plentiful. On the other hand, he may wish to buy certain things which cannot be legally obtained at any price, or at least not with any ease: certain books, films, records, foreign travel, and most Western-produced consumer goods.

The Growth of Consumption and the Question of Price Stability

East European consumers have experienced a generally rapid rise in consumption levels since the early 1950s. This has not been uniform for all the countries in question, nor for all major groups in each country's population; there was a distinct slow-down in the growth of consumption levels in the first half of the 1960s compared to the 1950s. For some major groups there have even been reversals, as for example for the Soviet collective-farm peasants from 1958 up to about 1964, or for most Jugoslavs after the belt-tightening reforms of 1965. But, overall, the growth of consumption levels has been impressive. The official figures for the various countries show average annual growth rates of material consumption (excluding most expenditure on services) per head of population, in the 1950s, of over 7% for Bulgaria, around 7% for East Germany and around 6% for Poland. Even allowing for some possible exaggeration in these figures, they are very respectable. The corresponding UK figure would be around 2%. The growth of consumption levels in Eastern Europe in the first half of the 1960s was less impressive, but there are signs of a partial recovery in the second half of the decade.

Another part of the East European consumer's experience is relative price stability. Prices in state and cooperative retail trade are generally set, or approved, or at least are subject to limits set at fairly high levels in the planning hierarchy. In most of the post-war period retail price increases have been avoided as far as possible. The official retail price indexes, except for Jugoslavia, show little overall change between 1958 and 1965, for instance, while the UK index shows a 21% increase. This does not necessarily mean that there was little or no change in the cost of living; these countries, typically, have peasant markets where food is sold at largely uncontrolled prices, and when there is inflationary pressure prices on the peasant markets rise. In the Soviet Union between 1958 and 1964 the general level of collective-farm market prices rose by at least 20%. However, these markets tend not to have a large share in total retail turnover, and price control has held the cost of living approximately stable in Eastern Europe, apart from Jugoslavia, from the mid-1950s to the mid-1960s. This price control has its disadvantages, as we shall see, but only an economist could be entirely blind to its charms.

Major Influences on the Supply of Consumer Goods

The supply of consumer goods and services has traditionally been a low priority in communist economies. This shows up in a variety of ways. To begin with, the share of resources allocated each year to producing goods and services for private consumption is less than is usual in the West. If this share is measured in the most sensible way—by the percentage of gross national product in current prices net of indirect taxes and subsidies—the typical Soviet post-war figure, for example, is of the order of 50%, while the corresponding shares in advanced Western countries range between 60% and 70%.

Second, the consumer sector has been treated in the past as a poor relation in comparison with heavy industry. By 'consumer sector' I mean those major branches of production which are geared, directly or indirectly, mainly to private consumption demand. They are agriculture, food-processing, the textile and clothing industries, and retail and wholesale distribution. In Eastern Europe this sector has probably tended on the whole to get lower-quality management, labour, equipment and materials than it would have done in a market economy. It has probably tended also to get a smaller share of investment and research and development funds than it would have in a market economy, even in a market economy saving and investing at an East European rate. Everybody has been accustomed to the idea that this sector goes to the back of every queue—for materials, for construction work or merely for central planners' attention. Moreover, this is a sector where small-scale operation, managerial autonomy and price flexibility are generally more desirable than in the rest of the economy, but it has been subjected to the same highly centralised planning system. (The main exceptions to this would be the Jugoslav system generally, Polish agriculture since the 1956 decollectivisation, the private plots and peasant markets throughout Eastern Europe and a small fringe of other more or less market-oriented activities.) This general bias against the consumer sector is being modified in the post-1965 reforms but vested interests, pecking orders and habits of mind cannot be reformed overnight.

Since imports of consumer goods from outside Eastern Europe have been kept to a relatively low level, the East European consumer is heavily dependent on his consumer sector. It is true that as his real income rises he spends an increasing proportion of his income on consumer goods produced in high-priority branches outside the consumer sector—watches, cameras, the larger durables and so on. But throughout Eastern Europe income levels are in a range where the products of the consumer sector, as defined here, are a very large part of private consumption. Hence the special urgency of economic reforms in this sector. And hence, since agriculture is a crucial supplier to the rest of the consumer sector, the critical importance of agriculture to consumption levels so long as the import of agricultural products from outside the bloc is not drastically increased.

The Planning of Consumption

Planning methods differ increasingly within Eastern Europe.[1] Here we will simply consider Soviet consumption planning, treating it as representative of Eastern Europe as a whole. It should, however, be borne in mind that

---

[1] See the chapters on the 'The Planned Economy' and 'Recent Reforms in the Planning System', p. 279 and p.291.

there are substantial national differences, with Jugoslavia making the most use of 'automatic' market mechanisms in place of detailed planning, and the recent Czechoslovak and Hungarian reforms, in particular, tending some way towards Jugoslav methods.

The problem, in practice, is to strike a balance of supply and demand, both for consumer goods supply and consumer demand in total, and for individual products and different regional and local markets.

The problem of overall balance should be relatively easy, one might suppose, in a system where the state is the predominant employer and central planners can determine the total wage bill, total consumer goods production, prices and taxes for each year all in one process. The planners have only to adjust these variables so that personal disposable money income, less a small margin for expected personal savings, equals total consumer goods supply at retail prices. And indeed East European countries have, by and large, avoided situations of inadequate consumer demand relative to the capacity to supply consumer goods. Difficulties in the opposite—inflationary —direction have been more of a problem, though for the most part this inflationary pressure is repressed by price control. There are several reasons for this. Agricultural production has tended to fall short of plan targets, with a resulting shortfall in consumer goods supply. Fluctuations in prices on the peasant markets affect the disposable money incomes of the peasantry in an unplanned way, generally reinforcing the first influence. The total wage bill in state employment may not move closely in line with the annual plan. (In the longer-run plans the errors are usually quite large, but the planners can adjust for this as they go along; thus inflationary pressure during the Soviet 1959-65 plan was contained to some extent by postponing the planned elimination of income tax and by increasing some official retail prices, notably of meat and dairy products in 1962.)

In detail, consumption planning has been often and substantially wrong. Some errors in planning lead to adaptive behaviour by consumers such that there may be no apparent discrepancy between plan and outcome. Thus there has been in the Soviet Union a chronic tendency to concentrate supplies of goods in urban shops and starve the countryside of many items. In the RSFSR in 1967 three times as much clothing and two-and-a-half times as many television sets *per head of population* were allocated to urban as to rural retail outlets. The result is an excessive amount of travel by country people to shop in towns. In other cases planned and actual balances simply do not coincide; those for the different Soviet republics, for example, and those for individual products. For instance, total retail sales of sugar in the Soviet Union in 1966 diverged by 24% from the annual plan target. Apparently this was because the plan had been based solely on supply potential, with no consideration of demand.

In general, plans for individual products, whether annual or longer-run, seem in practice, at least in the Soviet Union, still to be based primarily on extrapolations of recent growth in production, with little or no reference to expected demand. Projections of the pattern of demand are made in the Soviet Union on the basis of family budget surveys. They have not, however, been used in formulating annual plans up to and including that for 1967 or in the 1966–70 plan; and with good reason, since the samples used in the surveys are at present highly unrepresentative. Apparently an analysis of past trade turnover data would have been a good basis for projections, but it appears that this was only just beginning to be used for planning in 1967. 'Scientific' or 'rational' norms of consumption based on nutritional standards and such other-worldly concepts as 'the rational wardrobe' seem to have played some part in very long-run planning, but it is doubtful whether such planning has had any operational significance. Elsewhere in Eastern Europe, especially in Hungary, more use seems to be made of fairly sophisticated demand projections in planning.

As the supply of consumer goods has risen to levels at which consumers could no longer be relied upon to scramble for whatever was available, regardless of quality and assortment, the tightly centralised system of the 1950s tended to generate simultaneously surplus stocks and queues for different goods. In other words, it tended to get the assortment of consumer goods wrong, given the existing set of prices. In response, there has been a tendency to move towards a system in which supplies of consumer goods have been made more and more responsive to the evolving pattern of demand. The responsiveness has been provided either by basing annual and quarterly production plans on trade orders or simply by deviating from plans during the course of the year or by abandoning 'planning from above' in consumer goods production and leaving enterprise managers to arrange their own plans entirely on the basis of trade orders.

Central control over wholesale and retail prices has, however, been largely retained. Thus in the Soviet Union 'unsalable' items may be offered at cut prices, but in general only on the initiative of the local Soviet executive committee, not on that of the individual shop or trade organisation. However, even in the Soviet Union arrangements were beginning to be made in 1968 for some prices, for instance of rural craft items, to be set by agreements between shops and suppliers. Elsewhere in Eastern Europe there is in many cases greater decentralisation of consumer goods pricing, though generally subject to centrally imposed price ceilings.

The process of adjusting to 'equilibrium' supply-and-demand prices, while it helps to create balance in the markets for different goods, also has its costs. The political leadership can directly control the cost of living to a considerable extent, and naturally does not wish to be responsible for letting it rise. After all, the 1962 increases in official retail prices for meat and dairy products in the Soviet Union led to several outbreaks of riots.

There is something to be said for a system in which a little bit of rioting can keep down the cost of living. On the other hand, the reluctance to raise retail prices retards the introduction of more effective incentive systems in production. Thus profit incentive reforms have been delayed in sections of the Soviet food-processing industry because there is little or no profit for producers at existing prices. The planners must await long-run reduction of costs in agriculture before profit incentives can be most generally and effectively used with the existing retail prices.

MARKETING AND THE ECONOMIC REFORMS

The mechanisms by which supply is being made more responsive to consumer demand are varied and complex. The normal situation in Eastern Europe is that retailing and wholesaling are done by centrally controlled state and cooperative networks. Private small-scale retailing is important in Jugoslavia, but in most of the other countries is restricted to the peasant markets and some street vending, generally accounting for a small share of total retail turnover (about 3% in the Soviet Union in 1966).

The official retail network is sparse (2·8 outlets per thousand population in the Soviet Union in 1965, 2·2 in Rumania, 3·4 in Bulgaria, 4·8 in Czechoslovakia, compared to 9·3 in the UK in 1961). Although shops are relatively few, they are not correspondingly larger in terms of staff numbers than in Western Europe. There is, therefore, a substantial 'saving' in terms of the share of the labour force engaged in distribution as against production. This share is much below West European levels. State and cooperative retail and wholesale outlets, including catering, employed about 4% of the Soviet labour force in 1965 compared to something like 15% in the UK. This is one reason for the relatively low share of state and cooperative distributive gross margins in total retail sales (including catering), which was only 9% in the Soviet Union in 1965.

Since the early 1960s it has been increasingly accepted by policy-makers that the distributive network, both retail and wholesale, should be expanded, and service generally improved. Steps in this direction have been taken, and distributive costs have tended to rise faster than turnover as a result. There has been a squeeze on Soviet distributive profits, especially in the food trades and catering, such that it became hard to introduce the new profit incentives in retail trade. Retail gross margins were therefore revised upwards in mid-1967. Improvements in distributive techniques should help, but the introduction of self-service has long been hindered by a shortage of packaging.

The production of consumer goods is now supposed to be based on demand, rather than vice versa. In the Soviet case, distributors may place orders via 'direct links' to producers or via the wholesale bases, with considerable use of wholesale fairs at which preliminary agreements are made. These orders should provide the basis for production plans, both annual and quarterly, and within the limits set by producer-distributor contracts there can be subsequent amendments of detail so that distributors very often have a good deal of flexibility and can adjust supplies in response to shifts in the pattern of sales. This, however, refers mostly to fairly minor shifts between varieties of a given kind of good. In terms of broad categories of goods and sometimes even on points of detail, adjustment may be difficult or impossible because it may lead to a conflict with centrally planned allocations of goods and materials.

The extent to which consumer demand can induce major shifts in the pattern of supply, involving shifts in investment allocation, is uncertain. It may well be that political pressure is more influential here than economic processes. Thus, it is hard to explain the Soviet decision to embark on substantial production of private cars by 1970 in terms of demand pressures. Either the long waiting-list for cars could have been tolerated, or the prices of cars could have been lifted to astronomic heights. If it seemed better to give in and make more cars, the reasons would be primarily political, not economic.

The reforms in the Soviet Union have tended to put considerable weight on trade orders as a means of adapting supply to consumer demand. This has been a natural reaction against the old situation where supplies, dictated by rather arbitrary production plans, were unloaded willy-nilly on the distributive network. However, in the long run it is likely that more emphasis will be put on the moulding of demand by producers, as in the West. An all-union Demand Research Institute has been set up, and there is beginning to be a development of market research by specific industries, as in the new RSFSR Textile Industry Market Research Centre at Ivanovo. US motivation research and marketing techniques generally have been closely studied. The Soviet Union is just reaching that sophisticated stage of economic development where consumers will have to be researched and prodded into buying new things because otherwise they might not bother. If this is progress, East Germany, Czechoslovakia and Hungary are further ahead.

At the same time the unevenness of East European development shows up in the continued reliance on production from the small household plot. In the early 1960s about 100 million Soviet citizens lived in households—mostly rural but also in small towns and outer suburbs—with their own 'private plots'. In 1965 these yielded two-thirds of the total supply of eggs and two-fifths of total meat supply. In Hungary in the same year it was officially estimated that almost one-third of the total food supply in 1959 prices was from 'own production'. A minor part of this subsidiary-plot production (in Czechoslovakia in 1963, for example, an estimated 18%) is channelled to other households through the peasant markets. Post-Khrushchev policy in the Soviet Union has reversed previous trends by encouraging and stimu-lating private-plot production and the peasant markets.

Plans for 1965–70 in Eastern Europe show in general a shift to greater consumer orientation. The meeting of consumer demands is advanced more often and more prominently as a rationale for planning decisions. Not only are relatively high growth rates planned for consumption, but there seems to be a serious attempt to achieve them. Despite a modest 1967 harvest, Soviet official retail turnover in real terms in 1967 was about 9% up on 1966, although the planned increase was only about 7%; the gain in per capita real income was above plan. A rapid expansion of service activities is under way. The 1968 annual plan envisages a more rapid growth of industrial production of consumer goods than of producer goods, for the first time since the brief Malenkov era, and this was in fact achieved.

In the long run the maintenance of substantial growth in consumption levels and the attainment of levels more in line with the general level of industrialisation in Eastern Europe seems to depend on prior achievements in three fields. First, 'turning the corner' in agriculture; second, pushing the reforms of prices, incentives and enterprise autonomy to the point where short-run flexibility in producing and distributing consumer goods is com-parable to that of Western economies; third, finding sufficient stimuli to nnovation and major shifts in production patterns. A greater propensity to import consumer goods from the West would help, but does not seem crucial. Given these preconditions there may be scope for a fairly prolonged, rapid rise in consumption levels because of the technical and organisational back-log to be made up in the consumer sector.

A NOTE ON SOURCES

The international comparisons of consumption levels for 1960 were cited from Beckerman, Wilfred, and Bacon, Roger, 'International Comparisons of Income Levels', *Economic Journal*, September, 1966. Almost all the numerical data used are from official annual statistical handbooks for the countries concerned. Where my own estimates are referred to, these are given in detail in the book on the Soviet consumer listed below. Other data used here are from the Soviet press, and particularly from the weekly *Ekonomicheskaya gazeta*.

FURTHER READING

Goldman, Marshall I. *Soviet Marketing*, Free Press of Glencoe, New York; Macmillan, London, 1963.
Hanson, Philip. *The Consumer in the Soviet Economy*, Macmillan, London, 1968.

Hubbard, L. E. *Soviet Trade and Distribution*, Macmillan, New York and London, 1938.
Miller, Margaret. *The Rise of the Russian Consumer*, Institute of Economic Affairs, London; Transatlantic, New York, 1965.

PHILIP HANSON. Lecturer at the Centre for Russian and East European Studies, University of Birmingham. Has been Economic Assistant in the U.K. Treasury, Lecturer in Economics at the University of Exeter, and in 1967–8 Visiting Lecturer in Soviet Economics at the University of Michigan.

W

THE SOVIET TRADE UNIONS

MERVYN MATTHEWS

STRUCTURE AND ORGANISATION

THE Soviet trade unions differ fundamentally from those in the West both in their structure and functions. Formally, they are organised in a centralised manner, (somewhat like the Communist Party) and are very large: in 1968 there were only 21 of them—as compared with some 600 in the UK—though their membership embraced over 86 million workers and employees, or 96% of the total in all branches of the economy. They traditionally do not cover the country's 20 million peasants (or collective farmers as they are sometimes called). The policies of the Soviet trade unions are always in strict accordance with the state economic plan and the unions do not afford their members the right to strike. Workers join rather to gain better access to social insurance schemes and fringe benefits, or because failure to do so is now regarded as slightly unusual.

THE SOVIET TRADE UNIONS

Union	Membership (January 1967)
Aviation	—
Geological exploration	—
State trade and consumer cooperatives	5,031,482
State administrative offices	2,335,000
Rail transport	3,917,800
Local industry and communal services	4,398,000
Culture	1,560,000
Forestry, paper mills and timber	2,946,500
Machine building	—
Medicine	4,857,550
Metallurgy	—
Oil and chemicals	—
Food	3,187,000
Education and academic institutions	6,150,200
Merchant navy and river fleet	—
Communications, motor transport and highways	—
Agriculture (state farms only) and farm deliveries	13,864,000
Building and building materials	5,600,000
Textiles and light clothing industry	3,510,000
Coal	—
Electric power stations and electrical equipment	2,341,866

Source: *Spravochnaya Kniga o Profsoyuzakh*, Moscow, 1968. Listed in Russian alphabetical order. Figures for eight unions were not given.

Each union, as the table shows, caters for a whole branch of the economy (rather than for a trade or profession), so all the people employed in that branch, from the managers down to the doormen, are in the same union. According to the all-union statutes, the latest version of which was approved at the Thirteenth All-Union Trade Union Congress in November 1963, the supreme trade union organ is the Congress of Trade Unions of the USSR, which is convened every four years. (The last meeting, the Fourteenth, was held from the 27 February to the 4 March 1968, and attended by some 4,500 delegates.) This body elects the All-Union Central Council of Trade Unions (AUCCTU) which holds six-monthly plenums, and the Central Auditing Commission. This Council in turn elects a Praesidium which makes policy decisions for the whole movement between the plenums and is for this reason invariably headed by an important party figure. Current organisational and executive work is handled by a secretariat containing departments for wages, labour protection, social insurance, organisational problems, housing and living conditions, physical culture and sport, international relations, finance, and administration respectively. This pattern of organisation is retained, though in a simplified form, within each trade union and in each locality, from the union republics down. Coordination of the activities of all these bodies might appear difficult but in practice it presents few problems. The principle of 'democratic centralism' embodied in the union statutes ensures that decisions taken by the higher bodies are observed without question by the subordinate ones. The leaders of all unions are members of the AUCCTU, while in the localities officials are brought together in councils of trade unions, (Sovprofy) elected at inter-union conferences. The whole structure is therefore very close-knit.

The basic unit in the system is the primary trade union organisation, of which there were some 573,600 in 1967. The primary organisation consists of all the union members working in a given enterprise or institution. If there are less than 15 of them, they elect a trade union organiser to serve for one year: if there are more than 15, and this is usually the case, they set up a factory or works committee (FZMK), or, in non-industrial enterprises, a local committee (Mestkom), together with an auditing commission. The larger organisations may have a full-time official, but generally union work is done by unpaid part-timers, who fit in their extra duties between the demands of their job. All trade union members pay an entrance fee of 1% of their wage or salary when they join and thereafter $\frac{1}{2}$ to 1% of their earnings.

Relations with Party and State

The relationship of the trade unions to party and state is, to Western eyes, most unusual. The Bolsheviks took control of the unions, (which then embraced about a million-and-a-half workers), soon after they came to power, but the question of how these bodies were to function when the government was itself proletarian, and in conditions where the workers were said to own the means of production, was at that time largely unanswered. Was there a place for a trade union movement under the 'dictatorship of the proletariat'? Lenin proposed that the trade unions should continue to exist as a separate administrative entity, but be subordinate to the party and government. This plan was in fact adopted at the Tenth Congress of the Party in March 1921. However, the next ten years—the period of the New Economic Policy and the first Five Year Plan, saw a steady decline in the power of the unions to influence state policy towards labour or, indeed, affect the running of enterprises, which were all by now in the hands of state-appointed managers. In 1929 Stalin had Mikhail Tomsky, the chairman of the trade unions, removed because Tomsky objected to the bureaucratisation of his organisation and its decreasing capability to protect the workers' interests. By 1933, when the Commissariat of Labour was abolished and some of its functions, including managing social insurance and checking up on the observance of labour legislation, were transferred to the trade unions, the movement had in effect been reduced to the extremely subordinate status which Trotsky had envisaged for it before Lenin's formula was adopted. Union administration was badly hit by Stalin's great purges of 1936–8 and was unable, or unwilling to prevent a marked worsening in its members' working conditions, a fall in their real wages, and an increase of political pressure on them to produce more. The fact that the size and number of organisations grew quickly to match the expanding industrial labour force meant little in these circumstances. Indicative of the movement's decline was the fact that no all-union congress was held between 1932 and 1949, despite the four-year clause in the statutes. During World War II trade union concern with production, rather than with the workers' lot, was even more marked, while the post-war years up to Stalin's death in 1953 brought no real change.

Since then, however, there has been some improvement in their status. After the Twentieth Party Congress in 1956 union leaders began to place greater emphasis on the protective functions of the trade unions, and Khrushchev's decentralisation of industrial administration in March 1957 meant a definite, though limited increase in the responsibilities of the local union committees. New sets of statutes were introduced in 1954 and 1963 (though it must be admitted that they have changed little in form or spirit). The most recent amendments to these statutes, made at the Fourteenth Congress, are interesting insofar as they imply that members may now discuss union matters rather more freely at their meetings than was hitherto possible. Yet complete subordination of the unions to party policy is still *de rigueur*: Alexander Shelepin, chairman of the AUCCTU since July 1967 (and a full member of the Politburo of the party), reiterated at the Fourteenth Congress that the source of trade union strength lies precisely in party leadership, and that the aim and purpose of the movement is to serve the cause of Lenin and the Soviet state. The workers' own interests, by implication, take second place.

DAY-TO-DAY ACTIVITIES

The day-to-day functions of the unions are really determined by the structure of the movement and its dependence on the party and state. The statutes list the tasks of the key body, the AUCCTU, as follows. It:

> determines the immediate tasks of the trade union as a whole, and also deals with individual questions of trade union work: it participates in drawing up economic plans: it directs socialist competition and the movement for communist labour: it hears reports of committees and trade union councils, . . . state committees, ministries and departments, on questions of production, labour, cultural and communal services for workers and employees: it submits to the (state) legislative organs draft laws and decrees, takes part in preparing and examining government draft laws on wages, social insurance, labour protection, and cultural and communal services for the workers: it supervises the observance of government laws and decrees on these questions and issues instructions, rules and explanatory notices on the application of current labour legislation: it approves the trade union

budget and state social insurance budget: it determines the general structure of the trade unions and their staffs . . .

This list shows the AUCCTU as a body with apparently extensive administrative responsibilities in the field of labour policy, and far-reaching control over the unions subordinate to it. Yet its policy-making functions are, as far as we can tell, only formal. To judge from the past, it does not seem able to influence economic planning much to the benefit of its members. And although the wage bill both for the economy as a whole, and for individual branches of industry have, since 1957, been fixed jointly by the State Planning Commission, Gosplan, and the unions, there is no evidence that the AUCCTU (or, for that matter, individual union central committees) have ever acted as pressure groups to raise their allotments. Moreover, it is noteworthy that the 'protective' functions of the AUCCTU are listed *after* its duties to increase production.

The movement has, however, real authority in the field of social services. In 1967 its social service budget was 12,400 million roubles, or more than 10% of the entire state budget. It ran a network of rest homes and sanatoria to accommodate about seven million workers, and handled most of the country's 34 million disability and old-age pensions. The trade unions help in distributing housing, and organise many sporting and cultural activities: in 1967 they controlled 25 voluntary sports societies with over 17 million members, ran over 20,000 clubs and houses of culture, together with some 30,000 libraries. These are major benefits enjoyed by union members. In addition the trade unions organise schools and courses for their own officials. The AUCCTU has its own newspaper, *Trud*, and a publishing house which brings out trade union literature. The central committees of individual trade unions have a similar spread of activities, though they are rather more specific. The Soviet trade union leadership is anxious to develop links with unions in other countries, but the obviously political and official character of the movement has discouraged unionists in many non-communist states from associating with it. At present the Soviet unions play an active part in the communist-controlled World Federation of Trade Unions, and claim to maintain close and friendly contacts with unions in 110 countries.

At the factory, shop or office level, the FZMK or Mestkom has the right to conclude a collective agreement with the management, but this covers only the *application* of regulations on rates of pay, categories of skill, etc. which are already in force in that branch of the economy. Questions of working hours, working conditions or holidays, for instance, are covered in regular state laws, and therefore not open to discussion at this level. No reference is made in the trade union statutes, or indeed in the Soviet constitution, to the right to strike, and the state authorities have apparently taken the severest action against strikers in the few instances reported in the West (at Temirau, 1959 and Novocherkassk, 1962). Disputes between individual workers and the management are dealt with in the first instance by labour dispute commissions, consisting of equal numbers of representatives of the management and the trade union factory committee. The power of these commissions, is, however, fairly limited, questions of redundancy, wages and salaries, determination of length of service (important for calculating pensions), and the allocation of housing lying outside their competence. If the worker does not obtain satisfaction at a commission he may appeal firstly to the trade union factory committee itself, and then to a People's Court. Most of the work of the FZMK and Mestkoms seems in fact to be concerned with social services and cultural activities.

FURTHER READING

Brown, E. C. *Soviet Trade Unions and Labour Relations*, Harvard Univ. Press, Cambridge, Mass.,
    1966.
Deutscher, I. *The Soviet Trade Unions*, Royal Institute of International Affairs, London, 1950.
McAnley, Mary. *Labour Disputes in Soviet Russia, 1956–1966*, Oxford Univ. Press, London,
    1969.
Schwarz, S. M. *Labour in the Soviet Union*, Frederick A. Praeger, New York, 1951; Cresset
    Press, London, 1953.
The Trade Union Situation in the USSR, International Labour Organisation, Geneva, 1960.

MERVYN MATTHEWS. Lecturer in Russian Regional Studies at the University of Surrey.
    Studied at the Universities of Manchester and Oxford and did post-graduate work at the
    University of Moscow. At present writing a book on the sociology of the Soviet Union.

TRADE UNIONS IN EASTERN EUROPE

PETER MORAVEC

THE Leninist conception of trade unions was to regard them as one of the 'transmission belts' of the socialist system, whereby they were entrusted solely with the function of conveying party instructions to the workers. Because communist parties have tended to insist on the total monopoly of their power, they have, equally, regarded any attempt by trade unions to represent the closer interests of the workers with great hostility and as falling under the heading of undermining the leading role of the party. In a sense, this is paradoxical, for the communist party is supposed to be the vanguard of the proletariat and its rule the realisation of the aspirations of the 'toiling masses'. In practice, however, the interests of the party and of the unions have never coincided exactly and consequently trade unions have become totally subordinated to the rule of the party. In such circumstances, strikes were banned on the grounds that as the socialist state effectively represented the interests of the workers, a strike would be action by the workers against themselves. By the same token, the unions were systematically deprived of all power to protect the interests of their members against excessively high norms, low wages and poor conditions of work. The situation was especially unfavourable during the Stalinist period in Eastern Europe, when the Soviet concept was adopted wholesale. In 1953 in East Germany and 1956 in Poland and Hungary it became clear that the workers had lost all confidence in their official trade union representatives and in the latter two countries workers' councils or factory committees arose to replace them. However, after the parties had reconsolidated their rule, the powers of these factory committees were rapidly emasculated and the situation returned to the Leninist norm, though not, perhaps, with quite the same rigour that obtained during the Stalinist terror. The situation today varies with the extent of political liberalisation and pluralism in the countries concerned and is involved also with the degree of decentralisation in economic management.

BULGARIA

The traditional subordinate role of the trade unions has been steadfastly maintained by the Bulgarian Party. The constitution of the Bulgarian trade unions, adopted in 1966, made it clear that their role is seen to be 'to mobilise the workers for state and economic management'. This subordination has been confirmed subsequently, for instance, at the plenum of the Central Committee of the Bulgarian Party in July 1968, when it was stated that whilst the role of the unions must be enhanced, that of the party must be enhanced even more. The trend has, if anything, been intensified since the invasion of

Czechoslovakia, which appears to have brought about a freeze in most aspects of Bulgarian political life. At a plenary session of the Central Council of Bulgarian Trade Unions in February 1969, it was announced that the unions' functions should be restricted almost exclusively to carrying out party instructions. The unions were warned that they should not even regard conditions of work as falling within their sole competence. As against this, however, the unions have been permitted a somewhat more active supervisory role with regard to the powers of managers of enterprises and the unions will be required to be more active in promoting labour discipline.

East Germany

East Germany is another state which continues to adhere to a hard line in its labour policy and denies the unions much say in labour relations. East German unions are supposed, according to the Labour Law of April 1961, to 'mobilise the entire working class and the intelligentsia to fulfil economic plans' and to 'promote a high level of socialist work-morale and the rapid growth of labour productivity'. East German legislation has formally abrogated the right to strike in the 1968 constitution. The function of trade unions in the view of the party is to act as a transmission belt, the classical Leninist concept. In practice, this has meant the enforcement of a severe labour discipline, the justification of the retraining and redirection of labour —neither very popular—and, inevitably, ideological-political indoctrination.

Rumania

A similar Leninist concept of the role of the trade unions prevails in Rumania. The principal role of the unions, as outlined by the January 1969 plenum of the Central Council of the Trade Unions of Rumania, was 'the mobilisation of the working people . . . in order that they might fulfil and overfulfil their tasks under the plan'. However, that the situation in Rumania is not so totally quiescent as it is in Bulgaria or East Germany is suggested by one or two articles, calling for increased activity by, and a more democratic organisation for, the trade unions. There have also been criticisms of the poor quality of trade union officials, whose intellectual and educational qualifications are so low that they are unable to understand the needs of union members and are too easily overawed by enterprise managers. These are mere straws in the wind, however, and with the general slowing down of liberalisation in Rumania, as a result of the tense international situation in 1968 and 1969, the unions have been very largely denied any effective voice in the formulation of either economic policy or of labour policy. The educative function of the unions in Rumania not only covers ideology—as elsewhere in Eastern Europe—but, as befits a country pursuing nationalist policies, it also includes the propagating of patriotism.

Poland

In the aftermath of the upheavals of October 1956, the trade unions in Poland gained considerable powers, including the right to strike. In the years that have followed, however, these powers have been largely whittled away and the right to strike was formally abrogated in 1958—leaving the workers only with the right of holding token 'protest stoppages of work', lasting not more than a few hours. The Workers' Councils that sprang up in 1956 have also been emasculated. In December 1956 they were superseded by so-called workers' self-management conferences, consisting of the workers' council, the factory party organisation and the factory council appointed by the trade unions. In this way, because the party could always rely on the indirectly controlled factory council, the role of the workers' councils became rather irrelevant.

The role of the trade unions in Poland was most recently defined in 1968, when it was stated that their role in management—such as it was—was to ensure the best possible production. The trade unions were declared to have no business to adopt an independent role and make special demands for the workers, since that would be revisionism. The party would continue to be the only real protector of the workers by means of its ideological guidance offered to the trade unions.

In practice, the union leaderships have proved to be completely submissive to the party and have openly ignored protests from the rank and file against illegal (under the Labour Code) impositions by managements on various occasions. Specific complaints were directed at those managers who demanded work in excess of stipulated working hours and unpaid work in honour of some particular event. The union leaderships when faced with these protests referred to the paramountcy of 'Socialist competition' and the overriding need to fulfil production commitments. Hence it is quite clear that the unions in Poland behave as a classic Leninist transmission belt. Indeed the 1958 trade union statute lays down that the unions must be guided by the party in their activities.

CZECHOSLOVAKIA

Before the Dubček reforms the trade unions in Czechoslovakia were of the classic Leninist transmission belt model and, by the latter part of 1969, seemed to be reassuming this role. However, during the reform period, roughly from April 1968 to April 1969, the trade unions assumed a role that was radically different from the Leninist norm and not only defended workers' rights but participated actively in politics. This change was, in fact, provided for under the Action Programme of the Czechoslovak Party, which declared: ' . . . it is also necessary to reassess the present role of the trade unions . . . The central function of trade unions should be to defend, with increasing emphasis, the employment and interests of the working people, to act as an important partner in solving problems of economic management...' Strikes were accepted as a legitimate weapon, though only to be used in the last resort.

In the immediate aftermath of the invasion, the unions became much more politically active than before in supporting the reform programme. The powerful Metal Workers' Union threatened industrial action in support of Josef Smrkovský, when the campaign to eject him from the chairmanship of the Federal Assembly was unleashed in December 1968. At the Seventh Congress of the Czechoslovak Trade Union Central Council (4–7 March 1969) a charter and an action programme were adopted, fully supporting the reform programme, which was by then under severe pressure. These documents stressed the independent role that would be played by the unions in society, in particular, that they opposed any form of administrative pressure and that whilst the unions remained subordinate to the leading role of the party and to its ideology, they would nonetheless refuse to accept a passive role in society. The political role played by the unions was demonstrated most clearly over the dispute concerning the establishment of enterprise or workers' councils. The unions openly opposed the suggestion that instead of a workers' majority on the enterprise councils, these should be constituted of one-third workers, one-third management and one-third government representatives. However, after the April 1969 plenum of the Czechoslovak party (when Dubček was dropped), the bill on Enterprise Councils more or less fell into oblivion.

By mid-summer 1969 the independent role of the unions was largely disappearing, particularly after the accession of Karel Poláček, the Chairman of the Central Council, into the top leadership. However, the Metal Workers' Union remained restive even in June and the workers appeared to be carrying out a national go-slow in defiance of both government and union directives. It seems probable that with the tightening up after the anniversary of the invasion, the independent role of the unions will have been totally forgotten.

JUGOSLAVIA

The function of trade unions in Jugoslavia, alone in Eastern Europe, has been specifically declared to be 'an independent socio-political organisation of the working-class and working people' and their role is to assist in 'the construction of socialism on the basis of self-management'. Thus the Jugoslav party has rejected the Leninist view of the unions being a transmission belt and equally, although the right is not formally granted, the strike weapon is accepted in practice. Jugoslav ideologists have accepted that there may be a conflict of interests between workers and management and that this can result in stoppages of work, as the workers have the right to try and enforce their viewpoint on the management. However, given the generally decentralised system in Jugoslavia, strikes seldom extend beyond the enterprise level. Wage bargaining invariably takes place at this level, hence it can only be against the management of a specific enterprise that pressure can be brought.

The Jugoslav trade unions have, in fact, been acting much more independently since the Sixth Congress in June 1968 than before. It was made clear at the Congress that henceforth the unions would be willing to act as pressure groups supporting the interests of the workers, even to the extent of opposing the government. Thus in early 1969 the unions were caught between two sets of conflicting interests over a new pension scheme—those of the membership and of the government. The government was unwilling to accede to union demands that pensions should be 75% of wages, on the grounds that this would be an unacceptable burden on the economy. Instead, while giving in on the minimum pensionable period of service, it proposed that the relevant percentage remain at 67.5%. Eventually the unions put forward the compromise suggestion of 70%, after considerable pressure and bargaining. Likewise, the unions' independent role was demonstrated in the wage negotiations at the Zenica Iron Works, one of the largest enterprises in Bosnia, where thanks to union intervention a contract very favourable to the workers was reached with the management.

HUNGARY

A somewhat anomalous situation has arisen in Hungary with regard to the status and role of the trade unions. Although it has been recognised that the unions can usefully perform functions that go beyond the traditional transmission belt, nonetheless this new area of activity for the unions is severely restricted to the economic field. This innovation has come in Hungary with the institution of the new economic mechanism in 1968, which has given enterprise managers extensive powers of decision, some of which inevitably affect the interests of workers. Hence during the debates that preceded the introduction of the economic reform, it was tacitly accepted that the interests of the workers might diverge from those of the state. However, instead of reviving the right to strike, the Hungarian unions have claimed and been granted a right of veto over a certain range of management decisions. The purpose of the veto has been stated by trade union leaders to be the prevention of the infringement of the Labour Code or of the collective contract. Under the Labour Code the veto may be exercised either when there is a clear violation of regulations covering labour relations (i.e. in the collective contract or under the Labour Code) or when management decisions 'fail to meet the requirements of socialist morality'. Once the veto has been exercised, its effect is suspensory—a decision which has been vetoed cannot be implemented until the whole disagreement is settled.

The unions have chosen to interpret this right fairly broadly, in that it is regarded as a potential weapon against central institutions as well as against individual enterprise managements, even if it is likely to be employed mostly at the enterprise level because the extension of the rights of managers under the reform greatly widens the possible field of conflict. However, there are some restrictions on the use of the veto. First, a motion to employ it must be passed by the entire local union committee, in order, presumably, to lessen the chances of its being used irresponsibly. Second, once the motion has been passed the management concerned must be informed immediately and the higher union organs must be given full information on the decision to employ the veto, including a full statement of the reasons for its use. And finally, it has been repeatedly emphasised that the veto is a weapon of last resort and that unions must first attempt negotiation.

Armed with the right of veto, the Hungarian trade unions are in a fairly strong position to defend the interests of their members. The general area of competence granted the unions includes welfare of employees, working conditions, participation in the negotiations on the collective contract and some say in the appointment of managers. In general, the unions have a right to express an opinion on all matters of management, including purely economic decisions. There is, naturally, an overall provision that the unions must not attempt to usurp the leading role of the party. However, in practice it would appear that the party has genuinely delegated some of its authority to the unions and that the unions have begun to exercise their powers cautiously but firmly. By the summer of 1969 a number of cases had been recorded where the veto was invoked by the unions in the interests of the membership, including one case where work norms were involved.

FURTHER READING

Gamarnikow, Michael. 'New Trends in East European Trade Unionism', *East Europe*, New York, June 1969.

PETER MORAVEC. Trained as an engineer, he is currently working in West Germany on a study analysing the problems of labour efficiency in Eastern Europe.

AGRICULTURE

EVERETT M. JACOBS

INTRODUCTION

THE Soviet Union and the countries of Eastern Europe (except for Czechoslovakia and East Germany) were backward and overwhelmingly agricultural before the communists seized power. The major part of the labour force in these countries was engaged in farming, and exports consisted mainly of large, shipments of grain to Western Europe. However, little had been done to modernise the agricultural sector of these countries. As a result, farming methods remained generally primitive, rural areas suffered from acute overpopulation and most peasants lacked sufficient land to provide an adequate standard of living for their families.

Once in power, the communists' goal was to apply Marxist principles to transform these backward countries into advanced industrial societies. In effect this doomed independent small-scale peasant farming, since Marxist ideology demanded the collective ownership and large-scale use of the means of production. The new system of collectivised farming was first developed in the Soviet Union and was later adopted with some modifications by most of the communist countries of Eastern Europe.

THE SOVIET EXAMPLE

The Bolsheviks responded to the peasants' seizure and division of the landlords' estates by decreeing a land reform as soon as they took power in the Soviet Union. The New Economic Policy (NEP), adopted after the civil war, succeeded in restoring industrial and agricultural production to prerevolutionary levels by about 1927. However, agricultural production and deliveries were not rising fast enough to meet the economy's needs. The regime wanted to carry out rapid industrialisation with major emphasis on heavy industry and, under the conditions then prevailing, this required large quantities of cheap grain to feed the growing urban population and provide goods for export. At the same time agricultural investments had to be kept to a minimum. Stalin's solution was to force the peasants to join collective farms where their production activities could be more closely controlled by the state.

Almost 60% of the peasant households were enrolled in collective farms by March 1930, at which time strong peasant opposition forced a temporary decollectivisation. Recollectivisation began less than a year later and by the end of 1936, more than 90% of the peasant households and almost all of the country's sown area had been collectivised.

Three types of collective farms had been organised during the NEP period, but the simplest form, called the cooperative tillage association (TOZ), and the most radical form, called the commune, were eliminated during mass collectivisation in favour of the artel form of collective. In the artel (commonly called the *kolkhoz* after 1936) the peasant's land, machinery and most of his animals became the collective property of the farm's members, though the peasant was allowed to keep a small garden plot and a limited number of animals for his own use. Instead of receiving fixed wages, each peasant earned 'labour days' computed on the basis of his job classification and the number of days he worked. After all of the farm's obligations, excluding wages, had been met, the remaining income in cash and kind was distributed to the peasants in accordance with the number of labour days they had accumulated. The value of a labour day therefore varied from farm to farm and, if a farm did poorly, the peasants received little or no remuneration for their work. Because labour day payments were usually very low, minimum labour day quotas were established to force the peasants to work on the collectives.

The collective farm's first duty was to fulfil burdensome state production plans. In order to ensure this, a state-run system of Machine-Tractor Stations (MTS) was given responsibility for economic and political control over the farms. The MTS had a monopoly of farm machinery and carried out all mechanised work in return for a payment in kind. Political surveillance was maintained by the MTS political departments.

A number of state farms, termed *sovkhozes*, were also set up. *Sovkhozes* were much larger than *kolkhozes*, were financed by the state and received the most modern machinery and equipment. In contrast to collective farmers, *sovkhoz* workers were state employees and therefore received fixed wages (mainly in cash) and state pensions, and also belonged to a trade union. A *sovkhoz* worker's income was often several times higher than a collective farmer's, though lower than an industrial worker's. *Sovkhozes* were considered the highest form of socialist agriculture and were supposed to serve as models for the *kolkhozes*. However, they were expensive to run, and the government decided to concentrate on the expansion of the *kolkhoz* system in the pre-war years.

Soviet agriculture has been reorganised several times since the war, but only some of the changes have been of lasting importance. Among them, a campaign to create giant collectives by amalgamating smaller farms caused the number of *kolkhozes* to drop from 252,000 in 1950 to only 36,200 in 1967, when each had a sown area of 2,800 hectares.[1] By contrast, the number of *sovkhozes* has increased steadily after 1954, first as a result of the development of the Virgin Lands and then as a result of the conversion of many weak *kolkhozes* into *sovkhozes*. The number of state farms rose from 5,134 in 1955 to 12,773 in 1967, when each had an average sown area of 6,900 hectares. An experiment began in 1967 to end state subsidies to *sovkhozes* by making an increasing number of them fully responsible for their own profits and losses.

Another major change was the abolition of the MTS and the sale of their machinery to the collectives in 1958. Although this was done partly to give the farms more say in their production activities, state and Communist Party agencies still maintain control over the farms, and little real independence has actually been granted.

[1] One hectare equals 2·471 acres.

COLLECTIVISATION IN EASTERN EUROPE

The East European communist regimes have in general based their agricultural policies on the Soviet example, beginning with land reform and ending, except in Jugoslavia and Poland, with full collectivisation. One important difference is that in Eastern Europe the communists, not the peasants, initiated the post-war land reforms. The most radical reforms occurred in Czechoslovakia, Poland, Hungary and East Germany, countries in which there were large concentrations of land in private ownership. On the other hand communist land reform had almost no effect in Bulgaria, was of minimal importance in Jugoslavia and had only moderate impact in Albania and Rumania, since pre-war reforms had eliminated most inequalities in land ownership in these countries.

Collectivisation followed land reform much sooner in Eastern Europe than in the Soviet Union, though the pace and extent of collectivisation varied from country to country. In countries where land reform had little effect, collectivisation began almost immediately. Bulgaria started first, followed by Jugoslavia and Albania in 1945 and 1946. Most of the other countries began collectivisation in the early and mid-1950s in connection with programmes for rapid industrial development.

Collectivisation speeded up in Jugoslavia after the break with the Cominform, but a reversal of policy in 1953 brought with it the permanent dissolution of Jugoslavia's collectives. Meanwhile, Bulgaria, Czechoslovakia, Hungary and Rumania accelerated their collectivisation drives between 1950 and 1953, though the movement failed to make much progress during this period in Albania, Poland and East Germany.

Collectivisation came to a temporary halt in Eastern Europe during the 'new course' adopted after Stalin's death. The area collectivised actually decreased by one-third in Hungary and Czechoslovakia in 1953, but by 1955 the process had resumed on a moderate scale in most places except Bulgaria, which had begun rapid collectivisation. The disturbances in Hungary and Poland in 1956 caused a short-lived decollectivisation in the former, and the permanent breakup of the fledgling collective farm system in the latter. Albania, Czechoslovakia, Hungary and Rumania began mass collectivisation again after 1958, followed by East Germany in 1960. Collectivisation was completed by Bulgaria in 1958, by Czechoslovakia, East Germany and Hungary in 1961, by Rumania in 1962 and by Albania in 1967. Jugoslavia has remained uncollectivised, and only about 1% of Poland's agricultural land was farmed collectively in 1967.

Although the Soviet Union eliminated all other types of collective farms in favour of the *kolkhoz* during the period of mass collectivisation, most East European countries found it necessary to maintain from two to four different types of collective farms with varying degrees of collective ownership. The lower types resembled the Soviet TOZ, while the highest type was similar to the *kolkhoz*. Only Bulgaria adopted a *kolkhoz*-type farm as the sole form of collective.

The general policy in Eastern Europe has been to eliminate the lower types of collectives by upgrading them until they reach the *kolkhoz* level. The lowest type of collective has been abolished in Czechoslovakia and Hungary, and Hungary's middle type of collective and Rumania's lower type of collective are diminishing in importance. However, collectives below the *kolkhoz* level are still very important in East Germany. In 1967 they accounted for one-quarter of East Germany's collectivised area, but more than 54% of the total number of collectives.

Two types of collectives now operate in Poland's tiny collective farm sector. It has been reported that peasants with too much land for the size of their family's work force have been entering the lower type farms gradually since 1964, thereby facilitating the formation of new collectives. The socialisation of Polish agriculture is also proceeding through the development of the network of 'agricultural circles'. When the collective farm system collapsed in 1956, the circles were set up to acquire farm machinery and equipment for the collective use of the individual peasants. They functioned as collective machinery centres until 1964 when they were officially encouraged to take over cultivation of land and engage in a variety of collective production tasks, such as milk processing, livestock-breeding, drainage, etc.[1] The number of circles has been increasing by more than 15% a year since 1963, and by the end of 1967 they numbered 34,300, with more than two million members. However, only about 27,500 of the circles were active and of those only 21,000 formally covered their expenses. Nevertheless, the Polish government still seems determined to build the system into a mass organisation of the peasants and to transform the circles eventually into some sort of producers' cooperatives.

Each East European country has set up a state farm system based on the Soviet model. State farms are relatively more prominent in Czechoslavakia and Rumania, where they accounted for about one-third of the agricultural land in 1965. They are also important in Poland and Jugoslavia where they occupy only about 15% of the agricultural land but represent almost the only kind of socialist farming. State farms are less important in the rest of Eastern Europe, although giant collectives on Soviet lines have been formed in Bulgaria and East Germany to carry on large-scale farming.

Many of the East European countries have followed the Soviet example of abolishing the MTS and selling their machinery to the collectives. The exceptions are Albania and Rumania, where the MTS systems are expanding, and Czechoslovakia and Bulgaria, where most of the MTS machinery has been sold to the collectives but a number of MTS are being retained for backward farms and, in Bulgaria, also for hilly regions.

The Socialist Sector

The essence of collectivisation has been to take the most possible out of agriculture while putting the least possible into it. Because of the great emphasis placed on industrial development, investments in agriculture have been deliberately kept to minimum levels, resulting in very low mechanical and technical standards.

Although the number of tractors in the Soviet Union and Eastern Europe increased by almost 150% between 1956 and 1966 (in contrast to an increase of about 190% in Western Europe)[2], most of the communist countries are still badly under-mechanised. Only Czechoslovakia and East Germany have succeeded in reaching Western standards of general farm mechanisation with an average of one tractor (in 15-hp units) for 30 hectares of arable land. Most of the other countries had one tractor for between 60

[1] Andrzej Korbonski, 'Peasant Agriculture in Socialist Poland since 1956: An Alternative to Collectivization', in Jerzy Karcz (ed.), *Soviet and East European Agriculture*, Univ. of California Press, Berkeley, 1967, p. 426.
[2] *The State of Food and Agriculture, 1968*, FAO, Rome, 1968, p. 46.

and 75 hectares in 1966, though in Poland and Jugoslavia the ratios were over 1 : 100, among the highest in all of Europe (Table 1). The problem of under-mechanisation is even greater than the figures suggest since large numbers of tractors remain out of operation for long periods because of inadequate maintenance and repair facilities.

Production of mineral fertilisers more than doubled in the Soviet Union and Eastern Europe between 1960 and 1965, but supplies are still far from sufficient. In 1966–7, consumption of chemical fertilisers per hectare of arable land was 134 kg for Western Europe, 61 kg for North America, and only 39 kg for the Soviet Union and Eastern Europe[1]. Albania, the Soviet Union and Rumania had the lowest fertiliser consumption per hectare in all of Europe in 1965–6, followed by Spain and Portugal, and then Jugoslavia and Hungary (Table 1).

Although Albania now uses less fertiliser per hectare than any other country in Europe, it should be noted that Albania's level of fertiliser consumption was higher than Rumania's or the Soviet Union's until the break with the Soviet Union cut off a large portion of Albania's fertiliser imports. Despite some advance, Soviet fertiliser consumption is still only about one-fifth the European average, but the situation is likely to improve substantially due to the decision in June 1968 to expand mineral fertiliser production capacity by 48 million tons between 1968–72, with output reaching about 88 million tons a year at the end of 1972.

As in the cases of tractor and fertiliser production, the development of irrigation in the Soviet Union and Eastern Europe has been retarded by the lack of funds. Whereas about 20% of Bulgaria's cropland was under irrigation in 1966, the figure was no higher than 7% elsewhere. However, the Soviet Union and Rumania are carrying out programmes to increase the size of their networks.

Soviet and East European crop yields and overall production results have suffered considerably because of the low mechanical and technical standards. For instance, only East Germany and Czechoslovakia, the sole communist countries with a technically advanced agricultural sector, have been regularly able to equal or surpass the average wheat yield for European non-communist countries. Bulgaria has bettered this average since 1965 thanks to a significant increase in tractor power and fertiliser consumption (Table 2). As might be expected, there is an almost exact correlation among communist countries between rank in terms of fertiliser consumption and rank in terms of wheat yield. A strong link between general technical standards and milk yield is also apparent (Table 3).

Because Soviet and East European agricultural production was at a relatively low level in the past, the improvement in recent years has meant that communist agriculture has shown a faster rate of growth than Western agriculture. For instance, between a base period of 1952–6 and 1967, total agricultural production in the Soviet Union and Eastern Europe rose by 65%, while in Western Europe and North America it rose by 42% and 24% respectively. During the same time total agricultural production per capita rose by 40% in the Soviet Union and Eastern Europe, by 26% in Western Europe, and by only 1% in North America.[2] However, it should be kept in mind that the official government policy in the USA has been to limit the production of certain agricultural products in order to keep surpluses

[1] *Ibid.*, p. 44.
[2] Monthly Bulletin of Agricultural Economics and Statistics (FAO, Rome) XVIII, 1 (January 1969), 11-12.

TABLE I

TRACTOR POWER AND CHEMICAL FERTILISER CONSUMPTION, 1960–65

(*Tractors in 000s of 15 hp units; intensity of tractor use in hectares of arable land per 15 hp unit[1]; fertiliser consumption in kg of pure content per hectare of arable land*)

Country	Tractor power								Fertiliser consumption		
	1960		1962		1964		1965		1960	1964/65	1965/66
	units	*ha/unit*	*units*	*ha/unit*	*units*	*ha/unit*	*units*	*ha/unit*			
Soviet Union	1985	116	2400	96	2820	81	3050	70	11·9	19·5	24·8
Albania	4·5	105	5·9	80	7·6	66	7·7	65	15·0	12·8	16·0
Bulgaria	40·3	113	48·4	95	61·7	74	66·4	68	36·3	62·2	79·1
Czechoslovakia	94·3	56	137·6	40	164·5	32	179·5	29	97·1	152·3	166·3
East Germany	88·0	55	126·0	40	149·0	34	156·9	30	195·9	256·1	262·7
Hungary	47·9	110	61·1	89	83·1	68	91·5	59	31·5	60·7	62·5
Jugoslavia[1]	35·7	232	36·0	228			45·4	182		56·3	54·8
Poland	76·2	210	99·5	159	125·8	125	146·1	105	48·6	70·6	83·1
Rumania	65·3	160	86·0	120	120·3	87	133·0	74	7·4	22·0	25·4

[1] For Jugoslavia, tractors in 000s of physical units, and intensity of tractor use in hectares of arable land per tractor.

Sources: Statistical yearbooks; *Economic Survey of Europe in 1962* (UN, Geneva, 1963), part 1, chapt. I, p. 13; *Economic Survey of Europe in 1963* (Geneva, 1964), part 1, chapt. III, p. 34; *Economic Survey of Europe in 1966* (New York, 1967), part 1, Chapt. II, p. 22; *Economic Survey of Europe in 1967* (New York, 1968), part 1, chapt. II, p. 32; *Fertilizers: An Annual Review of World Production, Consumption, and Trade, 1966* (FAO, Rome, 1967), p. 22; *Fertilizers . . ., 1967* (Rome, 1968), p. 20.

TABLE 2

WHEAT YIELDS 1952–66
(100 kg/hectare)

Country	1952–56	1962	1963	1964	1965	1966
Soviet Union . .	9·1	10·5	7·7	11·0	8·5	14·4
Eastern Europe: .	13·4	17·0	17·6	17·4	22·1	22·0
Albania . .	10·3	10·5	7·1	9·6	8·0[1]	8·8[1]
Bulgaria . .	13·8	16·7	15·9	17·7	25·5	28·0
Czechoslovakia .	19·8	24·5	24·6	22·2	24·2	25·3
East Germany .	28·4	31·1	30·0	31·1	36·7	31·4
Hungary . .	13·9	17·9	15·7	18·6	21·7	21·7
Jugoslavia . .	10·5	16·5	19·3	17·6	20·6	25·1
Poland . .	13·6	19·4	19·9	18·7	20·6	21·5
Rumania . .	10·5	13·3	13·2	12·9	19·9	16·7
Europe, excluding Soviet Union .	16·2	21·1	19·7	21·1	23·4	22·4
Europe, excluding Soviet Union and Eastern Europe .	17·8	23·1	20·8	23·1	24·2	22·6

[1] FAO estimate.

Source: *Production Yearbook 1967*, 21, FAO, Rome, 1968.

TABLE 3

MILK YIELDS 1952–66
(Average annual yield in kg per milking cow)

Country	1952–56	1962	1963	1964	1965	1966	% increase between 1962–66
Soviet Union .	1479	1693	1600	1618	1853	1880	11
Albania . .	392[1]	550[1]	540[1]	540[1]	560[1]	560[1]	2
Bulgaria . .	621	1301	1375	1627	1741	1914	47
Czechoslovakia .	1614	1776	1812	1975	2015	2146	21
East Germany .	2267	2448	2650	2717	2982	3090	26
Hungary . .	1654	2178	2307	2359	2214	2410	12
Jugoslavia .	1040	1111	1125	1212	1221	1243	12
Poland . .	1798	2135	2083	2094	2252	2365	11
Rumania . .	1027	1385	1371	1435	1543	1686	22
France . .	2027	2423	2609	2622	2756	2912	20
UK . . .	2903	3708	3662	3676	3797	3779	2
West Germany .	2892	3443	3498	3572	3642	3649	6

[1] FAO estimate.

Source: *Production Yearbook 1967*, 21, FAO, Rome, 1968.

down to manageable levels—a problem certainly not encountered in the Soviet Union or Eastern Europe. In general, only East German agriculture approaches overall Western standards.

Large-scale socialist farming has failed to bring about the rapid upsurge in production foreseen by the communists. On the contrary, the rate of growth for agriculture has been exceedingly slow in the Soviet Union and most of Eastern Europe. According to the official figures, which are often inflated, the largest production gains throughout Eastern Europe between 1963 and 1966 occurred in Bulgaria and East Germany, where total agricultural output rose by an average of about 10% and 6% a year respectively. Uncollectivised Jugoslavia was next with an average annual increase of about 4%, but elsewhere advances in production barely kept pace with the growth in population. From about 1960 to 1965 total agricultural output in the Soviet Union, Hungary, Poland and Rumania rose by only 2% a year, while in Czechoslovakia it remained stagnant.

Total output has fluctuated a great deal from year to year and has depended to a large extent on the weather. In the favourable conditions of 1966, most of the countries registered significant gains. Production rose by about 15% in Jugoslavia and Bulgaria, and by about 10% in the Soviet Union, Rumania and Czechoslovakia. However, in Hungary, Poland and Albania the increase was only about 5%. The Soviet Union had a record harvest of 171·2 million tons of grain in 1966, but this dropped to 147·6 tons in 1967 when the weather was less favourable, and then rose to a reported 169·2 million tons in 1968.

The overall increases in 1966 generally resulted from large rises in crop production, with only small gains in livestock production. This disparity has been a persistent problem, caused largely by the inability of the governments to provide sufficient quantities of high-grade fodder. For instance, the Soviet Union has failed in its attempt to overcome the fodder shortage by greatly expanding maize production. Similarly, some East European countries have increased the area sown to fodder and industrial crops at the expense of grain crops, but this has not solved the fodder problem, though it has created further deficits in grain production.

The low productivity of the livestock sector can also be attributed to the inadequate development of livestock breeding by the communist countries. In the Soviet Union, any real advance in livestock breeding (or plant breeding) has been thwarted by the official acceptance of the genetic theories of Lysenko, who ignored Mendelian concepts of heredity and believed that environmental influences could bring about heritable changes. Most East European countries rejected Lysenkoism, and therefore did not suffer the heavy losses of the Soviet Union. Moreover, the Soviet Union itself has lately moved away from the doctrines of Lysenko, as was evidenced by his dismissal from high posts in February 1965, shortly after Khrushchev's fall.

Other factors have also contributed to the poor showing of Soviet and East European agriculture. For one thing, the enormous size of most collective and state farms makes them very difficult to manage. Moreover, the farm directors' freedom of action has been seriously hampered by constant inter-ference from central and local authorities responsible for seeing that the farms conform to centrally established plans.

The failure of socialist agriculture has been such that most of the countries are no longer able to export grain, and many have been forced to import part of their supplies. Between 1961 and 1965, Czechoslovakia, Poland and East Germany each imported an average of more than one million tons of grain annually, while Jugoslavia imported almost one million tons a year. Hungary, though able to meet its food grain needs since 1964, has had to continue importing about 10% of its fodder requirements. On the other hand, the Soviet Union and Rumania still export large quantities of grain, although the Soviet Union was forced to import grain from the West in 1963 in order to compensate for a disastrous harvest. Since 1963 the Soviet Union has continued to provide the bulk of the grain imported by the East European countries, though it still has difficulty in meeting its own domestic requirements. Similarly, Rumania has been able to maintain its large exports of grain, and also of sugar, only at the expense of domestic consumption.

THE PRIVATE SECTOR

Small-scale peasant farming has continued to make an important contribution to Soviet and East European agriculture despite the numerous official restrictions placed on the peasants' private plots. Although the regimes often claim that the private plots draw the peasants away from collective work and also encourage capitalism, they have hesitated to abolish them for fear of mass peasant opposition on the one hand, and a decline in overall production on the other. In the collectivised countries, the size of the plot is usually limited to half a hectare and strict controls are placed on the amount of livestock and the kinds of machinery that a peasant can own. Restrictions are less severe in uncollectivised Poland and Jugoslavia, where peasants are permitted plots of up to 40 and 10 hectares respectively, though the average size of plot in each country is slightly less than five hectares.

Because they lack sufficient means to compete with the socialised sector in the production of industrial or extensively farmed crops, the peasants have tended to concentrate on those items which the socialised sector is unable to supply in quantity or quality. They consume part of their output themselves and sell their surpluses either in the local market (at free market prices) or else to a cooperative or government agency. The plots thus provide the peasants with a vital source of income as well as food.

Private peasant farming has centred around producing potatoes, vegetables, fruits, eggs, milk, and meat. For example, private plots covered only about 3% of the Soviet Union's cultivated area in 1967, yet supplied more than 60% of the country's potatoes and eggs, more than 40% of the vegetables, and almost 40% of the meat. In Hungary in 1966 private plots covered about 13% of the cultivated area but accounted for 90% of the poultry, more than 60% of the fruit and more than 50% of the potatoes, milk and meat. Private farming of course predominates in Poland and Jugoslavia, but it is also very important in Rumania where it accounted for more than 40% of the total value of agricultural production in 1965. The share of the private sector is smaller elsewhere, though it still accounts for a considerable portion of agricultural output.

Continued stagnation in agricultural production has forced many of the governments to adopt a more lenient attitude towards the private plots in recent years. One of the first moves by the post-Khrushchev Soviet leadership was to remove the 'unfounded restrictions' which had been placed on the peasants' private production activities since 1956. Under the new policy the size of the peasants' private plots and the norms for private livestock ownership were restored to pre-1956 levels. Also provision was made to give the peasants assistance in acquiring livestock, together with pasturage and fodder.

In Bulgaria a decree in February 1963 made the ownership of plots permanent and hereditary and stipulated that all eligible peasants should have plots of the maximum legal size. However, this policy was modified somewhat in 1967 when it was decided that the size of the plots could be reduced under certain circumstances, and that the plots should be used mainly to grow fodder in order to encourage livestock production. Hungary has had a similarly ambivalent attitude towards private production. Attempts had been made for several years to convince the peasants that their plots would never be taken away, but legislation was passed in October 1968 to make the amount of social benefits and the size of the household plot depend on the degree of participation in collective work on the farm. As of 1 January 1969, men have to work 150 days and women 100 days annually on the farm before they have the right to social benefits (pensions, sick pay, etc.) and the minimum size private plot (about 0·3 hectares). For the maximum size plot (about 0·6 hectares), from 200 to 300 working days are needed. The clear intention of the new law is to increase the rate of growth of socialist agricultural production by making the farmers do more collective work, but the effect might be to cause an overall decrease in production through the restrictions imposed on the private plots. Both Bulgaria and Hungary sell insecticides to private farmers, and Poland sells fertilisers to them through the agricultural circles. However, such supplies are usually made available only after the needs of the socialised sector are met. Jugoslavia remains the only country in which a full complement of machinery may be owned by private farmers.

INVESTMENTS AND INCENTIVES

The slow rate of growth for agriculture has restricted general economic development in the Soviet Union and Eastern Europe. Since the mid-1960s Czechoslovakia, Poland, Rumania, Hungary and the Soviet Union have tried to remedy this by undertaking substantial agricultural investment programmes, but the level of investments in agriculture for the communist countries as a whole has remained low, averaging only about 15% of total state investments in the economy since 1963. Moreover, a number of countries have had to moderate their investment programmes because of demands on capital from other sectors of the economy. For example, the Soviet Five Year Plan for 1966–70 originally called for the state to invest a total of 41 thousand million roubles in agriculture, or more than twice the sum spent between 1961–5. However, the target was reduced by about 5·4 thousand million roubles at the end of 1967. Agriculture's share of total state investments also dropped in Hungary in 1965, in Poland between 1964 and 1967 and in Rumania in 1967.

Much of the new investments has been directed towards improving the technical standards of farming. As mentioned before, the number of tractors has been rising steadily in recent years, and greater attention is being paid to expanding fertiliser production and carrying out irrigation work. Developments along these lines will almost certainly increase productivity.

Along with increasing their investments in agriculture, most regimes have also taken important steps to provide better material incentives. Not only have compulsory deliveries been replaced by a less rigid system of contracts in all countries except Poland, but higher prices are now being paid to the farms for their produce, with substantial bonuses for the overfulfilment of plans. In addition farm managers in Bulgaria, Czechoslovakia, the Soviet Union and particularly in Hungary have been granted greater autonomy in planning their farm's output structure. It is too soon to tell whether these changes will greatly affect production, but they have gone a long way towards putting the farms on a firmer financial basis and encouraging farm specialisation to meet local conditions.

The farmers too have benefited from new incentive schemes. Bonus payments for above-plan production are now the general rule in the Soviet Union and Eastern Europe; Bulgaria and the Soviet Union have gone even further by introducing guaranteed minimum wages for collective farm work. In Hungary the Nádudvar system gives the farmers an incentive to work harder by providing them with a guaranteed percentage of the total harvest, regardless of results, plus a payment for their work based on labour-days. The feature of labour-days is what distinguishes the Nádudvar system from capitalist-style sharecropping.

Under the Nádudvar system, a specific piece of land is assigned to a farm member, collective farm family, or other small work unit for the cultivation and harvesting of highly specialised row crops (e.g., maize, sugar beets, potatoes), or for intensive farming (e.g., vineyards, livestock production). However, the Nádudvar system is not used for mechanised extensive farming, such as grain production. The guaranteed portion of the harvest ranges from 5 to 7% for apples, from 15% to 20% for sugar beets. So far the Nádudvar system has been introduced only in Hungary, where over 80% of the collectives had adopted it by July 1966, though farmers in Rumania began receiving a guaranteed part of the harvest of a number of crops in 1966.

Since the mid-1960s, Soviet policy has been to try and increase the farmers' sense of personal involvement in production by encouraging the replacement of large work brigades by small mechanised work teams called *zvenos*. Each *zveno* usually consists of about five or six highly skilled machine operators who cultivate and harvest crops on a specific piece of land. In addition to their guaranteed wages, they receive bonuses for the overfulfilment of plans. As under the Nádudvar system, mechanised *zvenos* are used for row crops and for intensive farming, though several instances of extensive grain farming by *zvenos* have been reported. Bulgaria's 'accord system' for small work units is very similar to the *zveno* arrangement, but the work is not necessarily mechanised. However, Bulgaria is also introducing mechanised *zvenos*.

Despite the recent improvements, collective farmers in Eastern Europe still earn less than state farm workers, and both earn considerably less than industrial workers. A gap still remains between incomes for Soviet collective farmers and state farm workers, even though their wages have been based on the same scale since mid-1966. This is because collective farmers on average are not as skilled as state farm workers and consequently earn less for their work. However, pay rises announced for the Ukraine in October 1968 will bring the monthly income of collective farmers on most farms up to the average monthly income of Soviet industrial workers, with farm equipment operators earning between 30% and 60% more. If the experiment is successful in the Ukraine, it might be copied in the rest of the Soviet Union. Czechoslovakia plans to equalise agricultural and industrial wage levels by about 1970, and Bulgaria plans to accomplish this by 1980.

Other measures to raise the farmers' standard of living, thereby providing incentives, include the introduction of pensions and the redevelopment of rural areas. Bulgaria was first to give its collective farmers pensions in 1957, followed much later by the Soviet Union and most of the other countries of Eastern Europe, but pension payments are low and are inadequate to meet the farmers' retirement needs. The Soviet Union and East Germany have announced plans for extensive rural construction, though little has been accomplished so far because of the enormous investments required.

Because conditions have been slow to improve, many farmers, especially the younger ones, have left the farms to seek work in the cities. As a result, the size of the agricultural labour force in Czechoslovakia, Hungary, Bulgaria, East Germany and the Soviet Union has declined rapidly, causing manpower shortages, while at the same time the average age of the farmers has risen steadily, creating problems for the future. On the other hand, Albania, Jugoslavia, Poland and Rumania are faced with manpower surpluses on the farms since industry is not sufficiently developed to absorb the rural over-population. Any rapid modernisation of agriculture would produce unemployment, which helps to explain why these countries have been slow to introduce technical improvements.

PROSPECTS

One should not be too optimistic about the future of Soviet and East European agriculture. In spite of the advances made throughout the 1960s, agriculture was still the Achilles heel of the Soviet and East European economies at the end of 1968. Any significant improvement in production will depend very much on whether the countries can carry out, and in fact exceed, their plans to increase investments and provide better material incentives. If history is any guide, the likelihood of this happening is rather remote. Nevertheless, some increase in production can be expected as a result of the programmes already implemented.

A serious dilemma faces the regimes in relation to incentives policy. The Nádudvar and *zveno* systems promise to stimulate the peasants' personal interest in production, but this cannot be allowed to go too far, lest socialist farming comes dangerously close to small-scale capitalist farming. Similarly, the peasants' activities on their private plots must be kept in check. Another difficulty is that further increases in farm wages or pensions will make it harder to finance industrial development, in addition to causing resentment among the industrial workers. Thus, the problem of providing better incentives without upsetting the political or economic bases of the socialist system will doubtlessly occupy the socialist governments for some time to come.

By the end of 1968 there was already evidence of departures from the more flexible line of the mid-1960s. For instance, the Soviet government set 'fixed and unalterable' grain procurement quotas for five years in 1965. However, by 1968 it was clear that these had become minimum quotas which had to be fulfilled and overfulfilled. Also, publication of new draft Model Statutes for the collective farms, originally scheduled for 1966, was delayed until April 1969. A meeting of the Third All-Union Congress of Collective Farmers was called for November 1969 to ratify the new Model Statutes. Many Soviet economists, administrators, and agricultural experts had campaigned for new Model Statutes which would give the farms much more say in their production activities than the old Model Statutes, adopted in 1935. However, this was not the case. While the continued existence of collective farms (and also peasants' private plots) was asserted in the Statutes, little was done to change the basic organisation or operation of the farms.

Even more important are the recent moves to socialise agriculture in Jugoslavia and Poland, the two uncollectivised countries. In Jugoslavia the socialist sector has been steadily acquiring land from the peasants since 1961 by means of its right to purchase land not properly cultivated by families having outside economic interests. Moreover, since 1963 any person wishing to sell his land has first to offer it to the socialist sector before selling it to another individual. In 1967 Jugoslavia's socialist sector covered 15% of the cultivated land and accounted for 40% of all the marketed agricultural produce. By 1970 it is planned that the socialist sector will occupy 28% of the land and provide 90% of all the marketed produce.

Although Poland is moving towards the socialisation of agriculture, no precise timetable for achieving this has yet been announced. In September 1967 the party decided that socialisation would proceed mainly through the development of state farms which in the future are expected to encompass about 30% of the agricultural land instead of the present 15%. In addition, it was indicated that the entrepreneurial activities of the agricultural circles would be extended and that control over them would be increased. As in Jugoslavia, the government is greatly concerned also about the trend towards subdividing already small farms. Since 1967 the authorities have had the power to take over farms of five hectares and upward, with compensation to the owner in the form of a pension and allowances applicable to old-age pensioners in the state sector, together with free use during the owner's lifetime of a house and a plot of land of up to one hectare. Along with this, district authorities may now order the sale by auction of farms with low productivity.[1] While the Jugoslav and Polish attempts to rationalise farming will probably prove beneficial in the long run, it is plain from past events that the governments of Eastern Europe and the Soviet Union must proceed cautiously with the socialisation of agriculture if they are to avoid renewed peasant opposition and a consequent decline in production.

[1] *The State of Food and Agriculture*, 1968, op. cit, p.59.

FURTHER READING

Brown, J. F. *The New Eastern Europe: The Khrushchev Era and After*, Pall Mall Press, London, 1966. (See chapter on agriculture.)

Conquest, Robert (ed.) *Agricultural Workers in the USSR*, Bodley Head, London; Frederick A. Praeger, New York, 1968.

Enyedi, György. 'The Changing Face of Agriculture in Eastern Europe', *Geographical Review*, LVII, 3, July 1967.

Gamarnikow, Michael. 'Reform in Agriculture', *East Europe*, XV, 11, November 1966.

Jasny, Naum. *The Socialized Agriculture of the USSR: Plans and Performance*, Stanford Univ. Press, Stanford, Calif., 1949; Oxford Univ. Press, London, 1950.

Karcz, Jerzy. (ed.) *Soviet and East European Agriculture*, Univ. of California Press, Berkeley, 1967.

Korbonski, Andrzej. *Politics of Socialist Agriculture in Poland 1945–60*, Columbia Univ. Press, New York and London, 1965.

Lewin, Moshe. *Russian Peasants and Soviet Power: A Study of Collectivization*, Allen and Unwin, London, 1968.

Mitarny, David. *Marx Against the Peasant: A Study in Social Dogmatism*, Collier Books, New York, 1962.

Sanders, Irwin T. (ed.) *Collectivization of Agriculture in Eastern Europe*, Univ. of Kentucky Press, Lexington, 1958.

EVERETT M. JACOBS. Research Fellow in the Centre of Russian and East European Studies at the University College of Swansea. Currently completing doctoral thesis on aspects of Soviet collectivisation policy. Since 1963 has specialised in Soviet and East European agriculture. Author of *Patterns of Control over Soviet Agriculture, 1946–1967*.

TRANSPORT IN THE SOVIET UNION AND EASTERN EUROPE

DAVID TURNOCK

INTRODUCTION

TOTAL traffic in the communist world is growing and the relative significance of the various prime hauliers is changing. Thus, in the Soviet Union the importance of railways for both passengers and freight is being modified as road and air transport make a greater contribution, especially in the movement of passengers (Table 1). In a technological sense transport is more highly developed in the 'Northern Tier' of Eastern Europe (East Germany, Czechoslovakia, Poland and possibly Hungary), as distinct from the Balkan countries of the 'Southern Tier'. While, for example, the proportion of the total national investment devoted to transport in Rumania rose from 3·8% in 1960 to 4·0% in 1965, these figures remained below comparable Polish rates of 5·3% and 6·2% respectively. This does not imply that recent developments in the north have necessarily been substantial everywhere; indeed it would appear that Czechoslovakia's system is badly overstrained in certain areas while in East Germany the post-war deterioration of the rail system following Soviet dismantling has not been fully made good. In the following discussion the contribution of each of the prime hauliers is examined.

TABLE 1

SHARE OF PRIME HAULIERS IN TOTAL TRAFFIC IN THE SOVIET UNION, 1940–67 (%)

Haulier	Freight				Passengers			
	1940	*1950*	*1960*	*1967 (plan)*	*1940*	*1950*	*1960*	*1967 (plan)*
Railway	85·2	84·4	79·7	66·3	92·4	89·5	68·5	51·8
Road	1·8	2·7	5·2	5·3	3·2	5·4	24·6	34·8
Sea	4·9	5·5	6·9	17·2	0·8	1·2	0·5	0·4
River	7·4	6·5	5·3	4·7	3·5	2·7	1·7	1·2
Air	0·0	0·2	0·2	0·6	0·1	1·2	4·7	11·8
Pipeline	0·7	0·7	2·7	5·9	—	—	—	—

Source: W. Grumpel *Das Verkehrswesen Osteuropas* (Transport in Eastern Europe), Verlag Wissenschaft und Politik, Köln, 1967.

349

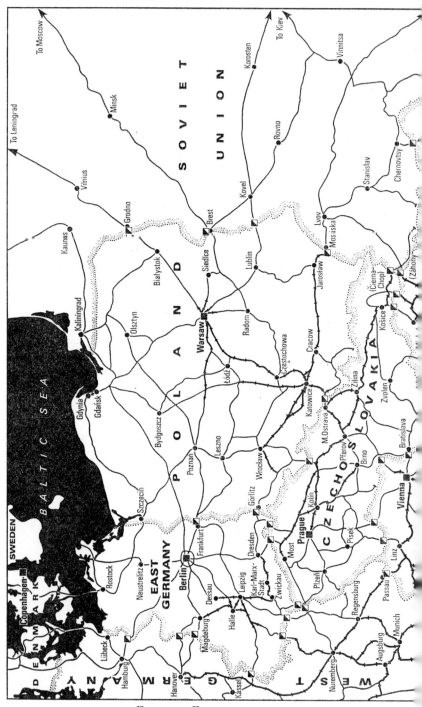

EASTERN EUROPE:

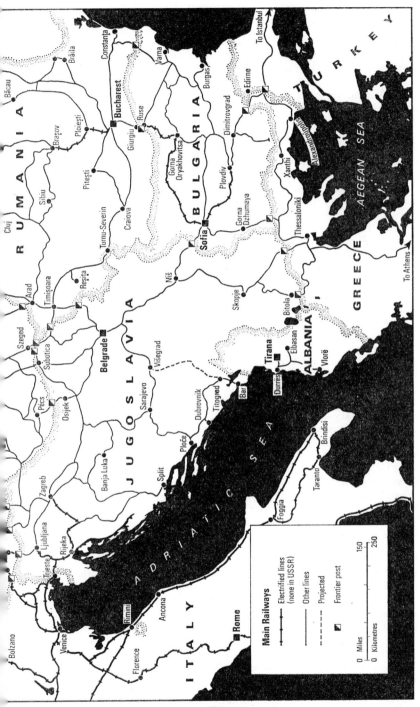

RAILWAYS

RAIL TRANSPORT

Growth of the System

Construction was generally delayed until the second half of the 19th century when lines were built to serve the needs of the three great empires of Austria-Hungary, Germany and Russia. In the case of Austria-Hungary lines were built from Vienna through the Moravian Gate to Southern Poland (1841–47) and also to Budapest and Prague (1845–50) while the 'Südbahn' to Trieste afforded an important maritime outlet to the south-west. From Budapest construction was extended to the Adriatic Coast at Rijeka and also to the Banat, Slovakia and Transylvania. The Germans attached great importance to links between the capital and the eastern provinces and completed railways from Berlin to Breslau (now Wrocław) in 1846, Danzig (now Gdańsk) in 1852 and Königsberg (now Kaliningrad) in 1853, not to mention the grandiose Berlin-Baghdad project. In Russia the first trunk lines were from Leningrad to Moscow (1851) and Warsaw (1861) with routes to the Black Sea opened in the following decade. The 'Trans-Siberian' route running entirely over Russian territory was developed from 1892 but was not fully opened until 1916. In Russia after the 1914–18 war further 'supertrunk' lines were built including the Turkestan-Siberian ('Turksib') with important links to the Vorkuta coalfield in the Soviet Arctic and to Soviet Harbour in the Pacific in anticipation of German and Japanese war action. But the territorial upheavals in Eastern Europe posed great problems for the emerging successor states. The new state of Poland, inheriting parts of the Austrian, German and Soviet systems, had to adapt the latter's broad gauge lines to accommodate standard gauge traffic and construct new lines in the centre between Warsaw and Poznań and Warsaw and Cracow as well as the coal line from Silesia through the 'corridor' to the Baltic. Elsewhere large developments were required to link the Czech lands more effectively with Slovakia, Transylvania with the Danube provinces of Rumania and Serbia with Jugoslavia's Croatian and Dalmatian regions. Very often the completion of these programmes was delayed until after 1945 when further territorial changes had to be taken into account. Even now, however, there are few areas where a really dense system exists, the Soviet Centre, Silesia, Bohemia and East Germany as a whole being the best examples. The historical legacy is still very considerable; while the 'Südbahn' and the Cracow-Bucharest routes now run rather illogically through corners of Jugoslavia and the Soviet Union respectively, former frontier cities like Łódź in Poland and Braşov in Rumania still lack the importance for rail traffic that their central positions would now suggest.

Operation

Except for Albania whose railways are completely isolated, the movement of goods by rail is of very great significance. In the Soviet Union 80% of the total freight was moved by rail in 1960 compared with 85% in Hungary and Poland and approximately 60% in Czechoslovakia. In the Soviet Union the length of the average haul is enormous by British standards although the contrast with East European practice is not, of course, so marked. In the Soviet Union exchanges take place between the main industrial bases of the Centre, Donbas, Ural and Kuzbas and the strain which such traffic has placed on the system has been a factor influencing the choice between regional policies of specialisation and self-sufficiency. Long distance hauls link the Soviet Union with Eastern Europe and here the differences in gauge have demanded the provision of elaborate facilities at Chop (for Czechoslovakia and Hungary) and at Brest and Mostiska (for Poland) where wagon loads can be readily transferred. Movements by rail within Eastern Europe concern timber, fruit and other raw materials from the Balkans in exchange for manufactured goods; Czechoslovakia and Hungary both play a key role in this international traffic by virtue of their central positions. Freight traffic to and from Western Europe is increasing and a number of lines formerly cut by the Iron Curtain have been reopened; routes through Czechoslovak territory, for example, are a useful alternative to the heavily used line through Passau for traffic from West Germany to Austria. Further east considerable use is being made of the Trans-Siberian railway by Japan to move goods to the Middle East. Passenger traffic by rail is still very heavy although road and air transport are carrying increasing proportions of short distance and long distance passengers respectively. Through trains from the Soviet Union are again affected by changes in gauge and here special arrangements are made to change the bogies of sleeping and restaurant cars at the frontier using systems and equipment developed in East Germany. Important routes link the East European capitals by way of Berlin and Prague through Budapest to Belgrade, Bucharest and Sofia, or from Warsaw to the Balkans through Lvov (Soviet Union) to Bucharest and Constanţa, whose sea link with Istanbul enables this route to be used as an alternative to the direct routes from Western Europe to Turkey. Tourist traffic to the Black Sea resorts from Czechoslovakia, Germany and Poland is heavy and, along with the Adriatic Coast of Jugoslavia, justifies augmented services from Western Europe, also, on the routes through Vienna and Trieste. The Soviet Union has rail links with Iran and Turkey as well as with China, Korea and Vietnam. Another interesting route developed recently is that from Moscow to Tokyo using the 'Rossiya' service over the 'Trans-Siberian' from Moscow to Nakhodka.

Current developments

In most countries the post-war programme of new railway construction has been considerable though there are still some outstanding projects (Table 2). In the Soviet Union numerous new branch lines have been opened to tap new raw material sources and additional 'supertrunks' are being provided in Siberia; these include the South Siberian ('Yuzhsib') already completed, the Central Siberian ('Sredsib') and the projected North Siberian ('Sevsib'). Links with China have been opened through Ulan Bator in the Mongolian Peoples' Republic and a new line from Aktogay is under construction through Sinkiang. Apart from the new railway built by East Germany to avoid transit through West Berlin, practically all post-war construction in Eastern Europe is restricted to the Balkans. Rumania has improved her links from Bucharest to Oltenia, Moldava and Maramureş; and Jugoslavia has completed the broadening of the narrow gauge line from Sarajevo to Ploče, with additional proposals for a new link from Valjevo to Titograd (which will give direct access from Belgrade to the Montenegrin port of Bar) recently financed by the World Bank. The main emphasis has recently switched from new construction to the increase in capacity of overloaded main lines. Recently therefore, the volume of traffic has increased much more rapidly than the route-milage especially in the Southern Tier (Table 2).

Provided power is available, electrification is proving to be preferable to the construction of more powerful steam locomotives (with attendant weight problems) or relief routes. In the Soviet Union electrification of the Kizel-Chusovaya-Sverdlovsk line in the Urals was completed in 1939 using thermal

TABLE 2

GROWTH OF THE RAIL SYSTEM AND RAIL TRAFFIC
IN COMECON COUNTRIES, 1950–63
(*1950 = 100*)

Country	Length of railway	Volume of traffic
Northern tier:		
East Germany	101	250
Czechoslovakia	100	260
Hungary	97	290
Poland	102	210
Southern tier:		
Bulgaria	104	330
Rumania	101	330
Soviet Union	110	290

Note: Figures are not available for Albania and Jugoslavia.

Source: W. Grumpel, *Das Verkehrswesen Osteuropas* (Transport in Eastern Europe), Verlag Wissenschaft und Politik, Köln, 1967.

power but hydro power was subsequently used on mountainous stretches of railway in the Caucasus and Kola Peninsula. The whole of the 'Trans-Siberian' is now being electrified but the work will not be finished until after 1970. In Eastern Europe a number of key routes have been electrified in recent years; these include the usual lines from Most to Čierna in Czecho-slovakia, Hegyeshalom to Žilina in Slovakia and Wrocław to Mostiska in Poland as well as radial lines from Warsaw to Katowice, Poznań, Łódź and Wrocław in Poland and the 'Saxon Ring' (Berlin-Halle-Dresden) in East Germany, where the partially completed inter-war Berlin-Munich electrifi-cation had been earlier dismantled by the Russians. Further south electrified sections are shorter: Ploieşti to Braşov in Rumania, Rijeka to Ljubljana and Zagreb in Jugoslavia and Sofia to Ruse and Plovdiv in Bulgaria. It is significant, however, that in very few cases do electrified lines cross frontiers and the selection of different systems is bound in future to frustrate the realisation of any international scheme.

ROAD TRANSPORT

Outside Eastern Europe and European Russia in particular, modern road systems in the Soviet Union have been very slow to develop through limited demands and high construction costs in areas of permafrost. The military requirements of the Russians were an important stimulus and the Georgian, Osetian and Sukhumi military roads are fine examples in the Caucasus. The Pamir and Uzbek roads in Central Asia and the Aldan and Ussuri roads in Eastern Siberia are other important examples of 'routes without rails'. The construction of such feeder roads is increasing as part of a new Soviet leap forward in road transport in places where initial costs are cheaper than those for rail construction. Roads are already taking a substantial proportion of the total passenger traffic in the Soviet Union and it is intended that eventually all short distance freight traffic (moving less than 50 km) will be handled by roads as well.

In Eastern Europe roads play an important part in most countries, especially in the industrial regions of Bohemia, East Germany and Silesia.

Local demands, as well as those of foreign tourists, are increasing and some new roads are being built where rail links would not be feasible; the Dalmatian Highway in Jugoslavia is a spectacular example. Generally, however, developments are taking the form of improvements to existing roads to provide more suitable motorways such as the 'Brotherhood and Unity' road in Jugoslavia from Slovenia to Macedonia. Once again, however, there is little evidence of an international motorway scheme. Indeed, the reverse is more demonstrable since the inter-war German autobahns from Berlin towards Stettin (now Szczecin) and Breslau (now Wrocław) now peter out short of the present frontier with Poland and the former autobahn in East Prussia is abandoned. Road passenger traffic is usually integrated with rail services and buses operate principally between towns and cities lacking a direct or speedy rail connection. In Poland the density of such services is very high in eastern Poland (former Russian-administered territory where railway network remains sparse), whereas in the former German and Austrian lands railways are much more important. In Rumania bus services operate on the several Carpathian routes which, on account of the old frontier with Austria-Hungary along the crest of the mountains, have never been followed by railways; the eastern Carpathians demonstrate the point especially well with one bus service operating from the railhead at Vatra Dornei along the Bistriţa Valley to Bǎcau and thence across Moldava to Iaşi.

INLAND WATERWAYS

There are many navigable inland waterways in the Soviet Union and Eastern Europe and the low terrain of the North European Plain reduces the cost of building link canals in places where the natural river systems do not coincide with the main lines of trading movements. In the 18th and 19th centuries, therefore, canals were built to link the Rhine with the Elbe, Oder, Vistula and Dnieper but, except in the case of the larger Mittelland Canal in Germany, their capacity is too small for them to be valuable in the context of current demands. To accommodate larger vessels much higher levels of capital investment are required. However, the potential traffic is being constantly reduced because the inherent slowness of water transport often makes road, rail or even air transport preferable. The 180 hours needed to travel from Moscow to Volgograd by express steamer may be compared with 20 hours by rail or less than three by air. Consequently, although many canal schemes suggest themselves on physical grounds, actual developments of large canals have been modest.

In the Soviet Union the Volga is well aligned for traffic from Moscow to the Black Sea and Donbas with the completion of the Volga-Don Canal and Volga-Moscow Canal and movement is possible further north to Leningrad via the Volga-Balt Canal completed in 1967. The Volga system in fact carried two-thirds of all the waterborne traffic in the Soviet Union, the other river systems are less helpful; the south-north flowing Siberian rivers lie transverse to the main line of movement east-west and enter an ocean which is frozen most of the year, so that their usefulness is restricted to feeding the railways at the main crossing points such as Krasnoyarsk where the Trans-Siberian railway crosses the Yenisey. Waterways are potentially important for Poland since in the context of its present frontiers the Vistula system is very central and the Oder provides a second north-south route on the western frontier. The Gliwice Canal (replacing the older Kłodnica Canal) links the headwaters of the two rivers in Silesia and the Bydgoszcz Canal links

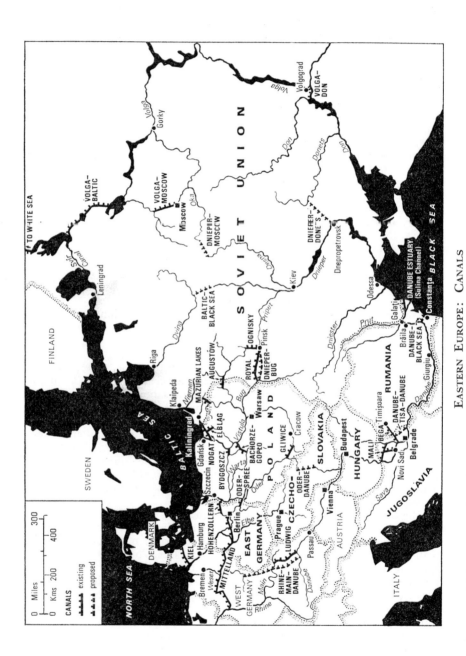

EASTERN EUROPE: CANALS

the Vistula with the Notec (a tributary of the Oder) in Central Poland. This has the effect of producing a circular waterway system which should be further improved by the completion of a new Central Canal from Silesia to the Middle Vistula to overcome problems of low water in the upper reaches of the river itself.

Elsewhere, however, a comprehensive waterway system is less feasible and the pattern resolves itself into a limited number of major rivers, where navigation often requires a measure of international cooperation. The Elbe was formerly important as an outlet for Czech goods moving northwards for export via Hamburg, but the incidence of the German inter-zonal frontier between Hamburg and Magdeburg has encouraged the transfer of traffic to the railways to Rostock in East Germany or Szczecin in Poland. A new canal project from Magdeburg to Rostock might restore the role of the waterways in this area. The Danube is certainly the most important system apart from the Vistula and Volga but limited traffic potential and lack of unified political control in the past often discouraged the necessary stimulus to overcome the main physical hazards. The removal of the Turkish economic monopoly in the 19th century and the expansion of the cereal and timber traffic prompted the scheme at the critical sections of the Iron Gates where the Sip Canal was built (through which vessels moved upstream against the strong current with the aid of a steam locomotive running on the Jugoslav bank) and the delta where the Sulina Canal was dredged. The political situation in Central Europe in the inter-war and early post-war periods was hardly conducive to further development but greater cooperation between the riparian states, including Austria and West Germany, has now been achieved and improvements to the river made still more appropriate by a combination of navigational requirements with hydromelioration schemes.

The Jugoslavs are involved with their Danube-Tisa-Danube Canal which will offer a more direct shipping route across the Vojvodina and provide valuable irrigation water. The vast Iron Gates scheme, being developed jointly by Rumania and Jugoslavia, will provide electricity while removing the remaining navigational hazards. More ambitious still are the outstanding plans from the Stalin era for a Baltic-Black Sea Canal using the Oder and Danube with new canals through the Moravian Gate (Oder-Danube Canal) and across the Dobrudja (Danube-Black Sea Canal) to avoid the delta. New port facilities would be installed at Szczecin and Midia (near Constanţa). Linked with the Volga system by means of a sheltered passage across the Black Sea or through the Baltic, a major ring waterway in Eastern Europe would be available to handle a large number of different shipping movements. The justification for the scheme, however, rests on very close economic association of all the countries involved with heavy movements of raw materials from the Soviet Union to Eastern Europe.

The proposed waterway, however, would be exposed to competition from rail transport offering a quicker and more direct service while the completion of the 'Friendship' oil pipeline system (see below) has robbed the canal of an important potential source of traffic. The determination of most East European countries to follow a national line with less emphasis on trade with their near neighbours in general and the Soviet Union in particular makes the completion of the whole project still more unlikely; certainly the Rumanians, who invested vast sums of capital and drafted forced labour to the Danube-Black Sea Canal until its abandonment in 1954, are unlikely to proceed in future with a project which is largely superfluous to their own requirements. The trade between the 'Southern Tier' and their northern neighbours may justify the Oder-Danube Canal, which is reported to be under construction, while the growing movement between the Balkans and Western Europe makes a case for the new Rhine-Main-Danube Canal which West Germany is building. Another international scheme is the Dnieper-Bug Canal which, in conjunction with the Vistula-Bug Canal in Poland would allow iron ore to move by water from the Ukrainian ore fields to the iron and steel works in Silesia, and also to Nowa Huta.

SEA TRANSPORT

Although the Soviet Union and its East European neighbours have a very lengthy coastline, the scope for transport by sea is much reduced by ice which poses major problems in the north beyond the port of Riga. Although reliable bases exist at Murmansk and Petropavlovsk-Kamchatsky the Northern Sea Route carries only 7·1% of the total Soviet sea traffic, since it is affected by ice from seven to ten months of the year and suffers from the additional liability of fogs during the short open season. The introduction of ice-breakers, including the atomic powered *Lenin* has increased reliability but the capacity is still very limited. Much of the sea traffic is, therefore, limited to individual seas where the problem of freezing is less severe. On the Black Sea, Odessa and Sebastopol can normally be kept open throughout the year as can the entry to the Sea of Azov, and a vigorous coasting trade has developed which embraces Bulgarian and Rumanian ports (Burgas, Varna, Constanţa, Galaţi and Brăila) with important coal and ore traffic. In the Baltic ice affects all ports, including those of East Germany and Poland, although most can be kept open if ice breakers are available. Riga suffers particularly from pack ice which accumulates during onshore winds. Leningrad is the most important port but has suffered from the difficulty of guaranteeing the security of the Gulf of Finland as well as the problem of ice; the acquisition of the former German port of Königsberg (now Kaliningrad) with its outport of Pillau (now Baltiysk) has improved the strategic situation in the Baltic from the Soviet standpoint, while Tallinn and Murmansk are now well placed to act as winter ports for Leningrad.

East Germany and Poland have developed their Baltic ports partly for their own requirements but also to attract traffic from Czechoslovakia and Hungary. East Germany's development of Rostock under difficult conditions and Poland's capacity at Szczecin and Gdańsk/Gdynia demonstrate the importance of the national component in development plans. Jugoslavia's principal Adriatic ports are Rijeka and Split which, along with Trieste in Italy, handle some of the transit traffic to and from the landlocked states. Additional capacity is being installed at Ploče and Bar as well as Gruz (Dubrovnik) backed up by the plans for better rail links across the Dinaric Alps already referred to. Albania's Adriatic port of Durrës (Durazzo) is largely isolated from its neighbours but the Greek port of Salonika is valued by Jugoslavia. The Greek Aegean port of Alexandroupolis (Dedeagach) is well placed for Bulgarian traffic, but links with that country are not very substantial today. On the whole the Comecon countries (including Czechoslovakia and Hungary) possess modern fleets and a number of their vessels are available for international charter.

PIPELINES

Oil pipelines

Pipelines have been important in Rumania since the late 19th century when oil was exported from Ploieşti through the Danube port of Giurgiu upstream to Hungary and Austria. The Rumanian network has been extended following the extension of drilling into Oltenia but the Soviet system is now much more important. In 1966 the Soviet Union boasted 29,000 km of pipelines carrying crude oil from the Caspian and Middle Volga oilfields to the refineries located at the ports and major centres of consumption, including Leningrad and eastern Siberia (Irkutsk). Much of the development is recent for the 1966 figure compares with one of 17,300 km in 1960, 5,400 km

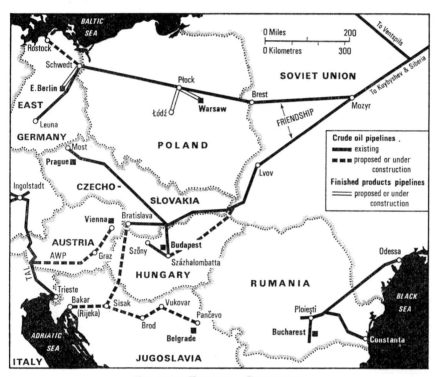

EASTERN EUROPE: PIPELINES

in 1950 and only 1,100 km in 1913, when the 800 km Baku-Batumi project was the main installation. After some initial post-war dependence on imported oil (taken as reparations from Rumania through the Ploieşti-Odessa pipeline) the Soviet Union has become an important exporter of oil. Japan is importing considerable quantities from Moskalvo in Sakhalin and a depot has been built at Ventspils on the Baltic for export to the West. Most important, however, is the 'Friendship' pipeline system to Eastern Europe; this takes the form of two arms, one of which runs through Poland to the East German frontier at Schwedt/Oder while the other extends to Százhalombatta near Budapest in Hungary and also to Bratislava and Záluží-Most in Czechoslovakia. Following this impressive symbol of Comecon integration, new refining and petrochemical complexes have emerged at Płock in Poland, Schwedt in East Germany and Bratislava in Czechoslovakia, areas removed from the older concentrations of industry. Bulgaria, Rumania and Jugoslavia import oil now by sea but not necessarily from the Soviet Union; this is partly for political reasons but also because the Soviet Union cannot be relied upon to meet Eastern Europe's requirements from its own resources indefinitely. Jugoslavia is building a pipeline from the Adriatic at Rijeka to Sisak and Belgrade and East Germany has plans for a link from Rostock to Schwedt where it would join the extension of the 'Friendship' system to Leuna in Saxony. A further extension to Czechoslovakia is a distinct possibility. Finished products pipelines are planned in East Germany from Schwedt to Berlin and in Poland from Płock to Łódź and Warsaw.

Gas pipelines

The Soviet Union and Rumania possess rich resources of natural gas and pipelines are again used for transport. In the Soviet Union pipelines have been built from Stavropol, Saratov and western Ukraine to Moscow, Gorky and Leningrad, and further extensions will serve the Centre and Donbas industrial regions as well as the Black Sea ports. Gas is also sent from Bukhara in western Siberia to the Urals. Rumania has built a comprehensive distribution system from her Transylvanian fields, first to the main towns of that province (Braşov, Cluj, Sibiu, Sighişoara, etc.), but more recently to Bucharest and the peripheral provinces as well. In the Banat the gas is used to increase the efficiency of the blast furnaces, while in Moldava and Oltenia large chemical plants based on gas supplies are helping to build new industrial nodes in formerly backward areas. Rumania exports gas to the Hungarian chemical town of Tiszapalkonya, but this is unlikely to increase in view of Rumania's strictures that its resources be used to support its own industrialisation programme rather than for the benefit of the more highly industrialised 'Northern Tier'.

AIR TRANSPORT

The Soviet Union and each East European country has its own international airline, though some of these appear to be mainly for prestige purposes. It is unnecessary to comment in detail on the various radial patterns of services which link capital cities with their respective provincial centres or upon the international traffic which is particularly heavy between Budapest, Prague and East Berlin. In the Soviet Union, however, air transport plays a more important role in view of the greater distances involved and has developed steadily since the first service was inaugurated between Moscow and Gorky in 1923. In the remote Soviet regions air transport is seen as the initial prime haulier. Services operate to centres such as Magadan and Norilsk and serve the scientific and military bases in the Arctic. In Central Asia aircraft are used to maintain contact with remote herding communities and to locate flocks in times of drought. However, the potential, especially in international traffic, has not yet been fully developed in the Soviet Union.

CONCLUSIONS

Organisation of material under the headings of prime hauliers has the disadvantage that a synthesis of the whole transport pattern in any one country only dimly emerges. Yet, there is considerable evidence to suggest that the national component is fundamental with international movements of secondary importance. Apart from pipeline flows and electricity passing through the 'Mir' international grid which can be centrally controlled, international systems are poorly developed except in the case of rail transport which accommodates 70% of the freight moving between Comecon countries. These countries operate a wagon pool system OPW (Obszczy Park Wagonow) to ease this traffic. Although the cohesion maintained by the Warsaw Pact allows coordination in the maintenance of strategic railways such as the east-west central line from the Soviet Union to East Germany through southern Poland via Mostiska and Görlitz, increasing competition in the economic field between individual countries is likely to continue.

FURTHER READING

Armstrong, T. *The Northern Sea Route*, Cambridge Univ. Press, Cambridge, 1952.
Gumpel, W. *Das Verkehrswesen Osteuropas* ('Transport in Eastern Europe'), Verlag Wissenschaft und Politik, Köln, 1967.
Khachaturov, T. S. 'The Organisation and Development of Transport in the USSR', *International Affairs*, XXI, 1945.
Mellor, R. E. H. 'Motive Power and its Problems on Soviet Railways', *Locomotive*, LXV, 1959. *Geography of the USSR*, Macmillan, London, 1964; St. Martin's Press, New York, 1965.
Nikolsky, I. V. 'Geography of Transport in the USSR', *Soviet Geography*, II, June 1961.
Taaffe, R. N. *Rail Transportation and the Economic Development of Soviet Central Asia*, Univ. of Chicago Press, Chicago, 1960.
Westwood, J. N. *Soviet Railways Today*, Ian Allan, London, 1963; Citadel Press, New York, 1964. *A History of Russian Railways*, Allen and Unwin, London; Soccer Associates, New York, 1964.

DAVID TURNOCK. Lecturer in Geography at the University of Aberdeen. Has visited most East European countries, especially Rumania which is now the subject of his research, covering the post-war pattern of economic growth. Publications are forthcoming on this topic as well as Highland development in Scotland.

ENERGY

RICHARD BAILEY

Energy Policies

Consideration of energy problems is important not only because of its contribution to the satisfactory development of the energy sector, but because this development is indispensable to economic growth. In common with other areas the East European countries will require growing amounts of energy up to 1980 and beyond to support economic expansion. As a whole, the group is well supplied with coal, oil and natural gas, but in an area so vast as that embracing the Soviet Union and the East European countries it is not to be expected that all regions will have equally ready access to internal supplies of all three of these fuels. Nuclear energy has not as yet made any significant contribution to energy requirements in the Soviet Union and Eastern Europe.

As in Western Europe in general it is clear that, even with rapidly rising demands for particular forms of energy, resources in Eastern Europe will be adequate in total. There are however, various ways of meeting this demand, and energy policies are concerned with achieving the right balance between different and sometimes conflicting objectives. In Western Europe the two principal objectives are: (1) the maintenance of adequate and secure supplies, and (2) the assurance of reasonable energy prices to the community as a whole and to the individual consumer. The first objective applies with full force in Eastern Europe, the second is applied in ways determined by the different content of the communist economic system. For example coal and oil enter into various barter arrangements both within the Soviet system and with non-communist countries. In the latter case there is often a very considerable difference between domestic and export prices.

Energy forecasts are notoriously difficult to make in any but general terms as they are affected not only by the varying fortunes of the different fuels but by factors influencing the development of the economy as a whole. Looking ahead to 1980 the OECD has forecast that Eastern Europe and the Soviet Union will together consume 26% of world energy requirements, compared with 53% for the OECD countries (including Canada and the USA), 8% for communist Asia, and 13% for the rest of the world. The significance of this forecast is that it represents a faster rate of growth in consumption of fuel of all kinds in the communist countries as a whole than in the rest of the world.

Distribution of Energy Resources

Albania is the smallest and poorest of the countries which compose the East European group. Although rich in minerals these are largely undeveloped. There is some lignite at Tirana, in the Korçë basin and elsewhere. Albania

EASTERN EUROPE: NATURAL RESOURCES AND ENERGY

has oilfields which were developed before World War II by Italian and other foreign oil companies. The chief fields now producing are at Kuçovë and Patos, but drilling is going on in various other localities. Supplies are piped to refineries in Rumania and the Caucasus. The refinery at Cërrik near Elbasan has a capacity of 300,000 tons, which is regarded as adequate to meet local needs. Natural gas is increasing in importance but the distribution system will have to be improved before its use becomes widespread. Hydroelectric schemes have been developed to raise electricity production; the largest of these are at Ulzës and Tirana. Electric power production is of the order of 250 million kw.

Bulgaria has an annual output of over 20 million tons of coal of which about half is lignite or brown coal. The latter has been extensively developed as the main fuel for electric power stations. The main centres of lignite production are the Maritsa Basin, the Struma Basin and the Sofia area. Oil was discovered in the Southern Dobrudja near Tulenovo in the early 1950s and production was sufficient to cover 40% of the country's needs by the early 1960s. Bulgaria lacks refinery capacity, however, and much of the crude oil produced has to be refined abroad. Electricity production in 1964 was 8,700 million kwh and there is an adequate transmission system to most parts of the country.

Czechoslovakia has bituminous coal at Ostrava and Karvina in Silesia but supplies of coking coal for steel-making are limited. Lignite is mined in northwest Bohemia and is an important fuel for electric power stations. Annual output of bituminous coal is of the order of 27 million tons, and of lignite 65 million tons. Production of oil in Czechoslovakia is inconsiderable. However, an agreement made at the end of 1959 with the Soviet Union and other countries of the Soviet bloc provided for the supply of oil from the Volga fields by a pipeline through Uzhgorod to Bratislava. In April 1968 Czechoslovakia signed a ten-year barter agreement with Iran, whereby Czechoslovakia is to receive approximately one million tons of Iranian crude per annum against deliveries of machinery and finished goods.

Electricity production is mainly dependent on lignite and coal but hydroelectric resources are now being developed especially in Slovakia. The annual production is of the order of 32,000 million kwh representing a doubling in output since 1953.

East Germany depends heavily on the deposits of lignite in the middle Elbe Basin and lower Lusatia. The total annual output is of the order of 225 million tons, making East Germany the highest lignite producer in the world. Electric power for the heavy industry, chemicals and textiles of lower Lusatia, is generated at very large power stations using lignite. There is some hydroelectric power development in the Erzgebirge and Sudeten areas, and a 70-MW prototype nuclear reactor is in operation. Generation of electricity in 1963 was over 47·4 million kw.

Hungary has an annual production of coal of some 33 million tons which satisfies some 75% of its energy requirements. Lignite mined at Dorog accounts for about three-quarters of coal production. Hard coal is mined in the Mecsek region. There is little potential water power so that electricity generation is predominantly based on lignite burnt in large capacity power stations. The Tiszapalkonya power station alone supplies 20% of the national electricity requirements. Natural gas is produced in increasing quantities and in the mid-1960s annual output had reached 612,000 million cu. ft. Oil production has been intensified in the last few years and runs currently at about two million tons per annum.

Poland is the best endowed with energy resources of the East European countries. Post-war boundary changes led to the inclusion of the whole of the Upper Silesian coalfield within Polish territory, along with the coking coal deposits of Wałbrzych and the lignite fields of Żagań and Zgorzelec. Annual production was over 104 million tons in 1966, but the proportion of lignite in the total is increasing rapidly. The main lignite fields are near Konin and Łęczyca in central Poland and the south-west. Electric power production, which has expanded rapidly since 1950 was of the order of 30,000 million kw in the early 1960s and scheduled to reach 41·6 million kw by 1970. Coal has continued to provide the overwhelming bulk of Poland's power needs, but there has been a rise in production of oil and natural gas with the discovery of new oil deposits in the Carpathians, and of natural gas in the Lubaczów region. Poland imports oil by pipeline from the Soviet Union for the refinery at Plock. Oil consumption in Poland is forecast to rise to nine million tons in 1970 from an estimated eight million tons in 1966.

Rumania has a variety of minerals but resources are large only in the case of oil. The main producing areas are in the Băcau, Buzău, Prahova and Dîmboviţa area. The major refineries are at Ploieşti with pipelines running to Constanţa and to Reni in the Soviet Union. Annual production is over ten million tons and is increasing. All the crude oil produced is now refined in Rumania. The country also possesses large reserves of natural gas with an annual production of some 12,000 million cu. metres. The gas is found in the Transylvanian Basin and along the Carpathian foothills. It is now widely used for heating and lighting and as a basis for the chemical industry. Rumania has small coal reserves, the most important being in the upper Jiu Valley in the southern Transylvanian Alps. Annual production was about ten million tons in 1966.

A ten-year programme of electricity production was launched in 1950 involving the building of new coal-fired stations and the development of hydroelectric schemes. By 1966 installed capacity of Rumanian power stations had risen to two million kwh.

The Soviet Union is abundantly supplied with mineral resources of all kinds, and there is every probability that further deposits especially of oil, will be discovered. Coal supplies in the Soviet Union account for about 53% of world resources, estimated at about 15,000 years supply at present rates of extraction. The coalfields are widespread and deposits of some kind occur in every major region of the Soviet Union. In the European parts of the country the principal fields are the Donets Basin in the east Ukraine, the Pechora field, the Moscow Basin centred on Tula, and the Kama River of west Ukraine. In the Urals there are coalfields in five main basins producing both lignite and hard coal. Siberia has the largest proportion of Soviet reserves. Many of these remain unexploited but the Kuzmetsk Basin is second in production only to the Donets region. Soviet output of coal is of the order of 555 million tons a year.

The Soviet Union is one of the oldest oil-producing countries in the world, and relies on oil for some 35% of its energy requirements. Known reserves are estimated to total about a quarter of known world supplies. The greater part of present oil production comes from the Volga-Urals field which contains a number of deposits totalling 80% of known Soviet reserves. The second major field is at Baku in Azerbaidzhan. This was formerly the main producing area but since World War II it has been surpassed by the Volga-Urals field. Other fields in the Soviet Union are much smaller but some of these are of considerable importance in meeting local needs and thus saving long distance transport by pipeline. Total Soviet output of petroleum is of the order of 260 million tons a year and the greater part of this is refined on the oilfields at Baku and Grozny in the Caucasus and at Ufa, Kuybyshev and Saratov in the Volga-Urals area. With the extension of the pipeline system more refineries are being built away from producing areas. Apart from internal distribution, the Friendship Pipeline opened in 1964 takes oil from the Volga-Urals field to refineries in Poland, East Germany, Czechoslovakia and Hungary.

Resources of natural gas have been developed only since World War II, but are now of considerable importance. The principal deposits are located

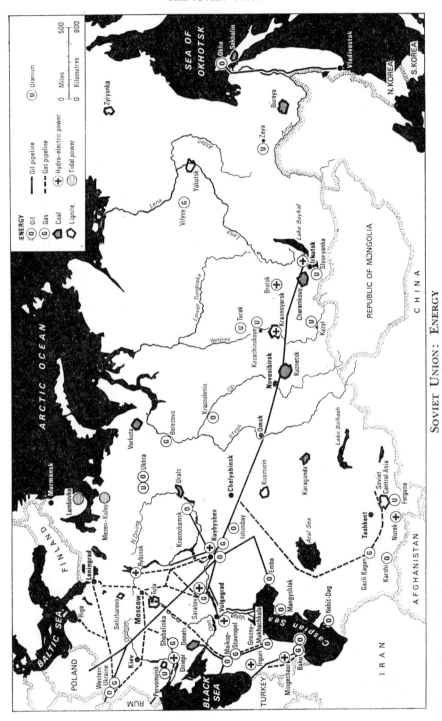

SOVIET UNION: ENERGY

on the oilfields and a widespread distribution network has been built up. The Soviet Union has enormous potential reserves of hydroelectric power particularly in the great rivers of Asiatic Russia. The production of energy in the Soviet Union in relation to industrial production with forecasts for output in 1980 are shown in Table 1.

TABLE 1
SOVIET ECONOMIC GOALS FOR 1970–80
(*Values at 1955 prices*)

Category	Unit	1960 output	1970 plan	1980 plan
Total industrial production . . .	Billions of roubles	155	408	970–1000
Heavy industrial production . . .	Billions of roubles	105	287	720–740
Consumer goods production . . .	Billions of roubles	50	121	250–260
Electric power . .	Billions of kwh	292·3	900–1000	2700–3000
Oil	Millions of tons	148	390	690–710
Gas	Billions of cu. meters	47	310–325	680–720
Coal	Millions of tons	513	686–700	1180–1200

Source: *Pravda*, 19 October 1961.

Jugoslavia has widely distributed deposits of coal and lignite mainly in upland areas. Annual output is of the order of 25 million tons. Oil is found near Zagreb and this is being increasingly exploited. The country has considerable electrical energy potential with an annual output of over 14,000 million kwh. Power stations are based on the coal deposits and are for the most part sited at the mines. The considerable hydroelectric power potential of Jugoslavia has still to be fully exploited.

THE GENERAL ENERGY SITUATION

The situation with regard to the principal fuels in Eastern Europe and the Soviet Union is analysed in the following sections. Nuclear energy does not as yet make any considerable contribution to total needs and is therefore not treated separately. Electricity production has been described in relation to the individual countries. The trade in fuels between OECD countries (which include the USA, Canada and Japan) and the Soviet Union and East European countries is summarised in Table 2. Exports of Soviet bloc coal are often made with the object of securing foreign exchange so that prices tend to be very variable and do not reflect production costs. The way in which prices vary is illustrated by the fact that between 1953 and 1963 Polish coal was offered to European countries at prices ranging from $6 to $21 per ton. On the whole Eastern bloc coal is generally sold more cheaply than indigenous coal or imports from North America. However, the amount of coal involved in this trade is small in relation to total consumption although imports from East European countries have sometimes been of the same order as those from the USA during the 1960s.

TABLE 2

TRADE OF OECD COUNTRIES WITH THE SOVIET UNION AND
EASTERN EUROPE 1963
(*millions of dollars*)

	Exports fob	%	Imports cif	%
Mineral fuels + related materials	10·6	0·4	600·5	21·0

Source: *East West Trade*, OECD, New York, May 1965.

Exports of Soviet oil and oil products to the OECD countries have risen during the 1960s and exceeded 25 million tons in 1965. It is probable that the surplus available for export to non-communist countries will fall and it might in fact disappear as demand rises in Eastern Europe and within the Soviet Union. However, the export of oil has been a major factor in Soviet trading policy, and as a means of securing foreign exchange. The construction of pipelines from the Soviet Union, and the heavy tanker building programme which had been undertaken in the 1960s indicate that it is likely that the export of oil will continue. At the same time it must be remembered that imports of Soviet oil are not essential for the needs of the OECD countries.

THE COAL SITUATION

A major difference between the consumption of primary energy in Eastern, as compared with Western, Europe is in the part played by coal. In Eastern Europe coal still accounts for 80% of total consumption as compared with 45% in Western Europe. Furthermore, as Table 3 shows, while the amount of coal used in the West is falling steadily, consumption in the East is in fact rising. However, it is important to note that taking Europe as a whole solid fuels are still the most important source of energy.

TABLE 3

CONSUMPTION OF SOLID FUELS
(*ooos of tons*)

	Solid fuels		
	1964	*1965*	*1966*
W. Europe	544	520	495
% of total energy . . .	53	48	45
E. Europe	270	272	276
% of total energy . . .	82	81	80

Source: *The Coal Situation in Europe in 1966*,
UN, New York, 1967.

The use of coal in Eastern Europe is fairly evenly distributed between power stations, coke-ovens and other industrial uses, with the domestic user taking a declining proportion. The increase in iron and steel production in the 1960s has been a major factor in maintaining demand for coal supplies for the coke-ovens. The consumption pattern varies between different countries largely as a result of availability of supplies. Consumption of coal for space-heating continues at a high rate in Poland and Rumania.

Production of coal in 1965 and 1966 rose in Poland by 3·2 million tons, but fell in Bulgaria, Czechoslovakia and East Germany. Brown coal is still important in Eastern Europe, especially in Poland, Czechoslovakia and East Germany.

The export of coal from Eastern Europe comes largely from Poland, which is the source of the cheapest coal available in Western Europe. A thorough appraisal of Polish export performance is hampered by lack of information on qualities and ports of destination. Imports from Poland into West European countries have averaged 9·3 million tons in the years 1964–6.

Exports of coal and coke from the Soviet Union totalled 16·75 million tons in 1966. The principal importers in both cases were East European countries, with East Germany and Bulgaria taking the highest tonnages (see Table 4). Exports to countries in Western Europe were less important, with only Italy taking more than one million tons of hard coal and France a similar quantity of anthracite. Other countries importing relatively large amounts were Austria (0·83 million tons), Denmark (0·6 million tons) and Finland (0·36 million tons). Exports of coke were concentrated in East European markets with Denmark (0·3 million tons) as the biggest importer in Western Europe.

TABLE 4

EXPORTS OF COAL AND COKE FROM THE SOVIET UNION TO
EAST EUROPEAN COUNTRIES IN 1966.

(000s of tons)

Country	Hard coal and anthracite	Coke
Bulgaria	2,905	158
Czechoslovakia . . .	2,059	5
East Germany . . .	5,876	1,487
Hungary	876	604
Poland	1,164	—
Rumania	358	592
Jugoslavia	1,067	—
Total:	14,305	2,846

Source: *The Coal Situation in Europe in 1966*,
UN, New York, 1967.

The situation in the coal industry in Eastern Europe can be summarised briefly as follows: the level of demand depends very much on activity in the iron and steel industry. Coal still provides the main energy requirements of the East European countries, the breakdown between fuels in 1966 was coal (80%), liquid fuels (11%) and natural gas (8%). The remaining 1% was supplied by hydroelectric power which is relatively much less important than in Western Europe. The picture varies from country to country, but in general the substitution of coal by oil and natural gas is going on everywhere with the exceptions of Poland and Rumania. The pattern of use of coal in East European countries is substantially the same as in Western Europe with electric power stations and coke-ovens as the main consumers, and with the level of demand falling in 'other' industry, transport and the domestic sector. The main difference between the two is that the running down of coal production is moving more slowly in Eastern Europe than in the major West European producing countries, notably the UK and West Germany.

THE OIL SITUATION

As a general policy the Soviet Union prefers to use its own oil rather than bring in supplies from outside. This policy is followed in spite of the fact that in many parts of the country it would be cheaper to bring in supplies from the neighbouring countries of the Middle East. Oil production in the Soviet Union is rising as new areas are surveyed and developed. It is forecast that by 1970 oil production will reach 350 million tons a year and 630 million tons by 1980.

A major difference between the Soviet Union and Western oil-producing countries is the fact that it has a much smaller number of motor cars in relation to the size of the population, and therefore a different pattern of demand for oil products. In 1966 car production in the Soviet Union was only 200,000 a year, about one-sixth of that of the UK or France. This position is changing and the Fiat and Renault companies are helping the Soviet Union to build up a modern motor car industry. However, it remains true to say that the greater part of Soviet oil will continue to be used as an industrial fuel or a feedstock for the petrochemical industry. In the export field oil is bartered for other products which the Soviet Union may need, in inter-governmental deals. Soviet oil accounts for only a small share of the world market: in 1966 this amounted to only 4% of the needs of the non-communist world. In Western Europe its principal markets are in Italy, West Germany and Sweden. As with other items traded abroad it is usually a shortage of industrial materials or commodities that prompts the Soviet authorities to negotiate export deals. In the 1950s the main compulsion to find outlets in the industrial countries for Soviet oil came from the shortage of steel pipe and other industrial materials needed to develop new oilfields. In the developing countries the Soviet Union has entered into a number of barter deals involving oil. The countries concerned include India, Ceylon and Cuba.

Sales of Soviet oil to the East European countries are organised on a more regular basis. A peculiarity of this trade is the differential pricing system under which the countries pay much higher prices than those negotiated in deals with non-communist countries. The Friendship Pipeline, opened in 1963 links centres in the East European countries to the Urals-Volga oilfield in Central Russia. Although dependent on the Soviet Union for most of their supplies some of the communist countries have begun to obtain some oil from outside sources. Rumania signed a barter agreement with Iran in November 1965 for a ten-year supply of oil in exchange for industrial goods. In 1966 a further agreement was made exchanging tractors and agricultural implements for oil. Other countries making barter deals of this kind are Bulgaria with Iran, and East Germany with Algeria. On grounds of geography and economics there are good reasons for the East European countries to regard the Middle East as possible trading partners. The oil-producing countries cannot sell their surplus oil in Western Europe and the USA except in competition with the international oil companies which are their main source of revenue. As the oil companies do not operate in Eastern Europe, the Middle Eastern countries are able to dispose of oil there without disrupting their relationships with them. Estimates show that by 1980 the local production of some 30 million tons a year in Poland, Rumania and Hungary will meet only about one-sixth of the demand in Eastern Europe. The Soviet Union will not be able to provide the balance because of its own increased requirements and its need to keep some oil for sale elsewhere to meet deficiencies in industrial products and raw materials. The signs are therefore that imports of oil from the Middle East into the East European countries will continue and involve increasing quantities.

NATURAL GAS

So far as natural gas is concerned the Soviet Union is both a buyer and seller. A contract worth 600 million dollars was signed in January 1966 under which Iran will supply natural gas at the rate of 6,000 million cu. metres a year from 1970 to 1975 and 10,000 million cu. metres in later years. As part of the arrangement Iran received a low interest loan to cover the cost and construction of a steel mill and related engineering plants. A contract has also been signed with Afghanistan for the supply of natural gas. In the opposite direction the Soviet Union has plans for building the largest natural gas pipeline in the world, to run to Trieste on the Italian Adriatic coast from the Ukraine. This would supply up to 12,000 million cu. metres a year. Once built the possibilities are that this pipeline would be extended to northern Italy and France connecting the Soviet Union to the West European gas pipeline system.

The largest proved reserves in the Eastern bloc countries are in the Soviet Union, and are assessed at 2,000 billion cu. metres or some 20 years production at present rates. Production is, however, planned to increase rapidly and there seems little doubt that the resources will be found to support the expansion. Among the East European countries natural gas is important in Rumania but the extent of reserves is thought to be relatively small compared to those of the Soviet Union.

TABLE 5

CONSUMPTION OF LIQUID FUELS AND NATURAL GAS IN EASTERN EUROPE AND THE SOVIET UNION
(*ooo tons coal equivalent*)

	Liquid Fuels			Natural Gas		
Eastern Europe:	*1964*	*1965*	*1966*	*1964*	*1965*	*1966*
Bulgaria	3,600	3,800	4,000	—	—	—
Czechoslovakia . .	7,000	7,400	7,800	1,229	1,139	1,321
East Germany . .	4,500	4,800	5,100	85[1]	104[1]	120[1]
Hungary . . .	3,936	4,268	4,600	1,198	1,520	2,204
Poland	6,186	7,112	8,100	1,858	1,860	1,870
Rumania	7,500	7,800	8,100	20,922	23,234	23,530
Total Eastern Europe .	32,722	35,180	37,700	25,292	27,857	29,045
Soviet Union . .	223,400	255,400	290,000	137,315	157,646	189,622

[1] Gross production.

Source: *The Coal Situation in Europe in 1966*, UN, New York, 1967.

ELECTRICITY IN THE EASTERN BLOC

The Soviet Union with several of the world's greatest rivers and high mountain regions has resources of renewable power in the form of hydroelectricity which have been calculated at 420 million kw, or 11% of the estimated total world potential. More than four-fifths of this figure is provided by the great rivers of Asiatic Russia. Even so, none of the power of the

Lena or Amur has yet been utilised. The principal hydroelectric stations that have been built in Siberia are those on the Angara an outlet of Lake Baykal, at Irkutsk. A third station on the Angara is at Ust-Ilim. Other large stations are at Krasnoyarsk on the River Yenisey and at Novosibirsk on the River Ob and at Kamensk, near the mouth of the same river. There are two big installations on the river Irtysh in Kazakhstan. All these are big plants with a capacity of four million kw and above.

In the republics of Central Asia the many rapid mountain rivers of the Tien Shan, Pamirs and other mountainous ranges provide huge potentialities. The power stations so far built are generally small and the resources are far from being fully utilised. The main plants are on the Chirchik near Tashkent, the Farkhadskaya river and the Kayrak-Kumskaya stations in the Fergana Valley and the Alma-Ata station on a tributary of the river Ili.

Although European Russia has only about one-fifth of the country's hydroelectric power, this has been much more fully utilised than the resources of Siberia and Central Asia. Under the GOELRO Plan launched in 1920, two stations were built near Leningrad and others on the Dnieper. The fullest utilisation has taken place on the Volga where there is a 'cascade' of seven stations completed, with others under construction. About 20 hydroelectric power stations have been built on rivers flowing from the Greater and Lesser Caucasus, of which the largest is at Mingechaur in Azerbaidzhan. In Armenia there is a group of power stations at Sevan-Razdan and there are other groups in the Karelian republic and the Kola Peninsula. The rivers flowing into the Baltic also provide hydroelectric power and there are power stations at Narva, Kegums and Kaunas. In 1962 the total hydroelectric capacity in the Soviet Union was over 18·5 million kw or about 4% of potential. Production in that year reached just under 72 million kwh representing 19% of total electricity production.

A high-voltage transmission line from the Krubyshev hydroelectric power station to Moscow was completed in 1955 as the first step towards a national high tension distribution grid. Lines connecting Volograd and Donets and Votkinsk and Sverdlovsk were opened in 1962. The integrated power grid of the European part of the Soviet Union has a capacity of over 50 million kw, and since July 1962 has been linked up with the Hungarian distribution system.

Since 1954 total capacity of nuclear powered generating stations has risen to over one million kw. New stations with about one million kw capacity are under construction on the eastern shore of the Caspian Sea and at Beloyarsk.

The seven year plan which ended in 1965 provided for the completion of hydroelectric stations with a total capacity of some ten to eleven million kw as well as for the construction of coal, gas and oil-fired power stations with a total capacity of some 50 million kw. Total output of electricity at the end of 1966 was estimated at 545,000 million kw.

CONCLUSIONS

In Eastern Europe and the Soviet Union the emphasis is still on the total level of energy supplies rather than the fuels entering into the total. Coal output continues to rise unlike Western Europe where the trend is for its substitution by oil, natural gas, and in the UK by nuclear energy also. This does not mean that oil and natural gas will not play as important a role in industrial development in Eastern Europe and the Soviet Union as in the OECD countries. The difference is in the urgency with which the problem is treated, which in turn arises from the differences in costing energy inputs and in the competitive situation. In the ECSC countries and in the UK the emphasis is on securing the cheapest fuel whether for manufacturing, transport or electricity generation. In the Soviet Union and Eastern Europe the main concern is with the provision and maintenance of adequate supplies of energy whatever their source, and this difference is likely to continue. In this situation in which capital is scarce, nuclear energy will continue to take a lower priority and the policy of utilising resources of the fossil fuels, particularly coal, will continue.

FURTHER READING

Chisholm, Michael. *Geography and Economics*, Bell and Sons Ltd., London; Frederick A. Praeger, New York, 1966.
Grzybowski, K. *The Socialist Commonwealth of Nations, Organisations and Institutions*, Yale Univ. Press, New Haven, Conn., 1964.
Ingram, David. *The Communist Economic Challenge*, Allen and Unwin, London, 1965.
Kaser, M. *Comecon—Integration Problems of the Planned Economies*, Oxford Univ. Press for the Royal Institute of International Affairs, London, 1967.
Kramish, A. *Atomic Energy in the Soviet Union*, (Rand Series), Stanford Univ. Press, Stanford, Calif., 1959; Oxford Univ. Press, London, 1960.
Spulber, Nicholas. *The Soviet Economy*, W. W. Norton, New York, 1962.

RICHARD BAILEY. Partner in an internationally known firm of industrial consultants. From 1964–6 Special Adviser to the National Economic Development Council. Member of the Senate of London University and author of *Problems of the World Economy*, 1967.

z

DEVELOPING AREAS

SOVIET CENTRAL ASIA[1]

VIOLET CONOLLY

CONDITIONS in the former imperial Russian colony of Turkestan and the adjacent Kazakh steppes (now Central Asian republics) undoubtedly inspired Lenin's theses on the necessity of raising the underdeveloped border-lands of Russia to the level of the more advanced areas of the country. The native masses were almost entirely illiterate and their living standards miserable. Being Muslims of Turkic-Iranian origin, they differed in religion and race from the dominant Russians. Industrialisation was in its infancy and confined to some rudimentary forms of metal-working, mining and cotton-ginning. The rich copper mines of Kazakhstan were worked by British and other foreign companies and southern Turkestan was known to contain valuable mercury, antimony and other rare metals, but prospecting had only scratched the surface of this mineral-rich country. Cotton was grown in increasing quantities for the Central Russian mills, but no cotton was manufactured in Central Asia before the Russian Revolution, though the people were skilled craftsmen in metals, wood-carving and the weaving of cloth and carpets.

The Revolution introduced far-reaching politico-economic changes into Central Asia which were at first bitterly opposed by the native peoples. Under a façade of federal institutions, they remained as firmly dominated by the central government as formerly. Thus, while the colonial regimes of the other Western countries were disintegrating into a number of independent governments, Soviet Russia maintained the imperial heritage intact. This hegemony, however, enormously facilitated the economic development of the Central Asian territories by providing an indispensable reservoir of financial and technical assistance for development.

POPULATION AND SOCIAL SERVICES

The post-war period has seen great demographic changes in Central Asia owing to the high birth rate of the autochthonous population and the large migrations of peoples from European Russia. The total population in 1965 was 29,080,000. Russian immigration alone, according to the 1959 census had leaped to over six million from a total Slav population of 2·6 million in 1926. This influx was most intensive in the cities and in the capitals both of the Kazakh and Kirgiz republics, Alma-Ata and Frunze, the Slav element now greatly outnumbers the native element and is rapidly overtaking the Uzbeks in Tashkent. The titular element has also been reduced though in

[1] Contrary to Soviet practice, Central Asia throughout this chapter includes Kazakhstan.

377

greatly varying degrees in all the republics. The most dramatic change was in Kazakhstan where the Kazakhs numbered only 30% of the entire population in 1959 (and may be even less at the present time). The need for skilled labour to man the new factories and industries of Central Asia, where, until quite recently, the native peoples had little or no knowledge of modern industrial processes, has been the main cause of this Slav immigration while the situation was aggravated in Kazakhstan by the added need for millions of migrants from all over the Soviet Union to work the Virgin Land farms set up by Khrushchev in 1953–4. There are various schemes for training native labour for industry, but the numbers forthcoming are still far from adequate. On the other hand, the skilled workers imported to develop the natural gas and oil and other resources often in particularly arduous climatic conditions (as for example the new oil-gas districts of Mangyshlak and Gasli) where little or no care was taken of their welfare, 'melt away' in thousands causing a severe labour problem.

Although industry has been expanding in all five Central Asian republics, the majority of the people are still engaged in agriculture. In Kazakhstan, where the industrialised sector has made most progress, the relative shares of the labour force engaged in industry and agriculture approximate most closely, while the least industrialised republic, Tadzhikistan, according to the to the 1959 census, had 63% occupied in agriculture and only 19·2% in industry. These percentages reflect the importance of cotton (Uzbekistan, Tadzhikistan and Kazakhstan), and of meat and grain (Kazakhstan) in the Central Asian economy.

Under the Bolsheviks education and public health made great strides in Central Asia, whereas before the Revolution the masses were virtually illiterate and medical services sparse and inadequate in the old cities like Bukhara. Modern sanitation was unknown, infant mortality was high everywhere in the region and diseases like malaria, trachoma and typhus were widespread. The small group of educated native families received their education for the most part in Muslim schools and life was deeply impregnated with Islamic beliefs and traditions. Sovietisation completely changed that picture. A massive campaign mounted against illiteracy has had resounding success. In spite of the great difficulties of creating a network of schools throughout the rural areas and the indigenous opposition to the education of women, the 1959 census showed that about 25% of the Central Asian population had received at least secondary schooling. The different nationalities have the right to national-language schools but the curriculum is otherwise identical throughout the Soviet Union. Marxist-Leninist ideology has replaced Islam as the official doctrine and all Islamic institutions (save a few mosques) have been ruthlessly swept away. Higher education which did not exist locally before 1917 was inaugurated by the establishment of the Central Asian State University (Tashkent) in 1920. In the post-war years higher educational bodies and especially technical institutes have proliferated but there is a strong concentration of such establishments in Tashkent, as for example the Polytechnical Institute, the Textile Institute, the Agricultural Institute, the Medical Institute, several Pedagogical Institutes, the Finance and Economics Institute and many more. These institutes turn out thousands of qualified teachers and technicians annually but the supply is still far below demand.

The new Soviet medical services have also been of the greatest benefit to the people. Many endemic semi-tropical diseases as well as tuberculosis have been virtually eradicated, while the spread of doctors and hospitals is relatively high, certainly by Asian standards. All treatment is free but the patient has to pay for the drugs and medicines prescribed by the doctor. In spite of the exceptionally high birth rate, infant and child mortality continue to fall in Soviet Central Asia, but the large rural populations spread over a vast area create many problems for the medical services. There are almost inevitably discrepancies and inefficiencies in these services but considering the low level from which they started a few generations ago, they deserve much praise.

INDUSTRIALISATION

The natural resources of the Central Asian republics are rich and varied but scattered over a huge area. Kazakhstan, the largest of the republics (some five times the size of France), is also the most highly industrialised. Though its mineral resources are still believed to be only partially prospected, Kazakh non-ferrous metals, in the first place copper, lead and zinc, coal and iron mines are of all-union importance and the recently discovered natural gas and oil deposits in the Mangyshlak peninsula in western Kazakhstan are rapidly increasing production in spite of major difficulties of exploitation. An important metallurgical complex is being built round the Karaganda-Ekibastuz coalfields and the very rich Sokolova-Sarbay iron reserves in the Temirtau-Karaganda district of north-west Kazakhstan. Some of the richest copper mines in the Soviet Union are in central Kazakhstan but, as no statistics of non-ferrous production are published, the exact state of the industry is a closely guarded secret. In recent years many new smelters and concentration plants have been built and there have been large-scale modernisation and mechanisation plans to promote production in this industry, notably at the rich Dzhezkagan, Balkhash and Altay mining combines. But there have also been official complaints of delays in developing ore-fields and exploitation of planned capacity, wastage in extraction processes and inadequate application of new technological methods.

In the southern republics there are considerable copper reserves in Uzbekistan and 'unique' deposits of mercury and antimony in Kirgizia and both industries are expanding. But the area is poor in iron ore, and the only steel plant in the south is at Bekabad in Uzbekistan. Its production is far below local requirements and metal has to be imported, at high cost, from the remote Ukraine, Urals and western Siberia. Unless domestic iron reserves come to light in the near future the situation is likely to become worse owing to the constantly expanding demand for metal for the industrialisation programme.

Electric power, a basic requirement for modern industry, has been developing rapidly since the war in all the Central Asian republics, though much still remains to be done to bring power to the rural districts. The southern Central Asian republics have the second greatest hydro-energy resources (after Siberia) in the Soviet Union and claim to produce the cheapest electric power. Some major hydroelectric stations are now being built to tap the huge resources of the Tadzhik rivers, the Vakshk and the Pyandzh, and are planned as the centres of new irrigation and chemical projects, etc. Thermal power is also being developed in Kazakhstan and Uzbekistan, both relatively poor in hydro-power, and are based respectively on domestic coal and the new gas-feed available from the Gasli natural gas fields, in Uzbekistan.

Central Asia, formerly regarded as having a deficient energy balance, is rapidly becoming one of the major sources of Soviet natural gas and oil owing to the successful strikes of both in Uzbekistan, Turkmeniya and most recently in western Kazakhstan at Mangyshlak. A large diameter pipe now carries this gas to the Urals and another completed in 1967 to central Russia. The export of large quantities of natural gas 'beyond the republic' aroused sharp criticism some years ago in Uzbekistan. Local authorities maintained that first priority should be given to domestic requirements but they were over-ruled in favour of the more highly industrialised regions in the Urals and Central Russia.

Among the new industries which are planned to meet all-union as well as local requirements are the chemical and aluminium industries. Khrushchev's 'Big Chemical' programme included a considerable expansion of chemical production in Central Asia with special emphasis on mineral fertiliser for the cotton plantations and, latterly, plastics. Uzbekistan, the union's largest cotton producer, now also ranks third among Soviet mineral fertiliser producers. The new Navoi chemical combine, the largest in Central Asia, and several other important plants have started to work on Uzbek natural gas. The largest phosphate works in the Soviet Union is being built at Chimkent in Kazakhstan (which has rich phosphate deposits at Karatau and Aktyubinsk) and there are several other works. Nevertheless, owing to delays and inefficiency in exploiting local resources apatite from Kola has still to be hauled hundreds of miles to supplement local supplies. Turkmeniya with vast mirabilite, phosphorite, potash and sulphur deposits is another expanding centre of the chemical industry.

Although a good start has been made with a modern engineering industry even in the most primitive parts of Central Asia such as Tadzhikistan and Kirgiziya, it has not yet to any extent reduced the heavy concentration of these industries in European Russia, the Urals and the Ukraine which export much machinery to these republics. But local needs are in certain cases satisfied by local plants. Thus, Uzbekistan now produces nearly 70% of all the spinning machinery and all the roving machinery made in the Soviet Union, and Tadzhikistan also has cotton textile machinery works. Alma-Ata builds machines for the Kazakh coal, metallurgical, power and agricultural industries. Karaganda has a modern steel-casting among a varied range of works and the first tractor works in Central Asia is being built at Pavlodar in northern Kazakhstan, and another is soon to be built at last in Tashkent. These industrial advances should not obscure the many defects that can be found in the planning and execution of industrialisation throughout Central Asia and perhaps in the first place in Kazakhstan. Heavy industry has been promoted often to the neglect of the light and food industries on which the welfare of the people largely depends. Central Asia, for example, is the cotton base of the Soviet Union, but the cotton textile industry has not fulfilled the great expectations aroused by the construction of the largest cotton mill in the world in Tashkent in 1934—the first in Central Asia. Complaints are now frequent in these cotton republics that the percentage of their cotton manufactured locally is far too low and the imports of cotton goods from the Central Russian mills far too high and expensive. In fact, only about 4% of the Central Asian cotton is manufactured there, though output of cotton cloth is constantly increasing. The creation of a big new textile mill in Alma-Ata is significant. The canning industry is growing, but both qualitatively and quantatively much more could be made of the excellent tropical fruit and vegetables grown in the lush Central Asian oases.

This brief survey of the main lines of development in the Central Asian republics should illustrate the great progress made in discovering and opening up local natural resources and establishing new industries in the Soviet period. Despite much unsuitable planning in housing, lack of co-ordination leading to unnecessary and expensive cross-hauls of raw materials and finished goods, excessive delays in completing construction sites and idling of machinery (much of which is endemic to Soviet industry every-where), in only two generations the economies of these countries have been completely transformed from the handicrafts' basis on which they previously depended.

AGRICULTURE

The primary products of Central Asian agriculture—cotton, grain, cattle and meat—are of major importance to the Soviet economy and are far from eclipsed by the rising role of industry. These items are very unevenly distri-buted throughout the republics owing to the great variations in climatic conditions. Cotton is grown in the southern areas, the chief producers being Uzbekistan and Tadzhikistan, with the result that the Soviet Union is now self-sufficient in cotton (at least for the rather meagre Soviet per capita consumption) and has some to spare for exports. Between them the five republics produced about 5·5 million tons in 1967. Output has been rising steadily since the better prices and grain incentives were introduced in 1963 and subsequently. All Soviet cotton is grown on irrigated ground and expansion has been promoted by a vast programme of irrigation canal construction involving Herculean labour and great capital outlay. The most notable of these canals are the Karakum Trunk Canal which will eventually link the Amu-Darya River with the Caspian Sea through hundreds of miles of waterless desert; the Amu-Bukhara and Karshi Canals. Apart from irrigation these canals have important industrial uses in desert areas now found to be rich in oil and natural gas but which require water for their workers and industrial development. Many Central Asian irrigation schemes have been accompanied by much inefficiency and wastage as well as success. A major cause of trouble has been the lack of skilled labour, including engineers to look after mechanisation. Irrigation is of course an age-old practice in Central Asia but new methods call for numbers of technicians who are in short supply. The expansion of cotton was long highly unpopular among the local people because it cut into their subsistence farming and often threatened their food supply when supplies from the centre were inter-rupted for one reason or another. The improved cotton prices have eased this situation and grain is usually supplied from the Virgin Lands of Kazakhstan for retail sale (apart from the bonuses to collective cotton farmers).

Since the ploughing up of millions of acres of former Virgin Land under Khrushchev's grandiose scheme to solve the Soviet grain problem, in 1953–4, northern Kazakhstan has become the 'second bread-basket' of the Soviet Union in spite of drastic fluctuations in output, due partly to drought and partly to bad management and cultivation. It is scheduled to produce some 26 million tons of grain in 1970 and has averaged 12% of total Soviet output for the last five years. The potential for substantial increases in grain pro-duction certainly exists in Kazakhstan but there must be fundamental improvements in methods of cultivation, machinery adjusted to the peculiar soil and climate conditions and better living conditions for the workers if it is to be realised. Soviet sources constantly complain of the large-scale 'flight' of migrants from these lands; the still primitive living conditions are not fully compensated for by the bonuses paid them for settling there.

On the whole the climate and arid land of the southern republics are not suitable for cattle-breeding (with the exception of sheep). However, Kazakhstan is a major cattle and meat supplier to the Soviet Union. Coercive collectivisation wrought havoc on the Kazakh nomads and their vast herds and it took many years for this once cattle-rich country to recover from the government's ill-conceived policies which reduced the rural population from 5·6 million in 1926 to 4·4 million in 1939 and the sheep and goats from 19·2 million in 1928 to 2·6 million in 1935. These official figures speak for themselves. The present large-scale meat exports to European Russia are hampered by inadequate refrigeration and processing plants or meat-combines, while output is constantly increasing and could increase much more according to local officials.

Conclusion

The foregoing analysis of the position in the developing republics of Soviet Central Asia shows how far they have progressed from their former backwardness and are getting in line with the older industrialised regions of the Soviet Union. Though they may still be regarded as 'under-industrialised' as regards per capita production of steel or electricity, for example, they have made great advances in a relatively short time in the establishment of a number of basic and other modern industries. Intensive prospecting has revealed some very valuable natural resources, oil and natural gas, hydro-electric power, gold and various rare metals of all-union importance. In spite of many difficulties these reserves are being developed in the framework of the centre's investment and reserve allocation policies, etc.

In fact, the rate of increase in investment in Kazakhstan where some major schemes such as the Karaganda iron and steel works and the Sokolovka-Sarbay mining combine have absorbed large capital funds, has been well above the Soviet Union average since 1950. But these increases in investment have not on the whole been accompanied by similar increases in industrial growth, though the latter were still well above the Soviet average for 1959–65.

The situation is less favourable in the four southern republics in these respects. Compared to the previous period, investment there was considerably increased during the seven year plan (1959–65) and even exceeded the Soviet annual increase of 8·6%. Many production plans were however not fulfilled during these years and gross output was considerably lower than the Soviet average. These results are scarcely surprising in an area which is really only now serving its apprenticeship to modern industry.

Against this background of social and economic development it may be tempting to regard the 'socialist' experiment in Soviet Central Asia as a model for the solution of the socio-economic problems confronting the newly independent countries of Asia and Africa. In considering this question it is all too easy to overlook (following the Soviet propaganda line) some fundamental features of the Soviet 'socialist' solution. In the first place the Central Asian republics form an integral part, politically and economically, of the larger and richer Soviet Union. All major decisions regarding the development of their economies, investment, etc. are made by the central authorities in Moscow at a level where local representation is either insignificant or non-existent. But, as part of the union, they are able to draw on the capital reserves and technical aid essential for the rapid transformation of their rudimentary economies. Both were invaluable economically. But politically the peoples paid a high price for this economic assistance. They were forced to accept Sovietisation with all its ramifications, i.e. nationalisation of the means of production with elimination of private industry and trade, collectivisation of agriculture, the destruction of Islamic institutions (with the exception of a few 'working' mosques) and of the nationalistic elements in politics, the arts and religion. As parts of the 'united economy' of the Soviet Union, with all that implies economically and politically, the Soviet Central Asian republics are in a completely different position from the newly independent countries of Africa and Asia which, having shaken off the shackles of western imperialism, have to rely on their own meagre capital resources or means of raising capital. The mere fact of adopting a socialist or communist form of government would not in itself help them to conjure capital out of the air. The Soviet 'solution' is thus dependent on the inclusion in a richer and more sophisticated unit for the provision of the necessary capital and technical aid, with or without strings.

FURTHER READING

Central Asian Review, London. The sections of Soviet Press Comment and the book reviews in this journal contain essential information on developments in the Soviet Central Asian republics.

Conolly, Violet. *Beyond the Urals, Economic Developments in Soviet Asia*, Oxford Univ. Press, London, 1967.

Nove, Alec. *The Soviet Economy*, Allen and Unwin, London; Frederick A. Praeger, New York, 1962, with Newth, J. A. *The Soviet Middle East*, Allen and Unwin, London; Frederick A. Praeger, New York, 1967.

Schuyler, Eugene. *Turkistan* (edited with an introduction by Geoffrey Wheeler), Routledge and Kegan Paul, London; Frederick A. Praeger, New York, 1966.

Wheeler, Geoffrey. *The Modern History of Soviet Central Asia*, Weidenfeld, London; Frederick A. Praeger, New York, 1965. *Racial Problems in Soviet Muslim Asia*, Institute of Race Relations, Oxford Univ. Press, London and New York, 2nd ed. 1962.

VIOLET CONOLLY. Russian specialist with long experience of Soviet Affairs. For many years a senior research expert in the Foreign Office, is a former Rockefeller Travelling Fellow and Hayter Research Fellow of London University (1964–6). Publications include: *Soviet Economic Policy in the East; Soviet Trade from the Pacific to the Levant; Soviet Tempo; Beyond the Urals*.

THE SOVIET NORTH[1]

TERENCE ARMSTRONG

THE northern land areas of this planet are climatically uninviting, sparsely inhabited and economically underdeveloped. They have long been thought to conceal riches, both mineral and biological, on plausible grounds of probability, and more recently this has been demonstrated to be the case. The pressure to make use of these territories is therefore bound to increase as the number of human beings in the world grows. In the Soviet Union, particular interest has been taken in this, because the government, motivated by the desire for a strong and self-sufficient economy, has made strenuous efforts to locate and exploit domestic sources of supply.

EXTENT AND CHARACTER OF THE NORTHLANDS

First, it is necessary to delimit, at least in broad terms, the territory to be considered. This is essentially the area north of all the major industrial and agricultural regions of the country. Soviet planners distinguish such an area, which they call 'the Soviet North'. It embraces both the Arctic and sub-Arctic as climatologists define them, and its southern boundary runs not far from latitude 60 in Europe, dropping to latitude 50 as it approaches the Pacific seaboard. Over half the country lies north of this line.

The territory is largely forested, broken by mountains in the east and giving place to tundra in the north. Permanent ice caps are found only on some of the off-shore islands in the Arctic Ocean. The climate everywhere is severe, in the sense that temperature extremes are great and the summers, though short, are often hot. There is abundant animal life. Virtually the whole area, apart from the off-shore islands in the Arctic Ocean, was inhabited, if sparsely, before the Russians moved in from the south and west over the last ten centuries.

TRANSPORT

In the last 40 years, the major concern of the Soviet Union has been the mineral resources, and the main prerequisite for gaining access to these (or anything else in the area) was a transport system. Historically the waterways had been the highways, usable whether liquid or frozen. It was the waterways that were selected first again—the rivers and the seas. Nature has provided a good network of rivers, remarkably free of rapids, and their mouths are joined by the offshore waters of the Arctic Ocean. The first major project, therefore, was to organise a northern sea route, which would

[1] An earlier version of this article appeared in *Survey* 67, April 1968.

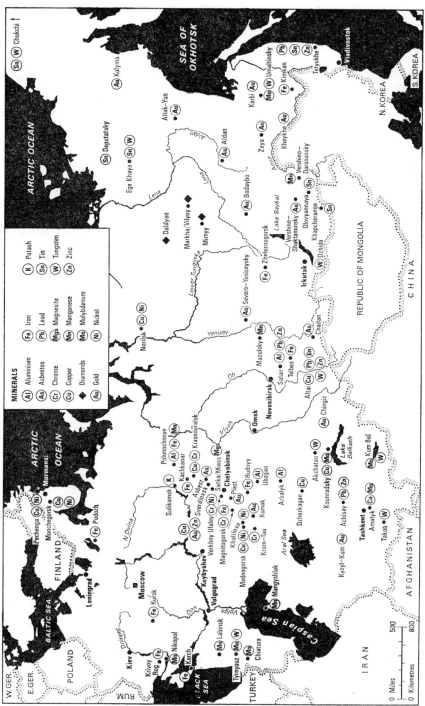

SOVIET UNION: NATURAL RESOURCES

permit access to the Siberian rivers from either the Pacific or the Atlantic. With the aid of icebreakers and a highly developed system of weather and ice reporting and forecasting, traffic built up to the present level of some hundreds of ships operating in these waters each season. The season itself has been extended from about two to about four months.

The sea route has never been of any significant economic use as a link between Atlantic and Pacific, although this is the role commonly ascribed to it. Only in 1967 did this aspect receive any prominence, when the Soviet Union invited foreign shippers to make use of Soviet navigational aids, for a fee, and to save perhaps 13 days sailing time between, say, Hamburg and Yokohama. None accepted the offer during the first season it was open, and the indications now are that it has been withdrawn—though no public announcement to this effect has been made.

On the rivers large fleets of powered craft and barges have been assembled. Latterly, hydrofoils have been extensively used, bringing down travel time from days to hours. The sea-river combination does provide a solution to at least some of the freighting problems, but its limitation in time is a serious drawback. The possibility of sidestepping this by use of submarine freighters —suggested in other Arctic areas—has apparently been considered but not taken up. Certainly the very wide continental shelf would cause difficulty.

A fortunate coincidence has been the advance in aircraft technology at just this period. Air transport has made all projects very much easier, and in some cases has been the decisive factor. A town such as Yakutsk, 5,000 miles from Moscow with a population of 100,000, has five direct daily flights to the capital. At the other end of the scale, a farming village of 500 people on the Yana River has two single-engined aircraft calling every day. Aeroflot also lets out aircraft on charter at very reasonable rates, so prospectors and scientists are well served. The helicopter has helped enormously, though distances are often too great for its economic operation. Hovercraft, curiously, are not in use, nor even, it would seem (despite protestations to the contrary), under very serious consideration.

On land the winter track has been the most widespread medium of communication and there is still little of greater sophistication. Very few all-weather roads exist and these are chiefly in the north-east, and a few spurs of railway line attack the southern fringe of the area. Much is being written currently of a 'northern Trans-Siberian', but this is a line which may in perhaps 20 years time parallel the existing line only a couple of hundred miles or so to the north; its route will be Tobolsk-Surgut-Kolpashevo-Maklakovo-Boguchany-Ust Ilim, and then along the line of the earlier projected Baykal-Amur Magistral, which loops around the northern end of Lake Baykal to rejoin the existing line at Komsomolsk. Even such a major centre as Yakutsk seems unlikely to have a rail connection in the foreseeable future. Perhaps it is possible for regions to achieve industrialisation, by-passing the railway stage, just as some Siberian peoples are said to be achieving socialism, by-passing the capitalist stage.

MINING

The transport system, despite its shortcomings, is a remarkable achievement in its context and it has permitted the growth of many major mining operations. The emphasis has always been, naturally, on minerals of exceptional value. If we take these in order of their importance to the country today, diamonds should come first. The country had virtually none until the spectacular discovery of not only alluvial but reef diamonds in the basin of the Vilyuy, a tributary of the Lena, in the 1950s. The mining centre, Mirny, today has over 20,000 inhabitants. Then there is gold, which historically was the first important mineral to be worked in the north, in the Yenisey valley. Now the workings are further east, around the Aldan, another tributary of the Lena, and in the far north-east, near Bilibino in Chukotka. Tin is probably the third most important, with working also in Chukotka, at Iultin, and at Deputatsky and Ege-Khaya, both between the Yana and Indigirka rivers. The ore at Deputatsky is so rich and accessible that the capital investment required was many times less than that at two major producing areas in the central regions. Next in order of importance comes nickel, which is mined at Pechenga, in what used to be Finland until 1944, and at Norilsk, close to the Yenisey estuary. This last is the most striking example of mineral based development in the wilderness, for the town of Norilsk, founded in 1935, today has over 130,000 inhabitants, although it stands 1,300 miles from the nearest mainline railway station. Of almost equal importance is apatite, a source of mineral fertiliser: one of the major deposits in the world is 100 miles south of Murmansk. To these should be added two notable sources of fuel. The Pechora coalfield was developed during World War II to replace lost Donbas coal, and now produces about 20 million tons a year, most of which is sent to the Leningrad region. The central mining town, Vorkuta, with its satellites, has 200,000 inhabitants. Finally, the most recent discovery is an immense oil and gas field across the Urals in the marshy basin of the lower and middle Ob. This is still in the process of exploration and development, but already pipelines are under construction to take both oil and gas to the Urals industrial region, where they will connect with pipelines to Moscow and Eastern Europe. Norilsk will obtain gas from this same field, which extends from the Ob to the Yenisey.

Production and reserve figures are not released in respect of these mining developments, apart from the fuel. We can only be guided by such comments as this by V. Uvachan, a regional party secretary, writing in 1967:

> The north contains virtually all the diamond resources of the country, nearly half the gold and tin, and a large part of the nickel, mica and apatites.

This alone justifies, in the past and in the future, heavy investment in northern development. It has given rise to ancillary industries. Local food production has been stimulated and now makes a significant contribution to supplying these northern settlements, though it will never, of course, free them from the need to import much from the south. Local sources of fuel are also tapped. A hydroelectric station on the Vilyuy serving the diamond industry is attracting special attention as the first of its kind in this environment.

BIOLOGICAL RESOURCES

The obvious primacy of mineral extraction must not obscure the existence of other important northern industries which exploit renewable resources. Fur, the original stimulus to Russian occupation of almost the whole of this area, is still hunted and ranched, and the annual Leningrad auction remains a highly significant event in the world fur trade. Timber is cut and processed in very large quantities. Much of this is done in the most southerly parts of the country, but the European north and part of central Siberia provide lumber of high quality and are the main sources of exports. Mention should also be made of the very large and fast growing sea fishery which, though not an exclusively northern undertaking, has two major bases in the north: Murmansk and Petropavlovsk-na-Kamchatke. Murmansk alone handles as much fish a year as all British fish ports combined (800,000 tons in about 1960), and is probably the busiest fish port in the world.

TECHNICAL PROBLEMS

The two main kinds of problem which may be distinguished in the development of the area are technical—how to build and operate the necessary plant, and human—how to get people to work there.

Examples of major technical problems are those posed by the existence of frozen subsoil (permafrost) in almost the whole of the area and by the presence of floating ice on the waterways. The permafrost problem is simply described. Any major structure, whether building, road, bridge or runway, will, unless precautions are taken, cause the soil temperature to change, with consequent differential settling of foundations and damage, up to and including the collapse of the structure, may result. The necessary precautions, therefore, have been studied in some detail. Geologists, geophysicists and soil mechanics specialists, working over the last 30 years chiefly in the Institute of Permafrost Studies, whose headquarters are now at Yakutsk, have evolved solutions in principle to most of the problems. This is a successful example of directing effective scientific enquiry to a practical field where results are needed urgently. The Soviet Union is, understandably, the world leader in permafrost studies. The emphasis now is on finding quicker cheaper solutions and on paring down the safety margin.

The floating ice problem was attacked in a similar way. A group of oceanographers and meteorologists was assembled at the Arctic Institute in Leningrad in the early 1930s and they have developed forecasting techniques which have given very real assistance to shipping. At the same time the construction of icebreakers has been pressed forward, often with use of Finnish yards and designers, and the first nuclear-powered icebreaker, Lenin, was completed in Leningrad in 1959. There has never been, as far as one can tell, any attempt to relate the cost of the scientific programme in an exact way to the income to be derived from the activities thus assisted. If there had been, it is doubtful if support would have been so generous.

These are two technical problems among many. The effective way in which they have been handled is repeated in some of the other cases, but not in all. A loudly voiced current complaint is that too much mechanical equipment used in the north was not specifically designed for that environment. It has been used because it was all there was, and the breakdown rate has been high. The work could be done in spite of this because conditions, both natural and man-made, are severe in much of the rest of the country. But it was and is demonstrably wasteful.

LABOUR

Human problems are generally more intractable than technical ones, and this is probably true of the Soviet north, even though men have at times been treated as if they were machines. The attraction of labour into an area which is undeniably less comfortable than other possible places of work has been attempted in various ways. From the 1930s to the early 1950s forced labour was widely used. This was inefficient as well as cruel and is not likely to be repeated for any economic reasons. Contemporaneously, but rising to a peak after the forced labour period, appeals to patriotism, sense of adventure and Bolshevik endurance were tried, and seem to have had a certain success. But ever since the early 1930s, and underpinning the other methods, there has been an elaborate system of incentive payments and privileges. These 'northern increments', as they are called, are scaled to vary with locality and length of stay. Every few years—in 1945, 1960 and 1967—the law in which they are embodied has been amended, and new rates introduced. The change last year was in the upward direction with emphasis on larger increments earlier in the immigrant's stay in the north. In addition, there is another set of wage differentials called 'regional coefficients', which are essentially cost-of-living allowances. These are paid as percentage increases on basic pay, and vary in the north between 30% and 100%, depending on locality. The northern increments and regional coefficients, taken together, have ensured that any worker who volunteers for northern service and stays on the job for, say, five years, is between two and three times better off in various ways than he would have been had he continued to work in a central region.

There is another possible source of labour in the indigenous peoples. The north, in this sense, contains about 950,000 'natives', belonging to some 20 different national groups. This is only about 20% of the total population (1959 figures), but it is the fraction with the greatest expertise at living in this environment. The most numerous groups—Karelian, Komi and Yakut, who between them account for all but 120,000 of the 950,000—are to some extent integrated in the industrial economy which has come in from the south and some of their number are employed in mining, transport and administration. The remaining peoples, in general more primitive, have continued to follow their traditional pursuits of hunting, fishing or reindeer herding. This has been Soviet policy, on the grounds that as long as food and fur are required, these peoples are the most skilled at producing them. The standard of living of the pastoral groups is below that of the industrial workers, so perhaps, it is argued, young people in the former group should be attracted into industry. An important factor is that since 1960 the native inhabitants of these regions have been eligible for the 'northern increments', and this has tended to reduce the disparity (*sovkhoz* workers therefore receive them whilst *kolkhoz* workers do not).[1]

Despite these measures, there is a labour shortage in places, and the turn-over of labour remains much higher in some regions than is consistent with efficient and economic running of the enterprises. The upward revision of the increments in 1967 was of course designed to ease these problems. To what extent it will do so will not become clear for some time; the higher rates only became effective on 1 January 1968.

The Future

What is quite clear is that solutions to all these problems are being energetically sought. The approval of the wage increments in 1967 must involve many millions of roubles, and so makes unlikely any abandonment or cutting down of the northern investment programme as a whole. It is true, however, that more and more is being written about the need to reduce costs. Furthermore, an idea novel in the Soviet context is being advanced: that northern development should be strictly limited to necessities; that big cities, like Norilsk, arose at least partly from prestige considerations and are not

[1] See chapter on Agriculture, p. 336.

economically justifiable; and that settlement in the north should be planned for the expected period of exploitation of the resource and no longer. The reason that these simple and logical views were not advanced long before seems to be that the motives for northern development had always previously been more than just economic. Confirming sovereignty over the area, Sovietising the northern peoples, making strategic dispositions—all these undoubtedly played a part. If serious thought is now being given to a policy of comparatively short-term settlement in the area, this must indicate diminishing relative importance of the other motives. At least it can no longer be considered grossly unpatriotic to suggest that the population of these remote areas might be permitted to stop rising. If this is to be the trend (and one should emphasise that these views are not yet dominant), then it will accord with the latest thinking on the American north. For there too the accepted idea that a continuously growing population is essential to economic development is being questioned: new transport media may be making it unnecessary and the rising value of wilderness and open space in an urbanised society may be making it undesirable. In the Soviet case, economic activities will still be at a high level, because the known resources happen to be very valuable, and continuing geological exploration will undoubtedly produce more of value. Development will thus proceed in any case, but its motivation may be more exclusively economic.

FURTHER READING

Armstrong, T. E. *Russian Settlement in the North*, Cambridge Univ. Press, 1965.
Botting, D. *One Chilly Siberian Morning*, Hodder and Stoughton, London, 1965.
Conolly, V. *Beyond the Urals*, Oxford Univ. Press, 1967.
Hooson, D. J. M. *The Soviet Union*, Univ. of London Press, 1966.

TERENCE ARMSTRONG. Assistant Director of Research at the Scott Polar Research Institute, Cambridge. Has travelled widely in the Arctic, and has visited northern Siberia several times. Author of *The Northern Sea Route*, *The Russians in the Arctic* and *Russian Settlement in the North*.

PART FOUR

SOCIAL

CHANGING SOCIAL STRUCTURE

FRANK PARKIN

THE social structure of contemporary European communist states has been fashioned by two powerful and often contradictory driving forces—Marxist ideology and modern industrialism. The tension between these two social forces has created a particular type of society that we are justified in calling 'East European', even though the countries that fall into this category do of course display important differences resulting from variations in cultural background and historical and economic development. It is natural enough that we should be more concerned with the similarities in social structure than with cultural differences, since the East European states share the unusual characteristic of having been consciously modelled on a distinctive set of political and social doctrines. Indeed, for most of these societies it was not always Marxism as such which provided the blue-print for their social institutions so much as the example of the original Soviet prototypes. But although the influence of the Soviet Union is obvious enough, it would be misleading to suggest that all major internal developments in the 'peoples' democracies' have come about through slavish imitation of Soviet precedents. Rather, they are partly to be seen as a response to the demands imposed on any type of society committed to rapid industrialisation, whatever its political ideology. Many social theorists, in fact, have been so impressed by the apparently growing similarities between advanced capitalist and communist states as to suggest that modern industrialism imposes its own 'logic' on the social structure. That is to say, once a society has reached a certain level of economic and technological development the actual range of social variation open to it becomes extremely narrow. The class structure in particular is held to be closely determined by the industrial system, so that the contrasting ideals of East and West European societies could not be expected to give rise to very different systems of social stratification.

But how true would it be to say that the class system of East European societies is becoming more and more similar to that of the West? Has Marxist ideology ceased to be a decisive factor in shaping the general hierarchy of rewards and privileges? Does the absence of private property affect the nature of communist élites? What is the position of the working class under the 'dictatorship of the proletariat'? These are questions that immediately spring to mind when we consider the problem of a socialist class system. The sociological evidence on Eastern Europe is not yet sufficient to provide authoritative answers to all these questions. But there are now perhaps just enough clues to enable us to make some tentative generalisations about the socialist class structure and the changes which have occurred within it since the seizure of power.

A New Social Order

The period of 'socialist reconstruction' in Eastern Europe following the end of World War II gave rise to a quite distinctive system of social stratification. The task of dismantling the old capitalist order and imposing a new political and social system on a generally unenthusiastic population, produced a highly fluid and unsettled class situation. Recruitment to, and expulsion from, positions of authority and responsibility were based upon a new set of political criteria—most commonly membership of the communist party or proven loyalty to its principles. Throughout the socialist states of Europe men who had served the party during the underground period of the pre-war years, or who had fought in its ranks as partisans during the German occupation, found themselves rapidly drawn up into positions of political, managerial and administrative responsibility. Very often they were men of lowly social origin, peasants and industrial workers, who lacked the formal education and training for their new positions. The members of the former ruling classes they replaced, businessmen, landowners and aristocrats, suffered a drastic social demotion as their property was confiscated and then political and economic power stripped away. Those who did not escape to the West, or who were not physically liquidated or imprisoned, were forced generally to find menial employment as best they could. The stock cartoon figures in the Eastern Europe of this early period were the semi-literate party boss in the director's chair and the ex-lawyer or businessman making a meagre living as a waiter. In some countries which had a well developed stratum of intellectuals, such as Poland, the situation was made more complex by the fact that this particular élite group could not automatically be equated with the former ruling class. Many had supported pre-war radical movements against the old regimes, and were often willing to throw their weight behind the new reforms. Unlike the aristocracy and the *rentier* class, the intelligentsia possessed important skills and abilities much needed in the establishment of a new social order, and their support was assiduously courted by party leaders. As a result the status of the intelligentsia was not undermined to anything like the same extent as that of other former élites. Indeed, many intellectuals felt that their personal and professional identities were greatly enhanced under a system which placed high value on science and learning, and which seemed, whatever the underlying political motive, to give art and culture a more elevated status than that allotted to it by bourgeois society.

Perhaps the most compelling and significant change in the class system concerned the position of the proletariat. Much has been written about the material and social status of the worker in socialist society, usually from a highly polemical viewpoint. Soviet and East European propagandists present their countries as 'workers' states', suggesting that the most privileged beneficiaries of socialism are the industrial proletariat. Western critics, by contrast, have often claimed that the position of the worker in these countries is a much less favourable one than in Western society. They cite the fact that trade unions do not properly exist in Eastern Europe, and that workers' wages are held down in order to finance crash programmes in industry. However, while this is undoubtedly the case, what has to be remembered is that the salaries of white-collar employees and specialists have also been kept low by Western standards, so that in *relative* terms the position of the manual worker has not necessarily been a disadvantaged one. The evidence suggests in fact that in the early years of socialist rule the proletariat were singled out for special benefits and privileges which greatly improved their condition in relation to other groups in society. Socialist incomes policies, for example, had a distinctly egalitarian flavour, and brought about a sharp reduction in wage differentials between blue-collar and white-collar workers. In Czechoslovakia, qualified engineers and factory directors earned only about 20% more than manual workers, while administrative and clerical staff earned considerably less than the workers. In Poland, the average earnings of industrial workers increased by 75% between 1937 and 1960, whereas the earnings of non-manual workers fell by 26%. Similar egalitarian policies had been introduced by Lenin's government in the Soviet Union during the first decade of socialist rule. Workers were also given special priority in the reallocation of flats and houses, in the granting of travel allowances and subsidised holidays, and in countries where food was rationed, such as Jugoslavia, men engaged in heavy manual work were given a larger share. The introduction of free comprehensive welfare and social services and the greater security of employment was especially beneficial to the formerly underprivileged.

REFORMS IN THE EDUCATION SYSTEM

The most significant of all improvements in the social situation of the working class was that brought about by educational reform. Soviet and other East European societies all made heavy investments in the provision of educational facilities, with the result that in a very short space of time the proportion of their populations receiving full-time higher education was considerably more than that of West European countries. The real significance of their educational programmes, however, lay not so much in the rapid expansion of numbers as in the social composition of the student population. Pre-war university and technical education in East European countries was very much a middle-class affair, and only small minorities of workers' and peasants' children were admitted to the student numbers. The socialist governments sought to reverse this trend by exercising policies of 'positive discrimination' in favour of children from proletarian or peasant families. Some countries, such as Hungary, East Germany, Bulgaria and Rumania, operated a quota system for middle-class university applicants to ensure that their numbers were kept down to a desirable minimum. In Jugoslavia and Czechoslovakia a similar aim was achieved by granting scholarships, hostel accommodation, subsidised meals and travel facilities only to children of poorer families. In faculties which had a heavy demand for places, a system of points was commonly used in deciding allocations; social origin of the applicant often accounted for more points than academic qualifications. In some countries the children of the middle classes sought to evade restrictions against them by misrepresenting the facts about their background, or by working in industry for a year or so to qualify for the label of manual worker. As a result of the policy of positive discrimination, the proportion of working-class students in East European universities and institutes of higher education soon became considerably higher than that commonly found in the West. In Hungary 66% of the university enrolment in 1949–50 were students from peasant and working-class families; the comparable figure for the pre-war period was 11%. In Jugoslavia 35% of students in 1951/52, were of manual background, a figure which had risen to 44% six years later. Comparable increases were recorded for other socialist states, which were, again, in line with what had occurred earlier in the Soviet Union.

This opening-up of the system of higher education to the sons and daughters of the proletariat was of vital importance in changing the old system of class stratification. In any type of industrial society the possession of educational qualifications is the most important prerequisite for upward social mobility and occupational achievement. But in socialist societies education takes on added importance because there are very few sources of reward available outside the arena of paid employment. There are almost no opportunities for individuals to take up business or entrepreneurial activities or to cultivate legitimately the money-making talents of the self-made man. Almost everyone is an employee of the state and, therefore, dependent upon certificates and formal qualifications in his occupational career. Under these conditions access to the means of higher education is decisive for material and social well-being, so that the relatively privileged position of the working-class in this respect was a source of fundamental change in the stratification order.

Educational reforms served to bring into being a new class of technocrats and white-collar experts which differed in important respects from the middle-class of the pre-socialist period. To begin with, its social and material privileges rest almost wholly upon the educational and occupational attainments of its members, and not upon inherited property and private wealth. Again, unlike the old bourgeoisie, a great many members of the new middle-class will have been drawn from the ranks of the proletariat—beneficiaries of the early educational reforms. Their own success within the system is thus liable to give it an extra patina of legitimacy in their eyes. At the same time, too, new recruits to the socialist middle-class will have been educated into the political outlook and values of the new order by the schools and the mass media. Consequently, they are not automatically defined as potential opponents of the system in the way that the former bourgeoisie certainly was. Quite the contrary in fact; they are decisive to the success of that system and their rewards have begun to reflect this fact.

THE NEW MIDDLE-CLASS

The creation of a new politically reliable middle-class was to pose certain ideological and political problems for the socialist rulers. For, whereas any industrialising society must place great emphasis on the skills and services of its middle-class experts, the values of Marxism single out the industrial workers as the key elements in the social and political system. In modernising societies in the socialist camp there has been, therefore, a certain tension between the values of the formal ideology and the values of industrial efficiency. The question has arisen as to how a society based on the 'dictatorship of the proletariat' can reconcile the goal of working-class supremacy with the day-to-day subordination of workers to the authority of factory managers and other white-collar specialists. Seen from the other angle, the question has been whether it is possible to relegate the new middle-class to a position inferior to that of the proletariat, given the crucial importance of their contribution to economic and technological progress. This contradiction between Marxist values on the one hand, and the demands of a complex industrial order on the other, lies at the root of many of the tensions found within socialist societies in the present day. Although there has inevitably been some variation in the way that East European societies have managed the relationship between the working-class and the new middle-class, the general tendency in all of them has been quite similar. What has happened is that the balance of material and social advantages has gradually but unmistakably shifted away from the working-class and in favour of the middle-class. This has come about by way of the progressive erosion of many of the egalitarian policies favoured in the immediate post-capitalist phase, as well as the abandonment of discriminatory practices against the middle-class in the field of education and elsewhere. Again, the experience of the Soviet Union was to set the pattern later to be followed in many other East European states.

Stalin's first Five Year Plan heralded the end of the equalisation policies undertaken during the first decade of Soviet rule. In a celebrated speech,[1] Stalin declared that no proletariat in history had managed without the aid of a white-collar intelligentsia and there were no grounds for assuming that Soviet workers could do so. He called for an end to the hostile attitude towards middle-class specialists, as well as to the system of payments which guaranteed them little more than that earned by manual workers. Sizable differentials were introduced between the wages of skilled and unskilled employees, in addition to a complex range of monetary incentives and bonuses designed to supplement the incomes of managers and technocrats. As a result of these reforms the Soviet Union had become, by the 1930s, a highly inegalitarian society, showing a range of incomes between the top and bottom occupational groups considerably greater than that found in many European capitalist countries. Later innovations included the reform of the tax and inheritance laws, which had the effect of removing restrictions on the accumulation of personal wealth, and the reintroduction of civilian ranks, titles and uniforms based on the old Tsarist system of *chiny*, or civil service grades. Stalin's concerted campaign against all forms of 'equality-mongering', and his insistence upon the need for wide salary and other differentials, led to the emergence of a large middle-class intelligentsia whose general status, privileges and authority were decidedly greater than those of the industrial workers.

Effects of the Economic Reforms

Although stratification in the new socialist states of Europe is by no means as marked as that of the Soviet Union, a similar shift in the direction of greater income differentials and middle-class advantages has become noticeable in recent times. In some cases, the move away from egalitarianism has been accelerated by the economic reforms introduced by several states in the 1960s. These were inspired by the need to make industry and the economy more efficient by placing greater emphasis on the role of market forces, and somewhat less on the dictates of central planners and bureaucrats. Many of the socialist states had begun to experience severe economic difficulties by the 1960s, partly as a result of inefficiencies and mismanagement of the planners. Factories were often badly run by incompetent directors and production targets were more commonly met by administrative manipulation, or covert malpractices, than by genuine output. It was also argued that the policy of wage equalisation had contributed to economic decline by failing to provide sufficient incentives for highly skilled people or for those with heavy responsibilities. In Czechoslovakia, for example, where by the early 1960s the economy had reached a state of critical decline, it was claimed that university graduates frequently preferred to seek employment as manual workers because the wages were almost the same as they could have earned in professional occupations, whereas their responsibilities were much lighter. A study published in 1963 showed that as many as 60,000 graduates were employed in manual occupations. A Polish survey had similarly shown that

[1] See Alex Inkeles, 'Myth and Reality of Social Classes', *Soviet Society*, Alex Inkeles and Kent Geiger (eds.), Constable, 1961, p. 559.

more than 80% of industrial workers who had been offered promotion to supervisory positions had declined to accept it on the grounds that the small difference in pay was inadequate compensation for the added duties.

The economic reforms sought to cure these various ills by making industrial enterprises more responsive to the demands of the market and by offering greater financial incentives to workers and employees. One effect of these changes was to increase the differentials between skilled and unskilled personnel as enterprises competed for their services. In Jugoslavia, where the reforms had come earlier and were more radical than elsewhere in Eastern Europe, extremely wide differences appeared in the wages of workers according to whether or not their factories were 'profitable'. Men employed by enterprises with a lucrative foreign market were paid exceptionally well, while those in inefficient plants tended to be paid badly for doing roughly the same kind of work. In Czechoslovakia the salaries of white-collar specialists showed a definite improvement in the two-year period following the 1966 reforms. The salaries of technicians increased by 5·2% and those of administrative personnel by 6·2%, whereas workers' wages rose by only 1·4%. This does not, of course, mean that countries like Poland, Bulgaria, Czechoslovakia and Hungary show the same degree of inequality as the Soviet Union or the countries of Western Europe. By comparison with these the people's democracies are still quite egalitarian. Nevertheless, the general trend towards better pay for professional and managerial cadres seems clear enough, no doubt reflecting official concern at the relative lack of material incentives for tasks carrying heavy responsibilities.

More recently the manual workers have found themselves disadvantaged in another way by the economic shake-up—through rising unemployment. Unemployment had hardly been conceived of as a possibility in socialist states; it was regarded as one of the distinctive hallmarks of capitalist society. In a centrally planned economy it is certainly possible to keep down or 'conceal' unemployment by hoarding surplus or inefficient labour, but this is less feasible when the economy is geared more towards market rationality and industrial enterprises are concerned with profitability. In Jugoslavia unemployment has become an especially acute problem; by the mid-1960s over a quarter-of-a-million men, mainly unskilled manual workers, were looking for jobs.[1] The problem would be even more serious had it not been for the government's policy of allowing large numbers of migrants to seek work in Western Europe. If this labour should no longer be needed by Western countries (West Germany in particular), the Jugoslavs will face a major domestic crisis. The Hungarians have arranged to meet their unemployment problem by sending large numbers of workers, especially school-leavers, to East Germany to help build up that country's depleted labour force.

SOCIAL COMPOSITION OF THE COMMUNIST PARTIES

The decline of egalitarian policies and the greater occupational uncertainties facing manual workers point to a general deterioration in their material position vis-à-vis the middle-class. But it is not only in the matter of pay and economic security that the latter have gained advantages. In the political sphere, too, the new middle-class has increasingly made its presence felt at the expense of the proletariat. The most telling illustration of this is provided

[1] The monthly average in the first half of this decade has been 236,000 unemployed, comprising between 6% and 7% of the total work force. See Robert G. Livingston, 'Jugoslavian Unemployment Trends', *Monthly Labour Review*, 87, July 1964.

by evidence of the changing social composition of the East European communist parties. The communist parties of the pre-war and immediate
post-war period were recruited largely from the ranks of manual workers and
peasants; leaders like Gottwald of Czechoslovakia, Gomułka and Tito were
not in the least unusual in having left school at an early age to serve industrial
apprenticeships. Although intellectuals have always played an important role
in the work of the party in every country, it has generally been accepted that
the industrial proletariat should be the dominant group within its ranks. But
however important this may be as an article of faith, the facts suggest that in
all East European states the new middle-class has gradually been edging out
the manual workers. A recent study of the communist party of the Soviet
Union calculated that one in every three white-collar 'specialists' with higher
education is now a party member, whereas among manual workers only one
in 22 is a member. Even in absolute terms the number of middle-class experts
in the party is greater than the number of workers, even though the latter are
of course much more numerous in the population as a whole. The author's
conclusion that Soviet workers are being 'steadily thrust into the background
within the communist party' would seem to apply no less to workers in the
other socialist states. A 1959 survey of the Jugoslav League of Communists
showed that peasants and workers comprised almost 80% of the party
membership in 1948 but by 1957 they made up less than half the membership. The decrease in manual representation, and the corresponding rise in
the proportion of white-collar members, has come about not simply by
differential class recruitment, but also by the pattern of resignation and
expulsions. In 1966 alone of the 13,488 members purged by the party more
than 52% were industrial workers, while of those who resigned of their own
accord, more than 54% were workers. In this same, not untypical, year the
number of economists and lawyers alone entering the party's ranks increased
by more than 3,600 over the previous year, while the number of technicians
and engineers increased by more than 4,400 in the same twelve-month period.
In Poland, white-collar workers constituted less than 10% of the party
membership in 1945; by 1961 they made up over 42%. Those with higher
education are now three times more likely to be party members than those
with only elementary schooling, while activists are even more likely to be
drawn from the white-collar segments of the population.

This progressive 'de-proletarianisation' of the Soviet and other East
European communist parties is symptomatic of the general erosion of
working-class power, status and privilege. The increasingly common trend is
to appoint individuals to positions of responsibility and authority more on
the basis of their formal qualifications and fitness for the task than as a
reward for political loyalty. This again is part and parcel of the growing concern with industrial and economic efficiency, which places great emphasis on
the rational use of managerial and scientific talent. Naturally enough, this
process has given rise to certain tensions between the old guard of political
appointees—often men of working-class or peasant origin—and the new
generation of middle-class technocrats and managers who are successfully
challenging them for key posts. As the European socialist societies become
politically stabilised, the role of the traditional old guard is rendered somewhat less important and men with new technological, as against political,
skills are more highly valued. This is not to say that political considerations
are always completely ignored in the appointment of men to top jobs,
especially in less developed countries like Bulgaria and Rumania. It should
be remembered that a great many of the young technocrats are themselves

party members, a fact which prevents there being too wide a political gap between them and the old partisan types. Both are able to employ the elaborate vocabulary of Marxism and both are skilled at justifying their positions by reference to sacred ideological tenets. Nevertheless, beneath this common language there is a very real difference in the businesslike and pragmatic outlook of the new graduates and the stubborn fundamentalism of the old guard. This fact alone would ensure that, given the increasing influence of the former, the aims and character of the socialist states will continue to depart from the early egalitarian model.

THE NEW TECHNOCRATS

The burgeoning power and influence of the new technocrats has raised in many minds the possibility that socialist societies have begun to spawn a new managerial class enjoying the same kinds of privileges as their counterparts in the West. Some have suggested that because *control* of the means of production, and property generally, is more decisive than mere legal ownership, the new class in socialist countries occupies an analogous position to the propertied bourgeoisie of the West. Writers like Milovan Djilas,[1] the former Jugoslav vice-president, and James Burnham, the American sociologist, have argued that men who control and dispose of material property are to be thought of as the effective owners of it, whether or not they can show legal title to it. Djilas, who was imprisoned for his views, claimed that the bureaucratic and managerial élites of socialist countries are able to use the collective property of the state for personal ends by virtue of their political offices. Whereas orthodox Marxists hold that economic control leads to political power, Djilas suggested that under communism the situation was reversed because those in office use political power to gain economic control. Few East European sociologists, though generally willing to acknowledge the existence of privileged and under-privileged strata in their societies, would agree with Djilas's analysis. They claim that the crucial difference between the stratum of well-to-do managers and bureaucrats in socialist society and the bourgeoisie in capitalist society is that although both may enjoy the fruits of property, the former cannot pass this property on to their offspring, whereas the latter can. Because under socialism property ownership is still vested in the state, men's privileges must derive from the *offices* they hold, and office is not transferable from father to son. The élite is continuously being replaced from outside its own ranks through the process of social mobility, and it is this fact which prevents the emergence of a hereditary property-owning class, having permanence over time and displaying a distinctive set of manners and rituals such as we find at the apex of capitalist society.

One must acknowledge the force of this argument that property relations have different implications for the class system of the two types of society. However, the fact that the managerial and bureaucratic élite in East European countries cannot hand on the property they control does not, of course, prevent them from conferring other advantages on their children. Most important of all, perhaps, are the advantages of higher education. Although the universities and colleges do, as we have seen, contain a relatively high proportion of students from poorer homes, there appears to be a definite tendency for those who come from privileged homes to fare better

[1] Milovan Djilas, *The New Class*, Thames and Hudson, 1967.

in the competition for academic honours. Working-class students tend to have higher failure rates and somewhat lower levels of achievement than students of white-collar background. This is partly a matter of differences in the ability to provide material support, and partly a matter of differences in motivation and cultural absorption. The fact that family or origin can have an important effect on a student's educational success (and hence on his occupational career) means that there will inevitably be some tendency for the élites in socialist countries to be self-recruiting. Lack of property notwithstanding, the likelihood of sons of well placed members of society ending up as manual workers is not very great. This is especially true now that East European states have gradually abolished the discriminatory practices in education that were such a distinctive feature of early socialist rule. Now that middle-class children are free to compete with the children of the working-class for academic honours, we may expect to find that the social composition of the student population will change over time as the former's material and motivational advantages begin to make themselves felt. In the Soviet Union this already seems to have occurred. Studies carried out in the mid-1960s have shown that children of peasants and unskilled workers not only have poorer academic records than other children, but also tend to enter less prestigious institutes, such as schools of mining and agriculture. Medical schools and the top scientific institutes in Moscow, Kiev and Leningrad, are more likely to be dominated by children of the middle-class élite. Low stipends and the fact that vacations are too short to enable students to work their way through college, puts those from poorer homes at a relative disadvantage. The evidence now suggests that, due to these and similar handicaps, working-class children in the Soviet Union are less upwardly mobile than they formerly were. As a result, the working-class (especially the unskilled) is virtually self-recruiting. An investigation in a large Leningrad factory revealed that of the 692 persons in the sample, 653 were offspring of workers and peasants. A survey in Sverdlovsk showed that 57% of workers' children themselves became workers, while 75% of white-collar specialists' children followed in their fathers' footsteps. All this suggests that the opportunities for those of lowly background to rise in the Soviet social order are gradually tailing off. No less important is the fact that the sons and daughters of the well-to-do seem to retain their positions fairly successfully, due in the main to their educational advantages.

As far as Eastern Europe is concerned, it seems unlikely that opportunities for upward mobility will be severely curtailed for some time to come. Industrial expansion in these countries will create far more white-collar jobs than could be filled by offspring of the present middle-class. Large numbers of bright and ambitious children from peasant and worker families will continue to be creamed off for middle-class careers, without there having to be a corresponding amount of downward mobility. This combination of high upward and low downward mobility is a feature of any society with an expanding industrial base, and may be seen as an important element making for internal political stability. Opportunities for movement up the social order serve as a kind of 'safety-valve' for ambitious or talented members of lower social strata who might otherwise express discontent if they were kept in an underprivileged position. An open opportunity structure encourages men to support the social system by demonstrating that rewards are available to those willing and able to make the necessary effort to succeed. In this respect European socialist states have created a source of political stability quite apart from that provided by the apparatus of coercion. As less and less use is made of the system of police repression, men's loyalty to the socialist order will have to be courted more and more by reliance on the system of material and social rewards, much in the way that it is in Western societies.

The Outlook for the Socialist Countries

The present stress on educational success and occupational achievement may in the long run pose certain problems for the socialist countries. The evidence suggests that high expectations of white-collar and professional employment are widespread among young people and their parents. A Jugoslav survey reported that about 70% of manual workers wanted their children to enter non-manual jobs requiring higher education, and similar ambitions have been implanted in the young themselves by the educational system. The danger for socialist societies is that, because of the large numbers entering universities and similar institutes of higher learning, well qualified people may be unable to find suitable posts. When rates of upward mobility begin to decline, through greater self-recruitment on the part of the middle-class and through levelling off in the expansion of the non-manual sector, then graduate unemployment could become a serious prospect. There is in particular the possibility that many low status youths will be frustrated in their high ambitions as a result of being 'over-socialised' in the ethic of achievement. If they begin to perceive their societies as marking them out as relative failures, with little prospect of advancement, then it is quite likely that the same kind of disenchantment and rebelliousness will occur among lower status youth in East European countries that is such a common feature in the West. Juvenile delinquency and 'hooliganism' have already appeared in the socialist states, although on a relatively limited scale. As in the West, this form of behaviour is typically a response of working-class youths to various social frustrations and deprivations, but it is a form of protest which has little real political significance. More serious perhaps is the type of protest behaviour shown by middle-class youths, university students in particular. This tends to be more political in character, aimed as it generally is against restrictions on free speech and civil liberties. In many of the East European states, including the Soviet Union, students and young intellectuals now appear to provide one of the major sources of opposition to authoritarian rule. In Poland, Hungary and Czechoslovakia students were in the forefront of the movement which brought down Stalinist leaders and had them replaced by more liberal elements. It is worth pointing out, in conclusion, that these opposition movements have rarely if ever contained demands for a return to the old pre-war order; almost always the political appeal has been for a system based on the more humanitarian and liberal ideals of 'pure' socialism. This suggests that political evolution in Eastern Europe is much more likely to take the form of variations on the socialist theme, rather than any drastic reversal to a capitalist type system. Jugoslavia has already suggested possible lines of development with its experiments in decentralisation and industrial democracy. Czechoslovakia was rapidly introducing the kind of social and political reforms which would have made it unique among socialist states. The Soviet intervention of August 1968 was not merely a tragedy for the Czechoslovak people; it was a tragedy for all those who looked to the new reforms as the first confirmation that socialism and democracy were compatible. If this experiment had been allowed to proceed, we might now have in Europe a type of society that could serve as a possible model of change for social systems on either side of the Iron Curtain.

FURTHER READING

Bendix, Reinhard and Lipset, Seymour M. *Class, Status and Power*, Free Press, New York, 1966.

Black, Cyril E. *The Transformation of Russian Society*, Harvard Univ. Press, Cambridge, Mass. 1960.

Djilas, Milovan. *The New Class*, Frederick A. Praeger, New York, 1957; Allen and Unwin, London, 1966.

Inkeles, Alex and Geiger, Kent (eds.) *Soviet Society*, Houghton Mifflin, Boston, Mass.; Constable, London, 1961; with Bauer, Raymond A. *The Soviet Citizen*, Harvard Univ. Press, Boston, Mass., 1959; Oxford Univ. Press, London, 1960.

Ionescu, Ghita. *The Politics of the European Communist States*, Weidenfeld and Nicolson, London; Frederick A. Praeger, New York, 1967.

Parkin, Frank. *Class Inequality and Political Order*, MacGibbon and Kee; Granada Books, 1970.

FRANK PARKIN. Lecturer in Sociology at the University of Kent at Canterbury. One-time Fellow at the Institute of Industrial Relations at the University of British Columbia. Author of *Middle Class Radicalism* (1968). His comparative study of capitalist and communist stratification systems, *Class Inequalities and Political Order* is to be published in 1970.

LAW, LEGALITY AND PENOLOGY

E. L. JOHNSON

LAW

General

In structure, terminology and technique the legal systems of Eastern Europe have an affinity with the legal systems of Western Europe and Latin America in that their basic concepts and principles are derived from the Roman Civil Law; systems so derived are known generically as civil law systems to distinguish them from the common law systems of England, Ireland, the USA and other English-speaking countries. In their content however, the civil law systems of Eastern Europe differ from those of Western Europe and Latin America in that they bear the imprint of the Marxist political and economic doctrines in favour with the ruling circles in their respective countries.

In the Soviet Union the old legal order perished almost completely with the Revolution of October 1917. In the other countries of Eastern Europe the break with the old legal order was not so drastic; as these countries were gradually Sovietised after 1945 there was no abrogation of the old laws *en bloc*, though many old laws were much amended by the new governments, and many others were replaced by new legislation, which often closely followed Soviet models. But even now the process is not complete; in most Eastern European countries other than the Soviet Union certain enactments originally promulgated by former regimes are still in force. The break with the past having been less violent, certain older traditions have still been preserved, particularly in Poland and Hungary. For example, in Poland the land has not been nationalised as in the Soviet Union and other East European countries in deference to the long Polish traditions of peasant ownership of the soil.

Court structure

Despite variations in detail the system of courts is essentially similar in all the countries of Eastern Europe. In each locality there is a court, usually termed a People's Court, which hears the majority of civil and criminal cases at first instance. A case is tried by a judge sitting with two People's Assessors, the latter being laymen who serve in that capacity for a period of about a fortnight each year, and who are considered to form the popular element in the administration of justice represented elsewhere by juries. Above the People's Courts are Provincial Courts, usually sitting in the provincial capitals. They hear particularly serious criminal cases and particularly important civil cases at first instance, and when sitting as courts of first instance the case is heard by a professional judge and two People's Assessors, as in the People's Courts;

they also hear appeals from the decisions of the People's Courts, appeals being determined by a bench of three professional judges. Above the Provincial Courts are the Supreme Courts: the Supreme Courts hear appeals from the Provincial Courts when sitting as courts of first instance, and also applications for the review of decisions of Provincial Courts when acting as courts of appeal from the People's Courts. Applications for review differ from appeals in four ways: (1) an appeal may be brought as of right whereas an application for review may be lodged only by certain official persons, such as procurators, or by judges of the reviewing court, though persons aggrieved by decisions against which no appeal will lie may petition such officials to apply for a review; (2) such an application may be lodged without the consent or against the wishes of the parties to the dispute; (3) an appeal may be brought on the grounds that the lower court either came to a wrong conclusion of fact or misapplied the law, whereas an application for review may generally be brought only on the grounds that the law was wrongly applied, and only in the most exceptional cases on the ground that there was a wrong determination of fact; (4) an appeal may be brought only within a limited period of time, whereas, subject to certain exceptions, an application for review may be brought at any time after the judgment or sentence has come into force. In some cases applications can be made for the review of a decision of a Supreme Court by a differently constituted bench of the same Supreme Court.

The Soviet Union and Jugoslavia are federal states, and each constituent republic has a Supreme Court: in addition there is a Supreme Court of the union, which hears applications for the review of decisions of the Supreme Courts of the republics, though such applications usually lie only where it is alleged that the Supreme Court of the republic has violated or wrongly applied all-union or federal legislation as distinct from the legislation of the republic concerned. (Details of the federal courts structure in the newly established Czechoslovak federation were not available at the time of writing. Doubtless, the Czechoslovak pattern will not have diverged significantly from the Soviet or the Jugoslav.)

Court procedure

Court procedure is of a kind more familiar to the civil lawyers of Western Europe than to common law lawyers. Prior to the open trial the court meets in closed session to determine preliminary matters such as the order in which witnesses are to be called. Witnesses are questioned by the judge more than by counsel for the parties, though counsel for the parties is afforded an opportunity for putting questions to them. If the judge and the two People's Assessors are not unanimous this dissent is not revealed in public, the opinion of the majority forming the judgment of the court. A dissenting judge or assessor, however, may write a dissenting opinion which will be attached to the official record of the case, and this will be available to an appellate or review court should the case go to appeal or review. Formal rules of evidence hardly exist, though hearsay evidence is recognised as unreliable. In criminal cases there is nothing equivalent to a plea of guilty: if the accused admits his guilt, evidence of the circumstances is heard from other witnesses before the court reaches its conclusions. There is no formal distinction between verdict and sentence, both being determined by the judge and the two People's Assessors acting together. In civil cases the compromise or settlement of a case pending trial sometimes requires the permission or approval of the court.

The legal profession

Unlike the position in West European countries, judges are in principle elected, though the elections have not always been held regularly. The appointment is not permanent, being usually for a period of a few years, though reelection or reappointment is possible. In most East European countries, though not in the Soviet Union, only persons with certain qualifications, usually including a university degree in law, may be elected.

In the Soviet Union and in some other East European countries the representation of parties in civil cases, and of the accused in criminal cases, is undertaken by advocates who are members both of a Bar Association and of a particular legal advice bureau established by the Bar Association. Clients usually pay the fee direct to the legal advice bureau and not to the particular advocate. In some countries advocates practise on their own as in Western Europe, in others both individual practice and practice as a member of a legal advice bureau is permitted. Because of party regimentation and possibilities of supervision and pressures afforded by the system of legal advice bureaux, the bar has not always managed to maintain high standards of independence and of ethical professional conduct; nevertheless, it has sometimes come under suspicion of lack of sufficient loyalty to the regime.

In addition to the advocates, there are two other kinds of legal practitioners prominent in Eastern Europe, notaries and jurisconsults. Notaries, organised in a state notarial service, are responsible for authenticating legal documents, such as contracts, wills, leases, sales of certain types of property (houses and cars), and gifts above a certain amount in value, for issuing the necessary documents of title to heirs who have inherited property, and for supervising the administration of the estates of deceased persons generally. An appeal can be taken from a notary's decision (for example, against a refusal to authenticate or issue a document) to the People's Court. In exceptional cases notaries may authorise the levying of execution without any court proceedings on a person who has failed to fulfil a contract, for example on a person who has not paid his telephone bill. The jurisconsults are the salaried legal advisers to government departments and to the public corporations responsible for the running of nationalised industries and commercial undertakings. The term, jurist, is used to denote anyone with a university degree in law whatever branch of the legal profession he may practise in: it therefore covers judges, procurators, advocates, notaries, jurisconsults and teachers of law.

The substantive law

The substantive law is officially divided into a number of branches, each of which has certain general principles running through the whole of that branch. These branches are in the Soviet Union: constitutional law, administrative law, civil law, family law, criminal law, criminal procedure, civil procedure, the judicial system, labour law, land law, collective farm law and financial law. In addition to 'branches' of law certain 'complexes' are generally recognised; these are fields of law relating to one specific subject, the rules being derived from different 'branches': for example, maritime law and air law are concerned with maritime and air navigation respectively, but their rules are drawn from different branches, in particular from administrative law, (for example, organisation of the shipping or air line) civil law (contracts for the carriage of passengers and goods) criminal law (breaches of safety regulations) and labour law (pilots' and crews' entitlement to holidays and rest periods, disciplinary liability for loss and damage caused to the line by their negligence). The most important 'complex' is economic law: this complex, derived from administrative and civil law, governs the state-controlled public corporations which are responsible for most industrial and commercial activities in socialist countries. The rules governing their organisation and administration (and their subordination to higher authorities, in particular the planning authorities) are derived from administrative law, while the rules concerning their contracts between themselves are derived from civil law. In Czechoslovakia and East Germany economic law is recognised as a separate branch of law as distinct from a complex, and a considerable body of legal opinion in the Soviet Union has long advocated the recognition of economic law as an independent branch of law. To the common lawyer, used to thinking of 'law' as a whole, and accepting only a broad distinction between civil and criminal law and regarding other classifications as having merely conventional or academic value, the division of the law into rigidly distinct 'branches' is unfamiliar: to the Western civil lawyer, more familiar with these distinctions, the most striking feature is the recognition of family law and land law as branches of law distinct from civil law.

The nationalisation of large (and, in the Soviet Union, virtually all) industrial and commercial enterprises and the entrusting of their management to state-owned public corporations has meant that a type of commercial dispute which often leads to litigation in the West (for example, a buyer's complaint that goods delivered by the seller do not come up to the contract specifications) commonly arises between the public corporations themselves. The settlement of disputes between public corporations has been withdrawn from the ordinary courts and submitted to special arbitration tribunals, which are of two kinds: departmental arbitration tribunals, which hear disputes between corporations both of which are ultimately subject to the same ministry or other governmental authority, and state arbitration tribunals, which decide disputes between public corporations subject to different administrative authorities. In so far as they decide cases arising from breaches of commercial contracts these arbitration tribunals may be compared to the commercial courts of countries such as France and Spain, except that they do not sit in public; they are unlike them, however, in that they have another function which exists by reason of the planned nature of the economy. Plans for production and distribution are decided by central planning authorities, and planning may require public corporations to enter into certain contracts with others. There may thus be a legal requirement, arising under administrative law, to conclude a contract with another public corporation. The planning directive is commonly of a general nature, and if the parties cannot agree on the details of their contract a pre-contract dispute arises between them which can be settled by the appropriate arbitration tribunal. Such pre-contract disputes commonly concern matters such as assortment and delivery dates: the prices at which goods must be delivered or services paid for are in most cases determined by the planning or other price-fixing authorities. In cases before the arbitration tribunals the parties are often represented by their jurisconsults. The arbitration tribunals have no jurisdiction over individuals: disputes between an individual and a public corporation (arising, for example, over goods bought in a nationalised retail shop) go to the ordinary courts exercising civil jurisdiction.

A second specific feature of the legal systems of Eastern Europe consists in the wide range of powers conferred on the procurators. Procurators in Western Europe are (and in Eastern Europe prior to Sovietisation were) salaried officials whose duty it is to prosecute in the courts persons accused of criminal offences, and to represent the state in civil proceedings where its interests may be concerned. They have little to do with matters of civil law affecting private individuals apart from cases in which it is alleged that a marriage is void (for example, because one of the parties was already married, or because the parties were within the prohibited degrees of consanguinity or affinity). Procurators in Eastern Europe, too, exercise these functions, and many others besides. It is their duty to bring all apparent breaches of the law to the notice of some higher authority, and the prosecution of persons accused of criminal offences is merely one aspect of this general duty. Another aspect, already mentioned, is their duty to apply to higher courts for a review of civil and criminal cases decided in lower courts where the procurator considers that the law was not properly applied; thus, in criminal cases the procurator may ask for a review on the grounds that the accused was wrongfully convicted or acquitted, or that the sentence was more severe or less severe than that permitted by law, or that the accused was convicted of a different offence from the one which it appeared on the facts that he had committed. The procurator asks for a review, not in the interest of either prosecution or defence, but in the general interest of legality. A third important function of the procurator is the protesting to higher authority of decrees and bye-laws where these exceed the powers of the authority purporting to issue them (in the terminology of the common law, protesting *ultra vires* decrees and bye-laws). It will be noted that the final decision does not in any case depend on the procurator: he prosecutes a person accused of crime, but the court decides the question of guilt; he applies for a decision of a lower court to be reviewed, but it is the reviewing court which decides whether the lower court's judgment was correct in law; he protests a decree to a higher authority, but it is for the higher authority to decide whether the decree is in fact *ultra vires* the lower authority. Where the procurator's protest is not sustained, it is open to a procurator of higher rank to protest to a still higher authority, should a higher procurator think fit to do so. Another function of the procurators is to visit prisons and detention camps to ensure that no one is detained in them after the term of his sentence has expired, and to satisfy himself that there are no other examples of illegality in such places. The procuracy is highly centralised and quite independent of all other authorities, its members being subject only to the legislature. This gives it in theory complete independence of ministries and local government authorities; this is considered necessary because it may be the duty of the procuracy to protest illegal orders and decrees issued by such authorities. In fact, however, it is often subject to party or police orders, especially in political cases. Preliminary investigations into cases of more serious crime are also conducted by the procurators (in less serious cases the preliminary investigations are conducted by the police or by some other authority). A career in the procuracy appears to be a common ambition among law graduates who have obtained high honours at university, particularly in the Soviet Union. The procuracy, therefore, usually has the cream of legal talent available to it.

The third specific feature of the East European systems consists in the degree of supervision and control which is exercised over the press, radio and television, stage and cinema. Strict censorship of the press is the rule, though press censorship has been much relaxed of late years in Jugoslavia, and, during the Dubček period, was also (28 June 1968) abolished in Czechoslovakia but was reintroduced after the invasion by the Warsaw Pact countries. Together with control of the mass media of information and entertainment goes control of societies and organisations. Permission usually has to be obtained for the formation of such societies and organisations, and for them to hold meetings and conferences. Religious organisations in particular are subject to strict legal control.

LEGALITY

Legality may be purely formal, in the sense that all acts of state agencies and officials are in conformity with the existing law. Material legality, or the rule of law as it is often termed, implies, in addition to formal legality, the existence of a legal system which is complete in the sense that there are no wide areas in which administrative discretion may interfere with the established legitimate interests of citizens, which contains adequate safeguards against illegal action by persons acting or purporting to act in the interests of the state together with adequate remedies of a political, judicial or administrative nature where such illegal actions have in fact taken place, and which gives effect to certain basic principles of modern civilised society, such as the equality of all citizens before the law, freedom from arbitrary arrest and detention, freedom of speech, the presumption of innocence, the independence of the judiciary, the openness of court hearings and the right of an accused person to be represented by defence counsel.

It is now accepted in both East and West that in the past the legal systems of the East European countries have failed to provide sufficient guarantees of both formal and material legality. In the Soviet Union the well known widespread breakdown of both formal and material legality under Stalin is now attributed to the 'cult of personality' then prevalent. There was a similar lack of legality in the other countries of Eastern Europe after communist governments had been installed during the period 1945–8.

Since 1953 the Soviet legal system has been largely remodelled; new Basic Principles of Criminal Law and Procedure on an all-union level appeared in 1958 and new Codes of Criminal Law and new Codes of Criminal Procedure replaced the older ones in all the union republics during the period 1959–61. The powers of the security police under the Committee on State Security (KGB) have been drastically reduced and the powers of the procuracy, the official body concerned with the protection of legality, have been increased. Yet it appears that the movement in the direction of greater formal and material legality had passed its peak by 1966: the reports available of the trials of the writers, Daniel and Sinyavsky, in 1966, and of many Ukrainian writers and intellectuals in the same year and of the administrative measures taken in the last three years against members of minority religious groups, such as Jews, Baptists and Pentecostalists, suggest that the authorities are now more prepared to disregard formal legality than they were in the opening years of the decade. It is significant that the protest movement of Russian and Ukrainian writers and intellectuals in the Soviet Union stresses legality strongly; the demand is not for new laws, but for the proper observance by the authorities of existing Soviet laws. Moreover, certain recent laws appear to be making inroads on material legality, though only to a very limited extent if comparison is made with the position during the Stalin era.

PENOLOGY

Marxism had no special theories of criminology or penology. In the early years after the Russian Revolution the Soviet authorities, influenced to a considerable extent by the writings of the Italian penologist, Ferri, tried to eliminate the concept of moral guilt from criminal law, for this was in accordance with the Marxist belief that the causes of crime lay in the exploitation of one class by another. At the same time it was necessary to protect society against anti-social acts and a double standard arose: offences committed by class enemies, genuinely or supposedly hostile to the Soviet state, were repressed with the utmost severity, while measures of reeducation were applied to delinquent workers. The Criminal Code of 1926 referred, not to punishment, but to 'measures of social defence' and explicitly stated:

> Measures of social defence shall not have as their object the infliction of physical suffering or personal humiliation. The question of retaliation or punishment does not arise.

In 1935 the term, punishment, came into use again and harsh measures of repression were widely used on the ground that crime was a form of the class-struggle directed against the Soviet state. The gross abuses of the Stalin period led to a thorough reshaping of the criminal law during the period 1958–61, the main features of which were the provision of lighter penalties for offences of comparatively little social danger, the abolition of some minor criminal offences altogether or their reduction to the status of mere 'disciplinary offences' to be dealt with by the offender's employer, or of 'administrative offences' punishable by a small fine imposed by a local government authority, with a right of appeal to a People's Court, and an extension of the powers of the judges to impose punishments below the legal *minima* where the social danger represented by the offender or the offence is negligible, and to impose suspended sentences (probation). The maximum period of deprivation of liberty was reduced, with a few exceptions, from 25 to 15 years. The trend was towards leniency with much emphasis on the reeducational role of punishment in enabling the offender to prepare himself for reintegration in society. As it was announced that society was about to enter a period in which there would be full-scale development towards communism, it was felt that crime would rapidly diminish as the conditions which favoured its existence disappeared, with greater rises in the standard of living and of further development of education. This did not happen: the leniency of the courts and their readiness to grant suspended sentences led to an actual increase of crime in some areas, and a reaction in favour of greater severity set in almost immediately (1961–2), and penalties were then increased for a wide range of offences. This was something of a disappointment for the theorists, who seem to have fallen victims of their own propaganda about the inevitable reduction in crime and the resulting possibility of relaxing severity as society moved into the period of constructing communism. In recent years serious attempts to study the causes of crime have been undertaken and, while 'survival of capitalism in the minds of the people' is still cited as one of these causes, it is no longer regarded as the only one. Low standards of housing and education are recognised as contributing to crime, and the misuse of alcohol is regarded as one of the most important contributory factors. Gambling, often associated with crime in the West, is seldom mentioned by Soviet authors in this connection, though they do refer to the excessive indulgence of parents towards their children, a factor which tends to be overlooked in the West.

Leniency is still widely extended towards first offenders and others whose offences are comparatively trivial, though the 'leniency' is relative to former Soviet practice; the sentences of Soviet courts commonly appear severe to those familiar with Anglo-American and West European practice; but very severe measures are applied to habitual criminals and to those whose offences appear to the authorities to have been motivated by political opposition to the Soviet regime, as for example, five years deprivation of liberty in a corrective labour camp with strict regime for Gerald Brooke, the English lecturer convicted of introducing anti-Soviet émigré literature into the country, seven and five years deprivation of liberty in a corrective labour camp with strict regime for the writers, Sinyavsky and Daniel, convicted of having conducted anti-Soviet propaganda by publishing fiction in Western Europe.

The death penalty

The death penalty requires a special note. It was little used in Russia in medieval times, but became the normal punishment for a wide range of offences during the 17th century. Enlightened opinion in the 18th century was strongly opposed to the death penalty, and it was abolished in 1754. Shortly afterwards it was restored, but for offences of a political nature only, and this remained the position until 1917. In 1917 the death penalty was abolished by the provisional government under Kerenski. It was restored by the Bolsheviks after the October Revolution of 1917, although in principle they were firmly against it. The following year it was first abolished and then restored. In 1919 it was again abolished and restored, but this time it was restored for political offences only, and this remained the position until 1932, when it was extended to large-scale thefts of state property. In 1947 the death penalty was again abolished, and this time the abolition was accompanied by widespread propaganda emphasising the humanitarian nature of the Soviet penal system. It was, however, restored again in 1950 for treason, espionage, sabotage, banditry and terrorism (political assassination), and extended in 1954 to murder with aggravating circumstances. It was extended to a much wider range of offences in 1961 and 1962, but nevertheless in principle the Soviet leadership remains opposed to it; the Programme of the Communist Party of the Soviet Union of 1961 promises its eventual abolition, and the Basic Principles of Criminal Legislation of the USSR and of union republics of 1958 refer to the death penalty as an 'exceptional penal measure, pending its complete abolition'. Despite theoretical objections on the ground that the purpose of punishment is the reformation of the offender, the maintenance of capital punishment is justified by the Soviet leadership on the ground of 'capitalist encirclement' with its attendant dangers to the whole Soviet system. As criminal statistics are not published in the Soviet Union, it is not known to what extent capital punishment is used in practice; but there is reason to believe that since 1961 over 200 persons have been executed for economic offences (large-scale thefts, frauds and currency offences) alone.

The punishments which can be imposed by Soviet criminal courts are of three kinds: basic, mixed and supplementary. Supplementary punishments are imposed only in addition to a basic punishment. Mixed punishments can be imposed on their own as a basic punishment or as a supplementary punishment. The basic punishments are death, deprivation of liberty, corrective labour without deprivation of liberty, and social censure. The mixed punishments are: exile, banishment, disqualifications from holding certain positions or engaging in certain occupations, fines, dismissal from office and making amends for the harm caused. Confiscation of property and deprivation of rank are the supplementary punishments.

Some of these terms require explanation. The death penalty is carried out by shooting, and can be imposed for 14 separate offences: in some of these cases it can be imposed only where the offence is of a particularly serious kind or where the perpetrator has a long criminal record. The death sentence is never mandatory; the court always has the option of imposing a sentence of deprivation of liberty.

Deprivation of liberty may extend from three months to 15 years, and the sentence is normally served in a corrective labour colony. There are four types of corrective labour colony, with increasingly severe regimes: general, strict, very strict and special. Most offenders are sent to corrective labour colonies of the general or strict type: those with the very strict regime are for political prisoners and offenders who have served at least two previous sentences in corrective labour colonies, and those with the special regime for particularly dangerous habitual criminals. There are also corrective labour colony-settlements, with a milder regime, to which offenders who have shown signs of reformation may be sent to complete sentences already partly served in ordinary corrective labour colonies. The conditions in camps vary widely, but can be extremely bad even in general regime camps, particularly as regards the inhumanly small rations (2,400 calories per day, 1,300 as the punishment ration).

Corrective labour without deprivation of liberty is an innovation of the Soviet regime, and is a punishment widely imposed for minor offences instead of fines, which are comparatively little used except in the case of disabled persons or those above working age. The period of corrective labour without deprivation of liberty may range from one month to one year: the offender is required either to continue in his ordinary occupation, or to take some specified job in his district of residence, and a proportion of from 5% to 20% of his wages is made payable to the state (the punishment thus having the effect of a fine), and the period of corrective labour does not rank as employment for purposes of apprenticeship or seniority based on long-term service. Supervision over persons serving such sentences is exercised either by special commissions or by trade union or other authorities at the place of work. Soviet authorities have recently shown great interest in the work of the probation officers in the UK, though as yet there is no exact equivalent in Eastern Europe.

A person sentenced to social censure may be required to have the fact advertised in the press or in other ways at his own expense.

Exile means an obligation to transfer one's residence to a specified area, commonly in Siberia or the Far North. The exile lives as a free person, though he may find the opportunities for employment in his place of exile limited to activities such as forestry or lumbering. The duration of the sentence is from two to five years, and this punishment is commonly ordered to follow a long period of deprivation of liberty in the case of persons convicted of very serious offences.

Banishment, which also may last from two to five years, means a prohibition from living in a certain place or places. This punishment often takes the form of a prohibition from residing in the five largest cities in the country for the period in question. Subject to the terms of the sentence, the offender may take up residence in any place where he can obtain employment. Exile and banishment are now less frequently employed than formerly, but still operate on a large scale.

Confiscation of property may be of the whole or of a portion of the property of the person convicted. Confiscation of the whole is commonly ordered when the death penalty or a long term of deprivation of liberty is imposed. On convictions for offences such as fraud and embezzlement that part of the accused's property which was acquired with the proceeds of the offence is commonly confiscated.

There are elaborate provisions concerning reduction of sentence where the person serving it gives evidence of reformation by conscientious work and exemplary conduct, though such reduction of sentence is not possible in all cases.

Prisons are used in the Soviet Union mainly for the detention of persons awaiting trial: however, certain categories of offenders, such as particularly dangerous habitual criminals, may be sentenced to spend the whole or part of their term of deprivation of liberty in a prison, and persons serving a sentence in a corrective labour camp who deliberately violate camp discipline may be condemned to serve up to three years of their sentence in a prison.

During the period 1945–53 the other countries of Eastern Europe followed Soviet patterns fairly closely. Since 1953, and particularly since 1960, they have diverged from the Soviet model, though not all in the same ways or to the same extent. A greater degree of sophistication and a closer contact with Western criminological and penological literature have resulted, in general, in more lenient treatment for the offender, particularly for the non-political offender. Detention in corrective labour camps and corrective labour without deprivation of liberty are, however, widely used as penal measures. Exile, banishment and fines are little used, and the death penalty is not provided for such an extensive range of offences as in the Soviet Union. Poland is exceptional in that ordinary prisons are used more than labour colonies, that life imprisonment is possible for some offences, and that fines are more extensively used than in the other countries concerned: corrective labour without deprivation of liberty is seldom imposed except in the case of non-payment of fines. Moreover, in Poland, deprivation of liberty may take the form either of imprisonment or of detention; the latter, from one week to five years, is a milder form of deprivation of liberty which apparently carries considerably less social stigma than actual imprisonment. In Poland, although there is a very wide range of offences for which the death penalty may be imposed, it appears that it is little used in practice; eight persons were sentenced to death in Poland in 1963 and six in 1964, and in some of these cases the sentence was later commuted. A Draft Penal Code published in 1968 greatly reduced the number of offences for which the death penalty may be imposed, though this Draft Code is still under discussion and may not be adopted in its present form.

Czechoslovakia and Hungary adopted new Criminal Codes in 1961 when new Criminal Codes were being introduced in the Soviet Union: Bulgaria and East Germany adopted new Criminal Codes in 1968 and Rumania followed suit in 1969. The new Rumanian Code abolishes life imprisonment, as does the Polish Draft Code of 1968, though life imprisonment remains possible under the new East German Code. In general it may be said that the new Criminal Codes follow the Soviet tendency of increasing the penalties for recidivists and professional criminals and reducing them for other offenders. Particular attention has been devoted to devising forms of punishment not involving imprisonment, similar in principle to corrective labour without deprivation of liberty under the Soviet Codes.

FURTHER READING

Berman, H. J. *Justice in the USSR*, Harvard Univ. Press, Cambridge, Mass.; Oxford Univ. Press, London, 1963. *Soviet Criminal Law and Procedure*, Harvard Univ. Press, Cambridge, Mass.; Oxford Univ. Press, London, 1966.

Conquest, R. (ed.) *Justice and the Legal System in the USSR*, (Soviet Studies Series), The Bodley Head, London, 1968.

Gsovski, V. and Grzybowski, K. *Government, Law and Courts in the Soviet Union and Eastern Europe*, (2 vols.), Stevens and Sons, London, 1959; Frederick A. Praeger, New York, 1960.

Hazard, J. N. and Shapiro, I. *The Soviet Legal System*, Oceana Publications, New York, 1962.
La Fave, W. R. *Law in the Soviet Society*, Univ. of Illinois Press, Urbana, Ill., 1965.
Labedz, L. and Hayward M. (eds.) *On Trial*, (on the Sinyavsky–Daniel case), Collins, 1967.
Lapenna, I. *State and Law: Soviet and Yugoslav Theory*, Athlone Press, London; Yale Univ. Press, New Haven, Conn. 1964. *Soviet Penal Policy*, Bodley Head, 1968.
Szirmai, Z. (ed.) *Law in Eastern Europe*, (14 vols., 1958–68), Humanities Press, New York, 1958–68.
'Law and Legality in the USSR', special issue of *Problems of Communism*, No. 2, Washington, D.C., 1965.

EDWARD L. JOHNSON. Until his death in 1969 he was reader in Soviet Law in the University of London. In 1967 was exchange scholar at the Faculty of Law, Leningrad University. Author of *Family Law* and co-author (with R. E. F. Smith) of *Russian Social Science Reader*.

SOVIET SOCIAL POLICIES[1]

DIMITRY POSPIELOVSKY

IDEOLOGY AND HISTORY

IDEOLOGICALLY the central aim of Soviet social policies is the withering away of the state and the moulding of the new Soviet man. Lenin in his *The State and Revolution*, written in 1917, predicted the beginning of the process of the withering away of the state *immediately* upon the seizure of power by the proletariat (or rather, by its 'vanguard', the communist party). Lenin emphasised that the very first act of the proletarian socialist state would be to give 'working-men's wages . . . (to all) technicians, foremen, accountants . . . as indeed *all* state officials'. The other principle 'of the first stage of communism (usually called socialism)' was: 'He who does not work shall not eat' (and) 'An equal amount of products for an equal amount of labour'.[2] The higher stage of communism and the complete withering away of the state will be achieved only when society adopts the rule: 'From each according to his ability, to each according to his needs'; i.e. when people become so accustomed to observing the fundamental rules of social intercourse and when their labour has become so productive that they will voluntarily work *according to their ability*. Nowhere does Lenin speak about the time-span between the primary and the final stages of communism. It must, however, have been conceived of as a very brief period, for already in the first stage the running of the state was to be reduced to simple 'accounting and checking . . . (requiring only) knowledge of the four rules of arithmetic'. Thus, Lenin envisaged the new Soviet man as a selfless being, devoted to the socialist society, living under an economically and socially egalitarian system, enjoying no personal privileges and yet being conscientious enough to give the utmost of his talents and energy to working under a system which provided no incentive.

Lenin tried to implement some of these ideas during the so-called War Communism of 1918–21, when money all but ceased to function, enterprises were run or controlled by workers' committees and foodstuffs were acquired from the peasants by the 'surplus-appropriation system'. This was effected by armed convoys which came from the cities to the rural areas, searched the

---

[1] The author of this article has relied heavily on published Soviet sources.

[2] This contradicts the first promise in the same book of equal working-men's wages for all in the first stage. It also contradicts the criteria by which the amount of work was to be measured. If by the narrow Marxist concept of calling only the work directly involved in the production of physical goods 'productive work', then the practice of the first years of Soviet rule, when manual workers received the highest rations and the intellectuals the lowest, is logical. Today the concept is still theoretically in force, but the practice is the reverse of the theory.

peasants' homes, confiscated everything they could lay their hands on and often punished (and sometimes shot) disobedient peasants. Equipped with the simplistic Marxist philosophy, according to which human behaviour can be totally moulded and changed by the socio-economic environment, Lenin believed that once capitalists were liquidated, human behaviour would immediately undergo a change. What followed, however, was industrial chaos with productivity dropping almost to zero and peasants reducing their plots of arable land so as to have no surpluses. In 1921 this situation forced Lenin once again to legalise a controlled market system with limited private enterprise and private farming. Wage differentiation according to skills began to grow, and reached the highest rate of stratification under Stalin, when it received full justification in the Soviet constitution of 1936: 'From each according to his ability, to each according to his work.'

Earlier, in 1931, Stalin had pronounced egalitarianism a heresy. By 1937 the basic wage differentiation between the highest and the lowest paid workers within the metal industry reached 360%.[1] Also, various systems of bonuses and premiums were introduced for fulfilling and overfulfilling the production norms. Improved housing, special rest homes and sanatoriums paid for by the trade unions were granted to the norm-exceeders, while party functionaries and managers became the beneficiaries of special stores with imported textiles at nominal prices and closed restaurants with unobtainable foodstuffs.

The best known of these norm-exceeding movements was the *Stakhanovshchina*, named after a Donets Basin coalminer, Stakhanov, reputed to have cut 102 tons of coal in one shift in 1935. This was, to a considerable extent, a fraud, as Stakhanov's pneumatic pick was assured of a constant supply of compressed air and two timberers were attached exclusively to him to do the pit-propping all the time, whereas under normal conditions the miner would do everything on his own. At regular intervals while working Stakhanov was also served hot food, not provided for ordinary miners. All these facts were concealed from the Soviet miners who were told (along with other workers) to emulate Stakhanov's production rates.

Since 1956 the minimum wages have been considerably raised, and the number of grades on the wage scale reduced from 2,000 to 12. Now the differential in the basic wage scales of industrial workers between the minimum and the maximum is 1 to 2. The fringe benefits mentioned above, however, increase the differences. The 1965 economic reforms, emphasising bonuses and premiums for quality of work fulfilled, the saleability and profitability of goods produced have caused a considerably greater increase in the incomes of administrative and engineering personnel than of ordinary industrial workers. In other words, the reforms are once again increasing income stratification.

Even more glaring are the contrasts between the income of the average person (108 roubles per month in 1968) and that of the 'new class': top university professors, scientists and academicians, high officials, outstanding musicians and leading party-line writers and artists. These incomes are often about 1,000 roubles a month, and in some cases may go up as high as 10,000 to 15,000 roubles a month, i.e. exceeding more than 100 times the wage of an industrial worker. Thus, after marching for 50 years towards communism, where the income distribution should be 'according to needs', the Soviet

[1] F. Hayenko, 'Labour Conditions in the Soviet Union', *Studies on the Soviet Union*, Munich, 1968, 3, p. 4; and Conquest, *Industrial Workers in the USSR*. See Further Reading.

Union can now boast the greatest contrasts in incomes of the whole socialist camp. Even Jugoslavia could hardly be called a competitor. There the highest incomes are earned by citizens engaged in legal private enterprise, whereas in the Soviet Union the contrasts are created by state distribution of wealth. The other East European countries are much more egalitarian. In Bulgaria, for instance, the average income is between 80 and 90 levas per month, while a university professor can earn some 200 levas and an academician up to 400 to 500 levas. In Czechoslovakia the differences used to be even less. A skilled worker could earn up to 2,500 crowns, and a full professor up to 3,000, or 3,500 at the most. (At the time of writing the economic situation in Czechoslovakia was rather unstable and inflationary.)

The Soviet taxation system increases these contrasts even further. Since there are no tax reductions for dependants, an average Soviet worker with three children pays 8% of his wage in income tax, whereas in the UK he would pay 5% and in the USA 7%. But the highest Soviet income tax is only 13% of the salary. The most important are the turnover taxes, which are particularly heavy on food and clothing and much lighter on most of the durables and luxury goods. Thus, the hardest hit of all is the lower income bracket.

This income stratification is also retained in sickness benefits and invalid and old-age pensions, since all these are set as proportions of the past salaries and wages of the recipient. These are discussed in greater detail below.

Medical Care

Undoubtedly Soviet achievements in medicine have been considerable when compared to pre-Revolutionary times. The Soviet Union graduates annually about as many physicians as there were in the whole of the Russian empire at the time of the Bolshevik Revolution, (a rate which is about three times greater than that of the USA). More than one in every five doctors in the world today is a Soviet physician. In 1966 there were over 21 physicians per 10,000 inhabitants in the Soviet Union, the second highest figure in the world after Israel, which in 1963 had 24 per 10,000. However, this figure may be misleading. First, the expanses of land and sparsity of population in the Soviet Union combined with very poor transport and communication facilities, require a considerably higher number of doctors than in the average advanced Western country. On the other hand, life is so difficult in the Soviet countryside and in the smaller towns that the majority try to find employment in one of the capitals or major cities. Hence, there is a constant shortage of professional people, particularly good ones, outside the main centres. This is equally true of doctors. In 1961 the urban average for the whole of the Soviet Union was 27·6 doctors per 10,000 inhabitants, but only 9·8 per 10,000 in the countryside. Further discrepancies exist between the different republics. In the Georgian republic, which enjoys a good climate and one of the highest standards of living in the Union, there are 34 doctors per 10,000 inhabitants. In Kazakhstan there are only 16 per 10,000 inhabitants, although it has a very sparse population, very great distances and poor communications, and thus should require a higher proportion of doctors than the tiny and more advanced republic of Georgia. The lowest rural rate is in Tadzhikistan, where there are seven doctors per 10,000 inhabitants.

The average Soviet doctor has a poorer education than his Western colleague. His training lasts only five-and-a-half years, with a ten-year primary and secondary school preceding. An internship system was started in

1968. As all the new graduates (with some exceptions in special cases or owing to highly placed contacts) are sent by the special state job allocation administration to work for three years in any part of the country, rural and small-town clinics are almost entirely staffed by young inexperienced graduates, who go to the bigger towns as soon as their terms are up.

All medical care is free of charge in the Soviet Union, except for the purchase of medicines; the same is true of the rest of Eastern Europe. The Soviet press is full of complaints about the constant shortage of medicines, particularly in the provinces. Besides working as employees in the state hospitals and clinics, physicians may, and do, keep privately paid practice after hours, and some famous doctors may charge as much as 30 to 50 roubles for such a visit.[1] There are also several private cooperative clinics and some 48 hospitals throughout the country, where the patients have to pay and where they get a much better service from the best doctors, who either work after hours or have retired from state service. Recently a Soviet author recommended the expansion of these hospitals together with the introduction of some nominal fees in government medical establishments, arguing that this would stimulate a more responsible attitude towards medicine on the part of the public and a better service on the part of the doctor, who would get a proportion of each fee. In other words Soviet socialised medicine suffers from the same handicaps as that of the Western welfare states.

In August 1968 a new decree was issued in the Soviet Union. Its two most important features were: medical graduates to undergo one year of internship before they have the right to practise; and tiny ill-equipped rural hospitals to be replaced by larger and better-equipped regional and district hospitals.

One of the most advertised features of the improved Soviet medical care has been the fall in the death rate and the rise in projected longevity. However, the official Soviet figures on these issues should not be taken at their face-value; the same applies to Poland. Both countries lost nearly 20 million of their population (mostly adult and male, who have a shorter natural span of life than women) in World War II, and both had very high bulges immediately after the war. Moreover the Soviet Union lost millions in the pre-war and post-war purges and famines. The figures are as follows[2]:

Country	Age distribution (%)		Death rate per 1,000	
	Below 40	Above 60	1925	1966
USA	65	14	11·8	9·5
UK	57	17	12·5	11·8
Czechoslovakia	60	13	12·2	10·0
Poland	68	11	17·0	7·3
Soviet Union	75	10	22·6	7·3

Obviously, a nation with 75% of its population below 40 years of age should have a record-breakingly low death rate. (Also, there are 20 million more women than men.) The longevity figures, which are a projection into the future of the life expectancy of the generation now being born and based on the past dynamics of deaths, are subject to the same bias.

[1] This is what Mrs. Pasternak had to pay for the visits of two famous doctors to her dying husband.

[2] These figures are based on the population-age data in the 1966 UN *Demographic Yearbook*.

PENSIONS

The Soviet Union is a newcomer to the field of old-age pensions. The current old-age pension system, with some later modifications and improvements, was introduced in 1956. Until then extremely meagre pensions were paid only to invalids and the disabled, or granted for special merit. In fact, a law of 1926 stated:

> Children must provide for the needs of their disabled parents . . . Disabled and needy grandparents have the right to receive support from their children . . .

Since 1956 the pensionable age is 60 for men and 55 for women, with further age privileges for particularly hard or physically harmful work. In order to qualify for a full pension a citizen is required to have had a 25-year employment record (20 for women). The size of the pension depends on the last basic salary scale of the pensioner, being 100% of a wage or salary not exceeding 35 roubles and gradually descending to 50% of the last pay scale if the salary had been 100 or more roubles. The maximum pension is 120 roubles, with the exception of 'personal pensions' granted for meritorious work and responsible office. In these categories are the 'peoples' artistes', 'heroes of labour', party and state officials, members of the Academy of Sciences and other important scholars. These 'personal pensions' have no upper limit and may include a free country house, a car with a chauffeur provided by the state, etc.

State pensions for collective farmers were introduced only with the law of 15 July 1964, which became effective from January 1965. The pensionable age for a male collective farmer is now 65 years, and 60 for females. The equalisation of the retirement age with that of the state workers applied only from 1 January 1968, when the following benefits were also introduced: the minimum annual holiday for workers extended to 15 working days; income tax lowered by 25% for those earning between 61 and 80 roubles (those below 60 pay no tax); those with a permanent working record of eight or more years to receive full pay when temporarily disabled (whereas before they received 90%); those who have worked from five to eight years to receive 80% of their full pay when ill; but the old provision that non-union members' sickness benefit be 50% of the above rate remained in force; the minimum pension for invalids to be raised to 30 roubles a month.

EMPLOYMENT POLICIES

Article 12 of the Soviet Constitution declares: 'Work in the Soviet Union is a duty and a matter of honour for every able-bodied citizen . . . ' This principle has officially been interpreted as the existence of guaranteed full employment by definition. The last official figure for unemployment to appear in the Soviet Union was that for 1 October 1930. There were then 240,000 unemployed persons (not counting the huge agricultural labour surplus). Less than three weeks later the Soviet Government declared that there were no more unemployed throughout the whole country. On 9 October unemployment benefits were suspended once and for all by a decree of the People's Commissariat of Labour. The same decree stated that the unemployed 'should be given jobs not only within their vocational qualifications, but also other work'. Another decree, issued in December 1930, stated that the only legally valid excuses for not accepting a job were illness, lack of dwelling space and separation from one's husband (valid for women only). Thus, a citizen could be forced to work out of his profession and be assigned to work in any part of the country. In addition, wilful departure from work (or refusal to accept a job, without having the above excuses) between 1940 and 1956 was punishable by up to four months' imprisonment.

Until the 1965 economic reforms (which gradually began to be implemented in 1966) enterprises were given orders by the central authorities as to the number of workers to be hired. It used to be advantageous to have constant labour surpluses to make it possible to fulfill the plans at very short notice,[1] as the exact wages were set centrally and funds were allocated to enterprises in accordance with the number of workers employed and the total volume of production in either aggregate nominal rouble value or in aggregate total weight (*valovaya produktsiya*) of goods produced. Thus, there were no incentives for the management to keep the labour force down or to intensify the production rate per worker. This is how 'full' employment was achieved in the Soviet Union.

In 1960 78% of the able-bodied Soviet citizens of working age were employed, in 1965 this rose to 87% and by 1970 the number should rise to 92%. The Soviet argument is that all these rates are above the US figure of about 72%. But the basic difference is that the average US wage is some five times higher than that of the Soviet Union (the UK rate is between two and three times that of the Soviet Union, or probably more, taking into consideration the British fringe benefits). A further consideration is that most US wives are neither working outside the home, nor are they seeking employment. The majority of Soviet university and technical school students work full time and study in the evenings or by correspondence, which adds several million to the working force. In the West the vast majority of students study full time. Nevertheless, the increasing proportion of people employed in the Soviet Union shows that there has been, and still is, some active unemployment there, if we define unemployment as the situation in which people desire work, but are unable to find it locally. In the past few years several Soviet studies have shown that, even in highly industrialised cities with diverse production, it takes an average industrial worker from 20 to 30 or more days to find employment, while he would be given only a two-weeks' pay at the time of release from his previous employment. At the same time heavy overstaffing has such bad effects on work and production morale that a Soviet sociologist recently wrote that it would be more profitable for the economy and national morale to have regular labour exchanges with unemployment benefits, rather than to go on supporting latent unemployment under the guise of full employment. In fact, in the Soviet Union in 1967 State Committees on the Use of Labour Resources were founded, whose functions are the same as those of labour exchanges in the West, with the sole difference that the Soviet committees do not pay any benefits but only help the unemployed to find work.

Although the economic reform makes it profitable for a manager to decrease the number of workers by increasing the quality and quantity of production per man through paying higher wages, it has not yet abolished the old regulation forbidding managers to release redundant labour solely on the grounds of redundancy. The continuing rigid staff-hiring regulations further increase overstaffing. A highly qualified staff member with a salary of

---

[1] This need is caused by the irregularity of supply in the Soviet Union, resulting in high rates of fluctuation in the availability of raw materials and parts arriving from other enterprises to be finished at the given enterprise. Therefore, when these arrive there is frantic activity in the enterprise to have the plan fulfilled after having lost probably several months waiting for the goods.

150 to 160 roubles per month may be hired only together with an additional structural cell (a bureau or a working group), although the latter is often unnecessary. In order to hire a senior engineer, two additional members of staff must be hired as well. But by using roundabout ways, managers have succeeded in rationalising a reduction of labour power since the introduction of the economic reforms, thus creating in the Soviet Union a type of technological unemployment. The only 'privilege' that an unemployed Soviet enjoys over his Western confrère is that his existence is not officially recognised by his own state; and, consequently, he receives no financial support. In Jugoslavia, Czechoslovakia and most other East European countries some unemployment benefits do exist, which is ideologically justifiable since they are still building socialism. However, in the Soviet Union the construction of socialism was allegedly completed in 1936 and the country is moving towards communism.

Conclusion

The official and specified commitment of the country to economic competition with the West, announced by Khrushchev and confirmed by the present leadership, necessitated an overhauling of the economic system of the country. The economic reforms, although severely curbed by the bureaucracy, are its chief expression. The revision of the economic system has created many socio-economic and socio-ideological problems, some of which have been raised and aired in the Soviet press. For instance, the recognition, although somewhat veiled, of unemployment under socialism contradicts almost all the basic ideological assumptions and premises of Marxian economics. The development of a new class structure in the stratification of jobs, wages, material and social incentives and privileges together with the increasing stabilisation of this *status quo* are other such developments totally incompatible with the Marxian ideological model.[1] The facts of life have proved that there is no such thing as the new Soviet man and that the Soviet citizen needs the same incentives as a citizen of any capitalist country. If the Soviet social conditions have changed the Soviet citizen, these changes primarily amount to having taught him how to dodge the multilateral state control of all spheres of human life, and how to bypass the multitudes of restrictive laws and bye-laws. The fantastic resourcefulness of the black market (as often reported in the Soviet press), with the direct or indirect participation of citizens from all walks of life, is the human response to the regimentation of human life, the ideological aim of which has been to mould the citizen into a different, new and socially super-conscious being. To curb the socially harmful effects of the black market the most advanced Soviet reformists have recently suggested the legalisation of limited private and semi-private enterprise.[2] But so far their advice has not been heeded.

One of the great problems about the implementation of the economic reforms, even in their limited form, is the shortage of independent-thinking technologists and administrators. For this the Soviet educational system has been bitterly criticised in the Soviet press for an authoritarianism which frustrates the development of independent thought and initiative.[3]

[1] Marx's universal communist man was to have been a person of many professions and preoccupations: a worker for a few hours, a farmer for a few more, then an artist, then a philosopher, etc. Division of labour was to cease to exist under communism.

[2] Among these proponents could be mentioned Lisichkin, Likhodeyev, Kvasha and many others.

[3] Among the most outspoken critics were Academician Kapitsa, the leading Soviet psychiatrist Academician Snezhnevsky, the leading economist Birman, etc.

It is hardly necessary to add that after 50 years the methods of Soviet state administration are far removed from Lenin's 'four rules of arithmetic'. Indeed, the common cry in the Soviet Union today is that the Soviet administrators, and particularly the economists, need more education, as economics and administration have become so much more complex with the technological revolution.

The other unfulfilled promise has been that of the disappearance of crime and alcoholism under socialism. These were officially claimed to be legacies of the bourgeois past and ever since the 1920s the crime and alcoholism rate is said to be gradually decreasing. In fact, if one added up all the statements to this effect, there should be no crime or heavy drinking left in the country. Yet, the observations of foreign travellers, careful reading of the Soviet press and the unofficial admissions of ordinary Soviet citizens create quite the opposite impression. Further evidence that the crime and alcoholism rate is at least not *decreasing* is suggested by the fact that there have been no absolute figures released on this subject by the Soviet statistical offices since the 1930s. One of the last statistics available showed an 100% growth in the crime rate in Moscow in the three years from 1931 to 1934. The usual Soviet practice is to conceal statistics of ideologically, politically or economically unfavourable phenomena. Still more evidence of the probable growth of crime in the Soviet Union today is the passage of several strict laws on 'hooliganism' and 'parasitism' in the last several years.

To sum up, the Soviet social policy has failed to solve its social problems any more successfully than the Western welfare states. In fact, policy makers have aggravated many of these problems by pretending not to recognise their existence. By pushing them underground they have allowed frustrations to accumulate and emerge 'illegally' without making a proper study of them or learning how to cope with them. Altogether, the Soviet man enjoys no more, and in some cases less, welfare and social benefits than a modern West European. Moreover, many of his problems and needs remain unrecognised by his state.

FURTHER READING

Conquest, Robert. *Industrial Workers in the USSR*, Bodley Head, London; Frederick A. Praeger, New York, 1967.
Field, Mark. *Soviet Socialized Medicine*, The Free Press, New York; Macmillan, London, 1967.
Hazard, John N. *Law and Social Change in the USSR*, Stevens and Sons, London, 1953.
Hendel, Samuel, (ed.) *The Soviet Crucible 1917–1967*, Van Nostrand, Princeton, N.J., 1967.
Juviler, Peter and Morton Henry. *Soviet Policy Making*, Pall Mall Press, London; Frederick A. Praeger, New York, 1967.
Kassof, Allen (ed.) *Prospects for Soviet Society*, Frederick A. Praeger, New York, 1968.
Lyons, Eugene. *Workers' Paradise Lost*, Funk and Wagnalls, New York, 1967.
Schapiro, Leonard (ed.) *The USSR and the Future*, Pall Mall Press, London; Frederick A. Praeger, New York, 1963.
Studies on the Soviet Union, No. 2. *Society and Culture*, Munich, 1967.
Treml, V. (ed.) *The Development of the Soviet Economy*, Frederick A. Praeger, New York, 1968; London, 1969.
Nove, Alec. *The Soviet Economy: An Introduction*, Allen and Unwin, London; Frederick A. Praeger, New York, 1965.

DIMITRY POSPIELOVSKY. Russian economic historian, lecturing at Stanford University and Research Associate at the Hoover Institute. Contributor to many periodicals, currently writing a book on Soviet society since Khrushchev.

SOVIET FAMILY POLICY

DIMITRY POSPIELOVSKY

THE CHANGING ATTITUDES

THE most authoritative Marxist classic on the family is *The Origin of Family, Private Property, and State* by Friedrich Engels.[1] In it Engels advocates marriage based solely on love, placing even temporary sexual infatuations on a pedestal above the principles of matrimonial stability:

> The duration of the urge of individual sex love differs very much according to the individual . . . and a definite cessation of affection or its displacement by a new love, makes separation a blessing for both parties.

He then speaks about:

> freedom in marriage . . . operative only when the abolition of capitalist production and of the property relations . . . has removed all these secondary economic considerations which still exert so powerful an influence on the choice of the partner.

But Engels was very vague on what kind of family, if at all, there would be under communism, stating that he was convinced only of one thing: that the bourgeois family would vanish 'with its hypocrisy'.

How then has the problem of love and marriage been approached in the Soviet Union?

A left-wing Bolshevik female leader, who was one of the foremost theorists on love and marriage at the time, A. Kollontai, wrote that sexual relations are to be carried out:

> *en passant*, in the course of other business, for the satisfaction of biological needs . . . so that the latter would not be in the way of the main business—the activities for the good of the revolution.

Indeed, free love was advocated by many leading Bolsheviks at the time, one of whom was Lenin's intimate lady-friend, Inessa Armand. Some local decrees were even passed attempting to propagate free love legally. One of the most extreme of these was a decree of the Vladimir Regional Council of 1918:

> After 18 years of age every (unmarried) girl becomes state property . . . and must . . . register at the office of 'free love' attached to the Commissariat of (Social) Care.

[1] The accusation in the advocacy of free love has often been advanced by anti-communist authors against the communists on the basis of this ambiguous treatise. But Soviet authors have emphatically rejected these accusations, claiming that Engels advocated only the destruction of the bourgeois family.

The registered girl is given the right to select for herself a cohabitant-husband in the age group of 19 to 50 . . . the right to select from among the girls of 18 years or older is also given to males. Males aged 19 to 50 have the right to select women for themselves, registered with the office, in the interest of the state even if the girls do not agree. Children born as the result of this sort of cohabitation become the property of the state.

Lenin himself opposed these extremist views. In his letters to Inessa Armand he disagreed with the concept of 'freedom of love' and with her statement that, 'even a fleeting passion and intimacy are more poetic and cleaner than kisses without love'. Lenin argued that the contrast is illogical: 'Would it not be better to contrast philistine-intellectual-peasant vulgar and dirty marriage without love, to proletarian civil marriage with love?' Much publicised in the Soviet Union are also Lenin's conversations with Klara Zetkin, in which he protested against the loose morals and promiscuity developing after the Revolution. However, nothing substantial nor authoritative was ever written by Lenin on the subject of sexual relations under socialism and communism or on the family and marriage, to counter the flood of propaganda for free love. A leading Soviet sociologist, A. G. Kharchev, explains this gap by the fact that Lenin had been too busy 'to make a comprehensive public statement on all these questions'. Should not this rather be understood as evidence that Lenin, although opposed to the disintegration of the family as such, never considered the issue sufficiently important to merit serious thought? Besides, how could Lenin convincingly defend the concept of a strong family, when he had once written: 'What is moral is that which serves the cause of destruction of the old society of exploitation'. Having undermined the religious moral values on which the family had been based, the new leaders found themselves unable to replace them by any positive new values which would have been sufficiently stable to strengthen the family. Apart from these ideological factors weakening family ties and morality, there have also been other forces at work with a direct disintegrative effect. On the one hand, the effects of the rapid industrialisation of the 1930s were similar to the experience of other societies. On the other hand, the purges, deportations and executions of whole classes[1] resulted in literally millions of fatherless families and orphans. Most of the latter became known as the *besprizorniki* (the uncared-for), who lived in the streets, dugouts or abandoned houses, engaged in juvenile delinquency and were used by professional criminals as aides or trainees.[2] Soviet dictatorship has further undermined family unity and parental authority by teaching school children to report on their parents if the latter were in any way opposed to the regime. The example of Pavlik Morozov, who denounced his parents and had them executed, is often invoked in Soviet propaganda as an example to be emulated by children.

The other demoralising effect has been the shortage of males which became worse from 1917 to 1945, owing to wars and purges.

[1] Professor Kurganov's calculations are that this resulted in the partial or complete destruction of some 1·5 million bourgeois families, 250,000 families of the intelligentsia, and up to 15% of the peasants, i.e. about three million families. I. A. Kurganov, *Semia v SSSR*, New York, 1967.
[2] Many stories and films appeared in the Soviet Union on this subject. Makarenko's *Pedagogic Poem* is one of the best works on the reeducation of the *besprizorniki*; and one of the best Soviet films on the subject was *A Start in Life*. Kharchev writes that in Petrograd alone 35,000 homeless children were registered between 1918 and 1924 'most of whom had no families'.

THE TOTAL POPULATION OF RUSSIA

1913	139,000,000
1917	143,000,000 (population still increasing despite war losses)
1920	137,000,000 (effect of the civil war, famine and terror; the heaviest losses were obviously in the male population)[1]

The breakdown by sex in the population of the Soviet Union in 1965 was 45·7% males, 54·3% females, i.e. there were roughly 20 million more women in the Soviet Union than men. This disproportion in the sexes has perhaps made it easier for a man to get a wife or a lover and has considerably lowered women's resistance to chance sex-relations. This in turn, aided by the family legislation of 1944 (which will be discussed below) resulted in a dramatic growth of illegitimate children after World War II.

SOVIET FAMILY LEGISLATION

The first Soviet laws on marriage were adopted in 1918. The Soviet minister (people's commissar) of justice, N. Krylenko, stated that the main purpose of this legislation was to undermine the religious marriage. This legislation made the actual procedure of marriage easier. Children were declared equal in rights whether they were born in or out of wedlock, although common law cohabitation of man and woman without a registered marriage was not given the status of legal marriage by this legislation. The reason for this was that at that time the majority of such 'unregistered cohabitations' were in fact church marriages of couples who did not want to undergo 'atheist' registration, particularly because the Russian Orthodox Church had officially 'expressed its negative attitude' to this form of civil marriage. The divorce procedure was greatly facilitated: if only one partner wanted divorce, his or her petition had to go through the local courts, whereas, if both partners wished to divorce, all they had to do was to send a joint statement to the local registry office that they desired a divorce, and it was automatically registered as accomplished. Marriage at the same time was declared free from interference by parents, relatives or any other interested groups. Fatherhood was established by a simple statement at the registry office by the mother or guardian of the child, or by the child itself. Furthermore, on 18 November 1920 abortions were made legal and free of charge if performed at the state hospitals.

The 1926 law on marriage and divorce largely repeated the earlier legislation, only broadening the concept of legal marriage by including under its heading 'factual marriages', i.e. unregistered cohabitations in which 'man and woman, live together and consider their union as being in wedlock, rather than in lewdness'. Professor Kurganov, states that this innovation was brought about by the many cases of church marriages not recognised by the state, where the husbands, married in church only, often left their wives and children for other women, without any legal responsibility for their actions. The 1926 legislation further facilitated the procedure for divorce: from then on it became sufficient for only one partner to send in a written statement of

---

[1] In 1897 there were about one million more women than men; by 1926 the number of women exceeded the number of men by five million; by 1939 the difference increased to 7·2 million, although there were no military conflicts in this period, therefore this last figure could be attributed only to purges. Kurganov, *op. cit.* p. 153.

desired divorce to the registry office, the courts ceased to participate in the divorce procedure.

Naturally, these laws, combined with the social, economic and political instability of the new order, resulted in a tremendous growth both of divorces and of abortions: in Leningrad alone the divorce rate rose from 1·9 per 1,000 inhabitants in 1920 to 11·3 in 1929; while in Moscow by 1934 there were three abortions for one live birth.

The 1934 average for the urban population of the Soviet Union was 375,000 abortions for 574,000 live births; while the countryside—which is normally much more conservative—averaged 324,000 abortions per 243,000 live births in the same year.[1] In 1936, however, abortions were made illegal by new legislation, imposing prison sentences on doctors performing abortions as well as on men encouraging women to undergo an abortion.

A substantial limitation on divorce was introduced in 1944. According to this new decree divorces could be performed only through the courts, whose first responsibility was to try to reconcile the applicants for divorce. At the same time divorce costs were raised considerably, and the court hearings (on two levels: the lower court tried to reconcile and then applied to the upper court for the actual divorce to be either granted or rejected) were made public with necessary witnesses and advance announcements in the local press. As a result of this legislation 'the number of divorces which had reached almost 20% of all the marriages concluded in 1939, fell after the promulgation of the new legislation by over 14 times'. Kharchev, however, admits that the other result of this legislation was 'a great discrepancy between the registered divorces and the number of factual disruptions of marriages'. Also the practice of unregistered couples living together as man and wife became more widespread due to the 1944 legislation which freed the father of all responsibility for an illegitimate child, i.e. a child born out of registered wedlock. Furthermore, a child born out of wedlock could be registered only under the mother's name, even if there was a man willing to give his name to the child. This practice is particularly distressing because of the use of the patronymic in the Soviet Union: a child born out of wedlock after 1944 had no patronymic and thus was doomed to be reminded of his illegitimacy for the rest of his life. As the result of this legislation 'thousands of tragedies have occurred, maiming the lives of women, who are known as "lone mothers", and of their children, who are regarded by the average inhabitant as illegitimate . . .'[2]

Soviet sociologists have since justified the 1936 abolition of legal abortions and the 1944 legislation freeing the male from all responsibility for his illegitimate children on the grounds that it was then necessary in 1936 to increase the birth rate and to make up for war losses. On the other hand, they proposed that as this necessity no longer existed the time had come to change the law. In fact, abortions were made legal again by a decree of 23 November 1955, which is still in force.

But the reforms demanded in the above letter and similar writings were slow to come. A decree of 10 December 1965 confined the divorce procedure

[1] *Izvestiya*, 12 July 1936.
[2] A joint letter demanding a reform in the status of unmarried mothers and their children, which was written by the leading Soviet intellectuals, S. Marshak, Professor Speransky, D. Shostakovich and I. Ehrenburg, in the *Literary Gazette*, 9 October 1956.

to the local court, abolished the necessity to announce the forthcoming divorce hearings in local newspapers, limited the number of written certificates that had to be presented to the court and permitted the courts to use their discretion in establishing the fees for divorce in any particular case.

Finally, on 10 April 1968 there appeared in *Izvestiya* the draft text of the new Soviet legislation on marriage and the family. This draft retains the principle that legality is accorded only to registered marriage. The main improvements are in the field of childbirth out of wedlock, where 'the fatherhood may be established through the courts'. Children born out of wedlock will now once more receive rights equivalent to those born of married parents. If there is no court decision on the identity of the father, the unmarried mother has the right to enter her family name and any patronymic of her choice into the registry rubric related to the father's identity.

The size of alimonies for children of divorced or separated parents remains the same as before—25% of the parents' income for one child, 33% for two children and 50% for three or more children—with the very important difference that the father of an illegitimate child now has to pay the alimonies from which he was exempt under the 1944 legislation.

There is, however, also a section in the new draft legislation which, if loosely interpreted, could be harmful to the integrity of the family. Article 18 asserts that parents 'are obliged to bring up their children in the spirit of the moral code of a builder of communism'. Article 19 gives the courts of law jurisdiction to deprive parents of their rights to their children and to entrust the latter to institutional guardianships if it is established that the parents 'do not fulfil their obligations as to the upbringing of their children'. But, communists and builders of communism by Soviet definition are expected to be atheists. Can, then, this legislation be interpreted as allowing the courts to deprive parents who are active religious believers of their parental rights? Several cases of confiscation of children from their religious parents and sending them to boarding schools were in fact reported in the main atheist journal of the Soviet Union, *Science and Religion*, in 1963–4.[1]

FAMILY LAW IN EASTERN EUROPE

In the other East European countries family law, like the rest of the legislation, has largely been modelled on the Soviet Union, but it has never been as severe on the unmarried mother as the Soviet Code of 1944. Abortions are also legal in all of these countries except Rumania, which, alarmed by its catastrophic drop in the birth rate, banned abortions towards the end of 1966 and virtually prohibited divorce (though these measures were coupled with the introduction of rather generous family allowances). Hungary, on the other hand, tries to combat the world's lowest birth rate by generous childcare allowances and paid maternity leave for working mothers.

[1] When this essay was already in print a document arrived from the USSR signed by nearly 1500 Baptist mothers. It states that the authorities are removing children from the care o believing parents, and depriving the latter of their parental rights on the grounds of the 1968 family legislation. The boarding schools for these children are stated to be full of lice and contagious disease, the children ill, cold and hungry. In other instances it was stated that believing children were not removed from their parents but remain in their original schools, where they are persecuted by their teachers and schoolmates. See Michael Bourdeaux in *The Times* (London), 6 November 1969.

TABLE I
MARRIAGE AND DIVORCE RATE AND POPULATION GROWTH

	Marriages per 1,000 inhabitants			Divorces per 1,000 inhabitants			Net population growth (i.e. death rates subtracted from birth rates)			
	1962	*'64*	*'66*	*1962*	*'64*	*'66*	*1950*	*'60*	*'66*	*'67*
Soviet Union	10·0	8·5	9·0	1·3	1·5	2·8	—	18·0	11·0	10·0
Bulgaria	8·1	8·1	8·2	1·0	1·0	1·0	15·0	9·7	6·6	n.a.
Czechoslovakia	7·8	7·9	8·1	1·2	1·2	1·4	12·0	6·7	5·6	n.a.
Hungary	8·1	8·7	9·1	1·7	1·9	2·0	9·7[1]	4·5	3·6	n.a.
Poland	7·5	7·4	7·2	0·6	0·7	0·8	19·0	14·8	9·4	—
Rumania	9·9	9·0	8·9	2·0	1·9	2·0	—	10·0	6·0	15·0
France	6·7	7·2	6·9	0·7	0·7	—	6·8[1]	6·5	6·8	n.a.
UK	7·4	7·8	8·0	0·6	0·7	—	4·2[1]	6·0	6·1	n.a.
USA	8·5	9·0	9·4	2·2	2·3	2·5	15·0[1]	14·2	9·0	n.a.
West Germany	9·2	8·6	8·0	0·8	1·0	0·9	5·4[1]	6·4	6·5	n.a.

[1] Average annual figure for 1950–54.

Source: The above data have been compiled by the author from several official statistical sources including the *UN Demographic Yearbook* and the Soviet *Narodnoye khoziaystvo* series.

However incomplete the above data may be, they are sufficient to show that the socialist countries can claim neither a higher rate of population growth or marriages, nor more stable marriages than the capitalist countries. Soviet authors have, however, claimed that the marriage rate in the Soviet Union is considerably above that of the capitalist countries and that divorce is dramatically on the increase in the UK. In fact, the rate of marriages has been steadily declining in the Soviet Union since about 1950, when it was 11·6 per 1,000; the slight increase in 1966 is directly related to the coming-of-age of those born in the bulge of the post-war years.

The fact that the net population growth more than doubled in Rumania in 1967 was the direct result of the anti-divorce and anti-abortion measures taken in 1966.

THE SOVIET WOMAN

The decree of 8 July 1944 introduced illegitimate child benefits for unmarried mothers, and these have remained unchanged up to the present time: 5 roubles per month for one child, 7·50 for two and 10 for three or more. The amount is payable only up to the child's twelfth birthday.

If the 'lone mother' is unable to support her children, her only option is to give them up to state orphanages. The decree of 1944 gave also priority places in state children's institutions (crèches, kindergartens, etc.) to children of 'lone mothers' and declared that mothers whose income is 60 roubles or less per month are to pay 50% of the regular fees for the upkeep of their children in these institutions. With the introduction of boarding schools illegitimate children also received priority there.

Soviet family legislation is most generous in its allowance for maternity leaves: as from 1 April 1956, 56 days prior to delivery and 56 days after delivery on full pay. Even the 1944 legislation stipulated prison punishments for employers refusing to employ pregnant women or breast-feeding mothers, or reducing their wages for these reasons. Under the latest decree on this subject (August 1968) 'women having infants will be granted, in addition to leaves on full pay for pregnancies or deliveries, paid leaves until the infants are one-year-old'. The earlier 1944 legislation also stipulated that 'parents earning 40 or less roubles a month and with three children should be freed from 50% of the fees for kindergartens or crèches, as well as parents with four children earning 60 roubles and those with five or more children independently of the size of their earnings'.

Otherwise, the regular family allowances in the Soviet Union are not very generous if compared with those in most West European countries. They start only with the third child, when the mother receives 20 roubles in a lump sum. When the fourth child is born, the mother receives an initial 65 roubles and then four roubles per month. The figures increase until the eleventh child, when the allowance goes up to 250 roubles and 15 roubles respectively for the eleventh and every child thereafter. These monthly allowances, however, are paid only between the child's second and fifth birthdays. Further, mothers of large families receive special titles and medals, the highest being the 'Heroic Mother' for ten or more children born and reared.

Nevertheless, the Soviet family is decreasing in size. In fact, whereas the average Soviet family went down from 4·1 in 1939 to 3·7 members in 1959, the average US family increased from 3·5 members in 1950 to 3·7 in 1961.

The following are the real causes for the steady, and in some cases, quite rapid decrease of the family size in practically every country of Eastern Europe: (a) rapid industrialisation and urbanisation not accompanied by a proportional rise in living standards; (b) overcrowded housing: the average dwelling space per urban inhabitant is only 10·3 sq. metres of which the actual living area is 7 sq. metres at best; (c) low wages and salaries which make it necessary for the wife to work full-time, combined with lack of facilities for part-time work; (d) instability of marriages, high rate of divorce combined with insufficient material incentives which do not ensure an adequate support of the children in case of divorce, alimonies also being very small. We have already seen how unfortunate the woman's position in the Soviet Union has been as far as unmarried motherhood is concerned. The position will have somewhat improved with the introduction of the 1968 draft legislation but even this legislation leaves the status of unmarried mothers in a less favourable position than that provided by the law of 1926. As for jobs and education, women have, in theory, attained full equality with men. But a look at the Soviet job-sex differentiation is sufficient evidence that in practice this is not the case. Women in the Soviet Union have almost monopolised medicine, teaching, communications and services, where their percentages are respectively: 85%, 72%, 66% and 73%. But even in these spheres the proportion of women will decrease now that there are proportionately more males in the younger generation. The same process is true of graduate studies; the rate of pay for post-graduates is considerably higher than for those with an ordinary diploma. The proportion of females in the graduate courses decreased from 39% in 1950 to 29% in 1956; no such figures are available since that date—a sign that the decrease has probably continued, as Professor Kurganov correctly remarks. The proportion of women in the medical faculties of the Soviet Union decreased from 65% in 1950 to 54% in 1965, and in the faculties of education from 71% to 66% in the same years; while in the total university student body the proportion has gone down from 55% to 44%, which is only 6% higher than that in the USA and France. Further evidence that the high rate of female students is not an exclusive achievement of the socialist system lies in the fact that the pre-war percentage of female students dropped from 37% in 1913 for Petersburg

(Leningrad) alone to 29% in 1925, to 27% in 1929, surpassing the pre-revolutionary level only in the 1930s, which was at least partially due to the great losses in the male population in the course of the purges (the rate of female students in 1940 was 58%).

As far as the working-class is concerned, women are predominantly employed in the unskilled heavy jobs, while men take either the skilled positions or those of foremen, supervisors, etc. Soviet writers have often protested against this situation. One of them, Larisa Kuznetsova, quoted in 1967 the official figures for the job-sex distribution at the Saratov hydro-electric station construction.

TABLE 2

LOW PAID MANUAL LABOUR

	Men	Women
Earth-diggers without mechanised instruments	17	119
Plasterers ,, ,, ,,	24	184
Painters ,, ,, ,,	21	156

HIGHLY PAID MECHANISED LABOUR

Assistant operators of excavators	.	.	.	60	2
Compressor operators	.	.	.	.	25	1
Crane operators	.	.	.	.	.	142	10

Source: *Literaturnaya Gazeta*, 15 February 1967.

In the professional field, as well, the proportion of women markedly diminishes in the more responsible positions. Thus, for instance, in the academic field 51% are women among the research and teaching assistants, but only 8·8% among the academicians and full professors. The same trend is evident in Communist Party and government posts: there are no women among the Politburo and Secretariat members of the party.

The position of the Soviet woman at home has also been the subject of serious sociological research in the Soviet Union in the last few years. While 53% of men spend less than two hours a day on domestic work, married women with full-time seven-hour employment work on an average 'almost 16 hours'. Even if this Soviet figure includes time spent on going to and from work, the domestic endeavours of a married Soviet woman must amount to at least another seven hours a day, i.e. to another full working day. This, then, must be another reason why the number of female students has lately been decreasing, particularly as, since the 1950s, the state has been increasing the proportion of part-time university education—evening schools and external courses—at which the student body has increased from 1940 to 1965 respectively 21-fold and 7·5 times, whilst that of the ordinary full-time day education has grown only 2·8 times. Obviously a woman working a 14-hour day can hardly find time for studies.

THE FUTURE SOVIET FAMILY

There are at least two major ways in which the woman's lot in the family could be improved. One would consist of increasing the incomes of wage-earners, family allowances for children, tax-exemptions for non-working dependants, and of opening up possibilities for part-time employment, so that more married women could stay wholly or partly out of work and devote most of their time to their homes and the upbringing of their children. The other method would be for the state gradually to take over most of the family responsibilities. Officially the Soviet policy makers have rejected the extremist ideas of the left-wing communists on the family nearly 50 years ago, and have announced their intention to 'strengthen the Soviet family'.[1] However, they still tend to prefer a solution of the problem of women's inequality which hands it over to the state. The eminent Soviet academician and over eighty at the time, S. Strumilin, wrote in 1960 that under communism the education of children will be taken over from the parents by the state almost entirely: the new-born baby will be taken to a day crèche; later on, the child would be transferred to a children's home with a 24-hour upkeep, and then to a boarding school. The state, he wrote, will be able to educate the children much better than the parents and the only ties that will hold the couple together under these conditions will be the ties of love between them. Although Khrushchev criticised Strumilin at the time, the Communist Party Programme adopted in the same year promised a development for the Soviet family similar to that suggested by Strumilin: broad-front introduction of day schools, boarding schools, whole day or 24-hour kindergartens and crèches, canteens with home delivery of warm meals to replace home cooking, etc.[2]

Life, however, dictates its own laws. The Programme promised that 'public catering will be able to take precedence over home cooking within 10 to 15 years'. However, in 1962

> 'the public catering facilities made 83 meals per person (in the whole year). This means the average Soviet citizen could be wholly fed by the public catering system for eleven or twelve days in the year.'[3]

It is not likely that the catering service has improved very markedly since 1962, as the total proportion of employees in commerce, public catering, supplies and storages has remained at a static 6% of the total since 1960 (before the Revolution it was 9%). Even the average eleven-to-twelve day feeding is a myth, as this includes all the travellers, holiday-makers, tourists, both domestic and foreign, who are fed almost entirely by the public catering services, as well as university refectories and workers' canteens and not to mention the Soviet 'aristocracy' who make use of the better restaurants regularly.

The situation of the state education of children is apparently little different. In 1964 out of a total of approximately 53 million school children, 2·4 million were either in 'extended day' schools, (i.e. spending the whole working day at school) or at the boarding schools, (just over 6%). Crèches and kindergartens of all types had nearly seven million children out of a total of nearly 40 million pre-school children, i.e. nearly 17%. And, according to Kharchev, nearly 100% of children at the boarding schools are either orphans or come from problem families.

Relatively little has been written lately on the boarding schools in the context of their being *the* schools of communist education. More and more the opinions of serious sociologists can be heard demanding a general introduction of part-time working facilities for mothers, so that they might devote more time to their children, which would in turn strengthen the family and protect children from the bad influences of the street. In other words, no state institution can replace the moral integrity passed on to children only by a

---

[1] Khrushchev in *Pravda*, 20 October 1961.
[2] The 1961 Party Programme, full text, *The USSR and the Future*, edited by L. Schapiro, Praeger, New York, 1963, particularly pp. 296, 305 and 306.
[3] *Kommunist*, 1964, 4, p. 42.

loving mother, with sufficient time to devote to them; and equally by that figure often ridiculed in the Soviet press, the *babushka*, (grandmother), who replaces the working mother during the day in many Soviet families, and is a substitute for the banned Sunday-schools introducing the grandchildren to some rudiments of religion and religious ethics.

Thus, once again, the system has revealed its inability to fulfil its promises. This is encouraging moderate humanists to demand a fuller recognition of the positive educative role of the family and the mother, and to demand not 'equality with men' but a special treatment for women which would allow them to perform their traditional functions in the family. It is hoped that these demands will be heeded. The alarming spread of 'illegitimate' and problem children, and of juvenile delinquency[1] has constrained the authorities finally to draft new and more humane laws in place of the 1944 legislation. Ideologically, such a change of emphasis in the official family policies should not be too difficult, since, except in the earliest revolutionary period, the only criteria that have determined the Soviet family and other social policies have been the pragmatic needs and considerations of the state. Invariably policies could then be ideologically justified *ex post facto*, however inconsistent they may be at any time.

[1] Professor Peter Juviler assumes that there were at least six million illegitimate children in the Soviet Union in 1962 under 18 years of age, as there were in 1962 approximately five million unwed mothers. And a Soviet lawyer, Vaxberg, wrote in 1964 that there were eight million illegitimate children, but he did not specify the ages. (Peter H. Juviler, 'Family Reforms on the Road to Communism', *Soviet Policy Making*, edited by P. Juviler and Henry Morton, New York, 1967, pp. 43–4).

63% of juvenile cases studied in the Soviet Union were either complete or partial orphans or illegitimate children, i.e. in many of these cases the upbringing responsibilities were taken over in whole or in part by the state institutions. Also 'Children brought up without family participation are much more in danger of a one-sided and retarded development than those children who are members of (normal) families', concludes Kharchev after referring to some examples of deficient upbringing of children in the Soviet full-time institutions for children. His position is that the role of the family will remain considerable 'even under Communism', but it will develop in harmony with the growth of state functions in helping the family to bring up the children, whatever this may mean. His view is, however, that the state should supplement the family and replace it only where the family is unavailable or where it is in such a moral disorder that its influence becomes harmful and dangerous. He remarks that even today to those families who do send their children to the state institutions, the government pays 80% of the costs. Kharchev, *op. cit.*, pp. 267–77.

EDUCATION IN THE SOVIET UNION

MERVYN MATTHEWS

Principal Characteristics

During the half-century of its existence the Soviet Union has made impressive progress in developing its educational facilities. The all-union census of January 1959 showed that the illiteracy rate for persons aged between nine and 49 was down to less than 2%, as compared with 44% in 1926, and according to the 1967–8 estimate some 76 million people, or nearly a third of the entire population, were engaged in full or part-time training of some kind (see Table 1).

Table 1

NUMBER OF PERSONS STUDYING IN SOVIET UNION[1]

(At the beginning of the academic year in ooos)

	1914/15	1940/41	1945/46	1960/61	1966/67	1967/68
All persons studying	10,588	47,547	37,385	52,600	73,559	75,924
Including:						
Full-time general school	9,656	34,784	26,094	33,417	43,529	48,901
Part-time general school	—	768	714	2,770	4,641	
Vocational and technical schools	106	717	945	1,113	1,961	2,130
Middle special educational institutions	54	975	1,008	2,060	3,994	4,166
Higher educational institutions	127	812	730	2,396	4,123	4,311
Training of all kinds directly at place of work	645	9,491	7,894	10,844	15,311	16,416

[1] This covers all types of institutions.

Sources: *Strana Sovetov za 50 Let*, Moscow, 1967.
SSSR v Tsifrakh v 1967, Moscow, 1968.

The Soviet educational system differs in many important respects from the systems of most non-communist states. Its aim is not so much to develop the capabilities of the individual, or help him compensate for his shortcomings, as to train him in a manner most useful to the state. Administratively the institutional network is highly centralised and although the Soviet Union is by no means unique in this respect, the Soviet authorities probably take the principle further than most. Major policy decisions lie with the Central Committee of the party, but day-to-day state control over all aspects of education is exercised through the union-republican Ministry of Higher and Middle Special Education, the union-republican Ministry of Education (for the general school), and the state committees (at republican level) for vocational and technical training. The ministries and committees operate through their representatives in the local soviets.

Pedagogical science maintains rather a conservative position, and intelligence tests are in principle disallowed, in deference to the general Marxist principle that the circumstances of an individual's existence are more important than hereditary factors in determining his consciousness. Teaching is imbued whenever possible with Marxist-Leninist philosophy, as currently interpreted, and seems generally to be aimed at imparting as much factual material as possible, rather than developing the pupils' critical faculties. Thus, there have in recent years been frequent complaints that school courses are overloaded and demand too much of the pupils' time. In the upper classes of the general school, for example, class work alone takes up to 36 hours a week, while compulsory lectures at establishments of higher education may be as numerous. Some attempts have been made to deal with this problem in the post-Stalin period, but with little success: a long school year and bulky textbooks remain characteristic of the system. On the other hand, not much provision is made for leisure activities. Clubs (especially sports clubs) and circles do indeed exist, but they tend to be large and somewhat impersonal. The small ephemeral student societies typical of West European universities are absent. Science subjects tend to be emphasised at the expense of arts, and there is also a tendency to underline the practical application of what is taught. Examinations are frequent and mostly oral: academic standards on the whole appear to be reasonably good. Part-time study is something of an exception in this respect, but is nevertheless widely encouraged. Since June 1956 education at all levels above the nursery school has been free, while a number of categories of pupils and students may claim maintenance allowances. Most of the taught belong to one of the country's political youth organisations—the Young Pioneers or Communist Youth League (Komsomol), while many teachers are in the party.

None of these characteristic features have changed fundamentally since Stalin's death in 1953, though the successive governments have introduced some noteworthy changes and modifications. Khrushchev took a keen interest in education, and his main contribution (apart from de-Stalinising the ideological content of the curriculum) was a massive 'polytechnisation' drive which reached its peak in the educational reform of December 1958. By this means the Soviet leader tried to change the nature of the school, making theoretical subjects more practical, introducing manual labour into the curriculum and even teaching the pupils trades. At the same time he abandoned the aim of ten-year education for all in favour of an eight-year school for most children, with an eleven-year course for a minority. Pupils from the reformed school would thus possess manual skills, be more fitted to start work immediately and possibly less anxious to get into the country's crowded universities and institutes (VUZy in the Russian abbreviation of the words 'higher educational institutions'). Another benefit envisaged by

Khrushchev would be a blurring of class distinctions which until then had been fostered by the Soviet school. In December 1958 this policy was reinforced by the reorganisation and expansion of the vocational school network, the introduction of sandwich courses at VUZ level, changes in VUZ intake rules so as to favour applicants who had been in full-time jobs for at least two years, and an extension of part-time courses.

Khrushchev's ideas were very unpopular and administratively difficult to implement, and from August 1964, if not before, there was a steady retreat from them. In August of that year Khrushchev's plan for an 11th class was rejected, and soon after the principle of a ten-year education for all reestablished. Polytechnisation schemes were watered down, so that by the beginning of 1968 only a third of the schools in the RSFSR were teaching their pupils manual trades. Khrushchev's scheme for a rapid development of boarding schools was quietly dropped. In a decree passed in November 1966 the Soviet authorities announced a withdrawal from the principle of standard courses for all pupils in the general school, and the toleration of some specialisation. At the same time a general revision of the curriculum was started (being due for completion in 1970/71) and a new drive launched to improve facilities in the most backward sector of Soviet education—the village school. As far as the VUZy are concerned, entrance rules approved in 1965 practically abolished privileges for candidates from full-time employment, and little is now heard about the sandwich courses. New interdisciplinary subjects of study have been introduced, and higher part-time education is to become relatively less important.

General Education

The first rung of the Soviet educational ladder takes the form of crèches for children aged from two months to three years and kindergartens, which admit children aged three to seven. In January 1967 they together catered for about eight million children, though there were half as many places again in temporary institutions in the summer. Altogether they would cover something like a third of the corresponding child population. Pre-school institutions in the Soviet Union are important in view of the fact that about four-fifths of all able-bodied women are in full-time employment—in fact it is perhaps surprising that the network is not bigger. The service has to be paid for at rates varying from about fifteen shillings to seven pounds a month (at the official rate of exchange)[1] depending on the type of school and the parents' income.

The Soviet complete general school (or general labour polytechnical school, to give it its full title) consists basically of ten forms or classes, though an eleventh is added in non-Russian areas where Russian is taught as a foreign language. The school is split up into three parts, classes 1 to 4, classes 5 to 8, (now being reorganised as classes 1 to 3 and 4 to 8), and the last two, classes 9 and 10. By 1962 Soviet educational authorities were claiming that eight years of schooling (covering young people from the age of seven to 15) had been introduced for everyone, and there are plans to extend ten years of general education, or its equivalent, to all young people, in principle, by 1970. This is, however, likely to prove very difficult in the countryside where settlements are scattered, schools small and teaching staff relatively scarce. The standardisation of courses mentioned above means that a child finishing four or eight classes in an 'incomplete' school (and these still

---

[1] See table of currency exchange rates, p. 19.

predominate in rural areas) can continue his studies without undue academic disruption at another. The teaching is apparently fairly efficient, the repeating rate in the RSFSR in 1967 being about 4%.

The curriculum of the eight-year school begins by concentrating on Russian language and literature and mathematics, with some music, physical training and manual work, but by the 8th class most of the subjects familiar to us have crept in. The school week contains 24 hours of obligatory classes in the first class, rising to 30 by the 8th class (on six days a week), and the school year lasts from 1 September until 30 June.

The last two classes of the general school, which in 1967 held 7·3 million pupils, deserve separate mention. They are still considered to be the high-road to a university education, as a general school leaving certificate, or *attestat zrelosti* is an essential VUZ entry requirement. Recent sociological studies have revealed that they tend to be filled by children of the intelligentsia, no doubt for this very reason. In 1968 a majority of all the young people in the corresponding age groups attended them, especially in the towns. The curriculum at this stage contains a number of new features. Sociology (of a Marxist-Leninist variety) and astronomy find a place in the 10th class, at the expense of Russian language and geography. Five hours of physics and mathematics respectively are supplemented by three hours of chemistry and two hours of biology. The basic work-load is again 30 hours a week, though two to four hours extra may be allotted for optional classes, as specified by the November 1966 decree. Two types of option are now permitted: first, many schools provide optional courses, from the 7th class on, according to the desires of the pupils themselves. Second, there is, for a limited number of schools only, intensive study of arts or science subjects in the 9th and 10th classes. M. I. Kashin, deputy minister of education for the RSFSR, in fact stated that there were some 200 schools of this type in the republic by the beginning of 1968. All this implies that in future there will be more built-in academic differentiation between schools. Up to the present the only special schools have been those catering for musically or artistically gifted children, together with a few schools with instruction in a foreign language and schools for the handicapped.

In 1967 some 4·6 million persons were studying at the country's four types of part-time general school: the Schools of Working or Rural Youth, the Schools for Adults and Correspondence Schools. Nearly all of these pupils were in the part-time equivalent of classes 8 to 10, many of them (according to a survey conducted in the industrial town of Ufa in 1965–6) young people aiming specifically at middle special or higher education, despite the fact that they were already in full-time employment. These schools offer basically the same curriculum as the day-school, and the courses require a rigorous 20 to 24 hours of study a week. Students who attend them may claim limited day release from their jobs, but even so the demands on their time are great. This, combined with often inadequate facilities, causes a fallout rate of between a quarter and a third over the course, a repeating rate of about 16% and a shortfall in recruitment plans. The authorities, nevertheless, see an important place for the system in the future as a long-stop for people who do not finish the full-time school, and intend to push enrolment up to ten million by 1970.

VOCATIONAL AND MIDDLE-GRADE SPECIALIST TRAINING

Vocational training in the Soviet Union is provided, in the case of about 20% of all new entrants to the labour market, by the 4,790 schools of the

TABLE 2
STANDARD CURRICULUM[1]

Subjects:	Classes (Forms) 1–10 No. of hrs per week										Total of hrs taught in each subject per week[2]	
	1	2	3	4	5	6	7	8	9	10	Current curriculum	1959 curriculum
Russian language	12	10	10	6	6	3	3	2	2/0	—	53	57
Literature	—	—	—	2	2	2	2	3	4	3	18	19
Mathematics	6	6	6	6	6	6	6	6	5	5	58	59
History	—	—	—	2	2	2	2	3	4	3	18	20
Sociology	—	—	—	—	—	—	—	—	—	2	2	2
Nature studies	—	2	2	2	—	—	—	—	—	—	6	2
Geography	—	—	—	—	2	3	2	2	2	—	11	12
Biology	—	—	—	—	2	2	2	2	0/2	2	11	11
Physics	—	—	—	—	—	2	2	3	4	5	16	17
Astronomy	—	—	—	—	—	—	—	—	—	1	1	1
Technical drawing	—	—	—	—	—	1	1	1	—	—	3	4
Chemistry	—	—	—	—	—	—	2	2	3	3	10	11
Foreign language	—	—	—	—	4	3	3	2	2	2	16	20
Art	1	1	1	1	1	1	—	—	—	—	6	7
Music	1	1	1	1	1	1	1	—	—	—	7	8
Physical training	2	2	2	2	2	2	2	2	2	2	20	22
Manual training	2	2	2	2	2	2	2	2	2	2	20	58
Total of obligatory classes	24	24	24	24	30	30	30	30	30	30	276	330
Optional classes	—	—	—	—	—	—	2	4	6	6	—	—
Total of all classes	24	24	24	24	30	30	32	34	36	36	—	—

[1] Approved in November 1966 for introduction into all schools by 1970–1.

[2] These columns show how the emphasis on different subjects is being changed by the post-Khrushchev leadership, involving an increase in the sciences and a massive reduction in manual training, which formerly meant an extension of the school year.

Source: *Narodnoe Obrazovanie v SSSR 1917–67*, M. A. Prokofiev and others, (ed.), Moscow, 1967, p. 91

state committees of vocational and technical training. The other 80% learn their skills in groups (brigades) directly at their place of work, although some tuition in modest skills like dressmaking or typing is available privately in the towns. Figures for trainees in factory, farm or office are not readily available, as they are usually combined with those for persons acquiring further skills (see table 2).

The vocational school system contained many different types of institutions up to the reform of December 1958, when they were all turned into 'vocational-technical schools', with a training period of from ten months to three years, designed primarily to take pupils from classes 8 to 10 of the general school, without examination. Most of the common industrial and agricultural trades are taught in them, and two-thirds of the pupils at present come from rural areas. On finishing the pupils are directed into a job, which they are not supposed to leave for four years. This requirement more or less precludes them from a full-time college education and this, together with the low grade nature of the training, means that the vocational schools are one of the less attractive sectors of the Soviet education system. But, according to some Soviet writers, the eventual expansion of educational facilities to cover all young people up to the age of 17 may mean that these schools will be partially combined with the ten-year school.

General school-leavers who wish to set their sights a little higher may take the examinations for one of the country's 3,820 middle special educational institutions, where they do a two- to four-year course, depending on their educational standard and choice of subject. These institutions are run on the same lines as the VUZy, offering much the same assortment of courses though at a lower level, with a similar procedure for the planned placement of graduates. They tend to be regarded as a *pis-aller*, and complaints on the relative shortage of middle-grade specialists whom they train are commonplace.

THE UNIVERSITIES AND INSTITUTES

The Soviet authorities are justly proud of the extent of higher education in their country. In 1967 the country's 767 VUZy provided the economy with some 479,800 graduates, and intakes are scheduled to rise to 940,000 by 1970. According to Soviet estimates the Soviet Union has more students per 1,000 of the population than any other country, with the exception of the USA and more than three times as many as the UK. Of course, such claims must be treated with caution, as over 2·3 of the 4·1 million students in 1967 were on part-time and correspondence courses, which, like the general-school courses of this type, are exceedingly demanding and suffer from heavy fall-out. Nevertheless, the achievement is considerable.

VUZy fall into two types, universities and institutes. The country's 42 universities offer training in a wide variety of specialities, as in the West, whereas the institutes, usually much smaller establishments, are limited to a few closely allied faculties. There are considerable differences in the standing of different VUZy, as might be expected, but as at present only about one ten-year school-leaver in five or six has a chance of a place in a full-time institution, the general level of competition is high.

Most institutions offer four to six-year courses, in 343 officially approved specialities, with arts subjects taking about four years, engineering and science five and medicine six. The academic year is divided into two semesters, and the students attend obligatory two-hour lectures and seminars for up to 36 hours a week. These include theoretical and (when necessary) practical work in their subject, up to four hours a week on socio-political studies, (Marxist dialectical and historical materialism, political economy, Communist Party history, etc.) and, for the boys, one afternoon a week of military training. The content of the courses is determined by the ministry, which also approves and publishes the textbooks. In their last year students write a short dissertation, choosing the exact topic from a list compiled by the faculty board.

Soviet VUZ courses cover most fields of endeavour and except for their political bias (primarily in history, economics, literature and the arts) are as extensive as those of Western institutions. Centralism is again in evidence insofar as all subjects taught are approved by one of the ministries and entered on a central register, which now contains some 400 items. The idea of encouraging faculties or departments to plan and offer their own options or experiment in combinations of different subjects is rather foreign to Soviet practice. Conversely, students have much less choice of subject than their counterparts in the UK or the USA, once they have picked their main field of study.

Higher education is free, and some 70% of the full-time students receive modest maintenance grants, family circumstances here being the deciding factor.

On graduating students receive a diploma (possibly 'with excellence'), and under the terms of regulations which have been in force since 1928 are obliged to spend three years at one of the jobs offered to them by the VUZ 'personal placement commission' which interviews them a few months before graduation date. In this way the state endeavours to get the best value for its investment. When a graduate arrives at his place of work he is, in most cases, expected to learn the job as he proceeds, for management training schemes as such are unknown in the Soviet Union. The many part-time students, however, will already have considerable practical experience, whilst many young people from full-time VUZy do some practical work at local enterprises during their years at college. Khrushchev was anxious to introduce sandwich courses at the higher levels of Soviet education, but this idea seems to have been neglected by his successors.

From the point of view of social origins, the Soviet student body is in many respects similar to that of Western industrial lands, since most students are drawn from the 'upper' classes of society, and have the same kinds of attitudes and aims. But the nature of Soviet education and the character of Soviet society itself inevitably leave a distinctive imprint. For example, the inability to travel abroad freely and restrictions on information about the outside world or certain events of the past make most of them rather limited in their outlook—while admittedly stimulating the curiosity of a minority.

There are two research degrees in the Soviet Union: the Candidate's degree, which is roughly the equivalent of an MA and takes three years, (two on specialised study for an examination, and one on a thesis) and the Doctorate, which is something rather more elevated than a British PhD, and requires a minimum of three years after the Candidate's degree. In 1967 there were 769,600 persons engaged in research of all kinds (including 18,300 Doctors and 169,300 Candidates) at VUZy and at over 2,000 research institutes under the general direction of the Academy of Sciences of the USSR. Soviet scholarship is generally recognised to be of very good quality. The authorities have been particularly concerned to promote research in the field of science and technology, and it is here that the most impressive gains have been made.

439

FURTHER READING

Azrael, Jeremy. 'Bringing Up the Soviet Man: Dilemmas and Progress', *Problems of Communism*, May–June, 1968.

De Witt, N. *Education and Professional Employment in the USSR*, National Science Foundation, New York, 1962.

Dodge, Norman T. *Women in the Soviet Economy*, (Chapter 5), Johns Hopkins Press, Baltimore, Md., 1966.

Grant, Nigel. *Soviet Education*, Univ. of London Press, London; Peter Smith, Gloucester, Mass., 1965.

Inkeles, Alex and Geiger, Kent. *Soviet Society*, Constable and Co, London; Houghton Mifflin, Boston, Mass., 1961.

Noah, Harold J. 'The Economics of (Soviet) Education', *Problems of Communism*, July–August, 1967.

Rosen, Seymour M. *Higher Education in the USSR*, US Department of Health, Education and Welfare, Office of Education, Washington DC, 1963.

Rudman, Herbert. *The School and State in the USSR*, Macmillan, New York, 1967.

Soviet Education (Translations of selected Soviet articles on education.) International Arts and Sciences Press, New York, monthly, 1958 onwards.

EDUCATION IN EASTERN EUROPE

BRIAN HOLMES

SIMILARITIES IN EDUCATIONAL POLICIES

THE educational policies pursued in the arc of East European countries bordering on the Soviet Union show similarities, first because of their common historical traditions, and second because of the influence of Soviet policy on them since the end of World War II. It would, however, be a mistake to suppose that, in spite of common features, considerable differences do not exist. For example, the traditions of education in East Germany are old and are shared by many countries including the Baltic republics of the Soviet Union and to some extent the RSFSR itself. Polish education, on the other hand, has been influenced by French modes of thinking. However, all these countries before World War II possessed features in education which were very typically West European. A system of primary schools from the age of six to ten or thereabouts was followed by a differentiated pattern of second level schools, including terminal classes. The highly academic schools were very selective and prepared pupils for the university faculties. They paid great attention to classical and modern languages and mathematics, and provided for the minority of young people who gained admission to them a broad education. By and large they were attended by children from the middle, upper and professional classes. Fees were frequently charged.

Less academic schools had developed to fill the gap between the university preparatory schools, the vocational and technical schools and the terminal elementary schools. Another feature of many of these pre-war systems was that primary school teachers were trained in secondary schools for teachers, academic secondary school teachers were educated in the universities and received a minimal amount of professional, pedagogical instruction.

Post-war changes of policy in all these countries have been based on the desire to extend compulsory schooling and to establish comprehensive or common second level schools and the need to reform and revise the curriculum in the second level schools. In general the reform policies have followed Soviet lines; the important period of discussion was the 1950s; proposals there radically to change the system of education were adopted in 1957–8. Since then Soviet policy has been modified in the light of experience.

Two features of it serve to focus attention on trends in East European countries. The first of these has been the tendency everywhere to democratise education by making it available at all levels to an increasingly large proportion of the population. The second feature has been the attempt made to break down the traditional dichotomy between intellectual training and manual instruction. Attempts to unify these aspects of education largely

441

failed in the Soviet Union through lack of general theories which could be easily understood and applied in the classroom by the average teacher.

One of the immediate post-war aspects of policy throughout the world was to regard education as a human right. The provision of universal primary and second level schooling on the basis of merit was embodied in the UN Declaration of Human Rights. In most of the East European countries new constitutions were drawn up proclaiming much the same thing. The East German constitution of 1949 guaranteed free general polytechnical and higher education. Private schools were abolished. Article 61 of the constitution of the Polish People's Republic stated that education was a human right. Article 80 of the constitution of the Rumanian People's Republic stated that every citizen had a right to a general and free education. Likewise, under Article 79 of the Bulgarian constitution every citizen was guaranteed the right to education. Similar provisions are found in the post-war constitutions of Czechoslovakia, Hungary and Jugoslavia.

Primary Schooling

Government policies were geared to expanding educational provisions. The numbers of kindergartens, primary schools and children enrolled expanded rapidly during the late 1940s and early 1950s. By 1962, in Bulgaria some 60% of all the three- to six-year olds were attending kindergartens—over 70% of the seven-year olds were in these schools. Later in all East European countries enrolments at the second and third levels of education expanded as a result as the post-war bulges passed into adolescence. Compulsory attendance became more effective as schools were built, consolidation of small schools took place and boarding schools were established. In Poland, for example, regulations (1968) provide for the opening of primary schools in all towns and villages containing at least 20 children of school age—15 in mountainous districts. In 1968 small schools in Czechoslovakia remained a problem and attempts were then being made to group small units together. The effective attendance of all pupils over the period of compulsory schooling, of course, varied.

Legislation has been passed in most countries to extend this period—some indication of the extent to which most children were attending primary schools. In July 1961 Poland amended a decree of 1956 by extending the period of compulsory attendance from seven to eight years. In the same year Rumania made the period of compulsory attendance eight years—from seven to 15. This move was regarded as a step towards twelve years of general education. In 1968 twelve-year schooling (ten years compulsory) was introduced, with the aim of having it fully implemented by 1973. Bulgaria has a period of seven to 16 compulsory attendance. In East Germany the period is ten years from the age of seven. Poland in 1961 raised compulsory attendance by one year to eight. All these moves reflect Soviet policy which in 1958 raised the period of compulsory attendance from seven to eight years. There is, of course, a general trend everywhere to extend education by raising the minimum school leaving age. The East European countries have followed this trend.

Secondary Education

In a similar way attempts have been made throughout Europe to reorganise the second stage of education. General policy in the East European countries

has been to develop a common school over the period of compulsory attendance. Such schools absorb into one unit the primary, terminal elementary
and lower secondary stages of education. For the most part the basic school
lasts eight years (Bulgaria, Hungary, Poland, and Jugoslavia) but in Czechoslovakia the period is nine years and in Rumania and East Germany it is ten
years. The starting age varies a little: in East Germany, Rumania, Czechoslovakia and Hungary, it is six, whilst in Bulgaria, Poland and Jugoslavia
children attend school from the age of seven.

The general pattern is a seven- to ten-year basic school—the usual
duration being eight years. Such policies are designed to abolish the traditional differentiated second level system of school organisation; another way
of regarding this move would be to say that the selection of pupils for different
school types has been deferred compared with the pre-war system from
ten to twelve to 14 to 16. After the age of compulsory attendance pupils in
most East European countries complete their general secondary school
education in courses lasting from three or four years. In these cases pupils
may, in fact, attend the same all-age school. These schools prepare pupils for
the universities and technological institutes of higher education. Another
group of pupils from the basic schools go on to technical or professional
schools which offer very specific training for a variety of occupations. Pupils
successfully completing these three- or four-year courses may find their way
into institutions of higher education. The majority leave for skilled occupations. Another group leaves the basic school for trade or vocational
secondary schools. There courses last two to three years and pupils move on
into industry. A proportion of pupils who have completed the basic school
course leave to take up jobs. The adult education system in most countries,
however, ensures the possibility that pupils who have not completed the
normal general secondary school course may enter universities and technological institutes.

The ten-year school introduced in 1964 by the East German authorities is
divided into three stages—the *Unterstufe* (ages six to nine), the *Mittelstufe*
(nine to twelve) and the *Oberstufe* (twelve to 16). Some pupils leave at the age
of 14. The choice for those completing the ten-year general polytechnical
secondary school lies between a two-year extended secondary school leading
to universities and institutions of higher education and a *Berufsschule* (vocational trade school), some of which prepare students for the university
entrance examination—the *Abitur*—while others prepare them for employment. Specialised professional schools (*Fachschulen*) offer a two-year course at
a level approximately equivalent to the first two years of a technical university (*Hochschule*).

Among the school types which follow the basic schools are secondary
schools for prospective teachers. Here students are trained as teachers in the
lower forms of the basic school. Present policies are designed to move this
type of training into the field of higher education. Indeed, many such
teachers now hold the school leaving certificate which qualifies them to enter
the university.

DIFFERENCES IN STRUCTURE OF SCHOOL SYSTEMS

In general East European countries have developed comprehensive basic
schools which have absorbed the old terminal elementary schools and the
lower classes of the former second stage of education. There has been everywhere an expansion of educational provision which has more than kept pace

with increases in the school-age population. Somewhat different emphases have been given to the structure of the school systems. In Czechoslovakia a nine-year compulsory primary school is followed by either a three-year general secondary school or a four-year vocational school, the latter covering a wide range of subjects. In Hungary the law of 1961 made the first stage of education eight years in duration. These basic schools were followed by a two-year terminal course or a three-year course for skilled industrial and agricultural workers. Vocational and technical schools offering a four-year course award a school leaving certificate from the general secondary school. In Rumania secondary education is provided in two-, four- or five-year courses in specialised secondary schools. After the basic eight-year school, however, pupils may go into apprenticeships, technical schools or to secondary schools training primary school teachers.

In terms of balance between the expansion of general secondary schools and technical secondary schools, interesting differences can be observed. Between 1954 and 1964 the expansion in enrolment in technical schools in Bulgaria was from some 53,000 students to almost 180,000; general enrolments in secondary schools remained steady. In the same period the number of secondary technical school students in Poland grew from just over a quarter-of-a-million to well over a million. General secondary school enrolments more than doubled. In Rumania, on the other hand, in 1964 there were four times as many students in general secondary schools as in 1954, while secondary technical school enrolments had barely doubled. A balanced growth can be discerned in Czechoslovakia. There is no doubt, however, that throughout Eastern Europe great attention has been given to the development of technical schools to meet the pressing demands of industry and commerce.

Reforms in Curricula

Policies of unification of the basic schools and differentiation of the upper secondary stages of education have been accompanied by attempts to reform curricula. The curricula of the basic schools are, for the most part, common to all pupils and include a range of traditional school subjects, such as the mother-tongue, mathematics, science, history, geography, a foreign language and fine arts subjects. In the early 1960s emphasis was given to science and mathematics, and in most countries provisions are made for instruction in the schools for minorities to be in their own language.

Less attention was paid in most East European countries in the early 1960s to the introduction of practical work in industry or agriculture into the general school curriculum as was the case in the Soviet Union. But in East Germany in 1962 three or four hours per week in production were provided in the 7th to 10th classes. By 1968 this number had been considerably reduced. This particular plan to break down the dichotomy between manual instruction and intellectual education was largely unsuccessful in the Soviet Union. The principle of polytechnical education which brings into close harmony these two aspects of education nevertheless dominates educational theory in all East European countries.

In the late 1960s experiments were being conducted with optional subjects. These were introduced at the 7th class or later and frequently included a modernised science subject or one of several foreign languages, for example in Bulgaria and East Germany. The intention, as in the Soviet Union, seems to be to offer to the most able students opportunities to move ahead rapidly on the basis of an enriched curriculum. The move is interesting insofar as it

444

breaks away from the older Soviet concept of a common ten-year school with a unified curriculum. In Soviet policy a trend to return to a common ten-year school with differentiation within the curriculum was apparent in the late 1960s. In Eastern Europe, excepting East Germany, a basic ten-year school had not been achieved by 1969. The general trend, however, to a basic school extending over a longer period of years (up to ten or eleven) with differentiation in the form of options within the curriculum was evident.

These changes in structure and content are difficult to bring about. General policy directives can easily be issued but the effective implementation of them in the schools depends upon the ability of individual teachers to do so. Teacher training is consequently important. A new college for science and mathematics teachers and for the training of kindergarten teachers was established in Bulgaria in 1962. In Czechoslovakia, as in most countries, colleges training primary school teachers have been brought into the ambit of higher education. Emphasis is also placed on in-service training and on the involvement of teachers' organisations in the discussion and formulation of policies in education. Nevertheless, the older European traditions of learning persist, and the effective integration of manual instruction and intellectual training remains a problem of considerable magnitude.

The centralised administration of education can, of course, effect some changes. Generally speaking, in Eastern Europe a Ministry of Education and Culture works out basic syllabuses and curricula and issues regulations and instructions. Traditional differences between the administration of primary and secondary schools continue to exist. Typically, in Hungary the local authorities were and are responsible for the general primary schools. In Poland the Ministry of Education is responsible for all branches and levels of education except higher education and art. The former is administered by the Ministry of Higher Education—a not uncommon feature of educational administration in East European countries.

HIGHER EDUCATION

Institutions of higher education in Eastern Europe operate on the basis of state legislation. Since the war, either in their constitutions or in special decrees, the structure, objectives and administration of higher education have been laid down by the governments of these countries. In East Germany the constitution of 1949 and decrees of 1951 provided a framework for education. Policies in Poland were laid down in 1958 and 1959; in Hungary the most important legislation was passed in 1961; in Rumania in 1953, and Czechoslovakia in 1950 and 1956. In all these countries universities, technological and pedagogical institutes and academies of fine arts constitute higher education. No sharp distinction is drawn between the universities and the technological institutes, although in many cases the former are much older and provide a range of courses which tend to be less applied than those offered in the Institutes. In East Germany, for example, Leipzig University was established in 1409 and Rostock in 1419. Charles University in Prague was founded in 1348 and served the countries of Central, Northern and Eastern Europe. The early technological institutes were creations of the 19th century. Rapid growth has taken place since 1945 in the number of and enrolments in both universities and technological institutes. Teaching and research are regarded as important functions, but at the level of secondary education every attempt is made by the authorities to reduce the dichotomy between theoretical and applied studies. There is evidence that the universities, with their more theoretical approach, remain the prestige institutions. Forms of administration have little effect on this situation.

DIRECTIONS OF POLICY DECISIONS

In 1960 policies of decentralising control and finance were a feature of developments in Poland. There is no doubt that the authorities wish to involve a great many educationists and the representatives of workers in the organisation of education. Professional traditions are strong and there is undoubtedly a built-in resistance to change from an élitist form of academic education, provided through a differentiated structure of schools to a more open form of provision. Evening classes, hobby circles in pioneer palaces, short courses and supervision through correspondence are designed to keep open the doors to further education for as many people as possible. But the crux of many shared problems is similar throughout Eastern Europe. How is it possible to modernise the curriculum in a mass educational system designed to serve a technological society? How does this affect the place of the traditional subjects? To what extent can diversity be provided in a unified structure? When is the best time, and what are the best ways of encouraging the special interests and abilities of individual children? How can the social purposes of education be achieved? And how can work and education be reconciled?

The educationists in Eastern Europe are faced with all these difficult policy decisions. They are meeting them from a broadly Marxist-Leninist pattern of theories. They are committed to the democratisation or opening-up of the school system and they hope to bring the schools 'closer to life'—which for communists means productive endeavour. They are also conscious of the ideological orientation of education and society. Against this background and the traditions of Europe it is fascinating to see how educational policy fluctuates and how differences of approach result from national differences.

FURTHER READING

International Year Book of Education, UNESCO and International Bureau of Education, Geneva.

Roucek, J. S. and Lottich, K. V. *Behind the Iron Curtain—The Soviet Satellite States—East European Nationalisms and Education*, Caxton Printers, Caldwell, Idaho, 1964.

Singer, G. *Teacher Education in a Communist State: Poland 1956–1961*, Bookman Associates, New York, 1965.

UNESCO World Survey of Education, Vols I–IV, UNESCO, Paris.

Vodinsky, S. *Schools in Czechoslovakia*, State Pedagogical Publishing House, Prague, 1965.

The World Year Book of Education, Harcourt Brace, New York; Evans, London, annual 1948 onwards.

Articles will be found in the *International Review of Education*, UNESCO, Hamburg; *The Comparative Education Review*, Comparative Education Society, USA; and *Vergleichende Pädagogik*, German Central Educational Institute, East Berlin.

BRIAN HOLMES. Reader in Comparative Education at the University of London's Institute of Education. Publications include *Problems in Education—A Comparative Approach* and (with T. Bristow) *Comparative Education through Literature*. Secretary-Treasurer of the Comparative Education Society in Europe since its inception.

HOUSING[1]

D. V. DONNISON

HOUSING PROGRAMMES IN EASTERN EUROPE

VIEWED from 1,000 miles away, the housing systems of Eastern Europe all appear very similar. Housing programmes form an integral part of successive economic plans, prepared in central planning commissions in accordance with the general directives of those in power. The state can readily acquire and redistribute such land and housing as it does not already own, and the rights of property owners have been so circumscribed that virtually no commercial profit can be derived from them. The building and distribution of houses in the programme is largely organised by regional and local units of government, and (until very recently) rents have been so low that they do not cover the full costs of repair and maintenance. In and around the bigger towns the building of houses—or more often flats—usually proceeds in the form of large projects on a scale resembling new towns and largest estates in the West. Housing conditions in Eastern Europe are cramped and new flats are by Western standards small, poorly finished, but fairly well equipped— centrally heated, averaging between two-and-a-half and three rooms per dwelling, with 400 to 550 sq.ft. of 'useful floor space'. Housing privileges and hardships are reasonably equitably distributed through rationing systems of various kinds which give priority to families with children and to the most urgently needed workers and industries. Meanwhile, the pace of economic development is rapid, productivity in building is rising and long-term perspectives reach ahead to a dawn of abundance that is expected to break some time after 1980.

NEEDS AND RESOURCES

As in the West, the countries with the longest industrial history and the most slowly growing populations have more old housing, larger houses, the most plentiful stock of houses, and the greatest opportunities for improving their situation. Although the populations of these more fully industrialised coun- tries are increasing slowly, the growing proportion of old people amongst them means that the numbers of households are growing a good deal faster than their rate of natural increase would suggest. Meanwhile, though shortages are less severe than elsewhere, much of the housing stock will have to be replaced before long. East Germany and Czechoslovakia are in this position. Hungary's situation is more complicated, combining a slow rate of

[1] This is a shortened version of a chapter in D. V. Donnison's *The Government of Housing*, Penguin Books, 1967.

population increase with a low but rapidly increasing degree of industrialisation. At the other extreme lie the predominantly rural countries. Data are
scarce for Jugoslavia, Bulgaria, Rumania and Albania, but all appear to
have more rapidly growing populations and severe housing shortages.
Between these two groups stand Poland and the Soviet Union with an
intermediate standard of housing but even faster rates of population increase.
The Soviet Union neglected its housing needs for many years, but having
established the heavy industrial foundations of its economy and repaired the
ravages of war, it turned in the mid-1950s to deal with its housing problems
and has for some years been building about half the dwellings going up
throughout the whole of Europe—14,234,000 out of a total of 27,370,000
during the peak period between 1958 and 1962, and slightly less since then.
But Poland, with a less advanced building industry, and other investment
priorities dictated by a frighteningly large generation of young people for
whom to find work in the coming years, has one of the smallest housing
programmes in Europe—building 4·6 houses per 1,000 inhabitants in 1962,
compared with averages of 7·5 for north-western Europe, 6·4 for southern
Europe, 11·7 for the Soviet Union, and 5·6 for the rest of Eastern Europe.

OWNERSHIP AND MANAGEMENT

The ownership and management of housing in the Eastern countries varies
widely. Owner-occupation is most common in rural areas, though this
depends partly on the extent to which agriculture has been reorganised into
state farms, cooperative or collective units, and the types of housing provided
for such units. In 1960–1 the proportions of housing that were owner-
occupied in Czechoslovakia (50%), Poland (over 50%), Hungary (62%)
and Jugoslavia (78%)—and probably in other East European countries too—
were appreciably greater than in the UK (about 40%). The Soviet Union
(39% in urban areas) must also have a proportion of owner-occupiers larger
than the UK. In the West owner-occupation is sometimes regarded as a
symbol of the bourgeois virtues; in the East it more often distinguishes the
rural population, living in separate houses, from urban flat-dwellers. In the
more rural economies new building is largely initiated and owned by private
households—often with help from the state. In 1964 building for owner-
occupation accounted for over half the output in Jugoslavia (58%), Rumania
(60%) and Bulgaria (77%) and a large though declining proportion of the
Soviet Union's (about 25% in 1963). Building by the state and its industrial
enterprises accounted for the largest proportions of output in East Germany
(51%), Poland (53%) and the Soviet Union (about 60%, including urban
cooperatives). Building by cooperatives, though still accounting for only a
small proportion of the total stock of housing, is now the most rapidly
growing sector in Eastern Europe—particularly in Poland (where it formed
18% of total output), Czechoslovakia (33%) and East Germany (41%). In
Czechoslovakia the building of houses by industrial enterprises has now been
stopped and a new form of cooperative housing is taking its place. The growth
of these cooperative forms of ownership is likely to have a major impact on
the development of housing policies in the centrally planned economies, as
will be shown.

THE EVOLUTION OF POLICIES

The first systematic attempt to legislate for rents in the Soviet Union, made in
1927 just before the first Five Year Plan, imposed standard levels of payment

that were reasonably high in relation to income and not very different from those to be found in capitalist countries at the time, although there were deductions to help families with low incomes. It was the freezing of these rents, coupled with the serious inflations that took place during the next 25 years—a period of slow building with an interval of catastrophic destruction —which reduced rents to a sum that became negligible. The basic law on rents today is still that of 1927. Low rents, leading eventually to the provision of free housing, were espoused as a principle of Soviet social policy in 1961. But this principle was not derived direct from the gospels, it emerged from the slow erosion of economic change under political pressures in a fashion not unfamiliar in regulated capitalist economies. Nevertheless, housing has clearly been accepted as the responsibility of the state, to be provided as a form of social service.

Table 1 shows how small a proportion of household spending is devoted to rent and related housing costs in the East European countries. Further inquiries made between 1959 and 1961 in five of these countries showed that the average annual rents of new dwellings ranged from 0·4% of the total cost of the dwelling in Poland, to 3·0% of the total cost in East Germany.

Governments of other East European countries generally began by following the Soviet example. In many of them wartime devastation had been appalling, wholesale migrations and frontier changes had taken place, and equally drastic redistributions of housing were required to provide shelter for the homeless and to eliminate the social injustices of earlier years. The state took over houses that had belonged to municipalities, the larger

TABLE 1

AVERAGE ANNUAL EXPENDITURE OF MANUAL WORKERS'
FAMILIES ON HOUSING AND RELATED ITEMS, AROUND 1960

		Percentage of expenditure devoted to:			
Country	Year of inquiry	Rent	Fuel and light	Furniture, upkeep and equipment	Total
		%	%	%	%
Bulgaria	1957	1·2	3·2	10·7	15·1
Czechoslovakia	1963	1·4[1]	2·9	6·2	10·5
East Germany	1957	6·7[2]	3·5	—	—
Hungary	1962	1·6	4·5	10·6	16·7
Poland	1962	1·2	3·0	5·6	9·8
Soviet Union	1958	3·7[3]		—	—
Jugoslavia	1961	4·9	5·7	6·7	17·3

[1] Raised considerably in subsequent years.
[2] In 1962, 4·1%.
[3] Inquiry in Leningrad only; very similar results were obtained from an inquiry in Moscow. It is estimated that rent is approximately 2% of expenditure.

Source: UN 'Major Problems' Study.

landlords and the dead and dispossessed—property that had belonged to Jews in Poland, and to Germans expelled from the Sudetenland, for example. In rural areas much of this housing was given or sold cheaply to individuals; in towns it was let by the state at low rents. The smaller landlords were in most places left with a formal title to their property, but their tenants were selected by the municipal authorities, their rents were frozen and mostly paid into special funds used for meeting maintenance costs, and the principal advantage conferred by their title to property was the opportunity of getting a flat for themselves somewhere within it. House building revived slowly. As in the Western countries, the first estimates of housing requirements made after the war tended to be too low; the effects of changes in the size and structure of the population and the pace of migration to the towns were not fully foreseen. The first official housing programmes often produced large houses, but far too few of them. Standards were gradually reduced and the quantity of dwellings built was increased. Under Stalin the Soviet Union built large and ornate flats worthy of the millennium to come, and placed two or three families in each of them. Thereafter, small flats were built, and since 1960 each new flat has been allotted to one family only. As a simple ratio of new dwellings to total population, Soviet output rose to the levels of Western Europe by the mid-1950s, and then beyond, but among the other countries of Eastern Europe only Rumania has attained the average quantitative output of the West.

CzECHOSLOVAKIA

In Czechoslovakia the existing stock of housing is rationed by allocation procedures determining the numbers of rooms which each type and size of household is entitled to, and by a system of rents which calls for increased payments for households occupying more space than their numbers justify. Private landlords—who usually own the oldest and poorest property—are expected to repair and maintain their houses, but the rigid restriction of rents renders it difficult to enforce their obligations and the decay that results in some neighbourhoods is frightening to behold. The property of landlords can be taken from them in default of repairs, but the state is in practice reluctant to do this since it would find it difficult to assume the burden itself.

PolAND

Housing policies and procedures in Poland are broadly similar to Czechoslovakia's. Differences arise from the fact that Poland is a larger country (with 31 million people, while Czechoslovakia has 14 million) and is less fully industrialised. Its more rapidly growing population is still heavily dependent upon small primitive and widely scattered farms, especially in the eastern and southern parts of the country. And although the greatest population increase has taken place in the towns—whose inhabitants rose from 9·6 million to 14·1 million between 1950 and 1960—the rural population figure has not yet fallen. Moreover, because Poland's industrial structure and the communications serving it grew up, before 1918, as offshoots of neighbouring economies, industry still tends to be concentrated around the fringes of its territory. The economic problem is thus twofold: to even out regional disparities and develop new industrial centres. Housing policy has a part to play in fulfilling these objectives.

In 1964 nearly 160,000 houses were built: 53% by the state (about two-thirds by local authorities and the rest by enterprises) and 18% by co-operatives (all at 'wholesale prices'); the remaining 29% were built for owner-occupiers (at prices about 9% higher) about half of them with the aid of government credits. In Czechoslovakia, where 83,000 houses were built the same year, 42% were built directly for the state, 1% for enterprises, 33% for cooperatives and 24% for owner-occupation.

In both Poland and Czechoslovakia it is the cooperatives that have been gaining ground most rapidly, mainly at the expense of enterprise housing and owner-occupation. But the enterprises' needs play a large part in this allocation: local authorities with expanding industries get the biggest allocations, 10% to 15% of the municipal programme is reserved for enterprises too small to build their own houses, and many enterprises make loans or grants to cooperatives housing their workers. The municipal authorities are also responsible for housing larger and poorer families. But in Poland the maximum incomes per head which entitle people to get on to the municipal waiting-lists had been reduced by the early 1960s to a level that excluded most of the single and childless and compelled all who could afford it to seek cooperative housing. Similar developments appear to have followed later in Czechoslovakia.

The Poles make greater use of the price mechanism in their town planning procedures than do the Czechoslovaks, partly because of the scarcity of properly equipped sites and the need to ration building land. The shape of new and rebuilt towns is noticeably different from that dictated by competition for sites in a 'free' market. Densities and building heights tend to be lower in central areas and more uniform throughout a town, because they reflect the cost of the buildings rather than the land, and industrialised building methods are most economical if heights are standardised.

ACHIEVEMENTS AND DILEMMAS

Determining the size of the housing programme in a centrally planned economy is a major political decision, made by the government in the course of working out long-term plans for the whole economy. In the short run the economy depends largely on the level of output attained in the previous year or two. Over longer periods housing forms a residual element within a general strategy that normally gives higher priority to other sectors of the economy—heavy industry, agriculture, mining, defence and education, for example. Thus, the scope for improving the housing situation depends, as in the West, largely on the economic and demographic 'climate' confronting the planner, and on the size and efficiency of the building industry—a complex and widely scattered industry which cannot be quickly changed.

Once the volume of resources available for housing has been determined, decisions have to be taken about the proportions of these resources that are to be devoted to increasing the stock of houses, to repair and maintenance work and to the replacement of obsolete property.

Here, the situation is confused by the side effects of major economic and social readjustments proceeding in these countries. Small-scale craft industries of many kinds have been discouraged or obliterated altogether, and such trades play an essential part in the repair and improvement of housing. The introduction of large-scale factory methods of construction, which reduces the costs of building a new house, increases—relatively at least—the costs of repairing and improving existing property. The latter is, therefore, less favoured and more likely to suffer cuts when adjustments have to be made to the programme. Moreover, although the state has greater resources for repairs and improvements than the private owner, it tends, by historical accident, to own the *better* old property. Thus, repairs and improvements are often concentrated on the property in which they are less urgently needed, and replacement programmes tend to be less ambitious and less promptly achieved than programmes that add to the existing stock.

The geographical distribution of house building presents further problems of choice. In the short run it depends heavily upon the distribution of building labour, equipment and materials and on the vigour and efficiency of municipal authorities and local building enterprises. However, in the longer run the natural increase and migration of population are the principal factors to be considered. For a while it seems to have been thought that a government which employs and houses most of the population, and regulates people's movements by a system of passes and permits only surpassed in South Africa, should be able to determine the population of each area by administrative decree. Attempts were in fact made to regulate the growth of Moscow, Leningrad, Belgrade and Warsaw in this way, and to restrict their populations to predetermined figures. Although this seems to have been achieved fairly successfully in Prague, experience elsewhere has shown that the population of an area depends on the regional distribution and growth of industry—and that can only be controlled or predicted in an approximate fashion. 'Temporary' residence permits are given and extended for successive years and, although the holders of these permits have no right to housing provided by the authorities, they—and many others—find living space in the homes of friends and relatives who moved to the city ahead of them.

The Soviet Union is the only country which has clearly declared its intentions of providing free housing, but other East European countries have sometimes appeared to endorse this policy—if only as a distant objective. However, practice is leading in other directions. Cooperative housing is now the most rapidly growing sector of new building in most of these countries. In Poland in 1964 it was provided, under various systems, for households who paid 15% of the capital cost, borrowing 45% to 52% from the state (interest free) and repaying these loans over 40 years. The rest of the capital was provided by the state as an outright grant. In Czechoslovakia in 1963 the members of cooperatives paid 20% to 40% of the capital cost, borrowing 30% to 40% from the state (at 1% interest) and repaying this over 30 years. Further extensions of this system took place the following year. In the Soviet Union in 1964 cooperative members paid no less than 40% of the capital cost, and were entitled to borrow all the remainder (at 1% interest) repaying this over the short period of ten or 15 years. Similar procedures operate in other East European countries. Meanwhile, houses are built for owner-occupation on terms that usually call for a still larger contribution from the household. The tenant of state housing is also being asked to pay more, first through sizable down-payments at the point of rehousing and through charges that cover the full cost of heating and other services, and more recently through higher rents; and it is already clear that a determined campaign to develop cooperatives soon leads to strong pressure for rent increases in the (almost exactly similar) state and enterprise housing with which the cooperatives are competing.

Moreover, after concentrating for many years on producing a larger quantity of housing, often at the expense of reductions in the size and quality of dwellings, there is growing pressure in the wealthier countries of Eastern Europe for *better* housing. In Poland the standards of new housing are still falling, but in Czechoslovakia they are rising. In the Soviet Union it is being argued that further improvements in building productivity should be used to raise standards rather than increase output. That would make a decisive break with previous traditions. As consumer goods grow more plentiful in the centrally planned economies some increase in the size of dwellings will be needed to accommodate the greater range of possessions people own. This development will bring growing pressure for an increase in the contributions people make from their incomes to the cost of their housing. As new flats are built to more generous dimensions, housing will become a much less uniform commodity, and those fortunate enough to get a new flat are likely to be asked for a higher rent.

In Jugoslavia, which has set an example of decentralisation and cautious use of price mechanisms that other East European countries have often followed, the government intends to rely increasingly on a system of publicly subsidised owner-occupation which will call for a fairly heavy contribution from personal incomes. It will probably penalise poorer households, but it may give others greater security and independence, and greater opportunities for choosing the sort of home they want.

FURTHER READING

Engels, F. *The Housing Question*, Lawrence and Wishart, London, 1936.

Michal, Jan M. *Central Planning in Czechoslovakia*, Stanford Univ. Press, Stanford, Calif., 1960; Oxford Univ Press, London, 1961.

Montias, John M. *Central Planning in Poland*, Yale Univ. Press, New Haven, Conn., and London, 1962.

Musil, Jiri, *Housing Needs and Policy in Great Britain and Czechoslovakia*, Univ. of Glasgow, Dept. of Social and Economic Studies, Occasional Papers, 2, Oliver and Boyd, Edinburgh, 1966.

Wiles, Peter. *The Political Economy of Marxism*, Blackwell, Oxford, 1962.

D. V. DONNISON. Professor of Social Administration at the L.S.E. Recently studied housing policies in Europe during a period as consultant to the U.N. Economic Commission for Europe. Publications include *The Government of Housing*, 1967.

SCIENCE AND TECHNOLOGY IN THE SOVIET UNION

RAYMOND HUTCHINGS

SPECIAL POSITION OF SOVIET SCIENCE

THE Russian word for science (*nauka*) signifies any branch of systematic knowledge. The term 'scientist' is used in this chapter consequently in a rather broad sense, to include social scientists and also technologists. Science occupies a special position and role in Soviet society; it does not simply mean the practice of science within a certain country. In the Soviet Union the prestige of science stands as high as in any country in the world. It is considered to be of great national importance, and its potential is regarded as virtually unlimited. Soviet ideology (Marxism-Leninism) professes a strong faith in science, and Soviet science responds by always sketching out optimistic vistas for public exhibition and by refraining from attacking the official ideology. A relatively high proportion of the Soviet leadership has had some scientific training. If any military interest is involved strict scientific secrecy is preserved; technology especially is often regarded as confidential. The sums spent on particular branches of science and the number of scientists working on particular major projects are also secret. A number of higher educational institutions even grant higher degrees secretly.

RUSSIAN SCIENTIFIC HISTORY

The Renaissance which reintroduced many scientific ideas to Western Europe did not influence Russia, which was still under Tatar domination. The transmission to Russia of scientific ideas began much later, in the reign of Peter the Great (1682–1725). A scientific Academy was set up at St. Petersburg as early as 1725, but at first this body recruited only foreigners, who for a considerable time held dominating positions; some of them broke new ground in their scientific researches. The Russian Orthodox Church delayed the spread of scientific teaching but ecclesiastical opposition to science was finally overcome by the end of the 18th century. The Romanov Tsars claimed a right to regulate science, or to prohibit the teaching of particular disciplines or doctrines which appeared to cast doubt on Christianity or the principles of autocracy, and this at times obstructed progress. However, a counter-belief in science developed, and, among intellectuals, this often became obsessive.

Although the volume of work done by Russians was smaller than that of advanced Western countries, its average quality was quite high and often very imaginative. Explorers of Siberia and Central Asia made important discoveries. The science of soils was created in Russia, which, together with

Germany, is the home of non-Euclidean geometry. Geography and mathematics merged in the work of Tsiolkovsky, the pioneer of space flight. Other great Russian scientific figures of the 19th and early 20th centuries include Mendeleyev (the periodic table of elements), Lebedev (pressure exerted by light), Mechnikov (microscopy), Butlerov (chemistry), Chebyshev (probability) and Pavlov (reflexology). Other distinguished names should be mentioned, as for example Kolmogorov (mathematics), Landau and Kurchatov (physics) and Strumilin (economics).

Under Stalin several pre-revolutionary Russian scientists began to be given credit for a number of inventions which elsewhere are attributed to others: for example, the first heavier-than-air flying machine (Mozhaysky), the radio (Popov), the steam engine (ascribed to 'Polzunov and Watt') and the military tank. Certain of these claims, such as Mozhaysky's, have since been abandoned, but others such as Popov's have been consolidated.

At times certain advanced theories, such as Einstein's theory of relativity, were rejected on ideological grounds, while other doctrines (notably that of Lysenko, in agricultural science) were unjustifiably favoured. Scientific necessity has compelled the eventual abandonment of such positions, but only after damage has been done and time lost.

The pre-revolutionary legacy has been important in that, for example, geography and mathematics are still areas of special strength. On a map of the Soviet Union the number of man-made lakes now rivals that of natural lakes. Much has been achieved in geological prospecting; the Arctic has been used as a scientific and meteorological laboratory. Exploration continues, although now (apart from Antarctica) the arena is the ocean and outer space, rather than the land.

IDEOLOGICAL INFLUENCES

The Bolsheviks were much more keenly interested in science than the Tsars had been, but were also more determined to subject it to their own ideology. 'Science has actually entered into our flesh and blood, being fully and genuinely transformed into a component element of our daily life', wrote Lenin. Although premature, his description is coming true in a limited sense. Under Stalin a number of branches of science, especially genetics and the social sciences, were prejudiced by ideological or political interference. Marxism-Leninism is still officially considered to be the pre-eminent science in the Soviet Union; even if it is a philosophy which most Western scientists would reject. Dialectical materialism (*diamat*) figures as a compulsory subject in both school and university curricula. There is, however, no evidence that this philosophy has any direct influence upon types of discoveries made by Soviet scientists. Probably, most often *diamat* is kept in a separate mental compartment. Ideology has not attempted to adopt a specific position in regard to all scientific advances. Because of its ideological overtones science tends to get (official) preference over other fields, whilst in return scientists are expected to strive towards objectives set by the party.

As is the case outside the Soviet Union, a scientific paper published within the Soviet Union must conform to various standard rules. The Soviet criteria are more uniform and are national rather than common to the international scientific community, and they include an ideological framework. In the physical or exact sciences there need be no direct allusions to Marxism-Leninism, provided that no denial of or slur on the ideology is made or is readily inferable. In the social sciences, where topics can be more directly related to the official ideology, an explicit debt to that ideology or to the Communist Party has usually to be professed. Any divergent proposition has to be phrased with particular circumspection, and written in such a way that it does not at once strike the reader's eye.

Recently there have been indications that some Soviet scientists are beginning to reject the role of specialised assistants to the regime in assigned fields, and to question basic dogmas, such as the clash between 'socialism' and 'capitalism'—or the necessity of censorship. A case in point is the remarkable manuscript by Andrey Sakharov (possibly the father of the Soviet hydrogen bomb) entitled *Progress, Coexistence and Intellectual Freedom* which has recently been published in the West.

Since the late 1920s an important influence of communist ideology has been the focussing of attention on the physical rather than on the social sciences. One obvious reason for this has been that the social sciences, such as economics, sociology, philosophy, history, could clash with the official ideology and doctrine. A further effect of the impact of ideology has been that students have been deterred from entering fields of study where ideological influences are strong, since the pressures towards uniformity are there overwhelming. Thus the most able students are attracted rather into branches such as mathematics, physics or medicine, where these influences are more remote. As a result the social sciences have tended to be neglected.

Among particular disciplines, pride of place is held by mathematics and physics. Mathematical virtuosity is specially useful at the present time, when virtually all scientific and arts subjects are becoming influenced by an increasingly quantitative approach and when computers are beginning to be widely applied. As is the international trend, biology is also gaining in importance. Ideology has encouraged team research, and consequently individuals can, and do, specialise narrowly.

PLANNING AND FINANCING

Like most aspects of national life, Soviet science is in theory 'planned' and conducted in a centralised manner. However, the plans are relatively loose. Quarterly, annual and quinquennial scientific plans have been formulated, but only the shorter ones, and perhaps not even these, could claim to be operational. Annual and long-term plans of financing of science within the framework of the national economic plans have been drawn up since 1962. From the outset Soviet science was supposed to contribute towards the solving of practical problems, but scientific plans differ significantly from economic plans for various reasons, including the fact that in science particular individuals are more influential whereas results are more uncertain.

The St Petersburg Academy was renamed the Academy of Sciences of the USSR after the Revolution and moved from Petrograd to Moscow in 1934. Other administrative changes followed and since 1963 the 'general direction of the development of the natural and social sciences' has been transferred from the political authorities back to the Academy, albeit subject to overall party and government control. Academicians enjoy a very high status and are elected for life—Khrushchev's suggestion that they be elected for a fixed period not having been adopted. The present chairman of the Academy is M. V. Keldysh.

The Academy of Sciences exists at the federal level (in Moscow) and in the union republics. Over the years all 15 republics, except the largest (the RSFSR) have formed their own academies. These academies have control over various other scientific institutions and institutes ranging from as few as twelve under the Lithuanian academy to as many as 215 under the Academy of Sciences of the USSR. The number of highest-grade scientists (academicians, full members and corresponding members) per academy varies from 0 to 586, and of all scientific workers from 236 to 29,987. Including the staff of academies of agricultural, medical and pedagogical sciences, and of the communal economy of the RSFSR, the Soviet Union at the end of 1967 had 2,298 highest-grade scientists, and in all 69,896 scientists within the network of the various academies of science.

The formation of republican academies has brought about some decentralisation although at one time its extent seemed to have fallen short of the government's intention. Khrushchev, especially, tried to move research bodies out of Moscow into the provinces, but was largely frustrated in his wish. One major step has been to set up, in 1957, a Siberian branch of the Academy of Sciences at Akademgorodok, near Novosibirsk. This body controls some 40 institutions in Siberia and the Soviet Far East. Headed by a mathematician, M. A. Lavrentev, it has taken the lead in the study of mathematical economics. Subsequently, however, the increasing number of scientific institutions established under the aegis of the Academy of Sciences of the USSR suggests a trend of increasing centralisation rather than decentralisation.

The number of Soviet 'scientific workers' has increased steadily from 10,200 in 1914 (on a comparable territory) to 14,000 in 1926, 354,000 in 1960 and 770,000 at the end of 1967—a more than 75-fold increase in 53 years. However, the great majority of 'scientific workers' might more correctly be termed technologists. The Soviet Union, which holds about 7% of the world's population, claims one-quarter of the world's 'scientists'. An interesting aspect of this is that in 1967 38·3% of Soviet scientists were women, whereas in the West there is a smaller proportion of female scientists, especially those married.

Scientists work mainly in 'scientific' (i.e. research) establishments (58·7% in 1965) and in 'higher educational establishments' (33·4% in 1965) where the emphasis is on teaching. The proportion employed in 'scientific establishments' has risen: this seems to have been unscheduled, and might be regarded as a Soviet version of the 'brain-drain'. In 1965 the average scientific establishment employed about 80 scientists. Enlargement of these establishments has been entirely a phenomenon of the post-war period.

DISTRIBUTION OF SCIENTISTS

The distribution of scientists in the various fields of science is known only very approximately. About 45% are in 'technical' sciences; a term which includes all engineering and so probably a large part of defence research. The 'technical' group has been continually growing, like the 'physical-mathematical' group which is the second biggest (though still much smaller than the 'technical' group). Against this, the 'medical-pharmaceutical' and 'agricultural-veterinary' groups and all humanities have failed to hold their own, even although since 1960 economics (particularly the mathematical variety) has been gaining ground.

With its huge population, the Soviet Union has a considerable pool of talent and ability to draw on. The proportion of students in each branch of learning is regulated by the government, through its control over scientific education, although naturally there is a time-lag in steering the output of graduates from one field to another. The main official concern has been to ensure a sufficiency of trained scientists in the most advanced natural or exact sciences, including those sciences which have military applications.

FINANCING OF RESEARCH

Scientific research is financed by the state, which has normally contributed about 71% of the cost of research through the budget (this proportion differs in different components of the total). The remainder is almost entirely made up by contributions from state enterprises. Budget appropriations increased 47-fold from 1940 to 1967, from 0·105 thousand million roubles to 4·931 thousand million roubles. The share of science in total budget expenditures rose during this period from 0·6% to 4·3%. The budget allocation is stated to cover 'research into cosmic space, the peaceful use of atomic energy, rocket construction, radio electronics, automation and other branches of knowledge'. No breakdown of expenditures is published, although total spending is sometimes divided under functional headings (for instance, capital investment or wages), and by republic. The budget finances the various academies of science, the ministries and any research by business organisations which is of a theoretical character or which is regarded as nationally important.

The budget contribution consists of a federal and a republican element (the latter being divided among the 15 union republics). The federal element rose from 45·8% of the total in 1940 to 80·0% in 1960, clearly indicating how scientific spending became more centralised. This trend was particularly striking as it conflicted with a decentralising trend in *total* budget spending. Federal spending rose especially during the years 1940–50, perhaps mainly in connection with defence and nuclear research.

Scientific spending from all sources has risen particularly rapidly from 1957 onwards (until 1965, at 17·4% annually). This is probably connected with space research (the first *sputnik* having been launched in 1957). It has been necessary to slow down its rate of growth (to 9% annually between 1965 and 1967) as the expenditure would have become too burdensome for the economy. Although there have been indications that pressures have been put on scientific bodies to economise, scientific spending in absolute terms will doubtless go on rising.

Since scientific research is directed from the centre it is not surprising that 'big science' has tended to have preference: space exploration and nuclear physics are perhaps the most imposing illustrations of this. The Soviet Union is building the world's largest astronomical telescope (the diameter of the mirror is 6m., i.e. 236 in.) and has constructed the most powerful hydrogen bomb. The supersonic TU-144 airliner made its maiden flight in advance of the *Concorde*—which it strikingly resembles. Similarly, the Soviet Union has achieved many 'firsts' in space exploration. A systematic programme is being pursued, and evidently voyages of long duration by astronauts are envisaged. Although these are natural spheres of activity for a scientific and economic super-power, many of them also harmonise with, or are even closely connected with, military purposes.

The costs of particular projects, even broad categories of expenditures, are not disclosed. However, the space component is likely to be extremely expensive, and might account for about 40% of the whole scientific programme (this would be somewhere between the West European and US figures). Reasons for researching into space are not declared: a totalitarian state is not accountable as regards its aims or expenditures. Achieving the leadership in what is seen as a competition with the USA is of obvious importance to the Soviet Union; the military interest is also, doubtless, considerable. 'Spin-off', or fall-out, is probably smaller than in the USA in view of the particular secrecy surrounding the Soviet effort and the consequent restrictions on the dissemination of scientific information even internally. And, because the Soviet Union is, in many respects, less advanced economically, such technological innovations would, in any event, be more difficult to utilise effectively. Total Soviet spending on science, including research and development, amounts to over 3% of GNP, which is about equal to the US proportion and exceeds that of Western Europe.

The introduction of new production techniques is financed from funds allocated for capital investment, from a fund for the assimilation of new techniques, from state bank credits and from other sources. Loans are of minor importance, but they have been increasing rapidly of late. Expenditure on the purchase of research equipment, instruments and appliances appears to have been kept low before 1961, perhaps because of the demands of space research, but has since caught up and now comprises about 15% of the overall expenditure on science.

ASPECTS OF SOVIET TECHNOLOGY

The Soviet Union has been relatively slow to adopt the latest advances in technology, but it is gradually catching up. Main directions of progress resemble those in other countries, but emphasis has been given to certain aspects. Thus, for example, there has been a preference for large-scale rather than small-scale appliances and for technical excellence and up-to-dateness, regardless of the needs of the economy. Consequently, technical progress has been uneven.

In particular, electrification was assigned a crucial role in Soviet industrial development. Lenin coined the slogan, 'Communism is Soviet power plus the electrification of the whole country'. Electricity was envisaged as a universal force capable of transforming the entire economy. The theoretical ability to control electricity generation and transmission from a single centre doubtless appealed to the Soviet leadership. Much has been achieved in electrification, but undue stress on hydroelectric power has had negative effects, notably that of excessive inundation. In general, land has not been used economically and large areas have suffered pollution.

Emphasis on continuity of progress is demonstrated by the efforts to develop the continuous casting of steel; in gasification of coal; in increases in shift-working; and in tendencies to restrict the variety of products and to change only rarely their style or specification.

Iron and steel were the stuff of Soviet industrialisation, much less attention having been paid in the earlier stages to non-ferrous metals or to chemicals. Among fuels, until quite recently, coal was favoured to the comparative neglect of oil and natural gas, while among textile fibres cotton was favoured and most synthetics neglected. Until lately 'large chemistry' (such as sulphuric acid and synthetic rubber) was preferred to 'small chemistry' (including pharmaceutical preparations and catalysts). There has been a bias in favour of using materials which are domestically available and largely doing without those which must be imported. Consequently, the opening up of new mineral deposits, industrial diamonds for example (within the last 15 years in Siberia), has permitted a great increase in domestic consumption.

Mechanisation and automation have been encouraged although the lip-service paid to them has often gilded reality. Stalin announced an objective of eliminating manual labour wherever it was physically strenuous, but despatched armies of forced labourers to dig the Baltic-White Sea Canal, and other still less justified projects. Mechanisation has, perhaps, been aided by the absence of any popular sentiment that hand-made products are intrinsically superior to machine-made ones. However, alongside a large and efficient machine one may find manual workers toiling at ancillary processes; thus, for instance, mechanical handling has tended to be neglected. Successive slogans of 'technique decides everything' and 'cadres decide everything' omitted the middleground of man-machine relationships. Only recently, after a 40-year interval, has interest been revived in the 'scientific organisation of labour'.

Control systems, computer technology, automation and measuring devices form a large and interconnected branch which is currently receiving great attention. Development of remote-control devices has been necessitated, *inter alia*, by space flight. Automation is favoured, as being more fool-proof than the human element: for instance, the Soviet space programme has relied on automatic devices to a greater extent than in the USA, although sometimes automation has been introduced without adequate economic justification. Like mechanisation, automation is helped by the lack of any organised opposition from Soviet trade unions, but hostility due to inertia may be encountered.

The Soviet Union has made great strides in nuclear research. A programme to develop nuclear weapons was suggested by Soviet scientists in the early years of World War II, though it was not then adopted by the government. After the war nuclear, and especially rapidly thermonuclear, bombs were made. The Soviet Union built the first nuclear-powered icebreaker and the first (very small-scale) atomic power station, although this was not followed by any rapid development of nuclear power generation. Soviet scientists have already suggested the possibility of harnessing nuclear fusion for generating power, although this will not be achieved in the near future.

TECHNICAL INNOVATION AND INTRODUCTION OF NEW TECHNOLOGY

Technical innovation and introduction of new techniques in production are the responsibilities of central government bodies, research institutes and state enterprises. A State Committee (*Gostekhnika*) was set up for this purpose in 1948 and, except during one four-year interval, it has continued to function, albeit with kaleidoscopic changes of title. Its present title is the State Committee of the Council of Ministers of the USSR for Science and Technology (GNTK of the USSR, currently headed by V. A. Kirillin, a thermophysicist). This body also has the function of collaborating with the Academy of Sciences in working out proposals for the main trends of development of science and technology.

The main work in research and development is done by research institutes, whose numbers grew quickly during the 1920s. Although under Stalin many institutes concerned with social sciences were closed, their total number increased to 2,084 at the end of 1965 ('scientific research institutes, their subsidiaries and divisions'). Smaller units, such as departments, have tended to proliferate. Institutes are narrowly specialised on a branch basis. In contrast to the situation in the USA, a smaller proportion of research is carried out at universities.

Institutes cannot always bridge the gap between the germination of an idea and its practical realisation. A fairly recent innovation has been the 'scientific firm' which is entrusted with all tasks of design, coordination, etc. Experimental works attached to institutes fulfil a somewhat analogous role.

Innovation is also seen as the duty of enterprises. When in October 1965 a branch system of administration was reintroduced, many advantages were expected in connection with introducing new techniques. Between 1966 and 1970 experimental output was supposed to develop faster than output generally.

Managerial inertia in introducing new methods is another factor militating against the introduction of new techniques and has long been recognised as such. It has three main sources: managers feel that current routines are disturbed, that extra costs are not reimbursed and that difficulties would be experienced in obtaining supplies. These factors stem from the rigidity of the economic system and its refusal to allow enterprises to make appreciable profits out of their own initiative. Certain non-economic incentives are available, though, and the hierarchical system may be used to compel the adoption of a new method. To favour such innovations, capital funds from the state budget have been (and to a large extent still are) a 'free good' to state enterprises. In the whole economy, an enormous number of technical innovations are claimed (about 4,000,000 annually, of which some 2,500,000 are actually introduced). These statistics seem less impressive, however, when averaged on a per-enterprise basis and in general innovation is hampered by red tape and departmental barriers.

Encouragement for improvements in quality and methods is provided by the state system of standards, an official system of specifications. The number of federal standards (GOSTs)—republican standards also exist—has increased slowly in recent years: there were 8,600 in January 1952 and only 'over 10,000' 13 years later. By 1970 the number is to be increased by 22,000 to 25,000, with 'radical' improvements in content. This increased attention to standards exemplifies the importance now attached to raising the quality of industrial output.

FOREIGN INTERACTIONS

Soviet technology has borrowed from many countries but from two especially: Germany and the USA. Between 1917 and 1931 these two were well in the lead. After the war Germany lost the capacity to supply the Soviet Union, but in compensation the latter seized German equipment and some scientists as reparations. East Germany has now taken over to a large extent the role of scientific adviser to the Soviet Union.

Since World War II the East European states have industrialised themselves and reorientated their trade towards the Soviet Union, by which they are regarded as valuable scientific partners. Among these states scientific collaboration has become an organised interstate activity on a greatly enlarged scale when compared with the pre-war situation.

Many foreign prototypes have been adopted by the Soviet Union for mass production. Generally, serviceability and ruggedness are preferred to an exquisite finish. Whenever a new process is introduced from abroad, or developed at home, the Soviet leadership insists that it should be the latest one. Among consumer goods, many foreign prototypes have been copied, often with faults and usually without acknowledgment.

Although Soviet scientists were cut off from Western developments for many years, information is now much more accessible. An elaborately organised department, the VINITI, formed in 1952, makes available to Soviet specialists translated excerpts from material published abroad. The scale of its work is huge, over 23,000 periodicals being scanned. Yet its activity does not satisfy all requirements, and Soviet (like Western) scientists have become convinced that they must adopt radically new methods if they are to keep pace with the constantly swelling flow of information.

The Soviet Union has not been a party to copyright agreements (although since July 1965 it has been bound by the Paris Convention to observe patents and trademarks), and the publication in translation of foreign works popularising science enables the Soviet public to be informed of general developments without any risk of compromise to Soviet military or technical secrets. In recent years, transmission of scientific knowledge *from* the Soviet Union has increased sharply. Russian, which itself has absorbed numerous foreign scientific terms, is now becoming an important scientific language and translations of Russian scientific texts are increasingly numerous.

Exchange of information takes place mainly through the activities of technical delegations. (The function of a delegation is to learn rather than to teach, although some do both.) What may or may not be shown in the Soviet Union to foreigners is no doubt coordinated in advance. Within the permitted limits, information seems to be provided willingly. Exchange of delegations within the Soviet bloc is on an especially large scale. Contact and collaboration are not equally good in all spheres: in particular, they are much weaker in the social sciences than in others. Scientific and technical information with Soviet bloc countries is exchanged under two main auspices: the Joint Technical and Scientific Commissions which have been set up by most pairs of bloc countries, or one or other of the 19-odd permanent commissions of Comecon to which these countries belong. In numbers of items the Soviet Union has apparently imparted much more than it has received, but there has been an approximate balance with East Germany and Czechoslovakia—the two most industrialised East European countries. Such exchanges are in principle free of charge, apart from clerical costs, so that they favour the less advanced countries in relation to the rest. As regards the whole Soviet bloc the Soviet Union has imparted the most, relative to what it has received, in technical documentation on capital construction, and the least in descriptions of production technologies.

Collaboration between academies of science of the Comecon countries is growing, and fruitful combined work is reportedly carried out, as for example in high molecular compounds, solid-state physics, the chemistry of natural and physiological active compounds and peaceful uses of atomic energy. Direct links between Soviet scientific research or design organisations and those of other bloc countries are being strengthened and extended. Multilateral scientific collaboration between member-states has developed also outside Comecon. Most prominent in this connection is the Joint Nuclear Research Institute at Dubna, in the Soviet Union, set up in March 1956. A bilateral scientific agreement has been signed with France.

Scientific congresses are frequently held in the Soviet Union and foreign experts are invited to them—just as Soviet scientists are invited to congresses held elsewhere. The Soviet Union has participated in international scientific projects such as the IGY (International Geophysical Year). Scientific exchanges tend to be rather impersonal. Particular Soviet scientists may not respond to invitations, or may be unable to attend. The Soviet Union regards itself as a scientific unit, so that if a foreign invitation is accepted the individual selected may not be the one invited, although it is claimed that an attempt is made to select the most suitable person. This is not how scientific relations are usually conducted among Western scientists, and disharmony or misunderstanding may result.

CONCLUSION

The virtues and vices of Soviet science and technology are those of a state-controlled system. The natural and exact sciences are far ahead of the social sciences. The huge scale of the Soviet scientific effort assures it of major importance in areas where that effort is concentrated.

FURTHER READING

Davies, R. W. *Science and the Soviet Economy*, An inaugural Lecture delivered in the University of Birmingham on 18 January 1967.

Fischer, George (ed.) *Science and Ideology in Soviet Society*, Atherton Press, New York, 1968.

Freeman, C. and Young, A. *The Research and Development Effort in Western Europe, North America and the Soviet Union*, OECD, Paris, 1965.

Gill, Richard Rockingham. 'Problems of Decision Making in Soviet Science Policy', *Minerva*, V, 2, Winter, 1967.

Graham, Loren R. *The Soviet Academy of Sciences and the Communist Party, 1927–1932*, Princeton Univ. Press, Princeton, N.J., 1967.

Science Policy and Organisation of Research in the USSR, UNESCO, 1967.

The Editors of *Survey*. *The State of Soviet Science*, M.I.T. Press, Cambridge, Mass., 1965.

United Nations ECE. *Policies and means of Promoting Technical Progress*, UN Publications, New York, 1968.

Vucinich, Alexander. *Science in Russian Culture* (2 vols.); *A History of 1860*, I, Stanford Univ. Press, Stanford, Calif., 1963; Peter Owen, London, 1965.

RAYMOND HUTCHINGS. Research Specialist in Soviet Studies at the Royal Institute of International Affairs, London. In 1964–8 Senior Research Fellow in Economic History, at the Australian National University. Has contributed many articles on Soviet economic and economic-historical themes to various academic journals.

RELIGION

THE ORTHODOX CHURCH IN THE SOVIET UNION AND EASTERN EUROPE

JĀNIS SAPIETS

THE Orthodox Church consists of about 70 million believers; of these the majority (over 30 million in the Soviet Union and another 30 million in East European countries) live under communist regimes—that is, under a government policy of militant atheism, anti-religious legislation and, sometimes, open persecution. In the 52 years since the Revolution, the Orthodox hierarchy of the Soviet Union have gradually evolved a compromise relationship with the state that has also been followed by Orthodox churches in Eastern Europe.

THE RELATIONSHIP BETWEEN CHURCH AND STATE

During 1917–18 there took place three events crucial to the later position of the Orthodox Church under communism:

1. The Patriarchate was restored in 1917, transferring influence among the hierarchy from the six-man Holy Synod to the one man elected as Patriarch; policy towards the state depends largely on the personality of the incumbent Patriarch.

2. In 1918 the Soviet constitution guaranteed 'freedom of religious and anti-religious propaganda', but

3. The decree on the separation of church and state deprived the church of its property, allowing churches to be used for worship only at the discretion of local authorities; convents, monasteries, seminaries and theological academies were closed.

The period 1918–26 was one of violent persecution, during which Patriarch Tikhon tried to remain politically neutral. After his death and the imprisonment of his nominated successors, the Metropolitan Sergei took over the leadership, though he was elected Patriarch only in 1943. In 1927 Sergei made a declaration avowing the Orthodox Church's absolute loyalty to the Soviet state—a declaration that forms the basis of the Orthodox hierarchy's relations with the state to the present. Statements were and are issued by the church in support of state foreign policy and claiming, against all evidence to the contrary, the existence of 'religious freedom' in the Soviet Union. Sergei's declaration achieved little at the time: in 1929 the constitution was amended to guarantee 'freedom of religious *belief* and anti-religious propaganda'; in 1936 'belief' was changed to 'worship'—which is the position now. The church exists in Soviet law solely for the purpose of worship: it is forbidden to organise charitable or social work, to give children religious instruction or to organise classes for adults. Even where believers are allowed to use a church for worship, the priest must get special permission from the local deputy of the Council for Religious Affairs to conduct services.

The Orthodox Church's wartime support of the Soviet government gained it a certain amount of toleration. The number of churches increased from 4,255 in 1941 to 22,000 in 1947 and the number of priests from 5,665 to 33,000. Eight seminaries and two theological academies were permitted to open. However, the church's legal position was little improved; and the authorities do not always act within the law. Churches are still closed against the wishes of the believers; militant atheists often disrupt services with impunity. Priests are still imprisoned, often on trumped up embezzlement and debauchery charges. The Orthodox Church's only regular publication is the strictly censored *Journal of the Moscow Patriarchate*. Bibles and prayer-books are almost unobtainable.

In contrast to this is the 'freedom of anti-religious propaganda'. *Science and Religion*, the official atheist magazine, is published in large editions throughout the country. The All Union Society for the Dissemination of Scientific and Political Knowledge, the post-war successor to the League of Militant Atheists, produces an annual programme of 660,000 atheist lectures. However, since the 1954 CPSU decree denouncing the inefficiency of anti-religious propaganda 'which only led to an increase in the number of citizens observing religious ceremonies', it has become steadily more obvious that atheist propaganda is not having its desired effect. In town churches, two liturgies are said on Sundays because of the numbers attending. The Soviet press regularly castigates members of the party and komsomol for taking part in baptism, marriage and funeral services. A more ideological campaign against religion was attempted from 1954–8; there was a lessening of direct pressure on believers and an intensification of atheist education programmes. This was admitted in 1957 by the chairman of the All Union Society to have achieved only 'a partial revival of religion'. 1958 marked a return to more direct methods, while keeping up the ideological attack. There have been much publicised attempts by the government to replace religious baptism, marriage and burial by secular ceremonies. Palaces of Weddings and of the Newly Born have been built in towns; but the press has drawn attention to couples who take part in both secular and religious ceremonies. *Science and Religion* has openly encouraged both the dismissal of believers from their jobs and direct interference with the legal right of parents to instruct their children in religion. In some districts children have been forcibly prevented from entering churches and even removed from the custody of their parents; priests have recently been forbidden to give communion to children.

In 1961–4 about half of the Soviet Union's 20,000 Orthodox churches were closed. Only three seminaries are still open and in many districts priests have been refused registration. The Bishops Sergei of Astrakhan, Mikhail of Smolensk and Job of Kazan have been imprisoned on charges of tax-evasion and embezzlement. Many monasteries opened after the war have been closed, for example the Caves of Kiev and St. Job's of Pochaev.

The Policy of the Hierarchy Towards the Government

All this has happened without an open protest from the Orthodox hierarchy. Recently, however, there have been signs that a considerable body of Orthodox opinion no longer agrees with the Patriarchate's submissive policy towards the government. In 1965, two priests of the Moscow diocese—

Nikolai Eshliman and Gleb Yakunin—sent open letters to President Podgorny, the Patriarch and all bishops, protesting against state infringements of the right to religious worship guaranteed in the Soviet constitution, and charging the church authorities with submitting to secret oral dictates from the government. They were banned from priestly activity in 1966 by the Patriarch 'for disrupting the internal peace of the church'. It now appears that this was only the tip of the iceberg: there has recently been a flood of petitions to church and state authorities about illegal state pressure on believers. This insistence on legality, citing the Soviet constitution and church canon law, is also the main characteristic of Archbishop Yermogen's debate with the Patriarchate. Yermogen was removed from his see at Kaluga after disputes with the local authorities. In his letters to the Patriarch, (1956–66) protesting about his enforced retirement, he accuses the Council for Religious Affairs of acting unconstitutionally against the church and implies that the Orthodox hierarchy, far from defending the church's legal rights, acquiesce in state illegalities—such as the closing of churches in 1961–4. Yermogen also accuses the hierarchy of breaking their own canon law in electing bishops without the participation of all existing bishops. He is far from being a solitary figure—in 1965 he was supported by eight bishops. The next Patriarchal election (Alexei is 91) may bring the question of uncanonical procedure into the open.

The writings of two Orthodox laymen, Anatoly Levitin and Boris Talantov, now illegally circulating in the Soviet Union, also reflect dissatisfaction with the present policy of the hierarchy. Talantov accuses the Patriarchate of betraying the church abroad—referring probably to the Orthodox delegation's denial of religious persecution in the Soviet Union at the World Council of Churches. Talantov calls for 'false pastors', especially the Metropolitan Nikodim, to be repudiated. Levitin warns that 'the patience of Orthodox believers is not unlimited: unworthy conduct may lead to schism'. This is no idle fear: in the 1930s, many Orthodox priests broke away from the Patriarchate, refusing to be registered and holding illegal services—these mostly returned to the Patriarchate after the war, but, more recently, the Baptists in the Soviet Union have divided on the question of submission to the state and a large number have rejected the official Baptist leadership. So far an open split has been avoided by the Orthodox Church, but there are serious divisions beneath the surface.

REGIONAL CHURCHES OF THE SOVIET UNION

The Orthodox Church of Trans-Carpathian Ukraine and Galicia, which was annexed in 1945 from Poland and Czechoslovakia, contains a large number of former Uniates, whose church was declared illegal in 1945. The number of churches in this region has been much reduced due to the allegedly nationalist Ukrainian character of its priests.

The other Orthodox Church of the Soviet Union—the Georgian Church—is completely subject to the Moscow Patriarchate; it has been much persecuted and is said to have only 100 churches and priests left. Services are often conducted in ruined churches by laymen. The Georgian Church has no seminary of its own: candidates for the priesthood have to study at seminaries where they receive little instruction in Georgian religious literature.

The Armenian Monophysites are in a much better position, with 3,500,000 believers, one seminary and discreet aid from Armenians abroad. The Armenian Patriarch is elected by the laity which includes all unbelieving

Armenians. Hence the government is able to exercise considerable direct pressure on the Patriarchal elections.

THE ORTHODOX CHURCHES OF EASTERN EUROPE

Apart from those of Serbia, Macedonia and pro-Chinese Albania, the Orthodox Churches of Eastern Europe have, until comparatively recently, been completely dependent on the Moscow Patriarchate and have followed a similar cooperative policy towards the state.

Rumania

This policy has paid off best in Rumania, with 12,000,000 believers the largest Orthodox Church after that of the Soviet Union. Because of the Patriarchate's cooperation with the party, the Orthodox Church remained the national church after 1945: there was no official separation of church and state. This gives the Orthodox Church certain privileges—for instance, salaries for the clergy and eight church publications—sometimes resented by Rumania's more oppressed denominations. A large number of churches are open (300 in Bucharest as against 55 in Moscow), but since 1958 over half of Rumania's monks and nuns have been forced to leave their religious houses, and the orders have been forbidden to accept novices. The Uniate Church is still illegal in Rumania. The largely Uniate region of Transylvania was forced to unite with the Orthodox Church under government pressure.

Bulgaria

Bulgaria's Orthodox Church of 6,000,000 is just as cooperative politically, but gets far less in return. The church retains one seminary and quite a large number of monasteries: but anti-religious legislation is severe. The Bulgarian Church gains some prestige from its position as a symbol of national sovereignty and Slav culture. On 24 May 1969 there was a national holiday in memory of Cyril and Methodius, the founders of the Bulgarian Church and inventors of the Cyrillic alphabet; it was marked by an Orthodox conference under the aegis of the Moscow Patriarchate.

Hungary

The small Hungarian Orthodox community of 40,000 is unique in having no national ecclesiastical jurisdiction. The Orthodox believers are divided between the four Patriarchates of Serbia, Rumania, the Soviet Union and Bulgaria, each section governed by the appropriate episcopal representative. Voluntary religious instruction for children has recently been introduced in Hungary.

Poland

The Orthodox Church of Poland is half composed of Uniates not entirely voluntarily absorbed in 1945. The Polish Orthodox hierarchy conforms to the policies of the Moscow Patriarchate and has had a head from the Soviet Union since 1959. The Orthodox, like other denominations, benefit from the allowing of voluntary religious instruction for schoolchildren—a concession to Poland's strong Catholic Church.

Czechoslovakia

Before 1968 the Czechoslovak Orthodox Church was in a similar position to that of Poland, with Moscow-orientated policies. The church was subject to severe pressure from the Novotný government and a large number of Uniates were forcibly incorporated into the Orthodox Church. The reforms initiated by Dubček in January 1968 marked a new church-state relationship which persisted even after the invasion by the Warsaw Pact countries in the August of that year. The church press is no more or less restricted than other papers. By public demand voluntary religious education, entirely supervised by religious authorities, has been restored in schools. Theological faculties have been restored and there is talk of reopening theological academies. Following a press campaign and a report by the Health and Social Committee on the valuable work done by religious orders in pensioners' homes and other institutions, convents and monasteries are to be allowed to receive novices once again.

The Uniate Church has been rehabilitated and 250,000 Uniates have left the Orthodox Church. There are still 100 Orthodox parishes (100,000 members) but the Czechoslovak Orthodox are probably handicapped by their previous connections with the Moscow Patriarchate—unpopular in Czechoslovakia since it was the only church in Eastern Europe to support the intervention of the Soviet Union.

Serbia

The Orthodox Church of Serbia, with 9,000,000 believers, has never been influenced by the Moscow Patriarchate to the same extent as other East European Orthodox. It underwent a certain amount of persecution by the communist government of Jugoslavia but retained much prestige because of its sufferings under the Nazis. There have been attempts to disrupt the church by territorial fragmentation—hence the creation of a separate Church of Macedonia. The Serbian Orthodox continue to show much independence of the state, however, and church-state relations have improved of late. Priests are allowed to travel to Western colleges and books are imported from the World Council of Churches. The Serbian Orthodox have also published the Bible in a large edition.

Albania

The isolation of Albania from the Soviet bloc makes information on its small Orthodox community (100,000 in 1945) scarce. There has been violent persecution and the government boasts of being the first to liquidate all religious survivals.

FURTHER READING

Conquest, Robert (ed.) *Religion in the USSR*, Bodley Head, London; Frederick A. Praeger, New York, 1968.

Kolarz, Walter. *Religion in the Soviet Union*, Macmillan, London, 1961; St. Martin's, New York, 1962.

Struve, Nikita. *Christians in Contemporary Russia*. Harvill Press, London; Scribner, New York, 1967.

Ware, Timothy. *The Orthodox Church*. Penguin, London, 1964.

ROMAN CATHOLICS AND UNIATES

MICHAEL BOURDEAUX

HISTORY

AT one time it was possible to talk of a communist 'policy' towards the Roman Catholic Church (and indeed towards religion in general). Stalin's rule aimed at removing all the best Christian leaders and holding the mass of church people in an iron grip of submission. Naturally, the Roman Catholic Church in Eastern Europe, both because it was by far the strongest denomination and because of its loyalty to a leader well beyond the confines of communist influence, was subjected to especially intense persecution. Cardinal Stepinac (Jugoslavia), Bishop Kaczmarek (Poland), Cardinal Mindszenty (Hungary) and Cardinal Beran (Czechoslovakia) were only some of the most prominent among the Catholic hierarchy who were arrested under Stalin and held without trial or sentenced to savage terms of imprisonment. The list of martyrs is a long one.

Since 1956, however, the various governments of Eastern Europe have been much freer to follow their own religious policies. As a result, there has been so much divergence that generalisations are no longer possible. The state of religion in each country is governed by prevailing national and cultural factors which affect to a surprising degree even such a homogeneous body as the Roman Catholic Church. One can say that in general the communist governments have decided that their policies of direct physical repression have been counter-productive and damaging to the national image in times when they have begun to seek a *rapprochement* with the West; yet at the same time one has to qualify this by saying that in two countries (Albania and the Soviet Union) the Catholic situation is certainly no better—and possibly worse—than it was during Stalin's time. While the Russian Orthodox Church and the Reformed Church of Hungary have signed purely political statements in support of Soviet intervention in Czechoslovakia, none of the Roman Catholic Churches in Eastern Europe was forced to take this step—a sign of their continuing resilience.

In this review we will, with certain exceptions, omit those countries in which Roman Catholics are only a tiny minority. We will treat the rest in a progression from those where a situation of persecution prevails to those with comparative religious freedom.

ALBANIA

At the time of the communist takeover, the Roman Catholic Church in Albania was a minority of about 11% of the population (the Orthodox community was twice as large as this, but the majority of the people were

Muslims). Now, together with China, Albania claims to be the first com-pletely atheist state in the world, i.e. one where no institutional religion exists. The situation there had been difficult for religious believers for years, but in February 1967 it became considerably worse. Those who persisted tenaciously in their faith had to face acts of extreme provocation and public humiliation.

In July 1967 four Franciscan friars were killed when a gang of hooligans set fire to their monastery at Arramadhe. This was most likely an officially inspired act, for the youth newspaper, *Zëri i Rinise*, had conducted an especially virulent anti-religious campaign. In November 1967 it claimed that the clergy were voluntarily handing over their buildings to the state to be adapted to more productive purposes, but it contradicted itself when it went on to complain that Catholic priests had 'returned to their towns and villages in secret' and were now reading mass, hearing confessions and per-forming baptisms in private houses.

The laws recognising the existence of the religious communities have now been repealed, so the Roman Catholic Church in Albania has lost its right to institutional existence.

THE SOVIET UNION

Although in the Soviet Union as a whole the Roman Catholics are a minority, in the west of Belorussia and of the Ukraine, and also in Lithuania, they are numerous. We concentrate here upon Lithuania, as it is traditionally one of the bastions of Catholicism in Europe, owning the allegiance of about 84% of the population in 1940.

The following statistical table is a revealing indicator of the way in which the visible organisation of the church has declined since Lithuania became part of the Soviet Union.

TABLE

RELIGIOUS CONDITIONS IN LITHUANIA

	1940	*1967*
Archbishops and bishops in office	10	1
		(and a second consecrated February 1968)
Priests	1,450	844
		(about 100 of whom are incapacitated)
Parishes and mission churches	717	610
Other churches and chapels	330	5
Theological seminaries	4	1
Theological students (diocesan seminaries)	425	29
Theological students (monasteries)	141	0
University theological faculty	1	0
Monasteries	37	0
Convents	85	0
Membership of Catholic organisations	800,000	0
Schools and kindergartens	72	0
Charitable institutions	49	0
Journals and daily papers	32	0

Source: adapted from *Religious Conditions in Lithuania under Soviet Occupation* (see Further Reading).

The Lithuanian Roman Catholics have been one of the hardest hit of all religious communities in the Soviet Union. There was no improvement in their situation at the time of the Second Vatican Council, even though the Soviet government then tried to convince religious public opinion in the West that it wanted better relations with the Vatican. At the same time, there is hard evidence that the decline in organised church life has not brought about a corresponding fall in religious adherence. As Antanas Snieckus, first secretary of the Communist Party of Lithuania wrote (*Kommunistas*, No. 4, 1964):

> The emissary who had been sent from Moscow to Lithuania in 1963 to ascertain religious conditions . . . observed the strange phenomenon that, even though churches and religious societies were decreasing, the number of religious customs and practices was still very great.

HUNGARY

Among the many demands popularly made during the Hungarian Revolution in 1956 was one for complete religious freedom. Yet as early as February 1957 there were signs that the Communist Party was again preparing for an ideological struggle with the Roman Catholic Church. Cardinal Mindszenty was released from prison, but had to find asylum in the American Embassy when the Soviet tanks put down the revolt. Since then, he has been unwavering in his resolve that the only condition upon which he will leave his refuge is that he should resume his active office as primate. This permission has never been granted. In recent years there have been trials of Roman Catholic priests and this pattern was not broken by a partial agreement with the Vatican concluded in 1964 on the administration of the church. For example, in July 1965 Fathers László Emődi, László Rózsa and seven other clergy were given sentences of up to eight years for 'conspiracy'. Details of the case are not known, but it is certain that several priests who have tried to organise youth work have fallen foul of the law. It is probably true to say that there are more people in prison for religious reasons in Hungary than in any other communist country, except the Soviet Union itself (and possibly Albania and China).

POLAND

About half of the Roman Catholics living under communism are Poles. Within this country of 32 million people, about 95% owe nominal allegiance to the Catholic Church, a high proportion of whom are active Christians. At their head stands Cardinal Wyszyński, possibly the most outspoken consistent critic of communism who is now at liberty in Eastern Europe. Despite a continuing press campaign to brand him as a reactionary and unsuccessful attempts to drive a wedge between him and the 'progressive' Catholics who support the resolutions of the Second Vatican Council, his leadership has continued to inspire the people. The Communists have also attempted to use the appointment of Wojtyla as Cardinal to split the unity of the church, but with little success. Indeed, there is now a growing amount of concrete evidence which demonstrates that Wyszyński is even being held up as an ideal by some members of the Russian Orthodox Church inside the Soviet Union who wish to see their own leaders taking a stronger line.

After 1956 religious education for children became possible, conditional on the specific request of parents, though since July 1961 this can take place only on church premises. There are 48 theological seminaries, with about

4,000 students. In 1966 there was a clash between church and state over the celebrations of Poland's 1,000 years of statehood and of Christianity. The government at this time attempted to reduce the number of seminaries, but the church stood its ground. There is provision for advanced theological study at the Catholic University of Lublin and the Warsaw Theological Academy. Both have been subjected to severe restrictions, but continue to function. For example, the courses at Lublin are supervised by the state and only 150 students can be accepted each year. The total enrolment has been reduced by nearly two-thirds since 1956. One of Cardinal Wyszyński's most vigorous campaigns has been in defence of the Warsaw Theological Academy and it has suffered less than its provincial counterpart.

Despite the steady erosion of freedom in Poland since 1956, the state has fought shy of reintroducing physical repressions against the Roman Catholic Church.

JUGOSLAVIA

Jugoslavia's special position in the communist world is clearly reflected in the religious sphere, and the Vatican has better relations with its government than with that of any other communist country. This situation was reflected in a formal agreement in 1966, which included an exchange of envoys and established the right of the Vatican to control diocesan appointments in Jugoslavia.

Even before this, there was a constant flow of seminarists across the Adriatic to study in Rome. The Vatican paid a remarkable tribute to the quality of Jugoslav church leadership when Cardinal Šeper, a close friend of the late Cardinal Stepinac, was appointed to succeed Cardinal Ottaviani as head of the Vatican Congregation for the Doctrine of the Faith in 1968. It was he who pioneered the teaching programme on church premises when all religious education in schools was abolished. More recently, he inspired a remarkable revival in religious publishing, developing the fortnightly *Glas Koncila* ('Voice of the Council') into what is probably the finest religious periodical in any communist country. Its chief aim is to guide the implementation of the decisions of the Second Vatican Council and it now sells more than 200,000 copies per issue.

CZECHOSLOVAKIA

Because of the extreme uncertainty of the present situation in Czechoslovakia, it does not readily fit into our spectrum. Among all the remarkable events which took place there in the first eight months of 1968, developments in the Roman Catholic Church occupy a place of high interest. De-Stalinisation of church life was telescoped into such a short period that transformations occurred with a suddenness truly remarkable in Christian history.

Other countries had their government-sponsored Catholic 'peace movements', but that in Czechoslovakia, under Josef Plojhár, a defrocked priest and minister of health under Novotný, was probably more widely despised than the equivalent anywhere else. In a masterly move, Bishop František Tomášek of Prague transformed it into a 'Movement for Post-Conciliar Renewal', while the compromised figures associated with the old framework of church-state relations have ceased to be a serious factor in either political or religious life.

The Czechoslovak press itself contained much striking evidence of the changes taking place. Almost at a stroke the past was revealed. For example,

Father Vladimír Rudolf described the compromises of the past in these terms (*Katolické Noviny*, 'Catholic News', 17 March 1968):

> The life of the church suffered under a great spell of manipulation, which most priests experienced very painfully. They were threatened that the state would deny them a permit to perform pastoral duties . . . I was assigned as a parish priest and immediately received a warning from two of my colleagues to be cautious in my relations to another who was our cadre priest (i.e. political agent) . . . Witless contributions to *Katolické Noviny* became the preconditions for obtaining a better parish.

83 Roman Catholics wrote a letter to *Literární Listy* (21 March 1968), asking for full restoration of the rights of thousands of priests who were still debarred from office. The signatories had between them served 472 out of the 734 years of prison sentences to which they had been convicted. By and large, religious freedom was restored to Czechoslovakia in the first part of 1968. At the time of writing, there is little evidence of direct Soviet interference with Catholic life—probably the invaders are far too preoccupied with political problems.

UNIATES

Uniates (Eastern-rite Catholics) preserve the visible forms of Orthodoxy, but owe allegiance to the Pope. After World War II several Uniate areas fell under Soviet domination. The main churches (in western Ukraine, Rumania and Czechoslovakia) were forcibly assimilated into the Orthodox Church between 1946 and 1950 in an obvious attempt by Moscow to exploit religion as a means of fostering political unity. All those bishops and priests who opposed this measure were removed to prison camps, including the Ukrainian, Cardinal Slipyi, who was released only in 1963 on the condition that he emigrate at once to the Vatican. Only in Hungary was the Uniate Church—with a very small number of adherents—permitted to maintain its separate existence. The Uniate Bishop of Hajdúdorog, Miklós Dudás, even attended the Vatican Council.

After 1956, in the Soviet Union, however, some of these priests began to return to their native areas after being released from detention. This had the effect of giving new inspiration to the illegal Uniate Church, which had probably continued to exist in some form of underground organisation. There has recently been considerable evidence in the Soviet press that the authorities are worried about increasing Uniate activity. In 1965 they even managed to hold an illegal congress in Lvov, a considerable feat in Soviet conditions. According to the Soviet Ukrainian youth newspaper, *Molod Ukrainy*:

> They attracted 'delegates' not only from all parts of the Ukraine, but also from Belorussia and Moldavia. They brought with them a brass band, sang hymns and spread information about the 'miracle of Serednaya'.

On 12 April 1968 the Communist Party newspaper, *Rudé Právo*, reported that the suppressed Uniates of Czechoslovakia had met. By the time of the Soviet invasion, 147 parishes and nearly 200 priests had formed the nucleus of the reconstituted church.

These events cannot but inspire the ex-Uniates of the Ukraine (who number over three million people) to press for the reconstitution of their rights also.

Although the Uniates are only a small proportion of all the Roman Catholics living under communism, their revival would cause problems to the relevant governments which could be out of proportion to their numbers.

FURTHER READING

Blit, Lucjan. *The Eastern Pretender—Bolesław Piasecki: His Life and Times*, Hutchinson, London, 1965.

Brizgys, Bishop Vincent. *Religious Conditions in Lithuania under Soviet Russian Occupation*, Lithuanian Catholic Press, Chicago, 1968.

Conquest, Robert (ed.) *Religion in the USSR*, The Bodley Head, London; Frederick A. Praeger, New York, 1968.

Kolarz, Walter. *Religion in the Soviet Union*, Macmillan, London, 1961; St. Martin's Press, New York, 1962.

Religion in Communist Dominated Areas, National Council of Churches, New York, fortnightly.

Shuster, George, M. *Religion Behind the Iron Curtain*, Macmillan, New York, 1954.

Wyszyński, Cardinal Stefan. *A Strong Man Armed*, G. Chapman, London, 1966.

MICHAEL BOURDEAUX. In 1969 became Visiting Lecturer on Religion in Eastern Europe at St. Bernard's Seminary, Rochester, New York. Publications include *Religious Ferment In Russia: Protestant Opposition to Soviet Religious Policy*, 1968, and *Patriarch and Prophets: Tensions in the Russian Orthodox Church Today*, 1969.

ISLAM IN THE SOVIET UNION
AND EASTERN EUROPE

GEOFFREY WHEELER

The Soviet Union

THE Soviet Union and the communist countries of Eastern Europe together contain a total of about 34 million persons who can historically be regarded as Muslims and whose culture is broadly speaking Islamic. There is, however, no means of determining what proportion of these are practising or acknowledged Muslims.

Of the total given above the vast majority, some 30 million,[1] live in the Soviet Union, where Islam occupies second place among the various religious communities. Islam is unique in the Soviet Union in the sense that it is the sole religion practised by over 30 more or less compact and distinct nationalities. Five of these nationalities constitute the majority nationality in the union republics which bear their names.[2] There are also seven ASSRs bearing the names of other Muslim nationalities.

The Muslims of the Soviet Union are distributed in three main areas: about three-fifths live in the five Central Asian and Kazakh SSRs, one-fifth in the Caucasus and one-fifth in the Ural and Volga regions. Islam became established in these areas at various times after the Arab conquests of the 7th and 8th centuries: it was widespread in what are now the Azerbaidzhan, Uzbek, Tadzhik and Turkmen SSRs by the end of the 9th century; it reached the north Caucasus, the Volga and Ural regions and what are now the Kazakh and Kirgiz SSRs much later, in some instances not until the 16th century.

Apart from small Arab (22,000) and Chinese (Dungans 21,000) communities, the Muslims of the Soviet Union fall into three ethnic groups: Turkic (80%), Ibero-Caucasian (9%) and Iranian (11%). Within these groups the strongest link, apart from Islam, is language rather than race. Intermarriage among the various nationalities was at one time rare but is now more frequent. Between Muslims and non-Muslims however, it remains extremely uncommon, and between Muslim girls and non-Muslim men almost non-existent.

The Muslim khanates of Kazan and Astrakhan were conquered and annexed by Russia in the middle of the 16th century; the remaining Muslim peoples of the Caucasus and Central Asia were incorporated in the Russian

---

[1] The Soviet census of 1959 indicated a total of about 25 million. With an annual natural increase of 3% the total is now not less than 30 million.

[2] These are the Azerbaidzhan, Kirgiz, Tadzhik, Turkmen and Uzbek SSRs. In the Kazakh SSR the Kazakhs only constituted 29% of the population in 1959.

empire during the 18th and 19th centuries. Although military government operated in most of the conquered territories, Tsarist rule was not oppressive. Muslim educational and other cultural institutions were free from interference and the great majority of the Muslim population, that of Central Asia, was exempt from compulsory service until World War I, when part of it was conscripted for labour duties. Moreover, their annexation by Russia brought peace and relative prosperity to regions which for centuries had been subjected to internecine warfare. But the Tsarist system of political administration took no account of national distribution and no plans existed for eventual self-government or even for regular central representation. The two Central Asian khanates of Bukhara and Khiva were reduced to a state of vassalage but enjoyed some degree of economic independence under their traditional rulers.

NATIONALITIES POLICY

During the chaos which followed the collapse of the imperial administration in 1917, various uncoordinated attempts were made to set up Muslim national governments in Transcaucasia and Central Asia. These were unsuccessful owing to the absence of indigenous armed forces or a nucleus of a trained civil service, the presence of a large Russian settler population,[1] and the determination of the new regime to retain central control over the former Tsarist empire. After overcoming often violent resistance, the Soviet government developed what has become known as its nationalities policy. This involved the classification of the larger Muslim nationalities, including those of them living in Bukhara and Khiva, as 'nations' and constituting those bordering on foreign countries—Kazakhs, Uzbeks, Kirgiz, Tadzhiks Turkmens and Azerbaidzhanis—as 'union republics'. The other nationalities were contained in ASSRs, or oblasts, affiliated to the union republics. The full sovereignty and self-determination officially claimed for the republics has not so far extended to such matters as foreign policy, foreign trade, defence, educational policy or finance.

An essential aim of the Soviet nationalities policy has been the breaking up of the old tribal and extended-family society which was prevalent among all the Muslim peoples of Russia and with which the Tsarist regime had hardly begun to interfere. The new social groupings were to be the 'nation' and the *narodnost* (community) on the way either to becoming a 'nation' or to becoming merged in an adjacent 'nation'. In spite of the cultural, and in many instances, ethnic and linguistic affinities among the Muslim peoples, the Soviet plan was to emphasise differences rather than similarities. This, so it is argued by Western critics, was in order to prevent the Muslims 'ganging up' with each other and with the peoples in the adjoining non-Soviet Muslim countries against the Soviet regime. The old social order has now to a large extent been undermined: the tribal and family structure has almost disappeared; and most of the large nomad element has been stabilised. However, the nationhood which the Soviet authorities evidently intended should remain notional, is fast becoming a reality.

ISLAM AND COMMUNIST IDEOLOGY

The general campaign of anti-religious propaganda and cultural regimentation instituted shortly after the October Revolution, and maintained with

[1] The greatest concentration of settlers was in Central Asia where it exceeded two million. This number has since increased to about nine million, or just under 40% of the total population of the whole region.

varying degrees of intensity ever since, has been directed with particular force against Islam. Whereas the Orthodox Church has always been regarded as an integral part of Russian culture, Islam and the Islamic way of life are considered to be not only merely backward, but exotic and positively inimical to Russian culture and to the Russians as people. This Soviet attitude towards Islam is similar to that adopted by the Tsarist regime, which at first followed the policy of ignoring Islam in the belief that, faced with the 'superior' Russian culture, it would die of inanition. The much more active measures taken by the Soviet regime do not seem to be any more effective. Many of the practices condemned, such as child marriage, seclusion of women and tomb-visitation, which have little to recommend them and elsewhere are dying out under the influence of enlightened Muslim opinion, are clung to by the Soviet Muslims as something of their own not to be wrested from them by their alien and atheist rulers.

The various restrictions imposed on Islam, though heavy, cannot be said to amount to persecution or suppression. The measures taken include the closure of mosques, of which the official total is now given as 400,[1] abolition of religious holidays, exclusion of religious instruction from state schools and the abolition of mosque schools and the limitation of pilgrims to Mecca to a handful of selected persons. Apart from these negative measures designed to reduce the overall spiritual and social influence of Islam, a large number of positive measures have been taken which have much improved the material condition of the Muslim population, particularly in the urban areas. Great strides have been taken in primary, higher and technical education, and the standard of living and public health have risen to a remarkable extent. In the total absence of facilities for first-hand observation it is hard to assess the effect of these negative and positive measures in reducing the status of Islam and in transforming the average Muslim into the standard *homo sovieticus*. Westernisation and modernisation have had a considerable effect on urban life throughout the Muslim world and probably nowhere so much as in the Soviet Union. Elsewhere, however, the change has been brought about by national governments, which have at the same time been intent on preserving the dignity and status of Islam. From the scanty information about the rural Muslim population available from Soviet sources, material conditions do not seem to be much, if at all, better than those in, for example, Turkey, Persia and Afghanistan, where progress during the past 20 years has been rapid.

The future of Islam in the Soviet Union must depend on the continued existence of the Muslim republics. At the time of the Twenty-second Party Congress held in 1961 there was clear evidence of a move towards abolishing the national principle from union administration. This, if it ever materialised, could have the effect of reducing and eventually removing the political and cultural distinctiveness of the Muslim peoples of the Soviet Union. Since 1964, however, there has been a marked decline in the emphasis on this plan, which probably encountered a strong undercurrent of opposition in all the national, and particularly in the Muslim, republics. During the past few years, too, there have been several indications that the Soviet authorities are beginning to take a much more serious view of what may be called Muslim cultural consciousness. Like its Tsarist predecessor, the Soviet regime began by underestimating the staying power of Islamic culture. It seems now to

---

[1] In 1900 it was estimated that in Turkestan alone, apart from the khanates of Bukhara and Khiva, there were 1,503 congregational and 11,250 parish mosques.

have realised that even the much more vigorous measures which it has taken with the object of eradicating Islamic influence have not yet had the desired effect, and that a less hostile approach might produce better results. An additional consideration is the Soviet government's desire to improve still further its relations with the Muslim countries of the Middle East and South Asia.

EASTERN EUROPE

The attitude towards Islam of the communist regimes in the countries of Eastern Europe is in theory the same as that of the Soviet Union. With the exception of Jugoslavia, information about the Muslim population in these countries is difficult to come by, even as regards their numbers. This is not only because, as in the Soviet Union, official censuses do not include details of religious profession, but because, unlike the Soviet Union, there is no historical association of Islam with complete nationalities. Thus, while it is generally assumed that three-fifths of the population of Albania is Muslim, it is impossible to say how far this proportion applies to the Albanian element of about 1·1 million living in Jugoslavia.

Although Islam as a religion incurs the same official communist disapproval as in the Soviet Union, it does not constitute the same political problem. A large part of the East European Muslim elements—about half that of Jugo-slavia—are ethnically of the same European origin as the national majority of the countries where they live and only one country, Bulgaria, borders on a non-communist Muslim country, i.e. Turkey. The Muslim elements in Jugoslavia and Bulgaria are by far the largest, amounting to about two million and one million respectively. Those in Poland and Rumania probably do not exceed 100,000 and are of marginal importance. The governments of all the communist East European countries conduct anti-Islamic propaganda, exclude religious instruction from the state schools and have expropriated the *waqf* (evkaf) lands formerly owned by the Muslim hierarchy. As regards freedom of worship the Muslim population of Jugoslavia is probably the best off, while that of Albania is subjected to most restrictions, Bulgaria coming a close second. In Jugoslavia the term 'Musulman' is officially applied in an ethnic rather than a religious sense to the Muslims of South Slav ethnic origin, most of whom live in Bosnia-Hercegovina and are the descendants of the Bogomil sect which embraced Islam *en masse* at the time of the Turkish conquest in the middle of the 15th century. The putative grand total of two million is reached on the assumption that the great majority of the 1·1 million Albanians and 200,000 Turks living in Jugoslavia are Muslims. Jugoslav authorities however, consider that the grand total is nearer two-and-a-half million.

Two instances of the relatively tolerant Jugoslav attitude towards Islam can be found in the number of mosques and in the number of persons permitted to undertake the pilgrimage to Mecca. Full details about mosques are not available for all the constituent republics, but the number of those operating in Bosnia-Hercegovina alone in 1958 was officially given as 836, or more than twice the number officially given as serving the 30 million Muslims of the Soviet Union. Moreover, the building of new mosques is frequently reported. Figures of attendance at the 1967 pilgrimage given in the *Islamic Review* included 1,539 from Jugoslavia compared with 14 from the Soviet Union.

In spite of the relatively liberal application of communist principles the long-term political and economic prospects of the Muslims of Jugoslavia may be less good than those of the Soviet Muslims. Whereas the artificially created Soviet Muslim republics have a prospect of developing into something real and lasting, Muslims are not in the majority in any of the Jugoslav republics and their largest group, the 'Musulmans' of Hercegovina, is not ethnically distinct from the predominant Serbs and Croats. In Bulgaria, where two-thirds of the Muslims are Turks, many of whom have already emigrated to Turkey, whilst the remainder are Pomaks (Bulgarian-speaking Muslims), there is even less prospect of the Muslims achieving any political individuality.

FURTHER READING

Bacon, Elizabeth E. *Central Asia Under Russian Rule: A Study in Culture Change*, Cornell Univ. Press, 1966.

Bennigsen, A. and Quelquejay, C. *Islam in the Soviet Union*, Frederick A. Praeger, New York; Pall Mall Press, London, 1967 (in association with Central Asian Research Centre). *Les Mouvements Nationaux chez Les Musulmans de Russie*, Mouton, The Hague, 1960.

Central Asian Review, London, quarterly since 1953.

Stuika, Vincenzo. 'La comunitá religiosa islamica della Jugoslavia', *Oriente Moderno*, Rome, January 1967.

Vaidyanath, R. *The Formation of the Soviet Central Asian Republics*, Peoples Publishing House, New Delhi, 1967.

Wheeler, Geoffrey. *The Modern History of Soviet Central Asia*, Weidenfeld and Nicolson, 1964. *Racial Problems in Soviet Muslim Asia*, 2nd ed., Oxford Univ. Press, London, 1962.

GEOFFREY WHEELER. From 1953–68 Director of the Central Asian Research Centre and Joint Editor of *Central Asian Review*. Author of *Racial Problems in Soviet Muslim Asia, The Peoples of Soviet Central Asia* and *The Modern History of Soviet Central Asia*.

THE PROTESTANT CHURCHES IN EASTERN EUROPE

JĀNIS SAPIETS

THE Protestants in Eastern Europe suffer from the same pressures as the Orthodox and the Roman Catholics, but their lack of liturgical and hierarchic traditions makes it even more difficult for them to preserve the continuity of their faith in an anti-religious state. Protestant worship is centred on the Bible and on preaching. The denial of free speech and the severe shortage of religious literature, including the Bible, deprives Protestants of the essential means of communicating their faith. This tends to obscure the doctrine and to put the brunt of the responsibility for decision-making on the individual believer. On the other hand, it is precisely this Protestant individualism, as a protest against the compulsory state ideology, which often attracts converts to the Protestant Churches.

The development of church-state relations has followed a similar pattern in all the East European countries: an initial period of severe persecution which left the church weakened and often leaderless has been generally followed by a church-state agreement on conditions dictated by the state. This guarantees the church its legal status in return for the church's undertaking to support the internal and external policies of the state. Since, however, it is the ultimate intention of every communist state to eradicate religion and to rid the people's minds of what it considers to be an obsolete and harmful prejudice, the permanent value of these agreements seems to be doubtful.

THE SOVIET UNION

The Baptist Church is the second largest Christian community in the Soviet Union, after the Russian Orthodox Church. In 1966 an official Baptist report stated that there were a quarter of a million adult baptised members and another quarter of a million non-adults and adherents in the church. Twelve years earlier, in 1954, the official Soviet Baptist magazine, *Bratsky Vestnik*, gave a considerably larger figure—half a million baptised believers,[1] with another three million adherents, including believers' families. The discrepancy between the two statements is probably due to the fact that many Baptist communities have been denied registration over the past few years. This, in turn, is connected with an inner schism within the Baptist Church, which goes back to 1961 when a 'reform' or 'initiative' movement began to develop.

[1] This figure was also quoted when the Soviet Baptists applied for membership of the World Council of Churches in 1962.

The Baptist reformers accused the official church leadership (the All-Union Council of Evangelical Christians and Baptists) of having betrayed the true faith by allowing the state authorities to exercise full control over the church and its activities. They demanded an end of state interference in church affairs and a strict application of the constitutional decree concerning the separation of church and state.

The activities of the Baptist reformers and their demand for a spiritual revival within the church were denounced by the Soviet authorities as anti-social and illegal. The 'initiative' communities have been subjected to considerable pressure and persecution, including some hundreds of long prison sentences. The reform movement continues, however, and has even provided the impetus for similar tendencies among the Orthodox churchmen, as well as for considerable recruiting to Baptism among the young generation.

Among the other Protestant bodies in the Soviet Union, the Lutheran Church is the largest. It is estimated that there are some 500,000 Lutherans in Latvia and about 350,000 in Estonia. Small Lutheran communities exist in other parts of the Soviet Union but, being without clergy, these have little hope of survival. The Calvinist Church in the Transcarpathian Ukraine has about 90,000 members, all Hungarians.

Other Protestant communities include the Seventh-Day Adventists, (c. 40,000), the Mennonites and Molokans (c. 25,000) and a number of smaller sects.

BULGARIA

The Bulgarian Protestants—Methodists, Baptists, Congregationalists and others—number about 33,000. The Protestant Churches were almost destroyed as organised bodies in 1949 when 15 Protestant leaders were put on trial on charges of illegal currency deals and espionage. The World Council of Churches was named as the 'foreign agency' responsible for collecting the secret information. The accused were sentenced to life or long-term imprisonment. The trial paralysed normal church activities and led to an almost complete severance of ties with the Protestant Churches in the West. Since about 1956 the situation has improved but detailed information is not available.

CZECHOSLOVAKIA

The Protestant Churches in Czechoslovakia include the Czech Brethren (Calvinists and Lutherans, united after 1918, membership 260,000), the Lutheran Church (50,000 Silesian Evangelical Lutherans, mainly Poles, and the Slovak Evangelical Church with 400,000 members), the Reformed Church in Slovakia (150,000 members, mainly Hungarians), the Moravian Church (10,000) and the Seventh-Day Adventists (18,733). There are also smaller groups of Baptists, Unitarians and the Assemblies of God. The Czechoslovak National Church, which came into being in 1920 as a break-away movement from the Church of Rome, has 500,000 members. Since the Protestant leaders in Czechoslovakia decided to give their full support to the state legislation on churches (1949), the relations between the Protestants and the state authorities in Czechoslovakia have been better than anywhere else in Eastern Europe. The clergy have to swear an oath of allegiance to the state but are comparatively free to maintain relations with other Protestant Churches abroad. The stipends of the clergy are paid by the state, religious instruction is available in the schools, and the churches can publish their own periodicals and other religious literature. There is a theological faculty at the

Charles University in Prague, where the students receive full state scholarships. The Protestants in Czechoslovakia have been among the most zealous supporters of the communist-organised peace movements, and, since 1958, Prague has been the centre of the Christian Peace Conference founded by the outstanding Protestant theologian, Josef Hromádka. The Peace Conference consistently supported the Soviet policies and advocated the necessity of a Christian-Marxist dialogue. Professor Hromádka has been equally active on the World Council of Churches, serving for many years on its executive council. After the occupation of Czechoslovakia by the Warsaw Pact forces on 21 August 1968, Professor Hromádka, together with other Protestant leaders, declared his loyalty to the Czechoslovak government and addressed a bitter protest to the Soviet authorities.

Until 1968 the state retained direct control over all the church activities, but after the government change in January 1968 these controls were largely removed, and the Czechoslovak Protestants enjoyed an almost complete freedom of action and expression—an unprecedented situation in a communist-governed country. The future of the Protestant Churches—as, indeed, of all churches—in Czechoslovakia will, however, depend on the further development of the political situation.

EAST GERMANY

The 14 million members of the East German Evangelical Church form the largest Protestant community in Eastern Europe. The relations between church and state have been tense ever since 1949, when the East German government began a violent propaganda campaign designed to prevent young people from joining the church. All schoolchildren were required to take part in secular youth consecration ceremonies (*Jugendweihe*), designed to replace the church confirmation. The church replied by denouncing the *Jugendweihe* as an atheist initiation ceremony and declared that it was incompatible with the confirmation: the parents had to choose between the two. The government's claims that its campaign has been successful do not seem to be substantiated by any decisive decrease in church membership.

The other cause of church-state tension was the determination of the East German Evangelical Church to preserve unity with its sister-church in West Germany. Both churches together constituted the All-German Evangelical Church, the only body which represented East-West German unity. The unrelenting pressure by the East German government, however, provoked a split among the church leaders, and the separation of the two bodies took place in September, 1969.

HUNGARY

The two most important Protestant groups are the Reformed Church (membership 1·9 million) and the Lutherans (500,000). In 1948 both churches signed an agreement with the state authorities, accepting government control over the church life in return for a legally recognised status. The agreement, which was renewed in January 1969, guaranteed state subsidies to cover salaries, running costs and normal upkeep of buildings. The Lutheran Bishop Ordas, who had insisted on greater freedom for the church to organise its own affairs, was charged in 1948 with illegal currency deals, sentenced to two and a half years' imprisonment and deposed in 1950. His rehabilitation and reinstatement in 1956 were of a short duration. Since the abortive Hungarian Revolution in 1956, the Protestant Churches have avoided all conflicts with the government, scrupulously observing the 1948 agreement. In September 1968 *Pártélet*, the Hungarian Communist Party Central Committee monthly, promised the churches continued coexistence and even 'lasting cooperation', provided they adhered strictly to the church-state agreements and dissociated themselves from 'reactionary elements' among the clergy.

POLAND

Before World War II there were about one million Protestants in Poland, most of them German Lutherans. After the war, mainly as a result of the deportation of the German population from Poland, the total membership of the Protestant Churches dropped to 165,000. Of these 109,000 are Lutherans and 27,000 Methodists, the rest being made up of the Reformed Church and the Baptists, and some smaller groups. The churches receive no financial help from the government but maintain lively relations with the World Council of Churches. The church-state relations are regulated on the basis of the agreements of 1946 and 1947.

RUMANIA

The total membership of the Rumanian Protestant Churches is about 1·2 million and their adherents are largely members of the Hungarian and German minorities. This figure includes 780,000 Reformed, 218,000 Lutherans, some 90,000 Baptists, 50,000 Pentecostals and 70,000 Seventh-Day Adventists. The Rumanian constitution of 1965 provides for the citizen's right to 'profess or not to profess a religious faith', but the government campaign of anti-religious propaganda has lost none of its vigour. The churches receive no state subsidies. They had few contacts with Western Protestants until 1961 when active association with the World Council of Churches was resumed.

FURTHER READING

Bourdeaux, Michael. *Religious Ferment in Russia*, Macmillan, London; St. Martin's Press, New York, 1968.

Conquest, Robert (ed.) *Religion in the USSR*, Soviet Studies Series, Bodley Head, London; Frederick A. Praeger, New York, 1968.

Coxhill, H. W. and Grubb, Sir Kenneth (eds.) *The World Christian Handbook, 1968*, Lutterworth Press, London, 1968.

Gsovsky, Vladimir. *Church and State Behind the Iron Curtain*, Frederick A. Praeger, New York, 1955.

Tobias, Robert. *Communist-Christian Encounter in Eastern Europe*, School of Religion Press, Butler Univ., Indianapolis, 1956.

JEWS

MICHAEL BOURDEAUX

GENERAL

THE following table gives a clear impression of the decline of the Jewish population in Eastern Europe and where the present weight lies. The Soviet Union contains ten times as many Jews as the other communist countries combined, while nearly half of the remainder are in Rumania. The city of Moscow alone contains more Jews than all those living in the countries other than the Soviet Union listed on following page.

A Jewish demographic map of Eastern Europe would therefore divide decisively into two, with the Soviet Union on the one hand and the rest of the communist countries on the other. The story of the former is of a great and unresolved problem, while that of the latter is of a diminishing feature which would dwindle almost to insignificance in the cultural development of the countries concerned, were it not from time to time artificially inflated for political reasons.

Two principal factors have determined sharp changes in Eastern Europe over the past 30 years: first, extermination of the Jews by the Nazis (and the exodus of refugees associated with it); second, legal emigration after the formation of the state of Israel in 1948. Poland is outstanding as the most dramatic example of the way in which these two have combined to reduce the Jewish population. The original community of over three million has been reduced to a 130th part of its former size and the great majority of all those alive in 1939 perished. There were also a few surviving Jews living in the Polish territories incorporated into the Soviet Union at the end of World War II.

This general decline in the Jewish population can be further piquantly illustrated by the fact that Jugoslavia's last rabbi, Menahem Romano, died in Sarajevo in November 1968 aged 87, thus leaving the country with no authority to decide Jewish religious questions, unless someone were to come from another country to take over.

The situation in the Soviet Union has been determined by a completely different set of factors. It is true that many Jews did perish in the Ukraine at the hands of the Nazis, but a number of cities with very large Jewish populations (Moscow and Leningrad, for example) were not captured by the invaders. Moreover, emigration to Israel has been limited to a handful, so total numbers have not declined in recent years.

TABLE

Country	Total population (1966)	Jews (before 1939)	Losses to Nazis	Present Jewish population	City	Present Jewish population
Albania	1,814,000	300	—	300	—	—
Bulgaria	8,144,000	50,000	7,000	7,000	Sofia	4,000
Czechoslovakia	14,058,000	315,000	260,000	12,000	Prague / Bratislava	3,400 / 1,500
East Germany	18,000,000	no separate figures	no separate figures	2,400	E. Berlin	850
Hungary	10,146,000	403,000	200,000	80,000	Budapest	65,000
Jugoslavia	19,511,000	75,000	55,000	7,000	Sarajevo / Zagreb	1,100 / 1,400
Poland	31,420,000	3,300,000	2,900,000	25,000 (halved in 1968)	Warsaw	5,000 (halved in 1968)
Rumania	18,927,000	850,000	425,000	100,000	Bucharest	50,000
Soviet Union: RSFSR, Ukraine, Belorussia	229,000,000 (whole Soviet Union)	2,100,000 (Nazi occupied areas only)	1,500,000	2,486,000 (whole Soviet Union)	Kiev	220,000
Lithuania		150,000	135,000		Leningrad	165,000
Latvia		95,000	85,000		Moscow	285,000
Estonia		no figures available				
		7,288,300	5,567,000	2,719,000		

Note: These figures, compiled by the author, are approximate and take no account of further emigration to Israel since 1966.

488

POLAND

The Arab defeat by Israel in the war of June 1967, in which the communists supported the Arabs morally and with supplies of weapons, had a detrimental effect on some aspects of Jewish life in Eastern Europe. This was particularly noticeable in Poland and the officially-inspired anti-Semitic campaign which followed has received considerable publicity in the world press, although public opinion in Poland was sympathetic towards Israel. In essence, the Polish communist party tried to cloak its own deficiencies by finding a scapegoat, which without foundation it dubbed 'the Zionist conspiracy'. The situation further deteriorated after the student disturbances of March 1968; hundreds of Jewish writers, journalists, scientists and university teachers were hounded from their posts. It is reported that some aspects of scientific research have had to be discontinued as a result. Many Poles were genuinely surprised to discover that the small Jewish community had furnished so many people in important positions. Several thousand of Poland's Jews are thought to have left the country as a result of these events. Poland has lost thereby and it is difficult to see that it has gained anything in compensation.

CZECHOSLOVAKIA

As in Poland, so too in Czechoslovakia there was a wave of public sympathy for Israel at the time of the June war. In the first half of 1968 the Czechoslovak press demonstrated the artificial nature of the anti-Zionist campaign by criticising Novotný's rupture of diplomatic relations with Israel at the time of the war and revealing ugly details of what was developing in Poland. Before the Soviet invasion, there were abundant signs of a reanimation of Jewish life.

In May 1968 the Council of Czechoslovak Jewish Communities drew up a 1,500-word document calling upon the Dubček regime to restore full civil and religious rights to all Jews of the land. A major exhibition in the Prague Jewish museum, planned for 1967 as part of the celebration of 1,000 years of Judaism in the city, was forcibly postponed by the government, but was opened in May 1968—a unique event in a communist country.

HUNGARY

There have been isolated reports of anti-Semitism from Hungary in recent years, but nothing comparable to the Polish campaign of 1967–8 seems to have taken place. There are indications that Jewish life is proceeding with some degree of normality. There is, for example, a small rabbinical seminary. At the 1966 World Jewish Congress in Brussels, two Hungarians presented a report in which it was stated that there were 14 synagogues in Budapest alone. It is revealing to compare it with Moscow and its environs, where there are only three synagogues but over four times the number of Jews. It is also indicative of the Hungarian situation that in March 1967 two young men, who had fled from the country in 1956, were inducted as rabbis after being allowed to return to the country to take the necessary examinations. The only Jewish school in Eastern Europe is also in Budapest.

RUMANIA

The outstanding Jewish leader of Eastern Europe is Dr Moses Rosen, head of the largest community outside the Soviet Union. He gained his present office in 1948 at the age of 36 and opinions were expressed at the time that he was merely a plant of the regime. However, the way in which he has guided his community through the first intensely difficult years and into a period of much greater freedom demonstrates the danger of making sweeping pronouncements on East European religious leaders without adequate evidence. From 1958 Jews began to leave the country for Israel in substantial numbers. Dr Rosen encouraged this, even though it meant a weakening of the remaining communities. About 650 rabbis emigrated in all, leaving only nine behind. The religious seminary in Arad had to close, because both its pupils and teachers decided to continue their courses in Israel.

Despite these handicaps, considerable Jewish activity in Rumania continues. There are about 20 synagogues in Bucharest. The government also supports a Yiddish theatre and permits a publishing house to operate for Yiddish books. The fortnightly Jewish journal is printed in about 10,000 copies.

THE SOVIET UNION

Anti-Semitism was rife in Tsarist Russia long before it ever became so in Germany (the word *pogrom* originated in the former). That the country which did so much to break German fascism should be unable to bring itself to a sufficient practical repudiation of Hitler's worst excess is a keen irony. Soviet policy towards the country's very large Jewish community (more numerous than all the Jews in Israel) has aroused considerable hostility in many sectors of world public opinion.

Two notorious instances were the murder in January 1948 of Solomon Mikhoels, director of the Moscow Jewish Theatre, and the 'Doctors' Plot' in January 1953, just before Stalin's death. In the latter, nine doctors, mostly Jewish, were accused of trying to cause the death of members of the Praesidium—a complete fabrication, as Khrushchev revealed in his speech at the Twentieth Party Congress in 1956. Even more inexplicable, in the light of Khrushchev's known views on the Doctors' Plot, was the anti-Semitic campaign which struck the Soviet Union in the early 1960s. At this time, Jewish religious communities were subjected to the same violent atheist attacks as those which engulfed many of the Christian congregations.

Several Soviet sources give the number of synagogues in 1959–60 as between 400 and 500. Yet by 1963 the Chief Rabbi of Moscow, Yehuda Leib Levin, gave the figure as 96, which is almost precisely confirmed by the 1965 edition of *USSR—Questions and Answers*, published by Novosti (the official Soviet press agency). Even more recently a group working at Brandeis University, Massachusetts, computed the number as 'at least' 62. While none of these figures may be precisely accurate, much supporting data for this destruction of Jewish religious life was published during these years in the Soviet press, where many articles were printed depicting synagogues as hotbeds of crime (as for example, the synagogue at Lvov which closed in November 1962 after a year-long campaign).

In one respect, Jews were worse hit than Christian communities at this time: Jews were brought before the courts for alleged economic crimes which had nothing to do with religious activities. An objective report by the International Commission of Jurists amassed the evidence on this subject in 1964. Part of its conclusions reads as follows:

> It is also clear that there has been an insidious and sometimes subtle propaganda campaign directed against the Jewish people of the Soviet Union, specifically against those charged with economic crimes and also against the supposed general

characteristics of Jews that have been reiterated for centuries. If the reports of trials for economic crimes are even reasonably complete, the number of Jews receiving death sentences and severe terms of imprisonment is greatly disproportionate to their number as a minority group.

There is also a positive side to Soviet Jewish life. It cannot, of course, be reported in the press, least of all in the sole Yiddish publication, the relatively ineffectual *Sovietish Heimland*. For this one must go to sundry reports by visitors and among these none is more notable than the eyewitness accounts of the famous Eli Wiesel, journalist and writer, who was present at the festival of *Simchat Torah* in Moscow in both 1965 and 1966. He describes how young and old prayed together in the synagogue. Then the young people, perhaps a hundred of them, left to hold their own festival in the street: 'Outside, the celebration was that of the Jewish youth of Russia, which sings that it may survive'. Fearful of the consequences, the synagogue officials switched off the outside lights and plunged them in darkness in the middle of their *hora*—upon which the young people improvised a torchlight procession. Next day they were back in the same street, more of them now, in the middle of a working day. The police had to close the road to traffic, while a boy stood up and gave a roll-call of all the well known Jews of the land, to the ecstatic applause of all those around.

There is perhaps not yet enough evidence to speak of a 'revival' of Jewish culture among the young, but neither can the Soviet leaders claim that their goal of assimilation is about to be achieved.

FURTHER READING

Brumberg, Joseph and Abraham. '*Sovietish Heimland*—An Analysis' *Ethnic Minorities in the Soviet Union*, Goldhagen, Erich (ed.), Frederick A. Praeger, New York, 1968.
'Jewish Aspects of the Changes in Czechoslovakia' (Staff study), Background Paper No. 11, Institute of Jewish Affairs, London. June 1968.
Korey, William. 'The Legal Position of the Jewish Community of the Soviet Union', *Ethnic Minorities in the Soviet Union*, Goldhagen, Erich (ed.), Frederick A. Praeger, New York, 1968.
'The Student Unrest in Poland and the Anti-Jewish and Anti-Zionist Campaign'. Background Paper No. 9 and No. 12. Institute of Jewish Affairs, London. April 1968, July 1968.

PART FIVE

CONTEMPORARY ARTS

THE POLITICAL AND SOCIAL SETTING
OF THE CONTEMPORARY ARTS

GEORGE GÖMÖRI

The Role of the Intellectual

SOCIETY creates culture; culture reflects, expresses and shapes society. Looking at the political and social factors that influence the character of the arts, especially literature, in European communist countries, we should perhaps begin our survey with the thesis that in the Soviet Union and Eastern Europe intellectuals, and writers in particular, have always played a much more important role than in other societies. This peculiarity is the consequence of the uneven, distorted and often interrupted course of development in the history of these countries. It is bound up with such facts as the non-existence of a proper middle class and the search for an independent nationhood or national survival. Traditionally the artist was a client of a rich patron, a town or a select social group and his task was to serve and delight his patrons. There were, of course, always artists and writers who criticised the social institutions of their age, but the scope of their criticism was on the whole limited. Only after the French Revolution and the ensuing social turmoil did the writer appear in the new role of a social 'prophet' and political leader. The great Romantics were the first to raise the banner of revolt against society, with different consequences in the East and West. While Shelley's, and even Victor Hugo's, revolt was of little significance in the context of English or French politics, the Russians Pushkin and Lermontov, the Poles Mickiewicz and Slowacki, the Hungarian Petöfi or the Bulgarian Botev left an indelible imprint on the collective national consciousness of their respective peoples. All these poets were alienated from the centre of power in their country, were opposed to the *status quo* for national or social or, as in the case of Eastern Europe, both reasons. Byron's or Shelley's hatred of tyranny expressed in their poetry was shared by many liberals and radicals in England who were free to voice their opinions through democratic channels. Literature in Russia and Eastern Europe has been able to play such a significant role in the past 150 years because writers, alienated from the assumptions upon which power rested, both expressed and intensified the frustrations felt, but *unexpressed*, by the educated majority of their society. This majority was either disenfranchised or intimidated by feudal tradition, religious obscurantism or political terror. The poet or writer became, in fact, the mouthpiece of a whole nation. Since no proper institutions existed, the writer became an institution. The intellectuals acted as substitutes for a non-existent or very weak middle class and at certain moments poets volunteered as political leaders. The classic example of the 'prophetic' poet-leader is the Polish poet,

Adam Mickiewicz, who within a decade twice left his civilian occupation and family to organise Polish military units to fight against Austria and Russia— enemies of his partitioned country.

The Soviet Union

Here it is necessary to distinguish between the Soviet Union on the one hand and Eastern Europe on the other, though even the countries of Eastern Europe differ amongst themselves. The source of these differences lies above all in national tradition. Russia's past weighs heavily upon its present: its religious, Byzantine and autocratic traditions are still very much alive under the veil of communism. 'Cosmopolitanism' is one of the dirtiest words in the Soviet vocabulary—it means lack of total commitment to the Motherland. There is still an almost religious adoration of 'Mother Russia'. The famous 19th century controversy between Slavophiles and Westernisers in Russia hinged on the questions: what is best for Russia? Should it preserve its separateness and ancient customs, or should it turn to the West for help and inspiration? This basic dichotomy in Russian life has been reflected in the creative sphere—the two attitudes sometimes coexisting in the mind of a single man. In the context of Tsarist Russia one could be a revolutionary émigré like Herzen or a Slavophile nationalist like Tyutchev, but the greatest Russian poet of all, Alexander Pushkin, behaved on occasion as a revolutionary (he was implicated in the Decembrists' unsuccessful plot) and yet still wrote occasional poems reeking of anti-Polish nationalism. In other words, in Russia the wish for social reforms did not always go hand in hand with a genuine international revolutionary attitude.

Another outstanding feature of the Soviet Union is the uncompromising nature of its demand for 'truth'. For the sake of the peasant masses everything had to be simplified to basic 'truths', to 'either-ors'. Petru Dumitriu, the Rumanian author, sardonically suggested that, for the ordinary Russian, literature is a ritual 'where virtue triumphs and evil is exorcised' and that the Russian demand for a 'positive hero' (a persistent feature of socialist realism) in the contemporary novel is the outcome of the traditional reading habits of Russian peasantry: its chief reading matter was the *Lives of the Saints*. This explains how it is that a Soviet writer need not be a Marxist-Leninist in order to glorify 'Mother Russia' (the Soviet Union) or conjure up a picture of perfect happiness in the *kolkhoz*—it suffices if he is a nationalist or a Slavophile. Those Soviet writers who step out of line and criticise Soviet society abroad, ignore this Russian tradition at their own peril: they are branded as 'traitors', and not only by their Stalinist colleagues. Pasternak's experience is the perfect example; the publication of *Doctor Zhivago* in the West was denounced in vitriolic terms by many of his fellow-writers (including some anti-Stalinists and anti-Westerners) and none of his friends had the courage to make a public statement in his defence. In this respect the Russian mentality (with the exception of the youngest generation) is still bound by 19th century concepts and prejudices, although since the Sinyavsky-Daniel trial of 1966 these have been noticeably weakening.

Poland and Hungary

In Poland and Hungary the position of the writer has been historically different. The Polish state was wiped out of existence at the end of the 18th century and there seemed little or no hope that this situation could be reversed. After the failure of the Polish uprising and war of independence of 1830–1 when Poland's best statesmen, writers and scholars emigrated to the

West, the importance of the written word increased enormously—it became the last refuge of those who could not accept foreign domination. The Polish obsession with national independence evident in the works of Mickiewicz, Slowacki and Krasinski is an outcome of the loss of independent statehood. The emphasis on the value of language in part explains the exalted position of the poet—the maker of words, the bard, the spiritual leader. His position, by and large, survived even after 1918 when Poland regained its independence. It was dramatically enhanced during the World War II years of German occupation, when all Polish schools and institutes of higher education were closed and publishing in the Polish language was disrupted by the Germans. 23 years after, the official ban imposed on Mickiewicz's drama 'The Forefathers' Eve' galvanised the Warsaw students into protests which ended in street fighting with the police.

The Hungarian 'national model' for the men of letters is also based on opposition to unrepresentative government and rule. Hungary was more fortunate than Poland: even if it was for centuries ruled from Vienna, most traditional Hungarian institutions were (not without recurring struggles) preserved and in the first half of the 19th century were able to evolve towards complete self-determination for the nation. Hungary's main problem before the 1848 Revolution was that its social grievances were inseparable from its lack of independence, since dependence on Austria perpetuated the country's agrarian structure and anachronistic feudal customs. The best thinkers and writers demanded both social reforms and national self-determination. This is why Sándor Petőfi, the most popular and one of the best poets of the age could be both an ardent Magyar patriot and a radical revolutionary. His dream was the realisation of the threefold slogan of the French Revolution— he was all for brotherhood and could not imagine freedom without equality or equality without freedom. His vision of 'Heaven on Earth' is certainly Utopian but the spirit of dedicated revolt that emanates from his work exerted a powerful influence on future generations. He saw the poet as a 'pillar of fire', a spiritual leader of the people towards a Canaan to be won by revolution. He was admired and his rebellion was kept alive by such outstanding Hungarian poets of our century as Endre Ady, and after Ady, Attila József and Gyula Illyés. Between the two wars Petőfi's demands—the demands of democratic revolution—were shared by the group of Populist 'village explorers' and by the socialists, in fact by the entire Hungarian left; even the communists when making a bid for power would pose as 'Petőfi's heirs' as his name (and that of Lajos Kossuth) meant the *authentic revolution* for many Hungarians who had never read a line of Marx or Lenin. But no dictatorship can contain the spirit of real revolution. Petőfi appeared once again in 1956 as the patron saint of the famous Petőfi Circle (a debating society of the young intelligentsia) which, together with the Hungarian Writers' Association led the first attacks against the bastions of Stalinism in Hungary. The important thing about Petőfi, and for that matter Ady and the entire 'revolutionary line' in Hungarian literature, was that in his case national aspirations could only strengthen social revolt (unlike the Russian experience) and that by trying to be more European, the Hungarian writer or artist would only become more, and not less, Hungarian. Whereas the conservative-radical split existed in Hungarian society as much as anywhere else, only the peculiar inter-war social and political situation actually produced conflicts between 'Hungarophiles' and 'Westernisers'. Since 1945 (when the democratic revolution was at long last carried out in Hungary) the 'national poetic model' has lost some of its relevance. However, the main problem of the communists has remained the achievement of a peaceful synthesis between the contradictory models of home-grown (national) and imported (Soviet) revolutions.

Czechoslovakia

In the case of Czechoslovakia national tradition produced another, perhaps more sophisticated, model. Whereas in Poland and Hungary (and to a certain extent in Bulgaria) poets were in the vanguard of national awareness, in the Czech and Moravian lands poetry did not play such a distinctive role. The Czech national character has changed much since the Hussite wars when the Czechs were regarded as the best soldiers in Europe; it has both been hardened and mellowed by circumstances, changing from being romantic, poetic and revolutionary to rational, matter-of-fact and evolutionist. Nonetheless, intellectuals have been an important force in Czech history. I have in mind people like the historian Palacký whose part in the new rise of Czech national consciousness cannot be exaggerated. The greatest Czechs were traditionally preachers, thinkers or educators—like Jan Hus, Chelcicky and Komenský, then Palacký and Masaryk himself. The independent Czecho-slovak state that came into being after World War I was an achievement of the intellectuals in which, however, the contribution of journalists, philosophers and historians was decisive. This is not to underestimate the influence of such figures as Čapek or Halas. But the specific cultural traditions of the Czech nation made it more receptive to an 'objective' mode of discourse while in its scale of values, time and again, priority was given to seeking the absolute truth as opposed to seeking one's own truth or own right. (This does not apply to the Slovak lands where historical tradition influenced cultural impulses which were similar to those in Poland or Hungary.) At the same time, the fact that Czech intellectuals fought for specific national rights as well enhanced their position and standing in the eyes of the nation. So in the Czech context, once again, there was little contradiction between 'universal' and 'national' ideals. Whereas in Poland and Hungary sharp conflicts developed after 1918 between the ideals of the progressive intelligentsia and the realities of actual power, this was not so in Czechoslovakia, the questions of national minorities excepted. The socialist and communist movements in Czechoslovakia enjoyed the support of the majority of the Czech and Slovak intellectuals, who were the most willing supporters of radical social reform. This is why the communist revolution in Czecho-slovakia was, and still is, a test case. If we accept the thesis that the full collaboration and support of the intelligentsia is indispensable to the success of socialism and if no civilised form of socialism can be created in this small Central European country with its strong left-wing traditions, then socialism has no real future in Europe.

Marxist-Leninist Ideology and Socialist Realism

Apart from national tradition and Western influences the third factor which shapes the thinking of writers and artists in the Soviet Union and Eastern Europe is Marxist-Leninist ideology. Neither Marx nor Engels had worked out a coherent system of aesthetics. This accounts for the fact, that behind Marxist aesthetics one usually finds Hegelian or positivistic views. From various notes and hints, however, one can see the nature of demands that Marx made on the artist: he should be progressive in his politics and a realist in his art, and if one of the two requirements had to be sacrificed, realism was the one to remain. In other words, the writer should try and grasp the essence of human and social relations and it is the truthfulness of his work that should impress the reader not the loftiness of his political ideas. Lenin's fateful addition to this rather sane theory was his much-quoted article of 1905, 'Party Organisation and Party Literature' in which he formulated the demand that literature should become 'party literature', 'part of the Social Democratic . . . party work'. I called this article 'fateful' because this was the base upon which the entire Stalinist-Zhdanovist superstructure of literary control was later erected. Significantly, such an eminent anti-Stalinist Marxist thinker as Georg Lukács has never ceased to oppose the theory of partiynost (party-mindedness) derived from Lenin's article. For 'party literature' in Stalinist terms meant not only administrative control over funds, publishing houses and art galleries but also literature and art geared to the immediate political aims of the Communist Party. For what the enforcement of partiynost meant was the total subordination of the arts to the interests of political power and their constant manipulation and inevitable debasement in the serving of the ruling bureaucracy, even though the furtherance of long-term political aims or ideals might detract from the authenticity of the work of art.

Socialist realism in the arts is simply the 'best' (and in the long run the only approved) method which ensures the realisation of Lenin's claim for litera-ture. In the dogmatic Stalinist interpretation of socialist realism which is still dominant, though by no means omnipotent, in the Soviet Union, the writer's task is to depict society truthfully, on a high artistic level *and* in a party spirit. The latter demand stipulates optimism and simplicity as well. All this is possible only if the party's interest is in every case compatible with the objective (social) truth or the writer's subjective truth. In fact, these coincide only by chance, so socialist realism (a blend of revolutionary romanticism and critical realism) is a contradiction in terms. The writer can choose between following his own taste and convictions, in which case he will 'deviate' towards 'bourgeois' realism or some other artistic 'ism' or else following the party line and thereby inevitably committing the sin of 'embellishing' reality.

This short description explains the dilemma of the artist both in the Soviet Union and in Eastern Europe during the period that is now called 'the heyday of Zhdanovism' (in the Soviet Union 1946–53, in Eastern Europe 1948–53). In the Soviet Union socialist realism had a nightmarish quality: artists were blacklisted if they rejected it and yet were not consistently able to realise it. It got into the system of many writers, like brine which they had to drink as though it were spring water, so 'vomiting' (to use Ważyk's phrase) became inevitable.

Recently another more contemporary concept of socialist realism was propounded by Georg Lukács. This interpretation puts the stress on the realist content instead of the socialist message, and hence regards socialist realism simply as realism under socialist conditions. Lukács goes back to Gorky for some ideological confirmation, but then he arrives at an extra-ordinary conclusion: for him Solzhenitsyn is the first true socialist realist in Soviet literature since Gorky and the early Sholokhov! If we take a closer look at this concept, it becomes clear that Lukács has dropped the earlier interpretation of partiynost and prefers truthfulness and objective social analysis to wishful thinking and propaganda. His value system in judging art is infinitely more Marxist than that of Zhdanov, but I suspect that his reinterpretation of socialist realism stands no chance of being accepted in countries like the Soviet Union or Bulgaria.

That socialist realism should reign supreme above all other methods of writing, painting or composing music is a constant *desideratum* of the cultural policy of communist regimes. Whereas in the 1950s socialist realism was discredited in Eastern Europe as a Soviet-inspired method of ruthless artistic regimentation, lately there has been less insistence on its exclusive merits. This reflects, of course, the political concessions which had to be made to the people after the crisis of de-Stalinisation in the Soviet Union, Poland and Hungary in 1956, in Czechoslovakia and, to some extent, in Rumania after 1963. As soon as the fiction of complete unity within the ranks of the ruling party was exposed and the 'unflinching support' of the population for party policy disappeared, a period of uneasy tolerance was ushered in. Standards for creative activity other than socialist realism began to be accepted as temporary alternatives. For example in Poland between 1957 and 1963 the whole issue was conveniently forgotten by writers and critics, although it periodically reappeared in party documents. If after the demonstrations of students and writers in March 1968 there is now a renewed but modified insistence on *partiynost* in Poland, it is more on the basically 'socialist' (pro-regime) content, than on the realist form. Even high party functionaries are greatly concerned not to force Polish culture back into the straitjacket of the 1950s. The same could be true for the Soviet Union where since 1956 a whole generation of young writers has appeared (Voznesensky is perhaps their best representative) whose creative activities go against the grain of orthodox socialist realism. The publication of Solzhenitsyn's *One Day in the Life of Ivan Denisovich*, a masterful indictment of Stalin's empire of forced labour, could hardly be regarded as a major contribution to party-mindedness, and it is symptomatic that Solzhenitsyn's other two novels *The Cancer Ward* and *The First Circle* have not been published in the Soviet Union to this day.

POLITICS AND CULTURE

Policy affecting cultural activities fluctuates in countries with communist regimes. The extent to which writers or composers are free depends on the overall political situation, the exigencies of the moment and the party men in charge of cultural affairs. There is a direct and obvious connection between 'hard' and 'soft' periods in politics and a 'freeze' or 'thaw' in the arts. Although the Soviet leaders regard literature merely as a superstructure, they are in fact well aware of the impact which writers can make on a nation in moments of crisis. Khrushchev is reputed to have stated to a group of Soviet writers in 1957 that had the Hungarians shot a few of their 'troublemakers' (i.e. rebellious writers) in time, there would never have been an uprising in Hungary. It is also significant that before and after the military intervention of the five Warsaw Pact countries in Czechoslovakia the Soviet press reserved its special wrath and invective for those writers and journalists who wanted 'to undermine Socialist achievements' in that country.

All this does not mean that in Eastern Europe *every* writer has to be politically committed. Post-Stalinist communism is by definition more flexible and less coercive in matters of secondary importance than its monolithic predecessor; composers, painters and even writers can now afford to be apolitical in most East European countries. So writers like Dygat and Odojewski in Poland, Magda Szabó and Ottlik in Hungary, Škvorecký and Páral in Czechoslovakia, to mention only a few, are tolerated if not actually encouraged in their preoccupations with apolitical interests, even if they might occasionally be criticised for their 'indifference to socialism' or seeming 'frivolity'. The growth of apolitical writing in Eastern Europe poses a problem for the party overseers of culture. On the one hand they would like to have writers taking an active interest in politics, but past experience has shown that communist and leftist writers often end up as revisionists. Perhaps it is better, after all, to deny the writer's competence in politics and support apolitical literature?

We have mentioned the demand for the supremacy of socialist realism as a constant factor in communist cultural policy. An equally important principle is the organisational control exercised by the state and party over artists. No wholly independent Writers', Composers' or Painters' Union is tolerated, for such an organisation would sooner or later represent an ideological challenge to the ruling bureaucracy. For example, the Hungarian writers' rebellion which led to the 1956 revolution began in the Writers' Association; the struggle to overthrow Novotný gained strength in 1967 when Czech and Slovak writers took a stand against him at the Fourth Congress of their Writers' Association. The role played by the Warsaw branch of the Polish Writers' Union in the student protest movement of February/March 1968 is also well known. The party wishes to have control over these potentially dangerous organisations even if in 'soft' periods it is willing to make compromises. In periods of political crisis the professional association can be suspended or closed down, as for example in 1957 in Hungary when, amongst others, communist writers like Tibor Déry and Gyula Háy were charged with incitement and imprisoned.

CENSORSHIP

Censorship is the most important method of negative control exercised by communist governments. The severity of censorship varies from country to country, and from one period to another; some East European countries claim not to have formal censorship at all. In any case, censorship operates on two levels: external and internal. The external forms of censorship are not the same in every communist country—for instance, in Czechoslovakia each editorial office has its own censor, whereas in Poland censorship is centralised, and a copy of each newspaper or periodical has to be sent to the censor's office for approval before publication. In all communist countries the editor of a literary review as well as the editor of a publishing house is a part-time political censor—this is, so to speak, written in to the responsibilities of the job. In countries which have no formal censorship like Hungary, editors are even more cautious and circumspect than elsewhere because they are liable to be reprimanded or sacked following the publication of an objectionable article. While in Poland, Hungary or Czechoslovakia there is no law to forbid publication abroad, in the Soviet Union this is immediately interpreted as 'anti-Soviet' and is punished by severe reprimand (as in the case of Yevtushenko) officially organised campaigns of vilification (Pasternak) or terms of jail or labour camp (Sinyavsky, Daniel). Since 1966 there has been a law in force in East Germany that forbids authors to publish abroad unless they obtain special permission from the Ministry of Culture. (This in itself is proof of the extreme orthodoxy of the East German regime and a telling sign of Ulbricht's fear of his own liberal or 'revisionist' intellectuals.)

Apart from the external machinery of censorship, the 'internal censor' has been very active in communist regimes. An artist who has lived in a society which for decades has had so little regular contact with foreigners as the

Soviet Union, must find it hard not to conform. It became second nature for many to question inspiration in terms of whether it was 'correct' or 'incorrect' from the party point of view. No one likes writing a poem or painting a canvas which will never reach its public. Yet the extraordinary resilience of those Soviet writers who survived the purges of the 1930s and the partial break-down of censorship after the Twentieth Congress of the Soviet Communist Party is a hopeful sign in itself. Akhmatova wrote her moving cycle of poems *Requiem*, Bulgakov *Master and Margarita* and Pasternak *Doctor Zhivago* in the worst years of oppression. It could be argued that they all belonged to the older generation of intellectuals born before the Bolshevik Revolution, so they were less prone to Tartuffism and servile opportunism. 1956 and the late 1950s saw the rise of a new and more daring generation (that of Yevtushenko and Voznesensky) and a slow but steady erosion of 'internal censorship'. However, the unprecedented flow of *samizdat*, of self-printed mimeographed periodicals and novels, from the Soviet Union in the course of the last few years indicates that if the Soviet government wishes to contain the wave of legitimate criticism from its young intellectuals it will once again have to resort to traditional autocratic methods of control, since the functioning of the 'internal' censor is becoming less and less reliable.

PARTY CONTROL IN EASTERN EUROPE

Poland

This is particularly true of Eastern Europe, especially Poland and Czecho-slovakia. In these countries socialist realism left less of an impression on literature than it did in the Soviet Union. Nevertheless, before 1953 the system of external and internal 'checks' worked quite well and it was only in the permissive atmosphere of the post-1953 thaw that important books critical of the system came to be published. Between 1954 and 1957 Poland enjoyed the greatest artistic freedom (with the exception of Jugoslavia). Apart from the politically charged works of Andrzejewski, Brandys, Marek Hłasko and Adam Ważyk, abstract painting, modern music and the experimental theatre flourished in Warsaw and Cracow. Polish films, especially the works of Wajda, Munk and Polański won the acclaim of Western juries and audiences. Gomułka's increasingly dogmatic rule, however, put an end to these develop-ments: first, by curbing intellectual freedom and exuberance, later by strengthening the censor's hand to the point of the absurd. This process which could be perhaps defined as the 'roll-back' of intellectual freedom, started in earnest with the suppression of the radical Warsaw bi-weekly *Po Prostu* in 1957, continued with the closure of two cultural periodicals, *Nowa Kultura* and *Przegląd Kulturalny* in 1963 and was temporarily halted by the protest letter of the 34 intellectuals sent to Cyrankiewicz, the prime minister, early in 1964. The next significant event in the tug-of-war between the writers and the party bureaucracy was Leszek Kołakowski's speech at War-saw University in which he drew up a negative balance sheet of the ten years of Gomułka's rule. Kołakowski's immediate expulsion from the party was followed by a voluntary exodus of writers and intellectuals returning their party cards. Relations deteriorated even further when the unjustifiable and provocative ban imposed on Mickiewicz's classic 'The Forefathers' Eve', sparked off the so-called 'March events' of 1968. Since then the retaliatory policies of the regime have driven scores of Polish writers and 'Zionist' intellectuals to emigrate; others like Andrzejewski and Mrożek are blacklisted in Poland (for having protested against the participation of their country in the occupation of Czechoslovakia). The historian Jasienica and the poet Słon-imski have also become 'non-persons'—in that they cannot get anything published in Poland. In spite of official assurances to the contrary, censorship is now more severe in Poland than anywhere else in Eastern Europe with the exception of East Germany, Bulgaria and, of course, Albania.

Czechoslovakia

In Czechoslovakia, after a short-lived glimmer of hope in 1956, artistic freedom has been slowly growing since about 1963, but the publication of such politically explosive books as Mňačko's *Delayed Reports* and *The Taste of Power* were fought by Novotný to the last moment of his unimaginative rule. After January 1968 censorship was first relaxed, then lifted completely: there were two or three months in Czechoslovakia during which practically any literary work of merit could be published. However, the Czechoslovak Communist Party, even when led by Dubček, did not entirely give up its right to a say in cultural affairs, even if the Action Programme of the party in April 1968 declared:

> We reject administrative and bureaucratic methods of implementing cultural policy . . . Artistic work must not be subjected to censorship.

Between January and August 1968 literary weeklies like *Literárni Listy* in Prague and *Kultúrny Život* in Bratislava were important rallying-points for progressive writers and journalists, though the Slovak writers, concerned with national unity, were not so united in their insistence on radical reforms as their Czech colleagues. After the military intervention of the five Warsaw Pact countries, *Literárni Listy* was closed down only to renew publication under the slightly different title of *Listy*. In spite of frequent threats by the 'dogmatists' and of not unjustified fears for their safety, most leading and politically exposed Czech and Slovak writers (Havel, Vaculík, Seifert, Tatarka, Jesenská) have remained in Czechoslovakia. The Czech temperament seems to prefer the oblique to the direct statement and as long as they are protected from police persecution, Czech writers will probably find ways to communicate with their readers, even through the bars of censorship reimposed by the government for 'geopolitical' reasons.

Hungary

Hungary also enjoyed a spell of artistic freedom between 1954 and 1957 which (as the Communist Party regained its controls temporarily lost in 1956) was reduced to a minimum in the following years. In the early 1960s, however, a new cultural deal and a more liberal cultural policy emerged which culminated in the publication of ex-prisoner Tibor Déry's short stories, László Benjámin's outspoken and polemical poems and József Lengyel's dramatic account of his experience in Soviet labour camps. Since then this policy has suffered some setbacks but its basic platform—the extension of artistic freedom to non-communist and non-realist literature—has not changed. There are still certain kinds of books which cannot be published in Hungary, for fear of offending the Soviet Union or for probing too deeply into the recent past, but by and large censorship is more relaxed and publishing policy more generous than in most communist countries.

Jugoslavia

Ever since Tito's break with Stalin and Soviet-type communism in 1948 the Jugoslav cultural scene has been dominated by a permissiveness unimaginable in other communist countries before 1956 and wistfully admired by them in recent years. The first major split which divided Jugoslav literature into rival camps of 'realists' and 'modernists' was followed by others. Now there exists a multitude of groups, schools and periodicals, each complete with its own artistic method and theory, most of them subsidised by state or local government funds. Socialist realism has long been buried and forgotten, and as long as the artist does not defy, or subject to open criticism, the basic assumptions of 'Jugoslav socialism', he is more or less safe from official interference. Though the Jugoslav writer's lot is envied by his less fortunate colleagues in other East European countries, his freedom too has its limits. To give some examples: *Hero on a Donkey*, a novel by Miodrag Bulatović on the Italian occupation of Montenegro in which black humour is mixed with exuberant pornography, although published in a literary periodical, was banned in book form in Jugoslavia. On a more serious level, years after Djilas's first trial other writers, namely the Slovenian Marjan Rozanc and the Zadar lecturer, Mihajlo Mihajlov, were put on trial for expressing opposition to party policies and, significantly, for criticising the Soviet Union too openly. (Rozanc's sentence was suspended but Mihajlov is still in jail.) In the two main centres of Jugoslav literary life, Zagreb and Belgrade, political dissent amongst writers and philosophers is a major headache to party leaders— their reactions to the Zagreb-based philosophical review, *Praxis*, show that, whether Marxist or not, intellectuals are always suspect when they deviate from the ideological line laid down by the party. Nonetheless, the fact that in spite of all its financial and political difficulties *Praxis* still continues publication means that its search for 'creative Marxism' is at least partly supported by the younger generation of party and state functionaries.

Rumania

As for Rumania the situation at the end of 1968 was rather fluid. In retrospect 1968 might look like an important year for Rumanian literature—this was the year when the crisis of socialist realism, masked and long delayed by political pressures, was exposed. The efforts of the Ceauşescu leadership to create a united front of intellectuals behind its (more nationalist than communist) programme could not be successfully implemented as long as the issue of creative freedom remained unresolved. This happened, in a fashion, when, after a meeting of the Central Committee with the writers, Eugen Barbu, a prolific writer and current leading spokesman of the regime, was dropped from his position of editor-in-chief of the literary paper, *Luceafărul*. His demotion was partly due to a lively debate which had been going on earlier between Barbu on the one hand and the writer, Marin Preda, and his younger friends on the other, a debate between 'traditionalists' and 'progressives' or 'modernists'. The latter insist that only the 'plurality of literary styles' can assure the development of Rumanian literature, badly retarded, if not crippled, by two decades of ruthless party control and manipulation. At the last Congress of the Union of Rumanian Writers in November 1968 Marin Preda spoke of the readers' loss of faith in the written word and of the writer's task to restore its prestige through writing the truth as he sees it. The question remains: to what extent can Rumanian literature live up to Preda's hopes and ambitions? Although cultural exchanges with the West have been expanding in recent years, censorship and party surveillance remain permanent features of Rumanian cultural life and it would be too optimistic to hope for their complete erosion in the near future. Decentralisation may yet lead to increasing 'plurality', more freedom of experimentation to a 'Jugoslav' situation. One thing is certain—future developments will be affected by changes in Rumania's foreign policy and its relationship to the Soviet Union.

Bulgaria and East Germany

This leaves us with Bulgaria and East Germany as the two countries in Eastern Europe where the Soviet model is still upheld and emulated. Of the two Bulgaria is the more volatile and restive at present. Though traditionally pro-Russian, Bulgarians have a long tradition of fighting for national independence and during two short periods of cultural liberalisation (1956-7 and again 1962-3) there were several indications that deep cracks had appeared behind the wallpaper of revolutionary happiness in literature. These signs did not encourage the Zhivkov regime to leave its artists alone—indeed, whenever the ideological discipline seems to slacken, the party raises its voice and tells the writers to fall back in line. All the same, socialist realism is now implicitly defied in the works of some younger poets and artists and it is only a matter of time before this defiance (like in Rumania) finds theoretical and organisational support among the writers.

East Germany, because of its peculiar position within the Soviet orbit, is the last outpost of Stalinism in the arts. It used to be an infinitely more interesting place in the 1950s with Brecht and others still alive; since then the philosopher, Ernst Bloch, Uwe Johnson, Manfred Bieler and other writers having fled to West Germany, the best East German poets being dead, silenced (Huchel) or drastically censored (Biermann), there is very little the regime can point to as a genuine literary or cultural achievement. Although it has successfully improved economic conditions since 1961, East Germany (apart from relative material comforts) cannot offer anything to the creative artist, its ideology is sterile, its everyday life is permeated by petty-bourgeois conformism and servility. This is why post-Novotný developments in Czecho-slovakia proved to be such a powerful magnet for East German intellectuals, many of whom in August 1968 protested against Ulbricht's return to those German military traditions which the communists used to detest most.

Until now we have dwelt only on the *negative controls* of the Communist Party over writers and artists. There are, of course, positive ones as well—incentives. Intellectuals can be enlisted into the service of communism not only by attractive ideas or veiled threats but by rewards as well. In countries where the state is the only employer the artists enjoy the benefits of other state employees. There are special funds established for them; for example, the Literary Fund gives loans and grants to writers, maintains 'creative homes' (retreats for creative work) at secluded beauty-spots in and around the country and supports writers' families in cases of need. Besides these altogether admirable funds (which support even artists who are not members of the professional association in their field of activity), the annual awards given by the state to outstanding artists represent a very strong incentive. In the Soviet Union the Lenin Prize (up to 1956 the Stalin Prize) is awarded to writers and artists; in Poland the State Prize, in Hungary the Kossuth Prize and some minor artistic and literary prizes serve the same purpose. In some communist countries the heavily subsidised system of royalties is designed to make the writer's occupation socially desirable and at the same time rather privileged. The fact that what the state gives to the artist in appreciation of his work can be, if political circumstances warrant it, easily withheld, undoubtedly helps to cement the solidarity of some artists behind the regime.

THE ARTIST'S POSITION IN COMMUNIST SOCIETIES

Socially and also materially, the artist is a privileged citizen in communist society, the successful artist being more privileged than the average party functionary because, for one thing, he has less to worry about. On the other hand, some artists may feel that the price of a good life—conformity and political 'good manners' in Eastern Europe, active political engagement in the Soviet Union—is too high for them. The more non-conformist the artist is by nature, the more rebellious he becomes when that authority which first seemed to encourage his youthful search for truth, frustrates his creativity under a different political situation. This is when the force of national tradition, the psychologically binding 'posture' of the writer or poet usually reasserts itself: for example Poland and Hungary in 1956 when even seasoned communist writers took an anti-Soviet stand, and Czechoslovakia in 1968.

An artist's loyalty towards the communist regime can be swayed for one or more of the following reasons: revolutionary, national, or aesthetic-individualistic discontent. When all three are mobilised together on a wide front the intellectual movement is capable of changing, if not the whole structure of the regime, at least its ugliest features. This is what removed Rákosi and Novotný from power and it could happen to others. Perhaps the Soviet leaders are aware of this danger and this is why they keep such a close watch on rebellious writers and intellectuals in Kiev and Vilnius as well as in Moscow. For apart from 'charismatic' politicians (at present non-existent in the Soviet Union) only intellectuals and, above all, writers can influence public opinion effectively and prepare the painful transition of the Soviet Union from Stalinism to the pluralism of modern 20th century society. If in coming years the protests and representations of Soviet intellectuals are ignored by the party leadership and once again punished by exile and hard labour then the stage will be set for a violent political confrontation in the Soviet Union.

FURTHER READING

Alvarez, A. *Under Pressure*, Penguin, London, 1965.
Blake, Patricia and Hayward, Max (eds.) *Dissonant Voices in Soviet Literature*, Pantheon, New York, 1962; Allen and Unwin, London, 1965.
Gömöri, George and Newman, Charles (eds.) *New Writing of East Europe*, Quadrangle Press, Chicago, 1968.
Swayze, E. *Political Control of Literature in the USSR 1946–1959*, Oxford Univ. Press, London; Harvard Univ. Press, Cambridge, Mass., 1962.

GEORGE GÖMÖRI. Born in Budapest. Lecturer in Polish language and literature at the University of Cambridge. Left Hungary in 1956 and completed his studies at St. Anthony's College, Oxford. Sometime Senior Research Associate at Birmingham University. Author of *Polish and Hungarian Poetry*, 1945 to 1956.

THEATRE

OSSIA TRILLING

THE THEATRICAL TRADITION

THE main difference between the theatres of Western Europe and those of the East lies in the revolutionary tradition which superseded older needs and habits. The theatre as a moral institution (to use Schiller's formulation) was on the whole taken for granted in the East, even before socialist and popular revolutions overthrew the old bourgeois cultural forms and institutions. The logical outcome of this combination was an unprecedented growth in theatrical activity and attendance everywhere and the establishment of theatres in many areas where none existed before. The Soviet Union boasts over 500 professional companies (the highest per capita figure in the world) and an attendance of over 103 million spectators throughout the country in the year 1968. There are 42 children's theatres alone, and 95 full-time professional puppet-theatres. The corresponding figures for amateur drama are equally imposing, namely over 800 groups, many of them assisted by artists from the professional theatre. Finland, alone in the West, has a comparable record. The pattern throughout Eastern Europe is identical.

Unlike its counterpart in the West, the theatre is no longer a minority pastime, though tastes are not, therefore, necessarily highbrow, and the tendency in the 1960s was for proportionately more light entertainment than before. Throughout the East the theatre has been nationalised or come under municipal or institutional control. This has meant that, like the other arts, it has been used as a ready-made vehicle for mass-persuasion and propaganda and its struggles have reflected the ups and downs and changes which the society that has bred it has undergone and is still undergoing. It has been used as a forum for ideological polemics, mirroring the conflicts of the Cold War, the rival claims of aesthetic dogmas and creeds, the differing viewpoints of warring factions and in the liberalisation of expression that came to a head in the 1950s and 1960s.

In practice, this has meant that the drama of the West, regarded with suspicion in official circles, has received a greater hearing in such countries as Jugoslavia, Czechoslovakia and Poland; in the Soviet Union for the most part only such plays as reflected the official anti-capitalist or anti-Western viewpoint have been tolerated; Rumania and Hungary were the last to open their doors to the plays of unorthodox Western drama; Albania still frowns on it and trend-setters in East Germany, despite the Marxist works of the controversial Bertolt Brecht, who could not be disowned, are sharply divided on that score.

The turning-point came with the Twentieth Congress of the Soviet Communist Party which 'ushered in a new social and political era . . . with beneficial effects' on the life of all the socialist East; it restored 'Leninist standards of social life, breaches of which had affected the development of literature and art'. These words from a Soviet publication on the theatre recall the aesthetic battles fought in the name of the doctrine of socialist realism, that resulted in the outlawing of non-conformist writers in the 1930s and 1940s. Notwithstanding a more tolerant attitude towards non-conformism in writing and production, a former director of the Moscow Art Theatre wrote in 1968 that, 'we have overcome tremendous difficulties but refuse to desert our basic aim, the building of a socialist society on principles of justice and beauty'. Plays from the West that reveal a 'spirit of hopelessness or scepticism' are still taboo; and so are the works of native writers that fail to 'reflect our confidence in the future'.

Though the dramatic theory of lack of conflict according to which the dramatic clash is not between good and evil but between good and better has been dropped, a play in which the hero is not a 'person of intellect and action with lofty moral principles and a response to the problems of the day' will find it hard to obtain an official imprimatur. The ideological battle-order at any moment determines the extent to which the theatre in any East European country is free to speak its own mind.

THE SOVIET UNION

The Soviet theatre is a vast apparatus; too vast, when one considers that plays are performed in over 45 languages throughout the land, to be covered adequately in a general review such as this. Apart from Russian-language theatres, which cater for some 55% of the population, there are theatres, dating from before the Bolshevik Revolution in Armenia, Azerbaidzhan, Georgia and the Ukraine, to say nothing of those of the three Baltic republics. There are today well established theatres in Bashkiria, Belorussia, Buryato-Mongolia, Daghestan, Kazakhstan, Kirghizia, Moldavia, Tadzhikistan, Turkmeniya and Uzbekistan; in recent years permanent professional theatres have been performing in the Avar, Bataki, Chuvash, Karakalpak, Komi, Kumyk, Lezghin, Mari, Mordvin, Tuva, Udmurt, and Yakut languages.

The best known Russian theatre is the Moscow Art Theatre, which celebrated its 70th anniversary in 1968, and was founded by Konstantin Stanislavsky and Vladimir Nemirovich-Danchenko as 'the first judicious, ethical and generally accessible theatre'. The main playhouse, decorated on its front curtain with the emblem of the seagull, from Chekhov's play of that name, is small and elegant in the 19th century manner. Of its personnel of 600, 150 are players; its policy has always been not to engage guest-artists; guest-directors, like the late Gordon Craig (who staged *Hamlet* there in 1911), are the exception. A new modern building is to replace its present two houses with their 2,400 seats. Many of its plays have run for decades, some for well over half a century, notably Gorky's *Na dnye*, 1902 ('The Lower Depths') and Maeterlinck's *Sinyaya Ptitsa*, 1908 ('The Blue Bird'). Although its directors claim that it has fulfilled Lenin's dream to 'bring the theatre nearer to the masses and their socialist ideals', the tradition they have inherited has not gone undisputed.

The famous Stanislavsky system, the 'science of how an actor should seek the way to absolute truthfulness', has been the basis of teaching and acting practice throughout the Soviet Union, the socialist East and, indeed, most drama schools the world over, not least in the USA, notably in Lee

Strasberg's Actor's Studio, where its adapted form came to be known as 'the Method'. Its abuse has led to controversy and the spiritual sclerosis which often attacks old-established theatres (and not only the Moscow Art Theatre) and has led some Soviet directors to fight shy of it, or at any rate of its literal acceptance. Mikhail Kedrov, a veteran actor and director of the company, has defended its adaptability and willingness to take account of the most recent psychological research. Younger artists, some of them former Moscow Art members, or students of its school, have been less sanguine. The dividing-line has usually rested on the interpretation of the term 'truthfulness'. Gorky, who, like Chekhov, was closely allied with the Moscow Art, which bears his name, defined the tenet of socialist realism, of which he is said to have been the originator, as 'the affirmation of life as an action, as a con-structive endeavour' and he demanded the 'fusion of artistic truth with the tasks of building a new world'. During the Stalinist period, referred to by theatre critics as a period of grey realism, this became an inflexible rule, against which anyone transgressed at his peril; or, as with the great director, Meyerhold, whose poetic imagination abhorred the photographic naturalism that sprang from it, he paid for such transgression with his life. Mikhail Bulgakov (1891–1940), assistant director and resident dramatist of the Moscow Art for a time, was another who saw through the cant of this inflexible dogma. Most of his plays were proscribed in his lifetime, and he left dozens unperformed. A spiritual disciple of E. T. A. Hoffmann and Gogol, Bulgakov—possibly the greatest Russian dramatist after Chekhov—depicted the absurdities of vanity and self-delusion in a whole canon of fanciful dramas, as well as some more straightforward historically inspired ones, like *Dni Turbinykh* ('The White Guard'), that have only been rediscovered since the Twentieth Party Congress of 1956, thereby ironically realising Gorky's prophecy that 'Bulgakov will be remembered'. Even so, his idiosyncratic non-conformism has been giving trouble, both to existing and intending producers of his works.

During the late 1950s and 1960s, four of his plays, two of them revivals, were seen in Moscow and Leningrad. The Moscow Art's revival of *The White Guard* (his only play to have been staged in the West) is of interest if only because the original production was cut short on the grounds that it depicted white officers in the civil war in a favourable light. His *Molière* shows the French dramatist as a toady of the king who lives to rue his reliance on the royal word and was one of the plays put on by Anatoly Efros in Moscow shortly before the young director fell from grace. *Byeg*, 1957 ('Flight'), a grotesque study of a group of émigrés, *Vosyem Snov*, 1958 ('Eight Dreams'), a surrealist fantasy, and *Ivan Vasilyevich*, 1968, in which a group of scientists is transported by a time-machine into the reign of Ivan the Terrible, were the other three. The strengthening of the hands of theatre directors after 1956 against the opposing arguments that might be advanced by the Board or the Literary Adviser, usually a party nominee, no doubt accounted for the resurgence of some rebel drama, if only for a limited spell.

Criticism of the defects of the regime or of social injustice avoided official censorship by the use of allegory or by the skilful tactic of knowing just how far one may go too far. Writing or directing for the children's theatre pro-vided an outlet for a playwright like Yevgeny Shvarts (1896–1958) or directors like Olyeg Yefremov (b. 1927) and Anatoly Efros (b. 1925). Shvarts wrote heroic satirical or allegorical plays, ostensibly intended for children, in which corrupt power and the evils of tyranny were satirised, some of them, like *Tyen*, 1940 ('The Shadow') or *Drakon*, 1944 ('The Dragon') staged at the Leningrad Comedy Theatre by the late Nikolay Akimov but immediately taken off, and not revived for nearly 20 years. The satirical vein practised by Mayakovsky in the 1920s was fully sapped with the coming of Stalinist dogma and not reopened until *Banya* ('The Bathhouse') was revived at the Moscow Theatre of Satire in 1954. This set the pattern for the more or less unbroken record of satirical dramas staged there ever since by Valyentin Pluchek (b. 1909). Yefremov, formerly a teacher at the Moscow Art school, broke away to found the Sovremennik ('Contemporary') Theatre as a laboratory-studio in 1956 and saw it turn into Moscow's most popular theatre. It attracted young and old with older plays, such as Shvarts's *Goly Korol* ('The Naked Emperor'), based on the Andersen fairy-tale and forerunner of the anti-Stalinist dramas that came to be written in the late 1950s by critics of the so-called personality-cult, and the wholly modern dramas, dealing with great sympathy and understanding with the problems of the young, by Viktor Rozov (b. 1913), Alexandr Volodin (b. 1919) and their like. These plays lacked the studiously pathetic style of performance associated with the Moscow Art and the much older Maly Theatre, even though they could not muster such heavy acting talent as made these two theatres unrivalled in that field.

Yuri Lyubimov (b. 1917), a former actor of the Vakhtangov Theatre and pupil of the late Ruben Simonov, who kept the standard of Stanislavsky's dissident disciple flying at the theatre that bore his name for nearly 50 years, also broke away to manage the Theatre of Drama and Comedy, nicknamed the Taganka (from its location). Here he staged plays by Brecht and the young poets and documentary dramas of the type that became fashionable in the late 1960s, with ideological fearlessness in the teeth of official disapproval. Efros, at the Komsomol Theatre, won a huge new youthful audience only to find himself treading on official corns with the sexually outspoken plays of Eduard Radzinsky (b. 1932) and his unorthodox handling of Chekhov. Demoted to a smaller out-of-the-way playhouse, he turned the tables on his critics, with an unrepentant revival of Chekhov's *Tri Sestry* ('Three Sisters') in the unapproved manner. It was soon banned. Ironically, this same play and an earlier one by Radzinsky were staged with no less originality by the eminent director of the Leningrad Gorky Theatre, Georgy Tovstonogov (b. 1915), who also had to fight against artistic prying.

Undismayed, the Moscow Art and the Maly hit back. They, too, staged documentaries, among them *Shestovo Iyulya* ('July 6th') by Mikhail Shatov (b. 1932), about the aftermath of the Peace of Brest-Litovsk. This play, as well as the author's *Bolsheviki* ('The Bolsheviks'), which dealt with the attempt on Lenin's life, was put on at the same time by Yefremov. Simultaneous productions are no novelty in Moscow, witness Jerome Kilty's *Dear Liar* at the Moscow Art and Mossoviet Theatres, or *Irkutskaya Istoriya* ('It Happened in Irkutsk') by Alexey Arbuzov (b. 1908) at the Vakhtangov and Mayakovsky Theatres, each defended hotly by their respective partisans. Vying with *Ten Days that Shook the World* at the Taganka was *John Reed* at the Maly, two differing versions of a similar theme. Yuri Zavadsky (b. 1894), veteran director of the Mossoviet (or Moscow City) Theatre, and a pupil of Vakhtangov, has been as boldly innovatory as the younger men and as willing to experiment with new forms and methods. Probably the most versatile and most easily exportable dramatist in the Russian language is Arbuzov, concerned as he is with the spiritual growth of young people, their unhappiness and their anxieties. He is, moreover, unhampered by doctrinaire theories of dramaturgy. He will use a chorus, as in *Schastlivyye Dni*

Nyeschastlivovo Cheloveka, 1968 ('Happy Days of an Unhappy Man') staged both by Tovstonogov and by Efros, in which Krestovnikov, the failed hero, apostrophises the freedom of man, or simple naturalistic means, as in the three-character psychological problem-play *Moy Byedny Marat*, 1965, performed throughout the rest of the world as *The Promise*. Among the new directors, Leonid Kheifits, (b. 1934) at the Central Soviet Army Theatre, is held in high esteem; so is, among the new authors, Leonid Zorin (b.1924), as adept at the anti-cult as at historical drama. But even the older school is not inactive and dramas pour regularly from the pens of Leonid Leonov (b. 1899), philosopher of Soviet patriotism, Konstantin Simonov (b. 1915), playwright of politics, Alexandr Shtain (b. 1906), noted anti-cultist, and protégé of the late Nikolay Okhlopkov, until his death in 1967 the foremost Soviet innovator, Samuil Alyoshin (b. 1913), orthodox writer with an enquiring mind, and the party faithfuls like Alexandr Korneychuk (b. 1905), stoical son of his Ukrainian fatherland, Anatoly Sofronov (b. 1911), worker-poet and author of country comedies, Isidor Shtok (b. 1908), author of heroic wartime dramas, or Valentin Katayev (b. 1897), best known as the author of the light comedy, *Kvadratura Kruga*, performed throughout the world as *Squaring the Circle*.

There are scores of dramatists besides, of varying merit. None are likely to find an audience beyond their native frontiers, but the large numbers of theatres spread throughout the RSFSR provide them with a ready market for their wares. Moscow not only has two dozen drama theatres, some with two stages, and the world-famous Bolshoi Theatre, home of opera and ballet and rival of its Leningrad counterpart, the Kirov, a second opera-house, named after Stanislavsky (as a mark of the close affinity in production methods between the two disciplines), and houses for lighter fare; it also boasts the world-famous Obrastsov Puppet Theatre, three children's theatres, and a unique playhouse, the Romen, that stages the drama of the gypsy people in their own language.

The drama of the constituent republics is regularly heard in the capital during festivals of regional theatre and the leading drama schools provide the education of their students; the State Theatre Institute (GITIS) runs regular courses for whole teams of students from every corner of the far-flung union. The 25 theatres in Armenia are typical of the situation in a republic whose theatrical history goes back centuries, though the Sundukian Drama Theatre in Yerevan is only 32 years old. Many Armenians work permanently in Russian-speaking theatres. Martiros Saryan (b. 1880), the impressionist painter, has also contributed much to Soviet scenic art both in Moscow and elsewhere. Like Khachaturyan in Armenia, Kara Karayev (b. 1918) is a composer and Azerbaidzhan's best known artist. Author of operas and ballets, he wrote the incidental music for Vishnevsky's *Optimisticheskaya Tragediya* ('An Optimistic Tragedy') for Tovstonogov's celebrated revival at the Leningrad Pushkin Theatre, which won golden reviews at the Theatre of Nations in Paris.

Georgia, another republic with a dramatic tradition centuries long, has 22 theatres with the Rustaveli, in Tbilisi, heading the list. Here, Tovstonogov, partly-Georgian by race, learnt his trade. Its principal dramatist, Georgy Mdivani (b. 1905), has written several plays of patriotic content, performed throughout the union, and a political drama about modern Cuba. A musical by Mikhail Dumbadze and Georgy Lordkipanidze, adapted from a popular film, and staged by Tovstonogov in Leningrad was brought by his company to the World Theatre Season in London and stood up well to the over-shadowing power of Innokenty Smoktunovsky in Dostoyevsky's *Idiot* ('The Idiot'). The Ukrainian theatre, though much younger than its Russian counterpart, has a solid tradition. Its principal author, Korneichuk, has been as widely played in both Russian and Ukrainian, and so has Ivan Kocherga (1881–1952). *Antey* ('Antheus') by Nikolay Zarydny (b. 1921) has also been done in the main Russian theatres. The dramatist, Mikola Kulish, (1892–1942) was one of the Soviet Union's many artists (Isaac Babel [1894–1941] was another) who died an anonymous death in political exile, only to be rehabilitated posthumously.

The three Baltic states are a case apart, having come under communist influence only during the war and after, when a good many of the surviving artists and writers fled the country and continued their dramatic activity against impossible odds, mostly in North America. Estonia's eight theatres, with directors of the calibre of Karl Ird (b. 1909) to lead them, are very active, and the plays of writers like Eugen Rannet (b. 1911), strongly nationalist in feeling, and Ardi Liives (b. 1929), based on contemporary themes, have also been seen in foreign countries. Latvia's ten theatres have to compete artistically with the Russian Theatre in Riga, which was 76 years old in 1969. The lyrical plays of Gunars Priedes (b. 1928) are performed not only in the Rainis Theatre in Riga but throughout the Baltic states and the Soviet Union. Lithuania, with 13 theatres, has the oldest dramatic tradition. *Gerkus Mantas* by Iozas Grušas (b. 1901) has been called the first original Lithuanian contemporary tragedy.

Belorussia, with eleven theatres, is similarly placed to the Ukraine. Its two most successful dramatists are Kondrat Krapiva (b. 1896) and his pupil, Andrey Makayenok (b. 1920), both of whose plays are performed in Russian theatres. If the standard of a regional writer's excellence is to be gauged by his exportability, mention can be made of the Kirghizian Chingiz Aitmatov (b. 1928), the Bashkirian Mustai Karim (b. 1919), the Kazakh Abdilda Tazhibayev (b. 1909), the Moldavian Iulius Edlis (b. 1925); and a new impetus has been given in the 1960's to their theatres by such directors and players, rapidly gaining a local reputation, as Voldemar Panso (b. 1920), founder of the Tallinn Youth Theatre, Azerbaizhan Mambetov (b. 1932), director of the Auezov Theatre in Alma-Ata, or Tovstonogov's pupil Mikhail Tumanishvili (b. 1921) in Tbilisi.

POLAND AND CZECHOSLOVAKIA

The Polish theatre, ravaged during the war, revived rapidly as a result of the state's cultural policy. Today (with over 80 playhouses) it flourishes in every corner of Poland, and frequent drama festivals allow the outstanding pro-ductions of the year to be reviewed. The work of the major theatrical troupes is well known beyond their own frontiers, having won distinction in many European cities at festivals and on tour. The resistance to the aesthetic dictates of the communist ideologues was strongest in Poland, where party writers, like Leon Kruczkowski (1900–62), independent-minded poets, like Slawomir Mrożek (b. 1930), and a Catholic playwright like Jerzy Zawieyski (1906–69) coexisted for a time. The visit of the Royal Shakespeare Company's production of *Titus Andronicus* brought its director, Peter Brook, and the Warsaw critic, Professor Jan Kott (b. 1915), together and the succeeding visit of Brook's *King Lear* left a profound influence on Eastern Europe by opening the doors to new ideas. Kott's seminal writings on the contem-

poraneity of Shakespeare in turn left their imprints on directors in the West·
After the death of Stalin, Poland's many articulate dramatists exploited their new-found freedom to examine the nature of tyranny. Long neglected, essentially theatrical, ideas from the past, legacies of the dramas of Poland's first absurdist, Ignacy Witkiewicz (1885–1939), were given new form in the works of his spiritual disciples, led by Mrożek. Mrożek's most powerful cautionary drama, *Tango*, 1965, staged the world over, embodies the threat to democratic ideals of the new Lumpenproletariat. Heeding his own warning, Mrożek preferred to reside abroad, and after the invasion of Czechoslovakia in 1968, became an exile against his will, all his allegorical plays banned from the stage and the published page. The eminent critic and dramatist, Adam Tarn (b. 1902), Ida Kamińska (b. 1899), head of the Warsaw Jewish State Theatre, and other intellectuals found it expedient to leave Poland; Kott remained in America and Kazimierz Dejmek (b. 1924), talented manager of the two-centuries-old National Theatre in Warsaw, was one of many who lost their jobs. Unaffected by the purges was Witold Gombrowicz (1904–69), possibly the most original contemporary Polish dramatist, who had never returned from pre-war exile, and wrote his latest neo-Pirandellian existentialist poetic drama *Opereta*, 1966 ('Operetta') in the security of southern France. Poland has many first-rate directors who carry on the tradition of the late Leon Schiller, among them Dejmek's replacement, Adam Hanuszkiewicz (b. 1924), and Erwin Axer (b. 1917), head of the Teatr Współczesny ('Contemporary' Theatre); Axer directed *Tango* both at home and abroad, and the remarkable Tadeusz Łomnicki (b. 1927), appeared in his outstanding productions of Brecht's *Arturo Ui* in Warsaw and Leningrad. Another original director whose influence has been felt in the West is Jerzy Grotowski (b. 1933), creator of the Wrocławł Laboratory Theatre, apostle of the theatre of violence and ritual, and Peter Brook's collaborator on the Royal Shakespeare Company's production of the anti-war documentary *US*. His former assistant, Eugenio Barba, runs a parallel workshop in Denmark.

Despite the Polish theatre's acceptance of the plays of Ionesco and Beckett and its own tradition of absurdist drama, supported by student groups and satirical cabarets, the centre of East European avant-garde activity was firmly established in Prague after the coming of the political thaw, partly through the original scenographic theory and practice of Josef Svoboda (b. 1920) and other artists of his school; partly through the birth of state-supported 'private' theatres, that is, theatres independent of the top-heavy and regimented national and municipal groups; and partly thanks to the firmly rooted tradition set by the late E. F. Burian. The National Theatre's former chief director, Otomar Krejča (b. 1921), founded the Divadlo za Branou ('Theatre Behind the Gate'), with the support of his resident dramatist, Josef Topol (b. 1935), a lyrical writer of great imagination; Jan Grossman (b. 1925), helped by the anti-bureaucratic satirist Václav Havel (b. 1936), who successfully ran the Divadlo na Zábradlí ('Balustrade Theatre'), until the invasion of 1968; others with similar aims were grouped in an alliance of small experimental groups. The socialist-orientated plays of Pavel Kohout (b. 1928) have been performed throughout the East, and so had those of the Slovak author from Bratislava, Peter Karvaš (b. 1920), until he wrote his devastating satire on racialism, *Veľká Parochňa*, 1965 ('Wigs'), which sailed too near the party wind for comfort. The country's 65 theatres (and 103 companies) include several opera-houses, the one in Brno having international status; plays are given in the two main languages of the two federal republics;

there are Hungarian-language theatres, too; and several designers (e.g. Svoboda and Zbyněk Kolář) and directors (e.g. Alfred Radok, who invented the 'Laterna Magica' with Svoboda) have been active abroad. Immediately after the invasion life changed utterly, with many artists on temporary leave of absence abroad, and, significantly, not a single play or opera in the repertoire in a single place of entertainment by any author belonging to the five invading member-states of the Warsaw Pact has been heard.

HUNGARY, RUMANIA AND JUGOSLAVIA

When the political thaw came to Hungary in the 1960s. the floodgates were opened to every sort of influence and a government publication proudly announced that 'there is no censorship in Hungary'. This claim is not far removed from the truth, since more non-communist writers are habitually performed in the 40 theatres there than elsewhere in Eastern Europe. Yet, though Hungary, like Rumania, and Jugoslavia long since, has now taken the measure of the misleading term 'socialist realism', and the allegedly decadent Pinter and Beckett are no more suspect than the works of less 'difficult' Western writers of controversial dramas, like Dürrenmatt, or Hochhuth, or Weiss, its sense of what is real in the theatre is as safe as the basic socialism that informs all fields of cultural activity. Hungary's most successful export has been István Örkény (b. 1912), whose *Tóték*, 1966 ('The Tót Family'), at the Thalia Theatre, a grotesque parable of the abuse of power, might be cited as an example of 'socialist surrealism'. However, Hungary's best known dramatist is Gyula Háy (b. 1900), a life-long communist and exile, who returned after the liberation only to be sent to jail for his part in the 1956 uprising, and now lives in Switzerland, his humanitarian though increasingly sceptical parabolic dramas are performed in the West but studiously ignored in his native land.

After Háy comes László Németh (b. 1901), a physician and philosopher, whose well made realistic and historical dramas revolve mainly round the dilemma of the uncomprehending and misunderstood idealist, and Gyula Illyés (b. 1902), poet of peasant life. The Madách and National Theatres have offered an interesting contrast, the former with Németh's *Az Áruló*, 1967 ('The Traitor'), the latter with Illyés's *Fáklyaláng* ('Torchlight'), since each views the historical clash between the Hungarian patriot, Kossuth, and his political opponent, Görgey, from opposing angles and each protagonist is played by the same actor, the National Theatre's Ferenc Bessenyei (b. 1919), with shrewdly drawn differentiation. The plays of the communist playwright, Lajos Mesterházi (b. 1916), have been done in most East European countries.

Like their Czech counterparts, Rumanians have been much in demand in the West since the thaw as guest directors. Liviu Ciulei (b. 1923), architect, actor, designer, film director and manager of the Bucharest City Theatre, has worked in Berlin and West Germany, as has David Esrig (b. 1935), who joined him after making a career under Radu Beligan (b. 1918), founder of the much-travelled and widely applauded Comedy Theatre, which reintroduced Ionesco to Rumanian audiences under his original name of Ionescu. The success of the West's arch-absurdist in his country of origin must be viewed against the historical origins of this type of drama, which had its roots not only in the French 19th-century school of Alfred Jarry but also in the writings of the Rumanian Urmuz (1883–1923) (pseudonym of Dem Demetrescu Buzău). His disciple, Gheorghe Ciprian (1883–1968), gave to the Comedy Theatre its biggest international hit in *Capul de Raţoi* ('The

Drake's Head'). Among the multilingual country's 82 companies, performing in 42 theatres, there are both German-speaking and Hungarian-speaking ones (including opera). They have a vast choice of native plays to draw from, few of which, however, not even those of the revered literary giant, Victor Eftimiu (b. 1889), have proved exportable; noted exceptions are the plays of Aurel Baranga (b. 1913), ingeniously satirical, especially his *Iarba Nea* ('Poisonous Grass'), Horia Lovinescu (b. 1917), a communist who is not downcast by man's inescapable mortality, and Al. Mirodan (b. 1927), whose *Celebrul 702* ('The Famous 702'), was a play of protest inspired by the tragedy of Caryl Chessman. Ciulei's contribution at home has been positive, especially in his radical approach to the classics and his encouragement of young directors. Dinu Cernescu (b. 1935), taking a leaf out of the Western theatre of cruelty school, staged Ghelderode auspiciously at the Nottara Theatre, which, together with its studio for new young drama, is managed by Lovinescu. The National Theatre, without a proper home, has been conspicuously unadventurous, in contrast with the ambitiously lyrical productions of Radu Penciulescu (b. 1930) at the Teatrul Mic('Little Theatre').

The first East European state to throw off the shackles of Stalinism and allow its theatre to develop relatively freely, Jugoslavia, had other problems to face: war damage, differing traditions and languages, and changing political and social circumstances. The main centres were Serbia (Belgrade), Croatia (Zagreb), and Slovenia (Ljubljana), each with its own theatrical tradition, by comparison with Macedonia and Montenegro, which lacked a drama until after the war. Jugoslavia brought into being 56 theatres: 19 in Serbia, 14 in Croatia, six in Slovenia, seven in Macedonia, six in Bosnia-Hercegovina, and four in Montenegro; they do not include opera houses, children's, puppet or minority theatres in Italian, Hungarian, Albanian, Turkish and Rumanian. There is also a Slovene Theatre in the Italian city of Trieste having close relations with its colleagues across the frontier. While Croatia had a copious dramatic literature, Serbia was poorly catered for by comparison. From the outset Jugoslavia's writers accepted Western influences with a degree of tolerance, while maintaining their own socialist viewpoint. The grand old man of Croatian letters, Miroslav Krleža (b. 1893), lyric poet, polemicist and philosopher, has been a Marxist humanist in outlook all his life, his many dramas expressing his protest against reaction and obscurantism of every kind, without expressly attacking the noxious personality-cult of other socialist lands. Marijan Matković (b. 1915), found expression for his ideology in mythological subjects, while non-political or satirical comedy writers abounded. Two Belgrade authors, Djordje Lebović (b. 1928), and Aleksandar Obrenović (b. 1928), attracted attention with the existentialist tragedy, *Nebeski Odred* ('The Celestial Squad') 1965, set among the killers of a Nazi extermination camp. Aleksandar Popović (b. 1929), is another writer in Belgrade vernacular: witness his modern satire on bureaucracy, *Razvojni Put Bora Šnajdera* ('The Progress of Bora the Tailor'), that Belgrade's experimental theatre, Atelje 212, managed by Mira Trailović, performed at the 1968 Lincoln Center Festival.

Bratko Kreft (b. 1905), who adapted the Russian novel, *The 41st*, for the National Slovenian Theatre, is one of several writers in Ljubljana, the youngest being Domenik Smole (b. 1929), with a modern morality based on the Antigone legend. Several Jugoslav directors have worked abroad, notably Vlado Habunek (mainly in opera), Marko Fotez, both former directors of the Dubrovnik Festival, Kosta Spajić (their successor), France

Jamnik, and Bojan Stupica, who has brought his original theatrical imagination (as well as his skill as a designer) to bear on the national theatres of all three main centres, and was a co-founder and prime mover of Atelje 212. Jugoslavia seems to have one dissident dramatist only, namely the Montenegrin Miodrag Bulatović (b. 1930), whose rebuttal of Beckett's pessimistic *Waiting for Godot, Godo je došao* ('Godot has Come') had its world première in West Germany in 1966 and was published at home but never staged there.

BULGARIA AND ALBANIA

It is convenient to list these two countries immediately after Jugoslavia, not only for geographical and ethnic reasons, but also by way of contrast; for their attitude to the drama of the West has been as intolerant as that of the Soviet Union, Albania's doubly so. Albee's *Who's Afraid of Virginia Woolf?*, the prize production of Atelje 212 since 1964 in Belgrade, did, however, reach the National Theatre in Sofia, the pioneer of Bulgaria's 38 professional theatres (to which should be added the Turkish State Music Hall in Haskovo) in 1967. The creation of the Theatre of Satire in 1957, and the revival of the 80-year-old 'Sulza i Smyakh' ('Tears and Laughter') Theatre (now re-named the Theatre of Poetry) a decade later helped to clear the air for the anti-cult and socio-critical dramas of Kamen Zhidarov (b. 1902)—best known for the anti-Ottoman historical play *Ivan Shishman*—and the comedy-thrillers of Andrey Gulyashki (b. 1914). The acceptance of Brecht made up-hill going against the Stanislavsky tradition of realistic acting, strengthened by the power wielded by actor and teacher Nikolay Massalitinov (1880–1961), the Moscow Art's 1911 King Claudius. Of dozens of playwrights active in the 1960s, the nature-loving satirist, Nikolay Khaytov (b. 1919), has been most successful at home and abroad, while the anti-cultist drama, *Prokurorăt* ('The Public Prosecutor') by Georgy Dzhagarov (b. 1925), was even done in London in a version by C. P. Snow and Pamela Hansford Johnson.

Twenty-four theatres inside Albania cater for the needs of the country's theatregoers, to say nothing of the 600,000 Albanians in Jugoslavia, who have a theatre in their language in that country. Czech and Russian influence gave way to Chinese tutelage in 1960, and the propagation of 'communist ethics' and a fervent patriotism colour the mostly unexportable though fast-growing dramatic and operatic repertoire. The world-famed Albanian actor of the pre-war German stage, Alexander Moïssi (1880—1935), gave his name to the Alexander Moisiu drama school in Tirana.

EAST GERMANY

Here ideological and aesthetic differences between opposing theatrical theories have been sharpest. Bertolt Brecht (1898–1956), who was strongly influenced by Meyerhold's anti-illusionist theatre, propounded his own theory of the 'Epic Theatre' in opposition to Stanislavsky's widely accepted principles of psychological self-identification. He demanded an objectively critical and intellectual approach to the performance on the part both of the actor and the spectator. This led to irreconcilable clashes during the Stalinist period, when Meyerhold and his writings were still anathema in the Soviet Union. Even after Meyerhold's rehabilitation in 1956, Brecht's plays took some time in gaining general acceptance, and they were often staged in a manner that traduced their author's intentions. However, this was at no time the case in East Germany; the East Germans were able to exploit them as a political weapon, never so effectively as when the fabulous Berliner Ensemble, founded by Brecht in 1949, took them abroad. Led by a young team of highly trained enthusiasts, the Ensemble continued Brecht's traditions under his widow, Helene Weigel (b. Vienna, 1900), and his main disciple, Manfred Wekwerth (b. 1929), though it lost his gifted collaborator, Peter Palitzsch (b. 1918), after the division of Berlin in 1961. When the wall went up, contact between East and West was reduced to a minimum. The brilliantly managed Komische Oper, under Walter Felsenstein (b. Vienna, 1901), with its unrivalled visual realism and deft actor-singers, alone avoided the restrictions of isolationism. After 1961, more attention than ever was given to the fostering of dramas with socialist themes and plays by 'worker-playwrights'. Many shared the Brechtian form as well as Brecht's Marxist outlook. Besides the communist writers, Hedda Zinner (b. 1907) and Helmut Baierl (b. 1926), whose *Frau Flinz*, 1961 ('Mrs. Flinz') gave Miss Weigel her greatest role since Brecht's Mother Courage, and the Brecht-Gorky Mother, only Rolf Schneider (b. 1932), Heiner Müller (b. 1929) and Peter Hacks (b. 1928), have written exportable plays. Two of Hacks's best plays encountered ideological hurdles; one under Wolfgang Langhoff (1901–66), manager of Max Reinhardt's old theatre, the Deutsches, and another when the masterly Swiss-born director, Benno Besson (b. 1922), staged the anti-heroic *Moritz Tassow* (1965) at the Volksbühne. After 13 years with Brecht, and seven at the Deutsches, Besson was given the Volksbühne in 1969. Hacks's last few plays, though seen in the West, have found no producer in the East.

Several of the country's 51 drama companies (there are 81 stages, with 45 opera and 41 ballet troupes besides) do excellent work outside Berlin, theatrical regionalism being the keyword here, as much as in West Germany, notably in Rostock, Leipzig and Magdeburg; the Handel opera productions in Halle are also noteworthy. Still, it would be hard to find anywhere else productions of such finish and precision or such histrionic and technical mastery or inventiveness as the Berliner Ensemble's *Coriolanus* (1964). Finally, East Germany has her minority theatre, too: there is a Wendish theatre in Lusatia and *Matka Jančová* ('Mother Jansch') by Jurij Břejan (b. 1916), about a Sorbian Mother Courage, has much dramatic merit.

FURTHER READING

Brecht, Bertolt. *Brecht on Theatre*, Hill and Wang, New York; Methuen, London, 1964. *The Messingkauf Dialogues*, Methuen, London, 1965.
Csato, Edward. *The Polish Theatre*, W. S. Heinman, New York, 1965.
Esslin, Martin. *The Theatre of the Absurd*, revised ed., Pelican, London, 1968.
Glenny, Michael. (ed.) *Three Soviet Plays*, Penguin, London, 1966.
Gombrowicz, W. *Princess Ivona*, Calder and Boyars, London, 1969.
Guernsey, Otis J. (ed.) *Best Plays of 1964–5* (published yearly, most recently in 1970), Dodd, Mead & Co., New York, 1965.
Hainaux, René. (ed.) 'Theatre in East Germany', XIV, 4, *World Theatre*, Brussels, 1965. 'Theatre in Rumania', Special Issue *World Theatre*, Brussels, 1964. 'Theatre in Yugoslavia', XV, 5, *World Theatre*, Brussels, 1966. 'Total Theatre', XV, 1, *World Theatre*, Brussels, 1966. 'Brecht 1956–1966', XV, 3–4, *World Theatre*, Brussels, 1966. 'Twenty Years of Theatre', XVII, 1–2, *World Theatre*, Brussels, 1968.
Hájek, Jiří. (ed.) *Universum*, quarterly review of Czechoslovak Literature and Arts, Czechoslovak Centre for Publishing and Book Trade and the Union of Czechoslovak Writers, Prague.
Hartnoll, Phyllis. (ed.) *Oxford Companion to the Theatre*, Oxford Univ. Press, London, 1967.
Houghton, Norris. *Return Engagement*, Holt Rinehart, New York; Putnam, London, 1962.
Kott, Jan. *Shakespeare Our Contemporary*, 2nd revised ed., Doubleday, New York, 1966; Methuen, London, 1967.
Maliarová, Edita. (ed.) *Theatre in Czechoslovakia*, Theatre Institute, Prague, 1967.

Palmer, Helen H. and Dyson, Anne Jane, (compiled by). *European Drama Criticism*, new ed., Shoe String Press, Hamden, Conn., 1968.

Piens, Gerhard. (ed.) *Theatre in the German Democratic Republic*, GDR Centre of the International Theatre Institute, East Berlin, 1964.

Popkin, Henry. (ed.) 'Eastern European Theatre', *Tulane Drama Review*, (T35), New Orleans, La., 1967.

Rumanian Quarterly, Bucharest, quarterly.

Shaoulov, L. *The Bulgarian Theatre*, Foreign Language Press, Sofia, 1964.

Slonim, Marc. *Russian Theatre*, World, Cleveland, Ohio, 1961; Methuen, London, 1963.

Stanislavsky, Konstantin. *Stanislavsky on the Art of the Stage*, with an introduction by David Margarshak, 2nd ed., Faber, London, 1967.

The Theatre in Poland, monthly bulletin of the Polish Centre of the International Theatre Institute, Warsaw.

Volodin, Alexander. (translated and with an introduction by Ariadne Nicolaeff). *Five Evenings*, Minnesota Univ. Press, Minneapolis, Minn., 1966; Oxford Univ Press, 1967.

Willett, John. *The Theatre of Bertolt Brecht*, Methuen, London, 1967.

Ossia Trilling. Drama critic. Vice-President of the International Association of Theatre Critics; Critics' Circle Councillor. Has been writing drama criticism since 1937 and is a regular contributor to *The Times* and other newspapers. Co-editor and contributor to *International Theatre* and *Dobson's Theatre Year Book*.

CINEMA

JOHN RUSSELL TAYLOR

THE STALINIST ERA

THE various and violent ups and downs undergone by the cinema in Western Europe since the war have been almost entirely the result of economic pressures. In Eastern Europe the pressures have been no less effective, but they have been primarily political. The end of the war saw the cinema industries (such as they had been) of nearly every country in Eastern Europe brought to a standstill, their talents dispersed, their studios and technical resources virtually non-existent. In the Soviet Union things were a little better than elsewhere, since though the war had disrupted the major centres of film production, production had continued after evacuation in various Central Asian studios and locations, and continuity had thus been preserved. Czechoslovakia had also derived one future advantage from the many disadvantages of German occupation and partition: the enormous and highly equipped Barrandov studios, which had become in the later stages of the war the main centre of production for German films, and had been elaborated accordingly; on the other hand, immediately after the war there was virtually no Czech cinema to make use of these facilities.

Redevelopment was slow. Not only were there the technical problems of finding equipment, getting the experienced film-makers to work again and training new talent to make the most of the resources to hand, but there was also the problem of what sort of films ought to be made. This was primarily a political problem: while the communist regime in the Soviet Union was long established, in all the other East European countries it was a new thing, bringing with it its own problems of what sort of film might and might not be considered acceptable in the new climate of opinion. Life was not easy either for the established talents in the Soviet cinema. In 1946 Eisenstein found his work on the second part of his intended *Ivan the Terrible* trilogy attacked on grounds of 'formalism', and before long many other artists in all media came under similar attack. From 1947 until Stalin's death in 1953 the range of subjects which might be treated by Soviet film-makers and the ways in which they might be handled were very closely circumscribed, and general uncertainty prevailed.

Nevertheless, an ever-increasing number of films were made in all the East European countries—except Albania, which has always been too primitive to support much of a film industry of its own, and has at best served only as a location for one or two elaborate Soviet films, known courteously, before Albania's break with the Soviet bloc, as co-productions. The first country in Eastern Europe to produce films after the war which achieved any sort of

notice internationally was East Germany, where under Soviet encouragement a number of gloomy anti-Nazi films were made in mostly very primitive
conditions, roughly comparable to those in which the contemporary Italian
neo-realists were working. This phase passed in a year or two, and then
nothing of obvious artistic stature was produced until 1954, when Andrzej
Wajda made his first feature film, *A Generation*, in Poland. This was taken to
be the herald of a new and lively school of Polish film-making, as in fact
proved to be the case: Poland went on during the next three or four years to
produce the first distinctive national school of film-makers to develop under
communist rule in Eastern Europe.

Hopes that something similar would happen in Hungary, where directors
of clear talent like Zoltán Fábri (*Merry-Go-Round, Professor Hannibal*) and
Imre Fehér (*A Sunday Romance*) were beginning to make a name for themselves,
were dashed for the time being when the 1956 Hungarian Revolution
proved abortive and all the arts were thereafter kept under a very tight rein
for several years. But in the Soviet Union itself the death of Stalin brought a
thaw in the cinema: some new freedom in the choice of subject-matter (in
particular a veering-away from the sort of stuffy historical biography of
national heroes which had been the staple of Stalinist cinema), and a greater
readiness to make technical experiments well over the edge of what would
recently have been considered 'formalism'.

CONTACT WITH THE WEST

The generally more relaxed intellectual climate of the mid-1950s brought
with it much more cultural interchange than had been possible before. To
begin with, it was largely a matter of film-makers in the East having a
chance to see and absorb what film-makers in the West had been doing
during the war and since. This sometimes gives a curious air of time-slip to
East European films of this era: there are many Soviet films in particular
which look as though their directors had just, some 15 years after the event,
discovered Orson Welles and *Citizen Kane*, and swallowed them both whole.
This stage past, however, the traffic soon became two-way. At last there were
Eastern films which could be seen and genuinely enjoyed in the West: some
Polish, some Hungarian, even some Soviet, notably Grigory Chukray's
Ballad of a Soldier and Josif Heifitz's *The Lady with a Little Dog* (both 1960). A
little later the Czech cinema was added to the list, first of all with Miloš
Forman's *Peter and Pavla* (1963).

When this happened, commercial pressures too began to play their part.
Previously, all the film industries of the East European countries had been
run along the line laid down in the Soviet Union before the war. All film production was nationalised and government-directed, the principal administrative unit being the studio, with its rota of actors, directors and technicians
who functioned with more or less freedom, more or less choice according to
their current standing but were, virtually at all stages, and certainly at the
beginning and end of film-making, directly accountable to the officials in
charge. Since not only the question of what films were made, but where and
when they were shown, was completely in the hands of the government,
commercial considerations as understood in the West played a very minor
role in framing production policy. With the opening-up of a Western market
for Eastern films, however, the situation has subtly changed. It is recognised
—to some extent in the Soviet Union itself, and certainly much more in other
East European countries—that films are highly marketable in the West,

which is always to the advantage of the governments concerned. Moreover, a critical success in the West often seems to bring in its train success, critical and commercial, in the East: there, as elsewhere, prophets are likely to receive honour only when their compatriots are assured that the rest of the world has already given it.

Such questions have led, subtly but perceptibly, to a certain internationalisation of the East European cinema. If the likely tastes of the West are not capital in the inception of a new film project, they probably play their part in its elaboration: it is unlikely, for instance, that a production on the scale of the recent four-part Soviet *War and Peace* would be conceived in such terms without at least one eye being consciously turned towards the West and the earnings such a film might reasonably be expected to make there. Attempts on the part of Polish and (in co-production) of Hungarian film-makers to meet the Hollywood spectacle on its own ground have been less successful, but the returns on Western showings of more modest productions like those of the new Czech school of 'intimists' must be a major consideration in the economy of one of the smaller East European states.

Furthermore, interest in Western markets has passed over into active collaboration with Western film-makers. In 1966–7, for example, two large-scale US productions were made partly or wholly on Eastern locations, *The Night of the Generals* in Warsaw and *The Fixer* in Budapest, while at the same time two Soviet films, *The Journalist* and *Anna Karenina*, made use of locations in Paris, Geneva and the Italian lakes.

THE SOVIET UNION

At the end of the war the three great figures of Soviet silent cinema, Eisenstein, Pudovkin and Dovzhenko, were all still alive and active. But in fact, owing to circumstances largely political, they were all at the effective end of their careers. Eisenstein had fallen foul of the Committee for Cinematography, and of Stalin personally, for his preoccupation in the second part of *Ivan the Terrible* with private squabbles at the Tsar's court rather than the great heroic sweep of history, and also for his formal experimentation. He was already a sick man, and died in 1948 without being able either to do some projected reshooting on part two or to complete work on part three of the trilogy. Dovzhenko's film biography of the scientist Michurin, *Life in Flower*, was rejected by the Committee in 1947, and after two years reshot with the help of his wife; he did not live to complete another film himself, though in the three films made by his widow, Julia Solntseva, according to his scripts after his death in 1956—*The Poem of the Sea*, *The Turbulent Years* and *The Enchanted River*—have been extraordinarily successful in capturing his own mystical vision of a life close to the Russian soil. Pudovkin, always a more amenable character, continued in official favour until his death in 1953, but had in fact made no film of real note since the end of the silent period.

Of the middle generation perhaps only Mark Donskoy and Sergey Yutkevich remained important throughout the period under review. Donskoy had produced a masterpiece before the war in his trilogy on the early life of Maxim Gorky, and has continued on and off to return to the simple lyrical humane style of those films, as in *The Village Teacher* (1947) and his version of Gorky's *Mother* (1956). Yutkevich, in many ways exceptional in the Soviet cinema as a Westernised sophisticate, has managed to combine his own brilliant technical virtuosity and cool intelligence with safe subjects—

a beautiful colour version of *Othello*, a charming glimpse of Lenin off-duty in *Lenin in Poland*. Of the other directors of this generation many remain active, but the only one to produce something really outstanding has been Josif Heifitz, whose Chekhov adaptations *The Lady with the Little Dog* and *In the Town of S.* show extreme sensibility and a remarkable gift of period re-creation.

The Soviet cinema has failed to bring forward any talents of a younger generation at all comparable with these, now all in their 60s. At first the Stalinist freeze might be blamed, but the thaw failed to show us any except quite minor talents, such as Grigory Chukray, whose *Ballad of a Soldier* was pleasant, warm-hearted and innocuous, rather like some American message-pictures of the early 1930s; Andrey Tarkovsky, whose *Childhood of Ivan* showed a lot of bravura camerawork and little else; Mikhail Kalatozov, an older man whose romantic drama *The Cranes are Flying* gained interest mainly by introducing an exciting new actress in Tatyana Samoylova; and the actor Sergey Bondarchuk, whose first film as a director, *Destiny of a Man*, suggested an ambitious talent which spectacularly over-reached itself in his vastly expensive *War and Peace* tetralogy (despite a few scattered felicities).

Standing slightly to one side of all this are two survivors from the 1930s, Grigory Kosintsov, whose strikingly imaginative version of *Hamlet* with Innokenty Smoktunovsky in 1963 scored an international success, and Sergey Gerassimov, whose *The Journalist* in 1967 had a certain dogged determination to be fair and reasonable about the West as it strikes an intelligent Russian. The products of the cartoon and children's film studios in the Soviet Union are often excellent, and all the smaller republics have their own studios and their own film production set-up in their own languages. (The total film production in the Soviet Union now is about 120 to 140 feature films a year, plus about 300 documentaries, 500 popular science films and various other specialised products.) There have even been some signs, in 1967, of a Soviet 'new wave' developing, the most talked-about new films being Tarkovsky's lengthy biography of the mediaeval ikon-painter *Rublyov* (which was held to be too gloomy for showing during the celebrations of the 50th anniversary of the Revolution) and Marlen Khutziev's *Rain in July*, which seems to show the direct influence of Godard and other French directors of advanced inclinations in its depiction of the aimless lives of the new Soviet intelligentsia.

POLAND

During the immediate post-war years the Polish cinema was known outside Poland only for the films of Alexander Ford, a veteran who had been directing since 1928. His *The Youth of Chopin* had some real romantic dash, and *Five Boys from Barska Street* dealt stylishly, if from the plot point of view rather stodgily, with the problems of youth in a shattered post-war world. But these films were nothing to get very excited about, and no great excitement was visible until the arrival on the scene of Andrzej Wajda in 1954. Wajda provided for some time the image of the 'typical' Polish film-maker—which is an over-simplification, but not perhaps entirely untrue. Certainly his qualities of visual extravagance, black humour, and a penchant for playing drama up to and sometimes over the edge of melodrama seem to characterise a number of Polish directors besides himself. His particular brand of 'Polish baroque' was seen to best advantage in his war trilogy *A Generation*, *Kanal* and *Ashes and Diamonds*, the last of which also had the advantage of introducing to the world the first great international star from the Eastern bloc, Zbigniew Cybulski and his dark glasses. Wajda's later career has been more uneven, including a couple of films made abroad; he seems, like other film-makers in the East, to have difficulty in getting away from the war as an obsessive subject.

This was clearly also a problem for Wajda's near-contemporary Andrzej Munk, who died prematurely in a car accident in 1961, leaving what seemed to be potentially his most interesting film, *Passenger*, unfinished. It is difficult to decide, though, how much of the effect of *Passenger*, a strange, dreamlike story of life in a concentration camp, derives from the mystery its unfinished state throws over the narrative; certainly none of Munk's other films, such as *Bad Luck* and *Eroica*, achieve anything like the same density. Other directors to have found favour in the West include Jerzy Kawalerowitz, with his showy historical drama *Mother Joan of the Angels*, and Wojciech Has, with his elegiac war-story *Farewells*. But the two young Poles who have created the most spectacular impression have been Roman Polański and Jerzy Skolimowski. Polański first captured attention with a rather surrealistic short parable, *Two Men and a Wardrobe*, and then with his first feature, *Knife in the Water*, an edgy comedy about an amorous triangle during a sailing expedition. His films since then have been made in Britain and the USA and are therefore beyond the scope of this survey. But *Knife in the Water*, for many his best film, was scripted by Skolimowski, who has since come forward as the writer, director and sometimes star of a series of obscure, powerful and often rather unpleasant films, among them *Walkover, Barrier* and a strange comedy about automania, *Le Départ*, made in Belgium.

Poland has also produced some of the most idiosyncratic and powerful of modern animated films in the dark, biting and wholly adult work of Jan Lenica and Walerian Borowczyk.

CZECHOSLOVAKIA

Though some directors from pre-war days, such as Otakar Vávra and Martin Frič, started making films again almost as soon as the war was over, for some years all the Czech cinema meant to the outside world was the inventive puppet and animated films of Jiří Trnka and Karel Zeman (the masterpiece of the group is probably Trnka's visually resplendent version of *A Midsummer Night's Dream*). But all that rapidly changed after 1963 and *Peter and Pavla*. In this film Miloš Forman at once leapt to the forefront of world cinema with his cool, wry and witty universal observations on what it is like to be young. He repeated his success a couple of years later with *A Blonde in Love;* but by that time it had become evident that he was not alone. A whole school of talented Czech film-makers came fast on his heels. Or to be precise, two schools. Most of them had affinities with Forman, in that they were interested in the minute notation of particular moments in everyday life, sometimes comic, sometimes sad, rarely tragic. This group of 'intimist' film-makers, with their quality of making the most ordinary occurrences seem somehow extraordinary, includes Pavel Juráček (*Every Young Man*), Ivan Passer (*Intimate Lighting*), Jiří Menzel (*Closely Observed Trains*) and Jaromil Jireš (*The Cry*). The second group is smaller, though of much the same generation: its principal members are Jan Němec (*Diamonds in the Night*) and Věra Chytilová (*Daisies*). Both of these were pupils of the veteran Otakar Vávra, whose evocative *Romance for Bugle* (1966) is recognisably along the same line: they all deal with heightened, almost dreamlike states in visually striking, sometimes extravagantly stylised terms.

Of all the cinemas in Eastern Europe the Czech is most Western in its outlook, and has had the most general success with Western audiences. This has even extended in recent years to some of its most conservative elements: *The Shop in the High Street*, (1965) a stolid and worthy but very old-fashioned story about wartime persecution of the Jews directed by Ján Kadár and Elmar Klos, even won a Hollywood Oscar as the best foreign film of its year. Since the invasion of August 1968 many of the film-makers mentioned have settled in the West, though whether temporarily or permanently, and what the effect of the new regime will be on the Czech film, it is too early to say.

HUNGARY

The development of Hungarian cinema as of more than local appeal has been very recent. The first signs of growth, with the films of Zoltán Fábri and Imre Fehér around 1956, were rapidly stifled by external events, and though both these directors have continued to make films none of their later works has lived up to the promise of their early work. But *The Round-Up* (also known as *The Hopeless Ones*, 1966) suggested that Miklós Jancsó might be a major talent, a guess amply confirmed by his earlier-made, later-seen *My Way Home*. His is a secretive obsessional cinema, very much preoccupied with the empty spaces of Hungary's plains and the empty spaces between men's minds.

A somewhat similar temperament was shown in András Kovács's *Cold Days* (1966), a sombre piece of research into men and motives in a famous massacre of the last war. István Szabó, the third of the new generation in Hungarian cinema to make his mark, is very different: his *Father* (1967), an intricate story of a boy's involvement with and gradual freeing of himself from a protective imaginary image of his father, is carried off with considerable skill and something at times approaching bravado.

OTHER COUNTRIES

The film industries of the other countries in Eastern Europe have mostly been negligible artistically and for the most part very limited in their output, having to depend mostly on relatively small local markets (hence the importance attaching to a successful breakthrough to international success in countries where the films can be subtitled or dubbed). The only film of importance in Albania has been Sergey Yutkevich's celebration of the Albanian national hero *Scanderbeg* (1954). Rumania has a small local production of films each year, mostly sentimental comedies and strong dramas, intended strictly for home consumption. Bulgaria is in much the same case, except that one or two films, such as *The Peach Thief* (1964), have made some reputation outside their country of origin, and *The Turning* (1967), an emotional drama shifting very cunningly between the present and the past, seems to suggest that its makers, the theatre director, Gricha Ostrovsky, and the cameraman, Todor Stoyanov have qualities of intelligence and sophistication which augur well for their future. The East German cinema had its short day of glory just after the war, with grim anti-Nazi films like Wolfgang Staudt's *The Murderers Are Among Us* and some equally grim classic adaptations like Georg Klaren's of Büchner's *Wozzeck*, but since then it seems to have stagnated, no doubt because the regime is still the most repressive in Eastern Europe; most of the film-makers of any talent in East Germany have moved Westwards.

The Jugoslav cinema has developed along somewhat different lines since Jugoslavia's expulsion from the Cominform in 1948. It has still produced mostly for home consumption, but it has evolved towards greater freedom and variety of organisation, until today it is ready to tolerate independent production units within the general structure of the nationalised film industry. During 1967 it made concerted attempts to follow the path blazed by Poland, Czechoslovakia and Hungary to international markets. The demonstrations offered by such films as Dušan Makavejev's *Switchboard Operator* and Zvonomir Berković's *Rondo* do not as yet entirely convince us that it is ready to do so, but they are certainly modern cinema, Western style, and it seems unlikely that Jugoslavia will stop trying for the big breakthrough until it has achieved it.

FURTHER READING

Bodak, Jaroslav. *Modern Czechoslovak Film 1945–1965*, Artia, Prague; Vanous, New York, 1965.
Contemporary Polish Cinematography, Polonia, Warsaw, 1962; W. Heinman, New York, 1963.
Houston, Penelope. *The Contemporary Cinema*, Penguin, London and Baltimore, Md., 1963.
Learn All About the Soviet Cinema, V/O Sovexportfilm, Moscow, 1967.
Leyda, Jay. *Kino: A History of the Russian and Soviet Film*, Allen and Unwin, London; Macmillan, New York, 1960.
Zalman, Jan. *Films and Film-makers in Czechoslovakia*, Orbis, Prague, 1968.

JOHN RUSSELL TAYLOR. Since 1963 film critic of *The Times*. Regular contributor to *Sight and Sound*, *The Listener*, etc. Author of numerous books, including *Anger and After: A Guide to the New British Drama; The Penguin Dictionary of Drama* and *Anatomy of a Television Play*.

THE ROLE OF THE PRESS AND BROADCASTING

EUGENE STEINER

ARTICLE 125 of the Soviet constitution of 1936 enshrines the principle of freedom of speech, association and the press, although these constitutional rights are subject to and 'in conformity with the interest of the working people in order to strengthen the socialist system'. However, Soviet party documents concerning the press and other mass media have never claimed to adhere to the view that their role was to inform the public by the presentation of facts in unbiased reporting and comment. They have never pretended to uphold the principle that facts are sacred, comment free.

Lenin saw the press as an instrument fulfilling three main functions: it was to be a 'collective organiser, propagandist and agitator'. This axiom was adopted by Stalin and his successors and is still inculcated into every journalist in socialist societies today. The mass media are supposed to act as a transmission belt. When it is in the interests of the party or state to propagate or agitate for a certain policy, any fact which might be disadvantageous to those interests must be suppressed whatever its news value and, indeed, often just because of its news value.

Lenin and other Soviet theoreticians have not spared sceptical comment on the freedom of the press in bourgeois democratic societies. Lenin declared that 'this concept of freedom is a lie for as long as the best printing works and the largest stocks of paper are in capitalist hands'. In his *Thesis on Bourgeois Democracy and the Dictatorship of the Proletariat* he argues that 'true freedom will be found in that future system in which any worker, or group of workers whatever their numbers, will be able to process and exercise the right enjoyed equally by all of using public printing works and public paper'. This statement however was intended more as an optimistic vision for the future than as a description of the existing situation in Russia in 1919 when he wrote his *Thesis*.

After more than 50 years of Soviet rule, during which time the working class and its natural ally the peasantry have overthrown the capitalist order, to what extent has Lenin's prophecy been fulfilled? In Lenin's day when the disturbing effects of the October Revolution were still being felt, it is only fair to point out that his vision had little opportunity of being realised. But in the Stalin era Soviet power and the Soviet state had consolidated, the civil war had been won by the Bolsheviks and foreign intervention had ceased. Instead of translating Marxist-Leninist theories into practice, however, Stalin chose to supplant them with his own ideas, and to implement them by means of his own personal dictatorship. In the successful elimination of most of his potential enemies and rivals for power, orthodox Marxist theory became more and more out of touch with Soviet reality and reality out of touch even with the theories which had been elaborated and developed by Stalin.

In the late 1920s the role ascribed to the press was extended to apply to the new mass medium—broadcasting. In the Soviet Union, a country still in the stage of semi-literacy, the new medium assumed even greater importance than the press in carrying out the functions of propagandist, agitator and collective organiser. The Soviet party and government used it extensively, but whether they did so effectively and efficiently is a different matter.

With the advent of radio the Soviet Communist Party became the master of an instrument which could reach not only the peoples of the Soviet Union, but those outside its boundaries. Moscow became the first capital of the world to use the ether to spread propaganda abroad, and for a relatively long time it was the only capital to do so. Foreign language broadcasts were officially directed by the Comintern. That it failed to become a very effective instrument in fomenting and fostering world revolution was in part due to the inept, often clumsy and unconvincing methods of the Soviet leaders and their international comrades. For all their philosophical and political training they were not necessarily experts in the science of psychology. It is interesting to note that in those countries where propaganda was and still is almost a dirty word the impact of the mass media is considerably greater than in those countries where it is almost an accepted fact of life.

Communist Propaganda Techniques

The study of human behaviour and motivation is noticeably lacking from communist propaganda techniques, which accounts for its dullness and, ultimately, its ineffectiveness. The material disseminated by the Soviet mass media, in particular, has a monotony in its prefabricated clichés which often betrays incompetence and ignorance. This is equally apparent in the newest mass medium—television. Technically the Soviet Union was very quick to develop and make use of the new medium; and millions of people in the Soviet Union own television sets. However, whereas the monopoly of Soviet propaganda on the radio may be broken by the occasional access to foreign broadcasts, television pours out an uninterrupted stream of indigestible programmes. This has the effect of inducing an apathy and indifference of mind, which is perhaps not wholly unwelcome to the Soviet authorities.

There is a feeling of frustration among the more intelligent of those who work for the mass media in the Soviet Union and other East European countries in that so little scope is allowed for personal initiative and ideas. Journalists, radio and television commentators, whatever their views about the subject matter of the official propaganda, feel that they should be permitted to experiment with better techniques of persuasion and presentation. However, the official approach to mass communications does not value originality highly and often even suspects it. Adherence to the party line means not only a faithful following of the arguments published in party documents and tracts, but actually using the identical phrases and idioms. The greatest crime is sensationalism, which is condemned as a harmful and dangerous vice, typical of bourgeois journalism.

Despite the limitations imposed upon them, the spread of the mass media is greatly encouraged in the Soviet Union and throughout Eastern Europe. In the Soviet Union, in particular, the conspicuous expansion of the press since the Tsarist days has been largely responsible for the eradication of illiteracy—one of the main achievements of the Soviet era. There is no doubt that in all the socialist countries this social deficiency is treated very seriously.

In 1913 there were, for example, 859 newspapers in Russia with a total circulation of 2,700,000. In 1951, according to official Soviet figures, there were 7,800 periodicals with a circulation of 36,000,000. In the 1960s the figures have again increased considerably, although the per capita consumption of print still falls far short of that in Western countries. It is, however, questionable as to whether these quantitative increases are accompanied by an increase in actual readership. In the first place not all the millions of copies of books, periodicals and newspapers reach their public. Thousands of daily and weekly newspapers are sent to factories and offices, often distributed free, but frequently prospective readers do not even bother to collect them. Although it is a mark of good conduct for a party or trade union member to order at least one daily paper, it is more difficult to control or coerce him to read it. In the Soviet Union and Eastern Europe more copies of political books and periodicals are printed than sold and more are sold than read.

In the late 1940s and early 1950s the works of Stalin were published in tens of thousands of copies throughout the socialist bloc. Considerable pressure was brought to bear, especially on white-collar workers and party members, to subscribe to the whole series (more than 30 volumes). However, thousands of copies never left the state book-selling warehouses and, after Stalin's dethronement from his position as the greatest exponent of modern Marxist thought, his masterpieces were disposed of *en masse* and removed from the shelves of public and even private libraries. Whereas the figures for printing books are freely quoted as an eloquent sign of culture, those for the sale of books are usually kept a confidential state secret.

CENSORSHIP

At the time of the Bolshevik Revolution censorship was minimal. However, all means of communication suffered a tightening of control during Stalin's reign. Censorship was intensified when strict measures were introduced in the late 1940s under Zhdanov who was in charge of this vital weapon of the Cold War. In December 1947 the Soviet government passed a law which prohibited all contact between Soviet institutions and their employees and those of foreign countries without the intermediation of the Soviet Ministry of Foreign Affairs. (Article 6 of this law listed certain exceptions which included the visiting of cinemas or calling the fire brigade.) Those mainly affected were foreign correspondents and journalists.

An organisation by the name of Glavlit took over many of the functions and duties of censorship. The censorship function of Glavlit was never officially recognised or admitted, and indeed it was even denied. In theory it was only concerned with book publishing, film production and broadcasting and, in particular, with the welfare of workers employed in these activities. Glavlit came into operation only in those cases where there was no central party control. For example all political publications are controlled directly by the government.

In fact most of the mass media in the Soviet Union falls outside the scope of Glavlit. The Soviet authorities recognise that by putting the onus of censorship on the editor of a newspaper, he is likely to act as a better guarantee of non-deviation from the party line than an inexperienced and ignorant outside official from the censor's office. The mechanics of censorship in the Soviet Union and in most East European countries are such that the actual manuscripts are not submitted to the judgment of the censor. The representative of the state's interests, who sits at the printing plant, reads the pages only after they have been set, corrected and are ready for press. The fact that the original copy itself is not read by the censors serves to keep up the pretence that no preventive censorship is operated—which would be 'illegal'—and that the editor or writer may write and send to press anything on his own 'free will'. It also safeguards against the possibility of an editor overriding the censor and subsequently printing an item of 'dangerous' content. It is a more reliable system to watch and control the final stages of printing than the writing itself.

The introduction of the office of censorship was never formally passed by law but was instituted in a clandestine way in inner-party instructions. It is, therefore, technically an illegal institution. Previously all material put out by the mass media came under the watchful eye of the state prosecutor. His presence was a sufficient guarantee to prevent trouble. His office and activities were closely linked, and even merged, with those of the secret police and were consequently dreaded. It was only after the removal of Beria and the curtailment of the power of the secret police that it was thought necessary to find a method of preventing unwanted material from reaching the public through the mass media. The voluntary exercise of 'self-censorship' was no longer considered a sufficient check, even to those conditioned by Engels's axiom that 'freedom is the appreciation of necessity'.

Generally, the decisions of the censor are accepted and complied with. There are, however, instances on record where the editor or his staff has challenged the censor's decision. Should the censor be unsure and hesitant, he may telephone his superior at the central office for confirmation. This is usually given, not least to uphold the censor's authority. There have been, however, cases in which the editor's argument has triumphed, often after considerable haggling. Then, the material in question is given the rubber stamp of approval with the reference number of the Central Administration of Press Control, as it is most commonly called in Eastern Europe.

The Czechoslovak Experience

The Communist Party of Czechoslovakia in its 1968 Action Programme recommended the abolition of censorship. For a few months before the invasion of Czechoslovakia in August 1968 the mass media enjoyed almost total freedom. Even under the latter stages of the Novotný era, there was a certain amount of freedom on the cultural front. The heads of the ideological departments of the party were changed almost every month and as a result quite a number of articles, books, films and television and radio features, which would have otherwise been stopped by the censor, were released for general consumption. Novotný himself is said to have intervened on occasion in favour of an author or writer.

In all socialist countries varying degrees of pressure are exercised by the party on the mass media. After the departure of Stalin and during Khrushchev's reign, there was a widespread relaxation. In 1961 Glavlit ceased to control the dispatches of foreign correspondents, although the office itself was not abolished. Under the editorship of Khrushchev's son-in-law, Adzhubei, the official organ of the USSR Supreme Soviet, *Izvestiya*, (which competed in dullness with the official organ of the Soviet Communist Party,

Pravda) became a relatively lively evening newspaper. It seemed for a while that the mass media were being directed into new and more reasonable channels, which would benefit not only the general public but the party itself. However, although these were the days when Ehrenburg's *The Thaw*, Dudintsev's *Not By Bread Alone* and the works of Solzhenitsyn were published with Khrushchev's approval, his cultural criteria were not always consistent. Whilst the Kharkov professor, Liberman, was permitted to experiment in economics, Pasternak, who was experimenting in the field of literature, incurred official displeasure by his novel, *Doctor Zhivago*.

All these changes in the Soviet Union had an immediate impact on those socialist countries which remained faithful to the Soviet pattern. The Czechoslovak events of 1968 were watched with great apprehension in the Soviet Union and throughout Eastern Europe. The Soviet leaders were aware that the main instigators of the movement were Czech and Slovak intellectuals, writers and journalists, and they witnessed anxiously the part played by the mass media in the Czechoslovak 'counter-revolution'.

All this did not happen in Czechoslovakia because the Novotný regime was too lenient, as was thought in Moscow. Nor was the Czechoslovak experiment a result of the fact that the censorship was insufficient or abolished too soon. Perhaps it might be more accurate to suggest that the revolution itself abolished censorship, which in any event had disintegrated even before its official abolition by law in June 1968.

Fearing that the Czechoslovak example might affect other East European countries, including the Soviet Union itself, L. M. Zamyatin of the Press Department of the Ministry of Foreign Affairs issued on 19 January 1968 a statement to foreign correspondents, in which he reminded them of the validity of the 1947 law and warned them that 'any violation of the established rule will result in severe measures against the violators'. Clearly Zamyatin was more concerned with his own journalists and writers than with foreign correspondents. The official occasion of Zamyatin's warning was the trial of the Soviet writer, Ginzburg, and his friends, and from the outset the Soviet and allied press, radio and television were hostile to the Czechoslovak experiment.

THE POSSIBILITIES OF DISSENT

Although official control over the press in Eastern Europe and the Soviet Union is usually strict enough to prevent the expression of dissent beyond the officially-approved limits, it does happen on occasion that a particular interest group or organisation or even a courageous editor can temporarily convert a paper into a vehicle of dissent. One clear instance of this was *Kultúrny Život*, the Slovak Writers' Union weekly, which in the years 1963–4 pursued a campaign for more consistent deStalinisation and in favour of the recognition of Slovak interests. There is no doubt that *Kultúrny Život* enjoyed a certain measure of unofficial backing from the Slovak party in Bratislava, which, presumably, saw its interests threatened by Novotný's obscurantism. It is not without significance that the first secretary of the Slovak party at the time was Alexander Dubček.

Another instance of the press being used to present a point of view diverging from that of the party leadership was the challenge mounted by the Partisans in Poland during the spring of 1968. A number of publications, notably *Kultura* and *Prawo i Życie*, were printing articles unquestionably unacceptable to the Gomułka leadership and putting forward the nationalist and anti-Semitic theses of Mieczysław Moczar, the leader of the Partisans. The Partisans had a considerable amount of popular support for their anti-Semitic campaign and they commanded a good deal of power in a number of the party organisations. With the failure of the Partisan challenge in the autumn of 1968, the Partisan-controlled papers tended once again to come under the control of the Gomułka wing of the party.

Then again, there is the case of the Hungarian provincial paper *Kisalföld*, published in the west Hungarian town of Györ. For much of the Dubček reform period the editor of *Kisalföld*, Sándor Lónyai, adopted a much more sympathetic attitude to what was going on in Czechoslovakia than the central party papers in Budapest. In particular *Kisalföld* carried a fairly full summary of the 'Two Thousand Words' appeal, issued at the end of June 1968, unlike any other Hungarian paper.

However, such divergence from official policy can seldom be maintained for any length of time. Sooner or later, the authorities will oblige dissenters to return to orthodoxy or be purged. Essentially the communist system, as practised in Eastern Europe and the Soviet Union, is simply not geared to accept wide divergence from official dogma. Even in Jugoslavia, where the press is considerably freer than elsewhere in Eastern Europe, certain areas remain taboo. Thus, foreign affairs are recognised by Jugoslav editors to be within the strict domain of party control and no word of dissent was expressed in print about Jugoslavia's support for the Arabs in the Arab-Israeli war of 1967, despite a measure of popular support for Israel.

Ultimately freedom of the press in Eastern Europe is possible only when the party itself accepts the values of pluralism, of an open society. This did happen during the Dubček era in Czechoslovakia and the freedom of the press was one of the first victims of normalisation soon after the Warsaw Pact occupation of the country.

Stalin once said that the role of the press in a socialist society was to be that of a state advertising agency. The present rulers in the Kremlin and their followers in Eastern Europe have not by their actions dissented significantly from that dictum.

E. STEINER. Was foreign editor of the Slovak Trade Union paper *Práca* until the Soviet invasion of 1968. Since then he has been working at the London School of Economics.

LITERATURE

CONTEMPORARY SOVIET LITERATURE

MICHAEL SCAMMELL

In order to get a fair picture of Soviet literature in recent times it is necessary to take into account some special features of the cultural climate in which it has developed. A major influence has been the traditional Russian insistence on the importance of literature as a social force and correspondingly on its role as an instrument and a means to an end, rather than an end in itself. This tendency is partly the result of secular Russian literature's comparative youth. Having come into being only in the second half of the 18th century, when Russian cultural life was under the influence of a didactic French classicism, it flowered most brilliantly during the middle 50 years of the 19th century, when religious fervour, moral earnestness and idealism dominated the scene. Another factor was the monopolistic character of the Russian state, which tended to try and bring all areas of Russian life under central control. In the case of literature its instrument was an official and state-controlled censorship, which automatically scrutinised literature for its ideological content and forced upon writers a high degree of political and social awareness. Soviet rule has certainly perpetuated and systematised these features of Russian cultural life and has so accentuated them as to produce a society which, in its close and continuous political control of literature, has no parallel in the West.

Effect of World War II on Soviet Literature

The impact of World War II on Soviet literature was much the same as in other engaged countries. Belles lettres virtually came to an end. Among the various diaries of wartime life in the Soviet Union some of the best are *Voyenniye dnevniki*, 1940–2 ('War Diaries') by Konstantin Simonov (b. 1916), *Voina*, 1941–2 ('Russia at War') by Ilya Ehrenburg (1891–1968), *Rodina*, 1942 ('Motherland') by Alexey Tolstoy (b. 1882) and *Leningrad v dni blokada*, 1944 ('Leningrad in the Days of the Blockade') by Alexander Fadeyev (b. 1901). Another outlet for literary talent was in the writing of patriotic and popular verse, much of it in the form of songs, in which writers like Simonov, Alexey Surkov (b. 1899), Olga Bergholtz (b. 1910) and Margarita Aliger (b. 1915) excelled. Simonov in particular achieved unheard-of popularity with romantic lyrics such as *Zhdi menya* ('Wait for Me'), the plea of a soldier to his beloved to remain faithful while he is away in the trenches, or *Ty Pomnish, Alyosha, dorogi Smolenshchiny?* ('Do you Remember, Alyosha, the Roads of Smolensk?') about the beginning of the war and the tragic defeats of the Red Army, while *Zoya*, 1941 ('Zoya'), by Margarita Aliger told of the real life Komsomol girl of the same name who had fought in the underground against the Nazis and then been caught, tortured and hanged. The most outstanding verse production of the war years was the long narrative poem, *Vasili Tyorkin*, 1941–5 ('Vasili Tyorkin') by Alexander Tvardovsky (b. 1910), the story of a good-humoured Schweik-like Russian soldier who goes through a series of tragic and comic experiences but always emerges buoyant and cheerful.

The war was not only important to Soviet literature in the years that followed but has remained an important theme even to the present day. One reason is the deliberate encouragement of war themes by the Communist Party as a means of siphoning off strong emotions and directing hostility against external forces that, in theory at least, are beyond the government's control. Second, there has been the continuing fluctuation in official attitudes to the war and to such burning questions as the role of Stalin, the efficacy of the Red Army, the extent and effectiveness of the various underground movements and the impact of the German occupation. Each new twist in policy and each set of revelations has as a rule triggered off a new wave of works about the war and its place in Soviet life.

Another effect of the war was to create an atmosphere of greater freedom in the cultural life in the Soviet Union. The era of terror and purges that had closed the 1930s was forgotten in an upsurge of patriotic fervour and unity. The churches were brought back into national life and cultural fraternisation permitted with the allies in the West. In this newly relaxed atmosphere emerged some of the best literary fruits of the war, notably *V okopakh Stalingrada*, 1946 ('In the Trenches of Stalingrad') by one of the most talented writers to emerge in this period, Viktor Nekrasov (b. 1915). Nekrasov's contribution was to offer sober, objective reporting of the day-to-day operations of war in a detached, almost estranged style, together with deft psychological portraits of the soldiers and officers involved, a literary method that evokes a comparison with Leo Tolstoy and Hemingway. The more heroic and traditionally Soviet approach, meanwhile, was reflected in *Lyudi s chistoy sovjestyu*, 1945 ('Men with a Clear Conscience') by Pyotr Vershigora (b. 1905) and Fadeyev's celebrated *Molodaya gvardiya*, 1945 ('The Young Guard') which for many years remained a symbol of the ideal communist novel as conceived by the party.

ZHDANOVISM

In 1946 occurred an event that was to have enormous significance on Soviet literature for at least the next ten years and has remained influential to the present day. This was a special decree on literature passed by the Central Committee of the Communist Party on 14 August 1946, written and introduced by Andrey Zhdanov (1888–1948) on the direct orders of Stalin. The immediate subject of the decree was a condemnation of two Leningrad literary magazines, *Zvezda* ('The Star') and *Leningrad*, for publishing works that were ideologically unsound and even 'harmful', together with a sensational and unprecedentedly scurrilous attack on two Leningrad writers of the older generation, Mikhail Zoshchenko (1895–1958) and Anna Akhmatova (1888–1966) who had been published by these magazines. Both were drummed out of the Writers' Union, which meant literary death in those days, while the magazine *Leningrad* was closed down and *Zvezda* completely reorganised.

Many of the attitudes underlying Soviet political control of literature can be traced back to *Zhdanovshchina*, or Zhdanovism as it came to be called. In its worst excesses Zhdanovism indulged in a shrill anti-Semitism and anti-cosmopolitanism that can be seen now as byproducts of foreign policy. At the core of Zhdanovism lay a determination to return to the doctrine of socialist realism in the arts, a celebrated method that has never been satisfactorily defined. Zhdanov had been active at the First Congress of Soviet Writers in 1934, when the theory of socialist realism was first formulated as follows:

> Socialist realism, being the basic method of Soviet literature and literary criticism, requires from the artist a truthful, historically concrete representation of reality in its revolutionary development. Moreover, truthfulness and completeness of artistic representation must be combined with the task of ideological transformation and education of the working man in the spirit of socialism.

The problem now was to reapply this doctrine to the literature of the post-war period; and it was Zhdanov's task to carry it through.

On the organisational level, this was accomplished by the usual purges of editorial boards and Writers' Union officials. Nikolai Tikhonov (b. 1896), a talented and liberal-minded poet, was replaced as General Secretary of the Writers' Union by the more orthodox Fadeyev. As for literary works themselves, books with any traces of vitality or independence were in the main suppressed in favour of machined products produced to carefully pre-set formulae. Two formulae in particular proved to be safe and popular. One was the anti-Western tract, expressing chauvinism and even xenophobia, and the other was a positive one in which the tenets of socialist realism were carried through to the letter. A past-master of the art was Semyon Babayev-sky (b. 1909), an expert winner of Stalin prizes whose name later became a synonym for sentimental rubbish. Perhaps the best example of this genre, however, is *Povest o nastoyashchem cheloveke*, 1947 ('The Story of a Real Man') by Boris Polevoy (Boris Kampov, b. 1908), also a Stalin prize-winner.

THE THAW

The gloom of the Zhdanov era in literary matters was finally pierced by another political event on 5 March 1953—the death of Stalin. Shortly after, articles in the literary press called for a let-up in the political pressure by writers. Ehrenburg in the magazine *Znamya* ('Banner') and notably Vladimir Pomerantsev in *Novy Mir* ('New World') called for new values and sincerity in literature, and in the following year came a real breakthrough: publication in *Znamya* of the first part of Ehrenburg's new novel, *Ottepel*, 1954 ('The Thaw'), which gave its name to a whole era. Although no masterpiece, *The Thaw* shocked contemporary readers by its open devotion to the themes of love and personal happiness and the problems of men and women whose emotions had become 'frozen' by years of repression. Also depicted was a conflict between two artists, one a politically safe and highly rewarded conformist hack, the other a true creator who had starved for lack of recognition and support.

In December 1954 the Second Congress of Soviet Writers took place—20 years after the First—in the course of which many changes were made. Akhmatova, for instance, was reinstated as a member of the Union and in the following year a whole group of leading Soviet writers from earlier years was officially 'rehabilitated', including Isaac Babel (1894–1941), Mikhail Bulgakov (1891–1940), Yuri Olesha (1899–1960), Nikolai Zabolotsky (1903–58) and the celebrated stage director, Vsevolod Meyerhold (1874–1942). *Den poezii* ('Poetry Day') was started in 1955, an annual event at which poets, mainly young ones, read their works to mass audiences and subsequently printed them in an almanac of the same name. Another almanac, *Literaturnaya Moskva* ('Literary Moscow'), simultaneously began publishing the work of older poets, notably Akhmatova, Boris Pasternak (1890–1960) and the outstanding émigré poet, Marina Tsvetayeva (1892–1941), who had returned to the Soviet Union in 1939 and two years later committed suicide. It was forced to close, however, after only two issues. Finally there was the establishment of an official journal, *Inostrannaya literatura* ('Foreign Literature'), devoted exclusively to translations and criticism of foreign literature.

Khrushchev's famous speech at the Twentieth Congress of the Communist Party in February 1956 had repercussions in every sphere of life; and perhaps even more significant for literature was a vehement speech to the Congress by a senior Soviet writer, Mikhail Sholokhov (b. 1905). Sholokhov accused writers of alienation from life and the masses and in particular launched a virulent attack on the Writers' Union and its secretary, Fadeyev. Fadeyev, basically an honourable man who had been led into dictatorial methods and even denouncing fellow writers by his zeal for political orthodoxy, was shattered by this attack. In 1951, in the worst years of Zhdanovism, he had meekly agreed to rewrite his famous novel, *The Young Guard*, in order to eliminate certain 'errors'. Now, in a more liberal atmosphere, his past policies were shown up as base and unscrupulous, and in May 1956 he committed suicide. The shock to his fellow writers and the reading public was immense, but even more was it a symbol of the change in the times. The same year also saw the publication in *Novy Mir* of the celebrated novel, *Ne khlebom yedinym*, 1956 ('Not by Bread Alone') by Vladimir Dudintsev (b. 1918). Although not very distinguished from a literary point of view, Dudintsev's novel caused a sensation by its implicit attack on the whole system of Soviet bureaucracy and the hierarchy of power within it, which he illustrated by pitting a lone, eccentric but idealistic inventor against the cruel bureaucratic machine.

In 1957 was published a truly great and original work, the novel *Doctor Zhivago*, by Boris Pasternak (1890–1960). As a literary creation, *Doctor Zhivago* was immediately recognised as standing head and shoulders above all other Soviet work of the post-war period and as possibly one of the great novels of this century. It is impossible, in a small space, to do justice to the extraordinary complexity and beauty of Pasternak's creation, but one aspect of it was to have fateful consequences for Soviet literature. Pasternak completed the novel about 1955 and there were hopes that, in the light of the thaw, it would be published in the Soviet Union. After interminable hesitations and delays, however, during which the novel achieved a tremendous underground notoriety, it was rejected. Copies of it, which were already being widely circulated, quickly found their way abroad and in the autumn of 1957 it was published first in Italy (in both Russian and Italian) and then in the other countries of the West. At first the news of its publication and huge success was kept secret from Soviet readers, but in October 1958 Pasternak was awarded the Nobel Prize for Literature and at once a storm broke over his head of unprecedented violence and ferocity. He was unanimously denounced by the press, publicly vilified by government leaders and subjected to wrathful demands for punishment and deportation. Appalled by this storm, Pasternak rejected the prize and begged to be allowed to stay, which request was granted, although he was simultaneously expelled from the Union of Writers and prohibited from publishing a word from then until his death in 1960.

THE NEW GENERATION

The Hungarian revolt at the end of 1956 had set off a period of freeze in foreign policy and at home orthodox and conformist writers began to call for closer control over literature again. But at the Twenty-first Communist Party Congress in January 1959, Khrushchev again denounced Stalin, and at the Third Writers' Congress in May the same year, Alexey Surkov, a hard-line communist, was replaced by the respected novelist, Konstantin Fedin (b. 1892), as first secretary of the Writers' Union. Meanwhile a whole new generation of younger writers was coming to the fore that had no knowledge of the terror of the 1930s and 1940s and that therefore had less fear for its actions. This was the generation to whom Pasternak and Ehrenburg (in his liberal phase) spoke most clearly and which was as inexplicable to its immediate elders as is the younger generation in the West.

The most brilliant representatives of this generation are the two poets, Andrey Voznesensky (b. 1933) and Yevgeny Yevtushenko (b. 1933). Yevtushenko came to prominence first with his long poem, *Stantsiya Zima*, 1956 ('Zima Junction'). Subsequently he took a leading part in the mass poetry readings that were beginning to sweep the country and within a few years had become famous not only in the Soviet Union but also abroad. He spoke out, was provocative on public issues and carried his views to the public. Perhaps the most striking examples of this were his long poems *Babyi Yar*, 1961, and *Nasledniki Stalina*, 1962 ('Stalin's Heirs') on the subjects of anti-Semitism and lingering Stalinism respectively. Both caused a political storm and subjected Yevtushenko to violent attacks and even reprisals, but such was his popularity and his skill in making certain concessions to the regime that he rode the storms and carried on writing. His personal life has been bohemian in a manner reminiscent of the Soviet 1920s and in his frequent journeys abroad he has been loud and flamboyant, rather than discreet and tight-lipped in classical Soviet style. In 1962 he took the unprecedented step of publishing *A Precocious Autobiography* in France without permission of the censorship, a work that to this day has still not appeared in the Soviet Union.

Voznesensky appeared slightly later on the scene and with less publicity. His first collection of poems was *Mozaika*, 1960 ('Mosaic'), published in the provincial town of Vladimir, and it was only his second, *Parabola*, 1961, published in Moscow, that brought him fame. Like Yevtushenko he participated with enthusiasm in the poetry readings of the period and soon was accompanying the latter on official visits abroad. It is partly as a result of these trips in tandem that their names have come to be linked. His poetry is quite different from Yevtushenko's however. Although he writes frequently on public issues, these form only a small part of his poetic universe; on the whole he is more personal, and also more oblique and elliptical in his approach. In 1962 the appearance of a small collection, *Treugolnaya grusha* ('The Triangular Pear'), based on his experiences in America, confirmed his growing reputation and since that time he has generally been regarded as one of the leading figures in contemporary Soviet poetry.

In prose the transition has been in some ways less public and sensational, but the forces behind it are similar. One of the leading members of the younger generation is Vasily Aksyonov (b. 1932). In his recent stories Aksyonov has turned away from his naturalistic chronicles of youth to a vein of fantasy and satire that involves quite a different approach. The other prose writers who made a break at about the same time as Aksyonov took rather a different line, seeking refuge from clichés and public sentiments in tender lyricism and a subjective approach to reality.

Interesting as these younger writers are, the relatively modest nature of their achievements was thrown into relief by the sudden appearance in 1962 of an extraordinary book by an extraordinary literary phenomenon. The book was *Odin den Ivana Denisovicha*, 1962 ('One Day in the Life of Ivan Denisovich') and the author, Alexander Solzhenitsyn (b. 1919), who soared from total obscurity to world fame within the space of a few months. Solzhenitsyn had been a political prisoner after the war, having been summarily deported to a labour camp for making some derogatory remarks about Stalin. After Stalin's death in 1953 he was exiled and later rehabilitated, and he settled in the provincial town of Ryazan as a mathematics teacher. In the years that followed certain books were permitted to be published about some of the abuses of the Stalin period. Solzhenitsyn's novel, based on his own experiences, was both one of the first and by far the most daring and most successful of this genre. In outline it is a simple tale of the events of one day in the life of Ivan Denisovich Skukhov, a political prisoner, from reveille to lights out

Apart from its sensational subject matter, one of the most striking aspects of the book was its literary sophistication. The unity of action achieved by filtering the story through Shukhov's thoughts and eyes added immeasurably to its impact and the racy, colloquial language, spiced with camp obscenities, was the most pungent to appear in Soviet fiction since the 1920s. A similar sophistication showed itself in the short stories that Solzhenitsyn published the following year, *Sluchai na stantsii Krechetovka*, 1963 ('The Incident at Krechetovka Station'), *Dlya polzy dela*, 1963 ('For the Good of the Cause'), and especially *Matryonin dvor*, 1963 ('Matryona's Yard'), a minor masterpiece. Suddenly, however, a blanket of silence was lowered over Solzhenitsyn's name and works, and apart from the story, *Zakhar-Kalita*, published in *Novy Mir* in 1966, nothing more by him has appeared in the Soviet Union.

The cause of this is to be sought outside the realm of literature and in the political sphere (a distinction, of course, that is not recognised in the Soviet Union). The Cuban crisis in 1962 shook up the Soviet political establishment in no uncertain fashion and slowly, as foreign policy froze, its effects were felt at home. At the end of 1962 Khrushchev made his celebrated attack on abstract art and modernism, a signal for new repressions. The following year Yevtushenko was viciously attacked, and Viktor Nekrasov, who had created a stir during the period of the thaw with his novel, *V rodnom gorode*, 1955 ('Home Town') and later his travel notes on America and Italy, *Pervaya vstrecha*, 1960 ('Both Sides of the Ocean'), was threatened with expulsion from the Writers' Union for his excellent psychological novel, *Kira Georgievna*, 1962 ('Kira Gheorgievna'). Fedin, the first secretary of the Writers' Union, also came out with a denunciation of the 'decadent bourgeois formalists', Joyce, Proust and Kafka, and socialist realism was again promoted as the only possible model for Soviet writers.

NEW REPRESSIONS

With the fall of Khrushchev in October 1964 there occurred an event with ominous overtones: the trial of Iosif Brodsky (b. 1940). Brodsky was accused of being an idler and a parasite who did no work. When he replied that he was a poet the judge sneered and denied this claim on the grounds that Brodsky was not a member of the Writers' Union. Brodsky was sentenced to five years' hard labour in exile, but his poems, which had been known to only a small circle of admirers in manuscript versions were now circulated in large numbers. They were also smuggled out to the West and published first in Russian, *Stikhotvoreniya i poemy*, 1965 ('Poems and Longer Poems'), and then in various translations into English. The texts revealed a sensitive, inward-looking poetic personality of great versatility and talent whose work differed considerably from that of his contemporaries both in theme and treatment. He seems to have been influenced by English poets, to two of whom (John Donne and T. S. Eliot) he has dedicated major poems, and there is no doubt that like Voznesensky he is among the best young poets in the Soviet Union.

That the trial of Brodsky was a travesty of justice seemed to have been recognised a year-and-a-half later when he was suddenly released and his sentence suspended. But in the same month, September 1965, a more significant arrest took place. Andrey Sinyavsky and Yuly Daniel were arrested simultaneously in Moscow for having published works abroad under the pseudonyms of Abram Tertz and Nikolai Arzhak respectively. This basic charge was not denied as such, since there exists no law prohibiting Soviet writers from publishing works abroad, but the prosecution also alleged that their works were anti-Soviet and came under the heading of anti-state propaganda. The arrests and charges aroused an enormous controversy both within the country and abroad, where the books by these two writers had already captured a large audience and were highly regarded, but the trial duly took place and in February 1966 Sinyavsky was sentenced to seven years hard labour and Daniel to five. Of the two writers, Sinyavsky (b. 1925) is the more interesting and talented. Himself a critic and teacher of literature, he is a highly sophisticated craftsman with an idiosyncratic view of the writer's role and a pronounced preference for fantasy and satire. This is revealed in his stimulating essay, *Chto takoye sotsialisticheski realizm*, 1959 ('On Socialist Realism'), which is one of the best articles ever written on that subject, and it comes through even more strongly in his short stories under the general heading, *Fantasticheskiye povesti*, 1961 ('Fantastic Stories') and in the stories, *Sud idyot*, 1960 ('The Trial Begins') and *Lyubimov*, 1964 ('The Makepeace Experiment'). Daniel (b. 1925) also has a penchant for satire, which is seen at its best in *Govorit Moskva*, 1964 ('This is Moscow Speaking') and *Iskupleniye*, 1964 ('Atonement'), but his style is often flat and realistic and his stories depend much more on content for their interest than the complex works of Sinyavsky.

A notable contribution to the literature of arrests, purges and camp life is the autobiography of Yevgeniya Ginzburg (b. 1907), the mother of V. Aksyonov. Her long and harrowing story, *Kruto Marshrut*, 1967, ('Into the Whirlwind'), recounts the incredible sufferings not of an enemy of the people or opponent of the Soviet regime, but a faithful and convinced communist and trusted member of the party. It is a chronicle, so she puts it, of the period of the personality cult.

At the time of writing the existence of two streams of literature seems to be hardening into a pattern. The orthodox and conformist writers continue to enjoy official support but little popularity with discriminating readers, while what one might call the 'official opposition' consisting of writers such as Voznesensky, Yevtushenko and Aksyonov has been strangely muted. The unofficial opposition, on the other hand, though sadly depleted by numerous trials, has gained a weighty recruit in the form of A. Solzhenitsyn. For several years, however, copies of two long novels of his have been circulating by hand and a bitter struggle has been waged over the question of whether to publish them or not. Now, they too have found their way abroad and have appeared in translation. *Rakovy korpus*, 1968 ('The Cancer Ward') is auto-biographical in subject matter and deals with a group of cancer patients in a Soviet hospital, while *V pervom kruge*, 1968 ('The First Circle') is about three days in a special prison in 1949 but conveys the author's thoughts about almost the whole of Soviet history.

FURTHER READING

Alexandrova, V. *A History of Soviet Literature 1917–64*, G. Bell, London; Anchor Books, New York, 1964.

Blake, P. and Hayward, M. *Dissonant Voices in Soviet Literature*, Pantheon, New York, 1962; Allen and Unwin, London, 1965. *Halfway to the Moon*, Weidenfeld and Nicolson, London, 1964; Doubleday, New York, 1965.

Bosley, K., Sapiets, J., and Pospielovsky, D. *Russia's Other Poets*, Longmans, London, 1968.

Field, A. *Pages from Tarusa: New Voices in Russian Writing*, Little Brown, Boston, Mass., 1964; Chapman and Hall, London, 1965.

Hayward, M. and Labedz, L. *Literature and Revolution in Soviet Russia 1917–62: A Symposium*, Oxford Univ. Press, London and New York, 1963.

McLean, H. and Vickery, W, *The Year of Protest, 1956*, Vintage, New York, 1961.

Markov, V. and Sparks, M. *Modern Russian Poetry*, MacGibbon and Kee, London, 1966.

Muchnic, H. *From Gorky to Pasternak*, Random House, New York, 1961; Methuen, London, 1963.

Newnham, R. *Soviet Short Stories*, Penguin Books, Harmondsworth, 1968.

Reavey, G. *The New Russian Poets, 1953–66: An Anthology*, Calder and Boyars, London, 1968.

Reddaway, P. *Soviet Short Stories*, 2, Penguin Books, Harmondsworth, 1968.

Slonim, M. *Soviet Russian Literature—Writers and Problems 1917–67*, Oxford Univ. Press, London and New York, 1967.

Stillman, L. *The Bitter Harvest*, Thames, London; Frederick A. Praeger, New York, 1959.

Tertz, Abram. (tr. George Dennis). *On Socialist Realism*, Pantheon Books, New York, 1961.

Yarmolinsky, A. *Literature Under Communism*, Russian and East European Series, 20, Indiana Univ. Press, Bloomington, Ind. 1957. *Two Centuries of Russian Verse: An Anthology From Lomonosov to Voznesensky*, Random House, New York, 1966.

MICHAEL SCAMMELL. A freelance translator currently working on Tolstoy's diaries. Taught for a year in Jugoslavia at the University of Ljubljana. Has spent two years with the BBC's East European service. Among the authors he has translated are Tolstoy, Dostoevsky, Nabokov and Fedin.

POLISH LITERATURE

PEER HULTBERG

POLISH LITERATURE FROM 1945–9

POLISH literature after 1945 and up to 1949 is dominated by the politically confused and economically desperate post-war situation, and by the profound changes taking place in the country's social structure. All Polish cultural activities, including education, had been completely suspended, indeed prohibited, during the war years, so the main task was to get them started again. This attempt to forge links with the pre-war culture was opposed by ever-increasing ideological demands which, in the case of literature, were finally formulated as directives in 1949 at a conference of the newly-formed Związek Literatów Polskich (Union of Polish Writers). The writers were called upon to take a directly active part in building up the socialist state and the literary programme laid down was 'socialist realism'. The period of ideological wavering was finally over.

The volume of very valuable literary works published during the years immediately after the war was considerable. Many of these works had been written during the war but had no chance of publication, except perhaps in the illegal cultural periodicals. Others had been written and, in certain cases, published abroad and were now printed in Poland while their authors returned from exile, or in some cases remained abroad. Others were written shortly after 1945 and treated the war in retrospect, either reflectively or by direct description.

The poetry of these years is dominated above all by writers of the older generation who had established themselves firmly as poets before the war. They continued writing in their previous manner and showed only a few significant changes. The oldest of these poets may be called roughly 'classical' as regards form. Apart from Leopold Staff (1878–1957) they had spent the war abroad and so their poetry naturally views the war from a different angle from those works written in Poland itself. The most important collections of poetry are: Staff's *Martwa pogoda*, 1946 ('Mortal Weather'); Władysław Broniewski's (1897–1962) *Drzewo rozpaczające*, 1946 ('The Despairing Tree') and other collections; Kazimiera Iłłakowiczówna's (b. 1892) *Wiersze wybrane 1912–47*, 1949 ('Selected Verses'); Antoni Słonimski's (b. 1895) *Wiek klęski: Wiersze z lat 1939–45*, 1945 ('The Age of Defeat: Verses from 1939–45'); Julian Tuwim's (1894–1953) *Kwiaty polskie*, 1949 ('Polish Flowers').

Two poets of the younger generation were killed in Warsaw during the uprising in 1944, Tadeusz Gajcy (1922–44) and the remarkably gifted Krzysztof Kamil Baczyński (1921–44). Besides these, the leading talents of this generation who established themselves after the war are Roman Bratny

(b. 1921) who is also known as a novelist and playwright, Zbigniew Bienkowski (b. 1913), and perhaps above all Tadeusz Różewicz (b. 1921) with the collections *Niepokój*, 1947 ('Anxiety') and *Czerwona rękawiczka*, 1948 ('The Red Glove'). Różewicz's poems have been described as 'anti-poems' and have found countless imitators; they are highly realistic and avoid all superfluous embellishments, relying on strict economy of words and on self discipline.

Almost all the prose of these years has as its subject-matter the war or closely related themes. In contrast to poetry new names in prose appear to a far greater extent in this period; of the older generation only a few important writers published any prose at this time, the most notable being Zofia Nałkowska (1884–1954) *Medaliony*, 1946 ('Medallions'), a collection of sketches mainly concerned with concentration camps, and the novel *Węzły życia*, 1948 ('Bonds of Life'); and Jarosław Iwaszkiewicz (b. 1894) known also as a poet, with the collections of short stories *Stara cegielnia, Młyn nad Lutynią*, 1946 ('The Old Brickworks, The Mill on the Lutynia') and *Nowele włoskie*, 1947 ('Italian Short Stories').

Many writers are one-book authors. It is as if the impact of events and personal suffering has made writers out of people who would otherwise not have thought of themselves in such terms. An excellent example of this is Stweryna Szmaglewska (b. 1916) *Dymy nad Birkenau*, 1945 ('Smoke over Birkenau') which was one of the first works to describe existence in a concentration camp: it still is one of the finest. The approach of this book is documentary and a similar treatment is seen in the works of many authors like, for example, the two very talented writers, Ksawery Pruszyński (1907–50) in *Droga wiodła przez Narwik*, 1941 ('The Road Through Narwik'), *Trzynaście opowieści*, 1946 ('13 Short Stories'); and Tadeusz Borowski (1922–51) in *Byliśmy w Oświęcimiu*, in cooperation with other authors, 1946 ('We Were in Auschwitz'), *Kamienny świat*, 1948 ('The World of Stone') and the more fictional *Pożegnanie z Marią*, 1948 ('The Parting with Maria').

In this period four important individual talents came to light. Jerzy Andrzejewski (b. 1909) published a collection of short stories *Noc*, 1945 ('Night'), and in 1948 one of the major Polish novels of the post-war period, *Popiół i diament*, ('Ashes and Diamonds'), which depicts people and problems in Poland in the days immediately following the German capitulation. Kazimierz Brandys (b. 1916) published the novels *Drewniany koń*, 1946 ('The Wooden Horse'), and *Miasto niepokonane*, 1946 ('The Invincible City') which gives a vivid description of Warsaw during the war. In 1948 he published the first volume of his cycle of novels *Między wojnami* ('Between the Wars'). Stanisław Dygat (b. 1914) treated the war as seen from outside Poland in the novel, *Jezioro Bodeńskie*, 1946 ('Lake Constance'), and published in 1948 another novel, *Pożegnanie* ('Parting'). Like Andrzejewski, Adolf Rudnicki (b. 1912) started writing in the 1930s. But some of his most important work, two very sensitive and penetrating collections of short stories, were published at this time, *Szekspir*, 1948 ('Shakespeare') and *Ucieczka z Jasnej Polany*, 1949 ('The Flight from Jasna Polana'). Two collections of his short stories have been translated into English: *Ascent to Heaven*, London, 1951; and *The Dead and the Living Sea, and other stories*, Warsaw, 1957.

IDEOLOGICAL DEMANDS OF THE PERIOD 1950–6

The strict ideological demands to which literature was subjected during the period from 1950 to 1956 resulted in a dearth of works of value according to present-day taste; and most works are more valuable as historical documents than as literature. The writers who were able to express themselves most freely were the very old poets like Staff in *Wiklina*, 1954 ('Willows') or Iłłakowiczówna in *Poezje 1940–54*, 1954 ('Poetry, 1940–54'). But even a poet like Broniewski felt that he had to abandon personal themes in favour of the concrete problems of building socialism. This predicament is well illustrated by his collection *Nadzieja*, 1951 ('Hope') which among other things contains a *sui generis* excellent panegyric to Stalin in honour of his 70th birthday, *Słowo o Stalinie* ('The Song about Stalin'). Some poets, like Iwaszkiewicz, Jastrun, Przyboś, Różewicz, Ważyk went on writing but others were silent. One leading poet Czesław Miłosz, chose to leave the country in 1951. Neither in poetry nor in prose did there emerge any exceptional talent.

The demands made on prose were perhaps even more severe than on poetry; most interesting are works dealing with the past, especially the war. The best example of a Polish socialist realist novel is probably *Pamiątka z celulozy*, 1952 ('Cellulose Toys') by Igor Newerly. An isolated event of importance was the publication in 1955 of a collection of short stories, *Gwiazda zaranna* ('A Village Wedding, and other Stories') by Maria Dąbrowska (1889–1965), a leading Polish novelist. She was regarded in Polish literary life as a person of great moral integrity and had published almost nothing since the outbreak of war, except translations: this new work was seen as her attempt to come to terms with contemporary Polish life.

Towards the end of this period some works appeared which reflected the change in the ideological climate of the country, Ważyk's *Poemat dla dorosłych i inne wiersze*, 1956 ('A Poem for Adults and other Verses'); K. Brandys's *Czerwona czapeczka*, 1956 ('The Red Cap') a collection of short stories, and later his novel, *Matka Królów*, 1957 ('Sons and Comrades'); and Andrzejewski's *Ciemności kryją ziemię*, 1957 ('The Inquisitor'). These works also won great acclaim outside Poland, less perhaps on account of their literary merits than because they were interpreted as signs of the political 'thaw'.

The political changes of 1956 soon resulted in the publication of a great number of interesting works. In this way a parallel may be drawn with the situation immediately after the war. Works were published which it would have been impossible to publish previously, and the general relaxation of restrictions seemed to give rise to an upsurge of creativity. This was perhaps especially noticeable in poetry. Established poets who previously had difficulty in directing their imaginations towards socialist goals appeared to make a fresh start. This was perhaps especially the case for Przyboś who has gradually returned to his former poetic experiments in *Narzędzie ze światła*, 1958 ('Tools of Light'), *Próba całości*, 1961 ('Attempt at Totality'), *Na znak*, 1965 ('As a Sign Of'); and for Różewicz who started writing prose and plays as well as poetry, often publishing them in the same volume, *Formy*, 1958 ('Forms') (poetry and prose), *Zielona róża/Kartoteka*, 1961 ('The Green Rose, The Register') (poetry and a play), *Głos anonima*, 1961 ('The Voice of an Anonymous Person') (two rather long poems).

Besides these established poets a wide new group of very gifted poets emerged. These cannot be considered a school, nor do they even roughly belong to the same generation. Some of them had already published a few, generally insignificant, works, but the majority made their debut in the latter half of the 1950s. Three of them are outstanding experimenters with language and poetic form, Stanisław Swen Czachorowski (b. 1920) in *Echo przez siebie*, 1958 ('Echo from Itself'), *Białe semafory*, 1960 ('White Semaphores'); Tymoteusz Karpowicz (b. 1921) in such works as *Kamienna muzyka*, 1958 ('Stony Music'), and *Wimię znaczenia*, 1962 ('In the Name of Meaning');

Miron Białoszewski (b. 1922) in *Obroty rzeczy*, 1956 ('Turns of Objects'), *Mylne wzruszenia*, 1961 ('Erroneous Emotions'). Others approach poetry in a more 'classical' manner and are often deeply concerned with moral problems; Wiesława Szymborska (b. 1923) in *Sól*, 1962 ('Salt'); Zbigniew Herbert (b. 1924) in *Studium przedmiotu*, 1961 ('Study of an Object'); and Tadeusz Nowak (b. 1930) who exploits folklore and village themes in *Ślepe koła wyobraźni*, 1958 ('The Blind Circles of Imagination'), *Ziarenko trawy*, 1964 ('A Grain of Grass'). What might be called a strong neo-classical approach is seen in the work of Jarosław Marek Rymkiewicz (b. 1935) *Konwencje*, 1957 ('Conventions') and the interesting manifesto *Czym jest klasycyzm*, 1967 ('What is Classicism'). Still others exploit the present-day taste for the grotesque: Jerzy Harasymowicz (b. 1933) *Cuda*, 1956 ('Wonders'), *Mit o Świętym Jerzym*, 1960 ('The Myth of Saint George'); and Stanisław Grochowiak (b. 1934) *Ballada rycerska*, 1956 ('Knightly Ballad'), *Agresty*, 1963 ('Gooseberries'). Andrzej Bursa (1932–1957) expressed in his *Wiersze*, 1958 ('Verses') an aggressive desperation which was typical of his generation and led him to suicide. Stanisław Jerzy Lec published his first poetry in 1933 and was a very prolific poet after 1956 but has become especially well known internationally for his two collections of aphorisms *Myśli nieuczesane*, 1957 ('Unkempt Thoughts') and *Myśli nieuczesane nowe*, 1964 ('More Unkempt Thoughts').

PROSE WRITERS AFTER 1956

The development of prose after 1956 was as rapid as that of poetry but the pattern was much more traditional. Typical of the mood of the middle and late 1950s were the superficially cynical but, in fact, sentimental short stories by Marek Hłasko (1934–69) whose talent unfortunately seems to have dried up after his departure from Poland. Among the numerous prose writers Jerzy Andrzejewski has gained the position of the leading novelist of his generation with his two novels *Bramy raju*, 1960 ('The Gates of Paradise'), a historical novel of unusual form about the children's crusade in 1212–3, and *Idzie skacząc nagórach*, 1963 ('He Cometh Leaping upon the Mountains'), a work about an old artist closely resembling Picasso. Otherwise it is a very peculiar phenomenon that many of the most important novelists appear to have turned from fictional prose to prose of a more essay-like and reflective character, like Adolf Rudnicki's series of *Niebieskie kartki*, 1956 ('Blue Cards') and Kazimierz Brandys's *Listy do Pani Z.*, 1958 ('Letters to Mrs. Z.'), and *Dżoker*, 1966 ('Joker'). Teodor Parnicki holds a unique position for his remarkable individual historical novels; such as his trilogy *Twarz Księżyca*, 1967 ('The Face of the Moon').

The prose of the younger generation may be illustrated by the work of Stanisław Stanuch (b. 1931) and Włodzimierz Odojewski both of them very original and highly talented writers of a somewhat conventional nature. 'Experimental' novels are decidedly rare, a surprising phenomenon when one considers the very advanced poetry, and the tradition in Polish literature for experiments in prose. The most important are *Pomarańcze na drutach*, 1964 ('Oranges on Wires') by Witold Wirpsza (b. 1918) who is known also as a poet, and *Upalne nocne godziny czyli Champs Elysées de Varsovie*, 1966 ('Hot Nocturnal Nights or Champs Elysées de Varsovie') by Jerzy Pytlakowski (b. 1916); both these last novels, especially the first, are perhaps somewhat derivative of the French *roman nouveau*.

The upsurge of creativity which is seen in Polish literature in the late 1950s and early 1960s seems now to have died down. Few works of importance either in poetry or prose have been published recently and the intellectual and literary climate seems, at the present time, calm, if not dull. One should not forget, however, that much valuable literature is being written in Polish outside Poland by first and second generation émigrés. Some of these writers, like, for example, Teodor Parnicki, are published in Poland itself, whereas others like Witold Gombrowicz, (d. 1969) probably the most important dramatist and Polish contemporary novelist, are not.

FURTHER READING

Andrzejewski, Jerzy. *The Inquisitors*, Weidenfeld and Nicolson, London; Alfred A. Knopf, New York, 1960. *The Gates of Paradise*, Weidenfeld and Nicolson, London, 1963. *He Cometh Leaping upon the Mountains*, Weidenfeld and Nicolson, London, 1965.

Brandys, Kazimierz. *Sons and Comrades*, Grove Press, New York; Allen and Unwin, London, 1961.

Folejewski, Zbigniew. *Maria Dąbrowska*, Twayne, New York, 1967.

Herbert, Zbigniew. *Selected Poetry*, Penguin Books, London, 1968.

Hłasko, Marek. *The Eighth Day of the Week*, E. P. Dutton, New York, 1958; Allen and Unwin, London, 1959. *Next Stop—Paradise and The Graveyard*, Heinemann, London, 1961.

Lec, Stanisław Jerzy, *Unkempt Thoughts*, St. Martin's Press, New York, 1962.

Miłosz, Czesław. *Postwar Polish Poetry: An Anthology*, Doubleday, New York, 1965.

Pruszyński, Ksawery. *Russian Year, The Notebook of an Amateur Diplomat*, Roy, New York, 1944.

Szmaglewska, Seweryna. *Smoke over Birkenau*, Henry Holt, New York, 1947.

Wieniewska, Celina, (ed.) *Polish Writing Today*, Penguin Books, London, 1967.

PEER HULTBERG. Since 1967 Lecturer in Polish language and literature at the University of Copenhagen. Studied Slavonic languages at the Universities of Copenhagen, Skopje, Warsaw and London. Author of *Styli Literacki Wacława Berenta*.

CZECHOSLOVAK LITERATURE

KAREL BRUŠÁK

Effects of World War II on Czechoslovak Literary Scene

In the years immediately preceding World War II Czech and Slovak writers in general and the novelists in particular were becoming more and more *engagés*, their work being characterised by a growing concern for social and political ideas which they treated from a left-wing standpoint. Subsequent events, the dismemberment of Czechoslovakia, enforced by the Munich agreement between Nazi Germany, France and the UK, the occupation of Bohemia and Moravia by the Nazis, the secession of Slovakia and the ensuing war, brought about profound changes, both physical and psychological. There was a deep sense of betrayal of a small nation by its Western allies; disillusionment with the former order based on vague ideas of humanism and democracy; and, finally, contempt for all social and political formulae. For the younger generation of writers, despairing of the present state of the world, only the individual as such, 'the naked man', as they called him, stripped of all social relations, seemed worthy of attention.

During the Nazi occupation there was no freedom of expression and no free choice of themes; the psychological novel and the historical novel, with the accent on psychology and fiction of pure adventure, remained the only genres open to writers. Most authors of the older generation who had written about topical social problems were either silenced or ceased publishing, and the younger writers who became known during the war years wrote minute analyses of man's inner self.

This interest in the individual would probably have continued after the liberation, especially as the critics were pointing out parallels in some respects with Camus, Sartre, Graham Greene and other Western authors who were then being translated into Czech for the first time. But in 1948, after the Communist Party came to power, the Czech and Slovak literatures were given a new direction.

Communist Party Control of Literature

The Union of Czechoslovak Writers, established under the patronage of the party, held its First Congress in March 1949. The minister of information and enlightenment, Václav Kopecký, defined the new criteria of literary judgment:

> A new criterion is the attitude of writers towards socialism. Every Czech and Slovak writer has to face the test of a positive attitude towards the working people . . . For their creative work writers have to arm themselves with deeper knowledge and the teaching of Marxist-Leninist criticism and the Bolshevik ideas contained in the statements of Comrade Zhdanov and in Soviet discussions on the ideological line.

Up to a point the writers were instructed to link up with the tradition of social protest, formed in the late 1920s and the 1930s by communist authors, some of whom, like the poet S. K. Neumann (1875–1947) or the novelists Ivan Olbracht (1882–1952) and Marie Majerová (1882–1967), were able to begin publishing again after the war. There was, however, an important difference; the new literature must be optimistic.

Thus, literature was allotted a special task within the general plan of building the new order. The writers grouped in the Union—and they formed an overwhelming majority—willingly became obedient servants of the regime, the more so because they were rewarded by privileged positions, both economic and social. Those who did not submit to the party line were finished not only as writers but also as free citizens; in the following years many were accused of anti-state activities and imprisoned. But the self-censorship practised by obedient writers was not enough and the regimentation of literature in Czechoslovakia was undoubtedly the most thorough in the whole Soviet sphere. Moreover, a central preliminary censorship was introduced, carried out by the Central Administration of Press Control. This institution, presided over by senior police officers, worked on the orders of the Ministry of the Interior and the Central Committee of the Communist Party. As the right to publish periodicals was reserved for public organisations approved and controlled by the regime, and the publishing of books concentrated in six publishing houses rigorously controlled by the party, no deviation from the Zhdanov line was possible. Caricaturing the first Czechoslovak republic and the West, glorifying the building of the new order, idealising the communist resistance during the war or reinterpreting history —these were the main and, indeed, the only permissible themes for authors for whom socialist realism was the compulsory mode of literary expression. Not even after the death of Stalin was there any liberalisation in Czechoslovak literature, and whilst in Poland, Hungary and in the Soviet Union a gradual process towards this end was taking place, all sporadic and isolated outbursts in Czechoslovakia were promptly suppressed.

A More Liberal Climate

Only after the Twentieth Congress of the CPSU in February 1956 were more outspoken voices heard, and at the Second Congress of the Czechoslovak Writers' Union in Prague in April 1956 the rule of party officials over literature was publicly revealed for the first time. The greatest impression was made by the speeches of two outstanding poets from the pre-war period, František Hrubín (b. 1910) and Jaroslav Seifert (b. 1901). Hrubín spoke of the great poet František Halas (1901–49), who was given a state funeral but whose work was condemned by official critics soon after his death; of the poet Konstantin Biebl (1898–1951) who was driven to suicide by bickering party propagandists; and of several other writers who had been silenced and persecuted. Seifert asked that the silenced writers should be allowed to publish again and that the fate of the imprisoned writers should be made easier.

The 1956 Congress of the Writers' Union was greeted as the harbinger of a more liberal climate. For a time it seemed that the ideological grip of the party on literature might become weaker. The first important change was a more tolerant attitude on the part of the regime towards Western literature; translations from Western authors such as Greene, Hemingway, Wilder,

Moravia, Pratolini, Hesse, Fallada, Vailland, Amis and others were published for the first time since 1948. In original literature the first signs of the thaw were felt in poetry, less carefully scrutinised by the pedantic party censors. A new ironical approach towards contemporary reality was reflected in the poetry of Oldřich Mikulášek (b. 1910), who in his *Ortely a milosti*, 1958 ('Verdicts and Amnesties') is deeply concerned with the fate of the individual during the period of the so-called 'personality-cult' and reintroduces the principle of Death the Liberator into the falsely optimistic 'progressive society'. Miroslav Holub (b. 1923), a biologist by profession, tries to realise in his terse, anti-sentimental and anti-heroic poems the trend propagated in the review *Květen* ('May') by the young writers who, in contrast to the pathos and emotion of the poetry celebrating the achievements of socialism, advocated 'a lyrical matter-of-factness'. Among prose works which reflect the new attitude, the novel *Romeo, Julie a tma*, 1958 ('Romeo, Juliet and the Darkness') by Jan Otčenášek (b. 1924), the simple and tragic story of a Czech boy who hides a Jewish girl from the Nazis, shows, for the first time since the war, young people acting like human beings and not like cardboard heroes corresponding to party requirements. The novel *Zbabělci*, 1958 ('The Cowards') by Josef Škvorecký (b. 1924) departs even farther from socialist realism. It is the story of a student and his fellow jazz-players during the last months of the Nazi occupation, written in a style which is almost a pastiche of the American flat factual method from Hemingway to Salinger. Its theme, the uncertainty and futility of life, which the main character accepts because 'he cannot change it', was hardly new but the novel introduces into Czech prose the anti-hero, representative of contemporary youth, ironical, bored with politics, drifting along without taking sides and interested only in jazz and girls. Perhaps the most outspoken prose work of this period is the book of short stories *Hodiny a minúty*, 1956 ('Hours and Minutes') by the Slovak author, Alfonz Bednár (b. 1914). In his preoccupation with moral relations between individuals at the time of the Slovak rising against the Nazis and later during the first phase of the building of socialism, Bednár concentrates on cowards and opportunists, cynics and the embittered official interpreters of socialism who do not believe in it, party functionaries turned into village dictators, doctors refusing treatment to politically suspect patients and many others of the same kind.

However, this period of relative liberalism did not last long. Sharp attacks on writers in the press, at public conferences and at meetings of the Central Committee, coupled with strict administrative measures in editorial offices, gradually restored party control. The works which deviated from the party line on literature such as Bednár's stories or Škvorecký's novel were condemned by both Czechoslovak and Soviet critics, in particular by Boris Polevoy, and removed from circulation. Two literary periodicals, *Květen* ('May') and *Nový Život* ('New Life'), which had been the mouthpieces of the non-conformist youth movement, were suppressed.

A New Wave of Writers

At the Conference of the Writers' Union in March 1959 and at the Congress of Socialist Culture in June of the same year, the ideas of the Second Congress of the Writers' Union were rejected and the writers pledged themselves once more to serve the party. But behind the façade things were far from calm. The short period of relative liberalisation had given to the writers, particularly those of the younger generation, a foretaste of artistic freedom.

The first important attempts to break away from the prescribed norm appeared on the stage rather than in print. During the late 1950s several small cabarets (such as *Divadlo na zábradlí*, 'Theatre on the Balustrade', 1958, and *Semafor*, 1959) were allowed in Prague by the regime. But, instead of restricting their satire to permitted subjects such as Western Imperialists or survivals of the bourgeois ethic, they started attacking the Establishment. Another force working for a greater freedom of expression were two main literary weeklies—the Czech *Literární noviny* ('Literary Gazette') in Prague and the Slovak *Kultúrný život* ('Cultural Life') in Bratislava—and the monthly *Host do domu* ('Guest in the House') in Brno. It was in particular the younger writers, formerly grouped round *Květen* and attached to *Literární noviny* after the former review had been banned, who, in spite of a constant struggle with censorship, succeeded in introducing a progressive and rebellious spirit into the official organ of the Writers' Union.

The opposition to dogmatism and the authoritarian control of literature began to gain force around 1962, but it would be wrong to suppose that there was any conscious protest behind it. The primary cause of the gradual liberalisation of literature was the fact that official culture was collapsing from within, simultaneously with the crumbling of the economy. The literature produced during the first decade following the communist accession to power in 1948 was so monotonous and so predictable that the public was losing interest in it. Far from fulfilling its propaganda role it became an unwanted commodity. Whilst the older and established writers might still have been ready to go on as before, the younger writers wanted to produce something more interesting. The first attempts at a new way of writing were inspired by a consideration for the public rather than by a genuine need for self-expression. The new authors began to imitate features and trends which, in their view, were most remote from the official stereotype. Without any distinct idea of what they really wanted, the younger writers of this transitional period produced motley assortments, indiscriminately mimicking whatever artistic styles came their way, from Apollinaire to Pasternak and Kafka to Mailer. A new, ideologically ambiguous writing began to emerge and it required a certain amount of courage both to force it through the censorship and then to defend it theoretically. The critics and writers of the new wave would, however, have been unable to induce a more tolerant climate without the support of certain elements at the ministries and in the Central Committee of the party itself. At that time a section of top party officials was beginning a struggle against the Stalinists, both in order to gain power for themselves and to preserve the communist regime. In this struggle the dissatisfied writers appeared as useful allies and the so-called progressive faction was all the more willing to help them towards a greater freedom.

In May 1963 the Third Congress of the Writers' Union took place. In the letter sent to the Central Committee of the party the writers promised to devote all their abilities 'to the service of the artistic truth, which means to the service of the party, to the service of the communist future of the people'. The discussions preceding and during the Congress marked a final break with the artistic dishonesty prevalent in the Stalinist era.

This new mood was most perceptible in the work of young dramatists, such as Milan Kundera (b. 1929), Milan Uhde (b. 1936), Ivan Klíma (b. 1931,) Josef Topol (b. 1935) and Václav Havel (b. 1936), who broke the compulsory convention by introducing personal moral problems of an individual facing the totalitarian society.

The view that creative artists should be free to choose their subjects and artistic methods as they please, and that all works of art should be judged strictly on their merits and not by their immediate social usefulness, was gradually gaining strength. The more liberal climate, which was more tolerant towards attempts to end the isolation of cultural life in Czechoslovakia by informing the public about contemporary trends in the West was due, at least in part, to a new policy, introduced in the Ministry of Culture and Education by Dr. Čestmír Císař (b. 1920) who was appointed in 1963. A new literary monthly, *Tvář* ('The Face'), founded in 1964, became a platform for younger writers in open deviation from the official line. The Marxist-Leninist doctrine on literature and arts in general, as applied by the ideological department of the party, was seriously eroded and the dogmatic party leadership stepped in once more to save the situation. The censorship intensified its activity; *Tvář* received an ultimatum to change its editors and orientation, and in November 1965 its editorial board decided to cease publication rather than to comply. In 1965 Císař was relieved of his ministerial post. The 5,000-word resolution on culture which was passed at the Thirteenth Party Congress held in June 1966, complained of the erroneous and harmful views being expressed in some literary papers and of the tendencies towards 'ideological appeasement, apolitical attitudes and pacifism', rejected 'the problematic views that culture and art should be independent of party policy', condemned both 'liberalism and dogmatism' in the arts, and reiterated the right of the party to guide and control culture.

The ferment amongst the writers was only part of the general unrest permeating all sectors of society, and as party directives were becoming ever vaguer and often contradictory, the appropriate organs were finding it ever more difficult to execute proper control and to suppress all manifestations of independence. The ideological department of the Central Committee of the party hoped that at its forthcoming congress the Writers' Union would proclaim 'its adherence to the October Revolution and socialism' and encourage writers 'to support the Communist Party in its efforts for a further democratisation of life'. The Union was repeatedly warned that it must remain an organisation committed to socialism and that it must bear in mind that it was the party and the government that gave it publishing houses, newspapers, magazines and funds.

CONFLICT BETWEEN WRITERS' UNION AND PARTY DOGMA

The estrangement had gone too far however, and at the Fourth Congress of the Writers' Union held in June 1967, there was an open clash between the writers and the party. Many writers, all of them party members, freely criticised the system which had caused literature to decline to the level of propaganda, proclaimed their determination to break out from 'the isolation in time and space' and demanded abolition of censorship and freedom for the writer to choose his theme and artistic methods. Even more unusual and important was the fact that political questions, both fundamental and topical, were openly discussed, such as the basic problem of the relationship between the citizen and totalitarian power, or the official Czechoslovak attitude towards the Arab-Israeli war. It was these speeches rather than the resolution which aroused the wrath of the conservative elements in the party. Although only short and distorted summaries were permitted to appear in the press, the spirit of the Congress became generally known and contributed much towards strengthening the determination of the forces which later brought about the political change.

For the time being the Central Committee of the party had recourse to repressive measures. In September it attacked the Union for not opposing non-Marxist tendencies in its ranks, disguised as experiments and aesthetic advancements, for allowing works alien to socialism to come to the forefront and for generally waging an anti-communist offensive which could not remain unanswered. The Union's paper *Literární noviny* was accused of propagating inimical political views, the entire editorial staff was removed and three of its members, Ludvík Vaculík, Ivan Klíma and the film-critic Antonín J. Liehm, whose speeches were the most outspoken at the Congress, were expelled from the party. The control of the paper was transferred directly to the Ministry of Culture and Information.

POLITICAL UNCERTAINTY

The struggle between the so-called progressives and conservatives within the Central Committee of the party was resolved, provisionally at least, by the removal of Antonín Novotný from the office of the first party secretary in January 1968 and from the presidency of the republic in the following March, and his replacement by Alexander Dubček as first party secretary and by General Ludvík Svoboda as president. In March 1968 the Writers' Union, after having successfully boycotted the ministry-controlled *Literární noviny*, began publishing a new weekly, *Literární listy* ('Literary Letters'), which continued in the rebellious tradition of their former paper. The expelled writers were welcomed back to the fold of the party. A new freer era opened for Czech and Slovak literature and in June 1968 the censorship and the central control of publishing were officially abolished.

LITERATURE AFTER THE INVASION

When surveying Czech and Slovak literature of the late 1960s, we find that the freer climate influenced the authors rather in the quantity than the artistic quality of their works. The works published are undoubtedly interesting as documents, both collective and personal, of a particular period in a particular country but, apart from a few exceptions, are hardly outstanding in the larger European context.

The poetry of the late 1960s reveals two streams. On the one hand there are the poems which comment on the contemporary reality in Czechoslovakia and in the world in narrative or rhetoric style, such as the works of Miroslav Holub (b. 1923), Jiří Kolář (b. 1914), Ladislav Novák (b. 1925) or Jan Zábrana (b. 1931). On the other hand, there are the poets who try to escape into a private world, either by way of the flesh, like Ivan Diviš (b. 1924) or through the magic gate of infantine imagination like Ivan Wernisch (b. 1942). Few of the Czech and Slovak poets of the late 1960s show any will to break away and find new means of expression; their poetry is permeated by the feeling that they are 'outside Europe'. Hence their almost pathetic endeavour to become part of some imaginary community of mind and sensibility, which results in their relying heavily on such incongruous supports as the French symbolists, Allen Ginsberg or the Czech popular poetry of the Baroque period.

In prose, as might be expected, the events of the Stalinist period provide most of the themes. Yet only a few authors attempted a new approach and tried to express the feeling of uncertainty which had had to remain camouflaged for so many years. There are many purely personal narratives, written in a conventional outmoded style, such as *Studené slunce*, 1968 ('Living and Partly Living'), in which Jiří Mucha (b. 1915) gives a testimony of his confinement in a labour camp. Equally numerous are factual reports in the superficial form of a novel, such as the Slovak *Ako chutí moc*, 1968 ('The Taste of Power') by the Slovak author Ladislav Mňačko, himself a staunch supporter of the regime during the Stalinist era, which tells the life story of a high-ranking Communist functionary. Whilst the young dramatists tend towards allegory, symbolism and absurdity, the novelists relinquish socialist realism mostly for a modified naturalism. This has obviously been revived under the impact of contemporary Western prose, and, but for a different background, it retains many characteristics of the old naturalism—exceptional individuals in exceptional, extreme situations, stress on the squalid and unpleasant (especially in the love scenes), and harsh language, overburdened with slang and vulgarisms. Other authors pay only scant attention to plot or abandon it altogether, and indulge in minute descriptions, detailed introspection, cogitation or inverted moralising. But they all share the predilection for emotional instead of social conflicts and a pessimistic attitude towards social organisation and not infrequently towards life itself. Shifty adolescents in the last stage of puberty, dishonest bureaucrats and spineless intellectuals narrate their stories in the first person with a masochistic glee strangely reminiscent of the self-incrimination of the accused during the trials of the Stalinist era. The most original novels of the late 1960s are *Žert*, 1967 ('The Joke'), by Milan Kundera (b. 1929). Kundera's novel describes with dry humour the emotional and moral decline of a young man, who has been victimised as a student for sending a mildly political joke on a post-card, and whose revenge on his persecutor, which he plans over several years, misfires as yet another bad joke. In Vaculík's novel the hero, a journalist who has lost his job because his conscience clashed with party discipline, analyses his moral and human position during a visit to his native village. His father, a worker and old-guard Communist, dies disillusioned after a life of sacrifice for a social Utopia which has turned into a nightmare.

During the spring and early summer of 1968 Czechoslovakia was in a mood of elation. An avalanche of discussion on the future form of socialism swept over the country. Whilst the leaders remained weary and irresolute, the writers and intellectuals, turned amateur politicians, became ever more unrealistic in their pronouncements and forgot the hard reality of the country's status in the so-called Socialist Commonwealth. The illusion that Czechoslovakia could act as an independent state in matters of political organisation, economy and even defence was shattered in August 1968 by the inevitable intervention of its co-members in the Warsaw Pact, even before the leadership had taken any concrete steps to change radically the existing structure. This was a traumatic experience for a people so far gone in its illusions and an almost manic revulsion sprang up not only for the Russians but also for its own leaders, in spite of the fact that there were no definite signs of a return to the Novotný era. The literary papers were publishing many articles of political character and very little material relating to literature. In April 1969 a preventive censorship of the mass information media was revived and *Literární listy* was banned in May, but no obvious attempts were made to interfere with creative writing. In June, following the introduction of the federal system, the Czech and Slovak writers each formed their separate Unions and old Jaroslav Seifert was elected chairman of the Czech Union. Whilst the Czech Union passed a resolution protesting against the reintroduction of censorship and the banning of its paper, the Slovak Union recognised the new situation in a more realistic way and stressed in their statutes that the Government had guaranteed freedom and support for artistic creation. Furthermore, in August 1969 it concluded in Moscow an agreement on co-operation with the Union of Soviet Writers. In the following October the new First Secretary of the Central Committee of the Czechoslovak Communist Party, Dr Gustáv Husák—who had replaced Alexander Dubček in the previous April—criticised the views of some of the writers belonging to the party but in no way attacked their literary work. Paradoxically, the new situation may even have a beneficial influence, inasmuch as writers may now perhaps be able to turn away from political discussion and devote themselves more to writing.

FURTHER READING

Brusak, K. Frozen Thaw, Czechoslovak Literary Scene Since 1956; *Christian Democratic Review*, London, December 1959, pp. 13–16.

East and West, *Times Literary Supplement*, 30 March 1967, p. 267.

Holub, M. *Selected Poems*, tr. Ian Milne and George Theiner, Penguin Modern European Poets, London, 1967.

Kucera, H. and Kovtun, E. *Literature in Czechoslovakia*, V. Bušek and N. Spulber ed., Praeger Publishers New York, 1957; Atlantic Books Publishing Co., London, 1957, pp. 173–98.

Novotný's Freedom, *Times Literary Supplement*, 14 September 1967, p. 819.

Součková, M. Marxist Theory in Czech Literature, *Harvard Slavic Studies*, vol. 1, 1953, pp. 335–61, Harvard Univ. Press, Cambridge, Mass.

Stern, J. P. Czechoslovakia and the Common Weal, *Times Literary Supplement*, 5 September 1968, pp. 939–40.

Theiner, G. (ed.) *New Writing in Czechoslovakia*, Penguin Books, London, 1969.

KAREL BRUŠÁK. Was born in Czechoslovakia and has lived in the West since the war. A specialist in Czech and Slovak literature, he has published several articles in these fields.

EAST GERMAN LITERATURE

MARGARET VALLANCE

Writers Who Returned to East Germany

East German literature has only just begun to exist in any meaningful form; with the division of Germany in May 1945 into two societies, one shaped by the Western allies, and the other by the Soviet Union, writers who had fled from fascism to various parts of the world were faced with the decision over which Germany they wished to live in, if at all. Most writers did return. Naturally those who were communists or who had left-wing sympathies mostly chose to return to the Soviet Zone, which was proclaimed the German Democratic Republic in 1949. These writers had made their reputation in the 1920s and 1930s; they had experienced the rise of fascism, Hitler's Third Reich and years of exile. They returned with the hope of helping to create a new society, and can be regarded as the 'father' generation.

The most renowned of these writers who returned was the dramatist, Bertolt Brecht (1898–1956), after considerable hesitation, for he feared party censorship. As a safety measure he retained his Austrian passport and thus ensured for himself a greater measure of freedom than he would otherwise have been allowed. Brecht's theory of the function of theatre, namely to force the audience to think about social questions and to take a position, his development of the technique of *Verfremdungsaffekt*, had a profound influence on the younger generation of writers, many of whom worked with him in the Berliner Ensemble.

Other distinguished writers who returned but who have written little of significance since then are Arnold Zweig (1887–1968), famous for his novels written during the 1920s about World War I, and the novelist, Anna Seghers (b. 1900). Zweig's novel, *Traum ist teuer*, 1962, ('The Cost of Dreams'), reflects his own feeling of homelessness. Anna Seghers's novels on the other hand portray the building of the new socialist society: *Die Entscheidung*, 1959 ('The Decision') during the period 1947–51 and in *Das Vertrauen*, 1968 ('The Trust') from 1951–3. She describes temporary setbacks but affirms basic optimism and faith in the future of East German society.

Johannes R. Becher (1891–1958) was a former expressionist poet who renounced his earlier work as a result of the influence of the critic, Georg Lukács. He wrote some very good poetry during his years of emigration in Moscow. After his return to East Germany in 1945 he founded the Aufbau Verlag in the same year and the literary magazine *Sinn und Form* in 1949. Together with the composer, Hanns Eisler, he wrote the National Hymn, and from 1954 he was minister of culture. As a poet he seems to have had little influence on younger writers who have mostly adopted a style directly opposed to his, one of a dry terseness. Wieland Herzfelde (b. 1896), another former expressionist whose greatest contribution to German literature lay in the productions of his Malik Verlag which he founded in 1917, returned in 1949 to become professor of sociology and contemporary literature at the University of Leipzig. His brother, John Heartfield, known for his brilliant photo-montages during the 1930s, was a much-beloved figure in East Berlin until his death in 1968.

Amongst active communist writers who returned were Erich Weinert (1890–1953), who translated the works of several Russian poets into German; Ludwig Renn (b. 1889) who wrote a novel about his experiences in the Spanish Civil War, *Der Spanische Krieg*, 1955, which was severely cut by political censorship; Willi Bredel (1901–64), who published the magazine, *Das Wort*, together with Brecht and Lion Feuchtwanger (1890–1958) during the war, and wrote the scripts for the films about the communist leader, Ernst Thälmann (made in 1953 and 1955); and the proletarian novelist Hans Marchwitza (1890–1965), who returned from the USA in 1946 and wrote a novel about the difficulties overcome during the building of the new steel town of Eisenhüttenstadt called *Roheisen*, 1955 ('Raw Iron'). The most important poet of this generation is Peter Huchel (b. 1903) who returned to Germany in 1945 after being a prisoner of war and became artistic director of Berlin radio, then editor of *Sinn und Form* from 1949 until his sudden dismissal at the end of 1962 for political reasons. He writes predominantly nature poems, situated against the background of Brandenburg, but human beings enter into this background and symbolise man's relationship to society. At first the cultural functionaries praised his work, for instance, the volume of collected poems published in 1948, *Gedichte* ('Poems'), but in the 1950s he was accused of showing resignation and self-isolation in his poetry. Later collections of his poems are *Chausseen Chausseen*, 1963 ('Highways, highways') and of poems written during 1925–47, *Die Sternenreuse*, 1967 ('A Pocketful of Stars').

The problem of political censorship and the requirements of socialist realism are very real for East German writers; it cannot be said that West Germany represents an alternative for them, even were they free to choose (which they were until the building of the wall in August 1961, after the worst years of Stalinism were over), for they are socialists who support their kind of government. Even those writers who finally chose to go to the West for the pertinent reason that they could not publish in their own country tend to feel isolated from that society. All writers must be critical, and East German writers are hampered by a government of a peculiarly narrow and petit bourgeois nature, which demands that they write *positively* about the life of the workers and peasants and the achievements of the new society. Problems may be mentioned now, but only insofar as they serve to show how they may be overcome.

The 'Middle' Generation

The 'middle' generation, represented by writers who only started publishing after 1945, is composed of writers such as the novelist, Erwin Strittmatter (b. 1912), the self-taught son of a peasant, who wrote novels about the changing life of the peasants under the new system. He did allude to some of the problems which arose, but pointed the way forward with unflagging optimism. *Katzgraben, Szenen aus dem Bauernleben*, 1953 ('Cat-ditch. Scenes from Peasant Life') a four-act verse comedy, was produced by Brecht in the Berliner Ensemble and portrayed some of the problems arising from the land reforms of 1947–9. The novel *Tinko*, 1955 was filmed in 1957, but *Ole Bienkopp* (1964) the most popular of his novels was criticised by the functionaries for portraying problems too realistically. *Schulzenhofer Kramkalender*, 1967, is a collection of impressions and episodes taken from his country surroundings.

A writer of far higher literary calibre who also suffered under narrow-minded censorship, is the poet, Stephan Hermlin (b. 1915), who returned to West Germany in 1945 after years abroad in Egypt, Palestine, Spain, England and France where he fought with the resistance. He moved to East Germany in 1947. His poetry, which shows the influence of Becher's early work, also reflects the tragedy of his time; he is deeply affected by the German baroque poets, by the English poet, Swinburne, and by French surrealism. His first volume of poetry was published in 1945, *Zwölf Balladen von den grossen Städten* ('Twelve Ballads of the Big Towns').

Franz Fühmann (b. 1922) in the Sudetenland, published his first poems during the war. He was brought up to be a Nazi, and afterwards, with great honesty, tried to portray the growth of fascism and the development of anti-Semitism in his novels. He experienced a great turning-point in his life during his time as a prisoner of war in the Soviet Union; his epic poem *Die Fahrt nach Stalingrad*, 1953 ('The Journey to Stalingrad') portrays this turning-point and its consequences. *Die Richtung der Märchen*, 1962 ('The Meaning of Fairy Stories') contains some of his best poems.

Günter Kunert (b. 1929) is one of the best writers at the moment living in East Germany, but now has difficulty getting his work published. His first volume of poems, *Wegschilder und Mauerinschriften*, 1950 ('Sign Posts and Writings on Walls') showed Brecht's influence in the spareness of style. A collection of satires, *Der ewige Detektiv und andere Geschichten*, 1954 ('The Eternal Detective and Other Stories') was followed by some volumes of poetry and novels.

Greatly loved and respected was the poet Johannes Bobrowski (1917–65). His poems were first published in *Sinn und Form* in 1954. The collections, *Sarmatische Zeit*, 1961 ('Sarmathian Age') and *Schattenland Ströme*, 1962 ('Twilight Streams') all convey memories of the past, and are often situated in an East European landscape. He wrote two novels also, *Levins Mühle*, 1964 ('Levin's Mill') and *Litauische Klaviere*, 1966 ('Lithuanian Pianos'). Several volumes of prose and poetry have been published by Klaus Wagenbach in West Berlin, the most recent being the poems, *Wetterzeichen*, 1967 ('Signs for the Weather') and the prose *Der Mahner*, 1968 ('The Admonisher').

The dramatist, Peter Hacks (b. 1928), came to East Germany from the West in 1955. His works show the influence of Brecht, and they try to convey complicated social processes. By the early 1960s Hacks was in trouble with the cultural authorities, and had difficulty in getting his works performed. *Die Sorgen und die Macht* ('Worries and Power') written in 1958 and first performed in 1960, ran into political difficulties; *Moritz Tassow* was first performed in 1965. *Fünf Stücke*, 1965 ('Five Plays') have been published in the West.

WRITERS WHO LEFT EAST GERMANY

The most famous writer who left is Uwe Johnson (b. 1934) who wrote his first novel, *Ingrid Babendererde* there, which was not published, and then *Mutmassungen über Jakob*, ('Speculations about Jakob') which was published in 1959 when he moved to West Berlin. That and his two following novels, *Das Dritte Buch über Achim*, 1961 ('The Third Book about Achim') and *Zwei Ansichten*, 1965 ('Two Views') are all concerned with life in East Germany and reflect Johnson's rebellion against the simplicity of style and content as officially required. The dramatist, Hartmut Lange (b. 1937), and the poet, Christa Reinig (b. 1926), and the novelist, Manfred Bieler (b. 1934), are others who left for the West. Bieler, whose ironical novel *Bonifaz oder Der Matrose in der Flasche*, 1963 ('The Sailor in the Bottle') has been translated into six languages, wrote the screenplay for the film, *Das Kaninchen bin ich* ('I am the Rabbit'), which was based on a novel he had written. The film was made in 1966, and banned before it was ever shown. Bieler went to live in Czechoslovakia in 1965. In August 1968 he left Czechoslovakia and went to Munich. His most recent publication of short stories is *Der junge Roth*, 1968 ('Young Roth').

Amongst the novelists who stayed in East Germany is Christa Wolf (b. 1929) whose novel, *Der geteilte Himmel*, 1963 ('The Divided Heaven'), caused a sensation with the boldness of its theme: a young scientist goes to the West; his girl friend follows but returns home without him. The novel was filmed, but not shown in public. Her next novel, *Nachdenken über Christa T.* ('Thoughts about Christa T.') was published, after some difficulties, in 1969. Erik Neutsch (b. 1931) wrote about experiences in industrial works in *Bitterfelder Geschichten*, 1961 ('Tales from Bitterfeld') and in *Spur der Steine*, 1964 ('Stony Path') about social and moral problems amongst a group of building workers and a party secretary, demoted for unparty-like behaviour, but who proves himself as a real worker.

THE YOUNG GENERATION

The most promising aspect of the oppressed literary scene in East Germany is in the field of poetry. Most well known, though officially ignored and unpublished in his own country, is the poet and ballad-singer, Wolf Biermann (b. 1936), who left Hamburg in 1953 to live in East Germany. His songs, at first gently humorous and gradually growing sharper and angrier, express the bitterness and exasperation of the generation of young communists who are impatient to express their own views and indignant at being suppressed by dry old bureaucrats. Biermann's songs, influenced by Brecht, by the French *chanson*, and by American blues, have been published in West Berlin, *Die Drahtharfe*, 1965 ('The Wire Harp') and *Mit Marx-und Engelszungen*, 1968 ('With the Tongues of Marx and of Engels'). His publisher, Klaus Wagenbach, also published a record of Biermann singing his songs, essential if his true quality is to be appreciated. Other promising young poets are Volker Braun (b. 1939) who works with the Berliner Ensemble. His volume of poems, *Provokation für mich*, 1965 ('Provocation for Me') was followed by another collection entitled *Vorläufiges*, 1966 ('For the Moment'). His poems show Brecht's influence in their attitude to social problems. His volume, *Wir und nicht sie*, 1968 ('We and Not They') takes concrete examples from life in East Germany.

It is with this generation which has grown up entirely within the society created by the Soviet Union and ruled by German communists that the future will eventually lie. The young lyric poets, at any rate, are proving themselves as creative writers: they are original and critical and determined.

FURTHER READING

Brenner, Hildegard (ed.) *Nachrichten aus Deutschland*, Rowohlt, Reinbek, 1967.
Bridgwater, Patrick (ed.) *Twentieth-Century German Verse*, Penguin, 1968.
Endler, Adolf and Mickel, Karl (eds.) *In diesem besseren Land*, Halle, 1966.
Hamm, Peter (ed.) *Aussichten*, Biederstein Verlag, Munich, 1966.
Keith-Smith, Brian (ed.). *Essays on Contemporary German Literature. German Men of Letters*, vol. IV, Oswald Wolff, London, 1966.
Middleton, Christopher, (ed.) *German Writing Today*, Penguin, London, 1967.
Reich-Ranicki, Marcel. 'The Writer in East Germany', *Survey*, 61, London, October, 1966.
Vallance, Margaret. 'Wolf Biermann: The Enfant Terrible as Scapegoat', *Survey*, 61, London, October 1966.
Wagenbach, Klaus, (ed.) *Lesebuch. Deutsche Literatur der sechziger Jahre*, Wagenbach, Berlin, 1968.
'Who is Afraid?', review in the *Times Literary Supplement*, London, 2 December 1965.

MARGARET VALLANCE. Translator and reviewer. At present writing a Ph.D. thesis on the works of Gustav Landauer. At one time worked on the staff of *The Times Literary Supplement*.

CONTEMPORARY HUNGARIAN
LITERATURE

MÁTYÀS SÁRKÖZI

HUNGARIAN literature is rich in traditions. Its origins can be traced back to the early 13th century, but its overall social importance dates from the 18th century. The period between 1910 and 1940 is regarded as one of the golden ages of Hungarian writing. On the eve of World War II Hungary lost many of her eminent literary figures and by far the most important of the young poets, Attila József, committed suicide.

LITERARY FORCES AFTER THE WAR

In 1945 the country was in ruins. A new society had to be built and writers wished to make their contribution to this process. In Central Europe literature is politically committed, writers play a forceful, often passionate role in society, a role that may strike Western observers as somewhat idiosyncratic.

There was no lack of talent, but the war had taken a tremendous toll. The poet Miklós Radnóti, (1909–44) was shot by the Nazis. He wrote his last poems in forced labour camps and the manuscript was found on his body in a mass-grave. Two of the leading Hungarian essayists, Antal Szerb (1901–45) and Gábor Halász (1901–45) were murdered together with the lyric poet György Sárközi (1899–1945). Károly Pap (1897–1945), a novelist who wrote on Jewish themes and Andor E. Gelléri, (1907–45) the author of vivid short stories on working-class subjects, also fell victim to persecution. The controversial novelist Dezső Szabó (1897–1945), who had an exceptionally strong influence on the younger generation of inter-war years, died in an air-raid shelter.

Surprisingly few writers and poets of any literary standing had cooperated with the Nazis. Those who had, were inspired by a kind of ultra-right-wing nationalism with anti-Semitic undertones. Two of these were talented poets, both the children of poor peasants and both known for their infusion of a strong folk element into poetry. A certain deep mysticism lent originality to their poems and it was the mystical ideology of the Nazis which attracted them to it. One, József Erdélyi (b. 1896) fled to Rumania after the war, but later gave himself up and was given a short prison sentence. In 1954 he started to publish again. The other, a one-time shepherd, István Sinka (1897–1969), waited almost 20 years before he reappeared on the literary scene.

Some Hungarian writers were in exile. Communist émigrés returned from the Soviet Union, whilst those in the West did not. The Muscovite communists returned in the baggage-train of the Red Army. They were mostly insignificant writers, ambitious for recognition and power. Most were conditioned

561

by the ten to twenty-five years they had spent in the Soviet Union. As at least half the émigré writers had perished in Stalin's purges, the struggle for survival had corrupted most of the other half.

The return of the philosopher, Georg (György) Lukács (b. 1885), of Béla Balázs (1884–1949) who made early contributions to aesthetics of the film, and of the dramatist, Gyula Háy (b. 1900), can be considered exceptional inasmuch as their contribution to Hungarian culture turned out to be of positive importance. Lukács and Háy later took part in the 1956 revolution. Háy was sentenced to six years in prison and in 1965 settled in Switzerland. Of the Moscow group Béla Illés (b. 1895) came back to Budapest as a major of the Red Army. In the Soviet Union he had gone through a terrible ordeal. Having been secretary to Béla Kun, the purged Hungarian communist leader, Illés nearly followed him to the gallows. Back in Hungary at first he excelled in the role of the self-assured party activist, but with age reverted to his more congenial pre-emigration image, that of the jovial companion and raconteur of unbelievable anecdotes. His novel *Kárpáti rapszódia*, (*Carpathian Rhapsody*) portrays life among the minorities in sub-Carpathia.

LITERARY JOURNALS

It is the usual practice in Hungarian literary life for writers to group themselves around literary journals. Georg Lukács edited the first important post-war journal, the *Fórum*. Lukács, a Marxist theorist, has an international reputation as a philosopher and his aesthetic theories on realism in literature are of a high standard of depth and originality.

Younger intellectuals, the modernists who preferred to keep out of politics, supported *Újhold* ('New Moon'). Catholics lined up behind *Vigilia* which was edited by the humanist priest-poet and professor of literature, Sándor Sik (1889–1963). But the most important literary journals of the period were *Valóság* ('Reality'), *Válasz* ('Response') and at the other, the left wing of the political spectrum was *Csillag* ('Star').

Valóság had the official backing of the universities, but it provided a general forum for all writers. It was edited by Zoltán Szabó (b. 1912), a member of the 'Village Explorers', a Narodnik-type group of pre-war writers whose aim was to publish 'sociographical' essays on rural life in Hungary.

Válasz took the most clearly delineated line, reflecting the political theories of István Bibó (b. 1911), an eminent scholar and a member of the Imre Nagy cabinet in 1956. *Válasz* was edited by Gyula Illyés (b. 1902). It had great left-wing traditions, between 1934 and 1938 the magazine put up a courageous fight for social reform and at the same time stood for the best literary values. The surviving pre-war contributors came together again. László Németh (b. 1901), a writer of analytical novels which aim to present not only their ostensible theme—the life of a certain middle-class family—but also to sketch the whole spectrum of Hungarian society. The best of Németh's novels is *Iszony*, 1947 ('Revulsion'). Other contributors to *Válasz* included Áron Tamási (1897–1966) from Transylvania, a peasant writer, Péter Veres (1897–1970), and the poet, Lőrinc Szabó (1900–57), whose autobiographical volume *Tücsökzene*, 1947 ('Grasshopper Music') is one of the most notable single volumes of poetry in this period. Other first-rate poets connected with *Válasz* were Zoltán Jékely (b. 1913) and István Vas (b. 1910). It was also in *Válasz* that Imre Sarkadi (1921–61) first appeared with his short stories which were considered to be among the best in post-war Hungarian literature. He subsequently committed suicide at the age of 40.

Csillag was the literary organ of the Communist Party. After 1949 it was the only magazine to survive as all the others were forced to stop publication. The Catholic *Vigilia* managed to continue, but in deep obscurity.

THE YEARS OF SILENCE

The period between 1945 and the so-called 'year of change' (1948) was a fairly fruitful one. Besides those already mentioned there were quite a few other important literary developments. The communist writer, Tibor Déry (b. 1894), was at last able to publish his novel *Befejezetlen mondat* ('Unfinished Sentence') written in 1935. It tells the story of an upper middle-class idealist, and of his conversion to communism. Gyula Illyés published his novel about Paris in the 1920s, *Hunok Párizsban* ('Huns in Paris').

In poetry this period saw the maturing of Sándor Weöres (b. 1913), and *Újhold* launched two important intellectual lyric poets, János Pilinszky (b. 1921) and Ágnes Nemes Nagy (b. 1922). Taking part in the liberation of concentration camps in Germany in 1945 was the most profound formative experience for Pilinszky. The theme of human suffering has continued to haunt his poetry. Ágnes Nemes Nagy paints disturbing visions in her surrealist-influenced poems.

Weöres is justly regarded as being the closest to the mainstream of Western tradition. To some extent influenced by surrealism he has nonetheless evolved a highly individual style, composed of diverse elements, including classical Indian and Chinese mythologies. His contribution is possibly the most challenging of all post-war Hungarian poets.

There followed one of the bleakest periods in Hungarian literature. Most writers refused indoctrination and the aridities of socialist realism. Instead they became librarians, publishers' readers, literary translators or teachers. As artistic freedom was more and more curtailed two extremely popular novelists, Lajos Zilahy (b. 1891) and Sándor Márai (b. 1900), settled in the USA; the essayist, László Cs. Szabó (b. 1905), went to London.

The new minister of culture was József Révai, an old-guard Muscovite whose bright intellect was clearly tarnished by his newly acquired power. He wanted communist revolution to succeed immediately and showed impatience when the literary élite refused to follow the road of socialist realism. By methods of strong persuasion he put some writers to work, but the outcome was nothing more than juvenile literature or historical novels. Hence it is to Révai, in a sense, that we owe the charming children's jingles by S. Weöres or L. Németh's excellent translations from the Russian classics.

Gyula Illyés wrote in 1950 in the poem 'One Sentence on Tyranny' which was published during the 1956 uprising:

> Where there's tyranny / there's tyranny / not only in the gun-barrel, / not only in the prison-cell / not only in the torture rooms, / not only in the nights, / in the voice of the shouting guards; / there's tyranny . . . in everything . . . / everyone is a link in the chain; / it stinks and pours out of you, / you are tyranny yourself.

Nevertheless Illyés remained in favour, his reputation protected him and he avoided committing himself to the wrong side. At the same time the party turned on its most respected members. Just as T. Déry finished his complex novel *Felelet* ('Answer') in 1952, Révai criticised him for the picture given of the earlier days of the communist movement. Lukács also received strong criticism for insisting on a less dogmatic interpretation of the dictatorship of the proletariat.

The way was open for the second-rate to climb to the top. There were a few exceptions like the poet, László Benjámin (b. 1915), and the party itself discovered two young poets, both of peasant stock. Their indoctrination started at the party Academy, but was not successful. All the party hacks succeeded in doing was to induce severe psychological disturbances in these two. Nevertheless, the two poets in question, László Nagy (b. 1925) and Ferenc Juhasz (b. 1928), are the most outstanding of their generation. Juhász writes ballad-like, somewhat compact verse; his images reflect the microcosm of nature. The long lines betray a kind of despair and at the same time one can sense his urgency in seeking the most suitable expressions for his feelings. The poems of L. Nagy can be described as modernistic. Like Juhász he also is striving for new forms.

THE THAW

The thaw began in 1954. The first signs were literary reports from the countryside in the tradition of the 'Village Explorers'. These were written by Imre Sarkadi, György Moldova (b. 1934), Ferenc Sánta (b. 1927) and others. Déry wrote about the 'new class'. By the autumn of 1956 the atmosphere had changed completely. Writers were beginning to attach themselves to the weekly *Irodalmni Újság* ('Literary Gazette') now published in Paris, and *Új Hang* ('New Voice') a monthly of the younger writers.

The grand old men of Hungarian literature were now beginning to publish again. Lajos Kassák (1887–1967), a veteran socialist and the editor of constructivist and Dadaist magazines in the 1920s, published his poems once more. Another veteran, Milán Füst (1888–1967), the first Hungarian poet to write free verse, was once again able to disseminate his ideas, being a professor at Budapest University, where, like Lukács, he became the centre of a group of younger intellectuals.

It was at this time, during the summer of 1956, that the *Petőfi Kör* ('Circle'), was formed. It became a meeting place for communists who were dissatisfied with the regime. Echoing the desires of Hungarian society they demanded abrupt changes, but these were delayed by a reluctant leadership.

On 23 October 1956 the revolution broke out. Though crushed, it was not in vain. In its gloomy aftermath scores of intellectuals suffered punishment for their part in the rising: Déry, Bibó, Háy and the communist poet, Zoltán Zelk (b. 1906), amongst others. Several writers fled to the West.

SINCE OCTOBER 1956

Severe reprisals followed, but the old order could not survive unchanged. The time came when more voices had to be given hearing. Lyric poets of the prewar generation, like Lajos Áprily (1887–1967) published volumes again. There was no attempt to silence Catholic poets like Pilinszky or György Rónay (b. 1913) and those who defied classification in Marxist terms and had therefore been previously suppressed. They were Weöres, Jékely among the poets, Iván Mándy (b. 1918), a nostalgic modernist who writes about the flotsam and jetsam of urban society, depicting the continuing alienation of the individual; István Örkény (b. 1912), a writer of bizarre stories, Miklós Mészöly (b. 1921) the avant-garde existentialist novelist and Gyula Hernádi (b. 1926), a writer of short stories of a scientific nature. Also belonging to this group is Géza Ottlik (b. 1912) who wrote what is possibly the most important novel in post-war Hungarian literature, *Iskola a határon*, 1959 ('School at the Frontier'). This psychological novel, set in the iron discipline of a military academy, explores the process of dehumanisation and the nature of the relationships formed in such a context. Ottlik's philosophy of the possibility of survival of human values in such conditions is sensitively conveyed.

The regime dislikes them, but knows that only they represent evolution in Hungarian literature. Direct criticism of official ideology is still forbidden, but truthful portrayal of existing conditions has become possible. The best analysis of society yet is to be found in Endre Fejes's (b. 1923) novel *Rozsdate-mető*, 1964 ('Scrap Yard'). Tracing the life of a proletarian family, Fejes portrays almost all aspects of Hungarian society from the 1920s to the present day, both under communism and its reactionary predecessors of the inter-war years.

Déry and Illyés use historical parallels or the obscurity of highly philosophical forms to express their humanist views. Déry's novel *Kiközösítő*, 1966 ('The Excommunicator') takes as its theme the corrupting force of absolute power. In Illyés's play *Kegyenc*, 1963 ('The Favourite') the conflict of loyalty to a tyrannical ruler and interest of the people is strikingly portrayed.

An interesting new voice is that of József Lengyel. An active communist, he emigrated to Vienna in 1919 at the age of 23. Later he settled in the Soviet Union, where during the purges he was arrested, interned and exiled to Siberia. In 1955 the Soviet authorities rehabilitated him and Lengyel returned to Hungary. He writes now about the misery and humiliation of the prison camps but there is no bitterness in his stories; he treats his subject unemotionally and with humility.

There is in Hungary today a great wealth of young talent awaiting maturity and given the right intellectual climate, there is little doubt that they will be able to live up to the standards set by the previous generation.

FURTHER READING

Aczél, T. and Méray, T. *The Revolt of the Mind*, Frederick A. Praeger, New York, 1959; Thames, London, 1960.

Déry, Tibor. *Niki*, Secker and Warburg, London, 1958. *The Portuguese Princess*, Calder and Boyars, London, 1967.

Gömöri, George. *Polish and Hungarian Poetry*, Oxford Univ. Press, New York and London, 1966.

Illyés, Gyula. *People of the Puszta*, Corvina Press, Budapest, 1967.

Keresztúry, Dezső. 'Two Centuries of Hungarian Short Stories', *New Hungarian Quarterly*, Budapest, IV, 9, 1963.

Lengyel, József. *From Beginning to End*, Peter Owen, London, 1966.

Németh, László. *Revulsion*, Eyre and Spottiswoode, London, 1965; Grove Press, New York, 1966.

Remenyi, Joseph. *Hungarian Writers and Literature*, Rutgers Univ. Press, New Brunswick, 1964. *Hungarian Short Stories*, Oxford Univ. Press, London, 1967.

Somlyó, György. 'A Short Introduction to Contemporary Hungarian Poetry', *New Hungarian Quarterly*, Budapest, VII, 23, 1966.

Tábori, Paul (ed.) Hungary Number, *The Literary Review*, Teaneck, N.J., Spring 1966.

MÁTYÁS SÁRKÖZI. Born in Hungary. Writer and journalist. Worked on the weekly *Hétfői Hírlap* until he came to London in 1956. Regular contributor of short stories and criticism to Hungarian émigré publications. From 1963–66 Editor, Radio Free Europe, Munich. Since 1966 has worked for the External Services of the BBC. Author of two volumes of short stories written in Hungarian.

JUGOSLAV LITERATURE

K. F. CVIIĆ

Two Literary Giants

Two writers of the older generation tower above the post-war literary scene in Jugoslavia. One of them, the Croat poet, playwright and novelist, Miroslav Krleža (b. 1893) had appeared on the Croat literary scene before World War I and had published his best work by the beginning of World War II. The other, the Serb writer from Bosnia, Ivo Andrić (b. 1892), also appeared with his early prose and poetry just before and during World War I. His most mature work, however, was published immediately after World War II. Krleža, the leading Marxist intellectual in pre-war Jugoslavia, spent the Occupation period, thanks to a kindly doctor, in a psychiatric hospital in Zagreb. Andrić, a pre-war career diplomat, whose last post was that of Jugoslav ambassador in Berlin in 1941, spent the war in relative obscurity in enemy-occupied Belgrade.

Andrić's two best novels, *Na Drini Ćuprija*, 1945 ('The Bridge on the Drina') and *Travnička hronika*, 1945 ('Bosnian Story') deal with his native Bosnia's past. The first is a beautifully written chronicle of three centuries of life in Višegrad, a small Bosnian town on the border with Serbia. The bridge in the title is a magnificent stone bridge built in the 16th century by the Grand Vizier, Mehmed Pasha Sokolović, himself a Bosnian, and destroyed at the outbreak of World War I in 1914. The second is a vivid and amusing account of life in Bosnia's administrative capital, Travnik, during the Napoleonic wars in the early years of the 19th century.

Andrić is a superb stylist and spell-binding storyteller. All his work is shot through with an oriental sense of fatalism. In many ways he is an old-fashioned writer without any inclination towards literary experiment, which is perhaps one of the reasons for his immense popularity with a wider reading public. The novels published after the war have sold hundreds of thousands of copies and are still as popular as ever. A supporter of the regime since 1945, Andrić has never allowed his politics to influence his style. Only once did he choose a contemporary theme from pre-war Belgrade in a novel called *Gospodjica*, 1950 ('Miss') and treat it in a manner which suggested an acceptance of the party line. Not surprisingly, this is his least satisfactory work. His novels and short stories have been translated into many languages. In 1961 Andrić was awarded the Nobel Prize for literature, the first writer from Jugoslavia to have been awarded this honour.

Like Andrić, Krleža is also fascinated by the past. In his case it is the past under that other great empire that had dominated the life of Croats and other southern Slavs for so many centuries—the Habsburg empire. The declining years of Austria-Hungary and the first chaotic years of the new

566

Jugoslavia which arose from its ruins are the subject of Krleža's only major post-war novel, *Zastave*, 1967 ('The Flags'). Perhaps the most important of his pre-war novels is *Povratak Filipa Latinovicza*, 1930 ('The Return of Philip Latinovicz*), a powerful and brilliant psychological novel that has influenced several generations of Croat and other Jugoslav writers.

Krleža's best known cycle of plays constructed round the Glembay family, representative of the small and rootless middle-class in a mainly peasant country, consists of three works: *U agoniji*, 1928 ('Agony'), *Gospoda Glembajevi*, 1929 ('The Glembays') and *Leda* ,1930 ('Leda'). Krleža's enormous output includes a number of expressionist plays, several volumes of short stories, including what is probably the most powerful work on a war theme in any of the Jugoslav languages, a short-story collection, *Hrvatski bog Mars*, 1921 ('The Croat God Mars'). In this collection Krleža draws on his personal experiences of World War I campaigns in Galicia in which he took part as an Austro-Hungarian officer. Krleža has also written a large number of essays and critical studies as well as several volumes of excellent expressionist poetry, which, like his prose, exercised a powerful influence on several successive literary generations in Jugoslavia. Perhaps his most remarkable poetic achievement is a superb volume of ballads written in the archaic idiom of the most northern Croat province, Zagorje. This collection called *Balade Petrice Kerempuha*, 1936 ('Ballads of Petrica Kerempuh') a Croat *Till Eulenspiegel* describes the lot of the ordinary people during the Turkish campaigns fought for centuries on Croat national territory.

Before the war Krleža edited several very influential Marxist literary reviews, but fell out with the official 'socialist realism' group in the Jugoslav Communist Party in the 1930s. This group, which after the war produced a number of powerful party figures including Milovan Djilas (b. 1912), never forgave Krleža his lack of orthodoxy, but he was able to carry on thanks to his friendship with President Tito. Since the late 1940s he has been in charge of a vast project in Zagreb which has so far produced a number of specialist and general encyclopaedias. In his capacity as chairman of the Jugoslav Academy's Literary Institute in Zagreb, he has been responsible for the launching of *Forum*, perhaps the most important literary magazine in Jugoslavia today.

THE NEW GENERATION

With Krleža, Andrić and several other older writers unable or unwilling to tackle the horrors of the last war in their literary work, it was left to the generation born just before or during World War I to come to grips with that theme. By general consent, the most harrowing and vivid poetic wartime work is *Jama*, 1943 ('The Pit'), a poem in ten cantos by Ivan Goran Kovačić (1913–43), a Croat poet and himself a participant in the war on the partisan side. *Jama*, published posthumously by one of Kovačić's friends, describes the experiences of a man blinded in a massacre of civilians during the occupation.

The most impressive prose work on a wartime theme is by a Serbian writer from Bosnia, Branko Ćopić (b. 1915), himself an ex-partisan. Ćopić combines the epic storyteller's gift with a remarkable insight into the psychology of people involved on both sides of the civil war. Indeed, in his excellent novel, *Gluvi barut*, 1957 ('Dead Gunpowder'), he portrayed the enemy *četniks* (Serbian royalist guerrillas) with so much understanding and sympathy that he aroused the suspicion of the authorities. Among other things he was accused of 'nihilism'. Čopič is also a talented humorist. Perhaps his most successful humorous work is a collection of short stories, *Doživljaji Nikoletine Bursaća*, 1958 ('The Adventures of Nikoletina Bursać') describing the experiences of a simple country boy during the war. In recent years Čopić has been turning increasingly towards satire on contemporary themes, thereby once again jeopardising his position with the authorities.

Socialist realism as an official ideology was forcefully expounded and rather indifferently practised in Jugoslavia in the immediate post-war years by a Montenegrin poet and essayist, Radovan Zogović (b. 1907). Zogović wrote propagandist poetry in the style of the Russian poet, Mayakovsky, and harassed other non-socialist-realist authors but when in 1948 Jugoslavia broke with the Soviet Union and Zogović opted for the Soviet line, his brief cultural dictatorship came to an end. After years spent in complete silence and obscurity he has recently reappeared, ironically enough in the Zagreb *Forum* published by Zogović's bitter pre-war enemy, Krleža.

A novelist who could not be classified as a pure socialist-realist, but who is more of a traditional Serbian realist in the 19th-century manner is Dobrica Ćosić (b. 1921), whose best known work is *Daleko je sunce*, 1951 ('The Sun is Far Away'). In recent years, however, Ćosić has, despite the genuine popularity of his early work tried to move away from that early realism. His latest novel, *Bajka*, 1966 ('The Fairy Tale') is a complex and not entirely successful allegory of modern man's predicament in a technocratic and totalitarian society.

On the Croat side, the traditional realist school is best represented by Vjekoslav Kaleb (b. 1905), author of several novels and short-story collections. Kaleb is a master of the short sentence and compressed imagery. His most successful story, and indeed one of the best short stories to emerge from the post-war partisan literature, is *Divota prašine*, 1954 ('The Glory of Dust'), an account of the wartime experiences of a man and a boy who roam round the countryside in search of food.

The period after 1948 was marked by a growing interest in Western literature. This was reflected in an enormous increase in the number of translations from contemporary English, American, French, Spanish and German authors. Hardly anybody was barred on ideological grounds and names like Orwell, Kafka, Eliot, Joyce, Graham Greene and Faulkner were being widely read in first-class translations. New magazines sprang up in the early 1950s, first in Zagreb and then in other republican capitals where Serbo-Croat is spoken—in Sarajevo, Titograd and, of course, Belgrade. Many younger critics, who had read modern languages at the university, began to introduce methods of contemporary Western literary criticism into their critical work on Jugoslav literatures.

THE POST-1948 PERIOD

The post-1948 period saw in Zagreb the emergence of a new talented group of poets most of whom were too young to have taken part in the war. Their organ was the first of the liberal literary magazines in Zagreb called *Krugovi* ('The Circles') which was published between 1952 and 1955. Its editor, Vlatko Pavletić (b. 1930) is now one of the best-known critics in Jugoslavia. One of the most outstanding poets of the group was a woman, Vesna Parun (b. 1922), whose first collection of poetry, *Zore i vihori*, 1947 ('Dawns and Gales') attracted a number of unfavourable notices from socialist realist critics, then still powerful. Among other things, Vesna Parun was attacked for 'formalism'. Now, with half-a-dozen volumes published, she stands out as one of the most accomplished members of that generation. Another prominent member of this Zagreb group is Jure Kaštelan (b. 1919). His poetry is dominated by the theme of death, symbolised by the riderless horse of one of his collections, *Pjetao na krovu*, 1950 ('The Cock on the Roof'). Kaštelan, who is a university lecturer in literature, has also published plays and literary criticism. Of the younger members of the 'Krugovi' group the most talented are Slavko Mihalić (b. 1928), Milivoj Slaviček (b. 1929) and Zlatko Tomičić (b. 1930).

The leading Croat prose writer to emerge after 1948 was, without any doubt, Ranko Marinković (b. 1913), a short-story writer and novelist. A master of biting satire and vivid characterisation, he has written a number of memorable short stories on themes from his native Dalmatia. His best collection is *Ruke*, 1953 ('Hands'). His prize-winning novel *Kiklop*, 1966 ('Cyclops') one of the most interesting post-war novels in Jugoslavia, shows clear Joycean influences in its structure and approach, but is a most original and powerful work. Also from the Croat province of Dalmatia is Peter Šegedin (b. 1909), novelist and essayist. Something of a writers' writer, he is master of a complex, intellectual style packed with psychological insight. His best novels are *Djeca Božja*, 1946 ('God's Children') and *Mrtvo more*, 1954 ('Dead Sea').

Outside the usual categories stands Matko Peić (b. 1923), an art critic who has emerged as the best travel-writer in Jugoslavia. His collection, *Skitnje*, 1967 ('Wanderings'), an account of several journeys through northern Croatia, has been acclaimed both by critics and by the public as a masterpiece of modern Croat prose.

In Belgrade after 1948 the literary scene was dominated for a number of years by a pre-war surrealist group, most of whose members had come out in favour of the communist regime. A member of that group, Koča Popović (b. 1908), even became Tito's chief of staff, and later foreign minister and vice-president of Jugoslavia.

The most talented and influential member of that group is undoubtedly Oskǎ Davičo (b. 1909), author of a stream-of-consciousness novel, *Pesma*, 1952 ('The Poem'), an account of a day in wartime Belgrade. Davičo has written other prose and several important collections of poetry. A bold innovator in rhythm and vocabulary, he has exercised a strong influence on younger Serbian poets.

An important member of the pre-war generation of poets who in fact published some of her best work after 1945 and has continued to be widely read by the younger generation of readers is Desanka Maksimović (b. 1898). Her most recent book of verse *Tražim pomilovanje*, 1966 ('I Crave Pardon') is a successful and moving synthesis of her early romanticism and her subsequent humanitarian preoccupations symbolised by the titles of some of the poems from the book ('For the Naïve Ones', 'For Barren Women', 'For the Misunderstood', etc.).

Of the younger post-war poets, perhaps the most remarkable is Miodrag Pavlović (b. 1925), a fine intellectual poet whose most recent poetry is inspired by themes from Serbian and Slav history. His exact contemporary, Branko V. Radičević (b. 1925), writes evocative and erotic poetry and is one of the leaders of the bohemian revival in post-war Belgrade. Another member of this early post-war group is Stevan Raičković (b. 1928), a poet with a fine feeling for atmosphere and landscape. His latest book of poems, *Prolazi rekom ladja*, 1967 ('A Ship Sailing Down the River'), shows an intense awareness of decay and death.

A slightly younger poet, Ivan V. Lalić (b. 1931), showed in his early elegant and accomplished verse influences of Milan Rakić (1876–1938), one of the most popular and widely read of the pre-war Serbian poets. Lalić's most recent work has lost none of the elegance and sense of form, and also shows a new sincerity and depth of feeling.

A young poet whose work is currently receiving a good deal of attention is Branko Miljković (1934–61). This is due not only to the high quality of Miljković's non-conformist poetry but also probably to the circumstances of his tragic death: he hanged himself following a number of attacks on his poetry by orthodox party ideologues.

Better-known in the West than any other members of the younger generation of Serbian novelists is Miodrag Bulatović (b. 1930). His frequent brushes with authority have made him something of a celebrity in Western Europe, particularly in France and Germany. In modern Serbian prose he represents the 'black humour' school and is occasionally accused of 'nihilism' and 'cynicism'. His best work is the novel, *Crveni petuo leti prema nebu*, 1959 ('The Red Cockerel Flies to Heaven'). His most recent novel *Heroj na magarcu*, 1967 ('Hero on a Donkey') has been attacked in Jugoslavia as a pornographic work.

Among the short-story writers the most interesting is Antonije Isaković (b. 1923) whose work, mostly on wartime themes, has been translated into several languages.

The literary scene in Belgrade has been greatly enlivened by the return from many years in political exile in the UK of Miloš Crnjanski (b. 1893), poet, playwright and novelist whose work is now widely read by the younger generation. A splendid stylist and writer of powerful imagination, he completed the third volume of his historical novel, *Seobe* ('Migrations') in 1965. The first two volumes of this impressive psychological portrait of the great migration of Serbs in the 17th century had been published over 25 years ago. His best known post-war play is *Konak*, 1958 ('A Hostelry').

Unlike Crnjanski, who is now freely read again, the works of Milovan Djilas (b. 1912) are still proscribed in Jugoslavia. His books are only available in English and other translations. His best known works in the literary genre are *Land Without Justice*, 1958, an autobiographical account of his youth in Montenegro, written between two prison terms. *Montenegro*, published in 1964, consists of three separate sections, two of which are episodes from World War I in Montenegro, while the third deals with post-war violence. Both works have an epic quality about them and reveal Djilas' sensitivities and talents as a prose writer. A more definitive judgement of his qualities must await the publication of the Serbo-Croat originals.

Bosnia

From Bosnia have emerged in recent years a number of excellent poets, novelists and short-story writers. Two deserve a special mention. One of them is the poet, Mak Dizdar (b. 1917), whose collection, *Kameni spavač*, 1966 ('Sleeper in Stone') has won him wide recognition and several prizes. It is a powerful evocation of Patharene Bosnia before Turkish rule. The stones in the title are the special tombstones (*stećci*) of Bosnian Patharene heretics who called themselves *Bogomils*.

The other is novelist Meša Selimović (b. 1910) whose novel *Derviš i smrt*, 1966 ('The Dervish and Death') became a best-seller overnight and has won several prizes. This powerful novel, acclaimed as one of the most important post-war novels to appear in Jugoslavia is a moving story of a Muslim monk or dervish, who after agonies of indecision decides to plead for his brother sentenced to death but only to meet the deaf ear of authority. Years later he finds himself in the same terrible predicament, only this time as a representative of authority who has to pronounce on matters of life and death.

Slovenia

Slovene literature after the war has been most successful in poetry. Perhaps the most important representatives of this post-war poetic generation, whose work has been translated into English, are Jože Udovič (b. 1912) and Cene Vipotnik (b. 1912). A much older poet who continued to write and publish till well into the post-war period was Alojz Gradnik (1882–1967). A former judge and a man of wide cultural interests who had translated Spanish, Italian, German, English and Chinese poetry into Slovene, Gradnik was a poet of great originality and power and deeply attached to the countryside. At the same time he was an urban intellectual with a great interest in philosophy and so his poetry reflects this basic conflict in his nature. One of the most interesting writers to emerge from the partisan war is Edvard Kocbek (b. 1904). His war diary, *Tovarišija*, 1949 ('Company') is a successful combination of vivid wartime reportage and lyrical reflection and evocation. His short-story collection *Strah in pogum*, 1951 ('Fear and Courage') was the first Jugoslav attempt to present wartime experiences in existentialist terms. It, therefore, attracted a good deal of attention and was bitterly attacked by party hardliners. Another prominent prose writer of the same generation as Kocbek is Ciril Kosmač (b. 1910). He represents the stream-of-consciousness trend in modern Slovene prose and is master of accurate exploration of unusual psychological states. In all his writings, novels and short stories there is a strong autobiographical element. Perhaps his most important novel is *Pomladni dan*, 1955 ('A Day in Spring'). The psychological trend is very successfully pursued by one of the most talented younger novelists, Andrej Hieng (b. 1925), author of several novels and short-story collections.

Macedonia

The young Macedonian literature has so far produced a number of talented poets who successfully experiment with traditional folk idiom in a modern setting. The first volume of Macedonian verse was published just before the war in 1939 in the town of Samobor, near Zagreb. It was called *Beli mugri* ('The White Dawns'). Its author, Kočo Racin (1908–43) who was killed during the war, is really the founder of modern Macedonian poetry. At the moment the most prominent Macedonian poets are Blažo Koneski (b. 1921) who was elected the first president of the newly founded Macedonian Academy of Arts and Sciences in 1967, and Slavko Janevski (b. 1920). Literary activity in Macedonia is receiving a good deal of official encouragement and the development of the young Macedonian language is vigorously promoted through work on the new dictionary of the Macedonian language, and through the publication of many translations from Serbo-Croat and Slovene as well as non-Jugoslav languages. Relations with Bulgarian writers remain difficult in view of the continued Bulgarian denials of a separate Macedonian nationality and language.

Post-war Jugoslav literature claims one bilingual author from the ranks of the Hungarians living in Jugoslavia—Ervin Šinko (1898–1967), a life-long revolutionary who had lived for many years before the war in Moscow and then settled down in Jugoslavia after the war. His Moscow experiences from the time of the purges were published under the title *Roman jednog romana*, 1955 ('The Novel of a Novel'). Another important novel is his *Četrnaest dana*, 1947 ('Fourteen Days'), the story of the Bela Kun revolution in Hungary after World War I.

FURTHER READING

Aćimović, Dragoljub R. 'Serbian Literature since the Second World War', *Review*, 3, London 1962.

Kadić Ante. 'Present-Day Croatian Literature', *Review*, 3, London, 1962; *Contemporary Croatian Literature*, Mouton, The Hague, 1962; *Contemporary Serbian Literature*, Mouton, The Hague, 1964.

Koljević, Svetozar (ed.) *Yugoslav Short Stories*, Oxford Univ. Press, London, 1966.

Lavrin, Janko (ed.) *An Anthology of Modern Yugoslav Poetry in English Translation*, Calder, London, 1962.

Some Yugoslav Novelists: A Selection with commentary translated by A. Brown, Jugoslavija Publishing House, Belgrade, 1963.

Vaupotić, Miroslav, *Contemporary Croation Literature*, International PEN-Club, Zagreb-Centre, Zagreb, 1966.

THE POST-WAR LITERATURE OF RUMANIA

D. ILIESCU

THE year 1940—the year in which a fascist regime was installed in Rumania —saw a great literary travesty: *The History of Rumanian Literature*, a monumental work of a vigorous subjectivism and a lively aestheticism, by George Călinescu (1899–1964), one of the most notable writers and critics of the inter-war years, was at once banned and confiscated by the authorities on account of its non-conformist ideas. It was, however, later on to have an increasingly strong influence, being considered as a document on freedom of thought.

In the same year the most important pre-war critic, Eugen Lovinescu, began to publish a series of monographs on Titu Maiorescu (scholar and aesthetician of the 19th century who fought against the intermingling of moral and political ideas in art), with the avowed aim of promoting freedom of the human spirit. During the war also, the lectures in logic and metaphysics of Professor Nae Ionescu were published posthumously. Nae Ionescu was a disciple of Kierkegaard, Max Scheler and Heidegger and a former political figure of the extreme right; of his pupils—all brilliant essayists—two are now living abroad: Emil Cioran in France and Mircea Eliade in the USA. Of those who remained in Rumania, Constantin Noica has published commentaries on Kant's *Critique of Pure Reason* and a *Philosophical Journal*, while Mihail Sebastian was obliged to remain silent owing to the anti-Jewish persecutions. Another essayist of remarkable originality—Eugen Ionescu—was also abroad during the fascist period.

While the greatest writers of the inter-war period continued their work, new stars began to appear on the literary horizon. While the psychological novel—more or less in the Proustian manner—had become an established formula, one suddenly began to notice the revival of traditional realism. In *Sfârșit de Veac în București* ('The End of the Century in Bucharest'), Ion Marin Sadoveanu takes up—but with greater subtlety—an ancient theme of the Rumanian epic: the disappearance of the aristocracy and the rise, through its greater vitality, of the bourgeoisie. Similarly, Radu Tudoran wrote with great public approval of social problems in the novel, *Flăcări*, ('Flames'), the subject of which is exploration for oil.

A more modern prose, however, is to be found in the stories of Eusebiu Camilar, and in his famous novel, *Revoluția* ('The Revolution') Dinu Nicodin revived in expressionist terms the revolutionary spirit which shook France in 1789.

In poetry the situation was similar. Whilst before the war, lyricism was achieved almost exclusively by metaphor, and pure, hermetic or metaphysical poetry was a required ideal, in wartime a more direct and traditional poetry was written which was nearer to everyday reality and experience.

The outstanding characteristic, however, of this period was the publication of innumerable reviews and articles extolling feats of arms and chauvinistic nationalism. A poet like C. Virgil Gheorghiu (author of 'The 25th Hour') switched suddenly to reportage of a violent anti-Semitic war. As opposed to this literature of an official nature, was the reappearance of the review, *Kalende* ('Almanacs') edited by the critic, Vladimir Streinu. Lucian Blaga (1895–1961), the great poet, dramatist and philosopher—who edited the philosophical review, *Saeculum* ('The Century')—was vehemently attacked by the representatives of the Orthodox Church for his anti-Christian metaphysics.

From the autumn of 1944 until the autumn of 1947 there was on the one hand renewed access to American, English and Soviet cultures, and on the other new political problems—the conflict between Western and Eastern political ideologies—were preoccupying everyone. In *Viaţa Românească* ('Rumanian Life'), the old-established review with a democratic tradition, Eugen Ionescu published *Scrisori din Paris* ('Letters from Paris') in which he virulently attacked the Rumanian bourgeoisie. Camil Petrescu, novelist, dramatist poet and essayist of great renown, contributed political articles regularly to the paper, *Fapta* ('The Reality'), while George Călinescu edited a left-wing daily paper. The bourgeoisie were vulnerable because they had collaborated with the fascist regime during the war, while the intellectuals, though not opposed to the bourgeoisie, did not defend them.

In this climate of affairs, three poetical currents evolved: poetry of spiritual revolt and demystification, represented by Geo Dumitrescu, *Libertatea de a Trage cu Puşca* ('Freedom to Shoot'), Ion Caraion, *Omul Profilat pe Cer* ('Man Outlined Against the Sky'), Constant Tonegaru, *Plantaţii* ('The Plantations'), Mihai Crama, *Decor Penitent* ('Penitent Adornment') and others. Reveries, moral ideals, social offences, the temptations of cosmopolitan life in the city and the condemnation of material misery are all expressed in verbal violence and imagery, according to the degree of intensity in the poet's conscience. But this poetic conscience hid within itself both the desire of mastery and the necessity to impose itself on the febrile, actual phase of history. The machine age is repudiated and the chaos which would follow on its destruction seems to these poets to be the means by which real freedom would be achieved: freedom as a state of perpetual revolution.

The poets of the literary circle of Sibiu, Radu Stanca, Stefan Augustin Doinaş and Ioanichie Olteanu, followed another path and returned to the old ballads as a gesture of refusal to accept the actualities of the day. The first two of these poets endeavoured to reanimate in a modern way the spirit of German and English balladry of the romantic era. Radu Stanca wrote as a troubadour and a dandy; always, however, with melancholy, obsessed by the vision of Death who appeared to him in the guise of a phantasmal, sensual being. Doinaş was attracted by the fabulous as such; by gods and historical personages; by landscapes formed by cosmic change and by the platonic idea of corporeal reintegration through love. To Ioanichie Olteanu, the ballad was a pretext to express his sarcasm, irony and scepticism of real life in which a dream intervened to cause dismay and unrest.

Then, thirdly in the post-war period, a new powerful wave of pure surrealism appeared, richer and more fully evolved than that which appeared at the end of World War I. Tempted by the world-wide poetical revolution and by cosmopolitanism, these recrudescent surrealists—Gherasim Luca, Paul Păun, O. Trost, Virgil Teodorescu, Gelu Naum—forgot that Rumania had been the country of Tristan Tzara, the founder of Dadaism, and also of Isidor Isou, the founder of Lettrism after World War II.

Many novels were being published at this time, but few are of much interest and none is of great originality. *Accidentul* ('Accident') by Mihai Sebastian—who before the war had taken on the painful task in *Două Mii de Ani* ('Two Thousand Years') of analysing anti-Semitic psychosis and the Judaist complex—was written in a vaporous, delicate style on the themes of adolescence and love. *Zilele nu se Intorc Niciodată* ('The Days do not Return') of Sorana Gurian is a deep psychological novel, in which the author shows a cruel and expert knowledge of souls subjected to the tortures of love. A special place in prose—as in the case of Nina Cassian in poetry—is occupied by Petru Dumitru, who made his début with *Eurydice*—a work which does not fit into any category, least of all into realism and in which stylistic virtuosity and elasticity of vision bear witness to the aestheticism of the author.

Lastly, a new generation of critics now appeared: Ovid Crohmǎliceanu, Virgil Ierunca, Adrian Marino, I. Negoiţescu, Al. Piru and Cornel Regman. All were competent aestheticians and well-versed especially in French and German culture, they conscientiously endeavoured to assess the character of the new Rumanian post-war literature by comparing it with that of the inter-war period.

THE PERIOD OF SOCIALIST REALISM

But, at the beginning of 1948, the state—on the Soviet model—decreed socialist realism and banned any other conception of literature. The connection with Western culture was broken. The great writers of the inter-war period who were still alive, G. Bacovia, Lucian Blaga, Tudor Arghezi, Ion Barbu, Adrian Maniu, Hortensia Papadat-Bengescu, Ion Agârbiceanu, Camil Petrescu, George Cǎlinescu, were obliged to give up writing and resort for their livelihood to translation or to the writing of socialist-realist literature. As Camil Petrescu and George Cǎlinescu were disposed to dabble in apologetic journalism, they were acclaimed as great writers even while their former works were withheld from the public or even considered as non-existent. It was possible only to write propagandist literature about the socialisation of agriculture and industry; about the class-struggle and about the role of the Soviet Union and of Stalin in contemporary history. Love, nature and sadness were considered dangerous bourgeois themes and were forbidden. The critics, particularly Ovid Crohmǎliceanu, Ion Vitner, Mihai Petroveanu and Savin Bretu, engaged in the denunciation of bourgeois infiltration into the writings of the poets, novelists and dramatists. Young writers appearing on the scene were trained in a 'School of Literature' under the aegis of the Writers' Union whose aim it was to create such propagandists. Real talent, like that of the young poet, Nicolae Labiş, was cramped and disfigured by that School. A great inter-war writer, Mihail Sadoveanu (1880–1961) deteriorated lamentably in his attempts to satisfy socialist realism in his novel *Mitrea Cocor*. Among the older writers who conformed and became socialist realists may be included Zaharia Stancu, Demostene Botez (b. 1893) and Eugen Jebeleanu (b. 1911). In order to create and encourage socialist realism, Mihai Beniuc, president of the Writers' Union, exercised a pitiless censorship in the realm of literature. The anomalous situation arose wherein well-known critics like Perpessicius and Tudor Vianu, retired from their scholarly profession, were nominated members of the

Academy on the merit of their former works, while at the same time those writings were totally banned.

It was only after the death of Stalin—although socialist realism remained the only approved literary doctrine—that, nonetheless, a few good novels began to appear. George Călinescu appeared as an intelligent novelist in *Bietul Ioanide* ('Poor Ioanide'), in which the university world is satirised in an admirable portrayal of scholars full of human weaknesses, but later on, in *Scrinul Negru* ('The Black Chest'), a satire on the decadent aristocracy, one can feel the socialist realist influence. Of great interest was the attempt of Ion Marin Sadoveanu to continue his old novel *Sfârşit de Veac în Bucureşti* ('The End of the Century in Bucharest') in *Ion Sîntu* ('St. John')—a detailed work, constructed with ability and patience, which avoids the clichés of socialist realism. It is a novel of the childhood of a scholar left over from World War I which bears the obvious stamp of autobiography, giving it an authentic character.

Within the framework of socialist realism, Petru Dumitru made an impetuous career. After several novels which conformed strictly to this doctrine, he published *Cronica de Familie* ('Family Chronicle') where, in the Balzacian manner, he was able to depict, in a convincing way, Rumanian aristocratic and bourgeois society in the 19th century. The novel was, however, too tedious and often too conventional. A lasting work is *Moromeţii* ('The Moromets') of Marin Preda, in which the mentality and life of the peasants before the war were investigated with a documental precision and a taste for the hard, grey and absurd of Italian neo-realism. It is a pity that the keenness of observation and the original stylistic daring of Marin Preda become engulfed in the artificial socialist realist constructions of *Risipitorilor* ('To The Squanderers'). In the second part of *Moromeţii*, Marin Preda tries to examine the problem of human responsibility during the period of Stalinist restrictions. *Groapa* ('The Trench'), the work of Eugen Barbu, is also a lasting work. It is a naturalist novel of the Bucharest suburbs written, however, with a feeling for the romantic. But like the author of *Moromeţii*, Eugen Barbu became submerged, in his turn, in a sea of socialist realism in his *Şoseaua Nordului* ('The Highway to the North'), to emerge later in the historical novel *Prinţul* ('The Prince') with adventures treated in the manner of the cinema. *Familia Calaff* ('The Family Calaff') written by Julia Soare is a novel inspired by Thomas Mann, but the originality of the *milieu*, described here with coolness and artistic probity (Jewish bourgeoisie in a Danubian port) gives the book a convincing note of unquestionable probability. The few sketches of Dominic Stanca in *Roata cu Sapte Spiţe* ('The Wheel with Seven Spokes'), in which the figure of the revolutionary character, Horia, of the 18th century is indirectly suggested, as he does not appear himself—thus preserving a mythical quality—comprise a little oasis of true literature.

One result of the death of Stalin was the rehabilitation of Tudor Arghezi. He reappeared first as translator of Krylov's fables and then as socialist realist author of the poem *Povestea Omului* ('The Story of Man')—a poem sustained only by the extraordinary popularity of the poet's early days. Over the years, Arghezi had come to be considered officially as the most notable Rumanian writer and thus his former works of a religious nature were re-printed, at a time when other well-known poets like Blaga or Barbu were still banned.

It was only towards the end of 1964 that socialist realism began to fade, while in 1965, this term completely vanished from the vocabulary of criticism and the theory itself was rejected. The great writers of the inter-war years were all gradually reinstated and they resumed their writing each according to his former artistic conception. In 1967 Al. Philippide published the best collection of verses of his whole literary career—*Monolog în Babilon* ('Monologue in Babylon')—a terrifying vision of the world of monsters with chains which dragged heavily on the imagination of the poet. Western writers began to appear in translation and to be reviewed objectively: Joyce, Proust, Gide, Kafka, Faulkner, Eliot, St. John-Perse, Michaux, Musil, Céline, Borges. The American beat poets, the English angry young men, the new French novel and new criticism in France now became the order of the day in the pages of the reviews. The poets of the immediate post-war generation now reappeared in the literary field with new volumes of their works.

In addition the critics Adrian Marino and I. Negoițescu reappeared in vigour, after a silence of many years while Al. Piru and Cornel Regman, who had passed through a period of conformism, readjusted to resume their original work.

THE NEW GENERATION

The most striking change, however, brought about by the wind of freedom, was the rise of a new generation of poets, critics and prose-writers, who, by their richness and variety soon filled the distressing vacuum. Poets like Nichita Stănescu *Elegii* ('Elegies'), Ion Alexandru *Infernul Discutabil* ('Debatable Inferno'), Ion Gheorghe *Nopți cu Lună pe Oceanul Atlantic* ('Moonlight on the Atlantic'), Grigore Hagiu *Sfera Ganditoare* ('Sphere of Thought'), Adrian Păunescu *Mieii Primi* ('The First Lambs'), Marin Sorescu *Moartea Ceasului* ('Death of the Hour'), Ilie Constantin *Clepsidra* ('The Hour-glass'), Sorin Mărculescu *Cartea Nuntilor* ('The Wedding Book'), discovered with an overwhelming enthusiasm, unplumbed depths of lyricism. Their thirst was not quenched by nature or by love, but their inspiration was sought in the very springs of existence, of thought and of feeling. Drawn by the irrational and metaphysical, they returned with the aid of metaphor, to the system of Ptolemy or to ancestral myths, to Pascal or Nietzsche. As a rule they preferred long poems like monologues without beginning or end, for they despised the rigorous forms of classical poetry. Doubt, restlessness, inner perplexity or ecstasy in face of a cosmos full of mystery, was also present in their lyrical discourses.

Two trends appeared in prose: on the one hand there was a realism now capable of discovering new facets of objective existence, preferably in the human field—social or otherwise. On the other hand an anti-realism appeared in which the influence of Alain Robbe-Grillet or of Nathalie Sarraute can be detected. The novel of Nicolae Breban, *In absența stăpânilor* ('In the Master's Absence'), seems to be composed of fragments without any other connexion between them than the spiritual disorder of the characters, depicted, not psychologically, but by their physical gestures. The mysterious significance of these physical gestures is revealed by the technique of delayed observation and description; between the eye of the story-teller who observes them and the characters there is, as it were, a magnifying-glass which enlarges and, at the same time, breaks the reality into fragments which are themselves autonomous.

The fact should also be mentioned that, after the war, there was a rich émigré literature; in Munich, Paris, and Madrid notable reviews were published such as *Prodromos* ('The Forerunner'), *Destin* ('Destiny'), *Revista Scriitorilor Români* ('Review of Rumanian Writers') and *Ființa Românească* ('Rumanian Being'). The literature of the exiles is closely bound up with the personality of their distant homeland. The critic, Virgil Ierunca, entitles his volume in which he examines the writers in his country: *Românește* ('Rumanianism'). All the stories of Mircea Eliade (who published recently a first volume of his memoirs in Madrid which recalls his youth in Bucharest) take place in Rumania. Mihai Niculescu relives his childhood on the banks of the Danube in *Carte de Vise* ('Book of Dreams'), while Leonid M. Arcade depicts in *Poveste cu Țigani* ('A Tale of Gypsies'), a fantastic Rumanian village of mediaeval magic. On the other hand, the essayist, George Uscătescu, anchors his Rumanian concerns in the universal, writing with the same detachment about Eminescu or Heidegger. The tendency can be seen in all prose-writers and poets who live in exile to return to a more archaic language; perhaps in their desire to preserve the closest possible bond with their native land.

D. ILIESCU. Studied at the University of Iași and at the Sorbonne. Has made an extensive study of the influence of classical Latin themes on the literatures of the modern Romance languages.

CONTEMPORARY BULGARIAN LITERATURE SINCE WORLD WAR II

VIVIAN PINTO

THE MODERN LITERARY TRADITION

MODERN Bulgarian literature was born in the 18th to 19th century *vazrazhdane* (national revival). From Father Paisy (b. 1722) and Bishop Sofrony (b. 1739) to Petko Slaveykov (b. 1827), L. Karavelov (b. 1835) and H. Botev (b. 1848) the modern literary language was forged in a variety of writings. With the *Osvobozhdenie* of 1878 (liberation of Bulgaria from five centuries of 'the Turkish yoke') a succession of distinguished writers, notably I. Vazov (b. 1850), Pencho Slaveykov (b. 1866), P. Yavorov (b. 1878), Y. Yovkov (b. 1880) and Elin Pelin (b. 1877), established a modern tradition of Bulgarian letters, despite the unsettling interruptions of the Balkan and World Wars. The contemporary communist period of literature dates from the end of World War II, in effect from the September 1944 coup. This, as surely as the *Osvobozhdenie*, marks the end of an era.

THE LITERARY REGIME AFTER SEPTEMBER 1944

Critical realism (literature reflecting inadequacies of pre-communist society) now no longer sufficed. Socialist realism, designated as national in form and socialist in content—and it was content that counted—'now had to, and steadily did, become the method for the whole of Bulgarian literature . . . which adopted Soviet literature as its model, taking the path charted by it and learning from its experience'.[1] To establish this the Writers' Union made its preserve the literary forum formerly represented by such reviews as *Zlatorog*, 1920–44 ('Golden Horn'), *Literaturen glas*, 1928–44 ('Literary Voice') and *Izkustvo i kritika*, 1939–44 ('Art and Criticism'). Its organs *Literaturen front*, 1944 ('Literary Front'), *Septemvri*, 1947 ('September') and *Plamŭk* ('Flame') (1948, a revival of G. Milev's journal of 1924–5), together with its publishing house, Bălgarski Pisatel, were created to serve and interpret the new ideology, applied now to literature with unprecedented authoritarian thoroughness by such Marxist pundits as T. Pavlov (b. 1890) and G. Dimitrov-Goshkin (b. 1912). All literature, past and present, had to be reinterpreted in 'scientific' Marxist terms. Printing, publishing and distribution, like the rest of the country's economy, were nationalised, and throughout the whole material apparatus of literature, cultural subsidisation was to promote spectacular growth. This ensured, too, that writers and artists

[1] Acad. of Sciences' 'History of Bulgaria', III, pp. 654–5.

fulfilled the 'activist' role unequivocably assigned to them in the regime's
political, social and economic programme.

LITERARY 'PARTIYNOST' IN THE 1950S

It was the proletarian school of writers, many of them stemming from the
original RLF (Workers' Literary Front) review of 1929–33 and its Smirnen-
ski circle, which after years of protest and at times persecution was now to
assume total literary authority. The writers began immediately to create the
heroic legend of their opposition years, dating from the 1923 rebellion and its
aftermath in such novels as E. Koralov (b. 1906), *Septemvriytsi*, 1945 ('The
Septembrists') and E. Stanev (b. 1907), *Ivan Kondarev*, 1958, to the wartime
partisan resistance in the verse of V. Andreev (b. 1918) and D. Ovadiya
(b. 1923) and the Bulgarian contribution to a final campaign of the war in
the stories of P. Vezhinov (b. 1914), *Vtora Rota*, 1949 (No. 2 Company).
Heroic retrospect was one facet of this literary *partiynost* (party-mindedness),
but the concept also included dedication to the Soviet proletarian homeland,
denigration of the *esnafshtina* (bourgeoisie) and of 'Western decadence' and
above all, the urgent current commission both to inspire and reflect 'the
building of socialism'.

This mobilisation of literary effort yielded a plethora of works in prose and
verse which were as predictably angled and unremittingly activist as their
titles suggest, thus renewing an older Bulgarian tradition of publicism and
extremism on these new criteria of *partiynost*.

Changes of the order undertaken in the Bulgarian communist five-year
plan of nationalism, industrialisation and agricultural 'cooperativisation'
invite reportage but entail such complexity as to be not readily assimilable,
much less to yield 'instant' great literature. Yet two works stand out. D.
Dimov's (b. 1909) novel of contemporary social upheaval *Tyutyun*, 1951
('Tobacco'), Marxist, yet in the human detail in its first edition, not Marxist
enough to escape the Writers' Union's censure on 'a hundred counts of
mortal sin' and above all—widely acclaimed and, significantly, set in non-
contemporary territory—D. Talev's (b. 1898) rich and vivid reincarnation
of his forbears, their whole Macedonian life and *mores* in his trilogy of novels,
Zhelezniyăt svetilnik, 1952 (*The Iron Candlestick*), *Ilinden*, 1953 (*St Iliya's Day*)
and *Prespanskite kambani*, 1954 (*The Bells of Prespa*).

REJECTION OF THE PERSONALITY-CULT

The 1956 Party Plenum in Sofia echoed the Soviet Communist Party Congress's retreat from Stalinism, though it took till the Eighth Congress of
November 1962 in Sofia finally to reject Bulgaria's own *kultovshtina* (personality-cult). The shock of P. Penev's (b. 1930) suicide in 1959 followed his
'*Dni na proverka*' (*Days of Reckoning*), the poem in which, with a new and
challenging candour, he proclaimed the toll taken of his generation by a
materialist epoch 'with which we don't rhyme, though our rhythm and beat
are the same'. Another 'harrowing document of our time' (to quote A.
Todorov, *Bulgarski pisateli*, 1964, ('Bulgarian Writers')) is N. Lankov's
(b. 1902) *Spomenăt*, 1963 (*The Memory*), dedicated officially to the Eighth
Congress. In this poem cycle, with the same ring of true fact and feeling, the
author recounts the grim inquisition which he, an old RLF guard, endured
under the cult, imprisoned this time 'by one's own [comrades]'. The whole

tale is bluntly and briefly told in S. Minov's (b. 1902) story 'The Man with a Tail', 1962.

THE PRESENT DECADE

However agonising this reappraisal, by 1962–3 it cleared the air for a range and quality of writing in the present decade which, with permissive state paternalism and a growing responsive readership, could prove to be of lasting value. The old guard has had to look to its shibboleths and the new generation, with an honesty and frankness unthinkable during the' blight' or 'smog' (as present critics dub the cult), is now questing and questioning in print. In the verse of P. Matev (b. 1924) and G. Jagarov (b. 1925) the party tribune's Muse is mellower, and in the retrospective meditations of V. Petrov (b. 1920), *V meka esen*, 1960 ('In a Mild Autumn') the old homages seem less raucous, even nostalgic, while B. Dimitrova (b. 1922) with warmth and skill makes a poetic exploration of life and the self sought also in her personal novel *Păt kăm sebe si*, 1965 ('Journey to Find Oneself'). The changes had been rung *ad nauseam* on Y. Vaptsarov's (b. 1909) heroic 'faith', but it now reappeared in quite new terms in her:

> Gone is the teacher's belief in the cane,
> the artist's—in an aesthetic code,
> the student's—in the old textbook,
> the designer's—in the model of yesteryear . . .
> And that's why I believe, unshakeably I believe
> in all these searching people.
>
> *Ekspeditsya kăm idniya den*, 1963 ('Expedition into tomorrow')

Yet more revealing is the personal 'lyrical hero' implicit in the verse— relatively free now not only in form—of the younger poets S. Tsanev (b. 1931), P. Karaangov (b. 1931), O. Orlinov (b. 1931), S. Karaslavov (b. 1932), L. Levchev (b. 1935), D. Damyanov (b. 1935) and V. Bashev (b. 1935). The originality of Y. Radichkov's (b. 1929) stories, the novels of A. Navoski (b. 1925) and G. Markov and, on a different level, A. Gulyashki's and B. Raynov's spy dramas also lend a universal interest to contemporary Bulgarian prose. Literary criticism in the recent work of E. Karanfilov (b. 1915), P. Danchev (b. 1915), S. Karolev (b. 1921), T. Zhechev (b. 1921) and M. Nikolov (b. 1929) no longer follows a narrow predictable line. The Writers' Union recently held an enquiry into national characteristics in literature and published a variety of its members' views in *Natsionalnoto svoeobrazie v literaturata*, 1966, ('National Idiosyncrasy in Literature').

A sense of humour is not the least gift regained for Bulgarian literature in the new political climate. By such gifted humorists of the Satirical Theatre as H. Benadov, (b. 1907), V. Tsonev (b. 1920), R. Ralin (b. 1923) the weekly *Starshel*, 1945 ('Hornet') has been revitalised.

PRESENT LITERARY PROSPECTS

For Bulgaria, a late 19th century entrant into the family of modern European national cultures, these last two decades have witnessed a steady strengthening and extension of the 'sub-structure' of literature. Much basic scholarship has been achieved in the Academy of Sciences' Institutes of Language and Literature and in many other fields which contribute to literature. Many authoritative complete works have been published and more recently there has been a harvest of memoirs and of anthologies, mercifully now less obsessed with the party and revolution. The 19th century *chitalishtë* (library-club) tradition has been enhanced by a network of local finely equipped Houses of Culture. Educational magazines, amateur groups and festivals of poetry-reading, drama and other arts are some of the cultural catalysts which have attracted subsidisation at many levels, including the fundamental one of book-purchase itself.

Such things are the logistics of literature. They affect the size of a reading public. If backed by outward-looking attitudes implicit in trade, tourism and cultural exchange, they are likely to affect, too, the reading public's horizon of critical appreciation—the horizon denoted, perhaps, by the title *Obzor*, 1967 ('Horizon'), the new quarterly review of literature and the arts (issued also in English) by the Bulgarian Committee for Foreign Cultural Relations and the Writers' Union.

For the state to become a permissive parent, while continuing to promote literature materially could promise an exciting future. The September 1944 coup could yet prove to have been not just the end of an era, but, despite a literary dawn judged dim now even by diehards, the harbinger of a new and worthy chapter in the long and tragically interrupted tradition of the original Slavonic literary tongue, which was founded by S. S. Kiril and Metodi more than a millenium ago.

FURTHER READING

Manning, C. A. and Smal-Stocki, R. *The History of Modern Bulgarian Literature*. Bookman Associates, New York, 1960.

Pinto, V. *Bulgarian Prose and Verse* (with an introductory essay). Athlone Press, London, 1957; Essential Bks., N.J., 1958.

VIVIAN PINTO. Since 1947 Lecturer in Bulgarian language and literature at the School of Slavonic Studies, University of London. Author of *Bulgarian Prose and Verse*.

ALBANIAN LITERATURE

S. E. MANN

AFTER the death of Albania's last defender, Skanderbey, in 1467 the oppressive rule of Ottoman Turkey inhibited the growth of any considerable literature.

Albania was liberated in 1912. A single alphabet unifying the rude and vigorous language of the Geg mountaineers in the north with the more polished speech of the Tosk plainsmen in the south did not emerge till 1909. The lack of schools and the almost universal illiteracy meant that there were few Albanian writers and a negligible reading public. Such writers as there were had to use alphabets of their own devising. Even so, the 16th century produced a single work of high linguistic value in Buzuk's Litany (1555). This was followed by homilies and verses by Budi (1566–1623), an Albanian and Latin dictionary by Bardhi (1606–43), and a bilingual miscellany, part religious, part ethnographical, by Bogdani (1630–88) in 1685.

After the annexation of Albania by Turkey many Albanian patriots fled to Sicily and Calabria, and here the literary tradition struggled on in the work of Matranga (1560–1619) of Sicily, author of a religious work interspersed with hymns, in the poetry of Variboba (b. 1735) of Calabria, author of a unique epic, 'The Life of the Virgin', 1762, and in the writings of De Rada (1813–1903), whose unhappy life was spent assembling fragments of lost national epics half-remembered by the descendants of the original refugees. This activity of rescuing ancient folklore was continued by the Sicilian Zef Schirò (1865–1927), author of an anthology of folk poetry and two historical dramas in verse.

A new impetus came to Albanian writing in 1878 as a result of the Bulgarian peace settlement, when Albania had hopes of achieving autonomy. This period saw the rise of three remarkable brothers from Frashëri in Southern Albania. Naim Frashëri (1846–1900), best-loved of the three brothers Abdyl, Sami and Naim, wrote poetry in a new lyrical and nostalgic vein calculated to rouse patriotic feeling, and showed an aptitude for word-music and rhythm. Refugees in Rumania and Egypt eagerly read his works, which in turn did much to inspire the collections of folk tales and folk songs made by Dine (1846–1922) and Mitko (1820–90). Mid'hat Frashëri ('Lumo Skendo') (1880–1949), a nephew of Naim, carried on the literary tradition in Sofia, where he joined K. Luarasi to produce a literary almanac of prose and poetry. In the 1880s the Rumanian school, swollen by refugees from Istanbul, continued publishing the work of Naim Frashëri and others, and produced a literary journal 'Dodona'.

The period from 1912 (the year of national independence) to 1939 saw the rise of two Tosk novelists, Grameno (1872–1931) and Postoli (1889–1927), the first concerned with the local struggles against the Turks before liberation, the second with the themes of love, intrigue, treachery and reaction during the upheavals that accompanied Albania's occupation by neighbouring powers. The period is also notable for the work of the dramatist, Floqi (b. 1873), a Tosk lawyer steeped in the Greek tradition, who wrote a large number of plays and sketches of a satirical and political character in the style of Pinero; and Koliqi (b. 1903), now in Rome, who has written many dramatic tales about his native highlands, in which native lore and custom are brought into sharp contrast with the influence of the towns. His historical tales show the results of an Italian education, and among his poetic works are translations of Dante and Petrarch. Noteworthy Tosk poets of the period are the nostalgic Drenova ('Asdreni') (1872–1947), the symbolist Poradeci (b. 1899), an individual stylist trained in the school of Eminescu, and Çajupi (1866–1930), the exiled lyricist of Egypt.

The Catholic north spans the wild and pristine ruggedness of the Albanian highlands. Dominated by the Church of Rome, this area developed a Latin script which became the vehicle of Prennushi (1885–1948), Xanoni (1863–1915) and Mjedja (1866–1937), lyricists on pious and didactic themes. Unique among the northern poets stands the ebullient Father Fishta (1871–1940), a monk who for many years edited the folklore journal *Hylli i Dritës* ('The Star of Light'), and whose racy epics in folk rhythms commemorate the stirring times between 1878 and 1912, when Albania was fighting for survival. These poems were published under the title *Lahuta e Malcís* ('The Highland Lute'). The emergence of a social genre is seen in the novels of Stërmilli (1895–1953), author of *Sikur t'isha Djalë* ('If I were a Boy'), and Migjeni (1911–38), author of *Luli i Vogël* ('Little Luli').

For many years the Albanians of the USA had their leader in Bishop Fan Noli (1881–1965), the exiled communist who collaborated with the ex-diplomat, Konitsa, in editing an Albanian newspaper *Dielli* ('The Sun') and a literary journal *Vatra* ('The Hearth'), both published at Boston, Massachusetts.

POST-WAR LITERATURE

The period of World War II was dominated by the Italian occupying power, and literary activity was confined largely to the compilation of anthologies and readers. The emergence of the present regime from the Tosk south in 1945 gave literary activity a new turn. The national language was switched from Geg to Tosk, and the chief themes were henceforward the partisan movement, the struggle of the poor against the rich, the rebuilding of the economy on socialist lines, the theme of world peace, and the leadership of Stalin and Mao Tse-tung. Dhimitër Shuteriqi (b. 1915) is the author of a two-volume novel, 1952, 1955, entitled 'The Liberators', an anthology of Albanian literature (1955), a collection of poems, *Mbi krahun e praruar të paqës*, 1950 ('On the Golden Wings of Peace'), five short stories (1953), and a collection of tales, *Rruga e Rinisë*, 1953 ('The Road of Youth'). Popular novelists on political and social themes are Gjata (b. 1922), Sako (b. 1912), Dushi (b. 1923), Spasse (b. 1914), and Bulka, a psychological novelist of cynicism and despair. There is a flourishing school of short story writers. Drama found a new awakening in the work of Jakova (b. 1917), founder of The People's Theatre. Postoli's novel 'Flower of Remembrance' has been adapted as an opera.

Poetry in the socialist vein is represented by Musaraj, author of *Dje dhe Sot* ('Yesterday and Today'), *Epopeja e Ballit Kombëtar* ('The Epic of the National

Front'), and the tale *Shtek më shtek me Partizanët* ('With the Partisans through the Land'). Liberation themes and the tasks of the new economy are represented by the poet and playwright Çaçi (b. 1916), the novelist Gjata (b. 1922), the Kosovar Ll. Siliqi (b. 1924) and many more.

Separated by a political boundary are the million or so Albanians of the Jugoslav republic of Kosmet (Kosovo-Metohija), who have developed a vigorous local literature cross-fertilised with that of Albania proper. With its own university at Prishtinë, its theatre, and its cultural journal *Jeta e Re* ('The New Life'), Kosmet produces plays, poetry and fiction in the one-time standard Geg dialect of Albania. Esad Mekuli (b. 1916), an editor of the newspaper *Rilindja* ('Rebirth'), is a veteran of the Spanish civil war, and an experimenter in free verse and onomatopoeic effects. The novelist Hasani (b. 1922) is author of a novel of domestic conflict *Rrushi ka nisë me u-pjekë* ('The Grape has Begun to Ripen'); Surroi (b. 1929) and Shkreli (b. 1938) are writers on partisan and social themes. Rela (b. 1895) is the author of *Nita*, a stirring drama of rugged highland love and hate, and the conflict between peasant and landlord. Peza (b. 1919) is the author of the plays *Nuk martohem me pare* ('I Don't Marry for Money'), and *Parajsi i Humbun* ('Paradise Lost').

The dominant motifs of Albanian literature are the savage extremes of wealth and poverty, and the struggle for independence against ruthless political enemies. These are but the reflexes of the harsh background of Albanian life, where memories of hunger and hardship are seldom far from the writer's thoughts. The lyrical ecstasy over Albania's modest economic achievements must be read in the light of Albania's war-torn past.

FURTHER READING

Mann, S. E. *Albanian Literature*, Quaritch, London, 1955.

STUART EDWARD MANN. Reader in Czech language and literature at the University of London.

INDEX

INDEX

References to maps and statistical tables are in *italic* figures;
'SU' means 'Soviet Union', 'EE' means 'Eastern Europe'.

ABM (Soviet anti-ballistic defence): 180, 181, 182
AUCCTU (All-Union Central Council of Trade Unions): 327–9 *passim;* tasks of (statutory), *quoted*, 328–9
Abortions: 425, 426, 427
Academy of Sciences of the USSR (*formerly* St Petersburg Academy): 454, 456–7, 460
Acculturation in the Soviet Union: 202
Afghanistan: 308, 310
Africa: 229, 302; aid to countries of, 307–14, *313–14*
Agaltsov, Air Marshal F. A.: 180
Age distributions (1966): *418*
Agriculture (*see also* Collectivisation): 336–48; the Soviet example, 336–7; collectivisation in EE, 138–9, 289, 336, 338–9; the socialist sector, 339–44; the private sector, 344–5; investments and incentives, 345–7; prospects, 347–8; 'socialised', 347 (*see also* Collectivisation); milk yields (1952–66), *342*; wheat yields (1952–66), *342*; tractor power and chemical fertiliser consumption (1960–5), *341*; land utilisation and production (1966), *24*; in Soviet Central Asia, 381–2
Aid to developing countries: 307–14; origins and purposes of, 307–8; nature of, 306–10; scale of, and the recipients, 310–12; conclusion, 312; donors, commitments and recipients, *313–14*
Air transport (*see also* Transport): 360
Albania and Albanians (*see also* Agriculture, Arts, Cinema, Eastern Europe, Education in Eastern Europe, Energy, Housing, Law, Legality, Penology, Press and broadcasting, Religions, Social structure, Theatre *and* Transport): communism in, 7, 147, 235;

political evolution (1918–44), 143; peasantry of, 138–9; independent of Soviet control, 148, 258; after Stalin, 152; and Warsaw Pact, 182, 183; planned economy in, 291, 292; Orthodox religion and persecution in, 471; Roman Catholic Church in, 472–3; Jews in, *488*; theatre, *q.v.*, in, 516; cinema, *q.v.*, in, 524
Albania (*basic information*): 37–42; constitutional system, 42; economy, 39–40; education, 41; geography, 37; history, recent, 37, 39; map, *38*; mass media, 41–2; population, 37; social welfare, 40–1
Albania (*external relations*): and China, 7, 238, 292; and Italy, 143, 144; and Jugoslavia, 7, 238, 292; and the SU, 7–8, 147, 148, 238, 291, 292
Albania (*statistics*): agriculture, land utilisation and production (1966), *24*; consumer price index (1960–6), *27*; consumption (internal) of basic products (1966), *27*; currencies (Comecon), exchange rates of, *19*; energy production (1966), *23*; exchange rates of Comecon currencies, *19*; exports, total (1960–7), *21*; health services (1965), *28*; housing (and domestic facilities), *28, 29*; imports, total (1960–7), *20*; industrial production (indices of (1960–7) and major products (1966)), *22*; inland waterways transport (1966), *26*; labour force, *16*; minorities, *q.v.*, *32*; motor vehicles in use (1967), *29*; national products, origins of and expenditure on (1960–6), *17, 18*; population (1967), *16*; radios, tv receivers and telephones in use (1967), *30*; railways (1966), *25*;

Berlin: blockade of (1948–9), 170; Congress of (1878), 234; crisis (1958), 171; East, 152; Wall (1961), 171, 174
Bessarabia: 140, 146, 235, 273
Bethlen, Count István: 141
Bierut (of Poland): 150, 152
BISON (Soviet intercontinental bomber aircraft, 110M-4): 180
'Black Hundred', the: 192
BLINDER (Soviet medium bomber aircraft, TU-22): 180, 181
Bohemia: 138, 139, 144, 261
Bolsheviks: *see* Russian Communist Party (Bolsheviks)
Book-publishing statistics: 215
Boris, King of Bulgaria: 141
Bosnia: 240, 255, 481
Brătianu, Ion: 142
Bratislava: 244, 266
Brezhnev Doctrine: 9, 165, 186
Brezhnev, Leonid Ilyich: 227, 229, 266
Brioni plenum (1966): 246, 247, 255
Broadcasting: *see* Press and broadcasting
Brodsky, Iosif: 540–1
Brussels Treaty (1948): 149
Bucharest Declaration of Independence (1964): 9, 272, 273
Budapest: 139, 227
Bukharin, Nikolai Ivanovich: 130, 280
Bukovina, Northern: 146, 235
Bulganin, Nikolai Alexandrovich: 258
Bulgaria (*see also* Agriculture, Arts, Cinema, Eastern Europe, Education in Eastern Europe, Energy, Housing Law, Legality, Penology, Press and broadcasting, Religions, Social structure, Theatre *and* Transport): after World War I, 138; political evolution of (1918–44), 141; peasantry of, 138–9; and Peace Settlement (1919), 144; intransigent, 144; 'genuine coalition' in, 148; goes communist, 148–9; after Stalin, 152; and invasion of Czechoslovakia, 226; in fourteenth century, 233; and Congress of Berlin (1878), 234; armed forces of, *see* Military potential; book production in (1966), 215; independent, 234; on losing side in wars, 234; after World War II, 235; plundered by SU, 235; Turkish minority in, 245; 'the pillar of the

Kremlin's Balkan policies', 273; central economic planning in, 292, 293; price fixing in, 297, 298; trade with EEC, *304*; trade unions, 331–2; Orthodox Church in, 470; Protestant churches in, 484; Jews in, *448*; the Arts, *q.v.*, 505; theatre, *q.v.*, in, 516
Bulgaria (*basic information*): 43–9; constitutional system, 48–9; economy, 44–5; education, 46–7; geography, 43; history, recent, 43–4; map *38*; mass media, 47–8; population, 43; social welfare, 45–6
Bulgaria (*external relations*): and Balkan Entente (1934), 144; and East Germany, 175, 274; and Germany, 144; and Jugoslavia, 141; and the SU, 146, 236; and Turkey, 245
Bulgaria (*statistics*): agriculture, land utilisation and production (1966), *24*; consumer price index (1960–6), *27*; consumption (internal) of basic products (1966), *27*; currencies (Comecon), exchange rates of, *19*; defence expenditure (1966–7), *18*; energy production (1966), *23*; exchange rates of Comecon currencies, *19*; exports, total (1960–7), *21*; health services (1965), *28*, housing (and domestic facilities), *28*, *29*; imports, total (1960–7), *20*; industrial production (indices of (1960–7) and major products (1966)), *22*; inland waterways transport (1966), *26*; labour force, *16*; minorities, *q.v.*, *32*; motor vehicles in use (1967), *29*; national products, origins of and expenditure on (1960–6), *17*, *18*; population (1967), *16*; radios, tv receivers and telephones in use (1967), *30*; railways (1966) *25*; shipping, merchant (1967), *25*; trade, external, totals (1967), *19*; transport (1966 & 67), *25*, *26*; working hours in manufactures (1961–6), *23*
Bulgarian Agrarian Union: 149
Bulgarian Fatherland Front Coalition: 149
Bulgarian literature since World War II: 579–82; modern literary tradition, 579; the literary regime after September 1944, 579–80; literary 'partiynost' in the 1950s, 580; rejection of person-